Respt Yours
E. W. Gould

FIFTY YEARS ON THE MISSISSIPPI;

OR,

GOULD'S HISTORY OF RIVER NAVIGATION.

CONTAINING A HISTORY OF THE INTRODUCTION OF STEAM AS A PROPELLING
POWER ON OCEAN, LAKES AND RIVERS—THE FIRST STEAMBOATS ON THE
HUDSON, THE DELAWARE, AND THE OHIO RIVERS—NAVIGATION OF
WESTERN RIVERS BEFORE THE INTRODUCTION OF STEAM—CHAR-
ACTER OF THE EARLY NAVIGATORS—DESCRIPTION OF FIRST
STEAMBOATS—STEAMBOAT NEW ORLEANS IN 1811, AND SIXTY
CONSECUTIVE BOATS, WHEN AND WHERE BUILT—THEIR
EFFECT UPON THE SETTLEMENT OF THE VALLEY OF
THE MISSISSIPPI—CHARACTER AND SPEED OF
BOATS AT DIFFERENT PERIODS—APPROPRIA-
TIONS BY CONGRESS FOR THE IMPROVEMENT
OF WESTERN WATER WAYS—FLOODS
IN THE MISSISSIPPI VALLEY FOR 150
YEARS—MISSISSIPPI RIVER COM-
MISSION AND ITS WORK.

Rapid Increase and Decline of River Transportation.

CAUSES OF THE DECLINE—DESTRUCTION OF STEAMBOATS ON WESTERN
WATERS—BIOGRAPHIES OF PROMINENT STEAMBOATMEN—
ILLUSTRATED BY PHOTOGRAPHS AND CUTS OF
STEAMBOATS AT DIFFERENT PERIODS.

By E. W. GOULD.

750 PAGES. ELEGANTLY BOUND.

SAINT LOUIS:
NIXON-JONES PRINTING CO.
1889.

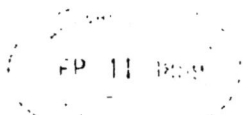

DEDICATION.

TO THE MEMORY

OF THOSE WHO,

AFTER STRUGGLING FOR YEARS TO OVERCOME THE EMBARRASSMENTS AND DANGERS INCIDENT IN THE LIFE OF A BOATMAN, HAVE BEEN WRECKED ON THE SHOALS OF TIME, AND WAFTED INTO A HAVEN OF REST ON THE SHORES OF THE BEAUTIFUL RIVER, WHERE THEY AWAIT THE ARRIVAL OF THEIR FRIENDS AND COTEMPORARIES, WHO ARE STILL CONTENDING WITH THE ADVERSITIES OF THIS LIFE BEFORE CROSSING THE RIVER THAT FERRIES BUT ONE WAY, THIS WORK IS DEDICATED.

THE AUTHOR.

PREFACE.

In compiling the following pages, the author is largely
indebted to individual friends, newspapers, periodicals and
historical works.

Notably J. W. Barker, H. H. Devinney, D. F. Barker, of
Cincinnati; J. W. Bryant, of New Orleans *Times-Democrat;*
James Kerr, New Orleans *Daily States;* Austin R. Moore,
Thomas H. Griffith, Joseph LaBarge, of St. Louis; *Missouri
Gazette*, 1808, its successors, *Missouri Republican* and the St.
Louis *Republic; Louisiana Gazette*, 1812; Memphis *Ava-
lanche;* Louisville *Courier-Journal;* Cincinnati *Commercial-
Gazette;* Cincinnati *Enquirer;* Pittsburgh *Dispatch; Hall's
West;* Internal Commerce of the United States, by Wm. F.
Switzler; Mark Twain's Life on the Mississippi; Commodore
Preble's History of Steam Navigation; Floyd's Steamboat
Directory; St. Louis *Scrap-Book;* Sharf's History of St.
Louis; Niles' *Register;* Potter's *American Monthly; Columbia
Magazine*, and libraries in Washington, New York, Cincinnati,
and St. Louis — also to Mr. T. Kytka, the artist who has
furnished the illustrations, among which will be seen some fine
pen and *ink* sketches from portraits.

(v)

GOULD'S HISTORY

OF

RIVER NAVIGATION.

CHAPTER I.

INTRODUCTORY REMARKS.

IN writing a history of navigation on the rivers of the Mississippi valley, it is so initmately connected with the settlement of the country, the character and habits of the early navigators — the modes of early transportation, the invention of steam — its application to navigation — the names and the peculiarities of its inventors and promoters, its effect upon the development of the valley, morally and physically, that to write intelligently of the one necessarily involves that of the others.

Therefore all will be considered as nearly in chronological order as the nature of the various subjects will permit.

While the writer can only speak from his own personal observations and experience from 1835 to the present time (1889), he has through the public records and the courtesy of friends secured reliable data sufficient to warrant an interesting book for the general reader and a valuable one as a book of reference to those more intimately connected with navigation.

It will not be necessary to remind those who are acquainted with the cares and duties of a *practical boatman* that but little time and less inclination to cultivate the faculty of *book making* or book writing remains.

Consequently this class of readers will expect but little beyond the careful compilation of facts, collected from the im-

ware river, at Philadelphia, about the 20th of July, 1786.
These trials were made with a steam engine of three-inch cylinder which moved a screw paddle—an endless chain having
paddles fixed upon it, and placed on the sides of the boat; and
they tested one or two other modes of propulsion. The skiff
was moved by the power of steam, but not so swiftly as to
satisfy the hopes of the inventors. They changed the method
of working by the employment of oars in the side of the skiff,
which were moved by cranks and beams. This skiff was then
propelled at the rate of seven miles per hour on the 27th of
July, 1786.

"The second vessel ever moved by steam was forty-five feet

FITCH'S FIRST SUCCESSFUL STEAMBOAT.

long with twelve feet beam. The engine was a twelve-inch
cylinder.

"Six oars or paddles working perpendicularly were on
each side of the boat. Of this boat we give a copy of an
engraving which appeared in the Columbia Magazine for December, 1786.

"In the same periodical appeared Fitch's account of this
steamboat, as follows:

"'PHILADELPHIA, December 8, 1786. _Sir._—The reason
for my so long deferring to give you a description of my steam
boat has been in some measure owing to the complication of
the works and an apprehension that a number of drafts would
be necessary in order to show the powers of the machine as
clearly as you could wish. 'But as I have not been able to

hand you herewith such drafts, I can only give you the general principals." " 'It is in several parts similar to the late improved steam engines in Europe, though there are some alterations. Our cylinder is too horizontal to work with equal force at each end.

" ' The mode by which we obtain (what I take the liberty of terming) a vacuum is, we believe, entirely new ; as is also the method of letting the water into it, and throwing it off against the atmosphere without any friction. It is expected that the engine, which is a twelve-inch cylinder, will move with a clear force of eleven or twelve cwt., after the friction is deducted.

" ' This force is to work against a wheel of eighteen inches diameter. The piston is to move about three feet and each vibration of the piston gives the axis about forty evolutions. Each evolution of the axis moves twelve oars or paddles five and a half feet, which work perpendicularly, and are represented by the stroke of the paddle of a canoe. As six of the paddles are raised from the water, six more are entered. And the two sets of paddles make two strokes of about eleven feet in each evolution.

" ' The cranks of axis act upon the paddles about one-third of their length from the lower end on which part of the oar the whole force of the axis is applied.

" ' Our engine is placed on the boat about one-third from the stern, and with the action and reaction, turn the wheel the same way.

" ' With the most perfect respect, sir, I beg leave to subscribe myself your very humble servant," JOHN FITCH.' "

" This Steam Boat was finished and tried upon the Delaware at Philadelphia, August 27th, 1787, in the presence of a large number of members of the convention to frame the *Federal Constitution*.

" They were all satisfied with the trip, and special certificates were given to Fitch by Governor Randolph of Virginia, David Rittenhouse, Dr. John Emering, provost of the University of Pennsylvania, Professor Andrew Elliott, of the same Institution, and many others.

" The third boat propelled by steam in the United States, was built by James Rumsey, of Virginia, and tried Dec. 3, 1787, at Shepardstown, Virginia.

" This boat was propelled by sucking in water at the bow and ejecting it at the stern. It moved at the rate of four miles per hour, but only made one trip, and probably did not go a half mile in distance. ,

"About the close of 1788 John Fitch organized a company in Philadelphia under whose auspices he built a small Steam Packet sixty feet long, and eight feet beam.

"This was the fourth steam boat. The oars or paddles on this boat were located in the stern and pushed against the water.

"The engine was of the same size as the one previously built by Fitch.

"Towards the end of July a trip was made to Burlington, New Jersey, it being probably the longest trip hitherto made by any steamboat.

"In October of the same year another trip was made to Burlington with thirty passengers, the time occupied being three hours and ten minutes.

"The average rate of this boat was about four miles per hour, which the company did not consider fast enough. They therefore determined to build another.

"This fifth boat was finished in 1789 and had an 18-inch cylinder. The rate of speed attained was eight miles per hour. During 1790 it was run regularly on the Delaware for the conveyance of both passengers and freight. But the company failed that year and the boat was withdrawn. About this time experiments were conducted on the Connecticut river by Samuel Morey, who built the *sixth steamboat* in the United States, which he propelled from Hartford to New York in 1794 at the rate of speed of five miles per hour.

"At the same time John Fitch tried his steamboat projects in France without success, the times being unpropitious on account of the excesses of the French Revolution.

"In 1796 he returned to New York where he built a yawl which was propelled by a *screw propeller*, at the stern. It was tried upon a fresh water pond called the Collect, under the patronage of Robert R. Livingston.

"In the following year Samuel Morey of Connecticut constructed at Bodentown, New Jersey, a steamboat with paddle-wheels at the sides, which was propelled to Philadelphia the same year and publicly exhibited.

"During subsequent years, other steamboats were built by Fitch, Oliver Evens and John Fox Stephenson, there being *eleven* in all previous to the year 1807."

CHAPTER III.

THEN came Robert Fulton with the *twelfth* steamboat, which was twenty-one years after Fitch's first experiments. So, contrary to the common impression, Fulton, instead of being the inventor of steamboats, was only the successful adopter of the discoveries and ideas of others who preceded him. We must not, however, underestimate the real service he has rendered to the science of steam navigation nor the value of his original experiments. While in Birmingham, England, he familiarized himself with the steam engine, then first improved by Watt. He had in September, 1793, addressed a letter to Lord Stanhope respecting the moving of vessels by the means of steam, and had been aided in France by Chancellor Livingston, who had procured an act by the New York legislature, giving to Fulton and himself the exclusive privilege of navigating the waters of that State by steam. In 1807 the "Clermont" was built and traversed the Hudson River at the rate of five miles per hour. That vessel was very unlike any of its successors, and even dissimilar in shape from which it appeared a few months afterwards. With a model like a Long Island skiff, it was decked for a short distance at the stem and stern. The engine was open to view, and from the engine aft, a house like that of a canal boat was raised to cover the boilers and the apartments for the officers. In these, by the addition of a few berths, the passengers were accommodated. There were no wheel-guards or covers. The rudder was like that used by sailing vessels, and worked by a tiller. The boiler was in form like that used in Watt's engines, and was set in masonry. The condenser was the size used on land engines, and stood in a large cold water cistern. The weight of the masonry and the great capacity of the cold water cistern, diminished very materially the buoyancy of the vessel. At this point, Fulton's ingenuity and versatility of invention, were called into play. To the eye of the world the experiment was successful, and yet was so imperfect as to be liable to continual accident and annoyance. The rudder had so little power that the vessel could hardly be managed and could not be made to veer around even in the whole breadth of the Hudson river at New York. The spray from the wheels dashed over the passengers, and the skippers of the river craft, taking advantage of the unwieldiness of the vessel, did not fail to run afoul of her as often as they thought they had the law on their side. Thus in several instances the steamboat reached one termini or the other of its route with but a single wheel. Before the season closed, the wheel was surrounded by a frame of strong beams, and the paddles were covered in. The rudder had taken the shape of a rectangle, of large iron of horizontal dimensions.

This rudder was worked by a wheel, the ropes of which were attached to the end next distant from the pivotals. The vessel of the last mentioned arrangement became so navigable as to be capable of veering at Albany, and was more likely to inflict than to receive injury, by an encounter with sailing vessels. During the winter of 1807–8 the Clermont was almost entirely rebuilt. The hull was considerably lengthened and covered from stem to stern with a flush deck. Beneath this two cabins were formed, and surrounded by double ranges of berths, fitted up in a manner then unexampled for comfort. The vessel was then advertised to run at stated periods, between New York and Albany, as a packet. The time of her first departure being the first Wednesday in May, 1808. On that day Fulton himself was on board. The first marked incident was leaving several passengers who had ventured to trust to the want of punctuality then usual in the departure of vessels.

The rule of starting at the exact hour was then enforced for the first time, and from that rule there was no deviation thereafter. The whole passage on this trip was made in less than forty hours, including a delay of two hours at Chancellor Livingston's seat — "Clermont." Symptoms of difficulty were manifested, however, on the upward passage. Mr. Fulton appeared anxious and abstracted. Finally steam began to make its appearance in very minute jets through the joints of a wooden trunk, that was at first considered by the passengers as the case of the boiler. It was at last found to be the boiler itself, and it was whispered that Fulton had been overruled by his associates and that a cylinder of wooden staves, containing fire place and flues of copper had been substituted for the boiler of Watt, instead of replacing by a new boiler of copper. This form of boiler had been proposed, but as far as we can learn had never been used by Watt. On the return voyage the leaks in the boiler continued to increase. The speed of the vessel, although aided by a flood in the river, became less and less, and after fifty-seven hours of struggling the engine ceased to work.

The vessel was then at the foot of Christopher street, New York City. The flood tide made itself felt in opposition to

CLERMONT AS ORIGINALLY BUILT.

its progress, and the passengers considered it better to make
a landing, and find their way on foot to peopled parts of the
city. On the upward passage the officer in command was
Captain Jenkins. During the downward passage Captain
Wesswell came on board and assumed command, replacing
Captain Jenkins. As the vessel approached upper Red Hood,
while Wesswell was trying his best to appear to advantage
before his owners, the boat grounded. Blame was laid by
him on the pilot, which led after a torrent of vituperation on
each side, to blows, in which one of the parties was knocked
down, and one received a black eye. This was the first and
last act of insubordination in that line. It took some weeks
to secure a new boiler, after the expiration of which the
Clermont resumed her proper trips.

In the month of September, in 1809, there occurred the exciting scene then first enacted of a steamboat race. A company had been formed at Albany for the purpose of competing with Fulton. The first vessel of the rival line was
advertised to leave at the same time with Fulton. Party
feeling ran high at Albany in the hotels and in all public
places. The partizans of Fulton were enrolled under Professor Kemp of the Columbia College — those of the opposition
under Captain Jacob Stout.

The victory was long in suspense, and it was not until after
the thirteenth hour of a hard struggle that the result was proclaimed by Dr. Kemp standing on the taffrail of Fulton's
vessel, and holding out in derision a coil of rope to Captain
Scott, for the purpose, as he informed him, of towing him
into port.

Fulton's second large boat on the Hudson was the "Car of
Neptune," which was also built in 1809. In 1809 he obtained
his first patent from the United States, and in 1811 took out a
second patent for some improvement in his boats and machinery. They were limited to the simple means of adapting
paddle wheels to the axle of the crank of Watt's engine.

In addition to the two vessels already mentioned, Fulton
constructed ferry boats, to run between New York and New
Jersey, a boat for the navigation of Long Island Sound, five
for the Hudson river, and several for different parts of the
United States, including a number for the Ohio and the Mississippi rivers.

CHAPTER IV.

IN THE *Missouri Gazette*, published in St. Louis, in 1808, an article appears by which it may be seen something of the feeling then pervading the public mind on the subject of Steamboat Navigation.

"The steamboat is certainly an interesting curiosity to strangers. To see this large and apparently unwieldly machine without oars or sails propelled through the element by invisible agency at the rate of four miles an hour would be a novelty in any quarter of the globe. As we understand there is none in Europe upon the plan upon which this is constructed. The length of the boat is one hundred and ninety feet, and her width in proportion."

The machine which moves her wheels is called, we believe, a twenty-four horse machine. Or equal to the power of twenty-four horses, and is kept in motion by steam from a copper boiler of eight or ten feet in length. The wheels are on each side similar to those on water mills and under cover. They are moved backward separately or together, at pleasure.

"Her principle advantage is in calms or against head-winds. When the wind is fair, light square sails, etc., are employed to increase her speed. Her accommodations are fifty-two berths, besides sofas, etc., and are said to be equal to any vessel that floats on the river, as all the space occupied by the machinery is fitted in the most convenient way.

"Between New York and Albany is a distance of one hundred and sixty miles, which she performs regularly twice a week; sometimes in the short space of time of thirty-two hours, exclusive of detention in taking in and landing passengers.

"On her passage last week she left New York with over a hundred passengers, and Albany with eighty or ninety. Indeed this aquatic stage from Albany, with the excitement, bids fair to attract the greatest part of the travelers which pass the Hudson, and afford them accommodations not exceeded in any other part of the world."

The following letters will be read with interest in this connection, showing the character and confidence of Mr. Fulton in this important motive power, then for the first time being practically applied in developing the great resources of the then almost unknown country.

The first letter was written on the return of the steamboat

"Clermont" from Albany, in August, 1807, and published in a New York paper. On this voyage Mr. Fulton had been a passenger on the boat. He writes:

"TO THE EDITOR OF THE AMERICAN CITIZEN :

"*Sir:*—I arrived this afternoon at four o'clock, in the steamboat from Albany. As the success of my experiments gives me great hopes that such boats may be rendered of great importance to my country, to prevent envious opinions, and to give some satisfaction to the friends of useful improvements, you will have the goodness to publish the following letter:"

"'I left New York on Monday at one o'clock, and arrived at Clermont, the seat of Chancellor Livingston, at one o'clock on Tuesday. Time, twenty-four hours; distance, one hundred and ten miles.

On Wednesday I departed from the Chancellor's at nine in the morning, and arrived at Albany at five in the afternoon. Distance, forty miles; time, eight hours. The total is one hundred and fifty miles, in thirty-two hours — equal to near five miles an hour.

On Thursday, at nine o'clock in the morning, I left Albany, and arrived at the Chancellor's at six in the evening. I started from there at seven, and arrived in New York at four in the evening. Time, thirty hours; space run through, one hundred and fifty miles, equal to five miles an hour.

Throughout my whole way, both going and returning, the wind was ahead. No advantage could be derived from sails. The whole has therefore been performed by the power of the steam engine.'"   I am, your obedient servant,

ROBERT FULTON."

Life of Robert Fulton, by C. D. Colden, 1817.

The second letter was addressed to Joel Barlow, a personal friend, living in Philadelphia:

"'NEW YORK, August, 2. 1807.

"MY DEAR FRIEND:—My steamboat voyage to Albany and back has turned out rather more favorably than I had calculated.

The distance from New York is one hundred and fifty miles. I ran it up in thirty-two hours and down in thirty hours. The latter is just five miles an hour.

I had a light breeze against me going and coming, so no use was made of my sails and the voyage has been performed wholly by the use of my engine. I overtook many sloops and schooners, beating to windward, and passed them as if they had been at anchor.

The power of propelling boats by steam is now fully proved. The morning I left New York there was not perhaps thirty persons in the city who believed the boat would ever be moved one mile an hour, or be of the least utility, and while we were putting off from the wharf, which was crowded with spectators, I heard a number of sarcastic remarks. This is the way, you know, in which ignorant men compliment what they call philosophers and projectors.

Having employed much time, money and zeal, in accomplishing this work, it gives me, as it will you, great pleasure to see it so fully answer my expectations.

It will give a cheap and quick conveyance on the Mississippi and Missouri, and other great rivers, which are now laying open their treasures to the enterprise of our countrymen, and although the prospects of personal emoluments has been some inducement to me, yet I feel infinitely more pleasure in reflecting with you, on the immense advantage my country will derive from the invention.

However, I will not admit that it is half as important as the *torpedo* defense and attack. For out of this will grow the liberty of the seas, an object of infinite importance to the welfare of America and every civilized country.

But thousands of witnesses have now seen the steamboat in rapid movement, and they believe. They have not seen a ship of war destroyed by a torpedo, and they do not believe.

We cannot expect people in general, will have a knowledge of physics, or power of mind sufficient to combine ideas, and reason from causes to effects. But in case we have war, and the enemies ships come into our waters, if the government will give me reasonable cause of action, I will even convince the world that we have surer and cheaper modes of defense than they are aware of.

Yours, etc.,
ROBERT FULTON."

Niles Register, vol. 33, 1822.

As an illustration of the fear and surprise manifested by those that were navigating the Hudson river, and the citizens living upon its banks, at the time the *Clermont* made her first trip, the following graphic account is found among the papers.

published at that time, and brings to mind a similar experience of the early boatmen on the waters of the Mississippi valley a few years later.

" The Clermont, on her first voyage, excited the astonishment of the inhabitants on the shores of the Hudson, many of whom had not even heard of an engine, much less of a steamboat.

There were many descriptions of the effects of her first appearance upon the people on the banks of the river. Some of them were ridiculous. But some of them were of such a character as nothing but an object of real grandeur could have excited.

She was described by some who had indistinctly seen her passing in the night, to those who had not had a view of her, as a monster moving on the waters, defying the winds and the tide, and breathing flames and smoke. She had the most terrific appearance from other vessels which were navigating the river when she was making this passage.

The first steamboats, as others still do, used dry pine wood for fuel, which sends forth a volume of ignited vapor many feet above the flue, and whenever the fire is stirred a galaxy of sparks fly off, and in the night have a very brilliant and beautiful appearance.

This *uncommon light* first attracted the crews of other vessels.

Notwithstanding the winds and tides were adverse to its approach, they saw, with astonishment, that it was rapidly coming towards them. And when it came so near that the noise of the machinery and paddle wheels were heard, the crews (if what was said by the newspapers was true), in some instances, sank beneath their decks, from the terrific sight, and left their vessels to go on shore, while others prostrated themselves, and besought Providence to protect them from the approach of the horrible monster which was marching on the tides, and lighting its path by its fire, which it was vomiting."

While it cannot be claimed that Mr. Fulton was the inventor or the first to apply steam to navigation, no one can deny that he is entitled to far more credit than any one else for its practical application for purposes of navigation, as well as for railroads and other modern inventions.

In fact, history gives no account of any other so brilliant and practical a genius as Robert Fulton, and posterity can never appreciate the loss of such a benefactor to the race.

He passed away in the zenith of his usefulness, in the city of New York, February 24th, 1815, in the fiftieth year of his age.

It seems surprising that so important and powerful an agent as steam should have lain dormant for so many centuries awaiting the advent of a mind with sufficient force and genius to control and utilize it.

While Watt, Fitch, Evens, Stephens, Morey, Ramsey, and others anticipated Fulton by several years in the application of steam, even in navigation, yet it remained for him to develop its wonderful power and utility not only as a motive agent in navigation, but in all branches of industry.

And hence it is that Robert Fulton's name is prominently associated with everything connected with the discovery and application of steam as a motive power.

It is claimed with some degree of probability, that a Spaniard by the name of Blasco de Gary, constructed in Spain, in 1543, a steamboat, under the patronage of King Charles the Fifth, and successfully tried her in the harbor of Barcelona.

From the fact that nothing further ever resulted from that experiment, so far as the record goes, it is hardly probable that it proved satisfactory.

At that period Spain was in position, and her commerce and enterprise was such that it seems strange an invention so important to her prosperity should have failed to attract the attention of the government or of her enterprising citizens.

CHAPTER V.

JOHN FITCH.

IT IS shown by the most irrefragable testimony that John Fitch was the first man, in America at least, and probably in the world, who ever carried this idea of applying steam power to the propulsion of vessels to any determinate result. A certificate from Dr. Thornton, of the Patent Office at Washington, states that Fitch took out a patent for the application of steam to navigation in the year 1788, before which time no similar patent had been issued in this country. The earliest ascertained experiments of Mr. Fulton in steam navigation took place about the year 1798, ten years after the date of John Fitch's patent. Oliver Evans, in 1804, propelled a mud-scow by steam on the Schuylkill river. Mr. Fulton's first experimental boat was built at Paris, in 1803. His first American steamboat was launched in the spring of 1807.

Fitch brought his plan to the test of experiment on the Delaware river a short time after he took out his patent. The following description is given of the machinery as contrived by Fitch: "The cylinder is horizontal, the steam working with equal force at both ends. The piston moves about three feet, and each vibration of it gives the axis forty revolutions. Each revolution of the axis moves twelve oars or paddles five and a half feet; they work perpendicularly and are represented by the strokes of a paddle of a canoe. As six of the paddles are raised from the water, six more are entered, and the two sets of paddles make their strokes of about eleven feet in each revolution. The crank of the axis acts upon the paddles about one-third of their length from the lower ends, to which part of the oar the whole force of the axis is applied. The engine is placed in the bottom of the boat, about one-third from the stern, and both the action and reaction turn the wheel the same way."

This description was written by the inventor himself, and was first published in Philadelphia *Columbian Magazine*, vol. I, for December, 1786.

Fitch's boat was tried, as previously stated, on the Delaware river, in front of Philadelphia. The boat was ordered under way at slack water, and, by the most accurate measurement, was found to go at the rate of eight miles per hour, or one mile in six minutes and a half. It afterwards went eighty miles in a day.

The Governor and Council of Pennsylvania expressed their satisfaction with the result of this experiment by presenting to the proprietors of the boat a superb silk flag, emblazoned with the arms of the State. But, after all this magnificent demonstration the most glorious achievement of American ingenuity was permitted to fall into utter neglect.

Dr. Thornton states that the company which had been formed under the Fitch patents to give the plan a proper trial — now, when the trial has been made, and when all reasonable doubts respecting the practicability and utility of the invention should have vanished — refused to advance any more money. It seems that those noble-spirited gentlemen, who constituted the first steamboat company ever organized, disbanded themselves because they were afraid to meet the "unceasing ridicule" which this project had excited. Not even the practical realization of the plan could prevent fools from laughing at it as an insane speculation; nor could the sight of a veritable steamboat, paddling along the Delaware, enable wise men to treat this idiotic merriment with contempt.

The company was dissolved, the boat was laid up in the docks, and the whole matter was abandoned, and John Fitch was fated to descend to the tomb without seeing the great object of his life accomplished, or the importance and value of his invention duly appreciated by his countrymen.

Justice to the memory of John Fitch forbids the admission of one particular incident of his life, which establishes beyond all cavil his claim to the invention of the steamboat. Before the dissolution of the company just referred to, Aaron Vail, Esq., one of the members who was then the American consul at L'Orient, sent over a request for Mr. Fitch to visit France, in order to have the steamboat experiment tried in that country. Fitch went over, accordingly, but on his arrival, owing to a scarcity of shipwrights, and other causes incident to the French Revolution, the enterprise failed, and Fitch returned to his own country, leaving his draughts and documents relating to his invention in the hands of Mr. Vail. These papers were exhibited by Mr. Vail to Robert Fulton, when that gentleman visited France several years afterwards and Mr. Fulton took copies, notes and memoranda which enabled him subsequently (he being more fortunate than John Fitch in finding assistance and resources) to complete the great work of which so considerable a part had already been executed by the ill-starred Fitch.

To the very end of his life John Fitch had unwavering confidence in his neglected and despised contrivance. He struggled manfully to bring it once more into the scope of public observation; but the public, when it had kindness to refrain from mockery, merely made an exclamation of sorrow and pity, like that of Ophelia—

"Oh, what a noble mind is here o'erthrown!"

Once, when he had been explaining the benefits of steam navigation to a party of gentlemen who heard his glowing description with significant smiles, one of the auditors remarked, after he had retired, "What a pity that the poor fellow is crazy!" When the experimental boat had been finally laid up, as aforesaid, Fitch, in a letter to Mr. Rittenhouse, wrote: "It would be much easier to carry a first-rate man-of-war by steam than a boat, as we would not be cramped for room, nor would the weight of the machinery be felt. This, sir, will be the mode of crossing the Atlantic in time, whether I bring it to perfection or not."

Fitch returned from Europe to his own country, destitute

2

and heartbroken. For two years he was obliged to depend for his daily bread on the kindness of a relation, Colonel George King, of Sharon, Connecticut. But having purchased some cheap lands in Kentucky, while he was surveying there in 1796, he now went thither to take possession of this little property in the wilderness. But even this gratification was not allowed him, for having been thrown into a fever by fatigue and exposure, he died two or three days after his arrival. According to his request, John Fitch was buried on the shores of the Ohio, where (to use his own enthusiastic language), "the song of the boatman would enliven the stillness of his resting place, and the music of the steam engine soothe his spirit." His manuscript journal contains the following prophetic exclamation:—

"The day will come when some more powerful man will get fame and riches from my invention, but nobody will believe that poor John Fitch can do anything worthy of attention!"

"I know of nothing so perplexing and vexatious to a man of feelings, as a turbulent wife and steamboat building. I experienced the former and quit in season, and had I been in my right senses I should undoubtedly have treated the latter in the same manner, but for one man to be teased with both, he must be looked upon as the most unfortunate man of this world."

The theory of steam navigation on water had been evolved and considered for more than 200 years before it actually took shape.

James Rumsey was engaged in experiments from 1784 to 1786, when he tried a boat on the Potomac, which made four miles an hour, propelled by a jet of water forced from the stern.

In the same year the paddle steamer, shown in the illustration, was invented and built in Philadelphia, Pa., by John Fitch, of Windsor, Conn. After many disappointments and misfortunes in applying steam to the propulsion of vessels, Mr. Fitch finally triumphed over repeated failures. Successful experiments on the Delaware river, at Philadelphia, were made in 1786, 1787, 1788, 1789, and in 1790 he ran a regular packet by steam for passengers and freight on the Delaware which, for more than three months, made regular trips between Philadelphia and certain towns on said river with ease and safety, and without material stoppage, accident or delay.

The propelling instruments used by Fitch were paddles suspended by the upper ends of their shafts and moved by cranks. The boat shown in the cut was sixty feet long, very lightly built.

The second steamboat in the world was invented by Mr. Symington in England.

It was tried in 1788, but only practically succeeded in 1801.

The third steamboat in the world was invented by Robert Fulton, and his first experiments were made in Plombieres in 1803, whilst his triumphs on the Hudson were delayed until 1807, twenty-one years after Fitch propelled his first skiff steamboat on the Delaware.

Patent-right granted to John Fitch. From G. H. Preble's "History of Steam Navigation."

' On the 26th of August, 1791, John Fitch obtained a U. S. patent for his invention which is signed by George Washington, president. Thomas Jefferson, Secretary of State, who also testifies that the patent was delivered to him August 30th.

The patent recites, " he having invented the following useful devices not before known or used, viz.," for applying the force of steam to a trunk or trunks, for drawing water in to the bow of a boat or vessel, and forcing the same out at the stern, in order to propel the boat or vessel through the water, for forcing a column of air through a trunk or trunks filled with water by the force of steam, and for applying the force of steam to cranks, paddles, for propelling a boat or vessel through the water.

The said John Fitch, his heirs, etc., were granted for the time of fourteen years the sole and exclusive right and liberty of making, using and vending to others the said inventions.'

JOHN FITCH'S WILL AND GRAVE.

The remains of John Fitch were interred in the village graveyard of Bardstown, Nelson county, Ky., in the rear of the court house and county jail, in 1798. Not a pebble of all the fine stone in the land marks his last resting place. But his last will and testament are on record, as copied by a correspondent of the Philadelphia *Evening Telegram*, viz.:

" I, John Fitch, of the county of Nelson, do make this, my last will and testament:

To Wm. Rowan, Esquire, my trusty friend, my beaver hat, shoe, knee and stock buckles, walking stick and spectacles.

To Dr. William Thornton, of Washington, D. C., to Eliza Vail, daughter of Aaron Vail, Council of the W. S. at L'Orient, to John Rowan, Esquire, of Bardstown, son of said William, and to James Nourse of said town, I bequeath all the rest of my estate, real and personal, to be divided among them share and share alike. And I appoint the said

John Rowan, Esquire, and James Nourse, Esquire, my executors, and the legacies hereby bequeathed to them, my said
executors is in consideration of their accepting the executor-
ship and bringing to a final close all suits at law and attending to the business of estate hereby bequeathed. Hereby
declaring this to be my last will and testament, this the 20th
day of June, 1798 — witness my hand and seal.
     Acknowledged, signed and sealed in presence of
                                   JAMES NOURSE,
                                   MICHAEL RENCH,
                                         her
                              SUSANAH + McCOWN.
                                        mark.
     On the 10th of July, following, the will was passed by the
executors and ordered to be recorded."

CHAPTER VI.

ROBERT FULTON.

WHILE we accord to John Fitch the credit which is justly
      due to him as the true and original contriver of the
steamboat, with equal justice we will make the acknowledgment, that the subject of the present sketch, by his firmness
of purpose and energy of character, no less than by his brilliant genius and correct judgment, carried the enterprise
through to a successful and glorious termination.   Robert
Fulton was born in the town of Little Britain, Lancaster
county, Pennsylvania (A. D. 1765). His father, a native of
Kilkenny, Ireland, was in very moderate circumstances, which
may explain the fact that Robert's early education was somewhat neglected. His earliest tastes inclined him to observe
the operations of different mechanics, in whose shops he
passed most of his leisure hours. Having a natural talent for
the use of the pencil he began at the age of twelve years to
cultivate this gift, and before he had reached his fifteenth
year, he became, in the estimation of his rural neighbors,
quite an expert artist. Two years later he practiced portrait
and landscape painting in Philadelphia. Here he soon acquired money enough to purchase a small farm in Washington
county, where he provided his widowed mother with a comfortable home, while he made preparations for a voyage to-

England, according to the advice of some of his friends, for
the purpose of exhibiting some of his paintings to his countryman, Benjamin West.   Mr. West, at this time, enjoyed the
favor and patronage of the British government, and his reputation as one of the first painters of the age was already established.   He received young Fulton with much kindness, gave
him all possible encouragement, and offered him a home in
his own house, where he remained for two years.   At the
end of that time Mr. Fulton traveled through different parts
of England, and became acquainted with several distinguished
men of science.

It is supposed that at this period of his life he began to
devote his attention exclusively to mechanical inventions.   In
his twenty-fifth year (A. D. 1793), he was actively engaged in
a project to improve inland navigation, and one year later he
obtained from the British government a patent for a double
inclined plane, to be used for transportation.   We have no
particular account of his transactions during several years
following, though in 1794 he submitted to the British Society
for the Promotion of Arts and Commerce, an improvement in
his invention of mills for sawing marble.   His patents for
two machines, one for spinning flax, and the other for making
ropes, are dated 1795.   In the next year he published at
London his treatise on the Improvement of Canal Navigation.
In this work he expresses his preference for small canals, and
boats of light burden, and contends for the use of inclined
planes instead of locks.   His plans were highly approved by
the British Board of Agriculture.

Mr. Fulton was now engaged in the profession of a civil
engineer, and employed the pencil merely to execute plans
and draughts of machinery in connection with his professional
duties.   He now visited France, for the purpose of introducing his canal improvements into that country.   In the year
1797 he became acquainted with the celebrated Joel Barlow,
who then resided at Paris.   In the family of this distinguished
American, Mr. Fulton took up his abode for several years,
during which time he studied the French, Italian and German
languages, and perfected himself in the high mathematics,
chemistry and natural philosophy.

In 1797 Messrs. Fulton and Barlow made experiments on
the river Seine with a machine which the former had constructed on the torpedo principle. the object of which was to
destroy an enemy's ships by submarine explosions.   These
experiments proved unsuccessful.   But not at all discouraged
by his first failure, Mr. Fulton pursued this object until his

plan for propelling and steering a boat under water was
brought to perfection. When this satisfactory result was
attained, he applied to the French Directory for pecuniary
assistance, but that body did not appreciate the invention. He
then applied to the British government, but met with similar
discouragement in that quarter. In the meantime, Bonaparte
had placed himself at the head of public affairs in France, and
he, not being one of the "old fogy" school, promptly responded to Mr. Fulton's application by appointing a commission to examine the new war-like machine. The examining
committee having made a favorable report, Mr. Fulton was
supplied by Napoleon with a sufficiency of funds to bring
some of his plans to the test of experiment. He first made a
trial of the "plunging boat" at Brest, in 1801. Notwithstanding many imperfections in the machinery, and other disadvantages incident to a first experiment, he demonstrated
that, by means of this contrivance, a sufficiency of light and
air could be obtained under water; that the boat could be
made to descend to any depth, or rise to the surface with perfect facility, and that she would tack or veer as rapidly as
any common sailing boat. On the 7th of August Mr. Fulton
descended with a store of air compressed in a copper globe,
and was thus enabled to remain under water nearly four hours
and a half. He next attempted to put this invention to its
proper use by blowing up English vessels cruising near the
harbor of Brest; for this purpose he provided his plunging
boat with a torpedo, or submarine bomb, and approaching a
small British vessel within a distance of two hundred yards,
he blew her to atoms. A similar attempt was made on an
English seventy-four, which saved herself at the critical
moment by an accidental change of position.

The advantages of a submarine warfare were not fully estimated in Europe, and Mr. Fulton having become disgusted
with the tardy action of several European governments in relation to this subject, returned to his own country in 1806.
He found the American government very propitious to his
undertakings, and a grant of sufficient funds was made to enable him to put the capabilities of his torpedo to a fair trial.
By means of one of these Jewels of Belona, he blew up, and
totally annihilated, a large hulk brig, which had been prepared for the purpose in the harbor of New York. In 1810
Congress granted $5,000 to meet the expenses of additional
experiments with Fulton's explosive apparatus, and a committee was appointed to superintend these trials. The old
sloop-of-war Argus, under the direction of Commodore

Rogers, was prepared for defense against the torpedoes, and that skillful commander did his best to make them ineffective. In these circumstances, Mr. Fulton did not succeed in his main design of blowing up the vessel, but he approached in his submarine boat near enough to cut off a fourteen inch cable attached to the Argus. He himself did not consider this experiment on the Argus a failure, attributing his want of success to various defects in the explosive machinery, for which it was easy to find remedies.

But the thoughts of Fulton now reverted to the subject of steam navigation, a subject upon which he had bestowed considerable study during his residence in Paris. In this enterprise he possessed one grand advantage over all who had preceded him, being enabled to avail himself of the great improvements which Watt and others had made in steam machinery. But for certain adaptations of the machinery to the object required, he was obliged to depend on his own inventive powers, in the absence of all precedent to direct his course. The paddle-wheel now used in steamboats appears to have been originally devised by Mr. Fulton. It should have been mentioned, by the way, that Messrs. Fulton and Livingston made an actual experiment with steam propulsion in France, in 1803. This experiment, however, was on a very small scale, and the result being not quite satisfactory, and as other objects demanded Mr. Fulton's attention, this project was temporarily set aside, nor was it resumed until some time after his return to this country.

Mr. Fulton took out his first patent for improvements in steam navigation on the 11th day of February, 1809, and on the 9th day of February, 1811, he obtained supplementary patents for further improvements in his boats and machinery. The pecuniary means required for carrying out these great designs were supplied by Mr. Livingston, a gentleman of great wealth and equal liberality, who had assisted Mr. Fulton in his steamboat experiments at Paris, and never at any time withheld his aid when the enterprise required it. The legislature of New York having passed an act which secured to Messrs. Fulton and Livingston the exclusive benefits of steam navigation on the waters of that State for the term of twenty years, the last named gentleman caused a boat of about thirty tons to be built, but her dimensions being found insufficient, she was soon abandoned. In 1807 a steam engine was ordered from the manufactory of Watt & Bolton, of Birmingham, England; it was constructed according to the specifications furnished by Mr. Fulton, who did not permit the manufacturers to know for what purpose it was intended. A suitable boat for the reception of this engine had been built at the ship-yard of Charles Brown, on the East river. The engine was put on board, and the boat was soon after moved by her machinery to the Jersey shore. This experimental trip was witnessed by a number of the principal citizens, including several men of science, whom Messrs. Fulton and Livingston had invited to be present on the occasion.

At this time it is difficult to believe that a great majority of the people of that day had no faith in this undertaking. The common belief was that the boat could not be made to move a foot from the wharf, and the crowd of spectators now assembled to behold the result very freely indulged in sarcastic remarks, aimed at what they were pleased to call the folly or insanity of the projectors. When, therefore, the boat actually left the shore, and began to plough her way through the still waters, the multitude for a while stood gazing in mute astonishment, mingled with awe, at what they considered a miracle of art. But when the boat, having reached the center of the river, turned her head down the stream and began to rush forward with increased velocity, the whole concourse, as if moved by one spirit, uttered a deafening and prolonged shout of applause and congratulation. Who can imagine the feelings of Robert Fulton at that moment? The day of recompense had arrived; his toils, travels, severe studies and frequent disappointments were unrequited no longer. He knew then that he had achieved a triumph which the world would acknowledge in all time to come. Here, then, for once, a public benefactor received, while living, the homage which his genius and his services to the cause of human progress had deserved.

This first boat, whose performance so electrified the spectators, was called the Clermont. When some errors in the construction of the machinery had been corrected she made a trial trip to Albany, and performed that voyage of one hundred and fifty miles in about thirty hours, against the wind. Soon after the Clermont became a regular passage boat between New York and Albany. Certain Quixotic persons conceived about these times that "pendulum power" might be made to rival steam as a propelling force, and a boat was actually built on that principle. As many had foreseen, however, the momentum of the pendulum could not overcome the resistance of the water, and this boat remained as stationary as the dock itself.

The exclusive right to steam navigation on the rivers of

New York, which the legislature had granted to Livingston
and Fulton, was not duly respected, for several opposition
boats were soon started. These were slightly varied from
Fulton's mode of construction, in order to avoid an obvious
infringement on his patent. Fulton and Livingston attempted
to assert their rights by recourse to the law, and applied to
the Circuit Court of the United States for an injunction; but
this court decided that it had no jurisdiction in the case. The
application was renewed in the Chancery of the State, but
after hearing the argument, the chancellor refused to grant
an injunction. The Supreme Court, however, reversed the
chancellor's decision, and ordered a perpetual injunction on
the opposition boats.

In the year 1812, two steam ferryboats for crossing the
Hudson river, and one for the East river, were built under
Mr. Fulton's directions. Thenceforth steamboats began to
increase and multiply, and improvements were gradually introduced by Mr. Fulton up to the time of his death. It has
been remarked in commendation of his progressive skill and
judgment, that the last boat built by him was always the best,
the swiftest and the most convenient.

About the beginning of the last war with England, Mr. Fulton exhibited to a committee of citizens of New York the
model of a steam man-of-war, provided with a strong battery,
furnaces for red hot shot, etc. Several distinguished naval
commanders had already pointed out the advantages which
must result from the employment of steam in propelling war
vessels, and Mr. Fulton's plan so well received, that in the
spring of 1814 Congress passed a law authorizing the President to cause to be built, equipped and employed one or more
floating batteries, for the defense of the ports and waters of
the United States. In conforming with this law, the steam
frigate Fulton the First, was built at New York, and on the
4th of July, 1815, she made her first trip to the ocean and
back, a distance of fifty-three miles in eight hours and twenty
minutes. Henry Rutgers, Samuel L. Mitchell, Thomas Morris, and Oliver Walcott, Esqs., commissioners of the navy,
were present. Mr. Stoudinger, successor to Robert Fulton
was engineer.

Before this vessel was completed Robert Fulton had ceased
to exist. While superintending the works on board of the
steam frigate, he exposed himself too long on deck, on a wet
and stormy day; an attack of pleurisy followed, which terminated his valuable life on the 24th day of[February, 1815.
Mr. Fulton was married, in the year 1806, to Miss Harriet

Livingston, a relative of Chancellor Livingston, his friend and associate in the steam navigation enterprise. He left four children, one son, Robert Barlow Fulton, and three daughters.

Capt. Samuel J. Morey of Connecticut, is *claimed* to be the inventor of the first practical steamboat ever built.

Rev. Cyrus Mann, of Oxford, New Hampshire, published in 1864 some account of Capt. Morey and of his steamboat.

Mr. Mann was a scholar and a man of integrity and spent a month's time with Morey in investigating the claims of Fulton, Morey and others.

The following is an extract from his book: —

"The credit of the invention of the steamboat is commonly awarded to Robert Fulton, but it belongs primarily and chiefly, it is believed, to a more obscure individual. So far as is known the first steamboat ever seen on the waters of America was invented by Capt. Samuel Morey, of Oxford, New Hampshire.

"The astonishing sight of this man ascending the Connecticut river, between Oxford and Fairlee, in a little boat just large enough to contain himself and the rude machinery connected with the steam boiler and a handful of wood for a fire, was witnessed by the writer in his boyhood, and by others who still survive. This was as early as 1793 or earlier and before Fulton's name had been mentioned in connection with steam navigation."

Writing to William A. Drier, in October of 1818, Morey says: "As near as I can recollect it was as early as 1790, that I turned my attention to improving the steam engine, and to applying it to the purpose of propelling boats. In June, 1797, I went to Bordentown, on the Delaware, and there constructed a steamboat and devised the plan of propelling by means of wheels, one on each side.

The shafts ran across the boat with a crank in the middle worked from the beam of the engine with a shackle bar.

The boat was openly exhibited in Philadelphia and I took out patents for my improvements."

He accused Fulton of adopting his models and if he had had the means would probably have prosecuted Livingston and Fulton for an infringement of his patents. As he insisted, he was fully entitled to them for the application of the side wheels."

It is difficult at this late date to determine who, if any one man, is entitled to the credit of first applying steam to navigation.

So far as the record goes, John Fitch is certainly entitled to a large share of credit and if he had been encouraged by men with pecuniary ability he would undoubtedly have secured the credit that finally was accredited to Robert Fulton.

CHAPTER VII.

DISCOVERY OF THE UPPER MISSISSIPPI.[1]

BY FATHER HENNEPIN, IN 1680.

THIS account is from his own narrative: —
" He set out from Fort Crevecœur, the 29th February,
1680. His party consisted of two Frenchmen and a few Indians,
with two large canoes. They embarked upon the Illinois river
and on the 8th of March reached the river (Colbert) *i.e.* the
Mississippi. The ice which floated down from the north delayed the expedition several days. We commenced to ascend
the great river in April. The first river we come to is Rock
river or Des Moines. Sixty leagues up we reach the Puntos,
fifty leagues above we reach the Lake of Tears, (Lake Pepin),
which we so named because some Indians who had taken us,
wished to kill us wept the whole night to induce the others to
consent to our death. Forty leagues above is the river St.
Croix by which striking northwest you can reach Lake
Condé (Superior). Continuing to ascend the Colbert (Mississippi) twelve leagues more the navigation is interrupted by
a fall, which I called St. Anthony of Padua's, whom we had
chosen patron and protector of all our enterprises. Eight
leagues above St. Anthony to the right we found the river
Issati, which you can ascend to the north for about seventy
leagues to Lake Issati where it rises. This last lake spreads
out into greater marshes and is probably the source of the
Colbert, *i.e.* Mississippi. We had considered the river
Colbert with great pleasure, and so far, without hindrance, to
know how far it was navigable up and down.

" On the 11th of April, 1680, we suddenly perceived thirty-
three bark canoes manned by a hundred and twenty Indians,
coming towards us. They soon surrounded us and took us
prisoners. After remaining captive for several months we
made our escape and descended the river one hundred and
twenty leagues distant from the country of the Indians who
had taken us. We met the Sieur de Luth, who came to the river
by the land route, with five French soldiers. Towards the end
of September we resolved to return to the French settlements.
We chose the route by the way of the Ouisconsin (Wisconsin).
After sailing up sixty leagues we came to a portage. After
sailing one hundred leagues we arrived at the bay of Fetid
(Green Bay). We then sailed a hundred leagues and reached

Miseilimackinac.   After many months we reached Montreal in
May, 1681."
Notes, Colbert is Mississippi river.
"   Issati is Itasca lake.
"   Ouisconsin is Wisconsin river.
"   Fetid bay, Green bay.
Fort Creve Cœur was a frontier fort of Canada.

THE MISSISSIPPI.

"The name of the Mississippi river is of itself worthy of
note.
If France ever had sufficient title to the Mississippi Valley
to convey ownership she undoubtedly had authority to name
the principle river.   If this follows then the technically correct name of the great river is St. Louis, for in 1712 the King
of France ordered in letters-patent to Crozat that the river
"heretofore called Mississippi be called River Saint Louis.'
But the people on its banks and on the western continent
gave no heed to the royal decree, though geographers, like
d'Auville, adhered for years to the name of St. Louis.
Mississippi is from the Ojibbeway tongue and signifies, according to Bishop Baraga, great river or rivers of water from
all sides, or by a liberal translation it may be interpreted as
the savage vernacular for the national motto, *E Pluribus
Unum.*"
The first commercial use of the stream was to carry the
skin-laden skiff, and from that to the row boat and barge the
transition was easy to the boatmen.   But little, however, is
known of the quantity or the character of traffic early in the
century.   Before the time of steam the barge afforded the
principle means of river transportation, and the methods of
its management were primitive, slow, and dangerous.   The
boats were from twenty-five to a hundred feet long   Breadth
of beam from fifteen to twenty feet, and the capacity from
six to one hundred tons.   The receptacle for the freight was
a large covered coffer, called a cargo box, which occupied
considerable portion of the bulk.   Near the stern was a small,
straightened apartment six or eight feet in length, in which
the captain and steersman, or patron were quartered at night.
Upon the elevated roof of this cabin the steersman stood to
direct the course of the craft.   There were usually two masts,
sometimes one served the purpose.   The main reliance was a
large, square sail forward, which when the wind was favorable, accelerated the progress of the boat and relieved the

hands, who at other times were compelled to use the most laborious methods.

Going down stream required watchfulness and some ingenuity, and a full knowledge of the fitfulness of the navigable currents, but no exhaustive exertion. Up stream, sometimes against the wind, through a land of savages, pirates and freebooters, the lot of a Mississippi navigator in modern phraseology was not a happy one.

About fifty men were employed. Sometimes all were rowing, sometimes they towed the boat, after the fashion of the old canal boat. But when the banks made this impracticable the "warp" was adopted. This was accomplished by sending a coil of rope forward to some tree on the shore, or snag in the river, toward which the hands on board pulled the boat. Then another tree or snag was selected, and so on to the end.

There was little poling on the Mississippi, though it was sometimes done on account of the depth of the water, the strength of the stream, and the yielding nature of the bottom. It was pole and warp, and tow and row, and row and tow, and pole and warp for months before a cargo from New Orleans reached St. Louis.

Buccaneers invested the mouths of rivers, and the bays, creeks and caves afforded places of concealment for them and their spoils till the close of the War of 1812, and every owner carried his own insurance against flood, robber and fire.

But it is recorded that the boatmen were scrupulous of their trusts, and would fight to protect the consignment, and seldom failed to account satisfactorily for everything entrusted to their care. For policy, perhaps, which had as much to do then with business rectitude as now.

The fates and fortunes of the traveler, however, who had that about him which excited the cupidity of fearless and unscrupulous men, who knew no law but their own wild wishes, and who recognized no higher consideration than expediency, were not so secure, and many an untold tale of murder and mysterious disappearance lies at the bottom of the Mississippi. Waves never babble or gossip. One, of many instances, must suffice: Cotton Wood Creek and Grand Tower were well known places of rendezvous for pirates who would attack voyagers from some such place, drive them off, and then appropriate their valuables.

Early in 1787 an event occurred which inaugurated severe measures by the Spanish government, resulting in dispersing the pirates.

One, Beausoliel, a New Orleans merchant, started for St. Louis with a richly laden barge. A strong breeze arose as she approached Cotton Wood Creek. The pirates were ready for an attack, but the rapid progress under a strong breeze frustrated their design, and they sent a body of men to head off the prize.

The point selected for an attack was an island since known as Beausoliel's Island, and was reached in about two days. The barge had landed and was easily captured and the crew disarmed. When the captors turned the boat down stream, soon after which a happy deliverance came from an unexpected source.

Casotta, a negro, who had effected great pleasure at the capture, was used by the freebooters as a cook. He kept up a secret understanding with Beausoleil, and at a given signal and an opportune moment the captured became the captors, and all the pirates were killed or secured. Vigorous measures followed. Trips were made in fleets, well armed for fight, and within a short time the robber haunts were vacated.

In those days of flat boats and barges and endless time, the freight from New Orleans to St. Louis was on an average about $6.75 per one hundred pounds.

After the establishment of military posts on the Ohio river, by Congress, no regular intercourse was kept with them by the government. Mail routes could not be contracted beyond Pittsburg. All communications of importance was made through expresses, either on land through the wilderness, by way of Virginia and Kentucky, or by transient boats on the Ohio river.

As this mode was slow, expensive and uncertain, Colonel Timothy Pickering, the Postmaster-General, deemed it advisable to establish a more regular and certain mode of communication with General Wayne and the army on the Western frontier. The first mail route across the Alleghany mountains was ordered by Congress in 1786, from Alexandria, in Virginia, to Pittsburg, in Pennsylvania, by way of Lewisburg, Winchester, Fort Cumberland and Bedford, also, from Philadelphia to the town of Bedford, and thence to Pittsburg.

On the 20th of May, 1788, Congress resolved that the Postmaster-General be directed to employ posts for the regular transport of the mail between the city of Philadelphia and the town of Pittsburg, by the way of Lancaster, York, Carlisle, Chambersburg and Bedford, and that the mail be dispatched once in each fortnight from the post-offices respectively.

CHAPTER VIII.

FIRST UNITED STATES MAIL SERVICE ON THE OHIO BY BOAT.

IN April, 1794, with the aid and advice of Colonel O'Harra, army contractor, and Mayor Isaac Craig, of Pittsburg, a plan was devised of transporting the mail in light, strong boats on the Ohio river, and put into operation early in the following June.

These boats were about twenty-four feet in length, made after the style of whale boats, and steered with a rudder. They were manned by five boatmen, viz.: a coxswain and four oarsmen. The men were all armed and their pieces kept dry in snug boxes along side of their seats. The whole could be covered with a tarpaulin in wet weather, which each boat carried for that purpose. For cooking and sleeping they generally landed on the beach at the head of an island, where they would be less liable to a surprise or an attack from the Indians.

In ascending, as well as descending, the boat was kept nearly in the middle of the river. The distance traveled against the current averaged about thirty miles a day, and double that down stream.

There were four relays between Wheeling and Cincinnati. The mail was carried by land from Pittsburg and Wheeling. The station where the boats met and exchanged mails, were Marietta, Gallipolis and Limestone, the distance between which was made in seven days both up and down; thus requiring about twelve days from Cincinnati to Wheeling, and about half that time from Wheeling to Cincinnati.

The transport by land only required one day and two fast riders who exchanged mails at Washington, Pennsylvania. Postmasters were appointed at each of these towns so that the citizens could have the advantage of the establishment as well as the military. The postmaster at Marietta was Captain Joseph Munroe, an old soldier in the "continental line," during the war.

This mode of carrying the mail was kept up until 1798. After the treaty with the Indians in 1798, the mail was landed at Graham's Station, a few miles above Limestone, and transported to Cincinnati on horseback. So cautious were the conductors of these boats generally that only one attack was made upon them by the Indians. This happened in 1794 to a boat commanded by Capt. Diegan, but at that time commanded by another man, employed for that trip. The packet was ascending the Ohio, and happened to have several passengers on board, as they sometimes did, and had reached within a few miles of the mouth of the Scioto, on the Indian shore. The man at the helm saw, as he thought, a deer in the bushes, and heard it rustling in the leaves. With the intention of killing it the boat had approached within a few rods of the bank, and the man at the bow had risen up with his gun to fire, when they received a whole volley from the Indians who lay in ambush, and had made these signs to entice them to the shore. One man was killed, and another desperately wounded. Several of the row-locks were shot off, and their oars for the time rendered useless. The Indians rushed down the bank and into the water, endeavoring to get hold of the boat and drag it to the shore. The steersman turned the bow into the current and one or two oars forced her into the stream, beyond the reach of their shot. One of the hands who had been a drummer in St. Clair's army, and had probably witnessed the effect of the Indian yell, became so alarmed that he jumped into the river as the boat was turning from the shore. A stout Indian dashed into the river and swam after him, with his drawn knife in his teeth. Wilbur's pantaloons being thick and heavy, impeded his swimming so much that the Indian gained rapidly upon him. He made an attempt to pull them off and got one leg free, but sank under the water while doing it. He was now worse off than before, as they dragged behind and nearly paralyzed all his efforts. The Indian was within a few yards of him, and escape seemed hopeless, when making another desperate effort he succeeded in freeing himself from the incumbrance. In accomplishing this last struggle he again sank entirely beneath the surface, and came up greatly exhausted, with the Indian within striking distance of him. As the enemy slackened his exertions to draw his knife from his teeth and give the fatal stab, Wilbur now having his legs free, and quickened by the sight of the gleaming blade upraised in the hand of the Indian, threw all his remaining strength into one convulsive effort, and forced himself beyond the reach of the descending knife, which plunged harmless into the water, within a few inches of his body. Before his enemy could repeat the blow he was several feet ahead of him and nearly in the middle of the river. The Indian now gave up the pursuit, and retreated to the shore. Nearly exhausted by fear and fatigue, and chilled by the coldness of the water, Wilbur reached the opposite bank with great difficulty.

In the meantime the boatmen, thinking him killed or drowned, pushed down stream and did not land until they reached the next station, some fifty miles below. Wilbur, however, made himself a raft, and descended to Graham's in safety. By this disaster, the line of communication was interrupted for a trip or two; but was soon after resumed and not broken again except by the ice in winter, when the boats were laid up for a few weeks until the system was abandoned in 1798, for the more feasible one by land.

CHAPTER IX.

THE FIRST VESSEL TO ENTER THE MISSISSIPPI RIVER FROM THE SEA.

JANUARY 6, 1700, M. d'Iberville, in command of the French frigate Rénommée, and the Gironde, anchored off Ship Island. In a few days he determined to enter the mouth of the Mississippi on an exploring expedition. He left the ships in three long boats, manned by sixty men, and after coasting along for thirty leagues entered the mouth of the river, the 15th. On February 19 we arrived at a large village of the Bayou Goula Indians, whom we found to be very friendly. They supplied us with Indian meal, fish and meats. After three days' rest we commenced the ascent against a strong current. About five leagues above, on the right hand side, came to the Manchac; five leagues above this stream we came to where the banks of the river are very high, called "Ecores," and in the Indian language "Istrouma," which signifies Baton Rouge, because at that place there is a post painted red, which the Indians have placed there to mark the boundary line of the territory of the two nations. About fifteen leagues from this place, we arrived at a large river called Sabloniere (Red River). On March 10 arrived at the great Natchez bluffs, where M. d'Iberville made a treaty of peace with this tribe of Indians. On April 12 left Natchez and, after hard rowing and cordelling, we arrived on April 16 at the Tensas.

As the period of M. d'Iberville's return to France was rapidly approaching, he resolved to descend the river. We set off the next morning. We progressed rapidly with the strong

3

current of the river, and in a few days arrived at the Bayou Goulas, where we found a gunboat which M. De Bienville had brought from Biloxi with material for the construction of a fort. M. De Bienville in descending from Natchez on his route to Biloxi met, on the 16th of September, a small English frigate careened in a bend of the river about three leagues in circuit. He demanded of the captain what he was doing in the Mississippi, and if he was not aware the French had already established themselves in this country. The Englishman was much astonished, and replied that he was ignorant of the fact and soon after retraced his steps to the sea. It was from this circumstance that the bend of the river was afterward called the English Turn. This frigate was commanded by Capt. Barr, and was fitted out in 1698 by the English with instructions to take possession of Louisiana and establish a colony on the banks of the Mississippi.

M. d'Iberville commenced at this place the building of a fort, and placing his brother, M. de Bienville, in command, he returned to Biloxi, followed by two of our long boats and five French Canadians, who, hearing of our establishment at Biloxi, had come to trade with us. He made us row night and day until we reached the ships. He set sail for France on May 3, 1700. But before his departure he recommended M. de Sauvol to place twenty men under the command of M. le Sueur to go to the copper mines in the country of the Sioux about nine hundred leagues from the mouth of the river, and above the Fall of St. Anthony. It was at the village Bayou Goulas that Iberville found the following letter from Tonti to La Salle, dated April 20, 1685, which the Indian chiefs had carefully preserved:

" Sir — Having found the column on which you placed the arms of France thrown down, I caused a new one to be erected about seven leagues from the sea. All nations have sung the Calumet. These people fear us extremely since your attack on their village. I close by saying that it gives me great uneasiness to be obliged to return under the misfortune of not having found you.'

Two canoes have examined the coast thirty leagues toward Mexico and twenty-five toward Florida. This chief of the Bayou Goulas had also some engravings, a New Testament, a gun and a letter which were given to him by M. de Tonti, all of which he had preserved with great care during these years from 1685 to 1700.

THE FIRST BOAT — 1541.

The following is given as an authentic account of the first vessel built upon the banks of the Mississippi River by white men : —

" Hernando DeSoto, in his expedition from Florida in 1541, discovered the Mississippi in this same year. He had with him 620 men and 223 horses. Upon his arrival at the great river he desired to cross to the western shore, and for this purpose he commanded his officers to have constructed four large pirogues, capable of carrying seventy or eighty men each and five or six horses. With these vessels he made the passage of the great river. DeSoto now determined to seek new Spain by traveling west, but after many months of great hardships he retraced his steps toward the great river, arriving at a point near the mouth of the Arkansas. Here, on may 21, 1542, he died. As soon as he was dead, Lays de Moscosa, his Captain General, commanded his body to be wound up in mantels, wherein he was carried in a canoe and thrown into the midst of the river. After the burial of DeSoto Lays de Moscosa de Alvarado called together his followers and they determined to seek the sea by way of the great river and find the coast of Mexico.

" The General then commanded them to commence building brigantines. He ordered them to gather all the chains together, which every one had to lead Indians in, and to gather all the iron which they had in the camp, and to set up a forge and make nails, and commanding them to cut down timber for the brigantines. A Portuguese of Centa had learned to saw timber with a long saw, which for such purposes they had carried with them, and he did teach others, which helped him to saw the timber. And a Geneves, who had learned to build ships, with four or five Biscayan carpenters, who hewed the planks and other timbers, made the brigantines. And two caulkers, the one of Geneva, the other of Sardinia, did caulk them with a tow of an herb like hemp, and because there was not enough of it, they caulked them with the flax of the country. A cooper they had among them made for every brigantine two hogsheads, to hold water. The provision of the vessels was maize, the flesh of horses and hogs, which they dried for the voyages. On the 2d day of July they departed from the Arkansas with seven brigantines and 322 Spaniards. After twenty days descending the river they reached the

sea, or Gulf of Mexico. The 18th of July, 1543, they went
forth to sea. From the time that they put out of the Rio
Grande or Mississippi until they arrived in the River of Panuco,
or Mexico, was fifty-two days. They came into the River
Panuco the 10th of September, 1543. They went up the
river, and in four days arrived at the town of Panuco; all of
them were appareled in deer skins, tanned and dyed a dark
color. After remaining at Panuco for some days the Viceroy
of Mexico, Don Antonio de Mendoco, sent an order that they
should be brought to the City of Mexico; upon their arrival
at the city every provision was made for them by the Viceroy,
and those that desired it were sent home to Spain.

" This is a narrative by a gentleman of Elvas in 1557.

WM. LONGSTREET ANTEDATES ROBERT FULTON SEVEN YEARS.

A correspondent of the Savannah (Ga.) *Recorder* writes as
follows: —

"ATLANTA, GA., Sept. 1.

" In looking over some of the letters on file in the archives
of the State, I find one from Wm. Longstreet, the grandfather of Judge Longstreet, which I copy and send you. It
will be seen by this letter that Wm. Longstreet, on the 25th
day of September, 1790, proposed and was running a steamboat on the Savannah River, near Augusta, Ga., and this date
was seven years before Fulton had his steamboat.

" If this be true, Georgia, and not New York, is entitled to
the credit of having the first steamboat in her waters: —

' "AUGUSTA, GA., Sept. 26, 1790.

" 'SIR—I make no doubt but you have often heard of my
steamboat, and as often heard it laughed at. But in this I
have only shared the fate of all other projectors, for it has
uniformly been the custom of every country to ridicule even
the greatest inventions until use had proved their utility.

" 'In not reducing my scheme to practice has been a little
unfortunate for me. I confess (and perhaps the people in
general), but until very lately I did not think that either
artists or materials could be had in this place sufficient.

" 'However, necessity — that grand source of invention —
has furnished me with an idea of perfecting my plan, almost
entirely with wooden materials, and by such workmen as may
be got here; and, from a thorough confidence of its success,
I propose to ask your assistance and patronage.

" ' Should it succeed agreeably to my expectation, I hope I shall discover that sense of duty which such favors always merit, and should it not succeed, your reward must lay with other unlucky adventurers.

" ' For me to mention to you all the advantages arising from such a machine would be tedious, and, indeed, unnecessary. Therefore I have taken the liberty just to state in this plain, humble manner, my wish and opinion, which I hope you will excuse, and I shall remain, either with or without your approbation, your Excellency's most obedient and very humble servant.   WM. LONGSTREET.

" ' To his Excellency Edward Telfair.' "

"ST. PAUL'S SHIP."

TALES OF SHIPS AND SHIPPING.

Under the above head Gath wrote in the Cincinnati *Enquirer* of a recent date as follows:

" The first boats we suppose to have been hollow logs and rafts, and the ingenious Mr. Lindsay, who has made a long history of merchant shipping and ancient commerce, thinks that the Ark, if it ever existed, was simply a raft of stupendous size, roofed with a big warehouse, and, as described by Scripture, no bigger than the ordinary sailing vessels on the North Atlantic at the present time. The registered tonnage of the Ark was less than 15,000 tons, and therefore the Great Eastern was a colossus in comparison.

" The old Assyrian monuments show people crossing rivers on inflated skins. The early Britians appear to have used basket-work, around which they had flannel wrapped, or leather. It is said that bitumen from the Babylon region was exported to Egypt in vessels 1500 years before Jesus. Among the earliest vessels known here was one called the Balza, on the west coast of South America, a raft of logs which carried twenty tons.

" The Homeric vessels were only large open boats, with a kind of a half-deck inside to shelter some people.

" Pounded sea-shells were first introduced into the seams and chinks of boats, and afterward pounded seeds, and finally pitch and wax. An old ship of Trajan, pulled up from a Roman lake, shows that the Romans also sheathed their ships. The names of punt and galley, skiff, etc., have a very high antiquity. The first vessels which carried horses were called Hipagogi. A picture of St. Paul's ship by Mr. Smith who was both a believer and a boat builder, shows that she was something like a life-boat or batteau, with a sort of railing around her top, and two masts; she carried a cargo of grain and 276 people; she probably had two decks besides a high poop and forecastle.

"They steered vessels for a long time by means of oars, and the first vessels had square sails. The first anchors were big stones, but St. Paul's ship carried four anchors. In the time of Alexander the Great they had chain cables for these anchors. The first important grain ships were built to carry Egyptian grain to Italy for the supply of the Romans.

"Ancient mariners used the gnomen to get the length of the sun's shadow at noon.

"The Phœnician galleys often had fifty oars in them, rower sitting above rower, with oars longer and longer, so that they all could pull at once; and they sometimes rowed twenty-six days without going ashore. * * * The river Nile has but few branches but many mouths; hence the mouths were worked out to make canals of them, and one of these canals was about 350 miles long, or about the size of the Erie Canal. The Egyptian sailors were Nile boatmen, and Herodotus says that there was 700,000 of these employed at one time, and they lived on the boats and held fairs and markets there.

"The habit the Egyptians had of using the double yard to keep the sail flat was unconsciously adopted by the Americans, who by the same process beat the English with the yacht America.

"The Egyptians put houses on their decks like American steamboats. After Alexander conquered Egypt the City of Alexandria became the New York of the Old World, and, like New York, a great lighthouse was put up, called Pharos, at Alexandria, which cost 800 talents. It had fires lighted in its top stories at night to guide ships. The port of Berenice was made on the Red Sea to facilitate shipments across to Alexandria on the Mediterranean.

"Though the Egyptians were poor sailors, they built some good vessels, and one of these, owned by Ptolemy, is said to have been 420 feet long, 57 feet beam and 72 feet in depth of hold, or about as big as the largest steamships of our day. A picture of this vessel represents her as steered by oars, with a straight gunwale, two or three decks on her poop and her bow rising high and elaborately carved. These figures are believed to be wrong, at least as far as the depth of hold is concerned.

"A fine galley was built by one of the Ptolemys, which

contained their bed-chamber, and this vessel was 300 feet long, luxurious as a North river steamboat and contained colonnades, marble stairs and gardens.''

A CONDENSED HISTORY OF STEAM.

'' About 280 years B. C., Hero, of Alexandria, formed a toy which exhibited some of the powers of steam, and was moved by its power.

A. D. 540 an architect arranged several cauldrons of water, each covered with the wide bottom of a leather tube, which rose to a narrow top, with the pipes extending to the rafters of the adjoining building. A fire was kindled beneath the cauldron, and the house was shaken with the effects of the steam ascending the tubes. This is the first notice of the power of steam recorded.

In 1543, June 17, Basca de Garay tried a steamboat of 200 tons with tolerable success at Barcelona, Spain. It consisted of a cauldron of boiling water and a movable wheel on each side of the ship. It was laid aside as impracticable. A present, however, was made to Garay.

In 1630 the first railroad was constructed at Newcastle-on-the-Tyne.

The first idea of a steam engine in England was in the Marquis of Worcester's '' History of Invention,'' A. D. 1663.

In 1701 Newermann made the first steam engine in England.

In 1764 James Watt made the first perfect steam engine in England.

In 1766 Jonathan Hulls first set forth the idea of steam navigation.

In 1778 Thomas Payne first proposed the application in America.

In 1781 Marquis Jouffrey constructed a steamboat on the Saone.

In 1785 two Americans published a work upon it.

In 1789 William Symington made a voyage in one on the Forth and Clyde canal.

In 1802 this experiment was repeated.

In 1782 Ramsey propelled a boat by steam at New York.

In 1789 John Fitch, of Connecticut. navigated a boat by steam on the Delaware.''

In 1784 Robert Fulton first began to apply his attention to steam.

In 1783 Oliver Evans, a native of Philadelphia, constructed a steam engine to travel a turnpike road.

The first steam vessel that crossed the Atlantic was the Savannah, in the month of June, from Charleston, S. C., to Liverpool.

In the New Orleans *Gazette* of July 23, 1807, may be found the following advertisement:—

"For Louisville, Kentucky.

"THE HORSE BOAT, JOHN BROOKHART, MASTER.

"She is completely fitted for the voyage. For freight of a few tons only (having the greater part of her cargo engaged), apply to the master on board or to

"SANDERSON & WHITE."

The trip was begun but never completed. Before arriving at Natchez some twelve or twenty horses were used up on the treadwheel, and the voyage was abandoned near that city. We republish this as an illustration of the expedients to which the earlier settlers of the Mississippi Valley were compelled to resort in carrying on commerce with the interior. It was easy enough to get from Louisville to New Orleans, and carry produce there, but getting the productions of the tropics to Louisville quite another matter.

"VIRGINIA CITY, September 19.
"TO THE EDITOR OF THE ST. LOUIS REPUBLICAN:

"*Dear Sir* — Will you please inform me through the columns of your valuable paper when and whereabouts the steamboat "Sultana," used for transporting of troops, was blown up.

"By so doing you will oblige yours, very respectfully,
"ERNEST BRAUN,
"Virginia City, Nevada."

In the early part of the spring of 1864 (it was about the 12th of March we believe), the steamer Sultana left Memphis late at night, with upwards of 2,400 souls aboard. When she had proceeded to a point just above a group of little islands called Paddy's Hen and Chickens, about seven miles above that city, it is believed the whole battery of five boilers exploded at the same time. Subsequently the boat took fire and was burned to the surface of the water, and the hull sank on a bar close to Bradley's Landing.   By this terrible catastrophe more than two thousand lives were lost.   It was the most destructive marine disaster that ever occurred since rivers and oceans have been sailed over by men.

CHAPTER X.

COL. PLUG, MIKE FINK AND OTHERS.

IN a book published at Louisville in 1852, " The History of Louisville," by Ben. Cassaday, may be found some interesting matter relating to the early navigation of the Ohio by barges and other primitive modes.

" In the winter of this year (1780) commenced the first of anything like intercourse between this part of the Ohio and New Orleans.

" Messrs. Tardinen and Honore, the latter of whom resided in this city until within a few years, made the earliest trip from Brownville to New Orleans and subsequently continued to make regular trips from Louisville to the French and Spanish posts on the Mississippi.

" Even previous to this, Col. Richard Taylor and his brother Hancock Taylor, had descended from Pittsburg to the mouth of the Yazoo, and Messrs. Gibson and Linn, in 1776, had made a trip from Pittsburg to New Orleans with a view of procuring military stores for the troops stationed at the former place.   These gentlemen succeeded in their expectations, having obtained 156 kegs of powder, which arrived at the falls in 1777, was carried around them by hand and finally delivered at Pittsburg.

" These early attempts at navigation were soon succeeded by the constant and regular trips of the barges.   Perhaps the most exciting and stirring scenes of Western adventure were connected with these peculiar craft."

The *bargemen* were a distinct class of people, whose fearlessness of character, recklessness of habits and laxity of morals, rendered them a marked people.   Their history will hereafter form the ground-work of many a heroic romance or epic poem.   In the earlier stages of this sort of navigation, the trips were dangerous not only on account of the Indians, whose hunting grounds bounded their track on either side, but also because the shores of both rivers were infested with organized bands of banditti, who sought every occasion to rob and murder the owners of these boats. Besides all this, the Spanish government had forbidden the navigation of the lower Mississippi by the Americans.

And thus hedged in every way by danger, it became these boatmen to cultivate all the hardihood and wildness of the pioneer, while it also led them into the possession of that recklessness and independent freedom of manner which, even after the causes that produced it had ceased, still clung to, and formed an integral part of the Western bargeman.

It is a matter of no little surprise that something like an authentic history of these wonderful men has never been written. Certainly it is desirable to preserve such history, and no book could have been undertaken which would be likely to produce more both of pleasure and profit to the writer, and none which would meet with a larger circle of delighted readers. The traditions on the subject are, even at this recent period, so vague and contradictory that it would be difficult to procure anything like reliable or authentic data in regard to them. No story in which the bargemen figure is too improbable to be narrated. Nor can one determine what particular person is the hero of an incident which is in turn laid at the door of each distinguished member of the whole fraternity. Some of these incidents, however, will serve so well to give an idea of the peculiar characters of the bargemen, and possess so much merit in themselves, that they cannot be omitted here.

Previous to referring to any of these anecdotes it may be interesting to introduce the following excellent description of the manner of navigating the Ohio and Mississippi prior to the introduction of steamboats. It is from the pen of *Audubon,* the celebrated ornithologist, whose death has caused a deep feeling of regret in all who know how to admire that union of simple goodness of character with greatness of mind and untiring energy of study, which he, perhaps more than any other American, possessed.

The keel boats and barges were employed, says this extract, in conveying produce of different kinds, such as lead, flour, pork and other articles. These returned laden with sugar, coffee and dry goods suited for the markets of Genevieve and St. Louis on the Upper Mississippi, or branched off and ascended the Ohio to the foot of the falls at Louisville. A keel boat was generally manned by a crew of ten hands, principally Canadian French, and a patroon or master. These

boats seldom carried more than from twenty to thirty tons.
The barges had frequently from forty to fifty men, with a.
patroon, and carried fifty or sixty tons.

Both these kind of vessels were provided with a mast, a
square sail, and coils of cordage known by the name of "cordelles." Each boat or barge carried its own provisions. We
shall suppose one of these boats under way, and having passed.
Natchez, entering upon what was called the difficulties of their
ascent. Wherever a point projected so as to render the course
or bend below it of some magnitude, there was an eddy, the
returning current of which was sometimes as strong as that of
the middle of the great stream. The barge, therefore, rowed
up pretty close under the bank and had merely to keep watch.
in the bow, lest the boat should run against a planter or
sawyer. But the boat has reached the point, and the current
is there, to all appearance, double strength, and right against
it. The men, who have rested a few minutes, are ordered to
take their station and lay hold of their oars, for the river must
be crossed, it being seldom possible that such a point can be
doubled and proceed along the same shore.

The boat is crossing, its head slanting to the current which
is, however, too strong for the rowers, and when the other
side of the river has been reached, it has drifted perhaps a
quarter of a mile.

The men are by this time exhausted, and as we suppose it
to be twelve o'clock, fasten the boat to a tree on shore.

A small glass of whisky is given to each when they cook
and eat their dinner, and after resting from their fatigue for
an hour, recommence their labors.

The boat is seen again slowly advancing against the stream.
It has reached the lower end of a sandbar, along the edge
of which it is propelled by means of long poles, if the bottom
be hard. Two men, called bowsmen, remain at the bow, to
assist, in concert with the steersman, in managing the boat,
and keeping the head right against the current. The rest place
themselves on the land side of the foot-way of the vessel, put
one end of their poles on the ground, and the other against
their shoulders, and push with all their might.

As each of the men reaches the stern, he crosses to the
other side, runs along it and comes to the landward side of
the bow, when he recommences the operation. The barge, in
the meantime, is ascending at the rate not exceeding one mile
the hour.

The bar is at length passed, and as the shore is straight in
sight on both sides, and the current uniformly strong; the

poles are laid aside and the men being equally divided, those
on the riverside take to the oars while those on the other side
lay hold of branches of willows or other trees, and thus
slowly propel the boat.

Here and there, however, the trunk of a fallen tree, laying
partly on the bank and partly in the water, impedes their
progress, and requires to be doubled. This is performed by
striking into it with the iron points of the poles and gaff
hooks, and propelling around it. The sun is now quite low
and the barge is again secured in the best harbor within reach
for the night, after having accomplished a distance of perhaps fifteen miles. The next day the wind proves favorable,
the sails are set and the boat takes all the advantages, and
meeting with no accidents has ascended thirty miles — perhaps
double that distance.

The next day comes with a very different aspect. The
wind is right ahead, the shores without trees of any kind, and
the cane on the bank so thick and stout that not even the
cordelles can be used. This occasions a halt. The time is not
altogether lost, as most of the men being provided with rifles
take to the woods and search for the deer, the turkey or the
bear which are generally abundant. Three days may pass
before the wind changes, and the advantages gained on the
previous five days are forgotten.

Again the boat advances, but in passing over a shallow
place runs on a log and swings with the current, but hangs
fast, with her lea side almost under the water. Now for the
poles; all hands are on deck, bristling and pushing. At
length, towards sunset, the boat is once more afloat and is again
taken to the shore where the weary crew pass another night.

I could tell you of the crew abandoning the boat, and of
numberless accidents and perils. But enough to say advancing in this tardy manner, the boat that left New Orleans on
the first of March often did not reach the falls of the Ohio
until the month of July — sometimes not until October —
and after all this immense trouble it brought only a few
bags of coffee, and at most one hundred hogsheads of
sugar. Such was the state of things as late as 1808. The
number of barges at that period did not amount to more than
twenty or thirty, and the largest probably did not exceed one
hundred tons burden.

To make the best of this fatiguing navigation, I may conclude by saying a barge that came up in three months had
done wonders, for, I believe very few voyages were made
in that time.

CHAPTER II.

IN this little history Mr. Audubon has said nothing of what was by far the most "dangerous danger," to which the crews of these crafts were exposed, This was the attack, open and fearless, as well as sneaking and treacherous, to the boatmen.

The country on both sides of the river from Louisville to the mouth of the Ohio, was almost an unpeopled wilderness. On the north side of the river from Fort Massac there lay a gang of these desperadoes, whose exploits need only the genius of a Schiller to render them the wonder of the world and the admiration of those who love to gloat over tales of blood. There was an independence and a recklessness of life and of danger connected with these fellows, with a dash of spirit and humor, that would render them excellent *material* in the hands of a skillful novelist. But they lacked that high sense of honor, and that gentlemanly bearing, which made heroes of the robbers of the Rhine, of Venice, or of Mexico. Their plan of action was to induce the crew of the passing "broadhorn" to land to play a game of cards (the favorite pastime of the boatmen), and to cheat them unmercifully. If this scheme failed they would pilot the boats into a difficult place, or, in pretended friendship give them from the shore such direction as would not fail to run them on a snag or dash them to pieces on some hidden obstruction.

If they were outwitted in all this, they would creep into the boats when they were tied up at night, and bore holes in the bottom, or scrape out the caulking. When the boat was sinking they would get out skiffs and crafts of all kinds and in the most philanthropic manner, come to save the goods from wreck; and save them they did, for they would row them up small creeks that led from swamps into the interior and no trace of them could afterwards be found; or, if some hardy fellow dared to go in pursuit of his *saved* cargo, he was sure to find an unknown grave in the morasses.

One of the most famous of these boatwreckers was Col. Fluger, of New Hampshire, who is better known in the West as "Col. Plug."

This worthy *gentleman* long held undisputed sway over the quiet wreckers about the mouth of Cash Creek. He was supposed to possess the keys to every warehouse between then place and Louisville, and to have them for his own privatt purposes on many occasions. He was a married man and became the father of a family. His wife's soubriquet was Pluggy, and like many others of her sex, her charms were a sore affliction to the Colonel's peace of mind. Plug's lieutenant was suspected of making familiarity with Mrs. Colonel Plug.

The Colonel's wise sense of honor was outraged, his family pride aroused.

He called Lieutenant Nine-eyes to the field. "*Dern* your soul, do you think this sort of candlestick ammer (clandestine amour, he meant) will pass? If you do, by gosh, I will put it to you, or you shall to me."

They used rifles. The ground was measured, the affair was settled in the most approved style. And they did put it to each other.

Each received a ball in some fleshy part, and each admitted that he was satisfied.

"You are all grit," said Col. Plug.

"And you waded in like a real Kentuck," rejoined Nine-eyes.

Col. Plug's son and heir, who was, very possibly, the subject matter of dispute, and who was upon the ground, was ordered to place a bottle of whisky midway between the disputants.

Up to this they limped, and over it they embraced, swearing they were too well used to these things to be plugged by a little cold lead. And Pluggy's virtue having been thus proved immaculate, the duel as well as the animosities of the parties ceased.

Col. Plug, man of honor as he was, sometimes met with very rough treatment from the boatmen, whose half savage natures could ill appreciate a gentleman of his birth and breeding.

An instance of this is recorded by the same historian, upon whom we have drawn for the greater part of the account of the duel. A broadhorn from Louisville had received rough usage from Plug's men the year before, and, accordingly, on their next descent, they laid their scheme of revenge. Several of the crew left the boat before they arrived at Plugs' domain, and quietly stole down the bank at its place of landing.

The boat with its small crew was quietly landed. The men hospitably received, and invited to sit down to a game of cards.

They were scarcely seated and placed their money before them, when Plug's signal whistle sounded in their ears for an attack. The reserve corps of boatmen also heard it, knew its import and rushed to the rescue. The battle was quickly over. Three of Plug's men were thrown into the river and the rest fled, leaving their brave commander on the field.

Resistance did not avail him.

Those worthless boatmen stripped him to the skin, and forced him to embrace a sapling about the size of his Pluggy's waist, they bound him immovable to this.

Then seizing the cowhide, each applied it until he was tired, and so they left him alone with his troublesome thoughts and with a yet more troublesome host of mosquitoes, which they could now get access to with ease.

Pluggy, finding her lord besieged with those troublesome little fellows, sought to relieve and sympathize with him, but the only response she received was a curse.

Not long after this Plug came to his untimely end. Just as a squall was coming up he was in a boat, whose crew had left it for an hour or two, engaged in the exercise of his profession, that is he was digging the caulking out of the bottom, when the storm came on rather prematurely, and broke the fastnings of the boat. It began to sink, and after several vain efforts to reach the shore the valiant Colonel sank with the boat and was seen no more.

This sketch of the character of the boatwreckers will prepare the reader for forming some idea of the boatmen who were their prey.

Among the most celebrated of those every reader of western history will remember *Mike Fink*, the hero of his class.

So many and so marvelous are the stories told of this man that numbers of persons are inclined altogether to disbelieve his existence. That he did live, however, does not admit of a doubt. Many are yet living who knew him personally.

As it is to him that all remarkable stories of western river adventures are attributed, his history will form the only example here given to illustrate the character of the Western bargeman.

It is necessary, however, to observe that while Mike possessed all the characteristics of his class, a history of all the adventures attributed to him would present these characteristics in an exaggerated degree. Even the slight sketch here drawn cannot pretend to authenticity.

For aside from the fact that, like other heroes, Mike has suffered from the exuberant fancy of his historians.

He has also had in his own person to atone to posterity for many acts which never came from under his hand seal.

As the representative, however, of an extinct class of men his ashes will not rise in indignation, even if he is again made the hero of " fields his valor never more."

Mike Fink was born in or near Pittsburg, where certain of his relatives still reside. In his earlier capacity he acted as an Indian spy and won great renown for himself by the wonderful facility by which, while still a boy, he gained knowledge of every moment and act of the foe.

But while in the exercise of this calling the, free, wild and adventurous life of the boatman attracted his youthful fancy. And the enchanting music of the broadhorn soon allured him away from Pittsburg to try his fortune on the broad Ohio.

He had learned to mimic all the tones of the boatman's horn, and he longed to go to New Orleans, where he learned the people spoke French, and wore their Sunday clothes every day. He went, and from an humble pupil in his profession, soon became a glorious master.

When the river was too low to be navigable, Mike spent his time in rifle-shooting, then so eminently useful and desirable an accomplishment. And in this, as in all his serious undertakings, he soon compassed his compeers. His skill with the rifle was so universally acknowledged that whenever Mike was present at a shooting-match for beef, which was then a common occurrence all over the country, he was allowed the fifth quarter, *i.e.* the hide and the tallow, without a shot. This was a perquisite for Mike's skill, and one he always claimed, always attained and always sold for whisky with which to treat the crowd. His capacity as a drinker was enormous. He could drink a gallon in twenty-four hours without its effect being perceptible in his language or demeanor. Mike was a bit of a wag, too, and had a singular way of enforcing his jests. He used to say he told his jokes on purpose to be laughed at, and no man should make light of them. The consequence was that whoever had the temerity to refuse a laugh when Mike intended to raise one, received a sound drubbing and an admonition for the future, which was seldom neglected.

His practical jokes, for so he and his associates called their predations on the inhabitants on the shores along which they passed, were always characterized by a boldness of design, and a sagacity of execution that showed no mean talent on Mike's part. One of the most ingenious of these tricks and one which affords a fair [idea of the spirit of them all, is told as follows: Passing slowly down the river Mike observed a large and beautiful flock of sheep grazing on the shore, and being in want of provisions, but scorning to buy them, Mike hit upon the following expedient:

He noticed there was an eddy near the shore, and as it was now dark he moved his boat into the eddy and tied her fast. In his cargo there were some bladders of Scotch snuff. Mike opened one of these, and taking a handful of the contents he went ashore and catching five or six of the sheep, rubbed their noses very thoroughly with the snuff. He then returned to his boat and sent one of his men in a great hurry to the sheep owner's home to tell him he had better come down and see what was the matter with his sheep. In going down hastily in answer to Mike's summons, the gentleman saw a portion of his flock very singularly affected. Floating, bleating and rubbing their noses againt the ground and against each other, and performing all manner of undignified antics.

The gentleman was very sorely puzzled and demanded of Mike if he knew what was the matter with his sheep.

"You don't know?" answered Mike very gravely.

"I do not," replied the gentleman.

"Did you ever hear of the black murrain?" asked Mike in a confidential whisper.

"Yes," said the sheep owner in a terrified reply.

"Well that is it," replied Mike. "All the sheep up the river has got it dreadful. Dyin' like rotten dogs, hundreds a day."

"You don't say so," said the victim. "And is there no cure for it?"

"Only one as I knows of," was the reply. "You see the murrain is dreadful catchen', and if you don't get them away as is got it, they will kill the whole flock. Better shoot them right off, they has got to die any way."

"But no man could single out the infected sheep and shoot them from among the flock," said the man.

"My name is Mike Fink," was the curt reply. And it was answer enough.

The gentleman begged him to shoot the infected sheep and throw them in the river. This was exactly what Mike wanted, but he pretended to resist. "It mought be a mistake," he said. "They will, may be, get well. He did not like to shoot many sheep on his own say so. He had better go and ask some of his neighbors ef it was the murrian sure 'nuf." The gentleman insisted and Mike modestly resisted until he was finally promised two gallons of old peach brandy if he would comply.

His scruples, finally thus overcome, Mike shot the sheep, and threw them into the eddy, and got the brandy.

4

After dark the men jumped into the water and hauled the sheep on board, and by daylight had them packed away and were gliding merrily down the stream..

(This incident is by some accredited to Wm. Creasy, a bargeman of the James river.)

CHAPTER XII.

ANOTHER story is told of rather a different character of this resolute man. It occurred on the Mississippi river. A negro had come down to the bank to gaze at the passing boat, who had the singularly projecting heel, peculiar to some races of Africans. This peculiarity caught Mike's eye, and so far outraged his idea of symmetry that he determined to correct it. Accordingly he raised his rifle to his shoulder and fired, carrying away the offensive projection. The negro fell, crying murder, believing himself to be mortally wounded. Mike was apprehended for this trick at St. Louis, and found guilty. But we do not hear of the infliction of any punishment.

A writer in the *Western Monthly Review*, for July, 1829, in a letter to the editor of that magazine, asserts that he himself has seen the records of this case in the books of the court, and Mike's only defense was, that the fellow could not wear a genteel boot, and he wanted to fix it so that he could.

One of the feats with his rifle, of which he used to boast of, occurred somewhere in Indiana.

Mike's boat was laying to, from some cause, and he had gone ashore in pursuit of game. As he was creeping along with the stealthy tread of a cat, his eye fell upon a fine buck, browsing on the edge of a barren spot, a little distance off. Repriming his rifle and picking the flint, he made his approach in his usual noiseless manner.

At the moment he reached the spot at which he went to take aim, he spied a large Indian intent upon the same object, approaching from a direction little different from his own. Mike shrank behind a tree with the quickness of thought, and keeping his eye upon the hunter waited the result with patience. In a few moments the Indian halted within fifty paces and leveled his piece at the deer. Instantly Mike presented his rifle at the body of the savage, and at the moment smoke issued from the gun of the latter the bullet of Fink

passed through the red man's breast. He fell dead, uttering
a yell at the same instant the deer fell. Mike reloaded his
rifle and remained in cover some minutes to ascertain whether
any more enemies were at hand.

He ascertained that the Indian and the deer were both
dead, when he took the choice parts of the latter and returned
to his boat, always thereafter claiming he had "killed two
birds with one stone."

After the introduction of steamboats on the western waters
Mike's occupation was gone. He could not consent, however,
altogether to quit his free, wild life of adventure, and accordingly, in 1822, he, together with Carpenter and Tolbert, who
were his firmest friends, joined "Henry and Ashley's" company of Missouri trappers, and with this company they proceeded, the same year, to the mouth of the Yellowstone
River. Here a fort was built and from this point parties of
hunters were sent out in all directions. Mike, with his two
friends and nine others, formed one of these parties, and pre-
ferring to live to themselves, they dug a hole in the river
bluff, and here spent the winter. While here Mike and Carpenter had a fierce quarrel, caused, probably by rivalry in
the favors of a certain squaw.

Previous to this time the friendship of these two had been
unbounded. Carpenter was equally as good a shot as Mike,
and it had been their custom to place a tin cup of whisky on
each other's head and shoot it off at a distance of seventy
yards with their rifles. This feat they had often performed
and always successfully. After the quarrel, and the spring
had returned, they revisited the fort, and over a cup whisky
they talked over their difficulty. and renewed their vows of
amity, which was to be ratified by the usual trial of shooting
at the tin cup. They skyed a copper for the first shot and
Mike won it. Carpenter, who knew Mike thoroughly,
declared he was going to be killed, but scorned to refuse the
test. He prepared himself for the worst. He bequeathed
his gun, pistols, wages, etc., to Talbot in case he should be
killed. They went to the field and while Mike loaded his
gun and prepared for the shot, Carpenter filled a tin cup to
the brim, and without moving a feature, placed it on his
devoted head. At the target Mike leveled his piece. After
fixing his arm, he took down his gun and laughingly cried.
Then raising the gun again he pulled the trigger and in an
instant Carpenter fell and expired without a groan.

The ball had entered at the center of the forehead, about an
inch and a half above the eyes. Mike coolly set down his

rifle and blew the smoke out of it, keeping his eye fixed upon
the prostrate body of his quondam friend.   "Carpenter,"
said he, "have you spilt the whisky?"   He was told that
he had killed Carpenter.   "It's all an accident," said he, "I
took as fair a bead on the black spot on the cup as ever
I took on squirrel's eye.   How could it happen?" and he fell
to cursing gun, powder, bullet and himself.

In the wild country where they were the hand of justice
could not reach Mike and he went unmolested.   But Talbot
had determined to revenge Carpenter, and one day, after several months had elapsed, when Mike, in a drunken fit, boast-
ing in Talbot's presence that he had killed Carpenter inten-
tionally, and that he was glad of it, Talbot drew out one
of the pistols which had been left him by the murdered man,
and shot Mike through the heart.   In less than four months
after this Talbot was himself drowned in attempting to swim
the Titan river, and with him perished "the last of the bargemen."

Mike Fink's person is described by the writer in the
Western Monthly, before referred to: His weight was about
one hundred and eighty pounds, height about five feet nine
inches, broad round face, pleasant features, brown skin, tanned by sun and rain, blue but very expressive eyes, inclining
to gray, broad white teeth, square brawny form, well pro-
portioned, every muscle of the arms, thighs and legs perfectly developed, indicating the greatest strength and activity.
His person, taken altogether, was a model for a Hercules,
except as to size.   Of his character, Mike himself has given
the best epitome.   He used to say: "I can out run, out hop,
out jump, thrown down, drag out, and lick any man in the
country.   I am a Salt River roarer, I love the wimen, and am
chock full of fight."

CHAPTER XIII.

[From Sharf's History of St. Louis and County.]

REFERRING to the character of the *vogageurs* or boatmen on the western rivers before the introduction of steamboats, is the following: —

"The boatmen were a class by themselves, a hardy, adventurous, muscular set of men, inured to constant peril and privation, and accustomed to severe and unremitting toil. For weeks, and even months at a time they saw no faces but their companions among the crew, or on some passing craft, and their days from daylight until dark were spent in constant toil at the oars, or poles, or tugging at the rope, either on the boat, or on shore, as they were employed, either at warping or cordelling.

At night, after "tying up" their time was spent either in gaming, carousing, story telling, etc. — the amusement of the evening being varied not unfrequently by a fisticuff encounter.

The labor performed in their occupation was of the severest kind, and the constant and arduous exercise produced in most of them extraordinary physical development.

So intense was the exertion usually required to propel and guide the boat, that a rest was necessary every hour, and from 14 to 20 miles was all that could be made against the current.

The sense of physical power, which naturally accompanied the steady exercise of the muscles inspired the average boatman, not merely with insensibility of danger, but a bellicoseness of disposition, which seems to have been characteristic of his class.

The champion pugilist of a boat was entitled to wear a red feather in his cap, and this badge of pre-eminence was universally regarded as a challenge to all rivals.

In summer the boatmen were usually stripped to the waist, and their bodies exposed to the sun were turned to the swarthy hues of the Indian. In winter they were clothed in buckskin breeches and blankets (capots), a grotesque combination of French and Indian styles, which gave their attire a wild and peculiar appearance.

Their food was of the simplest character. After a seven days' toil, says "Moneth," at night they took their "fillie," or ration of whisky, swallowed their homely supper of meat

half burned and bread half baked, retiring to sleep they
stretched themselves upon the open deck without covering,
under the open canopy of heaven, or probably enveloped in
a blanket until the steersman's horn called them to their
morning fillie and their toil.

Hard and fatiguing was the life of the boatman, yet it was
rare that any of them changed their occupation. There was
a charm in the excesses, in their frolics, and in the fightings
which they anticipated at the end of the voyage which cheered
them on.

Of weariness, none would complain, but rising from his bed
at the dawn of day, and reanimated by his morning draught,
he was prepared to hear the wonted order, " stand to your
poles and set off.''

The boatmen were masters of the winding horn and the fiddle, and as the boat moved off from her moorings, some, to
cheer their labors, or " scare off the devil and secure good
luck,'' would wind the animating blast of the horn, which,
mingling with the sweet music of the fiddle and reverberating
along the shores, greeted the solitary dwellers along the banks
with news from New Orleans.

Levity and volubility were conspicuous traits of the boatman's character, and while he was willing to perform long and
continued labor, he would render such service only to a " patroon '' whom he respected. In fine, the average keel-boat-
man was cool, reckless, even to the verge of rashness, and
pugnacious, but, notwithstanding certain grave shortcomings,
an unmitigated hater of all darker shades of sin and wrong-
doing, such as robbing, murdering for plunder, crimes in his
day that were frequently and boldly perpetrated along the
sparsely settled banks and lonely islands on the Ohio and Mississippi Rivers.

The departure of a boat was an important event in the uneventful life of the inhabitants of Western towns.

On such occasions it was customary for the friends to assemble on the banks to bid adieu to the *voyag-urs*. Sometimes
half the population of the village was present to tender their
wishes for a prosperous trip.''

For years it was believed that no keel-boat could ascend the
Missouri River. The rapidity of the current was supposed to
present an insuperable obstacle to the navigation with such a
craft.

The doubt was settled by the energy of George Sarpy, who
sent a keel-boat under Capt. La Brosse to try the difficult experiment of ascending the Missouri. The success of the un-

dertaking marked a signal advance in Western river navigation, and supplied the merchants of St. Louis with new facilities for the transportation of goods, while it greatly extended the operations of boatmen and increased their numbers.

Of the keel-boatmen, when classed by nativity, the Kentuckians bore the most unenviable reputation, on account of the fact that they were generally characterized by excessive recklessness and bellicoseness, and we are told that so gloomy was the reputation of the Kentuckians, that travelers were liable at every place (except at the miserable wayside taverns) to have the door shut in their faces on applying for refreshments or a night's lodging. Nor would any plea or circumstance alter the decided refusal of a matron or mistress, unless it might be the uncommonly genteel appearance or equipage of the traveler. For a similar reason, perhaps, badly built boats, with poor or injured plank in their bottoms, which had been sold to unsuspecting parties, were known as "Kentucky boats."

"In 1802," says a writer on "Early Navigators," in a St. Louis paper, "A Mr. Winchester's boat struck a rock in the Ohio river, below Pittsburg, and one of her bottom plank being badly stove in, she sank immediately, having on board a valuable cargo of dry goods.

The proprietor, not being on board at the time, conceived, when informed of the disaster, that it had been caused by the carelessness of the person to whom he had intrusted the care of the boat and cargo, and brought suit against him for damages. Indeed it was somewhat evident, from all that could be learned, that the patroon had no business in the neighborhood of the rock which sunk the boat, and could and should have avoided it.

The defendant's position was somewhat gloomy, but his resources were equal to the emergency. The suit was before (Dr.) Justice Richardson, of Pittsburg, who himself had had some sad experience with "Kentucky boats." The defendant knowing, or having been informed of this, hired two men, went down to the boat and procured some pieces of the plank that had given way. On the day of the trial, after the plaintiff had, as every one thought, fully established his charges and demands, the justice asked the defendant if he had any rebutting evidence to offer. "Yes, your Honor, I have;" and reaching down under the seat, he drew out the pieces of plank above mentioned, and said: "I have no evidence, your Honor, except these pieces of plank which I can prove to your Honor are a part of the same plank the breaking of which caused the sinking of the boat, which I say would not have occurred if the plank had been reasonably sound. Look at them; your Honor will find that it was my misfortune to have been placed in charge of one of these damned Kentucky boats."

Without in any way noticing the blasphemous expression, the justice examined the pieces, which proved to be thoroughly rotten and defective, unfit to be put anywhere, much less in the bottom of a boat. After hearing from the defendant's helpers, that those pieces were taken from the boat in question, and the identical place where she had broken, the court delivered its mind as follows: —

"This court had the misfortune once to place a valuable cargo on a Kentucky boat, not knowing it to be such; which sunk and went down in 17 feet of water, this court believed by coming in contact with a yellow bellied catfish, there being no snag, or rock, or other obstruction near her at the time. And this court being satisfied with the premises in this case doth order that the same be dismissed at the plaintiff's cost — to have included therein the expenses of the plaintiff's costs, in going to and returning from the wreck, for the purpose of obtaining such damnable and irrefutable evidence as this bottom plank has furnished." The bottom plank was deemed proof so conclusive and the prejudice against Kentucky boats in the minds of the public, and it was so extended and settled that it was thought inadvisable to urge the suit any further."

Whatever may have been the law and the practice in those days, all modern decisions in similar cases would have exonerated the defendant, as the boat in question was undoubtedly unseaworthy, although it would have been necessary, in the case cited by Justice Richardson, of the Pittsburg court, to have introduced some testimony to satisfy any court or jury as to the size and character of the yellow bellied catfish of that day.

CHAPTER XIV.

BESIDES the ordinary dangers of the treacherous currents, "cave-ins," shoals and snags of the Mississippi, and occasional assaults from prowling savages, the early boatmen were often called upon to face the more serious attacks of river pirates. Many a boat load of costly merchandise intended for the warehouses of St. Louis never reached its destination. The misdeeds of the robbers were not always limited to the seizure of goods. The proof of rapine was often extinguished by the murder of the witnesses.

The caves of the pirates were often rich with the spoils of a plundered commerce, and the depredations became more frequent in proportion to the impunity with which they were committed. At last the interruption of trade became so gross and the danger to life so eminent that the Governor-General of Louisiana was constrained to take more effective steps for the suppression of the bandits. An official order excluding single boats from the Mississippi granted the privilege of navigation only to *flotillas*, that were strong enough to repel their assailants. The plan succeeded; the pirates were ultimately driven from their haunts.

The arrival at St. Louis in 1788 of a flotilla of ten boats was a memorable occasion in the annals of the village. It was the last year of Don Francisco Cruzat's second administration.

In the year before, M. Beausoliel, a New Orleans merchant, had been captured by pirates, near the island that still bears his name, and subsequently escaping, killed the pirates and recaptured his boat. He then returned to New Orleans and reported his experience to the governor, who thereupon issued the order that all boats bound for St. Louis the following spring should sail together for mutual protection. This was carried out and the flotilla *des dix bateaux* made the voyage, capturing at Cotton Creek the camp and supplies of the pirates, with a valuable assortment of miscellaneous plunder which had been taken from many boats on previous occasions.

In an advertisement published in 1794, the patrons of an especial line of boats were assured of their safety. The statements which were made to allay apprehension, showed that the fear of the pirates was not then groundless. A large crew, skillful in the use of arms, a plentiful supply of muskets and ammunition, an equipment on each boat of six one-pound cannon, and a loop-hole rifle-proof cabin for the passengers, were the means of defense which were provided, on which were based the hopes of security.

So formidable an array of weapons was not well calculated to inspire timid natures with confidence in the safety of the voyage. The boatmen were very active in rooting out the nests of pirates, and not infrequently administered lynch law, in summary fashion. One of the most sanguinary incidents of this character was that which occurred in 1809. Island 94, or Stack Island, or, as it is sometimes called, "Crow's Nest," 170 miles above Natchez, was notorious for many years as a den for the rendezvous of horse thieves, counterfeiters, robbers and murderers. It was a small island in the middle of "Nine Mile Reach." From thence they would sally forth, stop passing boats, murder the crew, or, if this seemed impracticable, would buy their horses, flour, whisky, etc., and pay for them.

Their villainies became notorious, and several years pursuit by the civil officers of the law failed to produce any result in the way of punishment or eradication. But they were at length made to disappear by the application of lynch law, from several keel boat crews. The full history of this affair has never been unfolded, and perhaps never will be. But for terrible retribution and complete annihilation outside of any authorized decrees, it never had its equal in any administration of lynch law, the recitals of which cast so many shadows on the West and South.

The autumn of 1809 had been marked by many atrocities on the part of the bandits of the "Crow's Nest." Several boats and their entire crews had disappeared at that point, and no traces could be found of them afterwards. The country around and up and down the river, had been victimized and robbed in almost every conceivable form, by depredators, whose movements could be traced satisfactorily towards the Crow's Nest. At one time it occurred that several keel boats were concentrated at the head of Nine Mile Reach, within speaking distance of each other, being detained by heavy contrary winds.

The crews of these boats were well informed as to the villainies of those who harbored on the little island a few miles below them. Many of them had friends and comrades on the boats that had been among the missing ones. By what means it was brought about, or at whose suggestion or influence, it was never known. But one dark night, a few hours before daylight, eighty or ninety men from these wind-bound crafts, well armed, descended in their small boats to the Crow's Nest and surprised its occupants, whom they secured after a short encounter, in which two of the boatmen were wounded and several of the robbers killed. Nineteen men, a boy of fifteen, and two women were thus captured. Shortly after sunrise, the boy, on account of his extreme youth, and the two women, were allowed to depart. What was the punishment meted out to the men, whether shot or hanged, was never ascertained with any degree of certainty.

None but the boy, the boatmen and the two women, however, ever left the island alive, and by twelve o'clock noon, the crews were back to their boats, and, the wind having calmed the night before, they shoved out, and by sunset they were far down the river and away from the scene of the indisputably just, although unlawful retribution. Two years afterward came the terrible earthquake, which, with the floods of 1811 and '13, destroyed every vestige of the Crow's Nest, leaving nothing of it to be seen but a low sand-bar, and with it passed away from public sight and mind all signs of the bandits, their crimes, and the awful doom that awaited them.

Some years later a new type of desperadoes appeared, who, if history and tradition do not greatly belie them, were not much more exemplary in their conduct than the pirates and buccaneers that preceded them.

Mike Fink, in particular, was the model hero of the Mississippi boatmen, who has figured on the pages of popular romance, was a ruffian of surpassing strength and courage.

His rifle was unerring, and his conscience was as easy and accommodating as a man in his line of business could wish. His earliest vocation was that of a boatman, but he belonged to a company of government spies or scouts, whose duty it was to watch the movements of the Indians on the frontier. At that time Pittsburgh was on the extreme verge of the white population, and the spies who were constantly employed generally extended their reconnoissances forty or fifty miles west of that place. Going out singly, and living in Indian style, they assimilated themselves to the habits, tastes and feelings of the Indians.

In their border warfare, the scalp of a Shawnee was considered about as valuable as the skin of a panther.

Mike Fink, tiring of this, after awhile returned to the water life, and engrafting several other occupations on that of a boatman, put all mankind, except that of his employer, to whom he was honest and faithful, under contribution and be--

·came nothing more nor less than a freebooter. "Mike, having murdered Joe Stephens, was killed by one of Joe's brothers." — (See history of Mike in another chapter.)

CHAPTER XV.

JAMES GIRTY, another or the famous Mississippi boatmen, was represented as a natural prodigy, not constructed like other men, for instead of ribs, nature had provided him with a solid bony covering on both sides, without any interstices through which a knife, dirk or bullet could penetrate.

He possessed amazing muscular power, and courage in proportion, and his great boast was that he had never been whipped. The trade conducted by the these boats was of considerable importance.

As early as 1802 the annual exports of the Mississippi Valley amounted to $2,160,000, and the imports to $2,500,000. Up to 1804 the annual value of the fur trade of Upper Louisiana amounted to $203,750. The Province then exported lead, salt, beef and pork, and received Indian goods from ·Canada, domestics from Philadelphia and Baltimore, groceries from New Orleans, and hardware from the Ohio River.

Short notices in the newspapers of the day, announcing, "Wanted to freight from this place to Louisville about 1,600 weight. Apply at the printing office."

"Thirteen boatmen are wanted to navigate a fur boat to New Orleans, to start about the 15th of next month. Customary wages will be given."

"The barge Scott will start from St. Louis on the first of March, and will take freight for Louisville or Frankfort in Kentucky, on reasonable terms. Apply to John Steele."

FREIGHTING FROM NEW ORLEANS TO KASKASKIA IN 1741.

We doubt whether so unique or so old a bill of lading can be found in the Valley of the Mississippi as that which follows. It is a translation from a bill of sale executed the 18th of May, 1741, by Barois, a notary in Kaskaskia, Ills.

"And it has been further agreed that said Mettazer promises to deliver to said Bienvena, at the landing place of this town ·of Kaskaskia, at his own risks, the fortunes of war excepted, an iron kettle, weighing about 290 pounds, used for the man-

ufacture of salt, and which said Bienvena owns in New Orleans, and said Bienvena promises to pay to said Mettazer,
for his salary and freight, after the delivery of said kettle, a
steer in good order, three bushels of salt, two hundred pounds
of bacon, and twenty bushels of Indian corn under the penalty of all costs, etc."

[From *St. Louis Republican.*]

" Shipped by Peter Provenchere, of the town of St. Louis.
merchant, on board the boat 'Jas. Maddison,' whereof
Charles Quivey is master, now laying at the landing before
the town of St. Louis, and ready immediately to depart for
Louisville, Ky.

" F. T.   Six packs of deer skins, marked and numbered as
per margin. And a barrel of bear oil, containing about
thirty-two gallons, all in good order and well condition, which
I promise to deliver in like good order and condition, unavoidable accidents excepted, unto Mr. Francis Tarriscon or to his
assignees. And, moreover, I acknowledge to have of the
said Peter Provenchere a note of Peter Menard on Louis
Lorimer, inhabitant of Cape Girardeau, four thousand pounds
of receiptable deer skins, the said note transferred to my
order, and I bind and engage myself to ask of the said Louis
Lorimer the payment of the said note, and if I reclaim it to
deliver to the said Francis Tarriscon, or assign the one thousand
pounds of deer skins, together with the six packs and the
barrel now received, and in case of no payment to return the
note to Mr. Tarriscon, he or they paying freight.

" In witness whereof I have set my hand to three bills of
lading, all of the same tenor and date, one being accomplished, the others null and void.   CHARLES QUIVEY.

" Test. WM. C. CARR, ST. LOUIS, 8th, A. D., 1809."

CHAPTER XVI.

"THE WEST."

PUBLISHED IN CINCINNATI, 1848, BY JAMES HALL.

THE French, who first explored our Northern frontier, ascended the great chain of lakes to Huron and Michigan, and afterwards penetrated through Lake Superior, to that remote wilderness, where the head branches of the St. Lawrence interlock with those of the Mississippi. Adopting, and probably improving the bark canoe of the natives, they were enabled to traverse immeasurable wilds, which nature had seemed to have rendered inaccessible to man by floods of water at one season and masses of ice and snow at another, by the wide-spread lakes, and ponds, and morasses, which in every direction intercepted the journey by land, and by the cataracts and rapids, which cut off the communication by water. All difficulties vanished before the efficiency of this little vessel ; its wonderful buoyancy enabled it, though heavily freighted, to ride safely over the waves of the lakes, even in boisterous weather; its slender form and lightness of draught permitted it to navigate the smallest streams, and pass the narrowest channels; while its weight was so little, that it was easily carried on the shoulders of men from one stream to another. Thus when these intrepid navigators found the river channel closed by an impassable barrier, the boat was unloaded, the freight, which had previously been formed into suitable packages for that purpose, was carried round the obstruction by the boatmen, the boat itself performed the same journey, and then was again launched in its proper element. So, also, when a river had been traced up to its sources, and no longer furnished sufficient water for navigation, the accommodating bark canoe, like some amphibious monster, forsook the nearly exhausted channel and traveled across the land to the nearest navigable stream. By this simple but admirable contrivance, the fur trade was secured, the great continent of North America was penetrated to its center through thousand of miles of wilderness, and a valuable staple brought to the marts of commerce. If we regard that little boat as the means of bringing to market this great mass of the treasures of the wilderness, we may well remark, that never was an important object affected by means so insignifi-

cant. But the human labor, and peril, and exposure — the
courage, the enterprise, and the skill employed, were far
from insignificant. The results were great. Besides the vast
trade which was developed, the interior of a great continent
was explored, the boundaries between two empires were
traced out and incidently established, an intercourse with the
Indian tribes was opened, and valuable facts were added to
the treasures of science. And all this was accomplished, not
by the power of an empire, not by the march of a conqueror
impelled by military ambition or the lust of conquest — not
by a lavish expenditure of money, or the shedding of human
blood — but by the action of humble individuals acting under
the great stimulus of commercial enterprise.

Turning our attention to another part of the great theater
of early adventure, we see the bold explorers crossing from
the lakes to the Mississippi, passing up and down that river,
tracing its gigantic course from the Gulf of Mexico to the Falls
of St. Anthony — erecting forts, planting settlements, and,
in short, establishing a chain of posts and colonies, extending
from the mouth of the Mississippi, westward of the British
Colonies, to the mouth of the St. Lawrence. The adventurers to Louisiana sought the precious metals ; imaginary mines
of gold and silver allured them across the ocean, led them to
brave the terrors of the climate and the wilderness, and sustained them under the greatest extremes of toil and privation.
Though disappointed in the object of their search, they became the founders of an empire, they explored and developed
the resources of the country, they led the way to that flood of
emigration which had been gradually filling up the land, and
scattered the germs of that prosperity which we see blooming
around us, and promising harvests too great to be estimated.

" When the sagacious eye of Washington first beheld the
country lying about the head-waters of the Ohio, he saw and
pointed out the military and commercial advantages which
might be secured by its occupation. Had the annexation of
this country to the American colonies, or at a later period
to the States, been a political question, how various would
have been the opinions, how deliberate the discussion, how
slow the action, how uncertain the result. But this splendid
example of national aggrandizement was not achieved by the
wisdom of statesmen, nor by the valor of armies. No sooner
had a few daring pioneers settled in the wilderness, than the
eager spirit of trade, ever on the watch for new fields of adventure, discovered the rich promise of gain offered by a
region so wide and so fertile. Commerce did not then, nor in

any instance, in the settlement of our country, wait until
'grim visaged war had smoothed his wrinkled front,' as is
supposed to be her usual custom.   However specific in her
tendencies, she did not shrink from a full participation of the
perils of this glorious adventure.   Following the footsteps of
the pioneers, she came with the advance of the army of population.

"The first settlements in the West were made by the back-
woodsmen from Virginia and North Carolina, who were soon
after followed by those of Pennsylvania and Maryland.   New
Jersey came next in the order of population ; and from these
sources originated that gallant band of pioneers who explored
the country, drove back the savage, and opened the way for
civilization.   They were a daring, a simple, and an honest people, whose history is full of romance — but it is not with the
romance of history we have now to do.   Simple and frugal
as they were in their habits, they were still civilized men —
branches of the great social circle whose center glowed with
the brightest refinements of life — and they had some artificial
wants beyond the mere fruits of the earth and the products of
the chase, while the country abounded in the crude materials
which promised an abundant supply of articles of barter.

"Wherever there is a prospect of gain, there will the adventurous feet of commerce to thread their way, however dreary
the path, however difficult or dangerous the road.   While the
whole Alleghany ridge was still an unbroken mass of wilderness, trains of pack-horses might be seen climbing the mountain sides, by the winding bridle-path, threading the meanders
of the valleys and gorges, trembling on the brinks of preci-
pices, and sliding down the declivities, which scarcely afforded
a secure footing to man or beast.   They were laden with merchandise for traffic.   The conductors were men inured to all
the hardships which beset the traveler in the wilderness — men
who united the craft of the hunter to the courage and discipline of the soldier.   For the road they traveled was the
war-path of the Indian — it was the track that had been beaten
smooth by the feet of them that sought the blood of the white
man, and who still lurked in the way, bent on plunder and
carnage.   There was no resting place, no accommodation, no
shelter.   Throughout the day they plodded on, through the
forest, scaling steep acclivities, fording rivers, enduring all
the toils of an arduous march, and encamping at night in the
wilderness ; observing the precaution and the discipline of a
military party in a hostile country.   These are merchants,
carrying their wares to the forts and settlements of the West ;

they were the pioneers of that commerce which now employs the wealth and controls the resources of an empire. They deserve a high place among the founders of Western settlements, as they furnished the supplies of arms, ammunition, clothing, and other necessaries, which enabled the inhabitants of the frontier to sustain themselves against the hostilities of numerous tribes of Indians, incited to war by British influence, and supplied with the implements and appliances of savage warfare, by the agents of the same humane and enlightened people.

"The first boats used in the navigation of the Western rivers, were the flat-boat, the keel, and the barge, the first of which was only used in descending with the current, while the two latter ascended the streams, propelled laboriously by poles. Navigating long rivers whose shores were still infested by hostile savages, the boatmen were armed, and depended for safety upon their caution and their manhood. Mike Fink, the last of the boatmen, was an excellent marksman, and was as proud of his ability to defend his boat as of his skill to conduct it through the rapids and windings of the navigation. The Indians, lurking along the shore, used many stratagems to decoy the passengers and crews of the boat to land, and those who were unsuspicious enough to be thus deceived fell an easy prey to the marauder. Under the best circumstances these boats were slow, and difficult to manage, the cost of freight was enormous, and the means of communication uncertain.

"The application of steam power to the purposes of navigation forms the brightest era in the history of this country. It is that which has contributed more than any other event or cause to the rapid growth of our population, and the almost miraculous development of our resources. We need not pause to inquire whether the honor of the invention be due to Fitch, to Rumsey, or to Fulton, — for that inquiry is not involved in the discussion in which we are now engaged. But if we seek for the efficient patron of this all-powerful agent in the West — for the power that adopted, fostered, improved, and developed it — from an unpromising beginning, through discouragement, failure, disappointment — through peril of life, vast expenditure of money, and ruinous loss, to the most complete and brilliant success — we are again referred to the liberal spirit of commercial enterprise. Science pointed the way, but she did no more; it was the wealth of the Western merchant, and the skill of the Western mechanic, that wrought out the experiment to a successful issue. The first fruits of

the enterprise were far from encouraging; failure after fail
ure attested the numerous and embarrassing difficulties by
which it was surrounded. For although all the early boats
were capable of being propelled through the water, and although the last was usually better than those which preceded
it, it was long a doubtful question, whether the invention
could be made practically useful upon our Western rivers;
and it was not until five years of experiment, and the building of nine expensive steamboats, that the public mind was
convinced by the brilliant exploit of the Washington, which
made the trip from Louisville to New Orleans and back in
forty-five days.

"The improvements in this mode of navigation since then
have been surprising. The voyage from New Orleans to Louisville has been made in less than six days. The trip from Cincinnati to New Orleans and back is made easily in two weeks.
During the high water, in the spring of 1846, the trip from
Pittsburgh to Cincinnati was made in twenty-seven hours, and
the packet boats between these places have now regular days
and hours for departure.

"Explosions and other destructive casualties have become
rare, and the navigation is now safe, except only from obstructions existing in the channels of the rivers. All that skill, enterprise, and public spirit could do, to bring this navigation to
perfection, has been done by the liberal proprietors of steamboats. The wealth of individuals has been freely contributed,
while that of the government has been withheld with a degree
of injustice which has scarcely a parallel in the annals of civilized legislation, The history of man does not exhibit a spectacle
of such rapid advancement in population, wealth, industry,
and refinement, such energy, perseverance, and enlightened public spirit on the part of individuals, as is exhibited in the progress
of the Western people — nor of so parsimonious and sluggish a
spirit as that evinced toward us by the government. All that
we have, and are, are our own, created by ourselves, unaided by
a government to whose resources and power we are now the
largest contributors. We build and maintain a fleet of five
hundred steamboats, bearing annually a freightage of more
than two hundred million dollars — while we are subjected to
an immense yearly loss of life and property, from the narrow
and unwise refusal of the government to make a comparatively
small expenditure to remove obstructions from the channels of
rivers, over which it has the sole jurisdiction.

"By our own unaided exertions we have now actively employed in the transportation of passengers and merchandise

more than five hundred steamboats, worth ten million of dollars, having the capacity of one hundred thousand tons, and plying upon a connected chain of river navigation of twelve thousand miles in extent.

"The value of the exports and imports, floating on the Western waters annually, has been estimated at two hundred and twenty millions of dollars, consisting of the products of our soil and manufacturers on one hand, and of the fabrics of foreign countries upon the other, all bought with the money of our merchants, and by them thrown into the channels of trade.

" If the mercantile class had rendered no other service to our country, than that of introducing and fostering the agency of steam, in navigation and manufactures, they would have entitled themselves to more lasting gratitude and honor, than the most illustrious statesman or hero has ever earned from the justice and enthusiasm of his country."

CHAPTER XVII.

PREVIOUS to the year 1817, the whole commerce from New Orleans to the upper country was carried in about twenty barges, averaging one hundred tons each, and making but one trip in the year, so that the importations from New Orleans in one year could not have exceeded the freight brought up by one of our largest steamboats in the course of a season.   On the upper Ohio, there were about one hundred and fifty keel-boats, of about thirty tons each, which made the voyage from Pittsburgh to Louisville and back in two months, or about three such trips in the year.   That was about thirty years ago, and need I pause to inquire what would have been the probable condition of our country, at this time, had our commerce continued to be dependent upon such insufficient means of conveyance?

" The pioneers were a noble race, and well did they discharge the part assigned them.   They led the way into the wilderness.   They scaled the ramparts of the Alleghany mountains, that seemed to have been erected as barriers against the footsteps of civilized men.   They beat back the savage and possessed the country.   Their lives were full of peril and daring; their deeds are replete with romance.

" The farmers who have subdued the wilderness are hardy and laborious men, who have been well designated as the bone and muscle of the country. They have cheerfully encountered obstacles from which a less resolute body of men would have shrunk in despair, and have won the fruitful fields which they possess through toils and dangers such as rarely fall to the lot of husbandmen.

"But without detracting from the merits of either of these classes, what would this country have been now, without commerce? Suppose its rural population had been left to struggle with the wilderness without the aid of the numberless appliances which have been brought to their doors by the spirit of trade, to what point would their population and their prosperity have risen? Without money, without steamboats, canals, railroads, turnpikes, and other facilities for transportation, what would have been the destiny of our broad and fertile plains? Desert and blooming, they would have sustained a scattered population, rich in flocks and herds —a roaming, pastoral people, whose numbers would have grown by the natural increase; while the country would have remained unimproved, and its rich resources locked in the bosom of the earth. But commerce came, bringing them a market for their products, offering rich rewards to industry, and stimulating labor to the highest point of exertion. She brought with her money, and the various representatives of money, established credit, confidence, commercial intercourse, united action and mutuality of interest. Through her influence the forests were penetrated by roads, bridges were thrown over rivers, and highways constructed through dreary morasses. Traveling was rendered easy and transportation cheap. Through this influence the earth was made to yield its mineral treasures; iron, lead, copper, coal, salt, saltpetre, and various other products of the mine, have been taken from our soil, and brought into common use. Our agricultural products have increased, and are daily and hourly increasing in variety and value; while in every village is seen the smoke of the manufactory, and heard the cheerful sounds of the engine and hammer.

"Such have been the trophies of commerce; and still the same salutary spirit is abroad in our land. There is no page in the history of our country more surprising, or richer in the romance of real life, than that which depicts the adventures and the perils of the traders and trappers in the wilderness beyond our Western frontier. Leaving St. Louis in large parties, well mounted and armed, they go forth with the cheerfulness of men in pursuit of pleasure. Yet their whole lives are full of danger, privation and hardship. Crossing the wide prairies, and directing their steps to the Rocky Mount-

ains, they remain months and even years in those savage
wilds, living in the open air, without shelter, with no food but
such game as the wilderness affords, eaten without bread or
salt, setting their traps for beaver and otter in the mountain
streams, and fighting continually with the grizzly bear and
the Indian — their lives are a long series of warfare and watching, of privation and danger. These daring men secure to us
the fur trade, while they explore the unknown regions beyond
our borders, and are the pioneers in the expansion of our territory.

" So, too, of the caravans which annually pass from St.
Louis across the great plains to Santa Fe. Their purpose is
trade. They carry large amounts of valuable merchandise to
the Mexican dominions, and bring back rich returns. But like
the trapper, they go armed for battle, and prepared to encounter all the dangers of the wilderness. And here, too, we
see the spirit of trade animated by an intelligent enterprise,
and sustained by a daring courage and an invincible perseverance.

" There are many persons still living who bear in their
memories the records of the last fifty years, so fraught
with those momentous events, which have disturbed the
repose of the world, or advanced the progress of man.
The rise of Napoleon, the expansion of that gigantic military
power, which had nearly conquered Europe, the lavish expenditure of blood and treasure, by that mighty conqueror,
that man of brilliant genius and stubborn will, are still recent
events. Within that period, kingdoms were overthrown, nations conquered, crowns transferred ; — and who can forget
the pomp, the circumstances, the terror, the dreadful carnage,
that attended those great national changes?

" Within the same period the great plain of the Mississippi
was a wilderness, embracing a few feeble and widely scattered
colonies. Here also arose a mighty conqueror, more powerful than an army with banners. A vast region has been
overrun and subdued. The mountains have been scaled —
the hills have been leveled, and the valleys filled up, and the
rough ways made smooth, to admit the ingress of the invaders
The land has been taken. A broad expanse extending over
twelve degrees from north to south, and ten degrees from
east to west, has been rescued from the dominion of nature,
and from the hand of the savage, and brought under subjection to the laws of social subordination. A population of
seven millions has been planted upon the soil. Cities have
grown up on the plains, the fields are rich with harvests, and

the rivers bear the rich freights of commerce. This has
nearly all been effected without the horrors of war, without
national violence, without the domestic afflictions usually attendant on the train of conquest. The conquests of the war-
like emperor have vanished, and his greatness perished like an
airy fabric; while a commercial people, using only pacific
means, have gained an empire whose breadth and wealth might
easily satisfy the ambition of even a Napoleon. They have
gained it by labor, by money, and by credit — by the muscular exertion of the farmer and mechanic, aided by mercantile enterprise and fiscal ability.

"The great West has now a commerce within its own limits,
as valuable as that which floats on the ocean between the
United States and Europe. In that wide land, where so lately
the beaver and honey bee were the only representatives of
labor, and a painted savage the type of manhood, we manufacture all the necessaries of life, letters and the fine arts are
cultivated, and beauty and fashion bloom around us.

"We have, in the West and Southwest, an incorporated
banking capital of fifty millions of dollars, affording, with its
circulation of notes, a capital of about one hundred millions
of dollars for business; and however the demagogue may rail
against these institutions, there can be no question, that their
capital is so much actual power, wielded by the commercial
class, for the benefit of the whole country. The poor may
envy the rich the possession of that of which they feel the
want, the demagogue may decry credit, for the same reason,
but the truth is that this country has grown rich through the
money of banks and the enterprise of merchants. The
farmer has been the greatest gainer from the general prosperity. Commerce has supplied money to purchase his products; the building of mills, the creation of roads, canals, and
steamboats, are due to the enterprise of commerce, but they
bring a market to the farmer. The agricultural products,
which but a few years ago were not worth the labor of production, are now sources of wealth to the farmer — of vast
aggregated wealth to the State.

"In 1795, when the troops of Wayne triumphed over a
numerous Indian force, the whole territory of Ohio was a
wilderness; now we have a population of two millions, actively engaged in the various pursuits of industry, a country
rich in resources, highly improved, and intersected in every
direction by turnpike roads, railroads and canals; the aggregate extent of the artificial communications made by the State
being over fifteen hundred miles, and their cost more than

fourteen millions of dollars. And these are not military roads, constructed by the patronage of the government, neither are they the highways of a rural people, required for the purposes of social intercourse — they are the avenues of commercial system, through which wealth and property circulate throughout the broad land, nourishing its prosperity into healthful and lusty vigor — created by the wants, the influence, and the wealth of commerce.

" The introduction of steamboats upon the Western waters deserves a separate mention, because it has contributed more than any other single cause, perhaps more than all other causes which have grown out of human skill, combined, to advance the prosperity of the West. The striking natural features of this country are, its magnitude — its fertility — its mineral wealth — the number and extent of its rivers. Its peculiar adaptation to commercial purposes, is evident. The richness of the soil, and the abundance of all the useful minerals combine to render agricultural labors easy, cheap and greatly productive. The amount of produce raised for consumption, and for export, is great; and the people are therefore not only able, but liberally disposed to purchase foreign products. They do, in fact, live more freely, and purchase more amply, than the farmers of any other country. The amount, therefore, of commercial capital employed, as compared with the amount of population, is great; and the vast superficial extent of country, over which these operations may be extended with safety and facility, and whose products may be exchanged, concentrated, or distributed, is unexampled. There is nothing, in the topography of any other country, to compare with the Western rivers. The Mississippi and her tributaries may be navigated in various directions, to the distance of two thousand miles from the ocean; and every portion of this immense plain is intersected by these natural canals. In these respects nature has been prodigal; it was left to human skill and energy to turn her gifts to the best advantage, and never was the intellect of man more usefully employed than in the discovery and successful introduction of steam navigation. It was all that the Western country needed; and the name of Fulton should be cherished here with that of Washington; if the one conducted us to liberty, the other has given us prosperity — the one broke the chains which bound us to a foreign country; the other has extended the channels of intercourse, and multiplied the ties which bind us to each other.

" The rapidity with which new channels of trade have been

opened, and are now daily becoming developed, is astonishing;
but the improvements in navigation, and in the facilities for
transporting merchandise by land and water, have been infinitely greater and more remarkable.

"It is needless to do more than mention the Indian canoe,
the smallest and rudest of boats, but which, at a period but
little beyond the memory of living witnesses, was the only
vessel that navigated our western rivers. For the purpose of
commerce they were entirely inadequate, and were never used
in any regular branch of trade.

"Previous to their intercourse with the whites. the canoes
of the Indians must have been much more unwieldy, and imperfect, than any that are now in use. They had no tools except the clumsy axes made of stone, of which we see specimens in our museums, and their canoes were made of solid logs
by burning away the part intended to be removed. Some of
the most distant tribes, who have little trade with our people,
still pursue the same laborious and unsatisfactory process
When iron tools were introduced, the canoe assumed the
present shape.

"The birch canoe is peculiar to the northern regions, where
the tree which supplies the bark is found. These also were
probably of the most crude and awkward construction, previous to the visits of the French traders, under whose directions they acquired the lightness, strength, and beauty, which
have given them their celebrity.

"The earliest improvement upon the canoe was the pirogue,
an invention of the whites. Like the canoe, this boat is
hewed out of solid log; the difference is, that the pirogue has
greater width and capacity, and is composed of several pieces
of timber as if the canoe was sawed lengthwise into two equal
sections, and a broad flat piece of timber inserted in the middle, so as to give greater breadth of beam to the vessel. This
was probably the identical process by which the Europeans,
unable to procure planks to build boats, began in the first instance to enlarge canoes to suit their purposes. They were
often used as ferry boats, to transport horses across our
rivers, and we have frequently seen them in operation, of a
sufficient size to effect their object in perfect safety.

"These were succeeded by the barge, the keel, and the flat-
boat. Of the two first, the barge was the largest, had the
greatest breadth, and the best accommodations for passengers;
the keel was longer, has less depth, and was better fitted to
run in shallow channels. They were navigated by a rude and
lawless class of men, who became distinguished as well for

their drolleries, as for their predatory and ferocious habits. In the then thinly scattered state of the population, their numbers rendered them formidable, as there were few villages on the rivers, and still fewer settlements, which contained a sufficient number of able-bodied men to cope with the crew of a barge, consisting usually of thirty or forty hands; while the arrival of several of these boats together made them completely masters of the place. Their mode of life, and the facilities they possessed of evading the law, were such as would naturally make them reckless. Much of the distance through which they traveled in their voyages was entire wilderness, where they neither witnessed the courtesies of life, nor felt any of the restraints of law; and where for days, perhaps weeks, together, they associated only with each other. The large rivers whose meanders they pursued formed the boundaries of States, so that living continually on the lines which divided different civil jurisdictions, they could pass with ease from one to the other, and never be made responsible to any.

"One of the earliest attempts at an intercourse with New Orleans, by the river, is so remarkable as to deserve a separate mention. In 1776, Messrs. Gibson and Linn, the grandfather of Dr. Linn, now a Senator in Congress from Missouri, descended by water from Pittsburgh to New Orleans to procure military stores for the troops stationed at the former place. They completely succeeded in their hazardous enterprise, and brought back a cargo of one hundred and thirty-six kegs of gunpowder. On reaching the falls of the Ohio, on their return in the spring of 1777, they were obliged to unload their boats, and carry the cargo round the rapids, each of their men carrying three kegs at a time on his back. The powder was delivered at Wheeling, and afterwards transported to Fort Pitt.

"The character of Mike Fink, 'the last of the boatmen,' has been rendered familiar to most readers, by the pen of one of our best writers. He was a leader of the men of his own class; and was famous for his herculean strength, his contempt of danger, his frolics, and his depredations. He was a coarse, vulgar, desperate man — yet possessed a degree of humor, hilarity, and openness, that made him remarkable, and conciliated for him a sort of popularity, which caused him to be universally known, and still preserves his name in tradition. In his calling, as a master of a boat, he was faithful — a quality which seems to have belonged to most of his class; for it is a singular fact, that lawless and wild as these men were, the valuable cargoes of mer-

chandise committed to their care, and secured by no other
bond than their integrity, were always carried safely to
their places of destination and the traveler, however weak,
or however richly freighted, relied securely on their protection.

"In the earlier periods of this navigation, the boats employed in it were liable to attacks from the Indians, who employed a variety of artifices to decoy the crews into their
power. Sometimes a single individual, disguised in the ap-
parel of some unhappy white man, who had fallen into their
hands, appeared on the shore making signals of distress, and
counterfeiting the motions of a wounded man. The crew
supposing him to be one of their countrymen, who had escaped from the Indians, would draw near the shore for the
purpose of taking him on board; nor would they discover the
deception until, on touching the bank, a fierce band of painted
warriors would rush upon them from an artfully contrived
ambuscade. Sometimes the savages crawled to the water's
edge, wrapped in the skins of bears, and thus allured
the boatmen, who were ever ready to exchange the oar
for the rifle. But the red warriors were often sufficiently
numerous to attempt, by open violence, that which they
found difficult to accomplish by artifice, against men as wary,
and as expert in border warfare as themselves, and boldly
pursued the boats in their canoes, or rushed upon the boatmen, when the incidents or the perils of the navigation drove
them to the shore.

"These boats, but rarely using sails, and receiving only an
occasional impulse from their oars, descended the stream with
a speed but little superior, at any time, to that of the current;
while they met with many accidents and delays to lengthen the
voyage. A month was usually consumed in the passage from
Pittsburgh to New Orleans, while the return voyage was not affected in less than four months, nor without a degree of toil
and exposure to which nothing but the hardiest frames, and
the most indomitable spirits, would have been equal. The
heavily laden boats were propelled against the strong current
by poles, or, where the stream was too deep to admit the use
of those, drawn by ropes. The former process required the
exertion of great strength and activity, but the latter was even
more difficult and discouraging — as the laborer, obliged by
the heat of the climate to throw aside his clothing, and expose
to the burning rays of the sun, was forced to travel on the
heated sand, to wade through mire, to climb precipitous banks,
to push his way through brush, and often to tread along

the undermined shore, which giving away under his feet precipitated him into the eddying torrent of the Mississippi.
After a day spent in toils which strained every muscle to its
utmost power of exertion, he threw himself down to sleep,
perhaps in the open air, exposed to the cold damps and noxious
exhalation of the Lower Mississippi, and the ferocious attacks
of millions of mosquitoes, and reposed as unconscious of danger, or inconvenience, as the native alligator which bellowed
in the surrounding swamps.

"The flat-boat was introduced a little later than the others.
It is a strong boat, with a perfectly flat bottom, and perpendicular sides; and covered throughout its whole length. Being constructed to float only with the current, it never returns
after descending the river. These boats were formerly used
much by emigrating families, to transport themselves down
the Ohio, are still built in great numbers on the various tributary streams, and floated out in high water, with produce for
New Orleans.

"The French, who navigated the northern lakes, the Mississippi and its tributaries, adopted, in their trade, the use of the
Indian birch canoe. McKenny, in his "Tour to the Lakes,"
thus describes one of those boats.

"Its length was thirty feet, its breadth across the widest
part, about four feet. It is about two and one-half feet deep
in the center, but only about two feet near the bow and stern.
bottom is rounded, and has no keel.

"The materials of which this canoe are built are birch
bark and red cedar, the whole fastened together with wattap
and gum, without a nail, or bit of iron of any sort, to confine
the parts. The entire outside is bark — the bark of the birch
tree — and where the edges join at the bottom or along the
sides they are sewn with this wattap, and then along the seam
it is gummed. Next to the bark are pieces of cedar, shaven
thin, not thicker than a blade of a knife — these run horizon-
tally, and are pressed against the bark by means of these ribs
of cedar, which fit the shape of the canoe, bottom and sides,
and coming up to the edges are pointed and let into a rim of
cedar about an inch and a half wide, and an inch thick, that
forms the gunwale of the canoe, and to these, by means of
the wattap, the bark and ribs are all sewed; the wattap being
wrapped over the gunwale of the canoe, and to these, by
means of the wattap the bark and ribs are all sewed: the wattap being wrapped over the gunwale, and passed through the
bark and ribs. Across the canoe are bars, some five or six, to
keep it in shape. These are fastened by bringing their ends

against the gunwale, or edge, and fastening them to it with wattap. The seats of the voyageurs are alongside of, but below the bars, and are of plank, some four inches wide, which are swung, by means of two pieces of rope, passed through each end, from the gunwale.''

"These boats are so light, and so easily damaged, that precautions were necessary to be taken in loading them, yet the one described above carried not less than two thousand pounds. With these frail vessels the French navigated the Western rivers, and crossed the largest lakes, carrying on a most extensive traffic. The great peculiarity of this navigation is, that these light canoes are carried with facility from one river to another, or around the rapids and cascades, over which they cannot float. Their lading is accordingly made up into packages, each of which may be carried by one man, and these are transported over the portages, on the backs of the engages, by means of straps passed over the forehead. These boats are still used in the fur trade.

"As a curious illustration of the rapid improvement of our Western vessels, and the growth of our trade, I copy the following advertisement from a newspaper called *The Sentinel of the Northwestern Territory*, under date of Saturday, January 11, 1794, by which it will be seen that at that time four keel boats, carrying probably not more than twenty tons each, were supposed to be sufficient for the trade between Cincinnati and Pittsburgh, and that these were prepared to defend themselves against enemies.''

CHAPTER XVIII.

TWO boats for the present will start from Cincinnati for Pittsburgh, and return to Cincinnati in the following . manner, viz.: —

" First boat leaves Cincinnati this morning at eight o'clock, and return to Cincinnati, so as to be ready to sail again in four weeks from this date.

" Second boat will leave Cincinnati on Saturday, the 30th inst., and return to Cincinnati in four weeks as above.

"And so regularly, each boat performing the voyage to and from Cincinnati to Pittsburgh once in every four weeks.

" Two boats, in addition to the above, will shortly be completed and regulated in such a manner that one boat of the four will set out weekly from Cincinnati to Pittsburgh, and return in like manner.

" The proprietor of these boats, has naturally considered the many inconveniences and dangers incident to the common method hitherto adopted by navigating the Ohio, and being influenced by a love of philanthopy and a desire of being serviceable to the public, has taken great pains to render the accommodation on board the boats as agreeable and convenient as they could possibly be made.

" No danger need be apprehended from the enemy, as every person on board will be under cover made proof against rifle or musket balls, and convenient port-holes for firing out of. Each of the boats are armed with six pieces carrying a pound ball; also a number of good muskets, and amply supplied with plenty of ammunition; strongly manned with choice hands, and the masters of approved knowledge.

" A separate cabin from that designed for the men is partitioned off in each boat, for accommodating ladies on their passage. Conveniences are constructed on board each boat, so as to render landing unnecessary, as it might, at times, be attended with danger.

" Rules and regulations for maintaining order on board, and for the good management of the boats and tables accurately calculated for the rates of freightage, for passengers and carriage of letters to and from Cincinnati to Pittsburgh; also a table of the exact time of the arrival and departure to and from the different places on the Ohio, between Cincinnati and

Pittsburgh, may be seen on board each boat, and at the printing office in Cincinnati.   Passengers will be supplied with provisions and liquors of all kinds of the first quality, at the most
reasonable rates possible.   Persons desirous of working their
passage will be admitted on finding themselves; subject, however, to the same order and directions from the master of the
boats as the rest of the working hands of the boat's crew.

" An Office of Insurance will be kept at Cincinnati, Limestone, and Pittsburgh, where persons, desirous of having
their property insured, may apply.   The rates of insurance
will be moderate."

Such were the vessels in which the whole trade of the Western rivers was carried on, previous to the year 1811.   Nor was
the transportation by land farther advanced in improvement.
The few roads that crossed the mountains were so wretchedly
bad that wagons toiled over them with great difficulty, and a
large portion of the merchandise was carried on the backs of
horses.   Even that was considered a triumphant result of enterprise, and a rapid advance in improvement; for a few years
only had then advanced, since Mr. Brown, a delegate from
Kentucky, in Congress, had been smiled at as a visionary, by
the members of that august body, for asking the establishment of a mail to Pittsburgh, to be carried on horseback once
in two weeks.   He was told that such a mail was not needed,
that it would probably never be required, and that the obstacles
of the road were insuperable.   That venerable patriot has lived
to see the establishment of two daily mails on the same route ;
while the canals, the railways, and the turnpikes that lead, to
the West, have rendered it accessible with ease and safety, to
every species of vehicle.

We proceed now to give some account of the steamboat
navigation of these rivers, and shall first speak of some early
attempts towards the accomplishment of this object.

Mr. James Rumsey, of Berkely County, Virginia, invented a
plan for propelling boats by steam as early as 1782, and in
1784 obtained from the Legislature of Virginia the exclusive
right of navigating her waters with such boats.   In 1788, he
published his project, in general terms, together with numerous
certificates from the most respectable characters in Virginia,
among whom was General Washington, all of which assert,
that a steamboat was actually constructed which moved, with
her burden on board, at the rate of three or four miles an hour,
against the current of the Potomac, although the machinery
was in a very imperfect state.   In 1819, his brother, Dr.
Rumsey, of Kentucky, built a boat after this model; and at

that time it was said that the Rumsey plan united simplicity, strength, economy, and lightness in a degree, far superior to any other. The more complex machinery of Bolton and West, Fulton and Evans, have, however, been more successful.

In 1785, John Fitch, a watchmaker in Philadelphia, conceived the design of propelling a boat by steam. He was both poor and illiterate, and many difficulties occurred to frustrate every attempt he made, to try the practicability of his invention. He applied to Congress for assistance, but was refused; and then offered his invention to the Spanish government, to be used in the navigation of the Mississippi, but without any better success. At length a company was formed, and funds subscribed for the building of a steamboat, and in the year 1788, his vessel was launched on the Delaware. Many crowded to see and ridicule the novel, and, as they supposed, the chimerical experiment.

It seems that the idea of wheels had not occurred to Mr. Fitch; but instead of them, oars were used, which worked in frames. He was confident of success; and when the boat was ready for the trial, she started off in good style for Burlington. Those who had sneered began to stare, and they who had smiled in derision looked grave. Away went the boat, and the happy inventor triumphed over the skepticism of an unbelieving public. The boat performed her trip to Burlington, a distance of twenty miles; but unfortunately burst her boiler in rounding to the wharf at that place, and the next tide floated her back to the city. Fitch persevered, and with great difficulty procured another boiler. After some time, the boat performed another trip to Burlington and Trenton, and returned in the same day. She is said to have moved at the rate of eight miles an hour; but something was continually breaking, and the unhappy projector only conquered one difficulty to encounter another. Perhaps this was not owing to any defects in his plans, but to the low state of the arts at that time, and the difficulty of getting such complex machinery made with proper exactness. Fitch became embarrassed with debt, and was obliged to abandon the invention, after having satisfied himself of its practicability.

This ingenious man, who was probably the first inventor of the steamboat, wrote three volumes, which he deposited in manuscript, sealed up, in the Philadelphia library, to be opened thirty years after his death. When, or why, he came to the West we have not learned; but it is recorded of him, that he died and was buried near the Ohio. His three volumes were opened about five years ago, and were found to contain his speculations on mechanics. He details his embarrassments and disappointments, with a feeling which shows how ardently he desired success, and which wins for him the sympathy of those who have heart enough to mourn over the blighted prospects of genius. He confidently predicts the future success of the plan, which, in his hands, failed only for the want of pecuniary means. He prophesies that, in less than a century, we shall see our Western rivers swarming with steamboats; and expresses a wish to be buried on the shores of the Ohio, where the song of the boatmen may enliven the stillness of his resting place, and the music of the steam engine sooth his spirit. What an idea! Yet how natural to the mind of an ardent projector whose whole life had been devoted to the one darling object, which it was not his destiny to accomplish! And how touching is the sentiment found in one of his journals: "The day will come when some more powerful man will get fame and riches from my invention; but nobody will believe that poor John Fitch can do any thing worthy of attention." In less than thirty years after his death, his predictions were verified. He must have died about the year 1799.

"The first steamboat built on the Western waters," says a writer in the *Western Monthly Magazine*, "was the Orleans, built at Pittsburg in 1811; there is no account of more than seven or eight, built previously to 1817; from that period they have been rapidly increasing in number, character, model, and style of workmanship, until 1825, when two or three boats built about that period were declared by common consent to be the finest in the world. Since that time, we are informed, some of the New York and Chesapeake boats rival and probably surpass us, in richness and beauty of internal decoration. As late as 1816, the practicability of navigating the Ohio with steamboats was esteemed doubtful; none but the most sanguine argued favorably. The writer of this well remembers that in 1816, observing, that in company with a number of gentlemen, the long struggles of a stern-wheel boat to ascend Horse-tail ripple (five miles below Pittsburgh), it was the unanimous opinion, that " such a contrivance " might conquer the difficulties of the Mississippi as high as Natchez, but that we of the Ohio must wait for " some more happy century of invention."

We can add another anecdote to that of our friend which we have quoted. About the time that Fulton was building his first boat at Pittsburgh, he traveled across the mountains in a stage, in company with several young gentlemen from Ken-

tucky.   His mind was teeming with those projects, the successful accomplishment of which has since rendered his name illustrious — and his conversation turned chiefly upon steam,
steamboats, and facilities for transportation.   Upon these subjects he spoke frankly, and his incredulous companions, much
as they respected the genius of the projector, were greatly
amused at what they considered the extragavance of his expectations.   As the journey lasted several days, and the party
grew familiar with each other, they ventured to jest with Mr.
Fulton, by asking him if he could do this, and that, by steam;
and a hearty laugh succeeded whenever the singleminded and
direct inventor asserted the power of his favorite element.   At
length, in the course of some conversation on the almost impassable nature of the mountains, over which they were dragged
with great toil, upon roads scarcely practicable, for wheels,
Mr. Fulton remarked, " the day will come, gentlemen — I may
not live to see it, but some of you, who are younger, probably
will — when carriages will be drawn over these mountains by
steam engines, at a rate more rapid than that of a stage upon
the smoothest turnpike."   The apparent absurdity of this prediction, together with the gravity with which it was uttered,
excited the most obstreperous mirth in this laughter-loving
company, who roared, shouted, and clapped their hands, in
the excess of their merry excitement.   This anecdote was repeated to us by one of the party ; who, two years ago, on finding himself rapidly receding from Baltimore in a railroad car,
recollected the prediction of Fulton, made twenty years
before.

8

CHAPTER XIX.

IN a small book published in Pittsburgh, Pennsylvania, in 1811, called the "Navigator," is found about the first connected account of the intention and purpose of Fulton and Livingston to introduce steamboats on to the inland waters of the West. It says:

"There is now on foot a new method of navigating our Western waters, — particularly the Ohio and Mississippi Rivers. This is by boats propelled by the power of steam. This plan has been carried into successful operation on the Hudson River, in New York, and on the Delaware between New Castle and Burlington. It has been stated the one on the Hudson goes at the rate of four miles an hour against wind and tide, on her route between New York and Albany, and with five hundred passengers on board frequently. From these successful experiments there can be but little doubt of the plan succeeding on the Western waters, and proving of immense advantage to the commerce of our country."

A Mr. Roosevelt, of enterprise and who is acting, it is said in connection with Messrs. Fulton and Livingston, of New York, has a boat of this kind on the stocks at Pittsburgh, of 138 feet keel. calculated for 300 or 400 tons burden. And there is one building at Frankfort, Kentucky, by citizens, who will no doubt push the enterprise. It will prove a novel sight, and as pleasing as novel, to see a large boat working its way up the windings of the Ohio, without the appearance of sail, oar, or pole, or any manual labor about her, moving within the secrets of her own wonderful machinery, and propelled by a power undiscoverable."

FIRST TRIP OF THE NEW ORLEANS, 1811.

[From I. H. B. Latrobe's address before the Maryland Historical Society, 1882.]

" Prior to the introduction of steamboats on Western waters, the means of transportation thereon consisted of keel-boats, barges and flat-boats. The two former ascended as well as descended the stream. The flat-boat, or " broad horn," was broken up for its lumber on arrival at its place of destination. Whether steam could be employed on Western rivers was a question. Its success between New York and Albany was not considered as having been solved satisfactorily, and after the idea had been suggested of building a boat at Pittsburgh, to

ply between Natchez and New Orleans, it was considered necessary, investigations should be made, as to the currents of the
rivers to be navigated. These investigations were undertaken
by Nicholas J. Roosevelt, with the understanding that if the
report was favorable, Chancellor Livingston, Robert Fulton,
and himself were to be equally interested in the undertaking.
Livingston and Fulton were to supply the capital, and Roosevelt was to superintend the building of the boat and engine.

"He accordingly repaired to Pittsburg in 1809, accompanied by his bride, where he built a flat boat, which was to
contain all the comforts for himself and wife to float them
with the current from Pittsburg to New Orleans, and this boat
was the home of the young couple for six months. He
reached New Orleans about the first of December, 1809, and
returned home to New York by the first vessel. Mr. Roosevelt had made up his mind that steam was to do the work and
his visit was to ascertain how it could best be done upon the
Western streams. He guaged them and measured them at
different seasons and obtained all the statistical information
within his reach. Finding coal on the banks of the Ohio, he
purchased them and opened mines of that mineral, and so confident was he of the success of his project that he caused piles
of fresh fuel to be heaped up on the shore in anticipation of
the wants of steamboats whose keels had not yet been laid and
whose existence depended upon the reports he should make to
capitalists, without whose aid the plan would have temporarily
at least to be abandoned. Mr. Roosevelt's report so impressed
Fulton and Livingston, that in the spring of 1810 he was sent
to Pittsburgh to superintend the building of the first steamboat that was launched on the Western waters.

"On the Alleghany side, close by the creek and immediately under a bluff called Boyd's hill, the keel of Roosevelt's
vessel was laid. The railroad depot of the Pittsburgh and Con-
nelsville road now occupies the ground (1882). The size and
plan of this steamboat was furnished by Robert Fulton. It
was to be one hundred and sixteen feet in length and twenty
feet beam. The engine was to have a thirty-four inch
cylinder and the boiler, etc., was to be in proportion. To
obtain the timber men were sent into the forest to obtain the
ribs, knees and beams, transport them to the Monongahela,
and raft them to the ship yard. The ship builders, mechanics, etc., for the machinery department, had to be brought
from New York.

"A rise in the river set all the buoyant materials afloat,
and at one time it seemed as if the vessel would be lifted

from its ways and be launched before its time. At length
the boat was launched, at a cost of near thirty-eight thousand
dollars and was named "New Orleans," after the place of her
permanent destination. As the New Orleans approached
completion and it became known that Mrs. Roosevelt intended
to accompany her husband, friends endeavored to disuade her
from the utter folly, if not absolute madness of the voyage.
Her husband was told he had no right to *peril her life*, however reckless he might be of his own. The wife, however
believed in her husband, and after a short experimental trip
in September, the New Orleans commenced her voyage. There
were two cabins. One aft for ladies and a larger one forward
for gentlemen. In the former there were four berths. Mr.
and Mrs. Roosevelt took possession of the cabin, as they were
the only passengers. There was a captain, an engineer,
named Baker, Andrew Sack, the pilot, six hands, two female
servants, a man waiter, a cook and an immense Newfoundland
dog, named "Tiger." Thus equipped and manned the New
Orleans began the voyage which changed the relations of the
West and the East and which may almost be said to have
changed its destiny. The people of Pittsburgh turned out *en
masse* and lined the banks of the Monongahela to witness the
departure of the steamboat, and shout after shout rent the air,
handkerchiefs were waved and hats thrown up in "God
speed" when the anchor was weighed and when she disappeared behind the first headlands, on the right bank of the
Ohio.

"Too much excited to sleep, Mr. Roosevelt and his wife
passed the greater part of the first night on deck and watched
the shore, then almost covered with a dense forest, as beach
after beach, and bend after bend, were passed with a speed of
from eight to ten miles per hour. On the second night after
leaving Pittsburg the New Orleans rounded to opposite Cincinnati and cast anchor in the stream. Levees and wharf-
boats were things then unknown in 1811. Here, as in Pittsburg, the whole town seemed to have assembled on the bank,
and many of their former acquaintances came out in small
boats to welcome them. 'Well, you are as good as your
word, you have visited us with a steamboat,' they said; ' but
we see you for the last time. Your boat may go down the
river, but as to coming up, the idea is an absurd one.' The
keel-boat men crowded around the strange visitor and shook
their heads and bandied river wit with the crew, that had been
selected from their own calling for the first voyage. Some
flat-boatmen, whose arks had been passed a short distance.

above town, who now floated by with the current, seemed to
have a better opinion and proposed a tow in case they were
again overtaken. But as to the boats returning, all agreed
that *that* could never be.

" The stay at Cincinnati was brief, only long enough to
take a supply of wood for the voyage to Louisville, which was
reached on the night of the fourth day after leaving Pittsburgh.

" It was midnight on the first of October, 1811, that the
New Orleans dropped anchor opposite the town. There was a
brilliant moon. It was almost as light as day and no one
on board had retired. The roar of the escaping steam, then
heard for the first time, roused the population, and as late as
it was came rushing to the bank of the river to learn the
cause of the unwonted uproar. A letter written by one on
board records the fact that these were people who insisted
that the comet of 1811 had fallen into the Ohio and produced
the hubbub. A public dinner was given Mr. Roosevelt a few
days after arrival, complimentary toasts were drunk, and the
usual amount of good feeling on such occasions was manifested.
The success of the steamboat in navigating down stream was
acknowledged. But her return up stream was deemed impossible, and it was regretted that it was the first and the last
time a steamboat would be seen above the falls of the Ohio.

" Not to be outdone in hospitality, Mr. Roosevelt invited his
hosts to dine on board the New Orleans, which still lay anchored opposite the town. The company met in the forward or
gentlemen's cabin, and the feast was at its height, when suddenly was heard rumblings, accompanied by a very perceptible motion of the vessel. The company had but one idea —
the New Orleans had escaped from her anchor, and was drifting towards the falls, to the certain destruction of all on board.
There was an instant rush to the upper deck when the company found, instead of drifting towards the falls of the Ohio,
the New Orleans was making good headway up the river, and
would soon leave Louisville in the distance down stream. As
the engine warmed to its work and the steam blew off at the
safety valve the speed increased.

" Mr Roosevelt had, of course, provided this mode of con-
vincing his incredulous, and their surprise and delight may
be readily imagined.

" After going up the river a few miles the New Orleans returned to the anchorage. On leaving Pittsburgh it was determined to proceed as rapidly as possible to New Orleans and to
place the boat on the route for which she was designed between

that city and Natchez. It was found, however, on reaching
Louisville there was not sufficient depth of water on the falls
of the Ohio to permit the vessel to pass over them with safety.
The New Orleans therefore returned to Cincinnati convinc-
ing the most incredulous of her power to steam the current of
the river.

"The waters having risen, the boat returned to Louisville
and safely passed through the rapids, crowds collecting to see
her departure. Instinctively each one on board grasped the
nearest object, and with baited breath waited the result.
Black ledges of rock appeared only to disappear as the boat
flashed by them. The waters whirled and eddied and threw
their spray upon the deck, as a more rapid descent caused the
vessel to pitch forward to what at times seemed certain destruction. Not a word was spoken. The pilot directed the men
at the helm by motion of the hands. Even the great Newfoundland dog seemed affected by the apprehension of danger,
and crouched at Mr. Roosevelt's feet. The tension on the
nervous system was too great to be long sustained. Fortunately the passage was soon made and with feelings of profound
gratitude to the Almighty at the successful issue of the adventure on the part of Mr. and Mrs. Roosevelt, the New Orleans rounded to in safety at the foot of the falls. Hitherto
the voyage had been one of exclusive pleasure, but now were
to come, in the words of the letter referred to, ' those days of
horror.—— '

"The comet had disappeared and the earthquake of that
year which accompanied the New Orleans far on her way
down the Mississippi, the first shock of which was felt while
she lay at anchor, after passing the falls. On one occasion a
large canoe, fully manned, came out of the woods abreast of the
steamboat and paddled after it. There was at once a race,
but the steam had the advantage of endurance, and the Indians
with wild shouts soon gave up the chase.

"One night there was an alarm of fire. The servant had
placed some green wood too near the stove in the forward
cabin, which caught fire and communicated to the joiner work
of the cabin, when the servant, half suffocated, rushed on
deck and gave the alarm. By great exertion the fire was extinguished.

"At New Madrid, a greater portion of which had been engulfed, terror-stricken people begged to be taken on board,
while others, dreading the steamboat more than the earthquake,
hid themselves as she approached. Having an insufficient
supply of provisions for any large increase of passengers, the

requests to be taken on board had to be denied. The earthquake had so changed the channel of the river that the pilots
guided the boat more by luck than knowledge. As the steamboat passed out of the region of the earthquake, the principal
inconvenience was the number of shoals, snags and sawyers.
These were safely passed and the vessel came in sight of
Natchez and rounded to opposite the landing place.

" Expecting to remain here a day or two the engineer had
allowed his fires to go down so that when the boat turned her
head up stream it lost headway altogether, and was being carried by the current far below the intended landing. Thousands were assembled on the bluff and at the foot of it, and
for a moment it seemed that the New Orleans had achieved
what she had done so far that she might be overcome at last.
Fresh fuel, however, was added, the engine was stopped, that
steam might accumulate. Presently the safety valve was
lifted, a few turns of the wheel steadied the boat, a few more
gave her headway, and overcoming the Mississippi she gained
the shore amidst shouts of exultation and applause. The
romance of the voyage ended at Natchez, where the same hos-
pitalities were extended to Mr. and Mrs. Roosevelt that were
enjoyed at Louisville. From thence to New Orleans there
was no occurrence worthy of note.

" Although forming no part of the story of the voyage
proper, says Mr. Latrobe, as this has been called a romance,
and all romances end, or should end in marriage, the incident
is not wanting here. For the captain of the boat falling in
love with Mrs. Roosevelt's maid, prosecuted his suit so succes-
fully as to find himself an accepted lover when the New
Orleans reached Natchez. A clergyman being sent for a
wedding marked the arrival of the boat at the chief city of the
Mississippi."

(Mrs. Roosevelt was a sister of Mr. Latrobe, who seems to
have been a passenger on the New Orleans during this, her first
trip.)

The following reference to the voyage of exploration contained in a recent letter from Mrs. Roosevelt to the writer
may not be uninteresting:—

" The journey in the flat-boat commenced at Pittsburgh,
where Mr. Roosevelt had it built; a huge box containing a
comfortable bed-room, dining-room, pantry, and a room in
front for the crew, with a fire-place, where the cooking was
done. The top of the boat was flat, with seats and an awning.
We had on board a pilot, three hands and a man cook. We
always stopped at night, lashing the boat to the shore. The

row boat was a large one, in which Mr. Roosevelt went out constantly with two or three of the men to ascertain the rapidity of the ripples or current. It was in this row boat we went from Natchez to New Orleans with the same crew." * * * " We reached New Orleans about the 1st of December, 1809, and took passage for New York in the first vessel we found ready to sail. We had a terrible voyage of a month, with a sick captain. The yellow fever was on board. A passenger, a nephew of General Wilkinson, died with it. Mr. Roosevelt and myself were taken off the ship by a pilot boat and landed at Old Point Comfort. From thence we went to New York by stage, reaching there the middle of January, 1810, after an absence of nine months.

" Once, while in the flat-boat, on the Mississippi, Mr. Roosevelt was aroused in the night by seeing two Indians in our sleeping room, calling for whisky, when Mr. Roosevelt had to get up and give it to them before he could induce them to leave the boat."

The exploring voyage proper ended with the arrival of the flat-boat at Natchez, but Mrs. Roosevelt's account of the subsequent boat voyage to New Orleans is, perhaps, worth adding, if only for the sake of the comparison that it suggests: —

" By placing," says Mrs. Roosevelt, " a large traveling trunk between the stern of the boat and the first seat, it made a large level place on which we could spread a buffalo robe to sleep on. Our pilot, who had lived all his life as a boatman on these waters, assured us that there would be no difficulty in finding lodgings for the few nights we should be out. But it appeared that the inhabitants on the river had been so often imposed on by travelers whom they had received into their houses, that they refused all applications. A pouring rain came up one evening, and we tried to reach Baton Rouge, which we did at nine at night. It was a miserable place at that time, with one wretched public house; yet we felt thankful that we had found a shelter from the storm. But when I was shown into our sleeping room I wished myself on board the boat. It was a forlorn little place opening out of the bar room, which was filled with tipsy men looking like cut-throats. The room had one window opening into a stable-yard, but which had neither shutters nor fastenings. Its furniture was a single chair and a dirty bed. We threw our cloaks on the bed and laid down to rest, but not to sleep, for the fighting and the noise in the bar-room prevented that. We rose at the dawn of day, and reached the boat, feeling thankful we had not been murdered in the night. It is many, many years ago:

but I can still recall that night of fright. Our second night on shore was passed with an old French couple, who allowed us to spread our buffalo robes on the floor before a fine large fire, where we felt safe, though disturbed once or twice during the night by the people coming into the room we occupied, and kneeling before a crucifix which stood upon a shelf. They were Roman Catholics.

" The time actually occupied by the voyage from Natchez to New Orleans in the row-boat was nine days. Two of these nights were passed as above described, under a roof; four in the boat, partly drawn out of the water, and hearing the alligators scratch on the sides, taking it for a log; when a knock with a cane would alarm them, and they would splash down into the water; the remaining three nights were passed on a buffalo robe on the sand beach, feeling every moment, that something terrible might happen before morning.''

In the language of a very intelligent traveler of those days: " Many things conspired to make the year 1811 *the annus mirabilis* of the West. During the earlier months the waters of many of the great rivers overflowed their banks to a vast extent, and the whole country was in many parts covered from bluff to bluff. Unprecedented sickness followed. A spirit of change and recklessness seemed to pervade the very inhabitants of the forest. A countless multitude of squirrels, obeying some great and universal impulse, which none can know but the Spirit that gave them being, left their reckless and gamboling life, and their ancient places of retreat in the North, and were seen pressing forward by tens of thousands in a deep and solid phalanx to the South. No obstacles seemed to check their extraordinary and concerted movement. The word had been given them to go forth, and they obeyed it, though multitudes perished in the broad Ohio which lay in their path. The splendid comet of that year long continued to shed its twilight over the forests, and as the autumn drew to a close, the whole valley of the Mississippi, from the Missouri to the Gulf, was shaken to its center by continued earthquakes.'' — *C. J. Latrobe's Rambles in North America.*

CHAPTER XX.

EXTRACT of a letter to the editors of the *National Intelligencer*, dated Pittsburg, April 22, 1814: —

"*Messrs. Gales & Seaton, Washington:*

"This morning the steamboat Vesuvius, intended as a regular trader between New Orleans and the Falls of the Ohio, left Pittsburg. A considerable fresh in the river rendered it probable that notwithstanding the great size and draft of the vessel, she will pass the falls without difficulty, after which she will meet with no obstruction in the rest of the passage.

There is now on the stocks here, just ready to be launched, a boat adapted to the navigation of the Ohio above the falls, which will be finished in time to meet the Vesuvius, on her return from New Orleans, at the falls.

The boats are built by Fulton, under the agency of Messrs. Livingston & Latrobe, for companies who have vested very large capital in the establishment. The departure of the Vesuvius is a very important event, not only for this place, but for the whole Western part of the Union. And its influence will be felt over the whole United States.

In describing it it is not necessary to use the inflated language, which unfortunately for the credit of our trade too often renders real facts incredible, or at least lowers their importance by the manner in which they are puffed into notice.

It does not require the ornament of metaphor to impress upon the public mind the incalculable advantage of an intercourse by water, effected in large vessels which move with certainty and rapidity through an extent of internal navigation, embracing a space almost as large as the whole continent of Europe, and comprising in it the productions of almost every climate.

This intercourse, although now almost in its infancy, must in a few years become of immense magnitude.

About three years ago a steamboat of 400 tons burthen was built here, and now navigates the Mississippi between New Orleans and Natchez.

The Vesuvius, which, with another boat of the same size and construction now building, is intended to form the second link in this chain of navigation, is of 480 tons burthen, carpenter's measurement. She has 160 feet keel, and 28.6 inches

beam, but will, when loaded, draw from 5 to 6 feet of water.
The whole of her hold below deck, excepting a neat cabin for
ladies, and the space occupied for machinery, is appropriated
to the cargo.

On her deck is built what is known in a ship, and is called
a Round house, extending half her length, and elegantly fitted
up as a cabin, having twenty-eight double berths on a side.
Previously to her departure she had been several times tried
in going up and down the Monongahela and Ohio for four or
five miles and performed very satisfactorily.

This morning (Saturday, April 23), everything being in
perfect order, at ten o'clock she passed up the Monongahela,
in front of the town, to its eastern limits, and returning down
the opposite shore, went down the Ohio, firing a salute. Most
of the citizens were assembled on the bank when she
passed.

In order to witness and ascertain her speed, I crossed the
Alleghany and mounted a very elegant horse I endeavored to
keep pace with her along the road which skirts the river. But
she moved so rapidly that after riding three miles and a half
in nineteen minutes I gave up the attempt.

In one hour and thirty seconds she was at Middletown,
twelve miles below Pittsburgh, where several gentlemen, who
had proceeded on her thus far, came on shore. If, therefore,
the current of the Ohio be rated at four miles an hour in the
fresh, she has gone at the rate of eight miles an hour in
still water.

In coming up the rapids of the Ohio below the town, on
Monday last, she passed the shore at the rate of four miles
in an hour, a speed that would exactly agree with her descent
this morning.

The extent of the growing commerce of this town is, I believe, very inadequately understood to the eastward of the
mountains.

I am informed by one of the most respectable merchants of
this place that the amount of freight only of his consignments,
to and from New Orleans and the States below Penn, will be
this year $60,000 and every day adds to the extent and the
facilities of the business carried on through Pittsburgh.

The great difficulty which has rendered the transportation
by sea in time of peace from New Orleans to Philadephia and
Baltimore and thence by land to the immense country west of
the mountains, preferable to a voyage up the Mississippi and
Ohio, has been the slowness of the keel boats and barges
necessarily employed in the trade. The navigation by steam-

boats proves an end to that only objection to this course of
of trade, a course which in a few years will become the principal, if not the only one.

Situated as I am at present, on the spot where the advantages which the public will reap from the introduction of steam
navigation will be very sensibly felt, it is difficult to suppress the expression of feelings which arise towards the person to whom we owe it, that this mode of navigation, so often
before attempted and laid aside in despair, has become practicable, and its principles reduced to mathematical certainty.
But it is unnecessary in giving them vent. The obligation
which the nation, I had almost said the whole world, owes to
·him will be fully acknowledged by history, when the envy
and cupidity of his detractors will be remembered with disgust and reprobation.

It is worthy your attention in Washington and Georgetown
to consider that between New Orleans and Washington there
will be, when the road from Cumberland to Brownsville is
·completed, only seventy-two miles of land carriage, and that
over a capital turnpike road.

When the late Chancellor Livingston applied for his grant
for the exclusive navigation by steam on the North River to
the Legislature of the State of New York, for thirty years, on
condition that he should actually accomplish it, a very sensible member of the Legislature told me he could very easily
have had a grant of any further extent, as the navigation by
steam was thought to be much on a footing, as to practicability,
with the navigation of the *reindeer* in the Chancellor's park.
The case has altered since then, for many people have found
out that it is an old invention, open to every body who can
·read Mr. Fulton's specifications or look at his boats. — *Niles'*
Weekly Register, Vol. 6, 1814.

CHAPTER XXI.

STEAMBOAT BUFFALO

"OF 285 tons has been launched at Pittsburgh. She is designed to ply regularly between that place and Louisville once a month. And as she will draw when all her machinery is on board but two feet six inches, it is expected she will run all summer. If, however, she is found too large, other boats less bulky will be built, and she taken to a station below the falls, in the line to New Orleans.

The steamboat Enterprise, built at Bridgeport, on the Monongahela, arrived at Pittsburgh on the 8th, designed as a packet between that place and the falls of the Ohio. Her power was highly approved. She was tried against the current of the Monongahela, which was unusually high and rapid at that season, and made three miles and a half per hour. She returned with the stream that distance in ten minutes.

"ASTONISHING PASSAGE.

The steamboat Vesuvius made the following passage from Pittsburgh to New Orleans:—

From Pittsburgh to Shippingport, 67 hours and a half; from Shippingport to Natchez, 125 hours and a half; from Natchez to New Orleans, 33 hours. Total from Pittsburgh to New Orleans, 227 hours." — *Niles' Weekly Register, Vol. 6, 1814.*

"The steamboat Vesuvius went from Pittsburgh to Louisville, 767 miles, in 62 hours and 25 minutes, equal to 10 1-2 miles an hour.

"The city of New York is enjoying immense advantage from those vessels as packets and ferryboats. *Loaded wagons* are hourly seen in that city from Long Island and New Jersey."

"John L. Sullivan, of Boston, has obtained a patent for the use of steam engine power in towing luggage boats, being a a new and useful application of steam engines, and put in practice by him on the Merimack River. — *Niles' Weekly Register, Vol. 6, 1814.*

The steamboat Enterprise worked up from New Orleans to Bardstown, nearly 1,500 miles, in twenty-five days.

It is calculated that the voyage by steamboats from New

Orleans to Pittsburgh, about 2,300 miles, will be made in 36
days.

"How do the rivers and canals of the old world dwindle
into insignificance compared with this, and what a prospect of
commerce is held out to the immense regions of the West by
the means of these boats. It is thought that the freight from
New Orleans to Louisville (at the falls of the Ohio) will soon,
be reduced to $3.50 per hundred weight."— *Niles' Register*,
Vol. 8, 1815.

EARL OF LIVERPOOL.

"Lord Sheffield, if I mistake not, is now nicknamed the
'earl of Liverpool,' declared that the western part of the
United States never could become commercial. Let his
lordship take a map and trace the course of rivers from New
Orleans to Brownsville and then read the following from
a late newspaper published at the latter called the *Brownsville
Telegraph:*" —

"Arrived at this port (my lord-*port*), on Monday last the
steamboat Enterprise, Shrieve, of Bridgeport, from New Orleans in ballast, having discharged her cargo at Pittsburgh.

She is the first steamboat that ever made the voyage to the
mouth of the Mississippi and back. She made the trip from
from New Orleans to this port in fifty-four days, twenty days
of which were employed in loading and unloading freight at
the different towns on the Ohio and Mississippi. So she was
only thirty-four days in actual service in making her voyage,
which our readers will remember must be performed against
powerful currents, and is upwards of 2,200 miles in length."
Niles' Register, Vol. 8.

"Last Saturday evening steam was first tried on the steamboat 'Dispatch,' another steamboat lately built at Bridgeport,
and owned, as well as the Enterprise, by the Monongahela and
Ohio Steamboat Company. We are happy to learn she is
likely to answer the most sanguine expectations of the ingenious, Mr. French, the engineer, on whose plan she is constructed."

It is expected when her works are in complete operation,
she will pass through the water at the rate of nine miles an
hour. — *Niles' Register, Vol. 8.*

Whatever may be said of the wonderful achievements obtained by steam at that early date, judging from the above and
other records made at that time, no practical man at the
present period will fail to notice that there has been quite as
much improvement in the facilities for handling freight or in

the time consumed in handling it on a trip, as there has been in the speed of steamboats.

The idea of spending twenty days in taking in and putting out freight on a trip from New Orleans to Pittsburgh, and that with a boat of but 400 tons capacity, will hardly do justice to the well known reputation of Capt. H. M. Shreve, although he probably done more than any other individual in improving and developing the steamboat interests of the South and West.

CHAPTER XXII.

OHIO FALLS PILOT.

IN 1792, the office of *Falls Pilot* was created by law in consonance with the following preamble to the act, " Whereas great inconveniences have been experienced and many boats lost in attempting to pass the rapids of the Ohio, for the want of a pilot, and from persons offering their services to strangers to act as pilots, by no means qualified for this business.

The office was appointed at Louisville, Kentucky, by the Jefferson County Court, and the rate of pilotage fixed by the act, was two dollars for each boat, while all other persons were forbidden to attempt to perform this service under a penalty of ten dollars.

In *McMurtrie's Sketches of Louisville*, published in 1819, an interesting and valuable account is given of the introduction of steam navigation and its effect upon commerce and the settlement of the Mississippi Valley.

In chapter 8, page 193, on the subject of navigation and commerce, he says: —

" The increase of the navigation and commerce of Louisville and Shippingport since the year of 1806, is, perhaps, unparalleled in the history of nations. At that time six keel-boats and two barges — the one of thirty tons. belonging to Reed, of Cincinnati; the other of forty, belonging to Instom, of Frankfort, sufficed for the carrying trade of the two places. Whereas, at the present moment there are, exclusive of barges, keel-boats, etc., upwards of *twenty-five steamboats* employed in that business, whose united burthen is equal to six thousand and fifty tons.

This is a flattering and unequivocal proof of their prosperity, and gives us a glimpse of what they will be fifty years

hence. The application of steam for purposes of navigation
constitutes a brilliant and important era in the annals of our
country, and although Fulton was not the original inventor
(for it had been repeatedly essayed before his time in England, France, and in this country, but without success), yet
is his merit not the less on that account, as it requires more
courage to persevere in effecting an object, which, from the
constant failure of others seems to be impracticable, than to
try a new experiment.

Why has he not a statue?

Next to Fulton, the country owes a vast debt of gratitude
to Capt. H. M. Shreve, of Portland. It is to his exertions,
his example, and let me add, to his integrity and patriotic

STEAMER WASHINGTON.

purity of principle, that we are indebted for the present flourishing state of navigation.

Having been long convinced that the overpowering patent
of Fulton and Livingston, which granted them the exclusive
privilege of navigating by steamboats all the rivers of the
United States for fourteen years, no matter in what manner
the steam operated, was illegal, and consequently of no effect,
he determined to bring the point to issue. Accordingly on the
first of December in 1814, he embarked on the Enterprise for
New Orleans, where he arrived on the 14th of the same month.

Immediately on landing he applied to counsel and procured

bail, in case of seizure, which took place the next day. Bail was entered and a suit commenced against the vessel and owners in an inferior court, where a verdict was found for the defendants. The case was now removed by a writ of error to the Supreme Court of the United States, at which time the Enterprise left New Orleans and arrived at Shippingport. Before the question was decided by this tribunal, Capt. Shreve, returned to New Orleans with the Washington, a beautiful boat of 400 tons, which, as was expected, was also seized by the company to whom she was abandoned without any difficulty. Upon application, however, to the court, an order was obtained to hold the company to bail, to answer to the damages that might be sustained by the detention of the vessel.

To this it demurred, and began to feel the weakness of its case, and foreseeing the downfall of its colossal patent, it repeatedly offered through its counsel and individual members of the company to admit Capt. Shreve to an equal share with itself in all the privileges of the patent-right, *providing* he should instruct his counsel so to arrange the business that a verdict might be found against him. In vain this tempting bait, I had almost said bribe, was proffered.

It was rejected with scorn and indignation, and the affair left to justice, whose sword, with one blow, forever severed the links of that chain which had enthralled the commerce of Western waters.

Had Captain Shreve been weak enough to have accepted of this offer the result is obvious. No one would have dared to embark his fortune in vain endeavors to promote the best interests of his country by adding the wings of commerce to the feet of agriculture, because ruin would have been the inevitable consequence. The carrying business would have remained in the hands of the company, who would have continued just so many and no more boats in the trade as was necessary to keep up the price of freight, and consequently instead of paying two and half cents per pound for every article imported, the merchant, and ultimately the consumer (for upon his shoulders such things always bear at last), would have been compelled to have paid six, seven or eight, as best suited the convenience of the company.

Among the many advantages steamboats are to the community, is the extraordinary demand they create for provisions and fuel. With respect to fuel, that wood which heretofore cost the owners large sums of money to destroy will now bring from two and half to three dollars per cord, delivered anywhere on the banks of the river. As to provisions, anywhere in the vicinity of Louisville, the demand can hardly be supplied in consequence of the increasing population of the town.

Each steamboat employed in the trade of this place is obliged to disburse $600 per trip, at least three times in a year, or $1,800, which multiplied by the number of boats, gives us $45,000, a sum annually expended among owners of land at this place and along the river below.

But these are not only the advantages derived to the Western country by the introduction of steamboats. Their production has created good turnpike roads across the mountains as well as canals, thus diminishing the price of freight from Eastern cities, whose inhabitants, fearing the entire loss of their trade with the Western country, have been stimulated to counteract these effects by the means just mentioned."

CHAPTER XXIII.

THE NAVIGATOR, an old and rare book printed in Pittsburgh in the early part of this century, records many interesting facts concerning the early navigators.

From this source we learn something of the expense and profits of the "New Orleans" when running as a packet between Natchez and New Orleans.

This old chronicle says "her accomodations are good, and her passengers numerous, generally not less than from ten to twenty from Natchez at $18.00 each, and when she starts from New Orleans, generally from thirty to fifty and sometimes as many as eighty, at $25.00 each to Natchez.

According to the observation of Capt. Morris, of New Orleans, who attended her as a pilot several trips, the boat's receipts for freight upwards, have averaged the last year $700, the passenger receipts $900. Downward $300 for freight, $500 for passengers.

She performs thirteen trips in the year, which at $2,400 per trip amounts to $31,200. Her expenses are, 12 hands, at $20 per month, $4,320; captain, $1,000; seventy cords of wood each trip, at $1.75, which amounts to $1,586, in all $6,906. It is presumed that the boat's extra trip for pleasure or otherwise, out of her usual trade, have paid for all her repairs, and with the bar-room, for the boat's provisions, in which case there will remain a net gain of $24,294 for the first year.

The owners estimate the boat's value at $40,000, which gives an interest of $2,400, and by giving $1,894 more for furniture, etc., we have the clear gain of $20,000 for the first year's labor for the steamboat "New Orleans." She goes up in seven or eight days, and descends in two or three, stopping several times for freight and passengers. She stays at the extreme of her journey, Natchez and New Orleans, about four or five days to discharge or to take in loading."

"The first sea vessel on the Western waters was a brig built at Marietta, Ohio, called the "St. Clair," 120 tons burden. She was built by Commodore Preble in 1798 or '99, who went down the river on her to New Orleans, from thence to Havana, and to Philadelphia, and at the latter port he sold her.

From 1799 to 1805, there was built at Pittsburgh four ships, three brigs, and several schooners, but misfortunes happening to most of them in going down the rivers to the gulf, ship-building on the Ohio went into a decline until revived some years after in the shape of steamboat architecture.

One of these took out papers for Leghorn, Italy, and in illustrating the commercial habits and enterprise of the American people, Henry Clay, in a speech in Congress, related the following anecdote about her.

"When the vessel arrived at Leghorn, the captain presented his papers to the custom officer there, but he would not credit them, and said to the master, ' sir, your papers are forged, there is no such place as Pittsburgh in the world, your vessel must be confiscated.'

The trembling captain asked if he had a map of the United States, which he fortunately happened to have, and produced. The captain, taking the officer's finger, put it down at the mouth of the Mississippi, then led it a 1,000 miles up the river, thence another 1,000 to Pittsburgh, and said, 'there, sir, is the port whence my vessel cleared from.'

The astonished officer, who before he saw the map would have as soon believed the vessel had been navigated from the moon, exclaimed, ' I knew America could show many wonderful things, but a fresh water sea port is something I never dreamed of.' "

"The ' New Orleans ' was the first steamboat ever constructed on the western waters. She was 116 feet long, 20 feet beam. Her cylinder was 34 inches diameter, with boiler

and other parts in proportion. She was about 400 tons
burthen and cost in the neighborhood of ($38,000) thirty-
eight thousand dollars. There were two cabins, one aft for
ladies, and a larger one forward for gentlemen. The ladies'
cabin, which was comfortably furnished, contained four berths.
The ' New Orleans ' was launched in March, 1811. She left
Pittsburg October of the same year — passed Cincinnati Oct.
27th, and reached Louisville the next day in 64 hours' running time from Pittsburgh.

The water was too low for her to cross the falls, and while
waiting at Louisville for sufficient water, she made several
short excursions. She also made one trip to Cincinnati,
arriving there in 45 hours' running time from Louisville,
Nov. 27th, 1811. While here she made one excursion trip
to Columbia, charging one dollar per head. Shortly after
this, the river rising, she left this place for New Orleans,
December, 1811.

Her voyage down the river was perilous in the extreme, as
shortly after leaving Louisville the great earthquakes began.
[See full account in another chapter.] She ran between
Natchez and New Orleans, her trips averaging about three
weeks. July 13, 1814, she landed on her upward trip two
miles below Baton Rouge, on the opposite side, and spent the
night in taking on wood, the night being too dark to run with
safety. At daylight the next morning she got up steam, and
on starting the engine, it was found she would not move
ahead, but kept swinging around. The water had fallen during
the night and the captain found she was resting on a stump.
An anchor was put out on her starboard quarter, and by the
aid of her capstan she was soon hove off. But on clearing, it
was soon discovered she had sprung a leak, and was sinking
rapidly. She was immediately run into the bank and tied
fast, but sunk so rapidly her passengers barely had time to
get ashore with baggage.''

CHAPTER XXIV.

FROM SHARFS' HISTORY OF ST. LOUIS.

" The early history of steamboats following the New Orleans will be found interesting, as showing how quickly the innovation was felt, and how speedily the new system obliterated the old."

The second boat was the " Comet," of 25 tons, owned by Saml. Smith, built at Pittsburg by Daniel French, stern wheel and vibrating cylinders. French patent granted in 1809.

The " Comet " made a voyage to Louisville in 1813, and to New Orleans in the spring, 1814. Made two trips to Natchez and was sold and her engine put into a plantation and used to drive a cotton-gin. Third boat, the Vesuvius, 340 tons, built at Pittsburgh, by Robert Fulton and owned by a company belonging to New York and New Orleans. Left Pittsburgh in the spring of 1814, commanded by Capt. Frank Ogden. She started from New Orleans, bound for Louisville, first of June, 1814 and grounded on a bar 700 miles up the Mississippi, where she lay until December, when the river rose and floated her off. She returned to New Orleans, where she grounded a second time on the bature, where she lay until the first of March, when the river rose and floated her off. She was then employed several months between New Orleans and Natchez, under the command of Capt. Clemment, who was succeeded by Capt. John De Hart. Shortly afterwards she took fire near New Orleans and burned to the water's edge, having a valuable cargo on board.

The fire was supposed to have been communicated from the boiler, which was in the hold. The bottom was raised and built upon at New Orleans and she went into the Louisville trade, but was soon after sold to a company in Natchez.

On examination subsequent to the sale she was pronounced unfit for use, was libeled by her commander and sold at public auction.

Fourth boat, the _Enterprise_, forty-five tons. Built at Brownsville, Penn., by Daniel French, under his patent, and owned by a company at that place. Made two trips to Louisville in the summer of 1814, under command of Capt. J. Gregg. On the first of December, she took a load of ordinance stores at Pittsburgh, and left for New Orleans under command of Capt. Henry M. Shreve, and arrived at New Orleans on the 14th same month. She was then dispatched

up the river in search of two keel-boats, laden with small'
arms, which had been delayed on the river.   She got twelve
miles above Natchez, where she met the keels, took their
cargoes and masters on board and returned to New Orleans,
having been but six and a half days absent, in which she ran
624 miles.

She was there for some time employed entirely in transporting troops.   She made one trip to the Gulf of Mexico as
a cartel, and one trip to the rapids of the Red River, with
troops, and nine voyages to Natchez.   She left New Orleans
for Pittsburgh on the 6th of May, and arrived at Shippingport on the 30th, twenty-five days out, being the first steamboat that ever arrived at that port from New Orleans.

She then proceeded on to Pittsburgh and the command was
given to D. Worley, who lost her in Rock harbor, at Shippingport.

Fifth boat, the " Ætna," 340 tons, built at Pittsburgh and
owned by the same company as the Vesuvius, left Pittsburgh for New Orleans March, 1815, under charge of Capt. A.
Gale, and arrived at that port in April following; was placed
in the Natchez trade.   Was then placed under the command of
Capt. Robinson De Hart, who made six trips on her to Louisville.

The *sixth boat* was the "Zebulon M. Pike," built by Mr.
Prentice, of Henderson, Kentucky, on the Ohio River in 1815.
The Pike deserves especial mention, as she was the first boat
to ascend the Mississippi River above the mouth of the Ohio,
and the first to touch at St. Louis.

Her first trip was made in the spring of 1815 to Louisville,
Ky., two hundred and fifty miles in sixty-seven hours, making
$3\frac{1}{4}$ miles per hour against the current.   On her voyage to St.
Louis she was commanded by Capt. Jacob Read.

The hull, says Professor Waterhouse, was built on the
model of a barge.   (That is presumed to mean that she was
built on a barge.)   The cabin was built on the lower deck inside of the " running boards."

The boat was driven by what was called a low pressure engine, with a walking beam.   The wheels had no wheel houses
and she had but one smoke stack.

In rapid current the crew reinforced steam with the impulse
of their own strength.   They used the poles and running boards
just as in the push boat, navigation of barges.   The boat only
ran in daylight, and was six weeks in making the trip from
Louisville to St. Louis.   It landed at the foot of Market street
August 2nd, 1817.

The inhabitants of the village gathered on the bank to welcome the novel visitor. Among them was a group of Indians. As the boat approached, the glare from the furnace, and the volume of murky smoke filled the Indians with dismay. They fled to the high ground in the rear of the village, and no assurances of safety could induce them to go nearer the object of their fears. They ascribed supernatural to a boat that could ascend a rapid stream without the aid of sail or oar. Their superstitious imaginations beheld a monster breathing flame and threatening the extinction of the red man. In a symbolic sense their fancy was prophetic, the progress and civilization of which the steamboat may be taken as a type, is fast sweeping the Indian race into the grave of buried nations.

The first notice we have of the expected arrival of the " Pike " at St. Louis is the following announcement in the Missouri *Gazette* of 14th of July, 1817 : —

" A steamboat is expected here to-morrow from Louisville. There is no doubt but what we shall have regular communication, or at least with the mouth of the Ohio by a steam packet."

On the 2d of August the *Gazette* published this notice : —

The steamboat Pike will be ready to take in freight to-morrow for Louisville, or any town of the Ohio. She will sail for Louisville on Monday morning, the 4th of August, from 10 to 12 o'clock. For freight or passage apply to the master on board.

JACOB READ, Master.

The return trip of the Pike is also mentioned in the *Gazette* of September 2d as follows : The steamboat Pike will arrive in a day or two from Louisville. This vessel will ply regularly between that place and this, and will take in her return cargo shortly after her arrival.

Persons who may have freight, or want passage for Louisville, or any of the towns on the Ohio, will do well to make early application to the master on board. On her passage from this to Louisville, she will stop at Herculaneum where Mr. M. Austin will act as agent. Also at Ste. Genevieve and Cape Girardeau, at the former place Mr. Le Macellieu, and at the latter Mr. Steinbeck will act as agents, with whom freight may be deposited and shipped. Persons waiting passage on this vessel may apply as above. She will perform her present passage to and from Louisville in about four weeks and will always afford a safe and expeditious passage for the transportation of freight and passengers."

JACOB READ, Master.

Again on the 22d of November, the *Gazette* announced that
the steamboat "Pike," with passengers and freight, arrived
here from Louisville.

The Pike had capacity for thirty-seven tons old government tonnage. She made a trip to New Orleans and several
between Louisville and Pittsburgh, after which she was
engaged in the Red River trade and snagged in March, 1818.

The *seventh boat* on the Mississippi was the "Dispatch,"
twenty-five tons. She was built at Brownsville, Pa., by the
same company that owned the Enterprise and under French's
patent. She made several trips from Pittsburgh to Louisville,
and one to New Orleans and back to Shippingport, where she
was wrecked and her engine taken out. She was commanded
by Captain J. Gregg.

The *eighth boat* was the "Buffalo," 300 tons, built at Pittsburgh by Benjamin H. Latrobe, Sr., the distinguished architect of the Capitol at Washington. She was afterwards sold
at sheriff's sale, at Louisville, for $800.

We find in the *American Weekly Messenger*, published in
Philadelphia, July 2d, 1814, the following letter which relates
to the circumstances of the launch of the steamboat "Buffalo:" —

PITTSBURGH, June 3, 1814.

We omitted to mention that the steamboat "Buffalo" was
safely launched on the 13th from the yard of Mr. Latrobe.

This boat, which was intended to complete the line of steamboats from New Orleans to Pittsburgh, is a fine and uncommonly well built vessel, of two hundred and eighty-five tons
burden, carpenter's measurement, and is intended to trade regularly between Louisville and Pittsburgh, once a month, as
long as the water will admit. She has two cabins and four
state-rooms for private families and will conveniently accommodate 100 passengers with beds.

Should it be found that her draught of water, which will be
about thirty inches, when her machinery is on board, is too
great for the summer months, it is intended immediately to
put on the stocks another boat, or boats of smaller draught
and less bulky construction. It is expected the "Buffalo"
will be finished in time to bring up the cargo of the "Vesuvius" from New Orleans.

A succeeding number of the *Weekly American Magazine*,
contains the following items from St. Louis: —

ST. LOUIS (I. T.), July 2d, 1814.

" On Sunday last an armed boat arrived from Prairie du
Chien, under command of Capt. John Sulivan, with his com-

pany of militia and thirty-two men from the gunboat
' Governor Clark,' their terms of service (sixty days),
having expired, Capt. Zeizer, who commands on board the
' Governor Clark,' off Prairie du Chien, reports that his
vessel is completely manned, that the fort is finished, christened ' Fort Shelby,' and occupied by the regulars, and that
all are anxious for a visit from Dickson and his red troops.

The Indians are hovering around the village, stealing horses,
and have been successful in obtaining a prisoner, a Frenchman, who had gone out to look for his horses.

Ninth boat, the " James Monroe," one hundred and twenty
tons, built at Pittsburgh, by Mr. Latrobe, and owned by a
company at Bayou Sara, and run in the Natchez trade.

Tenth boat, the " Washington," 400 tons, a two decker,
built at Wheeling, constructed and partly owned by Capt.
Henry M. Shreve. The engine of the Washington was built
at Brownsville, Pa., under the immediate direction of Capt.
Shreve. Her boilers were on the upper deck, being the first
boat on that plan, a valuable improvement by Capt. Shreve,
which is still in general use.

The Washington crossed the falls of the Ohio in September,
1816, under the command of Capt. Shreve, bound for New Orleans, and returned to Louisville during the following winter.

In the month of March, 1817, she left shippingport a second
time and proceeded to New Orleans and returned to Shippingport, being absent only forty-five days.

This was the trip that convinced the despairing public that
steamboat navigation would succeed on Western waters.

Eleventh boat, the " Franklin," 125 tons. Built at Pitts-
burgh by Messrs Shiras & Cromwell, engine by George
Evens; left Pittsburgh in December, 1816, was sold in New
Orleans and was subsequently employed in the Louisville and
St. Louis trade.

She was sunk in the Mississippi, near St. Genevieve, in
1819, on her way to St. Louis, commanded by Capt. Revels.

Twelfth boat, the " Oliver Evans " (afterwards the Constitution), built at Pittsburgh by George Evans. The engines
of his patent. She was but seventy tons burden. She left
Pittsburgh for New Orleans December, 1816. She burst one
of her boilers in 1817, off Point Coupee, by which eleven men
lost their lives, principally passengers. Owned by George
Sultan and others of Pittsburgh.

Thirteenth boat, the " Harriot," forty tons. Built at
Pittsburgh, constructed and owned by Mr. Armstrong, of
Williamsport, Pa. She left Pittsburgh October, 1816, and

crossed the falls in March, 1871, made one trip to New Orleans and subsequently ran between that place and Mussel Shoals, Tennessee river.

Fourteenth boat, the "Kentucky," eighty tons. Built at Frankfort, Ky. Owned by Hanson & Beswell. Was engaged in the Louisville trade.

Fifteenth boat, the "Governor Shelby," ninety tons. Built at Louisville. Engines by Bolton & Ebolt, of England. In 1819 she was running very successfully in the Louisville trade.

Sixteenth boat, the "New Orleans," 300 tons. Built at Pittsburgh by Fulton & Livingston in 1817, for the Natchez trade. Sunk near Baton Rouge, but was raised, and sunk again near New Orleans in February, 1819, about two months after her first sinking.

Seventeenth boat, the "Vesta," 100 tons. Built at Cincinnati in 1817, and owned by Messrs Bosson, Cowdin & Co. She plied regularly between Cincinnati and Louisville.

Eighteenth boat, the "George Madison," 200 tons. Built at Pittsburgh in 1818, by Messrs Voories, Mitchel, Rodgers & Todd, of Frankfort, Ky. Was engaged in the Louisville trade in 1819.

Nineteenth boat, the "Ohio" 443 tons. Built in New Albany, Ind., in 1818, by Messrs. Shreve & Blair, in the Louisville trade.

Twentieth boat, the "Napoleon," 322 tons. Built in Shippingport, 1818, by Messrs. Shreve, Miller & Breckenridge, of Louisville. Engaged in the Louisville trade.

Twenty-first boat, the "Volcano," 250 tons. Built at New Albany by Messrs. John & Robinson de Hart in 1818. She was purchased in 1819 by a company at Natchez, and run from that port to New Orleans.

Twenty-second boat, the "General Jackson," 150 tons. Built at Pittsburgh in 1818, and owned by R. Whiting of that place, and General Carroll, of Tennessee; in the Northern trade.

Twenty-third boat, the "Eagle," 70 tons. Built in Cincinnati in 1818, and owned by James Berthoud & Son, of Shipping-port, Kentucky, in the Natchez trade.

Twenty-fourth boat, the "Hecla," 70 tons. Built at Cincinnati in 1818, and owned by Messrs. Honorus & Barbaror, of Louisville, Kentucky; in the Louisville trade.

Twenty-fifth boat, "Henderson," 85 tons. Built at Cincinnati in 1818, and owned by Messrs. Bowers, of Henderson, Kentucky, and run in the Louisville and Henderson trade.

Twenty-sixth boat, the "Johnston," 80 tons. Built at Wheeling, Va., in 1818, and in 1819 engaged in the Yellowstone expedition.

Twenty-seventh boat, the "Cincinnati," 120 tons. Built-at Cincinnati in 1818, and owned by Messrs. Paxton & Co., of New Albany, Indiana, in the Louisville trade.

Twenty-eighth boat, the "Exchange," 200 tons. Built at Louisville in 1818, and owned by David S. Wood, of Jefferson County, Kentucky, in the Louisville trade.

Twenty-ninth boat, the "Louisiana," 45 tons. Built at New Orleans in 1818, and owned by Mr. Duplesa, of New Orleans, in the Natchez trade.

Thirtieth boat, the "James Ross," 330 tons. Built in 1818 at Pittsburgh, and owned by Messrs. Whiting & Stackpole, of that place, and engaged in the Louisville trade.

Thirty-first boat, the "Frankfort," 320 tons. Built at Pittsburgh in 1818, and owned by Messrs. Vorrhies & Mitchel, of Frankfort, Kentucky, in the Louisville trade.

Thirty-second boat, the "Tamolane," 320 tons. Built at Pittsburgh in 1818, and owned by Bogart & Co., of New York, engaged in the Louisville trade.

Thirty-third boat, the "Perseverance," 40 tons. Built at Cincinnati in 1818, and owned at that place.

Thirty-fourth boat, the "St. Louis," 220 tons. Built at Shippingport, Kentucky, in 1818, and owned by Messrs. Herres, Douglass, Johnston and others; in the Louisville trade.

Thirty-fifth boat, the "General Pike," built at Cincinnati in 1818, intended to ply between Louisville, Cincinnati and Maysville as passenger packet, and owned by a company in Cincinnati.

She was the first steamboat built on Western waters for the exclusive conveyance of passengers. Her accomodations were ample. Her apartments spacious and convenient. She measured 100 feet keel, 25 feet beam, and drew only 39 inches of water. Her cabin was forty feet in length, and in breadth 25 feet. At one end was six state rooms, at the other end eight. Between the two state rooms was a saloon forty by eighteen feet, sufficiently large to accomodate 100 passengers.

The "Pike" was built as an opposition boat to the "Vesta," which was built in 1817.

The rivalry of these boats gave rise to a slang phrase, which held its place with the boys at that period, and outlived the career of both boats. There are old citizens of Cincinnati now living, if they will carry their memories back to the "twenties, " will remember the boys in the streets and through the commons crying, " go ahead, Vesta, the Pike is coming."

Thirty-sixth boat, the " Alabama, " 25 tons. Built on Lake Ponchartrain in 1818 for the Red River trade.

Thirty-seventh boat, the " Calhoun, " 80 tons. Built in 1818, at Frankfort, Kentucky, and afterwards employed in the Yellow Stone expedition.

Thirty-eighth and thirty-ninth boats, the " Expedition, " 120 tons, and the " Independence," 50 tons, built at Pittsburgh. Both of which were intended for the Yellow-stone expedition.

The Independence was the first steamboat that undertook to stem the strong current of the Missouri. They both arrrived at Franklin (Boons Lick), Howard County, 200 miles up the river from its mouth, in the month of June, 1819.

Fortieth boat, the " Maid of Orleans, " 100 tons. Built at Philadelphia in 1818, and owned by a company in New Orleans, and afterwards (in 1819), engaged in the St. Louis trade. She was constructed both for river and sea navigation, the latter by sails, and the former by steam power. She arrived at New Orleans schooner rigged, ascended the Mississippi by steam and was the first vessel that ever reached St. Louis from an Atlantic port.

Forty-first boat, the " Ramapo " 60 tons, built in New York in 1818, and in 1819 was employed in the Natchez trade.

Forty-second boat, the " M'bile " 150 tons, built in Providence, Rhode Island, in 1818, owned in Mobile, and in 1819 was engaged in the New Orleans and Louisville trade.

Forty-third boat, the " Mississippi, " 400 tons, built in New Orleans in 1818, arrived at Havana in February, 1819. She was intended to ply between Havana and Matanzas.

Forty-fourth boat, the " Western Engineer, " built on the Monongahela river in 1818 - 19, descended the Ohio river about the first of May, 1819, and afterwards ascended the Missouri river in connection with the government exploring expedition. The object of this expedition was principally to make a correct military survey of the river and to fix upon a site for the establishment of a military post at, or near the junction of the Yellow-stone and the Missouri, and to ascertain the point where the Rocky Mountains are intersected by the 49th degree of latitude, which formed the western boundary between the possessions of Great Britain and the United States, and to inquire into the " trading capacity and genius of the various tribes through which it may pass."

The officers employed on this duty were Major S. H. Long,

of the United States Engineers, Major Thomas Biddle, of the United States Corps of Artillery and Messrs. Graham & Swift. The boat was completely equipped for defense and was manned by a few troops. The " Western Engineer" drew only thirty inches of water. She was well built and the bottom was fastened with copper and had a serpent's head on her bow through which the steam passed, presenting a novel appearance.

This expedition was organized for the purpose of exploring the country on the Missouri river, and had a full complement of scientific officers of the government, among which were topographical engineers, mineralogists, botanists, geologists, ornithologists, landscape painters, etc. The " Western Engineer " was only 75 feet long, and 13 feet beam, and stern wheel.

Forty-fifth boat, the " Rifleman " 250 tons. Built at Louisville in 1819, owned by Butler & Bamers, and ran in the Louisville trade.

Forty-sixth boat, the " Car of Commerce " 150 tons. Built at Pittsburgh in 1819, owned by W. F. Patterson & Co., of Louisville, and engaged in the trade of that place.

Forty-seventh boat, the " Paragon," 376 tons. Built at Cincinnati in 1819, by Wm. Parsons, and owned by Wm. Noble and Robert Neilson, engaged in the Louisville trade.

Forty-eighth boat, the " Maysville," 150 tons. Built in 1819, and owned by citizens of Washington, Kentucky, and Maysville.

Forty-ninth boat, the " Columbus," 460 tons. Built at New Orleans in 1819, and owned there. She was employed in the Louisville trade.

Fiftieth boat, the " General Clark," 150 tons. Built and owned by a company in Louisville.

Fifty-first boat, the " Vulcan," 300 tons. Built at Cincinnati, 1819, for the New Orleans trade ; owned by citizens of Cincinnati.

Fifty-second boat, the " Missouri, " 175 tons. Built at Newport, Kentucky, 1819; owned by the Messrs. Yeatmans, and designed for the St. Louis trade.

Fifty-third boat, the " New Comet," 100 tons. Altered from a barge, owned at Cincinnati and intended for the New Orleans trade.

Fifty-fourth boat, the " Newport, " 50 tons. Built at that place and owned in New Orleans in 1819, and engaged in the Red River trade.

Fifty-fifth boat, the " Tennessee," 400 tons. Built at·

Cincinnati in 1819; owned by a company in New Orleans and Nashville and employed in the Louisville trade. She was sunk in 1823, in the Mississippi River, by which sixty odd persons were lost, some of them people of distinction.

This disaster caused great excitement through the country and deterred many from traveling on steamboats for a long time.

Fifty-sixth boat, the "General Robinson," 250 tons. Built at Newport, Ky., in 1819, for a company in Nashville, and run in that trade.

Fifty-seventh boat, the "United States," 700 tons. Built at Jeffersonville, Ind., for the Natchez trade in 1819, owned by Hart and others. She was the largest steamboat that had ever been built up to that time for Western waters.

Fifty-eighth boat, the "Post Boy," 200 tons. Built at New Albany, Ind., in 1819, owned by H. M. Shreve and others, and run from Louisville to New Orleans. She was one of the packets employed by the post-office department to carry the mail between those places according to an Act of Congress, passed March 1819. By this Act the expense was not to exceed that of carrying it by land.

Fifty-ninth boat, the "Elizabeth," 150 tons. Built at Salt River, Ky., in 1819, owned by a company at Elizabeth, Ky., and engaged in the New Orleans trade.

Sixtieth boat, the "Fayette," 150 tons. Built in 1819, owned by John Grey and others and engaged in the Louisville trade."

From the numerous lists of boats published by as many historians, I have selected the foregoing from "Sharf's History of St. Louis," as being more extended and probably quite as correct as that of any other, although it lacks detail in specifications; but it is sufficiently so for all practical purposes, I presume, at this late period.

A noticeable feature in this long list of pioneer steamboats is the numerous points that were selected to build them and the great number of persons that were ready to embark in the new enterprise.

Hardly any owners named, appear as such in any two boats. Even Fulton and Livingston who built the first boat, the "New Orleans," subsided very soon after the courts refused to legalize the authority they claimed, under some State enactments for the exclusive right to navigate the Mississippi, for the term of twenty-five years.

The same result occurred to them, in the claim they set up for the exclusive right to navigate with steam, the waters of the State of New York.

CHAPTER XXV.

CAPT. H. M. SHREVE seems to have been about the only one who figured in the different boats named, in the sixty heretofore mentioned.

The *St. Louis Republican* of March 7, 1851, thus notes the death of this eminent steamboatman:

"This worthy citizen died at the residence of his son-in-law in this city yesterday. He was for nearly forty years closely identified with the commerce of the West, either in flat-boat or steamboat navigation.

During the administration of Adams, Jackson and Van Buren, he filled the post of United States Superintendent of Western River Improvements and by the steam snag-boat, of which he was the inventor, contributed largely to the safety of Western commerce. To him belongs the honor of demonstrating the practicability of navigating the Mississippi with steam-boats. He commanded the first steamboat that ever ascended that river, and made several valuable improvements, both of the steam-engine and of the hull and cabins of Western steamboats.

While the British were threatening New Orleans in 1814–15 he was employed by Gen. Jackson in several hazardous enterprises, and during the battle on the 8th of January, served one of the field-pieces which destroyed the advancing column of Gen. Keane.

His name has become historically connected with Western river navigation, and will long be cherished by his numerous friends throughout this valley."

Up to 1817 there seems to have been but few boats built. But little confidence was felt by the public in the practicability of navigating these rivers by the use of steam, until Capt. Shreve made the trip from New Orleans to Louisville with the "Washington" in twenty-five days, in 1817, and the round trip from Louisville to New Orleans and back in forty-five days.

From that time forward there seemed no doubt of the result, and boats multiplied rapidly. Every town on the Ohio river, and some on the tributaries, were ready, and even anxious to establish a "boat yard." Many succeeded, and built one or more boats and the supply was soon greater than the demand. The result was as might have been expected and only the "fittest survived," and many of them were short lived. Still,

with few exceptions, there has never been a time when a con
tract could not be made at a reasonable price and for any
character of a steamboat and in a very short time. Neither
has there ever been a time on Western waters, when sufficient
capital could not be obtained to build more boats than the
commerce of the valley required.

The supply has always exceeded the demand, and, of course,
the natural result has followed with few exceptions. The exceptions are about enough to establish the rule.

Some boats and some trades have proved largely remunerative, at some period of their existence, and some boats have
even been successful to the end of their career; but that has
only stimulated their owners and others to duplicate them,
and the result has generally been disastrous in the end.

The same result has generally been realized by boat builders
as by the owners, and very few of either class have ever retired from the business rich men.

And where that has been the case, investigation shows that
the money made during prosperous periods has been with
drawn from the business and invested in something else.

The next vessel to arrive in St. Louis after the " Pike,"
was the " Constitution," Capt. Guzard, which arrived Oct.
2, 1817. The steamboat ceased to be a novelty on the Mississippi in 1818, and became a recognized agent of the commerce of the valley.

The arrival and departure of vessels about this time were
noticed by the *Gazette* as follows : —

" On Saturday last the steamboat ' Franklin,' of about 140
tons burden, arrived here from New Orleans in thirty-two
days, with passengers and assorted cargo.

The ' Franklin ' is admirably calculated for a regular passenger packet to ply between St. Louis and New Orleans. Her
stowage is capacious, and her passenger accommodations elegant." — *Gazette, June 12, 1818.*

" The steamboat ' Franklin ' left this place yesterday with
freight and passengers for New Orleans. The master expects
to arrive there in about eight days. Our common barges take
from twenty-five to thirty days to perform the voyage. —
Gazette, June 19, 1818.

" List of boats trading to New Orleans:

" ' Franklin,' 131 tons; ' Eagle,' ' Pike ' (sunk); ' James
Monroe ' (sunk, now repairing)." — *Gazette, Sept. 5,
1818.*

" The new steamboat ' Johnston,' of Kentucky, passed
Shawneetown the first of this month bound for New Orleans.

She is intended as a regular trader from Kentucky on the Mississippi, and the Missouri as high up as the Yellowstone river." — *Gazette, Nov. 6, 1818.*

" The arrival about March 1st, 1819, of the large and elegant steamboat ' Washington,' from New Orleans, which city she left on the first of February, was announced in the *Gazette* of March 3d.   The steamboat ' Harriet' arrived from the same port early in April.

" The ' Sea Horse,' which arrived at New Orleans from New York, and the ' Maid of Orleans,' from Philadelphia, early in 1819, were probably the first steamboats that ever performed a voyage of any length on the ocean.

" The ' Maid of Orleans ' continued her voyage to St. Louis, where she arrived about the 1st of May.   On the same day the steamboat ' Independence,' Capt. Nelson, arrived from Louisville."

The *Missouri Gazette* of 19th May, 1819, has the following steamboat memorandum : —

" The Expedition, Capt. Craig, arrived here on Wednesday last, destined for the Yellowstone.

The Maid of Orleans, Capt. Turner, sailed for New Orleans, and the Independence, Capt. Nelson, for Franklin, on the Missouri, on Sunday last.   The Exchange, Capt. Whips, arrived here ˎon Monday and will return to Louisville in a few days for a new set of boilers, she having burst her boiler in ascending the Mississipi.

The " St. Louis, " Capt. Hewes ; the " James Monroe," and the " Hamlet, " were advertised to sail for St. Louis from New Orleans about the middle of last month."

" In 1817, less than two years ago, the first steamboat arrived at St. Louis.

We hailed it as the day of small things, but the glorious consummation of all our wishes is daily arriving.   Already we have seen during the present season at our shores five steamboats, ˅ and several more expected.   Who would, or could have dared conjecture, that in 1819, we would witness the arrival of a steamboat from Philadelphia or New York ?   And yet, such is the fact."

" The Mississippi has become familiar to this great American invention, and another new arena is open."

" A steamboat owned by individuals, has started from St. Louis for Franklin, two hundred miles up the Missouri, and two others are here, destined for the Yellowstone.   The time is fast approaching when a journey to the Pacific will become as familiar, and indeed more so, than it was twenty years ago,

8

to Kentucky or Ohio. 'Illustrious Nation,' said a foreigner of distinction, speaking of the New York canal. "Illustrious nation, whose conceptions are only equaled by her achievements."

The "Independence" was the first steamboat that entered the Missouri River. Sailing from St. Louis, May, 1819, she reached Franklin, on the Missouri, after a voyage of thirteen days, of which four days were spent at different landings. Her voyage extended up the river to Old Chariton, from whence she returned to St. Louis."

The following announcement shows the appreciation of the citizens on the Missouri for the advent of steam navigation.

FRANKLIN, BOONSLICK, May 10, 1819.

ARRIVAL OF THE STEAMBOAT.

"With no ordinary sensation of pride and pleasure we announce this morning the arrival at this place of the elegant steamboat, 'Independence,' Capt. Nelson, in seven sailing days, but thirteen from the time of her departure from St. Louis, with passengers and cargo of flour, whisky, sugar, nails, castings, etc., being the first steamboat that ever attempted to ascend the Missouri river. She was joyfully met by the inhabitants of Franklin, and saluted by the firing of cannon, which was returned by the Independence. The grand *desideratum*, the important *fact*, is now ascertained that steamboats can safely navigate the Missouri."

"She was absent from St. Louis 21 days. This trip proves a proud event in the history of Missouri."

The Missouri river has heretofore almost effectually resisted all attempts at navigation. She has imposed every obstacle she could to the tide of navigation which was rolling up her banks and dispossessing her dear red children. But her white children, although children by adoption, have become numerous, and are increasing so rapidly that she is at last obliged to yield them her favor." — *Gazette, June 9th, 1819.*

In the same paper and the same date is the following announcement: —

"The United States Government having determined to explore the Missouri river up to the Yellowstone, and for the purpose as elsewhere stated, Major H. S. Long had built at Pittsburgh the steamboat "Western Engineer." To Col. Atkinson had been entrusted the command of this expedition, and starting from Plattsburgh, New York, in the latter part of 1818, he arrived at Pittsburgh in the spring of 1819. The Western Engineer was completed soon after, and arrived at St. Louis, June 8, 1819. On the 21st the expedition started for the Missouri. It was accompanied by three other United States steamers and nine keel boats, bearing a detachment of government troops.

The names of the steamboats and of their commanders were "Thomas Jefferson," Capt. Offord; "R. M. Johnston," Capt. Coalfax, and the "Expedition," Capt. Craig.

The little fleet entered the Missouri with martial music, display of flags and firing of cannon. In honor of the statesman who acquired the territory of Louisiana for the United States, the precedence was accorded to the "Thomas Jefferson."

But some disarrangement of her machinery prevented this boat from taking the lead, and the "Expedition" secured the position of being the first steamer in the flotilla to enter the Missouri.

The Jefferson was doomed to a worse mishap still, for not long after she ran upon a snag and sunk.

"The steam escape of the Western Engineer was shaped like a great serpent, coiled on the bow of the boat in the attitude of springing, and the steam hissing from the fiery mouth (which was painted red), filled the Indians with terror. They thought the wrath of the great spirit had sent this monster for their chastisement." — (Professor Waterhouse.)

The *Gazette* of June 2d, 1819, contains the following: —

"Arrived at this place on the first, the fast sailing and elegant steamboat "St. Louis," Capt. Hewes, 28 days from New Orleans. The captain has politely favored us with the following from his log book: —

On the 5th of May left New Orleans at 3 p. m. Passed steamer "Volcano" bound down; on the 10th passed steamer James Ross; at 11 p. m. passed steamboat "Rifleman" at anchor, with shaft broken.

On 15th passed steamboat "Madison,"

Six days from the falls of the Ohio.

Twentieth passed steamboat "Governor Shelby" bound for New Orleans; 22d ran on a sand bar, and was detained until next day.

Twenty-sixth at the grand turn below Island No. 60 passed nine keel boats, with the sixth regiment, United States Infantry, commanded by Col. Atkinson, destined for the Missouri.

At quarter past 11 o'clock ran aground and lost anchor and part of cable.

Twenty-second steamboat "Harriet" passed; while at anchor 28th, at 3 p. m., passed steamboat "Jefferson," with

United States troops, having broken her piston. At 4 p. m. repassed steamer "Harriet."

THE FIRST "EXCURSION" TRIP ON THE MISSISSIPPI.

The same paper on 9th of June announced that "Capt. Hewes, of the "St. Louis," had gratified the citizens of St. Louis with a sail to the mouth of the Missouri, and that the company on board was large and genteel, and the entertainment very elegant.

The return of the "Maid of Orleans," 28th July, and the departure of the "Yankee," early in December, for New Orleans, complete the record of steamboating for 1819."

The first steamboat that ascended the upper Mississippi was the "Virginia," which arrived at Fort Snelling in May, 1823.

The Missouri and upper Mississippi had now been opened to regular navigation, and the steamboat traffic of the great river and its tributaries developed rapidly.

On the 22d of August, 1825, the *Republican* announced that two steamboats, the "Brown" and the "Magnet," now laying here for the purpose of repairing, and added :
" We believe this is the first instance of steamboats remaining here during the season of low water."

On April 19th, 1822, the *Republican* remarks : —
"During the past week our wharf has exhibited a greater show of business than we recollect ever before to have seen, and the number of steam and other boats arriving and departing has been unprecedented. The immense trade, which has opened between this place and Fever River at the present time, employs, besides a number of keel boats, six steamboats, to wit: the "Indiana," "Shamrock," "Hamilton," "Muskingum," and "Mechanic." The Indiana and Shamrock on their return trip have been deeply freighted with lead, and several keel boats likewise have arrived with the same article. Judging from the thousands of people who have gone to make their fortunes at the lead mines this spring, we should suppose that the quantity of lead produced this year would be tenfold greater than heretofore."

Again, on the 12th of July, same year, the same paper remarks : —
" It must be gratifying to every citizen of St. Louis to witness the steady advancement of the town, the number of steamboats that have arrived and departed during the spring being cited as the best evidence of the increase of business."

CHAPTER XXVI.

THE following quotations are from " Hall's West," published in 1848 at Cincinnati, and are interesting as well as instructive, which fully justifies their insertion in these compilations: "The General Pike, built at Cincinnatti, in 1818, and intened to ply as a packet between Maysville, Cincinnatti and Louisville, is said to have been the first steamboat constructed on the Western waters for the exclsive convenience of passengers. Her accommodations were ample, her apartments spacious and superbly furnished, and her machinery of superior mechanism. She measured one hundred feet keel, twenty feet beam, and drew only three feet three inches water.

The length of her cabin was forty feet, the breadth twenty five feet, in addition to which were fourteen state rooms. The boats previously built had been intended solely for the transportation of merchandise: these objects have subsequently been successfully united.

The Calhoun, eighty tons, built at Frankfort in 1818, the Expedition, one hundred and twenty tons — the two last built at Pittsburgh — were constructed for the exploration of the Missouri river, in what was popularly termed the Yellow Stone Expedition, projected by Mr. Calhoun, while Secretary of War. The Independence was the first steamboat that ascended the powerful current of the Missouri.

The Post Boy, two hundred tons, built at New Albany, by Captain Shreve and others, in 1819, was intended for the conveyance of the mail between Louisville and New Orleans, under an act of Congress, passed in March, 1819. This was the first attempt on the Western waters to carry the mail on steamboats.

The Western Engineer was built near Pittsburgh, in 1818, under the direction of Major S. H. Long, of the United States topographical engineers, for the expedition of discovery to the sources of the Missouri, and the Rocky Mountains. which was afterwards so honorably accomplished by himself and his companions. This boat ascended as high as the Council Bluffs, about six hundred and fifty miles above St. Louis, and was the first steamboat that reached that point.

The following remarks are from the pen of Morgan Neville, Esq., and were written in 1829.

" The average cost of a steamboat is estimated at $100 per ton; the repairs made during the existence of a boat amount

to one half the first cost. The average duration of a boat
has hitherto been about four years; of those built of locust,
lately, the period will probably be two years longer. The
amount of expenditure in this branch of business on the Western
waters, then, for the last ten years, will in some measure be
shown by the following calculation:

```
56,000 tons, costing $100 per ton, amount to.....................$5,600,000
Repairs on the same.................................................. 2,800,000
                                                            _____
Expending in building and repairing in ten years................ $8,400,000
```

The annual expenditure of steamboats is very difficult to
be arrived at; the importance of this expenditure, however, to the towns on our rivers, and to the whole extent of
country running along their shores, may be estimated from
the following calculation of the item of fuel alone, for one
year — take the present year, 1829. We have now in operation about two hundred boats, the tonnage of which may be
stated at thirty-five thousand tons.

It is calculated that the business of each year lasts eight
months; deduct one-fourth for the time lost in port, and we
have six months, or one hundred and eighty days, of running
time. Each boat is presumed to consume one cord of wood,
for every twelve tons, every twenty-four hours.

```
The 35,000 tons then consume, per day...................... 2,917 cords
Or, during the six months.................................525,060 cords
```

" The price of wood varies from $1.50 to $5 per cord; a
fair average would place it at $2.25 per cord. This makes
the expenditure for fuel alone, on the banks of our rivers,
$1,181,385 for this year. The other expenditures, while run-
ning are calculated, by the most experienced and intelligent
owners, to be equal to $1,300,000, which gives the total ex-
penditure for 1829, at $2,488,385.   •

" This calculation and estimate, then, which are both made
lower than the facts justify, presents these results:

```
The amount of first cost of steamboats, since 1817...............$5,600,000
Repairs on the same........................................... 2,800,000
                                                           _____
Total amount of expenditure, produced by the introduction of
steamboats, for building and repairs...........................$8,400,000
```

We cannot better illustrate the magnitude of the change in
every thing connected with eastern commerce and navigation,
than by contrasting the foregoing statement, with the situation of things at the adoption of steam transportation say in
1817. About twenty barges, averaging one hundred tons
each, comprised the whole of the commercial facilities for

transporting merchandise from New Orleans to the " Upper Country," each of these performed one trip down and up to Louisville and Cincinnati within the year. The number of keelboats employed in the upper Ohio cannot be ascertained, but it is presumed that one hundred and fifty is a sufficiently large calculation to embrace the whole number. These averaged thirty tons each, and employed one month to make the voyage from Louisville to Pittsburgh, while the more dignified barge of the Mississippi made her trip in the space of one hundred days, if no extraordinary accident happened, to check her progress. Not a dollar was expended for wood, in a distance of two thousand miles, and the dweller on the banks of the Ohio thought himself lucky if the reckless boatman would give the smallest trifle for the eggs and chickens which formed almost the only saleable articles on a soil whose only fault is its too great fertility. Such was the case twelve years since. The Mississippi boats now make five or six trips within the year, and are enabled, if necessary,|within that period, to afford to that trade one hundred and thirty-five thousand tons. Eight or nine days are sufficient, on the upper Ohio, to perform the trip from Louisville to Pittsburgh and back. In short if steam has not realized the hyperbole of the poet in " annihilating time and space," it has produced results scarcely surpassed by the introduction of the art of printing."

From another valuable article of the same gentleman, we copy the following very interesting remarks : —

" On the first day of January, 1834, an official list of steamboats, from an authentic source, gives the whole number of two hundred and thirty, then in existence, whose aggregate amount of tonnage is equal to about thirty-nine thousand tons.

Allowing the cost of building at a rate much lower than the rule adopted three years since, the capital now invested in this stock will exceed $3,000,000. The expense of running may be put down nearly as contained in the following scale : —

60 boats over 200 tons, 180 days at $140 per day..............$1,512,000 00
70 boats from 120 tons to 200,240 running days, $90 per day.... 1,512,000 00
100 boats under 120 tons, 280 running days, $60 per day...... 1,620,000 00

    Total yearly expenses................................$4,644,000 00

" This sum may be reduced to the different items producing it in the following proportions, viz. : —

For wages 36 per cent, equal to $1,671,840 00
For wood 30 per cent, equal to............................... 1,393,200 00
For provisions, 18 per cent, equal to.... .... 835,920 00
For contingencies 16 per cent, equal to....................... 743,040 00

" This result is truly striking to those who were accustomed
to the state of things on our rivers within twenty years. The
difference in the amount of wages paid is in itself very considerable; but the item of fuel is one created exclusively by
steamboats; and when it is considered that nearly $1,500,000
is expended every year, at a few points on the Mississippi valley, it presents a vast field for speculation. The immense
forests of beech and other timber, unfit for agricultural purposes, were, before, not only useless, but an obstacle to the
rugged farmer, who had to remove them before he could sow
and reap. The steamboat, with something like magical influence, has converted them into objects of rapidly increasing
value. He no longer looks with despondence on the dense-
ness of trees, and only regrets that so many have already been
given to the flames, or cast on the bosom of the stream before
him.

"At the present period, 1848, the steamboats may be considered as plying as follows, viz.: —

25 over 200 tons, between Louisville, New Orleans and Cincinnati,
    measuring...... .... 8484 tons.
7 between Nashville and New Orleans, measuring................. 2,585 "
4 between Florence and New Orleans............................ 1,617 "
4 in the St. Louis trade...................................... 1,002 "
7 in the cotton trade.. 2,016 "
57 boats not in established trades from 120 to 200 tons........... 8,641 "
    The balance under 120 tons in various trades.............14,655 "

                                   89,000 tons.

" In the New Orleans and Louisville trade, the boats over
two hundred tons make about one hundred and fifty trips in
prosperous seasons; those of smaller size make from fifty to
sixty trips. But to go into an estimate of the number of voyages made by the boats in the different trades is impossible,
because no regular dates are furnished, and the result depends
upon a variety of contingencies."

Previous to 1817, about twenty barges afforded the only
facilities for transporting merchandise from New Orleans to
Louisville and Cincinnati. These, making but one trip in the
year, gave the means of bringing up only two thousand tons.
The present tonnage in this trade exclusively having been
stated to be eight thousand eight hundred and eighty-four
tons, gives the amount employed calculating one hundred and
fifty trips in the season, to be fifty thousand nine hundred and
four tons; a cause capable of producing a revolution in sixteen years hardly equalled in the annals of history. The effects upon Western commerce have been immense. The moral

changes alone which are felt throughout the West on price are almost incalculable; the imported article has fallen in a ratio equal to the increased price of Western products. In looking back at the old means of transportation, we cannot conceive how the present demand and consumption could have been supplied by them.

To those who have been acquainted with the early merchantile history of our country, when it was no uncommon thing for a party of merchants to be detained in Pittsburgh from six weeks to two months, by low water, or ice, the existing state of things is truly gratifying. The old price of carriage of goods, from the Atlantic seaboard to Pittsburgh, was long estimated at from $5 to $8 per hundred pounds. We have an instance in the last five years, of merchandise being delivered at the wharf of Cincinnati for $1 per hundred pounds, from Philadelphia, by way of New Orleans.

It may not be useless, or uninteresting to give an idea of the mortality among the steamboats in a given time. It is not pretended that any decided inference can be drawn from this statement, or that the facts go to establish any fixed rule. But under the present situation of steamboat discipline and regulation a tolerably fair conclusion can be drawn from it. Taking the period then of two years, from the fall of 1831 till that of 1833, we have a list of boats gone out of service of sixty-six; of these fifteen were abandoned as unfit for service; seven were lost by ice; fifteen were burnt; twenty-four snagged; and five destroyed by being struck by other boats. Deducting the fifteen boats abandoned as unseaworthy, we have fifty-one lost by accidents peculiar to the trade. In number this proportion is over twelve per cent, per annum; in tonnage the loss is upward of ten per cent. Amount snagged, three thousand three hundred and thirty tons.

A curious fact was ascertained by a committee of gentlemen, who were appointed a few years ago, by a number of steamboat owners, to investigate the whole subject. They satisfied themselves, that although the benefits conferred on our country, by steam navigation, were incalculable, the stock invested in boats was, as a general rule, a losing investment. In few cases, owing to fortuitous events, or to the exercise of more than usual prudence, money has been made; but the instances are so few as not to effect the rule. One gentleman, who has been engaged for years in the ownership of steamboats and has been peculiarly fortunate, in not meeting with any loss by accident, assured the writer, that his aggregate gain, during the whole series of years, was only about six per

cent per year, on the capital invested. These facts go towards accounting for the enormous proportion of accidents
and losses which occur upon our rivers.   A few instances, in
which large profits were realized, induced a great number of
individuals to embark in this business, and the tonnage had always been greater than the trade demanded.   The accidents,
which are almost wholly the result of bad management, were
set down as among the unavoidable chances of the navigation,
and instead of adopting measures to prevent them, they were
deliberately subtracted from the supposed profits, as matters
of course.   As the boat was not expected to last more than
five or six years, at best, and would probably be burned up,
or sunk within that period, it was considered good economy
to reduce the expenditures, and to make money by any means,
during the brief existence of the vessel.   Boats were hastily
and slightly built, furnished with cheap engines, and placed
under the charge of wholly incompetent persons; the most in-
excusable devices were resorted to, to get freight and passengers, and the most criminal indifference to the safety of the
boat and those on board, observable during the trip.
    The writer was once hurried from Louisville to Shippings-
port, two miles below, without his breakfast, and in the rain,
to get board a boat which was advertised to start at eight
o'clock on that morning.   During the whole day, passengers
continued to come on board, puffing and blowing — in the
most eager haste to secure a passage — each having been assured by the captain or agent, that the boat would start in
less than an hour.   The next day presented the same scene;
the rain continued to fall; we were two miles from the city,
lying against a miry bank which prevented any one from
leaving the boat — the fires were burning, the steam hissing
and the boat only waiting for the captain, who would be on
board in a few minutes.   By and by the captain came —
but then we must wait a few minutes for the clerk, and when
the clerk came, the captain found that he must go up to town.
In the meantime, passengers continued to accumulate, each
decoyed alike by the assurance that the boat was about to depart.   Thus we were detained until the third day, when the
cabin and deck being crowded with a collection nearly as miscellaneous as the crew of Noah's ark, the captain thought
proper to proceed on his voyage.   It was afterwards understood that when the captain began to collect passengers, a part
of his engine was on shore, undergoing repairs which could
not be completed in less than two days, yet during the whole

of those two days fires were kept up, and gentlemen and
ladies inveigled on board, in the manner related.

We mention this to show the kind of deception which has
been practiced. This, it is true, was an extreme case, but although the detention is not usually so great, nor the deceit so
gross, it is not uncommon for steamboat captains and agents
to deceive passengers by the most egregious misrepresenta-
tions.

The fact is important, not merely as showing the inconveniences to which travelers are exposed, but as explaining one of
the causes of the numerous accidents on the Western waters —
which is, bad faith. The man who will do one dishonest act,
will do another. The agent or officer, who will deliberately
kidnap men, by the assurance that he will start to-day, when
he knows that he will not start till to-morrow, and the owner
who will permit such conduct, will not shrink at any act by
which he may think his interest likely to be promoted — and,
having insured the boat, will risk the lives of the passengers
by running at improper seasons, and other hazards, by which
time may be saved and the expenses of the trip diminished.

The great danger to boats from snags has now become
greatly diminished on the Mississippi, and has almost entirely
ceased in the Ohio, in consequences of the measures adopted
for the removal of these obstacles.

The burning of boats must be the result of carelessness;
and the dreadful consequences arising from the collision are
produced by negligence and design. There is scarcely a conceivable case in which boats may not avoid running against
each other in the night; and there are many instances in
which the officers of steamboats have been induced, by a ferocious spirit of rivalry, or some other unworthy motive, to run
against weaker boats in such a manner as to sink them instantly.

It is proper however, to state, that the accidents occurring
on steamboats have been greatly magnified by premature and
inaccurate newspaper reports, and that they have been much
fewer and less fatal than has generally been supposed.

It is also true, that much of the evil alluded to is attributed
to the precipitancy and culpable negligence with regard to their
own safety and comfort of the passengers. The accidents are
almost wholly confined to insufficient or badly managed boats,
and the traveler who would be cautious in embarking only in
those of the more respectable class would almost uniformly
insure himself against danger. A choice of boats, embracing
every variety, from the best to those that are wholly unsea

worthy, is presented at all of our principal places of embark-
ation. Yet such is the feverish impatience of delay, evinced
by most travelers in our country, that the great majority has-
ten on board the first boat which offers, regardless of her
character, and only anxious to the moving forward, under
any discomfort, and at every hazard. The bad boats receive
undue patronage, the best do not meet the preference to which
they are entitled, and are not compensated for the extra expenditure bestowed upon their outfit and management; and the
inducements to accommodate the public well being weakened,
neither the owners or officers of their boats, nor the same
degree of responsibility, which would occur if the public
patronage was more judiciously bestowed.

The following remarks occur in a letter to the Secretary of
the Treasury, from Mr. William C. Reffield, agent of the steam
navigation company at New York, and are considered as embracing the steam navigation of the whole Union.

"The contest for speed, or practice of racing, between rival
steamboats, has been the cause, and perhaps justly, of considerable alarm in the community. It is remarkable, however,
that as far as the information of the writer extends, there has
no accident occured to any boiler which can be charged to a
contest of this sort. The close and uniform attention which
is necessarily given to the action and state of the boiler and
engines, in such contests, may have had a tendency to prevent
disaster. But this hazard, as well as the general danger of
generating an excess of steam, is greatly lessened by the known
fact, that in most steamboats the furnaces and boilers are not
competent to furnish a greater supply of steam than can be used
with safety, with an ordinary degree of attention on the part
of the engineers.

" The magnitude and extent of the danger to which passengers in steamboats are exposed, though sufficiently appalling,
is comparatively much less than in other modes of transit with
which the public have been long familiar. The accidents of
which, if not so astounding, are of almost every day occur-
ence. It will be understood that I allude to the dangers of
ordinary navigation, and land conveyances by animal power
of wheel carriages. In the former case, the whole or greater
part of both passengers and crew are frequently lost, and
sometimes by the culpable ignorance or folly of the officers in
charge, while no one thinks of urging a legislative remedy for
this too common catastrophe. In the latter class of cases,
should inquiry be made for the number of casualties oc-
curing in various districts in a given number of years, and

the results fairly applied to our whole population and travel, the comparitively small number injured or destroyed in steamboats would be matter of great surprise to those not accustomed to make such estimates upon passing events. It is also worthy of notice, that if the annual average loss of life by the electric stroke were ascertained in the manner above proposed, the results would probably show a loss of life by this rare casualty far exceeding that which is occasioned by accidents in steamboats."

In the year 1832 it was estimated that, besides the steamboats, there were four thousand flatboats annually descending the Mississippi, whose aggregate measure would be one hundred and sixty thousand tons. As these do not return, the loss on them would amount to $420,000, and the expense of loading, navigating and unloading them $960,000 — making the whole annual expenditure upon this class of boats, $1,380,000.

In the same year the aggregate cost of steamboats, the expenses of running them, interest, wear and tear, wood, wages and subsistence of crews and passengers, was estimated at $5,906,000.

The total expenditure on steam and flatboats was, according to this calculation, $7,286,000.

The value of produce exported in these boats, together with the labor expended in and about them, was estimated at $26,000,000.

The different descriptions of boats navigated on the Western rivers, in that year, were supposed to give employment to sixteen thousand nine hundred men, namely : —

To mechanics and laborers employed in building 20 steamboats, and repairing others	$1,700
Wood cutters	4,400
Crews of steamboats	4,800
Building flatboats	2,000
Navigating flatboats to New Orleans	4,000
Total	$16,900

But adding to those who are directly engaged the much larger number who are indirectly employed in making engines and in furnishing, supplying, loading and discharging boats, the whole number of persons deriving subsistence from this navigation, in 1832, was supposed to be ninety thousand. That number has since been greatly increased. During the last season there was built at Pittsburgh and the neighboring towns·

.about twenty-five steamboats, at Cincinnati and its neigh borhood about twenty-five.

From 1822 to 1827 the loss of property on the Ohio and Mississippi, by snags, including steam and flatboats, and their cargoes amounted to $1,362,500. Loss in the same items from the same cause, from 1827 to 1832, $381,000.

CHAPTER XXVII.

WE close this part of our subject with the following extracts from two very interesting articles published in the Wheeling *Gazette*, since our table of steamboats was compiled:

" We are informed on good authority that the number of boats built the present year between Louisville and Pittsburgh, including those places, will not fall short of fifty. About thirty-five of these are for distant parts of the country — for the southern and westernmost states: the remaining fifteen will be added to our river trade, increasing the number of boats thus employed to about sixty. Supposing the amount of freight conveyed in each boat to be forty tons down and twenty up, some opinion may be formed of the amount of merchandise transported yearly upon the Ohio. The river may be estimated to be navigable from six to eight months in the year, and each boat to perform twelve trips from Wheeling to Louisville and back. Each boat, then transports twelve times forty tons down, and half this quantity up, equal to seven hundred and twenty tons. This multiplied by sixty, the number of boats, gives forty-three thousand two hundred tons as the gross amount of merchandise transported yearly in steamboats upon the Ohio.

To fix the value of this merchandise is not so easy. Yet something like accuracy may be obtained. It is said that a wagon load of dry goods, weighing two tons, will cost about $4,000, and that western merchants that purchase $8,000 worth receive them generally in two wagon loads. This would make a ton of dry goods worth $2,000. As grosser and heavier articles, however, are sent down the river in large quantities, the value per ton may be rated at $500. Forty times five hundred gives $20,000 as the value of each cargo; this, multiplied by twelve gives $240,000 as the amount conveyed by each boat during the season; and this multiplied by sixty, the number of boats, gives the sum of $14,800,000 as the value of the down freight in a single year. This is independent of the merchandise conveyed in keel and flatboats, and the immense amount of lumber which almost covers the face of the river in the spring season. The value of the merchandise transported up the river may be estimated at $1,500,000. Making the total value of merchandise transported in steamboats yearly on the Ohio, upwards of $16,000,000.

The number of steamboats employed in 1842, in navigating the Mississippi and its tributaries, was four hundred and fifty. The average burden of these boats was two hundred tons each, making an aggregate of ninety-thousand tons, and their aggregate value at $80 per ton, $7,200,000. Many of these were fine vessels, affording the most elegant accommodations for passengers, and comparing favorably, in beauty of model, completeness of finish, and all other particulars, with the best packets in any part. of the world.

The number of persons engaged in navigating our steamboats varies from twenty to fifty to each boat. The average is about thirty-five persons, which will give a total of thirty-five thousand seven hundred and fifty persons embarked in this navigation.

It appears, from the reports of the Louisville and Portland canal, that more than seven hundred flatboats have passed that canal in one year. At this rate there cannot be less than four thousand descending the Mississippi, and allowing five men to each boat, there are twenty thousand persons engaged in this branch of the navigation. The cost of these boats is $420,000, which, as they do not return, is an annual expense, and the expense of loading, navigating and unloading them is $960,000, making the whole annual expenditure upon this class of boats $1,380,000.

In 1834, the number of steamboats in existence, on the Western waters, was two hundred and thirty, and they were estimated to carry thirty nine thousand tons.

Previous to the adoption of steamboat navigation, say in 1817, the whole commerce, from New Orleans to the upper country, was carried in about twenty barges, averaging one hundred tons each, and making but one trip a year. The number of keel boats employed on the Upper Ohio could not have exceeded one hundred and fifty, carrying thirty tons each, and making the trip from Pittsburg to Louisville and back in two months, or about three voyages in a season. The tonnage of all the boats ascending the Ohio and Lower Mississippi was then about six thousand five hundred.

Iu 1834, the number of steamboats was two hundred and thirty, and the tonnage equal to about thirty-nine thousand tons; and in 1842, the number of boats was four hundred and fifty, and their burden ninety thousand tons.

In 1832, it was calculated that the whole number of persons deriving subsistence from this navigation, including the crews of steam and flatboats, mechanics and laborers employed in building and repairing boats, was ninety thousand. As the number of boats had doubled since that time, the number of people directly engaged in and about this navigation in 1842, was not less than one hundred and eighty thousand; but who shall place a limit to the numbers who are beneficially interested, in a business which distributes its millions of dollars for wood, its millions for wages, its millions for provisions, its millions for machinery and the labor of mechanics, and which transports a commerce whose value can only be computed by hundreds of millions?

The cost of building and of running boats has not changed essentially within the last few years. The price of some items have risen, but others have been reduced, so as to leave but little difference in the general results.

In the construction of the boats there has been a progressive and very decided improvement. Their models have been changed to suit the exigencies of the navigation. The great objects have been to obtain speed and capacity for carrying freight, with power to stem the heavy currents of our rivers, and the less possible draught of water. In all these respects our boats have been improved from year to year, and are still improving. The most marked changes consist in a great increase in the length and decrease in the depth of the boats, adding to their speed and lightness of draught.

Boats are constructed now more than formerly for particular trades, and are specially adapted for the purposes for which they are intended. Lines of packets have been established, between all the more important places, which run regularly, and which have attained a commendable degree of punctuality in their departures and arrivals. All these are comfortable, many of them very fine, and a few of them very superior. The large passenger boats, running between New Orleans and Vicksburgh, St. Louis and Louisville, are inferior to nothing of the kind in any part of the world. The cabins are spacious and elegant, the state rooms commodious, and the tables equal to the ordinaries of the best hotels and far superior to those of any but the very best. The officers are not only accommodating, but generally kind and hospitable, treating the passengers as their guests, and taking pains to render the voyage agreeable. The company on board these boats is usually good, and it is an admirable peculiarity in our Western traveling, that fellow travelers avoid the exclusive and selfish deportment which is seen elsewhere, and mingle freely together, seeking the acquaintance and society of each other, and all contributing to the common comfort and amusement. A trip to New Orleans in one of our best boats often resembles a party of pleasure, and combines in its incidents much variety, and no small degree of luxury.

The men of business in the West, and all who are in easy circumstances, travel often and very extensively, and are thus very decidedly acquainted with each other. Besides the crowds who go annually to New Orleans upon business, there are other crowds who seek to while away a few of the weeks or months of the winter, in festivity, amid the gay and novel scenes of that busy metropolis, large and cheerful parties thus meet on board the steamboats, and, as they must necessarily be several days together, they endeavor to accommodate themselves to each other, and to pass the time agreeably; and it often happens that the greater portion of the cabin passengers form one circle, in which affability and freedom from constraint are chastened by perfect decorum and good breeding. Music and dancing are the chief amusements; and at night, when the spacious cabin of one of our Leviathan boats is lighted up, enlivened by the merry notes of the violin, and filled with well dressed persons, it seems more like a floating palace than a mere conveyance for wayfarers. These fine boats are safe as well as speedy, making the trip from Louisville or St. Louis to New Orleans in four or five days, and the upward voyage in six or seven days.

The mailboats between Louisville and Cincinnati are also very fine boats. Messrs. Strader & Gorman, the original proprietors of this line, have the merit not only of having been the first to establish a regular line of packets in the West, but of carrying out their plan with eminent success, with profit to themselves, and with great advantage to the public. They were the first to have fixed hours of departure, and to adhere to them with punctuality. Their boats have always been of the first class, the accommodations excellent, and the officials skillful and obliging; and it is with pleasure that we record the fact, so creditable to all concerned, that in more than twenty years, during which this line has been in existence, no accident

9

has occurred by which the life or limb of a passenger has been endangered. This line has lately passed into the hands of other owners who run a morning and evening line, and under whose management the boats have maintained, and we have no doubt will continue to maintain, their high character.

There is also a daily line of packets between Pittsburgh and Cincinnati, deserving of the highest commendation. There are few boats anywhere finer than the most of those engaged in this line. They are large vessels, with fine accommodations and are well managed. The proprietors, in a recent advertisement, assert that in the last six years they have carried two millions of people annually. The character of the persons who make this statement, and the acknowledged excellence of their boats, leave no room to doubt its correctness, and from our own observation, we feel no hesitation in giving implicit faith in it. *The New York Courier and Enquirer*, commenting on this fact, has this pointed remark : —

What a movement is here of human beings, each intent upon his own well being, and acting in obedience to his own views of self interest ! — what a future is unfolded for such a country, so replenished, and with such safe and rapid means of inter-communication !

" When, too, it is considered that there are various other avenues to the Western paradise, each crowded by its thousands, and its tens of thousands, one can hardly exaggerate the growth of such a country, or the responsibilities which devolve upon its general government to provide, by all adequate and constitutional means, for adding to the security of the great avenues and ports which are thus annually thronged by emigrants and travelers.

" The fact that two millions of persons, to say nothing of property, have been transported on the waters that connect Pittsburgh with Cincinnati, should be conclusive with the general government in favor of the exercise of all its legitimate power to improve the harbors of these cities, and the channels of the far-descended rivers which connect them."

St. Louis is one of the oldest places in the West, having been settled by the French in 1763; Pierre Chouteau and other Frenchmen were very successful in conciliating the confidence of the Indians, and extended the barter of merchandise for furs and peltry, throughout most of the Western tribes. The whole of the Indian trade of the country lying upon the Mississippi and its tributaries, centered at that point ; at which was also the depot for all the military posts on the Western frontier, and the headquarters for most of the officers and agents of the government having transactions in the far West. The lead mines in Missouri and the inexhaustible beds of the mineral more recently discovered in Illinois and Wisconsin render this the principle market for that article, of which immense quantities are annually exported. Wheat, corn, pork, tobacco and hemp, are largely produced in the vast region of fertile land lying around, of which St. Louis is, and must ever be, the emporium.

St. Louis has, therefore, always been a place of great resort, and of remarkable activity in business; and its geographical position seems to insure for it a continuance of that pre-eminence. Its central position in relation to New Orleans on the one hand, and the vast expanse of country on the other, gives its natural advantages, as a commercial place, which are unrivaled, and these advantages are well appreciated and improved by a sound and enterprising population. St. Louis holds the same rank in respect to the region of the Upper Mississippi that Cincinnati occupies in relation to that of the Ohio — east of them is the mart and commercial metropolis of a wide area, in which they are each unrivaled.

We have before us a valuable report, "prepared by authority of the delegates from the City of St. Louis, for the use of Chicago convention of July 5, 1847," from which we select the following passages:

" At the first census (1790), the population of the Valley of the Mississippi did not exceed two hundred thousand. In 1800, it had increased to about five hundred and sixty thousand ; in 1810, to one million three hundred and seventy thousand; in 1820, to two millions five hundred and eighty thousand; in 1830, to four millions one hundred and ninety thousand ; in 1840, to six millions three hundred and seventy thousand ; and in 1847, according to the present average ratio of increase, it exceeds ten millions five hundred and twenty thousand. In the year 1850, according to such ratio, it will exceed twelve millions, and be about equal to the population of all the Atlantic States.

The history of Missouri alone, however, exhibits a still more extraordinary increase. In 1771, the population was seven hundred and forty-three; in 1799, it was six thousand and five; in 1810, it was twenty thousand eight hundred and forty-five; in 1820, it was sixty-six thousand five hundred and eighty-six; in 1830, it was one hundred and forty thousand four hundred and forty-five; in 1840, it was three hundred and eighty-three thousand seven hundred and two; and according to the same ratio of increase (one hundred and sev-

enty-three per cent decenially), it is, 1847, eight hundred
and twenty-five thousand and seventy-four, being an increase
of sixteen per cent per annum. But while the decenial increase of Missouri was one hundred and seventy-three per cent,
that of Illinois was two hundred and two, Mississippi, one
hundred and seventy-five, and Arkansas, two hundred and
twenty-one per cent.

The commerce and agriculture of this valley exhibits a
growth as surprising as that of its population.

The first schooner of the northern lakes, the " Griffin," in
1679, was freighted with the first commercial enterprise and
settlement that reached the Valley of the Mississippi. Thus,
the rivers of the valley owe to the great lakes the introduction
of commerce and population.

From that period up to the purchase of Louisiana in 1803,
and even later, the fur trade of the French emigrants with the
Indians constituted a leading pursuit of the inhabitants,
especially of the upper half of the Valley of the Mississippi.
These immense rivers and lakes were navigated from Quebec,
on the St. Lawrence, to the Yellow Stone, on the Missouri, by
bark canoes, and the Fox and Wisconsin Rivers, connecting
the lakes with the Mississippi, were a chief thoroughfare of
the trade.

Next to the canoe came the Mackinaw boat carrying fifteen
hundred weight to three tons, and then the keel boat or barge
of thirty to forty tons. The first appearance of the keel boat
in the Mississippi, above the mouth of the Ohio, of which we
have any account, was in 1751, when a fleet of boats, commanded by Bossu, a captain of French marines, ascended as
far as Fort Chartres. This enterprise, also, was the first to
ascertain, by experience, something of the nature of the navigation of the Mississippi. One of the boats, the " St.
Louis," struck a sand bar above the mouth of the Ohio, was
unladen and detained two days. Three days after, says the
Traveler, " my boat ran against a tree, of which the Mississippi is full; the shock burst the boat, and such a quantity of
water got into it that it sunk in less than an hour's time."
This was probably the first boat snagged on the Mississippi.
From three to four months was the time consumed at this
period, and for many years afterwards, in a voyage from New
Orleans to the settlements in the vicinity of St. Louis; a
voyage occupying a steamboat, in 1819, twenty-seven days;
but which of late has been accomplished in less than four days.

The city of St. Louis is the base of the navigation of all
the Upper Mississippi and its tributaries, and the head of

navigation for the larger boats of the Ohio and Lower Mississippi. Here is concentrated all the trade of the Upper Mississippi, Missouri, and the Illinois rivers, and a large portion
of the Ohio, and the Lower Mississippi. Hence is exhibited
as busy and as crowded a wharf as can any where be seen,
upon which are commingled people of many nations, and
products of every clime, and every species of industry. The
city was built upon a limestone bluff, of moderate elevation,
fronting on the Mississippi, whose waters washed its base with
a convenient depth. From the condition of a fur trader's
post, it has grown to the quality of a city, promising soon to
be of the first class. From a mere boat load of traders, its
population has gone on multiplying until it has reached the
number of fifty thousand. From a trade of a few thousand
dollars in furs and peltries, a commerce has arisen which
counts its millions. It has grown to be the greatest steam
boat port, next to New Orleans, in the world." Its enrolled
and licensed tonnage was, in

1844..16,664
1845...20,424
1846...28,800

At $65 per ton, its tonnage, for 1846, was worth $1,547,000·
But this tonnage of its own is not all that is required by its
trade. The total number of steamboat arrivals at St. Louis
was: —

In 1839, 1,476 with 213,193 tons.
In 1840, 1,721 with 244,185 tons.
In 1841, 2,105 with 371,691 tons. .
In 1842, 2,412 with 467,824 tons.

Besides eight hundred and one flatboats, and is exclusive of
the daily packets to Alton. During the month of May, 1846,
there were twelve steamboat arrivals per day."

CHAPTER XXVIII.

THE FIRST WAR STEAMBOAT.

[From Preble's' Steam Navigation.]

NEAR the close of 1813, Robert Fulton exhibited to the President of the United States the drawing of a proposed *war steamer* or floating battery, named by him the Demologus. He contemplated in addition to the proposed armament on deck, she should have four submarine guns. Two suspended at each bow, to discharge a hundred-pound ball into an enemy ten or twelve feet below her water line, and that she should have an engine for throwing an immense column of hot water upon the decks or through ports of an opponent. Her estimated cost was $300,000, which was about the cost of a first-class sailing frigate.

Fulton's project was favorably received, and in March, 1813, a law authorizing the President to cause to be equipped one or more floating batteries, for the defense of the waters of the United States. The construction of the vessel was committed by the Coast and Harbor Defense Association, to a sub-committee of five gentlemen appointed by William Jones, Secretary of the Navy. Robert Fulton, whose soul animated the enterprise, was appointed the engineer, and on the 20th of June, 1814, the keels of this novel steamer were laid, at the ship yard of Adam and Noah Brown in the city of New York.

The blockade of our coast by the enemy enhanced the price of timber and rendered the importation of lead, iron and copper and the supply of coal from Richmond and Liverpool difficult. These obstacles, however, were surmounted, and the enemies blockade only increased the expense of her construction.

With reference to the mechanics and laborers there was no difficulty. Shipwrights had repaired to the lakes in such numbers that comparatively few were left on the seaboard. Besides, large numbers had enlisted as soldiers. By an increase of wages, however, a sufficient number of laborers were obtained and the vessel was launched on the 20th of October, 1814, amidst the hurrahs of assembled thousands.

The river and bay was filled with steamers and vessels of war, in compliment to the occasion. In the midst of these was the floating mass of the Demologus, or Fulton, as she was afterwards named, whose bulk and unwieldy form seemed to render her as unfit for motion as were the land batteries that were saluting her.

Captain David Porter, writing to the Secretary of the Navy, under date of the 14th October, 1818, says, "I have the pleasure to inform you that the "Fulton the First," was this morning safely launched. No one yet has ventured to suggest any improvement that could be made in the vessel, and *to use the words of the projector, 'I would not alter her if it was in my power to do so.'*

She promises fair to answer our most sanguine expectations, and I do not despair in being able to navigate in her from one extreme end of the coast to the other. Her buoyancy astonishes every one. She now draws only eight feet three inches of water, and her draft will be ten feet when her guns, machinery stores and crew are all on board. The ease by which she can now be towed by a single steamboat, renders it certain that her relaxity will be sufficiently great to answer every purpose, and the manner it is intended to secure her machinery from the gunners' shot, leaves no apprehension for its safety. I shall use every exertion to prepare her for immediate service. Her guns will soon be mounted, and I am assured by Mr. Fulton that her machinery will be in operation in about six weeks."

On the 21st of November, 1814, the "Fulton" was moved from the wharf of Mess. Brown on the east river to the works of Robert Fulton on the North river to receive her machinery. The steamboat Car of Neptune made fast to her port and the "Fulton" to her starboard side, towed her to her destination at the rate of three and half miles an hour.

The dimensions of this the *first war steamer* were: Length, 150 feet, breadth, 56 feet, depth, 20 feet, water-wheel, 16 feet diameter, length of bucket, 14 feet, dip, 4 feet, engine, 48 inch cylinder, 5 feet stroke; boiler 22 feet length, breadth 12 feet, and depth 8 feet. Tonnage 2,475. She was the largest steamer by many hundreds of tons that had been built at the date of her launch."

The commissioners to examine her in their report say: "She is a structure resting on two boats, keels separated from end to end by a canal 15 feet wide and 60 feet long. One boat contains the cauldrons of copper to prepare her steam. The vast cylinder of iron with its pistons, levers and wheels occupies a part of its fellow. The great water-wheel revolves in the space between them. The main or gun deck, supporting her armament is protected by a bulwark four feet

ten inches thick, of solid timber. This is pierced by thirty
port holes to enable as many as thirty-two pounders to fire red
hot balls. . Her upper or spar deck, upon which several thous-
andmen might parade, is encompassed by a bulwark which a f-
fords safe quarters. She is rigged by two short masts, each
of which supports a large lateen yawl and sails. She has two
bowsprits and gibs and four rudders, two at each extremity
of the boat so that she can be steered either end foremost.
Her machinery is calculated for the addition of an engine
which will discharge an immense column of hot water, which
is intended to throw upon the decks and all through the ports
of an enemy. If in addition to all this we suppose her to be
furnished according to Mr. Fulton's intention, with one hundred pounder Columbiads, two suspended from each bow, so
as to discharge a ball of that size into an enemy's ship, ten or
twelve feet below the water line, it must be allowed that she
has the appearance at least of being the most formidable engine of warfare that human ingenuity has contrived."
    Such is a correct description of this sea monster of 1814.
But exaggerated and fabulous accounts of her got into circulation. Among others the following was published in a Scotch
newspaper, the writer stating that he had taken great care to
procure full and accurate information.
    ' Her length, he writes, on deck is three hundred feet, thick-
ness of sides *thirteen feet*, of alternate oak and cork plank, carries 44 guns. Four of which are 100 pounders. And further
to annoy an enemy attempting to board, can discharge 100
gallons of boiling water, in a minute, and by mechanism
brandishes *three hundred cutlasses* with the uttermost regularity over the gunwales. Works also an equal number of iron
pikes of great length, darting through from her sides with
prodigious force every quarter of a minute.
    The War having terminated, after many trials of speed, and
to improve the ordinance and machinery on board of her,
"Fulton the First," was taken to the navy yard at Brooklyn,
and moored at the flats abreast of that station, where she was
used as a receiving ship, until the 4th of June, 1829, fifteen
years after the laying of her keels, when she was accidentally
or purposely blown up."
    By this explosion 24 men and women were killed, 19
wounded, and five missing and probably killed."
    As there was but little powder on board (only two and half
pounds and that damaged) it was evidently the work of incendiarism.
    Thus ignominiously ended the first steam vessel of war ever

constructed for that purpose. But from that crude and unwieldy mass of wood and iron, the finest specimens of naval architecture sprang rapidly into existence — and the great inventive mind that gave it life has long since ceased to be remembered with the admiration due to his great genius.

CHAPTER XXIX.

FIRST TOWNS ON THE OHIO AND MISSISSIPPI.

REMINISCENCES OF MANUEL WHITE, ESQ., OF NEW ORLEANS.

IN the year 1801, Louisville, or Falls of Ohio, was a small village of 500 or 600 inhabitants. Small as the place was, it witnessed the arrival and departure of great numbers of barges, keel-boats and flat-boats, as, every boat whether bound to New Orleans or down the river, was obliged to stop here in order to be piloted through the rapids. Wonderful were the tales told by the Western boatmen of hairbreadth escapes from flood and field, and the prowling Indians who infested the banks of the Ohio and Mississippi. Early in the month of May, 1800, the keel of a large brig was laid, which in the course of the year was launched, but did not arrive in New Orleans for a considerable time after. The writer, then a youth, employed by Wilson and Eastin, assisted in loading thirteen flat-boats with tobacco, flour, etc., and in company with one of the owners, set out about the first of June, 1801, for New Orleans. The fleet did not land in New Orleans until about the first of August, having been upon the voyage sixty days. The population of New Orleans was rated at that time about six thousand, including blacks and colored. There was not to be seen on the banks of the Ohio from the foot of the Falls to the mouth but a small settlement called Red Banks, another called Yellow banks, Fort Massac, and a cabin below the cave in rock. From the mouth of the Ohio to Bayou Sara, there were only two inhabited places, on the right bank, New Madrid and Point Chicot.

On the left side all the human habitants that were seen until we arrived at Point Coupee were Brownsburg, Natchez, and Fort Adams. All the rest was a dreary waste, over which the bear and the crocodile held their sway, unless interrupted by the occasional sojourn of an Indian tribe. Upon our arrival at New Orleans, the men composing the crew of those

A COPY OF THE WHARF REGISTER AT NEW ORLEANS FROM 1812
TO 1820 INCLUSIVE.

GIVING THE DATE OF THE ARRIVAL OF THE ORIGINAL STEAMBOATS, ALSO
THE NAME OF THE CAPTAINS.

STEAMBOAT.	YEAR.	MONTH.	CAPTAIN.
New Orleans	1812	Jan. 12	J. Baker.
Vesuvius	1814	May 16	R. De Hart.
Enterprise	"	Dec. 14	H M. Shreve.
Etna	1815	April 24	John De Hart.
Dispatch	1816	Feb. 13	
Gen'l Pike	"	Oct. 2	Benj. Booth.
Washington	"	Oct. 7	Henry M. Shreve.
Franklin	"	Feb. 10	E. Younge.
Constitution	1817	April 17	R. P. Guird.
Harriett	"	May 6	J. Armitage.
Buffalo	"	May 10	S. Claugh.
Kentucky	"	Nov. 12	B. Bosworth.
James Monroe	"	Nov. 26	J. A. Paulfrey.
George Madison	1818	Jan. 1	J. A. Holton.
Vesta	"	Jan. 24	J. Shackelford.
Governor Shelby	"	Mch 23	John T. Gray.
Gen'l Jackson	"	April 1	B. Hopkins.
Cincinnati	"	May 23	C. Paxon.
Ohio	"	Jan. 9	H. M. Shreve.
Napoleon	"	Jan. 19	I. Gregg.
Eagle	"	July 19	Nicolas Berthoud.
Louisiana	"	August 6	F. Duplises.
Newport	"	August 26	Benj. Booth.
Johnson	"	Oct. 25	Silas Craig.
Henderson	"	Dec. 30	Jonah Winters.
Volcano	1819	Jan. 4	Robinson De Hart.
Alabama	"	Jan 7	George Hauxhurst.
Hecla	"	Jan. 17	Francis Honorie.
Exchange	"	Jan. 20	Thos. Sturges.
James Ross	"	Feb 6	John Paulfrey.
Maid of Orleans	"	Feb. 12	Wm. Morris.
Maysville	"	Feb 18	John Campbell
Tamerlain	"	Feb. 26	Stephen Vail.
Frankfort	"	Mch. 1	J. G. Voohries.
Rifleman	"	Mch. 27	S. M. Barner.
Rising States	"	Mch. 31	Jas. Pierce.
St. Louis	"	April 14	T. W. Hews.
Ramapo	"	May 4	H. Reed.
Paragon	"	May 14	S. Cummings.
Mobile	"	May 29	D. Paul.
Gen'l Clark	"	July 6	John Sowers.
Yankee	"	Dec. 10	P. A. Oliver.
Feliciana	1820	Feb. 9	P. A. Oliver.
Fayett	"	Feb. 20	Wm. Anderson.
Car of Commerce	"	Feb. 21	Jas. Pierce.
Beaver	"	Feb. 21	D. Prentis.
Gen'l Robertson	"	Feb. 26	Luke Douglas.
Tennessee	"	Feb. 26	Jos. Smith.
Rifleman	"	Feb. 27	S. M. Barner.
Comet	"	Mch. 1	J. M. Byrne.

STEAMBOAT.	YEAR.	MONTH.	CAPTAIN.
United States	1820	Mch. 17	S. Hart.
Columbus of New Orleans	"	Mch. 25	J. Forsyth.
Gen'l Green	"	Mch. 25	G. M. Towers.
Missouri	"	Mch. 26	A. Gross.
Manhattan	1819	Nov. 27	D. Jenkins.
Rapids	"	Nov. 29	Thos. Sturges.
Columbus of Kentucky	"	April 4	L. Stephens.
Cumberland	"	April 16	Wm. Walker.
Vulcan	"	April 28	A. Ruter.
Fayett	"	April 29	John Mills.
Telegraph	"	May 16	J. Armitage.
Independence	"	Oct. 22	J. Jenkins.
Arkansas	"	Oct. 22	G. Rearick.
Mississippi	"	Nov. 7	Daniel McMeal.
Velocipede	"	Nov. 29	Jacob Beckwith.
Hornet	1821	Jan. 1	S. Brandenberg.
Osage	"	Jan. 13	N. Bliss.
Thos. Jefferson	"	Jan. 22	H. J. Offut.
Olive Branch	"	Jan. 23	J. Sanders.
Hero	"	Feb. 12	B. Land.
Alexandria	"	April 10	Wm. Waters
Gen'l Clark	"	May 7	J. W. Byrne.
Post Boy	"	May 22	H. N. Breckenridge.
Courier	"	Jan. 6	J. Beckwith.
Elizabeth	"	Jan. 9	J. B. Enlow.
Dolphin	"	Jan. 24	C. Whiting.
Providence	"	Dec 4	J. Lonsdale.
Henry Clay	"	Dec. 21	John Shalcross.
Rocket	"	Dec. 28	W. H. Keer.
Eliza	"	Dec. 28	B. Booth.
Mandan	"	Dec. 28	Wm. Lynn.
Gen'l Green	"	Dec, 29	Theophilas Minor.

CHAPTER XXX.

EMBARGO ON THE NAVIGATION OF THE MISSISSIPPI.

THERE were three periods in the history of the Mississippi River, when the free navigation of this river was prohibited.

First in 1785. During the Spanish occupation under Governor Miro an active trade from the population on the Ohio had forced itself down the Mississippi to every part of Louisiana, and the people of the Western settlements claimed the natural right to the use of the river through the province of Louisiana, although in the eyes of Spain they were unquestionably citizens of foreign power. It had early become a matter of great interest to the Spanish authorities to derive a large revenue from the trade by the importation of transit and port duties. A revenue officer, with a suitable guard, and a military post, was established at New Madrid, Chickasaw Bluffs, and other points, at which all boats were required to make land and comply with the revenue laws; which were enforced with vigor, even to the seizure and confiscation of the cargo.

The Western people believed these duties exorbitant and unjust towards those who possessed a natural right to navigate the river free of all such impositions. The whole people of the West determined to resist this unjust taxation and a military invasion of Louisiana was devised for redressing the wrongs of the Western people and seizing the port of New Orleans.

At the same time the Western people, indignant at the neglect of the Federal Government in not securing them the free use of the Mississippi, were strongly tempted to separate from the Atlantic States and to secure for themselves an independent government. The Spanish authorities, becoming alarmed at this threatened invasion, and knowing the power of the Western people, agreed to make the necessary concession of the free navigation of the river. It was under these circumstances that Col. James Wilkinson, of Kentucky, made an arrangement with the Spanish authorities to descend to New Orleans with several barges and flat-boats loaded with flour and other articles of Western produce. Having reached New Orleans, he obtained an interview with the Governor and at length succeeded in securing for himself and the people of the West permission to trade with the city and to introduce free of duties many articles of Western produce adapted to the Louisiana market.

From this time forward the free navigation of the Mississippi was opened until 1812. — *Monett's History of the Valley of the Mississippi.*

SECOND PERIOD WHEN THE FREE NAVIGATION WAS PROHIBITED.

In 1812, Livingston and Fulton obtained a grant from the Legislature of Louisiana for the exclusive right to navigate the waters of this State with steamboats belonging to their company. The first steamboat coming to the port of New Orleans that did not belong to the company of Livingston & Fulton, was the Enterprise, Captain H. M. Shreve, in December, 1814; immediately upon her arrival she was seized at the instigation of Livingston and Fulton, for infringing upon their rights to the exclusive navigation of the river within the boundaries of Louisiana; Captain Shreve, as agent of the owners of the Enterprise, gave bond in the suit, and proposed to test the legality of any such law, or grant. The next independent steamboat that appeared at this port was the Dispatch, in 1815; she was also seized while, loading with a cargo of sugar and molasses for the Ohio, the cargo was forcibly taken out of her, and she was ordered to leave the waters of this State and not return, under threats of confiscation. The captain not being prepared with bail was compelled to obey this unjust order, and departed without cargo for the Ohio, glad to save his boat. The next boat seized for trespassing upon the waters of Louisiana was the steamboat Constitution, that arrived at this port in 1816. She, like the Dispatch, was compelled to depart from the waters of Louisiana without cargo. The people of the West hearing of these outrageous proceedings of the authorities of Louisiana, held meetings at Cincinnati and Louisville and denounced the authorities of Louisiana for making any such grant to Livingston and Fulton, and demanded from the Congress of the United States that they should immediately abrogate and set aside any such grant to the free navigation of the Mississippi River, and if it was not done they would send an armed expedition to open up the river. Whilst this excitement was progressing, Captain H. M. Shreve arrived at this port in 1816, with the steamer Washington, a large and fine steamboat of her time. She also was immediately seized at the instigation of Livingston and Fulton for trespassing upon their waters. Captain Shreve this time had the case placed in the United States court. and after waiting some months it was finally decided that the State of Louisiana had no right to grant to

Livingston and Fulton the exclusive right of navigating the
waters within her territory, and that all the rivers, lakes and
bayous of the United States shall be free and open to all citizens of the United States, who might wish to navigate them
with any kind of vessel. Thus ended the second attempt
to prohibit the free navigation of the Mississippi. The
third period when the free navigation of the Mississippi was
interrupted was in 1861, shortly after the Civil War broke
out between the United States and the Confederacy. A fort
was established at Columbus, Kentucky, and no vessels of
any kind were permitted to pass up or down. This blockade
continued until 1862, when Columbus was evacuated, also
Memphis, Tenn., when the navigation was opened as far
down as Vicksburg, and after the fall of Vicksburg and Port
Hudson, was again opened to New Orleans

SOUTHERN CONFEDERATE CUSTOM HOUSE REQUIREMENTS — C. G. MEMMINGER, SEC.

Among the amusing relics that have been preserved from
the result of the late Civil War, none will afford coming generations of Western boatmen more amusement than to read
the following order issued by the Secretary of the Treasury, — C. G. Memminger.

As the Confederate line was drawn at *Norfolk*, on the Mississippi, a point just below Cairo, all floating craft of every
description were required to land there, and report to the Confederate officer, who was always prepared to enforce the
order.   And as all masters of vessels were soon convinced
that resistance to Confederate authority, when they got below the line, was not only useless but *dangerous*, Norfolk
soon became a point of great importance, although before
the war and the location of the revenue officer there, it was
hardly known even to river men as anything more than a
wood-yard and a warehouse.

The requirements, although much condensed, were as follows:

"Masters of flat-boats with coal in bulk intended for points
as above, must give, under oath, to the collector at Norfolk,
a schedule in duplicate, setting forth name of boat, master,
owner, where from, quality, quantity and value, and the fact
of its being intended to be landed at places other than ports
of entry or delivery.   On these schedules the collector will
estimate the duties payable; and on payment of the duties at
Norfolk, will endorse on the original schedule (to be returned

to the master) a certificate of payment, and a permit to land the goods. Should any portion of the goods arriving, as aforesaid, composed of dutiable or free articles, be destined to ports of entry or delivery, other than the port of final destination, permission may be given to land the same under the following regulations:

"The master shall present to the revenue officer at Norfolk a schedule in triplicate of the goods, describing them by their marks and numbers, number of packages and contents corresponding with the description in the general manifest of the vessel. Also stating the name of consignor and name of port of destination of the merchandise."

"On the arrival of the vessel at an intermediate port, the master or commander is to present to the revenue officer the original schedule and will receive a general permit to land the goods upon their being duly entered and special landing permits issued, as now provided by law, for the landing of imported merchandise.

Should the vessel out of business hours, or should circumstances compel it, the master is permitted to deposit the goods either in a bonded warehouse or the custody of a revenue officer, and shall receive a receipt containing all the particulars of the schedule and the original schedule shall be delivered to the person with whom the merchandise is deposited and by him delivered over to the collector or chief revenue officer as soon as the opening of the custom house will permit."

On the arrival of the vessel at the port of final destination the master or commander shall make due entry at the custom house by delivering his original manifest together with all schedules enclosed, with the permits to land at intermediate ports, and the receipts of officers to whom any goods may have been delivered or any other document showing the disposition of any portion of the cargo, and the residue of the cargo shall be delivered on permits similar to those provided by law for the landing of imported merchandise. And the total cargo as shown by the original manifest, shall be delivered at this port, with the exception of such as shall be shown by documents presented at the time of entry to have been landed elsewhere, under the penalties now provided by law, for discrepancies existing in the cargo of vessels arriving from foreign ports."

In order to relieve vessels in this branch of importing trade from embarrassments, all goods imported therein, remaining unclaimed, or for which no entry shall be made or permit granted, within twenty-four hours after arrival, may be taken

possession of by the collector, and deposited in a bonded warehouse on a general permit issued by him for that purpose.''
To afford further facilities in the event of vessels in this trade arriving at the port of final destination before the opening, or after the closing of the custom house for the day and a necessity exists for discharging the cargo, it shall be lawful to deposit same, or any part of it, at the risk and expense of the vessel, on the levee, in charge of the inspection service, of the customs, or in any bonded warehouse in the port, such portion of said cargo as may be practicable.

The master or commander of said vessel obtaining for the goods so deposited, a receipt from the inspection officer, on the levee, or the custom officer, in charge of the warehouse, which receipt shall be delivered to the collector of customs as soon thereafter as the business hours of the custom house of said port will permit.

"Any goods, wares or merchandise imported as aforesaid may be entered at the port of destination, on presentation to the collector of the bill or bills of lading, together with the other documents now required by law, on the entry of imported merchandise, before and in anticipation of the arrival of the importing vessel, and the necessary permits for the landing shall issue on the completion of these entries.

And on the presentation of these permits to the surveyor, it shall be his duty and is hereby required of him (if the vessel by which the goods are imported has arrived at the port), to detail an inspector of the customs to superintend the landing of the merchandise as described therein, and such landing is authorized before entry has been made by the importing vessel at the custom house when the interest of commerce or circumstances attending such arrival, shall render it necessary.

It must, however, be distinctly understood that it is unlawful to discharge any portion of the cargoes of these vessels, except under the inspection and supervision of the custom officer.

CLEARANCES.

Before the departure of any vessel navigating the Mississippi or others rivers, destined to a foreign port or place beyond the southern limits of the Confederate States of America, the master or person having the charge thereof, shall deliver to the collector or chief officer of the customs at the port from which the vessel is about to depart, a manifest of the cargo on board the same, in the form and verified in the manner now provided by law for vessels to a foreign port, and obtain from said collector a clearance as follows: " —

" CONFEDERATE STATES OF AMERICA.'

Here follows the usual clearance certificate of vessels bound to a foreign port and then follows: —

" It shall be permitted to vessels engaged in navigation and commerce provided for by those regulations, after clearance, to take on board at the port of original departure, or any other place within the limits of the Confederacy, any goods, wares or merchandise, and to proceed therewith to a destination beyond the Confederate limits on delivering to the collector or chief revenue officer at the port of Norfolk, on the Mississippi, or at the port nearest the frontier of the Confederacy, or any other river, a schedule describing all the goods on board — the quality, the value and destination, not declared in the manifest delivered at the time of clearance at the custom house of the original port of departure. The schedule thus received to be forwarded to the port from which the vessel may have originally cleared."

Lastly, it is made the duty of the collector at the port of Norfolk, or at the other frontier ports, at which masters of outward-bound vessels are required to deliver schedules, to board all vessels bound to places beyond the Confederacy, in the same manner and at the hours heretofore provided for inward-bound vessels."

It will be observed that these requirements are addressed to flat-boat masters with coal in bulk, etc. But there was no distinction made between flat-boats, steamboats, or any other craft. All were required to land and to conform to the regulations. But no great embarrassment or inconvenience was felt by the " regulations." For until Memphis was taken there was no business transacted by the river after the blockade was established at Cairo. Even before that was officially announced, the Confederates established a sort of guerrilla blockade at points along the river where they had troops stationed and provisions were not very plenty.

The writer calls to mind a case in point. In the early spring of 1861, returning from New Orleans with the steamer Empress, and passing " Fort Wright," a temporary fortification a few miles above Memphis, we were brought to about daylight one morning by a shot across our bows from a cannon on shore, entirely obscured from view. As we were not at that early period accustomed to that kind of " hails " but little time was lost in responding to the hail. It was a cold, wet morning, and the officer and file of soldiers that stepped on board as soon as the boat landed looked as if they had been on duty all night and that the easiest way to a compromise would be through the bar-room. I fortunately struck the key-note the first time, and sent for the barkeeper, and while it was a little early for me, I saw I was on the right road to an early release, and insisted that soldiers exposed to the inclemency of such nights were entitled to more than *one drink*, in which they freely concurred. Looking through our cargo, they saw nothing contraband or that would be useful to the Confederacy, except some hogsheads of sugar, marked *Chicago*. Nothing could have been more opportune ; rye or corn coffee without sugar was an abomination to a soldier of the Confederacy, and although, later on, it was often a luxury, but at that early date, with hogsheads of " Yankee " sugar in sight it was no use talking, remonstrance was in vain, and the Chicago sugar rolled on shore and the Empress and her crew were permitted to pursue their winding way north, realizing for the first time that they were in the " enemy's country " and hostilities had already commenced. We felt that we were fortunate in getting " through the lines," even with the loss of a few hogsheads of sugar. Other steamboats a day or two behind the Empress, were less fortunate and never returned to their home ports. Later on, the Empress made many narrow escapes from masked batteries and guerrilla attacks.

CHAPTER XXXI.

THE WATT & BOLTON ENGINE.

[Written for the N. O. Democrat.]

THE Watt & Bolton engine as originally used carried steam at a pressure very little above the boiling point. The difference between them and the high pressure was in the use of a condenser. On the Western waters the early low-pressure boats carried steam very seldom exceeding 10 pounds to the inch, but gradually, by the introduction of stronger boilers, this amount was increased to 30 and 40 pounds. The first boat — the New Orleans — had but one cylinder, 34 inches in diameter, and without a walking beam. The engine was what is known as a steeple engine, vertical, with the piston attached to a cross iron beam, something on the order of a saw mill engine. Many of the early boats had horizontal engines, low pressure, but single. The Caravan and Mechanic of 1820 had high pressure engines with cross-heads. In 1824 the Hibernia and Philadelphia had also high pressure engines on the cross-head principle, but they were horizontal, and the pitmans and cross-heads ran under the boilers. All the early boats had their cabins on deck, and it was of importance for the engine to occupy as little space as possible. The steeple engine took up but little more than the diameter of the cylinder. None of the low pressure boats had two engines up to 1823 except the United States, whose cylinders built in England on the Watt & Bolton principle had walking beams. French's engine was the oscillating; the Comet had one of these engines. She was sold at Natchez, in 1813, and her machinery put in a saw mill. After the Comet, came the Enterprise, a larger boat, in 1814, and then the Dispatch. These three boats were built at Brownsville, Pa., by the Monongahela Steam Navigation Company, and had the oscillating engine. The Washington, built by Capt. H. M. Shreve, in 1816, had high pressure engine and four single flue boilers. Trevithick invented the high pressure engine, and inasmuch as there was a saving in the use of a condenser, and as high steam and expansion were also found good qualities, Wolf conceived the idea of combining the two qualities in the same engine and introduced the compound engine, the principle upon which the Hartupee engine is built. Oliver Evans never built any engines for Western boats, but his son George established a shop at Pittsburgh and built a few high-pressure engines.

THE FIRST STEAMBOAT.

" A friend has favored the *Times-Democrat* of New Orleans with a copy of a letter that appeared in the *Louisiana Gazette* of the twentieth of October, 1810, from which it would appear that this city can claim the proud distinction of having built the first steamboat, and that, too, three years before Fulton built the Clermont for the Hudson River. The letter was written by Oliver Evans, of Philadelphia, the man who built and patented the first high pressure engine, and read as follows: —

" In the year 1802 or 1803 Capt. Jas. McKeaver and Louis Valcourt, having been in Kentucky, saw a letter which I had written to a gentleman there explaining how my improvements would apply to steamboats in the water, and agreed to construct a steamboat to ply between New Orleans and Natchez. The captain superintended the building of the boat, and Mr. Valcourt came to Philadelphia in the fall of 1803 and had the engine built at my shop, while I was in Washington, and they met at New Orleans, fitted the engine to the boat, ready for experiment, but the water had left them high and dry, and not likely to rise again to float the boat in less than six months. They having expended about $15,000, their money was exhausted and they were left in a sad dilemma. Mr. Wm. Donaldson, of New Orleans, furnished them with money on condition they would take the engine out of the boat and apply it to drive a saw mill. This they did and began to saw 2,000 feet of boards in twelve hours, when incendiaries set fire to the mill and reduced it to ashes. They have both written to me frequently, that they were confident that the power of the engine was quite sufficient to have insured success in propelling the boat. The engine for this boat was only nine inches in diameter, the stroke of the piston three feet. I believe my principle is the only one suitable for propelling boats up the Mississippi. This engine is ten times more powerful than the best English engine of equal dimensions. It has no equal, excepting the one I have since erected at Pittsburgh for Mr. Owen Evans; the cylinder is 9 feet 2-10 inches in diameter and 3 feet 2 inches stroke, and will grind 480 bushels of wheat in twenty-four hours.

OLIVER EVANS.

NOTE. — This engine was the first one used in the territory of Louisiana. The boiler consisted of cylinders of sheet iron, 3 feet 6 inches in diameter, 8 feet long, with flues.

OLIVER EVANS ON THE STEAM ENGINE.
[From Niles' Register, Vol. 13, 1817.]

" Citizens attend. Surely the sum of death and misery, occasioned by the explosion of the boilers of steam engines on the boats is now enough to arrest your attention, if you ever intend to travel on steamboats. This discovery has recently been so openly attacked, that the inventor is compelled to defend it.

Therefore, I announce that more than forty years ago, I discovered the principles and afterwards the means of applying the great and advantageous principle in nature of the rapid *increase of the elastic power of steam*, by geometrical progression and by the small increase of heat in the water by arithmetical progression, and thereby lessen the consumption of fuel, the size and weight of the steam engine to suit for steamboats.

For double heat in the water produces 128 times the power, and double force consumed produces sixteen times the effect. I have since got into operation seventy or eighty steam engines constructed on the unimitable and eternal principles and laws of nature, so combined and arranged that it is nearly beyond the art of man, either by neglect, design, ignorance or malice, to explode them by *the elastic power of steam*. He can only make them yield to the inevitable power, in a small degree, so as to let the power escape until the steam extinguishes the fire, and the danger ceases, by the regular operation of the engine itself. No accident has ever happened with any of my engines to do any injury."

I published in 1805 a laborious and difficult work (produced by long intense study) on this new and abtruse subject, describing and demonstrating those principles and directing their application to mills, and also to boats, by means of the very paddle wheels, since adopted, which mode of application I had conceived, or understood well, for about thirty years before.

To this book I now refer, "The Young Steam Engineer's Guide." It is to be seen in the Philadelphia library.

My cylindric boilers, 15 inches in diameter with the ends closed, with half globes, will hold about 1,300 pressure to the inch area of its inner surface.

If twenty inches diameter, about 1,000 lbs., if thirty inches about 700, and if sixty inches diameter, they will bear about 350 lbs. when constructed with wrought iron sheets one quarter of an inch thick, thoroughly riveted together, and that with as much safety as any other form will bear, ten pounds to the inch.   Double diameters will hold but half the power. But, further in my cylindric boilers the stress to make them yield, is equal in every part, and because it is impossible for any workmen to construct any boiler to be equal in strength, in all its parts, but that some part, or rivet, of a thousand, will be weaker than the rest, and yield first by a small open- ing, to let the power escape inside the furnace, and steam enough to extinguish the fire.   Thus the operation of the engine itself stops all danger.''

" Then we may safely conclude, and say, that it has been proved in practice that *these boilers cannot be exploded* to do any serious injury.   Not in such a degree, as to force through the furnace wall of a mill, and much less to force through the sheet iron covering of the boiler in the steamboat Ætna, by the elastic power of them.   I defy contradiction or any person to explode one of my boilers by steam.''

CRITICISMS ON OLIVER EVANS'

theory of non-explosion of the cylinder steam boiler.

While he is very positive that his boilers can not be ex- ploded by the elastic power of steam, later experiences show that he was sadly mistaken.

Without knowing the kind or character of his furnace it is impossible to say what would be the effect of a leak in the boiler.   The assertion he makes that a leak would extinguish the fire and thus make an explosion impossible would not hold good in more modern experience.   If a weak place in the boiler sheet, or an imperfect rivet was always on the bottom of the boiler, or on the part exposed directly to the fire, what he anticipated would sometimes occur.   But unfortunately for his theory, and for our experience, cylinder boilers have not been so considerate as to give timely warning before ex- ploding in many instances.

Still the name of *Oliver Evans* will long be remembered among the foremost of the enterprising and practical engi- neers of the age in which he lived, and probably no one did more to develop the power of steam and make it practical than did Oliver Evans.   No inventor in any age excelled Mr. Evans in his efforts before Congress and the public at large, to secure recognition and pecuniary assistance to enable him to extend his experiments and to advance the cause and pro- mote the science of steam engineering.

He predicted in 1794, that steam wagons would travel from Philadelphia to Boston in one day, and that the man was then living that would see the Ohio and Mississippi Rivers crossed with steamboats.

CHAPTER XXXII.

[Niles' Register, Vol. 16, 1819.]

THE YELLOW STONE EXPEDITION is to be one of the most respectable and imposing character.

It seems probable that 900 or 1,000 men will be stationed at the upper posts on the Missouri. A large steamboat has been launched to supply them with stores, etc., and a small boat called the " Western Engineer," built by the United States, to draw only nineteen inches water with all her machinery, etc., on board, is ready at Pittsburgh, if not already left, to take out Maj Long and an exploring party consisting of several learned gentlemen whose business is to collect information of all things relating to the great river Missouri, and the parts adjacent.

THE WESTERN ENGINEER,

As described in *Niles' Register*, Vol. 16, while laying at the landing in St. Louis, previous to her departure on the " Yellowstone Expedition," 1819 :—

" The Western Engineer is moored at the landing at the upper part of the city of St. Louis, where she lies waiting for orders.   In passing the Independence and the St. Louis, then at anchor before the town, she was saluted by these vessels.

The bow of this vessel exhibits the form of a huge serpent, black and scaly, rising out of the water from under the boat, his head as high as the deck, darting forward, his mouth open, vomiting smoke, and apparently carrying the boat on his back. From under the boat at its stern issues a stream of foaming water, dashing violently along.   All the machinery is hid. Three small brass field-pieces mounted on wheel carriages stand on the deck.   The boat is ascending the rapid stream at the rate of three miles an hour.   Neither wind nor human hands are seen to help her and to the eye of ignorance the illusion is complete that a monster carries on his back smoking

with fatigue and lashing the waves with violent motion. Her
equipment is at once calculated to awe and to attract the
savage.   Objects pleasing and terrifying are at once before
him — artillery, the flag of the Republic, portraits of white
men and an Indian shaking hands, the calumet of peace, the
sword through the apparent monster with a painted vessel on
his back, the sides gaping with port-holes and bristling with
guns — taken altogether and without intelligence of her com-
position or design, it would require a daring savage to approach and accost her with Hamlet's speech:—

> " Be thou a spirit of health, or goblin damned,
> Bring with thee airs from heaven, or blasts from hell?
> Be thy intents wicked, or charitable?
> Thou comest in such questionable shape,
> That I will speak with thee."

THE LONGEST BOAT ON THE MISSISSIPPI — STEAMBOAT MISSOURI.

Probably no steamboat owned at St. Louis has ever created
more curiosity in the minds of its citizens than did the " Big
Misssouri " on her arrival at the wharf in April 1841.   Her
size was phenomenal and her fame had so far preceded her
arrival, that everybody was on the *qui vive* to see her.   She
was 233 feet long, which was longer than any previous boat,
30 feet beam, 8 1-2 feet hold, 59 feet over all.   She drew
5 1-2 feet light, wheels 32 feet diameter with 12 feet buckets,
cylinders 26 inches, 12 feet stroke, two engines and seven 42
inch boilers, her capacity was 600 tons.   She was built at
Pittsburgh under the direction of Capt. J. C. Swan, her commander, and cost $45,000.   There is no public record of her
performance, as she was burned at the wharf in August of the
same year.   But there is no doubt if she had been given a fair
chance, she would have made the trip from New Orleans to
St. Louis about as soon as it was made by the " J. M. White "
three years later.

MAMMOTH STEAMBOAT.

The following extract taken from the *New Orleans Times-
Democrat* will show the difference in views between now and
then:—

A MAMMOTH STEAMBOAT BUILT SIXTY-FIVE YEARS AGO.

The steamboat United States was built at Jeffersonville,
Ind., 1819; sole owner, Edmund Forstall of New Orleans;
Samuel Hart, master; measures 645 82-95 tons; enrolled at

New Orleans, January, 1821. Mr. Vandusen, a ship builder of New York, contracted to build this boat, and he brought out from New York fifty mechanics and ship carpenters to do the work, as there were very few ship carpenters in the West at that period. After finishing the hull and upper works she was floated or worked by sweeps to New Orleans for the purpose of receiving her machinery in 1820. The engine was built in England upon the Watt and Boulton plan of low pressure engine with walking beam. Her planking and timbers were of immense thickness, twenty inches of solid wall so as to make her snag proof. She made several voyages between New Orleans and Louisville, but was of so heavy draft and slow speed that she did not prove a success. In 1823, while lying up at Withers' saw mill, just above the city, the batture caved in and sunk her. There is only one steamboat man living in this city, Capt. Louis Choat, who remembers this boat, as he was here at the time she was lost; he says she was the wonder of the Western world, and was thought to be the largest steamboat in the world. Thirteen years time elapsed before another steamboat of so great a tonnage was built in 1832.

OLD TIMER.

STEAMBOAT ENTERPRISE, 1814.

The Enterprise was the fourth boat built, and though only a small boat of 75 tons was a very remarkable one in many respects. She made two trips in the summer of 1814 between Brownsville and Louisville, and in December of that year came to New Orleans with a load of ordnance stores, and on arrival was pressed into service by Gen. Jackson. She afterwards made five trips to the Balize towing vessels, made a trip to the rapids of Red River, and ran to Natchez. The distance to Natchez was then called 313 miles; this distance she used to make without the use of sails in four days. In August of 1815 she went to Pittsburgh in 54 days, 20 days of which time was consumed in handling freight, all of which was considered a very remarkable trip. In 1812 Livingston and Fulton obtained from the authorities of this State a grant or charter for the exclusive navigation of the waters of the Mississippi River for a period of 20 years. As the Enterprise was built by other parties, she was seized while here at the instance of Livingston and Fulton, who claimed that they alone had the right to navigate the Mississippi River by steam and that she was infringing on their rights and violating the law. She was bonded out and the case carried to the Supreme Court. After

In an issue of that paper of July 1816, is the following announcement:

"The steamboat ' Vesuvius ' burned at Natchez. She was to have set out for her place of destination on Sunday morning.

In the afternoon of Saturday Captain De Hart raised steam and started up the river.

The machinery did not work well, and while examining the cause she was discovered to be on fire, and the crew had to abandon her. She floated down the current in a majestic blaze. This is an immense public calamity.

The estimated loss of boat and cargo is $200,000."

DIFFERENT VERSIONS NOT TANTOLOGY.

While these desultory scraps of history are by no means satisfactory, they are undoubtedly reliable as far as they go, and serve to illustrate to some extent the situation and the feeling created by the introduction of steam in navigation.

By collating the items, or scraps of history as they are interspersed through these pages, a general knowledge may be arrived at, although if chronologically arranged would be more enjoyable, but that seems difficult to do with the meager records there is to draw from. This will be apparent from the discrepancy in the records often ; and without reflection, may look like tautology, and might be obviated to some extent by slight changes in the text. But as it is not important it is thought best to preserve the text in the main, and quote the history as found.

STEAMBOAT ARRIVALS IN NEW ORLEANS.

[From a New Orleans paper.]

THE BEGINNING.

" In 1804 the amount of tonnage to this city was very small. Commerce was carried only by means of flat-boats and barges. There seems to have been no record kept of these arrivals until the year 1812. From 1812 to 1824 the record gives the number of arrivals but not the tonnage. They increased rapidly, however, as quantities of sugar and molasses were shipped to the Ohio. This was a long and tedious voyage indeed, as the boats were propelled almost entirely by hand. As a general thing, though, these boats were sold here for their lumber, and the owners, with the proceeds of their venture in their pockets, would cross the lake, and, striking the Natchez trail, would start a-foot for their homes 1,000 miles away. In 1812 a new era in transportation appeared. This year the first steamboat, the New Orleans, arrived at our landing. She was a low pressure boat of 371 tons.

In 1814 the second boat, the Vesuvius, of 340 tons, arrived and in 1815 the Enterprise, of 100 tons, the first boat to make the return trip to Pittsburgh, and which took her fifty-four days to accomplish. The Vesuvius also made a trip to Louisville this year. The fourth boat, the Etna, of 360 tons, arrived here in 1815. In 1816 there arrived the Dispatch of 90 tons, the Washington of 412 tons, the Franklin of 131 tons, and the Constitution of 112 tons. The Washington was the first boat to be called fast. In 1817 there arrived the Harriet of 54 tons, Buffalo of 249 tons, Kentucky of 112 tons, James Monroe 140 tons, James Madison 148 tons, Vesta 203 tons, and the Gov. Shelby 106 tons.

In 1818 the Gen. Jackson 142 tons, Pike 51 tons, Cincinnati 157 tons, Napoleon 315 tons, Eagle 118 tons, Newport 59 tons, Hecla 124 tons, Johnson 140 tons, Exchange 212 tons, James Ross 269 tons, Ramapo 146 tons, Tammarlane 214 tons, Maysville 209 tons, Maid of Orleans 193 tons, a total for the year of 14 new boats, with an aggregate tonnage of 2,347 tons. In 1819 there arrived the Ohio, Volcano, Alabama, Rifleman, Rising States, St. Louis, Paragon, Mobile, Gen. Clark, Yankee, averaging 150 tons each. In 1820 the Feliciana, Frankfort, Car of Commerce, Vulcan, Gen. Roberts, Tennessee, Comet, Hornet, United States, Columbus, Gen. Green, Missouri, Elizabeth, Beaver Rapids, Fayette, Cumberland, Arkansas, and the Independence, nineteen boats, whose tonnage aggregated 2,850 tons. In 1821 there arrived the Manhattan, Mars, Velocipede, Olive Branch, Hero, Dolphin, Osage, Telegraph, Rapides, Post Boy, Alexandria, Courier, Columbus, President, Rocket, Gen. Green, Elizabeth, seventeen boats, tonnage 2,550 tons. In 1822, Henry Clay, Rifleman, Neptune, Favorite, Expedition, Mandan, Nashville, Providence, Teche, Robt. Thompson, Indiana, eleven boats, 1,540 tons; and in 1822, the Leonard, Calhoun, Gen. Pike, Congress, Hope, Fidelity and the Robt. Ray, 7 boats with a total tonnage of 1,050 tons.

Colonel Aaron Burr's Expedition with a fleet of Flat-boats down the Mississippi River in 1807, with the intention of invading Mexico, as he had a large force of armed men with him.

1807. Early in January one of the coldest winters ever known in Mississippi, Col. Burr, with nine boats arrived at the mouth of Bayou Pierre and tied up on the western or

Louisiana shore.   The Governor issued an order to the military authorities to arrest Col. Burr and his fleet, as he was charged with high treason.   Lieutenant Patterson, of the militia, immediately marched to the point where Colonel Burr's fleet was moored and demanded a surrender of men and boats. The terms were accepted and he surrendered to the civil authorities of Mississippi.   In addition to the military force the Governor had induced Commander Shaw, in command of the naval forces at New Orleans, to concentrate the most of his vessels at Natchez to oppose the tremendous flotilla of Col. Burr reported to be coming down the river.

The following armed vessels were anchored in the Mississippi opposite Natchez, January, 1807.

Schooner Revenge, 12 guns.   Ketch Etna, 14 guns.
Ketch Vesuvius, 14 guns.   Gunboat No. 11, 2 guns.
Gunboat 12, 2 guns.   Gunboat 13, 2 guns.
Gunboat 14, 2 guns.   Gun Barge Victory, 2 guns.

NOTE.— This was probably the first fleet of United States war vessels that ever ascended the Mississippi River as high up as Natchez.

EXTRACTS FROM CLAIBORN'S HISTORY.

NEW MADRID EARTHQUAKE, 1811.

"An account of the great earthquake at New Madrid on the Mississippi River.   By Capt. John Davis, of Natchez, Mississippi.   We arrived at night on the 15th December, 1811, at Island 25, and on the 16th at 2 a. m., we were surprised by the greatest commotion of the boat, which I could compare to nothing more than of a team of horses running away with a wagon over the most rocky road in our part of the country. There were forty flat-boats, barges and keel-boats in the company, and each thought his boat adrift and running over the sawyers; but a man on board a boat lashed to us hinted it to be an earthquake.   An old navigator of the river just above, hailed us and said it was occasioned by the banks falling in. We were under a bluff bank which immediately cast off and fell in about a quarter of a mile, which drew us into the current on the right side of the island, where we staid till day; but in the meantime, we experienced fifty partial shocks, which shook our boat with great agitation.   At 7 o'clock we heard a tremendous distant noise, and in a few seconds the boats, island and main land became perfectly convulsed, the trees twisted and lashed together, the earth in all quarters was sinking, and the water issued from the center of Island 25, just on our left, and came rushing down its side in torrents. The shocks at this time became more frequent, one every fifteen minutes. The water rose from the first shock till about 8 o'clock that day eight feet perpendicular, and the current ran seven or eight miles an hour, as we ran from Island 25 and landed on Flower Island, a distance of thirty-five miles in five hours and twenty-five minutes. The logs, which had sprung up from the bottom of the river, were so thick that it appeared almost impossible for a boat to find ι. passage. There were a large number of boats sunk and destroyed, among them two boats of Mr. Jas. Atwell, of Kentucky. The logs and roots we passed had the sand and mud on them, which probably for many years lay in the bottom of the river, and which gave the appearance of timbered fields. We experienced shocks of earthquake for eight days. The whole country from the mouth of the Ohio to the White River country felt the terrible effects of this earthquake for many years — as many persons, houses and cattle were drowned or swallowed up by the opening of the earth. There were also several islands that disappeared, and many flat-boats and barges were wrecked. The town of New Madrid was a complete wreck and many of the people lost their lives. Our barge escaped and we arrived at Natchez, Jan. 5th. 1812.

NOTE. — This was the same earthquake that the first steamboat New Orleans encountered on her first voyage down the Mississippi."

11

CHAPTER XXXIII.

[From Floyd's S. B. Directory, 1856.]

"FROM the year 1786 to 1811, the only regular mode of transportation on the Western rivers was such as we have described in the preceding article. The entire commerce of those rivers was transacted by means of those clumsy contrivances called barges and flat-boats, which consumed three or four months in making the trip from New Orleans to Louisville, a trip which is now made by steam power in five or six days, and has been made in a little over four. The price of passage from New Orleans to Pittsburgh was then $160; freight $6.75 per hundred pounds. The introduction of steam has reduced the price of passage between these two cities to thirty dollars, and merchandise is carried the whole distance for a price which may be regarded as merely nominal. Besides this great saving of time and money effected by steam navigation on these waters, the comparative safety of steam conveyance is an item which especially deserves our notice. Before the steam dispensation began, travelers and merchants were obliged to trust their lives or property to the bargemen, many of whom were suspected, with very good reason, to be in confederacy with the land robbers who infested the shores of the Ohio, and the pirates who resorted to the islands of the the Mississippi. These particulars being understood, we are prepared to estimate the value and importance of the services which the steam-engine has rendered to the commerce and prosperity of the Western States.

The earliest account we have of the navigation of the Mississippi, refers to a period more than three hundred years ago, when Ferdinand De Soto, the first discoverer of that mighty stream, was engaged in his famous and fantastic exploring expedition in search of "the fountain of youth." About one hundred years later, Father Joliet, a Jesuit ambassador and envoy from France, again disturbed these waters, by launching on their bosom a bark canoe which had been transported by his fellow adventurers on their shoulders across the territory between the Fox and Wisconsin rivers.

The first vessel ever built on the waters of the West was the brig Dean, which derived her name from her builder and original proprietor. She was launched at the present site of Alleghany city, near Pittsburgh, in 1806. She afterwards made a voyage from Pittsburgh to the Mediterranean.

After the purchase of Louisiana from Napoleon, in 1803, some Eastern capitalists sent out mechanics, and built several ships on the Ohio. In 1805, Jonas Spoir built the ship "Scott" on the Kentucky River, twenty miles above Frankfort, and near the residence of that celebrated Western pioneer, General Charles Scott. This ship was the first that ever made a successful trip to the falls of the Ohio. She remained there for several, months before the occurrence of a rise in the river sufficient to float her over. In the meantime, two other vessels from Pittsburgh, built by James Berthone & Co., had arrived at the Falls, and in the attempt to get over, the longest one was sunk, and soon after torn to pieces by the violence of the current. This accident was so discouraging that no further attempts at ship-building were made on the Ohio.

In 1811, Messrs. Fulton and Livingston, having established a ship-yard at Pittsburgh for the purpose of introducing steam navigation on the Western waters, built an experimental boat for this service; and this was the first steamboat that ever floated on the Western rivers. It was furnished with a propelling wheel at the stern, and two masts; for Mr. Fulton believed, at that time, that the occasional use of sails would be indispensable. This first Western steamboat was called the Orleans. Her capacity was one hundred tons. In the winter of 1812, she made her first trip from Pittsburgh to New Orleans in 14 days. She continued to make regular trips between New Orleans and Natchez, until the fourteenth day of July, 1814, when she was wrecked near Baton Rouge, on her upward-bound passage by striking a snag."

"The first appearance of the vessel on the Ohio River produced, as the reader may suppose, not a little excitement and admiration. A steamboat, at that day, was to common observers, almost as great a wonder as a flying angel would be at present. The banks of the river, in some places, were thronged with spectators, gazing in speechless astonishment at the puffing and smoking phenomenon. The average speed of this boat was only about three miles per hour. Before her ability to move through the waters without the assistance of sails or oars had been fully exemplified, comparatively few persons believed that she could possibly be made to answer any purpose of real utility. In fact, she made several voyages before the general prejudice began to subside, and for some months, many of the river merchants preferred the old mode of transportation, with all its risks, delays, and extra expense, rather than make use of such a contrivance as a steamboat, which to their apprehension, appeared too marvelous and

miraculous for the business of every-day life. How slow are
the masses of mankind to adopt improvement, even when they
appear to be most obvious and unquestionable.

The second steamboat of the West was a diminutive vessel
called the " Comet." She was rated at twenty-five tons.
Her machinery was on a plan for which French had obtained
a patent in 1809. She went to Louisville in the summer of
1813, and descended to New Orleans in the spring of 1814.
She afterwards made two voyages to Natchez, and was then
sold, taken to pieces, and the engine was put up in a cotton
factory.

The Vesuvius is the next in this record. She was built by
Mr. Fulton, at Pittsburgh, for a company, the several mem-
bers of which resided at New York, Philadelphia, and New
Orleans. She sailed under the command of Capt. Frank
Ogden, for New Orleans, in the spring of 1814. From New
Orleans she started for Louisville in July of the same year,
but was grounded on a sand-bar, seven hundred miles up the
Mississippi, where she remained until the 3rd of December
following, when, being floated off by the tide, she returned to
New Orleans. In 1815–16, she made regular trips for several months, from New Orleans to Natchez, under the command of Captain Clement. This gentleman was soon after
succeeded by Capt. John de Hart, and while approaching
New Orleans with a valuable cargo on board, she took fire
and burned to the water's edge. After being submerged for
several months, her hulk was raised and refitted. She was
afterwards in the Louisville trade, and was condemned in
1819.

The Enterprise was No. 4 of the Western steamboat series.
She was built at Brownsville, Pa., by D. French, under his
patent, and was owned by several residents of that place. The
Enterprise was a small boat of seventy-five tons. She made
two voyages to Louisville in the summer of 1814, under the
command of Captain J. Gregg. On the first of December, in
the same year, she conveyed a cargo of ordnance stores from
Pittsburgh to New Orleans. While at the last named port,
she was pressed into service by General Jackson. Her owners were afterwards remunerated by the United States government. When engaged in the public service, she was eminently useful in transporting troops, arms and ammunition to
the seat of war. She left New Orleans for Pittsburgh on the
6th of May, 1815, and reached Louisville after a passage of
twenty-five days; thus completing the first steamboat voyage
ever made from New Orleans to Louisville. But at the time

the Enterprise made this trip, the water was so high that the banks in many places were overflowed; consequently there was no current. The Enterprise was enabled to make her way up without much difficulty, by running through the "cut-offs," and over inundated fields, in still water. In view of these favorable circumstances, the experiment was not satisfactory, the public being still in doubt whether a steamboat could ascend the Mississippi when that river was confined within its banks, and the current as rapid as it generally is.

Such was the state of public opinion when the steamboat Washington commenced her career. This vessel, the fourth in the catalogue of Western steamboats, was constructed under the personal superintendence and direction of Capt. Henry M. Shreve. The hull was built at Wheeling, Va., and the engines were made at Brownsville, Pa. The entire construction of the boat comprised various innovations, which were suggested by the ingenuity and experience of Capt. Shreve. The Washington was the first "two-decker" on the Western waters. The cabin was placed between the decks. It had been the general practice for steamboats to carry their boilers in the hold; in this particular Capt. Shreve made a new arrangement by placing the boilers of the Washington on deck; and this plan was such an obvious improvement, that all the steamboats on those waters retain it to the present day. The engines constructed under Fulton's patent had upright and stationary cylinders. In French's engines vibrating cylinders were used. Shreve caused the cylinders of the Washington to be placed in a horizontal position, and gave the vibration to the pitman. Fulton and French used single low-pressure engines, with cranks at right angles; and this was the first engine of that kind ever used on Western waters. Mr. David Prentice had previously used cam wheels for working the valves of the cylinder; Capt. Shreve added his great invention to the cam cut-off, with flues to the boilers, by which three-fifths of the fuel were saved. These improvements originated with Capt. Shreve.

On the 24th day of September, 1816, the Washington passed over the Falls of Ohio, on her first trip to New Orleans and returned to Louisville, in November following. While at New Orleans the ingenuity of her construction excited the admiration of the most intelligent citizens of that place. Edward Livingston, after a critical examination of the boat and her machinery, remarked to Capt. Shreve, "You deserve well of your country, young man; but we (referring to Ful-

ton and Livingston monopoly) shall be compelled to beat
you (in the courts), if we can.''

An accumulation of ice in the Ohio compelled the Washington to remain at the Falls until March 12th, 1817. On
that day she commenced her second voyage to New Orleans.
She accomplished this trip and returned to Shippingsport, at
the foot of the falls, in forty-one days. The ascending voyage was made in twenty-five days, and from this voyage all
historians date the commencement of steam navigation in the
Mississippi valley. It was now practically demonstrated to
the satisfaction of the public in general, that steamboats could
ascend this river in less than one-fourth the time which the
barges and keel-boats had required for the same purpose.
This feat of the Washington produced almost as much popular excitement and exultation in that region as the battle of
New Orleans. The citizens of Louisville gave a public dinner
to Capt. Shreve, at which he predicted that the time would
come when the trip from New Orleans to Louisville would be
made in ten days. Although this may have been regarded as
a boastful declaration at that time, the prediction has been
more than fulfilled; for in 1853 the trip was made in four
days and nine hours.

After that memorable voyage of the Washington all doubts
and prejudices in reference to steam navigation were removed. Ship-yards began to be established in every locality,
and the business of steamboat building was vigorously prosecuted. But a new obstacle now presented itself, which, for a
time, threatened to give an effectual check to the spirit of enterprise and progression which had just been developed. We
refer to the claims made by Mr. Fulton and Livingston to
the exclusive right of steamboat navigation on the rivers of
the United States. This claim being resisted by Capt. Shreve,
the Washington was attached at New Orleans, and taken possession of by the sheriff. When the case came for adjudica-
tion before the District Court of Louisiana, that tribunal
promptly negatived the exclusive privileges claimed by Liv-
ington and Fulton, which were decided to be unconstitutional.
The monopoly claims of Livingston and Fulton were finally
withdrawn in 1819, and the last restraint on the steamboat
navigation of the Western rivers was thus removed, leaving
Western enterprise and energy at full liberty to carry on the
great work of improvement. This work has been so progressive that, at the present time, no less than eight hundred
steamboats are in constant operation on the Ohio and Mississippi and their tributaries, and this mode of navigation has

there been carried to a degree of perfection unrivaled in any other part of the world."

STEAMBOAT ENGINES FROM 1812 TO 1826.

By Old-timer.

[Compiled for the Times-Democrat.]

"Almost all of the first boats upon the Western waters were designated as "low pressure." This was a misnomer, they had merely non-condensing engines, exhausting the steam into the air, although they were provided with condensers. Very few of the boats built for the Mississippi river had walking beams. They had what is called steeple engines, the cylinder being placed vertical; the piston was attached to a beam of iron running crosswise, something on the style of an old saw-mill engine. Some of the boats were provided with horizontal cylinders, like those of the low-pressure Richmond; these engines seldom made more than fifteen or twenty pounds of steam, from the fact that they could obtain only a partial vacuum. All of these original engines were built on the Watt & Bolton plan, several were imported from England. The United States had two walking beam engines, and was probably the first steamboat to have two engines. The New Orleans, Vesuvius, Etna, Buffalo, Ramapo, Fanny, Feliciana, and the Natchez, had the Watt & Bolton engine. The first high pressure engine was built in 1813 by French, at Brownsville, Pa., and was placed on the Comet. It was an oscillating engine, but not working well, was taken out and placed in a saw mill at Natchez in 1814. Afterwards French put his engines on the Enterprise, Capt. H. M. Shreve, the first boat to enter Red River, and the Dispatch. The first regular high pressure boat was the Washington, built for Capt. Shreve in 1816, at Wheeling. She had one horizontal cylinder twenty-four inches in diameter, six-foot stroke, four single flue boilers. The cut-off cam invented by Capt. Shreve was first used on this boat. French and George Evans built many high-pressure engines, also the Stackhouse family, who succeeded them, and after them the Longs, who became celebrated as engine builders. It has been stated that the originator of the high pressure engine was Trevithick, but Oliver Evans, the father of George, claimed that distinction, the one that he placed upon a dredging machine in the Delaware river, and which was propelled by steam years before Robert Fulton built and ran his Clermont on the Hudson River. The improvements made to these engines were due to an engineer named Wolf. He conceived the idea of combining the two systems in the same engine, which gave us the compound engine. Hartupee followed the plan of Wolf. These compound engines are now in use on some of the most powerful tow-boats on the river, and it is claimed for them a saving of fuel and an increase of power. The first engineers came from England, New York and Philadelphia. Very few of them had a theoretical idea of steam; about the only thing they knew was that they had a safety valve with a weight upon it, indicating so many pounds pressure of steam. They also knew that the water should be kept at a certain depth in the boilers. When any of these boats raced the engineers placed extra weights on the safety valves, and really couldn't tell in many instances within a hundred pounds of the amount of steam they were carrying. Within the last thirty years all this has changed, as engineers then commenced to receive both a theoretical and practical education of their calling. The first invention to guard against explosion was the Evans' safety guard. This invention has so been improved upon that an explosion has become a rare exception. The pilots of those days were the keel and bargemen. They knew from a hard-earned experience the sandbars, islands, and many of the worst obstructions in the river. In those days they did not run the river much at night, the danger from snags and sawyers being too great. They were a hardy, fearless set of men, whose former life had forced them to face every danger, and to stand up against fatigue. The captains were chosen mostly from the seafaring class, because they were thought to have greater command of the men under them. All of the first boats had their cabins on deck aft of the engine; the ladies' cabin was in the hold aft. They also had a bow-sprit and figure-head, like a ship. It is worthy of remark that the first steamboat, the New Orleans, on her first trip carried a lady passenger, Mrs. Roosevelt, the wife of the captain, and one of the owners of the New Orleans.''

LOUISVILLE CANAL.

[Louisville Courier, March 21.]

" The Louisville and Portland Canal will be opened as a great free water-way on the 1st of July, and the commerce of the loveliest valley of the world will steam through it without toll. For sixty years the canal has been one of the most important improvements on the Western rivers. It was conceived when steamboats were conceived, and the two have considerable history in common. There were some stirring events in those days, and in search of reminiscences a reporter called upon Capt. Joseph Swager. Capt. Swager is in his eighty-eighth year, but he is blessed with good health, a vigorous mind, and a memory which enables him to review the men and incidents of sixty or seventy years ago with the most graphic particularity.

"The first boat," said Capt. Swager, "which descended the Ohio and Mississippi Rivers, was the New Orleans in 1811. She was built by the Fulton Company of New Orleans and had an experience in the earthquake of that year, which caused the water in the river to run up stream. The Fulton Company built two other boats after that, the Etna and Vesuvius, and were endowed by the Legislature of Louisiana with the exclusive right to navigate by steam the waters of the State. In 1814 a company at Brownsville, Pa., with Capt. Henry M. Shreve as manager, built two boats, the Enterprise and the Dispatch, which made in all five boats west of the Alleghany Mountains.

"When the Enterprise reached the Falls at Louisville on her return from her first down trip her machinery proved too weak to bring her over. There were quite a number of us watching her make the attempt, and when she failed we volunteered to warp her over. We sank the anchor at the head of the Falls and connected it by a two-inch cable, with the capstan on the front, and wound her over by hand. Both of Captain Shreve's boats were at New Orleans in 1815, and were pressed into Government service by General Jackson. After the fight they were released, but the Fulton Company brought suit against Capt. Shreve for infringement on their exclusive right to navigate the waters of that State by steam. Shreve gave bond, and his boats were released, but the battle was long and fierce over the infringement of the Fulton Company's rights. Capt. Shreve finally won the fight. In 1815 he built another boat at Brownsville, and called her the George Washington. In coming down the river she got aground ten miles below Maysville, and in the effort to get her off the bar the boilers blew up and killed ten or twelve men. This, however, did not discourage the Captain. He repaired the boilers and came on down the river. He was a man of great ability and perseverance, and accomplished so much for navigation that in 1817, when he reached Louisville from New Orleans, having made the run in twenty-one days, a public dinner was given him, at which he said in his address that he had no doubt the day would come when the run would be made in half the time.

"John T. Gray and George Gretsinger built the Governor Shelby, the first boat that was launched at Louisville. They commenced in 1815, but did not complete her until 1817, owing to the failure of the engines, which were built by Dr. Ruble. The work was delayed until engines could be brought from New York. Steamboats continued to increase in number, and in a few years the risk incurred in going over the falls and the impossibility of getting over at all when the water was low led to the agitation of a proposition to construct a canal around the falls. The agitation developed a division in the sentiment of the people on the subject, many thinking that it would work a great injury to the prosperity of Louisville.

"The first charter for a canal was granted by the Legislature January 30, 1818, to the Kentucky Ohio Canal Company, and on February 10, 1820, an amended charter was granted them, more liberal than the first, but nothing was done under either. The time in which the canal was to be completed was extended from time to time by the Legislature, until the matter was taken up by two gentlemen from Philadelphia, named Ronaldson and Hulme, and Captain Shackelford of St. Louis. [From the published proceedings of the Legislature it seems that those men secured the franchise of the old company and applied for an amendment, which was granted them December 20, 1825. The name of the company was changed to the Louisville and Portland Canal Company, and on January 20, 1826, they purchased from John Rowan ninety acres of land, extending from the foot of Ninth street to Portland.—REP.]

"Great opposition was encountered when it became evident that a determined effort was to be made to build the canal. Petitions were circulated for signatures, praying the Legislature not to grant the new or amended charter. I was running a packet between Louisville and St. Louis at the time, and when I got into port they came to me with the petition for my signature, but I told them I couldn't sign it.

"They expressed great surprise at my refusal, and asked me if I, a citizen of Louisville, interested in her prosperity, was willing for them to build the canal around the falls, and make Louisville a way landing. I told them that what the city wanted was men and capital, and the way to bring them is to inaugurate public enterprises; that a million dollars invested in the canal was safe — it couldn't be taken away, and would bring men with more money.

"It took them four or five years to get the canal so boats

could pass through, and even then it was a very difficult undertaking. The sharp rocks stuck out from both banks and cut the boats up terribly, and it was necessary to hold a boat well in hand and go very slow to keep from tearing her sides to pieces.

"I don't remember who took the first boat through. The first one I saw go through I had charge of myself. It was in 1829 or 1830. I was in port with the Don Juan, and Capt. D. S. Benedict was running the first Diana, of which I was part owner, and he was not willing to run the risk of going through the canal. I told him to get everything ready and I would take the risk and run her through, which I did; but I don't remember whether that was the first boat that went through or not. But it was a dangerous piece of business for ten or fifteen years to take a boat through. The engineer made a mistake in the depth of the ditch, and gave only six feet in the canal, when there was nine feet on the falls. This mistake rendered necessary the construction of the lock and dams.

"Mr. Ronaldson, the prime mover in the canal project, was a bachelor, rich and philanthropic, and was very kind to the men working on the canal. Those digging in the ground began to sicken and die from the unhealthy nature of the work. Mr. Ronaldson bought heavy flannel, and employed the wives of the workmen to make it up into shirts, which he gave to them to keep them from getting sick. He was very particular, too, about the way the shirts were made, and examined them very closely. When he found one badly made, he would not accept it. When he returned them on account of the sewing, the women asked him what made him so particular, he was going to give them away, anyhow. This enraged him, and he scolded them terribly, saying, 'it's none of your business what I'm going to do with them; I pay you to make them, and you must make them right.' That was sixty years ago, however."

[From Louisiana Gazette.]

THE MANHATTAN.

Nov. 27, 1819. A portion of the manifest of the cargo of steamboat Manhattan from New York to Louisville, Ky. (Falls of Ohio).

10 boxes dry goods and clothing to Ramsey & Holmes, Natchez; 32 packages dry goods to H. Postlewaith, Natchez; 18 packages merchandise to I. G. Gates, Shawneetown, Ill.; 35 packages of merchandise to W. Foster, Evansville, Ind.;

24 casks of iron-mongery to M. Dewitt, Louisville, Ky.; 2 cases merchandise to W. C. Barker & Co., Louisville, Ky.; 13 cases merchandise to T. Jones, Louisville, Ky.; 2 pipes of wine and 81 bars iron to T. Jones, Louisville, Ky.

NEW YORK, Nov. 4th, 1819.—The elegant and powerful steam vessel Manhattan, Capt. Jenkins, started at 10 o'clock yesterday for New Orleans and Louisville, Ky. (Falls of Ohio), and in less than two hours after leaving the wharf, she discharged her pilot, having run 28 miles in one hour and 50 minutes.

The steamboat Manhattan, Capt. Jenkins, arrived at this port yesterday from New York. She is on a voyage to Louisville, Ky. She passed the town in handsome style, giving a gratifying specimen of her speed and power of her engine. We are informed by Capt. Jenkins, that he experienced a violent gale of wind on the second day out, attended with heavy cross sea, and during the whole of its continuance her engine was kept going. She proved herself a good sea boat. She is intended as a regular trader from this port to Louisville.

SATURDAY, March 24th, 1820.—Arrived from Louisville, Ky.,the steamboat Manhattan.— Log: —

Passed, on the 19th, near the mouth of Cumberland, steamboats Car of Commerce and James Ross. On the 22d, at Grand Cut Off, steamboat Vulcan, 10 days out. The Manhattan has run the distance from Louisville to New Orleans in 142 hours and 10 minutes. This we believe has not been surpassed or equaled by any steamboat. She was detained 35 days on her voyage up on account of low water and ice. Manifest of cargo, 330 hogsheads tobacco, 100 barrels pork, 150 barrels flour, 30 barrels beans, 100 kegs lard, 50 kegs tobacco, 50 barrels apples.

CULTIVATION OF COTTON.

1742. About this time a cotton gin, invented by M. Dubreuil, which facilitated the operation of separating the cotton fiber from the seed, created an epoch in the cultivation of cotton in Louisiana, and it began to enter largely into the products of the plantation. — *Extract De Bow's Review.*

1783. The first arrival of American cotton at Liverpool was witnessed by Mr. Maury, the first American consul at Liverpool, whose death recently took place at New York, witnessed the first importation at Liverpool of American cotton, and which was seized under the impression that it had been grown in India. — *Extract from Hazard's Register, 1840.*

EXPORTATION OF COTTON.

[Extract from United States Gazette, Philadelphia, 1828.]

An idea generally prevails that the cultivation of cotton in this country, as an article of export, commenced subsequently to the establishment of the Federal Constitution. This is an error. It appears from the following extract taken from an old work now in the city library, entitled " Present State of Great Britain and North America," London, 1766, that it was cultivated in Virginia as early as 1746.

PHILADELPHIA, April 14th, 1828.

" Some of the cotton from Virginia was sent to Manchester in the year 1746, where it sold for 18 pence per pound, and the workmen who had it on trial, reported to the merchants, who sent it to them, that it was as good as any they had, and that they would take any quantity of it."

" Upon this, several trials were made to plant cotton, both there and in the Carolinas as a standard commodity to send to Britain."

GROWTH OF COTTON.

The first notice of cotton growing in Mississippi is by Charlevoix, who states that he saw some planted at Natchez in 1722, in the garden of M. de Noir.

Bienville wrote, in 1735, that it grew well on the Mississippi, and Vandreuil in 1746, informed the French government that cotton had been received at New Orleans from the Illinois.[1]

It began to be cultivated as a crop in Louisiana in 1760, from St. Domingo seed and Maurepas, the French minister, recommended the importation of machinery from the East Indies for the separation of the seed and lint. In 1722, Captain Roman, of the British army, was at East Pascagoula and saw the black seed cotton growing on the farm of Mr. Krebs, with a machine of his own invention for its conversion into lint. This was the Roller gin and no doubt the first ever in operation in this country.

In 1796, David Greenleaf, a very ingenious mechanic, was constructing gins in the vicinity of Natchez. He built the first public or toll gin on the land of Mr. Richard Curtis, at Selsertown, conducted for many years afterwards by Edmund Andrews. 1807, Eleazer Carver commenced building gins at the

---

[1] All the country above the mouth of Yazoo was then called the "Illinois." The cotton referred to probably came from the Post of Arkansas, which had been early settled by the French.

town of Washington, where he erected the first saw mill
to supply his shop with materials. He commenced in a primitive style but did good work. He removed to Bridgwater,
Mass., and to this day his gins maintain their reputation.

1801. The first screw press was made in Philadelphia for
Sir Wm. Dunbar, after a model sent by him in 1799 to Mr.
John Ross. On its receipt, he wrote to his correspondent : I
shall endeavor to indemnify myself for the cost by making
cotton seed oil. This is the first suggestion of that product
which has now become a great article of commerce.

1711. The planters around Natchez turned their attention
to raising cotton on a larger scale, the seed having been procured from Jamaica and other West India islands. It was a
black seed, of fine fiber and good staple, and was the only variety planted in this quarter until 1811. After this date, what
is known as the Petit Gulf seed were introduced, it was commonly said from Mexico, by Dr. Rush Nutt, † a distinguished
planter and scientist. The variety was very prolific, with a
long, fine and strong staple.

**EARLY PROPHESIES ON THE CAPABILITIES OF THE MISSISSIPPI
AND OHIO VALLEYS.**

An illustration of the adaptability of the West to populate
the country rapidly is found in *Kramer's Navigator*, published in Pittsburgh in 1818, tenth edition.

" Mr. Charles Wells, Sen., resident on the Ohio River fifty
miles below Wheeling, related to me while at his home, in October 1812, the following circumstances : —

That he has had two wives (the last of which still lives, and
is a smart, hale-looking woman), had *twenty-two children,*
sixteen of whom are still living, healthy, and many of them
married and have already pretty large families. That a tenant of his, a Mr. Scott, a Marylander, has had *twenty-two,* the
last now being at the breast of its mother who is yet a gay
Irishwoman, being Scott's second wife. That a Mr. Gordon,
an American-German, formerly a neighbor of Mr. Wells, now
residing on the Muskingum, State of Ohio, has had by two
wives *twenty-eight children.* Mr. Gordon is eighty years old,
active and in hale health. These three worthy families have

---

† Dr. Rush Nutt was the first to perceive the advantage of regular
motion for the gin so as the better to detach the motes or false seed. And
with this object was the first to substitute, in 1830, the steam engine for
horse-power. This was the first steam power ever used in the ginning of
cotton.—*Ext. Claiborn's History of Mississippi.*

had born to them *seventy-two children* — a number, perhaps, unexampled in any other country in the world, and such as would make Buffon stare, when he generously asserts as well as several writers of Europe — "that animal life degenerates in America." Mr. Wells further states, that a tenant of his son Charles, has a family of *fifteen children.* The last year, 1811, within a circuit of ten miles around him, ten women had born to them *twenty children*, each having had twins.

The banks of the Ohio seem peculiarly grateful to the propagation of the human species, and perhaps stronger evidences could not be produced than the anecdotes just related. Indeed, an observation to this effect can hardly be missed by any person descending that river and calling frequently at the cabins on its banks. Children are the first object that strikes the eye on mounting the bank, and the last thing he hears on leaving the not unfrequently ragged-looking premises."

The following just observations were addressed to the Earl of Hillsborough in 1770, when Secretary of State for the North American Department: —

"No part of America will need less encouragement for the production of naval stores and raw materials for the manufacturers of Europe, and for supplying the West India Islands with lumber, provisions, etc., than the country of the Ohio, and for the following reasons: —

1st. The lands are excellent, the climate is temperate. The native grapes, silk worms and mulberry trees abound everywhere — hemp, hops and rye grow spontaneously in the valleys and lowlands. Lead and iron are plenty in the hills.

Salt springs are innumerable, and no soil is better adapted to the culture of tobacco, flax and cotton than the Ohio.

The river Ohio is navigable at all seasons of the year for large boats, like the West country barges, rowed only by four or five men.

And from the month of February to April large ships may be built on the Ohio, and sent to sea laden with hemp, iron, flax, silk, cotton, tobacco, pot-ash, etc.

All the articles may be sent down the river Ohio to the sea at least fifty per cent. cheaper than they are carried only sixty miles by land carriage in Pennsylvania, where wagoning is cheaper than in any other part of North America.

Whenever the farmers and merchants shall properly understand the business of transportation, they will build schooners, sloops, etc., on the Ohio suitable for the West India, or European markets, or by having cherry, black walnut, oak, etc., properly sawed for foreign markets and formed into rafts in the manner it is now being done by settlers near the upper parts of the Delaware, and in Pennsylvania, and thereon stow their hemp, iron, tobacco. etc., and proceed with them to New Orleans. The river Ohio seems kindly designed by nature as the channel through which the two Floridas can be supplied with flour, not only for their own consumption, but also for the carrying on an extensive trade with Jamaica and the Spanish settlements on the bay of Mexico.

Mill stones in abundance can be found in the hills near the Ohio, and the country is supplied with abundance of water power for grist mills, etc.

The passage is seldom made from Philadelphia to Pensacola in less than a month, and sixty shillings per ton freight (consisting of sixteen barrels), is usually paid for flour, etc., thither.

Boats carrying 800 to 1,000 barrels of flour may go from Pittsburgh in about the same time as from Philadelphia to Pensacola, and for half the amount of freight and arrive there in much better order.

This is not mere speculation, for it is a fact that about the year 1746 there was a great scarcity of provisions at New Orleans, and the French settlements at the Illinois, small as they then were, sent thither in one winter upwards of eight hundred thousand weight of flour."— From "Internal Commerce of the United States."

CHAPTER XXXIV.

[From Carnegie's "Triumphant Democracy."]

"Nature has done much for America as regards facilities for transportation. Her inland seas, containing one-third of all the fresh water in the world, and her great rivers lie ready at hand awaiting only an application of steam to vessels to render them magnificent highways. A vessel sailing round the edges of these American lakes traverses a greater distance than from New York to Liverpool.

The rivers of America are also the largest in the world. After the Amazon and the LaPlata comes the Mississippi, with an outflow of over 2,000,000 cubic feet per hour. This mighty river, which the Indians called, in their picturesque language, Father of Waters, is equal in bulk to all the rivers of Europe combined, exclusive of the Volga. It is equal to three Ganges, nine Rhones, twenty-seven Seines, or eighty Tibers. "The mighty Tiber chafing with its flood," says the master. How

would he have described the Mississippi on the rampage after
a spring flood, when it pours down its mighty volume of water
and overflows the adjacent lowlands?   Eighty Tibers in one!
Burns' picture of the pretty little Ayr in flood has been ex-
tolled, where the foaming waters come down " an acre braid.''
What think you of a tumbling sea 20 miles " braid " instead
of your " acre," dear Robin? The length of the Mississippi
is 2,250 miles, while its navigable tributaries exceed 20,000
miles.   The Father of Waters collects his substance from
water-sheds covering an area of more than 2,500,000 square
miles.

"The early history of navigation in America presents as
many curious contrasts and interesting facts as do other divisions of the history of American progress.   From the begin-
nings which to us seem ludicrously small and crude, the greatest
results have come.   At the beginning of the century a successful steamboat had not been built.   For twenty or thirty years
inventors in France, Scotland, England, and America had been
working and planning to apply a principle which they saw
was perfectly applicable; but lacking knowledge of one or two
little essentials, they only passed from failure to failure, yet
constantly getting nearer and nearer to success.   John Fitch
and Oliver Evans are the names of the earliest representatives
of America in this great struggle.

"After each experimenter had contributed some new light,
an American engineer, Robert Fulton by name, gathered, in
1807, the multiplicity of lights into one great flame, and made
practicable by the help of all what each had tried in vain to
achieve by himself.   Fulton's *Clermont* was the first commercially successful steamboat ever built.   A boat of 160 tons
burden, she was launched on the Hudson in 1807, and ran over
a year as a passenger boat between New York and Albany.
The first steamboat of the Mississippi Valley was built by
Fulton in 1811, and was called the *Orleans*.   She had a stern
wheel, and went from Pittsburgh to New Orleans, more than
2,000 miles, in fourteen days.   The next year Henry Bell, of
Scotland, built the *Comet*, of 30 tons, which plied, between
Glasgow and Greenoch, and in 1813 sailed around the coasts
of the British Isles.   In 1819 the *Savannah*, 380 tons burden,
crossed the Atlantic from America, visited Liverpool, St. Pet-
ersburg, and Copenhagen, and returned.''

"The traffic floated upon these Western rivers will surprise
many.   Take the Ohio, for instance; a competent authority
has stated that the total of its trade from its head at Pittsburgh
to its mouth at New Cairo, about 1,000 miles, exceeded in 1874

12

$800,000,000, or £160,000,000, a sum greater than the total
exports of the nation about which we hear so much. It is
upon the Ohio that the cheapest transportation in the world
exists. Coal, coke, and other bulky articles are transported
at the rate of one-twentieth of a cent, one-fortieth of a penny,
per ton per mile. This is made possible by means of barges,
many of which are lashed together and pushed ahead by a
steam tug. The current, of course, carries along the floating
mass. The steamer has little to do but to guide while descending and to tow the empty barges back. The records of 1884
show that there were owned in the one city of Pittsburgh for
use on the river 4,323 vessels, including barges, with a tonnage
of 1,700,000 tons. One hundred and sixty-three of these were
steamboats. Twenty-thousand miles of navigable water-ways
lie before these Pittsburgh craft, and many thousand miles
more are ready to be opened by easily constructed improvements in the lesser streams. This work the General Government is steadily performing year after year, as well as improving
the existing navigation. Even to-day, a boat can start from
Pittsburgh for a port 4,300 miles distant, as far as from New
York to Queenstown and half way back, or as far away as the
Baltic ports are from New York."

CHANGES AND FLUCTUATIONS IN RIVER BUSINESS.

There are several eras, somewhat vaguely divided from
each other in the commercial history of the Lower Mississippi.
1. The French and Spanish dominion, when the mouths of
the river and a large portion of its course was controlled by
France or Spain. It is only in the last few years of the Spanish dominion, when the American settlers had poured over
into the Ohio valley, that the river trade attained any importance whatever.
2. The period of flat-boats and barges, extending from
1803, the year of the purchase of Louisiana, to 1816, when
the steamboat was an acknowledged success, not only in going
down, but up stream against the current.
3. The early steamboat period, 1816 to 1840, when the
river found its first competitor for the traffic of the Mississippi Valley in the canals built westward from the Atlantic
seaboard.
4. From 1840 to 1860, when the river route came into competition with railroads.
5. The war period of almost total suspension in river traffic.

6. The *post-bellum* period of active rivalry between river and rail.

These different eras are marked by changes in trade lines, and means of transportation, and by the vessels used in navigating the river; first, bark canoes, then pirogues, bateaus, barges, flat-boats, keels, and finally steamboats.

THE FRENCH AND SPANISH DOMINION.

Although the early French settlements were made altogether on the Mississippi or its chief tributaries, like Red River and Bayou Lafourche, and travel from point to point was by the river, the Mississippi was of no importance whatever as a commercial factor. The great valley which to-day clothes and feeds so large a proportion of the world, was actually not self-supporting. The imports were larger than the exports, and but for the assistance given by the original grantee of Louisiana, Crozat, and afterwards by the French government itself, the colony would have died out from actual starvation, the records noting no less than three serious famines.

The early mode of traveling on the river is described by Bienville in his exploration in 1699, which ascended nearly as high as Natchez. The Frenchmen used the ships' boats of the fleet, and canoes made of bark or hollowed from the trunks of trees, almost similar in style and build to those of the Indians.

He left a fair record of the topography of the river at the time, and has thus enabled the engineers of later days to note what changes have taken place in the channel of the river in the past two centuries. He himself was a witness of the beginning of the Pointe Coupée cut-off, and notices in his account of his first trip there, the river was trickling around a point just below the mouth of Red River.

At that day the Indians along the Lower Mississippi, the Houmas, Bayagoulas, Natchez, and Tensas, were dying off as fast as they could—they are all extinct to-day — and the river was as dead commercially as it is possible to conceive. The Indians carried on no buisness or commerce whatever with each other; indeed on account of the overflowing of the banks, the settlements directly on the Mississippi were few, the aborigines seeking the highlands or mounds which are to be found here and there some miles back of the river. M. Bienville went for miles and days without seeing an Indian, but notices that the eastern bank of the river near the Baton Rouge was crowded with buffaloes.

The subsequent explorations of the Mississippi and the se-

lection of New Orleans as a location for the future capital of
the colony were made in French men-of-war and yawls. The
early colonists adopted the Indian bark canoe, which was exceedingly light and, even when freighted, easily handled.
When any difficulty was encountered in the river, either in
snags or on account of the current, or when it was found
shorter to cut across a point rather than take the long circuit-
ous trip around it, these boats were hauled out of the water,
just as Bienville had done, and carried by the Indian or negro-
slaves until the river was reached again.

The settlement of Lower Louisiana, however, and the increasing demands of trade required vessels of a different
character and greater carrying capacity than these canoes, and
the pirogue — a vessel peculiar to Lower Louisiana — came
into play to supply the need. The pirogue is simply a log-
canoe — a solid log of cypress or live-oak which has been cut
out in the center, and is propelled by paddles rather than oars,
worked first on one side and then on the other. It is astonishing how long this primitive boat continued in use. Pirogues,
indeed, exist to this day in Louisiana, but only for hunting,
never for commercial purposes. The modern pirogue is small
and holds at best two men. The propeller of the vessel stands
erect, using his paddle with skill and agility, for it requires
but the slightest tilting of the boat to overturn it. The commercial pirogue of early Louisiana was generally somewhat
larger, from 2 to 5 tons, and propelled by negro slaves, a mast
and sail being occasionally used when the wind was favorable.
In one of these as many as 20 bales of cotton or 30 barrels of
molasses could be floated down to New Orleans, the light vessel being entirely paddled back to the plantation. Although of
the most primitive character, and the first craft used on the
Mississippi, unless we except the bark canoe of the Indians,
the pirogue survived in river commerce for over a century,
and as late as 1830 a considerable amount of the produce of
Louisiana reached the market in these log canoes.

Besides these pirogues, the river craft in use in these early
days were the bateaux (French for boats,) and various non-
descripts. The bateaux were generally in use in the upper
country, and meant for longer voyages than the pirogues.
They were of rough plank, long in proportion to their breadth,
and something in the shape of a coffin. They were never very
popular on the Lower Mississippi, and died an early death,
although even as late as 1825 an occasional bateaux reached
New Orleans from some extreme point in the wild Indian
country west of the Mississippi.

The French settled the Mississippi Valley both at its head and at its mouth about the same time time. After Bienville had made his exploration of the Mississippi, but before New Orleans had been founded, or indeed dreamt of, they had made several settlements within the limits of Pennsylvania, Ohio and Indiana.

FIRST SHIPMENT BY THE MISSISSIPPI.

The first shipment down the Mississippi was made in 1705, when the French *voyageurs* in the Indian country around the Wabash collected from the several hunting posts in the neighborhood some 10,000 deer and 5,000 bear skins and shipped them down the river. The experiment was a success, although the cargo had a long and dangerous voyage to make. The *voageurs* traveled in their boats 1,400 miles without seeing a white man, through a country the population of which was mainly hostile. The trip was successfully made down the Ohio and Mississippi to the mouth of Bayou Manchac, which then opened into the river some 15 miles below Baton Rouge, but which has been closed to navigation since Jackson's day. Instead of going down the Mississippi to the mouth — there was no settlement below and no point at which the cargo could be loaded on ocean-going vessels — these early merchants went down Bayou Manchac and the Iberville River (now the Amite), thence through lakes Maurepas and Ponchartrain to the French settlements on Mississippi Sound at Biloxi (now Ocean Springs). From there the produce of the chase in Ohio and Indiana was sent to Mobile, whence it was shipped to France. It arrived there safely and the transaction proved a profitable one.

The *voyageurs*, however, who had made the long trip down the river never returned home, but settled in Louisiana. From the forests in Central Ohio these hides had been conveyed, mainly in open boats, some 1,400 miles by river and lake and 4,500 by sea, it taking more than half a year for them to reach their destination. This is the first reported commercial transaction on the Mississippi, and it is gratifying to know that it was a successful one to all those interested. It was the beginning of a trade that grew with years, and which, indeed, was the largest item of commerce at New Orleans for many decades of its early history. By 1720, when the Illinois country, both on the Illinois and Mississippi rivers, was settled by the pioneers from French Canada, the shipments down the river in-

cluded some other articles besides those of the chase, and agricultural products were shipped by the Mississippi, mainly for
use on the Gulf coast, which did not produce enough food for
its support during the first half century of the colony's existence. A small amount of these food products was shipped to
the West Indies.

The French Western Company, under Crozat, had been
granted a monopoly of the trade of the Mississippi for twenty-
five years, but this was so unprofitable that the company, after
holding it for fifteen years and sinking a large amount in the
experiment, surrendered its monopoly, and Louisiana, which
then includded the entire Mississippi Valley, became a crown
colony. The total exports from the valley amounted at that
time to $62,000, of which 65 per cent. were skins shipped from
the upper river country. Under the French crown there was
little improvement, and the colony was never self-supporting
while in French possession, the Government being compelled
to make good a large deficit each year.

EXPORTS FROM THE MISSISSIPPI VALLEY.

In 1763, when Louisiana was transferred to Spain, the total
export trade of the colony was estimated as follows: —

Indigo	$100,000
Deer skins	80,000
Lumber	50,000
Naval stores	12,000
Rice, peas, and beans	4,000
Tallow	4,000
Smuggled trade	54,000
Total	304,000

The deer-skins and tallow came from the upper country; the
indigo was mainly from Louisiana; the naval stores were produced in the Mississippi Sound country, which, although a
part of Louisiana at the time, is not within the limits of the
Mississippi Valley.

Under the Spanish rule Louisiana rapidly advanced commercially. The importance of the Mississippi was beginning
to be recognized, and the great powers of Europe soon became
involved in a game of intrigue for its possession. The population of the Lower Mississippi country — what is now Louisiana — advanced rapidly and the commerce doubled every few
years. For the first time in the history of the Mississippi
large shipments were made up the river, and it was through

New Orleans and by the river route that the struggling American colonies received through the connivance of the Spanish Government the arms and gunpowder they needed so sorely in the Revolutionary war. The fur trade of New Orleans had reached a high figure by this time, some $100,000 a year, nearly all of it the produce of the trappers in the Northwestern forests. It was from the Mississippi Valley also that Cuba got much of its lumber and a majority of the boxes in which the sugar crop of the island was packed. By 1770 the commerce of New Orleans and the Mississippi Valley had increased to exports of $631,000 a year — mainly furs, skins, indigo, and lumber. New Orleans, which had possessed no commerce worth speaking about before and no merchants — the articles consumed in the colony being obtained mainly from the Government vessels and only so many ships being allowed to enter the river each year — begun to talk of trade and to complain that the British were engrossing the commerce of the Mississippi Valley. In 1778 the merchants of New Orleans, who had grown to be of some importance, were granted special privileges by the Spanish Government on account of the loyalty and courage shown by the Louisiana troops, who had, under Governor Galvez, captured Baton Rouge, Pensacola, and other important points, and driven the British out of West Florida. In return for their courage and loyalty, New Orleans was granted the privilege of sending each year so many ship-loads of goods to France instead of being compelled to ship all its products to Spanish ports.

This marks the opening of the Mississippi to the commerce of the world. Previous to this grant there was no freedom whatever. Under Crozat, under the French and afterwards under the Spanish, the trade was regulated and controlled by the government; the people were not allowed to ship where they wanted to or what they wanted, and no vessel of a foreign power, whether friendly or not, was allowed to enter the river for commercial purposes.

In the meanwhile a settlement was growing up on the Ohio and its tributaries that soon changed the future of the entire Mississippi Valley. When the United States became possessor of the Ohio basin, as the legatee of Great Britain, the total white population of the vast region was only a few thousand, almost wholly of the French origin, and engaged more in hunting than in agriculture. About the time the Revolutionary war opened a new immigration set in from the English colonies on the Atlantic, over the Alleghanies into the Valley of the Ohio. The story of Daniel Boone and the settlement of Kentucky, Tennessee, and Ohio has been told already in full. Within twenty years after the first white American was settled in the basin of the Ohio, its population was producing large surplus crops of all kinds and seeking for an outlet by which they could be shipped to market. During the Revolutionary war the United States had stationed an agent in New Orleans for the purchase of guns and ammunition for the Continental forces and their shipment up the river to Pittsburgh and thence overland to Philadelphia. In 1788 the settlers in Kentucky and Tennessee were shipping a large quantity of produce down the Mississippi ; and several Philadelphia merchants found it profitable to establish themselves in New Orleans for the purpose of handling this trade, which amounted at that time to some $225,000 a year.

THE RIGHT OF DEPOSIT.

One of the first diplomatic acts of the young Republic was to secure greater facilities for its citizens settled in the Mississippi Valley in the shipment of their surplus crops. Nearly half the country lay in the basin of the Ohio or the Mississippi and dependent upon " the Father of Waters" to reach the seaboard. No one at that time, save Washington and a few others, dreamed of sending goods over the Alleghanies by canals or other means; and it was deemed absolutely necessary for the prosperity of the great region lying between the Blue Ridge and the Mississippi that the river should be neutralized as the Suez Canal is to-day and the settlers on its upper tributaries allowed to ship their produce through it without paying toll to the country of Spain, which happened to own its mouth, just as has been done with the Danube. Negotiations to this end were begun with Spain, and in 1795 the treaty of peace between that power and the United States made the Mississippi free to the commerce of the Western people, who were given for three years the right of deposit for their produce at New Orleans. If, at the end of three years, Spain desired to fix another place of deposit it was at liberty to do so.

The result of this treaty opening the Mississippi to the commerce of the Western Territories had the effect that might have been expected; and the river trade suddenly sprang forward with startling rapidity, and reached what was deemed in those days an immense figure.

It is interesting to note the traffic on it then, so as to see what advance there has been in the past hundred years.

The exports of New Orleans at that time were estimated by an expert, who made a careful examination of the matter, as: —

Cotton (200,000 pounds)	$50,000
Furs	100,000
Boxes (for sugar, 200,000)	225,000
Sugar (40,000,000 pounds)	320,000
Indigo (100,000 pounds)	100,000
Tobacco (200,000 pounds)	16,000
Timber	50,000
Rice (2,000 barrels)	50,000
Western produce (flour, tobacco, etc.)	500,000
Total	**$1,421,000**

The furs came from the upper country; so did some of the cotton; the sugar, indigo, rice, and timber from the Spanish possessions in Louisiana; the rest from Kentucky and Ohio. In 1798 the receipts of produce from the American settlements on the Ohio reached $975,000, and were increasing some $300,000 a year with the new population pouring into the country. The three years during which New Orleans had been agreed on as the depot for Western produce, according to the treaty between Spain and the United States had elapsed. The attention of the Spanish Government was called to this, and it was urged by the Kentuckians that if Spain desired to make a change, another point be selected ; but nothing was done. It remained for the Spanish intendant, Morales, to interpret the treaty as meaning that with the lapse of these three years the Americans lost all right of deposit at New Orleans or any other point in the Spanish possessions, and that the Lower Mississippi was thus virtually closed to them. It was a fatal decision for Spain, and if Señor Morales had seen the consequence or understood the feeling that his action aroused in Kentucky, Ohio, and Tennessee, he would never have been guilty of it, for his decision lost Louisiana to his government. The neutrality and freedom of the Mississippi became at once the aim of American diplomacy, and the United States was convinced that the stability of the Government and the commercial necessities of the West required the possession and control of the Mississippi. For the next four years the Mississippi problem and the purchase of Louisiana were the chief subjects of discussion in Congress, and American statesmen at home and abroad worked and intrigued zealously to prevent the Mississippi falling from the hands of a weak power like Spain into those of a strong one like England or France, both of whom had their eyes on this rich, fertile, and productive valley, whose wealth was just beginning to be recognized.

As for the Western people, the Kentuckians and Tennesseeans, they were wild with fury when they heard that their only outlet to market was closed to them by Morales's order. An expedition to New Orleans to capture the city and drive the Spanish out of the Mississippi Valley was seriously discussed. An account was taken of the men available for military service, who were estimated at 20,000, and the preliminary organization begun, when the President sent three regiments to the Ohio to prevent such a filibustering expedition, and assured the people that the matter would be settled by diplomacy. Petitions poured into Congress demanding that it take some action to open the Mississippi to the commerce of the Western Territories. The following, which is one of the petitions presented at the time, gives an idea of the Western sentiment on this subject: —

PETITION OF THE PEOPLE OF KENTUCKY TO CONGRESS, 1798.

"The Mississippi is ours by the law of nature; it belongs to us by our numbers and by the labor which we have bestowed upon these spots, which before our arrival were desert and barren. Our innumerable rivers swell it and flow with it into the Gulf of Mexico. Its mouth is the only issue which nature has given to our waters, and we wish to use it for our vessels. We do not prevent the Spanish and French from ascending the river to our towns and villages. We wish, in our turn, to descend it without any interruption to its mouth, to ascend it again, and to exercise our privilege of trading on it and navigating it at our pleasure. If our most entire liberty in this matter is disputed, nothing will prevent our taking possession of the capital (of Louisiana,) and when we are once masters of it, we will know how to maintain ourselves there. If Congress refuses us effectual protection, if it forsakes us, we will adopt the measures which our safety requires, even if they endanger the peace of the Union and our connection with the other States. No protection, no allegiance."

There is no doubt that this threat of secession was very popular among some of the pioneers of the West. It must be remembered that the Federal Union was less than ten years old; that the settlers along the Ohio were cut off from the Atlantic sea-coast by mountains through which no roads of any kind ran; that their sole dependence was the Mississippi, and their crops were of no value without the use of that stream.

The Government recognized the justice of these plaints, and Mr. Madison himself, while Secretary of State, in writing to the American minister at Madrid, said of the Western people: " The Mississippi River to them is everything — it is the Hudson, the Delaware, the Potomac, and all the navigable waters of the Atlantic States formed into one stream."

In the meanwhile this embargo had caused considerable trouble in New Orleans, where it threatened to create a famine. The lower river country, as to-day, raised articles like indigo, sugar, and cotton, mainly for export, and not enough provisions for the supply of the population. As a consequence of the stoppage of the shipments from the Ohio, there was a dearth of flour and other Western produce in New Orleans.

The discussion over the trade of the Mississippi found its way into Congress, and served as the chief subject of debate.

Mr. Ross, of Pennsylvania, representing the Western element, offered the following resolution: —

" *Resolved*, That we have an indisputable right to the free navigation of the river Mississippi and to a convenient place of deposit for the produce of the country and its merchandise in the island of Orleans.

"*Resolved*, That the President be authorized to take immediate possession of the country and to call into service the militia of the Western States."

The difficulty was finally definitely settled by the action of President Jefferson in purchasing Louisiana; and in 1803 the people of the Western States were satisfied by having the Mississippi not only thrown open to them, but actually belonging to the United States of America.

SHIPMENTS FROM THE OHIO.

The increase that had taken place in the population of the Upper Mississippi Valley in two decades is well shown in the shipments from that region to New Orleans during this period of contention.

These shipments were, for 1801, for the districts of Kentucky and Mississippi alone, $1,626,672, and for all the American possessions $2,111,672.

In 1802 the shipments from Kentucky alone were $1,182,-864, and for the Ohio Valley and that portion of the Mississippi basin possessed by the United States — all from Bayou Manchac up — including all Mississippi and portions of Louisiana and Tennessee, $2,637,564.

Adding what is known of the products of Louisiana, the

commerce of the Lower Mississippi Valley, that is the shipments down the Mississippi toward New Orleans, either for
consumption in the lower river country or for export, was in
the first two years of the present century as follows:—

	VALUE OF EXPORTS BY RIVER.	
	1801.	1802.
American territories:		
Pennsylvania and territory northwest of Ohio....	$485,000	$700,000
Kentucky and Tennessee and Mississippi........	1,626,672	1,522,064
Mississippi territory..........................	....	412,500
Spanish possessions:		
Upper Louisiana..............................	115,000	120,000
Lower Louisiana..............................	1,422,650	1,720,800
Total......	$3,649,322	$4,475,364

There are no records of the shipments up the river, but
they were small as compared with the down trade, except for
the country immediately around New Orleans.   The imports
at that city about equaled the exports of the Spanish possessions, and included such manufactured articles as could not be
obtained in the colony.   These were brought to New Orleans
from France and Spain, and distributed among the towns and
planters by barges, pirogues and plantation boats.   Less than
10 per cent of the imports found their way above Red River.
    The shipments from New Orleans consisted of the follow-
ing articles: 34,500 bales of cotton of an average weight
of 300 pounds each, a much smaller bale than to-day; 4,500
hogsheads of sugar of 1,000 pounds each; 800 casks of
molasses of 125 gallons each, equal to 2,000 of the barrels
used to-day in shipping molasses; 4,000 casks of tafia or
rum made from Louisiana molasses, each of 50 gallons; 3,000
pounds of indigo, the cultivation of which had proved a failure in Louisiana, and which was rapidly giving place to sugar;
lumber and boxes to the value of $300,000; peltries and
skins to the value of $120,000; rice and other miscellaneous
products to the value of $80,000.
    These were the products of Louisiana.
    Among the chief articles of Western produce received from
the American territory were: 50,000 barrels of flour; 2,000
barrels of pork; 1,200 barrels of beef; 2,400 hogsheads of
tobacco; 25,000 bushels of corn.   Besides, there were butter,
hams, meal, lard, beans, hides, staves and cordage.
    From Pennsylvania, and, indeed, from some portions of
Western New York, the woodsman or pioneer of that era
loaded his flat-boat with the products of the season and began
his voyage down the river to New Orleans.   It was a trip of

months of danger and exposure, for at least nine-tenths of the distance was wholly uninhabited by whites, and the Indians through all the river country were sullen and hostile. The Ohio Falls were passed with difficulty — generally during the high water — pilots being specially employed for this portion of the route. In the Mississippi itself were snags and dangers innumerable. When New Orleans was reached the produce was sold for, say, $2,000 to $3,000, which was about the average value of a cargo. In the earlier days the land route was seldom followed home, as the Indians held all northern Mississippi; but later this trail was popular, and the flatboatman returned home across Lake Ponchartrain and thence northward through Nashville — a trail marked to this day. In the first years of the century, however, he generally went by sea to some of the American cities on the Atlantic coast, Baltimore and Philadelphia being the favorites, laid in a supply of calicoes and other manufactured goods there, and got home six months after his departure, just in time to plant another crop.

VESSELS EMPLOYED IN RIVER TRADE.

The vessels employed in the river trade had changed considerably during this period of development, and the rude pirogues and bateaux of the early French settlers had given place to the flat-boat or Kentucky boat and barge, and afterward to the keel-boats of the Americans. The flat-boat of that day was a small affair, not one-tenth the size it attained half a century later. It averaged nearly 30 tons, and made the trip from Louisville or Cincinnati to New Orleans in 60 days. The professional flat-boat men made but three trips a year, selling not only their produce in New Orleans, but their boats as well, when they were broken up for lumber. The cheapness of this means of transportation — for the building of one of these boats cost but $20 — made it admirably adapted to the condition of the country at the time. The flat-boat man, after selling out his cargo and boat in New Orleans, and probably having a spree there, returned home by way of Philadelphia, or, at a later day, tramped overland with what money he had left strapped around his waist.

The first boats were built in the Mississippi Valley in 1787 near Pittsburgh, when 30 bateaux, 40 feet long by 9 wide, were constructed for the Government for the transportation of troops and provisions.

The trade of the Lower Mississippi, as will be seen, went almost wholly down stream. There were some few light ship--

ments up the river from New Orleans, but the bulk of the manufactured goods and supplies needed by the settlers on the Ohio were obtained, not through New Orleans, but in the American cities on the Atlantic.

To carry the produce brought from the Western States away from New Orleans, there arrived at that port during the year 1802, the last but one of Spanish Dominion, 265 vessels of an aggregate of 31,241 tons. These vessels, it is needless to say, were generally small sloops and schooners, the average being under 118 tons each, which would be looked on with contempt to-day. Yet it is gratifying to note that, although the government of Louisiana was in the hands of a European power, alien to the population, not only the Kentuckians, but the Louisiana creoles as well, the outward trade of New Orleans was in the hands of the American merchant marine. Of the vessels arriving there 158 were American, 104 Spanish, and 3 French. The departures for the same year were 258 vessels of 23,725 tons, of which 170 were American, 97 Spanish, and 1 French.

The next year, during which French and Spanish rule came to an end in the Mississippi Valley, saw still greater improvement, the total tonnage entering New Orleans being 42,817 tons, and all of the vessels being filled with Western and Louisiana produce.

The down commerce of the Mississippi during the three first years of the century and the last of European control over the mouth of the great river, was as follows:—

Year.	Freight received.	Value of products received.
	Tons.	
1801	38,325	$3,649,322
1802	45,906	4,475,364
1803	49,660	4,720,015

In the latter part of 1803 an event occurred which was destined to completely change the political and commercial future of the Mississippi Valley, and with it the whole history of the river changes.

THE PURCHASE OF LOUISIANA.

On Monday, December 20, 1803 Mr. Laussat, the French commissioner, turned over the province of Louisiana to the American representatives; and the United States became the owner of the entire Mississippi Valley, of which it had formerly possessed barely a third. The news brought satisfaction everywhere in America. At the last moment the European powers recognized the importance of Louisiana, and the possession of the Mississippi. Napoleon, who arranged the sale for France, expressed great regret that he had to surrender its possession, and predicted that it would make the United States one of the leading powers of the world.

In this country the sentiment which seemed strongest was rejoicing, not over the possession of the land so much as of the Mississippi, the control of its navigation and its outlet. To the Western people it was everything. With the millions of acres of public land then owned by the Government, there was no need, and indeed no desire for additional territory. What the people of the West wanted was the Mississippi. Without its possession the settlement and advance of the great interior country must have been slow until some outlet was found to the Atlantic sea-board. With it there was no limit to its development.

President Jefferson himself took the Western view of the importance of the Mississippi, and thought its control would change the industrial and commercial condition of this country if not of the whole world. His prediction as to New Orleans as the port of the Mississippi Valley was credited by the merchants of that city for years; and indeed it might have proved true but for the discovery of railroads. Writing to his newly appointed Governor of Louisiana, Claiborne, the President prophesied as follows: —

"New Orleans will be forever, as it is now, the mighty mart of the merchandise brought from more than a thousand rivers, unless prevented by some accident in human affairs. This rapidly increasing city will, in no distant time, leave the emporia of the Eastern World far behind. With Boston, Baltimore, New York and Philadelphia on the left, Mexico on the right, Havana in front, and the immense valley of the Mississippi in the rear, no such position for the accumulation and perpetuity of wealth and power ever existed."

If this prediction has not been fully realized in the eighty-odd years that have since passed it must be attributed to that accident which Mr. Jefferson foresaw.

The receipts of produce by the river showed less increase during the first four years of the American dominion than was to be expected.

1804	$4,275,000
1805	4,371,545
1806	4,937,323
1807	5,370,555

The arrivals of sea-going vessels during the latter year
were 314, and the departures 350, with a tonnage of 43,220.
The keel-boats and barges arriving numbered 340, and the
departures 11. The flat-boat arrivals were estimated at 1,500,
but this is probably an exaggeration. Besides these there
were in use on the river ocean scows, pirogues, skiffs and
floating lumber rafts.

FLAT-BOATS AND KEEL-BOATS.

The Kentucky boat of that day, in which much of the
produce was carried to market, was nicknamed an ark, and
the title was most appropriate, as in shape it was much like
the ark seen in children's toys. Large oars or paddles were
used, not to control or propel the boat, but to partially direct
its course. These arks encountered many dangers and difficulties in their trips down the river, and the calculation is
that at least one-fourth of them were lost en route. Above
the mouth of the Arkansas, where the navigation of the river
was worst, and where snags were plentiful, the arks were tied
to the shore each night. In the lower river, however, where
it was free from obstructions, they floated down as well by
night as by day. The large oars were used mainly to keep
them clear of the snags and sawyers.

For the transportation of freight up stream various kinds
of boats were used, but none of them can be said to have
proved successful, and the tonnage up was barely 10 per
cent. of that floating down. The system of rowing up the
river and against the current was tried. It was slow, tedious
and expensive. The boats coasted along the shore so as to
avoid the full force of the current, but it required one oars-
man for every 3,000 pounds of freight, and the work was so
tiresome that the men rested every hour. To travel from 14
to 30 miles a day was considered very good work. The river
was crossed at the lower end of each bend, and in the crossing
the current carried the boat down a half a mile or so. It is
said by old boatmen that they were compelled to cross the
Mississippi 390 times between New Orleans and Saint Louis.
On some of the tributaries of the Mississippi, however, where
the current was not so strong, as, for instance, the Ohio, a
considerable traffic was carried on up-stream, no less than
fifty boats of a tonnage of thirty tons each trafficking between
Pittsburgh and Cincinnati and making six trips a year.

The keel-boat was of a long, slender and elegant form, and
generally carried from 15 to 30 tons. Its advantage lay in its

small draught of water and in the lightness of its construction. Its propelling power was by oar, sail, setting poles, the cordelle; and when the water was high and the boats ran on the margin of the river, " bushwhacking," or pulling up-stream by the bushes.

The scow was used as a boat of descent for families travel-ing down the river for settlement, and had a roof or a cover-ing for it. These boats were frequently known as " sheds " in the vernacular. The Alleghany or Mackinaw skiff was a covered skiff carrying from 6 to 10 tons, and much used in the Illinois trade and the upper Mississippi and Missouri. Pirogues were sometimes hollowed from one very large tree or made from the trunks of two trees united and fitted with a plank run. They carried from 1 to 5 tons. There were common skiffs, canoes and dug-outs for the convenience of crossing the rivers, and a select company of a few travelers often descended in them to New Orleans. Besides these were a number of anomalous water craft that can scarcely be reduced to any class, used as boats of passage or descent, such as flat-boats worked by a wheel driven by cattle being conveyed to the New Orleans market. There were horse-boats of various constructions, used for the most part for ferry-boats, but sometimes as boats of ascent. Two keel-boats were connected by a platform. A pen in the center held the horses, which by a circular movement propelled the wheel. The United States troops frequently ascended the river by boats propelled by tread-wheel, and more than once a boat moved rapidly up-stream by wheel, after steamboat construction, propelled by a man turning a crank.

But the boats of passage and conveyance most in fashion were the keel-boats and the flats. The flat-boats were called, in the vernacular, Kentucky flats or broad-beams. They were simply an oblong ark, with a roof slightly curved to shed the rain, about 15 feet wide and from 50 to 100 feet long. The timbers of the bottom were massive beams, and they were intended to be of great strength and to carry from 200 to 400 barrels. Great numbers of horses, hogs and cattle were conveyed to market in them. Family boats of this description, for the descent of families to the lower country, were fitted up comfortably with apartments, and in them ladies, servants, cattle, horses, sheep, dogs and poultry, all floating in the same bottom and under the same roof, were carried down the river. The largest barges, which were the best boats of these days, resembled a modern canal boat in appearance. At the stern was the poop-deck, which covered the cabin, and a stand for the patron or captain at the tiller-head. There were two high masts and either hermaphrodite brig or schooner sail rigging. When the barge traveled up river it carried a large crew of from 30 to 40 men, who propelled it against the current, by the use of warnifs, anchors and cordelles, at the rate of 15 miles a day, using canvas when the wind was fair. The 1,200 miles from New Orleans to the mouth of the Ohio were made in 100 days, and when a barge made it in 96 days it was regarded as very quick time. The price of up-freight was 6 and afterwards 5 cents a pound, and there was not much profit in it at these figures. These barges were owned at the Ohio River towns, mainly at Pittsburgh, Wheeling, Marietta, Maysville, Cincinnati and Louisville. At Marietta several sea-going vessels were built and floated down the river to the Gulf of Mexico.

The flat-boat men were generally Kentuckians or Tennesseeans, and they became to the Louisiana Creoles the type of an American, so that " Kaintuck " (Kentuckian) was used as a synonym for American among the native population. They were a sturdy race of men, of splendid physique, indomitable energy and courage, somewhat wild, and ready for a spree when they reached New Orleans.

In those days just above the corporation limits of the town of New Orleans, where land has since formed, and where the wholesale trade of the city is principally carried on, the fleets of barges and flat-boats from the West moored and unloaded or retailed their contents at the water's edge. Farther down and immediately abreast of the town, between the upper limits and the Place d' Armes (now Jackson Square), at what is the sugar and ship landings of to-day, lay the shipping, averaging some 20 or more vessels of from 100 to 200 tons each.

THE TRADE OF THE MISSISSIPPI.

The Western people who shipped their produce down the river via New Orleans had many complaints to make against the tolls and charges at that city, and found that they did not enjoy all those advantages from the possession of the Mississippi which they had expected.

The matter found its way into Congress, where Mr. Poindexter, of the Committee on Ways and Means, inquired into the expediency of prohibiting by law in " the corporation of the City of New Orleans from exacting any tax or duty on vessels, boats or other craft descending the river Mississippi having on board articles the growth or manufacture of the

United States, or such articles of foreign growth or manufacture as have been regularly imported into the United States." The resolution was carried and the City of New Orleans prohibited from exacting these tolls. A couple of years afterward the Legislature of Louisiana, with the same idea that the State had some control of the Mississippi because it lay within Louisiana territory, attempted to give a monopoly of the steam transportation of the river to a company, in which it also was defeated by a ruling of the Supreme Court.

The Western produce trade had grown each year to be a large proportion of the total commerce of New Orleans.

Between October 5, 1810, and May 5, 1811, there passed the Ohio Falls bound down stream to New Orleans, 847 vessels of one kind and another, mainly flat-boats, and the number passing during the season is calculated at 1,200, with the following cargoes: —

Articles.		Quantity.
Flour	barrels,	206,855
Bacon	pounds,	1,008,026
Whisky	barrels,	15,797
Cider	do	4,198
Pork	do	22,602
Apples	do	4,200
Oats	do	6,700
Corn	bushels,	79,795
Merchandise		$ 592,640
Cheese	boxes,	8,569
Beans	barrels,	1,010
Lumber	feet,	2,825,210
Live hogs	number	1,518
Cider, royal	barrels	2,250
Butter	pounds	41,151
Lard	do	775,692
Onions	barrels,	364
Potatoes	do	3,019
Hemp	cwt.	1,050,492
Dried fruit	barrels	442
Yarn and cordage	pounds	189,020
Fowls	number	2,012,224
Shoe thread	pounds	4,820
Country linen	do	13,066
Horses		489
Beer	barrels,	459
Tobacco	hogsheads,	3,891

These statistics, which were taken by the pilots engaged in piloting the vessels over the Ohio Falls, for three-fifths of the vessels passing that point of danger, and estimated for the remainder, which went over the falls during extreme high water without a pilot, are in some respects more complete than many made afterwards when statistics of the river trade were much more carefully collected, for the later figures kept no record of the number of fowls, horses, etc., sent down the river.

The list of articles now sent to market gives some idea of the advance and development that has taken place on the Lower Mississippi with the advent of American rule.

CHAPTER XXXV.

THE STEAMBOAT.

The result of the transfer of Louisiana to the United States has been to greatly increase the population of the Mississippi Valley, as well as its trade; it was destined to still further change its condition by that great invention of American genius, the use of steam as a means of moving vessels in water. Fulton had tried this with success on the Hudson, and aimed to experiment with it on that greater river, the Mississippi. Great doubts were expressed as to the possibility of navigating it, on account of the velocity of the current, the many eddies and whirlpools, the danger from snags and other obstructions. An agent, Nicholas Roosevelt, was accordingly sent ahead to make a preliminary survey of the river between Pittsburgh and New Orleans, to find whether the obstructions were of a serious character, such as were likely to prevent the passage of a small steamer. He reported that there was nothing to prevent the trip. The Orleans, or New Orleans, which was under construction at Pittsburgh, was accordingly completed and made ready for the trip in the latter part of 1811. In this first steamboat the idea of marine architecture was preserved. She was built after the model of a ship, with port-holes on the side, had a long bowsprit, and was painted sky-blue. Her cabin was in the hold.

The steamboatmen of the Mississippi still delight to tell the story of this first cruise of a steamer down the "Father of Waters." The New Orleans was built at Pittsburgh in 1811, at a cost of $38,000; was 116 feet long and 20 feet beam, with a 34-inch cylinder, and was a stern-wheeler. The trip commenced in September, with Roosevelt as superintendent, Mrs. Roosevelt — it was regarded as a very hazardous journey for a woman — the captain, engineer, pilot, and a crew of six. All Pittsburgh turned out to bid the boat *bon voyage*, and when it reached Cincinnati on the second night and cast anchor there — for there were no regular wharf-boats or regular landings then — she was welcomed by the entire population. The New Orleans reached Louisville, October 1, when it was found that she could not safely descend the Ohio Falls, as the water was too low. She accordingly returned to Cincinnati, thereby proving that she could go up stream as well as down. In November, the river having risen, the New Orleans safely crossed the falls. She entered the Mississippi just about the time of the New Madrid earthquake, and arrived at Natchez in December, where she took on her first freight and passengers — she had been built for the Natchez and New Orleans trade — and arrived at New Orleans on the day before Christmas, 1811. The New Orleans at once regularly entered the Natchez trade, and until she was sunk by striking a snag in the winter of 1814, ran regularly between the two places, making a great deal of money for her owners. On her first year's business she cleared $20,000 net — not bad on an investment of $38,000. Natchez at that time was the great depot on the Mississippi for the overland trade from the North and East.

In Kramer's Almanac in 1813 is given a letter describing a trip up the river on the New Orleans, in which it is said : —

"The present boat does business to real advantage, and is owned by Fulton & Livingston, of New York. She performs a regular route from Natchez to New Orleans in three days, and returns in four. The passage descending is $18, and ascending $25. I descended in the boat in March, 1812, in thirty-two hours."

The first experiment with steam in the navigation of the Western rivers created surprise and excitement, but it did not give complete satisfaction. The truth is that it was neither a perfect success, nor yet a failure. The growing commerce of the river demanded something better than the flat-boats and barges, and the merchants and mechanics of the valley having the necessary means and animated by the spirit of enterprise, did not hesitate to continue to experiment in the hope of finally solving the problem of steam navigation, the Mississippi and its tributaries. The experimental period lasted for five years. In that time nine expensive steamboats were built, and while each succeeding boat was a decided advance on that which preceded it, defects and improvements being suggested by practical experience, steam navigation was not regarded as an assured success until 1817, when the steamboat Washington made the trip from New Orleans to Louisville in twenty-five days. The trouble all along had been to stem the current successfully, and this trouble the indomitable pluck and energy of the merchants and the skill of the mechanics finally accomplished. With 1817, therefore, may be said to begin the era of successful steam navigation on the Mississippi.

The difficulty of vessels stemming the current of the river

induced those who were interested in steam navigation to suggest a system of relays such as Fulton and Livingston had
originally designed, the river being divided up into sections.
Then one boat was to run from Pittsburgh to Cincinnati, another from Cincinnati to Louisville, a third from Louisville to
Smithland, a fourth from Smithland to Natchez, and another
from Natchez to New Orleans, the passengers and freight to
be transferred at each point. This ingenious plan of continually loading and unloading was never carried out, for before
it had been perfected the problem of stemming the current
was solved. The Washington, to which this solution is due,
was the sixth boat built on the Mississippi River. She was a
high-pressure steamer, with four single-flue boilers, and was
built at Wheeling, in 1816. She left there July 5 and arrived
in New Orleans October 17, 1816. It was on her return trip
to Louisville that she demonstrated very clearly the possibility of ascending the river with steam. The trip of the Washington to Louisville was by far the most rapid made, up to
that day. The following is her record: Left New Orleans,
March 24; reached Natchez, March 29; reached mouth of
Arkansas River, April 5; reached Chickasaw Bluff (Memphis), April 7; reached New Madrid, April 10; reached mouth
of Ohio River, April 11; reached Falls of Ohio (Louisville),
April 17.

The trip of the Washington established another point of the
very greatest advantage to the river country — that the Mississippi was the heritage of the people and could not be monopolized by any one. A company had been formed, at the
head of which were Fulton and Livingston, who had made the
first experiments with steam on the Ohio and Mississippi. This
company obtained from the Louisiana legislature an act giving
them the exclusive right of navigating the waters of Louisiana with steam-vessels for fourteen years, with the privilege
of renewing their charter at the end of that time. Any one
violating this monopoly was subject to a fine of $500. The
company owned the Ætna, Vesuvius, and Orleans, and had
arranged for a system of transfers at Louisville. The trip of
the Washington to New Orleans was in defiance of this law,
and that steamboat was accordingly seized when she arrived at
"the Crescent City." The United States court swept away
the monopoly, declared that the river was the heritage of the
whole people, that the State of Louisiana could not control it
and give its navigation to any company or monopoly. This
decision naturally gave a great impetus to steamboat building,

and the next few years saw all the Ohio towns turning out steamboats.

At the end of 1813, there were, according to Kramer's Almanac, eleven steamboats in the whole country, three building about Pittsburgh to complete the line between that town and New Orleans, and one small boat to carry wheat and corn on the Monongahela. The closing career of the New Orleans was in carrying reinforcements and munitions to Jackson's army, just before the battle of New Orleans. In 1814, three years after her construction, the New Orleans was sunk by a snag. She was tied to the bank at night. The river fell, and in the morning, it was found that the boat was snagged.

Following the Comet came the Vesuvius built at Pittsburgh in April, 1814, by Robert Fulton. She was of 480 tons burden, and made the trip to Louisville, 767 miles, in sixty-seven hours, from Louisville to Natchez in one hundred and twenty five hours, and from Natchez to New Orleans in thirty-three, making the whole distance in two hundred and twenty-seven hours, or 9$\frac{1}{4}$ miles an hour, not bad speed when the circumstances are considered. The Vesuvius also figured at the battle of New Orleans.

In 1814 the fourth steamboat on the Mississippi, the Enterprise, was built at Brownsville, reaching New Orleans the latter part of December, just in time to be pressed into service at the battle of New Orleans. The Enterprise was the first boat to reach Cincinnati from New Orleans, getting there in 1815, in twenty-eight days. She was a small vessel of only 35 tons. Some idea of the times is given by the fact, that the price of passage on this boat from New Orleans to Cincinnati was $130, and from Cincinnati to Pittsburgh, $30.

RIVER TRAFFIC.

The river traffic of 1814 shows that the steamboats had so far made but little impression. Transportation by steamboat was still an experiment. There arrived at New Orleans that year:—

	Number.	Tonnage.
Flatboats	598 }	88,850
Barges	324 }	
Steamboats	21	2,098

These steamboats were three in number, the New Orleans, Vesuvius, and Enterprise. The steamboat tonnage of New Orleans was but little over 2 per cent. of the total.

The sea-going vessels, leaving New Orleans that year, numbered 351, of 81,180 tons, as follows: Ships, 188; brigs, 95; schooners, 52.

The principal products received from the interior were as follows: —

Articles.		Quantity.
Cotton	bales	58,220
Corn	bushels	116,872
Flour	barrels	73,820
Sugar	hogsheads	11,640
Molasses	gallons	482,500
Pork	barrels	7,226
Rice	do	7,500
Tafia	gallons	142,800
Tobacco	hogsheads	6,210
Whisky	barrels	16,200

In 1815 still another steamer, the Buffalo, was built at Pittsburgh, which Livingston and Fulton proposed to run to the Falls of the Ohio, where she could connect with their large steamer Vesuvius, from New Orleans.

A curious fact, in regard to the river and its tributaries at this time, is, that the navigable streams are estimated as of so much greater extent than to-day. Notwithstanding the fact that the Federal Government has been at work improving many of them, the mileage considered opened to navigation in the year 1816 was much greater then, than now. In a book published at this time the total extent of rivers tributary to the Mississippi, entirely within the area of Louisiana, is estimated at 5,762 miles, double what it is to-day. Indiana is put down for 2,487 miles of tributary streams, Illinois, 3,094; Kentucky, 2,487, and Mississippi 2,902, a total of these five States of 13,732 miles of navigation, whereas, they are estimated to-day, as possessing only 7,650 miles. Streams never used by vessels now were then regarded as navigable because, during certain seasons of high water they were able to float flat-boats out to the main river, the produce being thus carried to market.

The return trade, that is a supply of the articles of European make, still came principally by way of the East from New York, Philadelphia, and Baltimore overland from Pittsburgh. Nor did the discovery of steam as a motive power for river boats cause much change. New Orleans increased its shipments up the river when a better means of stemming the current was discovered, but the bulk of its shipments were cheap and heavy products. The Southern States received supplies of Western produce, pork, grain, flour, etc.; the Western towns, like Cincinnati and Saint Louis, coffee, sugar, etc. The trade in dress goods, and the finer manufactured articles was mainly with the East. Thanks to steamboats, however, the business of New Orleans in this direction, although much less than it ought to be, considering its receipts of produce, showed great increase, and one singular fact is observable in this trade, showing how much influence the origin of a people will have upon their commerce. With the exception of some Philadelphians, who established themselves in New Orleans just before the purchase of Louisiana, a majority of its merchants, particularly the importers, were Creole or French, who preferred to get their goods from France rather than from England. As a result, the Kentuckians and Tennesseans of seventy years ago were supplied from New Orleans, mainly, with French print, broadcloths, and other dress goods, whereas the bulk of the people on the Atlantic wore almost wholly the produce of British looms. The early French influence made itself felt throughout the Lower Mississippi Valley until about the time of the outbreak of the war, and in many portions of the river country the demand was for French rather than English goods.

CHAPTER XXXVI.

IMMIGRATION INTO THE MISSISSIPPI VALLEY.

IT was just about the time of the discovery of steam as a motive power for steamboats that a new tide of immigration started from the Atlantic coast to the river country. There had been a rapid growth of the population of the valley from the date of the purchase of Louisiana, but between 1810 and 1820 that movement received a new impetus — probably due to the war of 1812. This movement went down the Ohio and into all the region tributary to it and to the Mississippi, both the upper and the lower portions. The immigrant guide-books of those days — of which there were many — declare the river route preferable, as being cheaper, more rapid, and more satisfactory than traveling across the country where there were few, if any roads. The river bottoms both of the Ohio and Mississippi Rivers were then regarded as very unhealthy and dangerous sections, and the immigrant was advised not to start on his trip until in the fall, after the frosts had killed the malaria. The guide-books describe the rivers as being very unpleasant during the summer season, with offensive odors coming from the shores. The immigrants were also warned against drinking river water before filtering or boiling it. On flat-boats and pine rafts, the latter being deemed the better plan, thousands of settlers drifted down the rivers each year, and in the short space of a decade the population of the Mississippi Valley doubled.

RECEIPTS OF PRODUCE.

The receipts of New Orleans during the first year of successful steam navigation, 1816, amounted in value to $8,062,-540. The character of produce received will furnish an excellent comparison for subsequent years by showing the lines of goods in which a trade was developed.

Articles.		Quantity.
Apples	barrels	4,253
Beef	do	2,459
Beans	do	439
Bagging	pieces	2,579
Bacon and hams	cwts	1,800
Butter	pounds	509
Candles	boxes	358

Articles.		Quantity.
Cheese	cwts	80
Cider	barrels	646
Cordage	cwts	400
Cordage baling	coils	4,798
Corn	bushels	13,775
Corn-meal	barrels	1,075
Cotton	bales	37,871
Flaxseed oil	barrels	85
Flour	do	97,419
Ginseng	do	957
Hair	bundles	356
Hemp-yarn	reels	1,095
Hides	number	5,000
Horses	number	375
Hogs	do	500
Lead	cwts	5,500
White lead	barrels	188
Linens, coarse	pieces	2,500
Lard	barrels	2,458
Oats	bushels	4,065
Paper	reams	750
Peltries	packages	2,450
Pork	barrels	9,725
Potatoes	do	3,750
Powder	do	294
Saltpeter	cwts	175
Soap	boxes	1,538
Tallow	cwts	160
Tobacco	hhds	7,282
Manufactured	barrels	711
Tobacco	carrots	8,200
Whisky	gallons	320,000
Bear-skins	number	2,000

Besides horned cattle, indigo, muskets, grindstones, pecan nuts, and beans.

This is independent of the produce raised in Louisiana, such as cotton, corn, indigo, molasses, rice, sugar, tafia or rum, and lumber. These were brought to the market in the planters' crafts, and often taken from the plantation direct in foreign-bound vessels, a ship loading directly with sugar and molasses, which thus never went through New Orleans. But little account was taken of this system in the commercial reports of the time, although sea-going vessels ascended the river as far as Natchez for cargoes. They were, of course, of small size, of but little more tonnage and draught than the steamboats themselves.

The value of receipts shows to what extent the produce of the West passed through New Orleans. Cotton, which in later days rose to be 60 and even 75 per cent. in value of all the receipts, was then barely 12 per cent. At least 80 per cent of the articles came from the West, that is, from the Ohio and the Upper Mississippi, above the Ohio. They represented the surplus products of the Mississippi Valley, for but little found any other exit to market. Much of the produce shipped from the West to New Orleans was lost en route. A rough estimate places the loss from disasters, snags, etc., at 20 per cent. Many boats, moreover, stopped along the river on their way down to sell supplies to the planters. Thus, at Natchez, flour, grain, and pork were purchased from the Kentucky boats.

From these losses and sales the shipments down the river in 1816, including the products of Louisiana, may be estimated at $13,875,000.

The river traffic required 6 steamboats, 594 barges, and 1,287 flat-boats, of a total tonnage of 87,670.

The effect of the use of steamboats in the river trade was soon seen in a large increase in the shipments of produce. The value of the receipts at New Orleans shows the following advance in the next half-dozen years : —

VALUE OF PRODUCE RECEIVED AT NEW ORLEANS FROM THE INTERIOR.

Years.	Amount.
1815–16	$ 9,749,253
1816–17	8,773,379
1817–18	13,501,036
1818–19	16,771,711
1819–20	12,637,079
1820–21	11,967,067

From 1802 the down commerce of the lower river had grown in 1818, sixteen years, more than fourfold. The trade up the river during the same period had been multiplied threefold.

The year succeeding the introduction of steamboats, 1817, New Orleans chronicled a large increase in its receipts of produce, as follows : —

Articles.		Quantity.
Cotton	bales	59,826
Sugar	hogsheads	10,642
Molasses	gallons	486,320
Tobacco	hogsheads	7,412
Do	carrots	9,862
Flour	barrels	95,325
Rice	do	9,820
Beans	do	3,896
Beef	do	5,122
Pork	do	4,382
Bacon	pounds	718,382
Bagging	pieces	9,825
Whisky	gallons	262,338
Gin	do	50,250
Tafia (rum)	gallons	18,600
Beer	barrels	826

Articles.		Quantity.
Cider	barrels	925
Apples	do	562
Potatoes	do	5,642
Lard	pounds	256,600
Soap	boxes	9,860
Candles	do	2,200
Castings	kettles, etc.	226,000
Lead	cwts	6,213
Bark	cords	4,000
Tar	barrels	6,580
Pitch	do	3,263
Hogs	number	1,227

The receipts for the following year show an improvement in nearly all lines, and a greater variety in the class of articles received, or at least noticed, for in these first commercial reports many products were altogether overlooked : —

Articles		Quantity.
Beans	barrels	3,643
Cotton	bales	65,223
Sugar	hogsheads	21,115
Bacon	cwts	18,620
Pork	hogsheads	813
Do	barrels	22,225
Bark	cords	4,000
Beef	barrels	5,142
Beer	do	306
Butter	kegs	1,825
Candles	boxes	2,150
Cider	barrels	520
Corn	bushels	145,200
Cordage	cwts	4,350
Flour	barrels	197,620
Gin	gallons	50,250
Ginseng	barrels	1,200
Hay	tons	40
Hides	sides	6,200
Hogs		1,200
Lard	barrels	412
Lard	cwts	6,738
Molasses	gallons	1,126,500
Oil	barrels	4,200
Onions	barrels	4,220
Paper	reams	426
Peltries	packages	3,550
Pitch	barrels	3,200
Rice	do	9,265
Skins, bear's	number	3,000
Soap	boxes	2,576
Starch	do	125
Tafia	gallons	42,026
Tallow	cwts	206
Tar	barrels	837
Tobacco	hogsheads	8,642
Do	carrots	1,600
Tobacco, manufactured	boxes	154
Wax, bee's	cwts	320
Wheat	bushels	95,650
Whisky	gallons	256,610

This includes, it will be seen, the produce of Louisiana as well as that of the upper country. The Louisiana products amount in value to 28 per cent of the whole. Of the remainder, fully 61 per cent. come from what is known as the West. In the last few days of Spanish rule in Louisiana over 40 per cent. in value of the receipts at New Orleans had come from that colony. The West was rapidly increasing in population, and New Orleans was securing all the new trade thus opened. It was as much a Western as a Southern city.

The commerce of the upper States was monopolized by the Americans. Indeed, before the colony was purchased by the United States a large proportion of the merchants of New Orleans were citizens of that country. The first American merchants had come from Philadelphia, and the commercial interests of New Orleans and the Mississippi Valley were in consequence more closely allied for years with " the Quaker City."

STEAMBOAT BUILDING.

From the day that the problem of successful steam navigation not only down the stream with the current, but up stream, was solved by the Washington, steamboat building was actively carried on, and new steamers were added each year to the river fleet.

The steamer Ramapo was built in New York in 1820. She was originally a schooner of 146 tons burden. She had a low-pressure engine, and was the first boat to run between New Orleans and Baton Rouge. The Manhattan, of 426 tons, was built also in New York, and had low-pressure engines. She ran for several years between New Orleans and Louisville. The Feliciana, 407 tons, low-pressure, was built in Philadelphia, and was the first regular packet to Bayou Sara. In 1821 the Mobile, 145 tons, low-pressure, was built at Amesbury, Mass., to run between New Orleans and Mobile. The United States, 645 tons, was built at New Albany. She was floated to this city for her machinery, which had been received from England. She was the wonder of her day, and was called The Mammoth. She was not a paying investment, owing to her complicated machinery. The Car of Commerce, 221 tons, was built at Freeport, Pa. She was considered remarkable in her day, having made the run to Shawneetown in twelve days. The Henry Clay, built at Newport, Ky., and the Paragon, built at Cincinnati, were also fast, making Louisville in sixteen days. The Mississippi, 372 tons, was built at Blakely, Ala., in 1820. Capt. H. S. Buckner was her commander. Finding her too heavy and unwieldy for the lake trade, Captain Buckner brought her around and ran her to points on the Mississippi.

Besides the above boats mentioned there was built the Eclipse, Phœnix, Florence, Scioto, Pennsylvania, Andrew Jackson, Fanny, Caledonia, Fidelity, Mars, Leopard, Bell Creole, Swan, Superior, Venture, Natchez, Robert Fulton, Balize, Spartan, Magnet, Steubenville, Missouri, Rambler, General Pike, Fayette, Rob Roy, Paul Chase, Robert Emmet, Belvidere, George Washington, William Penn, Bolivar, Congress, General Wayne, Tecumseh, Paul Jones, Tuscumbia, Philadelphia, Hibernia, Hercules, Commerce, Aerial, Liberator, Planter, Helen McGregor, Post Boy, Marietta, Louisville, Columbia, Huntress, General Coffee, Virginia, Ontario, Decatur, Lexington, Messenger, Governor Hamilton, Dolphin, Patriot, Emerald. The Fanny was a schooner propelled by steam. The Natchez was built at New York. Capt. H. S. Buckner bought and run her to Natchez. She made the run there in three days. The Hercules and Post Boy were tow boats between New Orleans and the Balize.

The three packet-boats were the Paul Jones, Tecumseh, and Philadelphia. They were single-engine boats, and their time to Louisville was twelve days.

In 1821 there arrived at New Orleans —

387 steamboats of a tonnage of..54,120
And flat-boats, barges, etc., of a tonnage of 52,750

This made the total river tonnage 106,870. The barges and flat-boats had fallen off both in numbers and tonnage, and the steamboats were in a lead that they have since kept.

Within a decade the steamboat had firmly established itself on the river, and was an acknowledged success.

The *Louisiana Advertiser* speaks as follows on the subject in 1823:—

" It is now nine years since the first steamboat was evolved at the port of New Orleans, since which period up to the present time eighty-nine different steamboats have been evolved at this port. The first boat was lost in 1814, and up to the present time there have been twenty-three other boats lost, either by sinking, destroyed by fire, decayed or condemned, forming in the aggregate about 4,000 tons, and leaving a balance, say, of 14,000 tons. This 14,000 tons does not employ more than 1,000 men and can do more in a given time than 50,000 tons could have done in barges, keel-boats, or any other kind of vessels employed ten years ago with 20,000 hands. The rapid increase of steamboats had very soon the natural tendency of reducing freights, and, although the owners suffer severely from this cause in the consequent diminution in the value of the vessels, yet the country at large has been greatly benefited by their introduction, and it is to be hoped the number in existence can be more beneficially employed."

The amount of products that descended the Ohio during this time was estimated at 68,932 tons.

Of the goods that went down the Lower Mississippi, one-half came from the Ohio and its tributaries. Indeed, up to this time the settlements in the West and South had been restricted mainly to the Ohio basin, and comparatively few persons had yet established themselves on the Lower or Upper Mississippi, or on the Missouri, Arkansas, White, or other tributaries on the west.

It cannot, however, be said that they were a success or proved themselves equal to the emergencies of the river. There was a decided disposition in the early days of the river navigation to follow too closely the habit of the sea, and to pretend that the Mississippi was an interior ocean. The captains, for instance, having been accustomed when at sea to issue their orders through a trumpet, necessary there, to make them heard in the roar of the waves and the storm, still insisted upon using the trumpet upon the quiet waters of the Mississippi, and shouted stentoriously through the trumpet at their mates but a few feet distant, with all the worst nautical oaths and expressions. It was not until years afterwards that the simple process of giving orders by means of bells was adopted.

The boats were small compared to those which now do the carrying trade of Western rivers. Indeed, there does not seem to have been a very great increase in their size for many years. It is mentioned by reliable authority that as late as 1846 the smallest boats were about 120 tons burden, and the largest, not more than 500 tons. The largest boats now are from 2,500 to 3,000 tons burden. Although the increase in the size of boats was slow, great pains were taken to make them attractive to passengers. The travel on the river was then very large and profitable, and it became necessary to cater to the wants of the traveling public. The saloons were elegantly furnished, and the table was provided with every delicacy which the season and the market afforded.

The accommodations and comforts of the boats of a quarter a century and more ago are still remembered and spoken of in glowing terms. They were no doubt very superior for those times, but they were hardly equal to those of the boats of the present day. The wants of the traveling public are greater now than then and their tastes more luxurious.

It is somewhat strange to hear the papers talk of the great cheapening of freights caused by the first steamboats, when we learn the rates from points above to New Orleans in 1819 was 3 cents a pound; a few years previous they had ranged from 4 to 6 cents. Passage by steamboat from Louisville to New Orleans was $100 when money was worth twice what it is to-day. Deck passage was $18, but the economical passenger could make it less by helping to wood the boat at the wood-yards scattered along the bank.

The flat-boats on the river increased in size with the steamboats. About four-fifths of them reached New Orleans, the others being lost en route or selling out at some way town. The hay flat-boats of Indiana of 1820-26 were 50 feet long, 16 feet wide, and carried about 30 tons of hay, ranging in price from $15 to $30. In 1832-33 the size of these boats began to increase; one 90 feet long and 18 wide, carrying 102 tons, cost $170 to build. They finally reached the size of 150 feet long by 24 wide, carrying 300 tons of produce. Flat-boats, when run to New Orleans for years, were broken up and houses built of them, the gunwales being cut up, and the streets and sidewalks paved with them. Some time between 1855 and 1860 the boats began to be towed back from all the ports along the river, especially the coal-boats and coal barges. The empty boats sold in New Orleans for from $30 to $200, increasing in price from $30 up to $200 in 1861, when the war stopped flat-boating. The price of hands to go down on flat-boats from Aurora to New Orleans was $10 to $30 per trip, the pilots usually receiving from $50 to $200. This was the price from the commencement of boating to the commencement of the war.

In the early days of boating, boatmen received gold and silver for their produce. Later they received gold, silver, and United States paper, and in bringing home their gold and silver, they messed together and put their money in a barrel, and one stood watch over it at a time, day and night, on the deck of a steamboat, as nearly all boatmen traveled " on deck."

Nearly half the cotton, all the tobacco and most of the provisions came through the Ohio. The Upper Mississippi furnished most of the furs and skins, the lead, etc.; the Lower Mississippi cotton, sugar, molasses, etc.

Of these products, the majority came from the Ohio basin,

14

then the most thickly settled part of the Mississippi Valley. Taking the period 1822–26 as a basis, the following would be about the proportion of the traffic enjoyed by the several districts constituting the great valley: —

Ohio basin..49
Upper Mississippi... 9
Lower Mississippi...42

These dry statistics tell the story of the settlement of the Mississippi Valley, its civilization, development and advance and the commercial changes that have taken place in it. The deer skins, the venison hams, the bear oil, peltries and furs, which form so important an article in the early receipts, soon disappear to give place to agricultural and afterwards to manufactured products. During the days of the French dominion the most important exports of the valley were the produce of the chase. Next came rough lumber for the manufacture of sugar boxes for Cuba; then raw agricultural products; afterwards articles like pork, flour and others that required some process of treatment. As yet the manufactured articles exported were few, being of the simplest character, such as bagging, rope, twine, candles.

PRINCIPAL SHIPPING TOWNS.

At this date the most important lines of trade — those requiring the most vessels — were with Nashville, Bayou La Fourche, Natchez and Louisville. Natchez was a more important river point than Vicksburg, being the center of a populous district, and gave employment to three times as many steamboats. Nashvillle, as the center of the rich tobacco country of Tennessee and Kentucky, sent more steamboats to New Orleans than any town in that section. On the Ohio, Louisville was the most important point, very few steamers ascending higher on account of the falls. If a steamer went above Louisville she generally continued up to Pittsburgh.

The Saint Louis and Upper Mississippi River trade with New Orleans was as yet insignificant, but few persons having penetrated into that region. On the Tennessee River boats ran as high as Florence, but when the water rose flat-boats poured out by the hundred, laden with the cotton of north Alabama and the tobacco of Tennessee.

On the Mississippi the other most important shipping points besides Natchez were Bayou Sara and Baton Rouge. Vessels ran up the Ouachita, but no higher up the Red than Natchitoches on account of the raft.

The flat-boats came from all the upper country. The great majority of them were from the Ohio and its tributary. The Cumberland and Tennessee sent out hundreds laden with cotton and tobacco, the Ohio proper with apples, corn, flour, coal, etc. A majority of the flats at this time were from the Southern States, but this soon changed, and Indiana and Ohio were in the lead. The flat-boat traffic, except that of the districts immediately around New Orleans, was confined to a few months of the year. The boats waited for a rise in the river and came down with the high water. During January and February two-thirds of the flats arrived in New Orleans, as many as 75 in a single week. The flat-boats were cheaply made, and were broken up and sold for lumber in the city. Keel-boats were going rapidly out of favor. The up-freight of the river was much smaller than that down, and the steamboats could easily handle all of it; hence the keel-boats were superfluous and were no longer needed to carry freight up the country. A few still ran in the rivers of Arkansas and some of the States west of the Mississippi, but they were disappearing. The batonux were altogether gone, save in the very wildest and most rugged portions of the Indian country, and but few of these arrived at New Orleans, with their cargoes of deer and bear skins. The market-boats were of the flat-boat order, dropping down the river from point to point, and trading, selling the planters and farmers Western provisions or trading it off for cotton and the products of the country.

The sugar, rice, etc., of the country immediately around New Orleans was brought to the city in pirogues, skiffs or boats made from solid logs. Each planter had his boat, and, although it was small, he could send his crop to market in it — a few hogsheads or bales at a time. But little record was kept of these arrivals at New Orleans, and hence the earlier records, while showing accurately how much corn, beef and other produce of the Upper Mississippi Valley was received, gave no record whatever of the receipts of Louisiana sugar, molasses or rice. A striking incident of the river commerce of those days was the large number of sailing vessels, sloops, schooners, and afterwards luggers, engaged in it. Nearly all the produce of the country below New Orleans was brought to the city in this way: and the sailing vessels ran even as high as Natchez, bringing down cotton and sugar from "the upper coast."

In 1825, nine years after the success of the steamboat, it had passed all competition, and the greater portion of the produce of the lower Mississippi Valley was brought to market

in it. In 1826 57 per cent. of the freight was carried to New
Orleans by the steamboats and only 43 per cent. by other
means.

The following arrivals during the season 1825–26 (the
commercial year then began in New Orleans and throughout
the South October 1; it has since been changed to September
1) gives some idea of the variety of crafts employed upon
the river: —

ARRIVALS IN 1825–26.

Class.	Number.
Steamboats....	715
Flat-boats.......	981
Keel-boats........	57
Schooners and sloops........	108
Pirogues	101
Market-boats	25
Bateaux........	13
Total........	2,000

While the steamboats had greatly increased in number —
threefold in four years — it will be seen that they had not yet
driven out the flat-boat. Quite the contrary. The flat-boats
also had increased largely. On the other hand, there was a
material falling off in the number of keel-boats in use. The
flat-boats were cheap, offered a cheap means of carrying
bulky freight to markket, and, moreover, they carried out a
great deal of produce from the smaller streams where the
steamboats could not go or where they did not care to take
the risk of snags and sawyers.

The average tonnage of the river vessels in 1831 was 240
tons, and of the sea-going vessels running from New Orleans,
437. The steamboats, however, were constantly and rapidly
increasing in size, whereas the sea-going vessels increased
more slowly, so that in 1845 the two were about the same
tonnage, and a ship could carry away from New Orleans just
the cargo that one steamboat could bring there.

LOSSES ON THE RIVER.

From the very start the steamboats had met with many
disasters. The sixth boat built for the river traffic, constructed at Brownsville in 1815, ran aground on her way
down the river and burst her boiler — a disaster by which ten
or twelve lives were lost.

Even more disastrous were the snags with which both the
Ohio and the Mississippi were filled. An appeal was made to

Congress in 1820 to remove them, but it declined to take any action.

From 1822 to 1827 the loss in the Ohio and Mississippi Rivers by snags alone, including steam and flat-boats and their cargoes, amounted to $1,362,500. From 1827 to 1832, when quite a number of snags were removed, these losses were greatly reduced, and did not exceed $381,000. In the latter year, 1832, in consequence of the successful working of the snag-boats, not a single boat was lost.

From 1833 to 1838 the Secretary of the Treasury reported that 40 steamboats had been snagged on the Mississippi, and damage inflicted amounting to fully $640,000. This was probably far below the true figures.

In 1839 the total loss of boats in the river was 40, of which 2 were snagged, 7 struck on rocks and other obstructions, the total loss amounting to $448,000.

The first steps taken by the Government to improve the navigation of the river were in 1829, when Captain Shreve, a prominent steamboat man, was employed to remove the snags which had caused such a heavy loss of vessels. The system pursued in their removal was to run down the snags with a double steamboat, the bows of which were protected with heavy beams plated with iron. A heavy head of steam was put on and the snags run down.

Captain Shreve did good work with this improvement, but he followed it up soon afterwards with a very unfortunate improvement that has given trouble ever since. Filled with the idea generally current at the time that it would be well to straighten out the river and shorten navigation, a channel was cut across one of the great bends just above the mouth of Red River, by which a distance of 30 miles was saved. This was known as Shreve's cut-off. Five days afterwards bars were formed at the mouth of Red River, at both entrances of the bend, leaving only 3 feet on one and 3½ on the other. On these bars dredge-boats were brought to work, but the bars have proved troublesome to this day.

RIVER TRADE OF NEW ORLEANS, 1813–1841.

Year ending September 30.	Arrivals of steam boats.	Freight received.*	Value of produce.†
		Tons.	
1818–14	21	67,560	....
1814–15	40	77,220	....
1815–16	....	94,560	$9,749,253
1816–17	....	86,820	8,773,379
1817–18	....	100,880	13,501,036
1818–19	191	186,300	16,771,711
1819–20	198	106,706	12,637,079
1820–21	202	99,320	11,967,067
1821–22	287	136,400	15,126,420
1822–23	392	129,500	14,473,795
1823–24	436	136,240	15,063,820
1824–25	502	176,420	19,044,640
1825–26	608	193,300	20,446,320
1826–27	715	235,200	21,730,887
1827–28	698	257,300	22,886,420
1828–29	756	245,700	20,757,265
1829–30	989	260,900	22,065,518
1830–31	778	307,300	26,044,820
1831–32	813	244,600	21,806,763
1832–33	1,280	291,700	28.238,432
1833–34	1,081	327,800	29,820,817
1834–85	1,005	399,900	37,566.842
1835–36	1,272	437,100	39,237,762
1836–37	1,372	401,500	43,515,403
1837–38	1,549	449,600	45,627,720
1838–39	1,551	399,500	42,263,880
1839–40	1,573	537,400	49,763,825
1840–41	1,958	542,500	49,822,115

During all this period, and despite all these difficulties, the number of arrivals at New Orleans and the amount of river business on the Lower Mississippi continued to steadily increase. The growth of the river traffic is well shown in this table.

In regard to the steamboats, it should be remembered that the steady increase in arrivals each year does not fully express the increase in tonnage, because the boats were not only growing more numerous, but were increasing in size each year, and thus while they doubled in number between 1825 and 1833 they more than trebled in their carrying capacity.

In regard to the flat-boats and other craft, there is no sufficiently definite information for most of this period. It should

* This does not include articles rafted down of which no record was kept.
† This includes the small amount of produce received by Lake Pontchartrain, from 1 to 6 per cent. of total. It is impossible to separate it from the receipts by river, since no separate account was kept, except for cotton and a few other articles.

be said, however, that while the steamboats supplanted the flat-boats in many lines of trade, they did not entirely drive them off the river for fifteen or twenty years afterwards. During all this period when the Western cities were building steamboats, the flat-boats also were increasing in numbers. They were found serviceable in carrying hay, coal, etc., and in reaching the interior streams. The Mississippi counted some hundreds of tributaries. On some of these the settlements were sparse, and the surplus products afforded at best one or two cargoes a year, and these were sent much more conveniently and cheaply in flat-boats than in steamers. The steamers had passed the flats between 1820 and 1830 in the business transacted and the freight handled, and from this time they increased the lead steadily. The number of flats, however, arriving at New Orleans kept but little, if any, behind the steamers, and as late as 1840 nearly a fifth of the freight handled in the Lower Mississippi went by flat-boat, keel, or barge. The early flat-boats had depended altogether on the current of the river to carry them down. The system of towing was tried in 1829, and a small steamer, which would be called a tug to-day, was successfully used in towing keel-boats up and down stream. The idea did not seem, however, to meet with much favor, the flat-boat men having a superstition that their conjunction with a steamer was not favorable to them, and it was reserved for a later generation to definitely try in the barge the system of towing freight up and down stream.

In but little more than a quarter of a century the steamboat had secured a practical monopoly of the traffic of the Mississippi, and developed an interior commerce of immense proportions. It was during this period that the river country fared its best. Between 1830 and 1840 the river cities increased rapidly in population, wealth, and trade, and New Orleans, the port of the valley, advanced more rapidly than any city in America. The commerce of the river — and all its commerce was carried on the Mississippi, except an infinitesimal amount that came through Lake Pontchartrain and the Carondelet Canal.*

STEAMBOAT DISASTERS.

From the very first day that steamboats had begun to navigate the Mississippi they had met with accidents during their

---

* Imported through Lake Pontchartrain.

first forty years.   The following total of losses are counted against them: —

GREAT TOTALITY AND LOSS OF LIFE.

	Lost.
1810 to 1820	3
1820 to 1830	37
1830 to 1840	184
1840 to 1850	272
Boats, the dates of whose loss is unknown	576
Total in forty years	1,070
Tonnage	85,256
Cost	$7,113,940
Killed at accidents	2,299
Wounded	1,881
Killed and wounded	4,180

Of the accidents, 166 boats were destroyed by fire, 209 by explosion, 45 by collision.

In 1840 the number of boats snagged was 21, valued at $330,000.   In 1841 the number snagged was 29; loss, $464,-000; in 1842, 68.   In one month of that year 11 vessels were lost between Saint Louis and the mouth of the Ohio, a dif-tance of only 175 miles, the loss being $234,000.   In the sev-enteen months succeeding 72 boats were lost, valued at $1,200,000.   In 1846 36 vessels were lost, of which 24 were by snags, sunken rocks, or logs; damage, $697,500 ; lives lost, 166.   In consequence of these many accidents the cost of run-ning a vessel on the river was estimated at three times that on the lakes.   In his report to the Memphis convention, in 1845, Mr. Calhoun estimated the loss of steamers on the Western water ways at 11 per cent. of the entire number, the average life of a vessel being only nine years.   In the six years be-tween 1840 and 1846 no less than 225 steamboats were lost on the Western water ways, an average of 56 per year.   The record of 1846 is bad enough.

Steamboats lost, 1846	120
Snagged	46
Sunk	38
Burst boilers	16
Collision	15
Destroyed by fire	13
Shipwreck	10
Cut down by ice	7

The following gives the actual losses in life of two average seasons of river business: —

Years.	Number of accidents.	Number of killed.	Number of wounded.
1853	31	319	158
1854	48	587	228

The most active year in steamboat business and the one ✝ ᵀ
chronicling the heaviest losses was that immediately preceding the war.
The following is the record for 1860:

Number steamboats destroyed and damaged..............................299
Number canal-boats and barges..................................... 48
Coal and flat-boats..... 208
Steamboats totally destroyed................... 120
Causes of disasters:—
Sunk.. 111
Burned..... 81
Exploded... 19
Collisions... 24
Snagged and damaged... 44

RAPID GROWTH OF NEW ORLEANS.

While the Mississippi Valley was listening at the Memphis convention to the story of its glories to come, and river men were calculating on the immense traffic that was assured the future, New Orleans was confident of the future. Few of its people anticipated any danger of its future and it was predicted not only in American papers but in the *British Quarterly Review* that it must ultimately become, on account of the Mississippi, the most important commercial city in America, if not in the world.

That eminent statistical and economical authority, *Debow's Review*, declared that " no city of the world has ever advanced as a mart of commerce with such gigantic and rapid strides as New Orleans."

It was no idle boast.　Between 1830 and 1840 no city of the ⅃ ⅃ United States kept pace with it.　When the census was taken it was fourth in population, exceeded only by New York, Philadelphia and Baltimore, and third in point of commerce of the ports of the world, exceeded only by London, Liverpool, and New York, being indeed, but a short distance behind the latter city, and ahead of it in the export of domestic products.　Unfortunately, its imports were out of all proportion with its exports.　It shipped coffee, hardware, and other heavy articles like this up the river, but it left the West dependent on New York and the other Atlantic cities for nearly all the finer class of manufactured goods they needed.

Later on, when the West began to go into manufacturing itself, and Cincinnati and Pittsburgh became important manufacturing centers, New Orleans imported their goods and reshipped them to the plantations.　Of these shipments upstream over 75 per cent., strange to say, were articles which had previously been sent down-stream.　Cincinnati sent its

lard, candles, pork, etc., to New Orleans to be carried up by
the coast packets to Bayou Sara and Baton Rouge. From
these latter towns were shipped so many hogsheads of sugar
and barrels of molasses to New Orleans to be thence sent by
the Cincinnati boats to the Ohio metropolis. There was no
trade between the Western cities and Southern plantations, very
little even with the towns; it all paid tribute to New Orleans.

SHIPMENTS OF COTTON TO OTHER POINTS.

The upper Mississippi had from 1850 become the center of
immigration and production, and New Orleans, which had
formerly depended on the Ohio River country almost wholly
for its supplies, now largely got them from Saint Louis.
About 1850 the traffic with Saint Louis exceeded that with
Cincinnati. In 1859, 32 steamboats of 48,726 tons were required for the Saint Louis and 36 of 26,932 tons for the
Cincinnati trade.

Next in importance to New Orleans among the lower river
towns was Memphis, which had steadily increased its traffic,
as follows: —

1851	$ 4,978,000
1853	6,377,000
1854	8,266,500
1857	11,938,959

The boats landing at Memphis the latter year were: Steamboats, 2,279; flat-boats, 379; a total tonnage of 901,214. The
shipments were nearly entirely to New Orleans. There were
shipped 223,081 bales of cotton, of which 204,281 went south
to New Orleans, 786 north to Saint Louis, and 28,014 to the
Ohio River. The other shipments were wheat, flour, tobacco,
furs, peltries, etc.

Vicksburg had passed Natchez, the levying and settling of
the Yazoo delta having made it the point at which the cotton
floated down the Tallahatchie, Coldwater, Yalabusha, Sunflower, and Yazoo Rivers on flats was transferred to steamers.
The construction of the Southern Railroad to Jackson had
made it also the river port for the shipment of the cotton of
central Mississippi to market.

Natchez continued an important social center and the shipper of cotton in the rich districts of southwestern Mississippi.

Bayou Sara, as the most western point of sugar production
on the Mississippi, was the terminus of what is known as the
upper coast packets, and has continued so to this day.

Baton Rouge was important as the State capital of Louisina,
but its shipments of produce were small. Below Baton Rouge

the steamboats loaded directly from the plantations; the towns were small and of little commercial importance. During all this period the Mississippi River steamboat had improved in size, in speed, and in appearance. Discarding the idea of making the river craft like those of the sea, a new genus of vessel had developed, especially to the needs of the Mississippi and its tributaries, adapted to both passenger and freight traffic, of light draught and great speed, and good carrying capacity. Changes had been made from time to time in the machinery employed and in the shape and appearance of the boat until finally a standard was reached that has been changed little in the last half century.

The first boat with a saloon and state-rooms, was applauded by the press as luxurious in the extreme. These cabins were steadily improved until they became really the equal of the finest ocean steamers on the Atlantic. The passenger business of the steamboats was very large; indeed, they carried all the passengers in the Mississippi Valley, and it was one of the surest sources of profit.

In size there had been a steady advance. In 1839 but 9 steamers on the Mississippi were over 500 tons, and 13 between 400 and ·500. The average tonnage of a steamboat was only 164. In 1846 108 steamboats were built a cost of $1,450,000 and of a tonnage of 51,660, an average of 479. One of these was a steamer of 887 tons, another of 750. They were built almost wholly on the Ohio River. Of the first 418 there were built at —

Pittsburgh...112
Cincinnati.. 70
Louisville, New Albany, and Jeffersonville........................... 55
Wheeling... 20

The others were at Brownsville, Marietta, Portsmouth, and other points.

RIVALRY BETWEEN WESTERN CITIES.

Although not relatively the most prosperous period in the history of river commerce, this period 1840–1860, is in the view of most steamboatmen, the flush time of river commerce. In these twenty years its volume had increased fivefold, and the steamboats had made a wonderful advance in beauty, size and ornamentation. If the railroads and canals had carried off some of the produce of the valley, the river towns still kept up a large traffic, and New Orleans, Cincinnati and Saint Louis competed with each other as to who should stand at the head of the list.

While the two latter sometimes passed New Orleans in the

GREAT ACTIVITY AMONG STEAMBOATS.

number of arrivals of steam vessels, in the tons of freight, and value of produce, the Crescent City was never distanced until war closed it to commerce. It had regular lines to all the important towns, Pittsburgh, Cincinnati, Louisville, and St. Louis, and it controlled, to a great extent, the commerce of the Tennessee, Cumberland, Arkansas, Red, Yazoo and other streams.

In the period 1840–1850 the steamers running between New Orleans and Louisville were the Gen. Brown, William French, Diana, Ed. Shippen, and others. Later on came the Bell Key, Bostona, Grace Darling, Peytona, Atlanta, Niagara, R. J. Ward, Eclipse, and Shotwell, with a tonnage of 1,200 tons.

Between New Orleans and the Tennessee River were the Huntsville, Knoxville, Mohican, Cherokee, Choctaw, East-port, and others which brought out 180,000 bales of cotton each year and 15,000 hogsheads of tobacco that afterwards found the way by rail to the Atlantic ports.

On the Cumberland were the steamers Old Hickory, Helen Kirkwood, Harry Hill, and Tennessee running to Nashville and bringing to New Orleans each year some 120,000 bales of cotton and 12,000 hogsheads of tobacco.

The Yorktown, Monarch, Duke of Orleans, and ten other vessels ran regularly between New Orleans and Cincinnati.

The lines to St. Louis included the George Collier, Auto-crat, Maria, Alex Scott, Hevry of the West, Meteor, Maria Denning, Imperial, E. J. Gay, Charles Chouteau, Illinois, and John Walsh.

The Memphis trade between 1848 and 1861 included the Bulletins No. 1 and No. 2, the John Semond, H. R. W. Hill, Ingomar, Prince of Wales, Ben Franklin, and other steamers, and brought down to the Gulf 325,000 bales of cotton.

The Ouachita river trade between 1850 and 1861 included the Rockaway and D. S. Stacey, Farmer, Paul Jones, Cora, Lizzie Simmons, R. W. Kimball, Frank Pargoud, and others, and brought out of the river and its tributaries 150,000 bales of cotton.

The Red River lines between 1848 and 1861 included the Caddo, Latonia, St. Charles, Compromise, H. M. Wright, R. W. Powell, R. W. Adams, B. L. Hodge, Duke, Grand Duke, and Dubloon. These steamers ran to Shreveport; other pack-ets running above to Jefferson, and above the raft which here impeded navigation.

Another line to Alexandria and Natchitoches included the
P. F. Kimball, Peter Dalena, Prota, and Rapides.

These vessels brought annually out of Red River some
250,000 bales of cotton and miscellaneous products of all kinds.

The Arkansas trade included the Gem, the Thirty-fifth Parallel, the Arkansas, which brought out some 150,000 bales of
cotton, running as high as Little Rock to Fort Smith in high
water, and sometimes even above that point into the Indian
Territory when the season was very favorable.

THE BEST YEAR ON THE RIVER.

· The season before the civil war (1859–60) was inaugurated
showed the largest receipts at New Orleans of produce and the
heaviest business the lower river has ever handled; indeed it
stands on record to this day as the maximum of river prosperity. The number of boats arriving at New Orleans was
not as great as in 1846–47, but the boats had in the meanwhile
more than doubled in size and the steam tonnage reaching
New Orleans was the largest that city ever saw and it has
never equaled it since. Nor was the total of value of the produce as high as in one or two subsequent years. On the other
hand, the prices of these latter years are the inflated prices of
a paper currency. Reduced to a gold basis they will not
amount to anything like the business of the year 1859–60,
which stands to this day the best on record in the Lower Mississippi. There reached New Orleans that season by river
2,187,560 tons of freight; and the total trade of the city in
the receipt and shipment of produce and in the export and
import coastwise or to foreign ports was: —

River trade $289,565,000
Ocean trade.. 183,725,000

Total................................. ....$473,290,000

Not only in its amount, but in the stretch of its river trade,
the season 1859–60 has never since been equaled. The arrivals of steamboats that season at New Orleans shows this,
and indicates the change in the river traffic that came in the
next quarter of a century: —

NUMBER OF STEAMBOATS ARRIVED AT NEW ORLEANS DURING THE SEASON
ENDING AUGUST 31, 1860.

Trade in which engaged.	Number.
Atchafayla River.....	29
Arkansas River.....	30
Barataria Bayou.....	30
Bœuf Bayou.....	12
Cairo.....	12

Trade in which engaged.	Number.
Cincinnati	206
Coast: Lower	180
Upper	605
Courtableau Bayou	91
Cumberland River	66
Des Glaises Bayou	16
Evansville	8
Grand River	8
Grosse-Tete Bayou	20
Greenville and Bends	118
La Fourche Bayou	90
Louisville	172
Macon and Tensas	83
Memphis	110
Ouachita River	224
Pittsburgh	526
Paducah	4
Red River	488
Saint Louis	472
Tennessee River	16
Teche Bayou	94
Vermillion Bayou	15
Vicksburg	211
Wheeling	9
White River	4
E. Yazoo	59
Other streams	22

BOATS BEING WITHDRAWN.

Of this trade, that of the Arkansas, White, Tennessee, and
Cumberland may be said to be entirely gone. To-day no vessels run up Bayou Vermillion or Grosse Tete. The Yazoo
trade is now transferred at Vicksburg instead of going direct
to New Orleans. Evansville, Paducah, and Wheeling are
ignorant of special New Orleans lines. The Cincinnati trade
has fallen off three-fourths. The Lafourche trade is less,
since many of the planters now send their goods by way of
the railroad. The same is true of the Teche, along which
stream now runs the Southern Pacific Railway. The Red
River trade is less than one-fourth what it was then. The
Texas and Pacific strikes the Red at Shreveport, Alexandria
and other points, and diverts a large traffic from it. The recently completed Vicksburg, Shreveport, and Pacific carries
a large amount of cotton across the country to Vicksburg, to
be thence distributed by railroad. The Red River is seldom
navigated above Shreveport, and whereas in those days vessels
ran through to Jefferson, and even to White Oak Shoals, this
is rare and almost unknown to-day. From the Ouachita and
its tributaries a considerable amount of cotton is taken by the
Vicksburg, Shreveport and Pacific at Monroe. The Greenville and Bend trade has dropped one-half in the last few

years. The Memphis trade does not call for one-fourth the vessels then in use. One line of steamers suffices for the traffic of Louisville and Cincinnati with New Orleans.

The only improvement perceptible is in the coal trade with Pittsburgh, which has greatly increased in tonnage and importance, and which defies all railroad competition; in the lower river traffic, which shows a slight advance in consequence of the increased production of the lower parishes; and in the barge and mainly the grain trade with St. Louis, which has been somewhat spasmodic, but which has grown to much larger proportions than it was at any time before the war.

The extent of the commercial area governed by the river traffic of New Orleans in 1860 will show what was lost in the four years of war that followed, and never fully regained.

CHAPTER XXXVII.

(From Internal Commerce of the U. S.)

HOW LEVEES ARE BUILT.

"THE first advent of the white man into the Mississippi Valley shows the necessity for levees or dikes of earth-work to prevent the low bottoms on both sides of the river from being overflowed. LaSalle found the banks under water at several points when he came down the river in 1684, and Bienville in his exploring expeditions similarly found them overflowed.

At several points on or near the river were mounds erected by the Indians presumedly as a refuge from extraordinary high water. One of the highest points encountered by Bienville during his explorations of the Mississippi in 1699–1700 was New Orleans. The Metaerie ridge which runs back of the city rises from 6 to 7 feet higher than the surrounding country, and the front land facing on the river, especially that extending from Bayou St. John forward, is high enough to escape the flood in ordinary years. It is to this fact that the selection of this location as the future capital of Louisiana was due. Seeing that the land here was out of water when nearly all the surrounding country was flooded, Bienville came to the conclusion that it was above overflow and selected it for the city which he had then in view.

The flood that he saw, however, was but a small one, the river not rising its usual height that year.

THE FIRST LEVEE.

The water of 1718 was much higher and interfered seriously
with the men employed in laying the foundations of New Orleans, they being compelled by it to stop work and devote
themselves to the construction of a rude levee in front of the
town and for some short distance above it, which sufficed to
keep it clear of water. This was the first levee in Louisiana,
and was constructed under the auspices of Sieur LeBlonde de
la Tour, chief of engineers of the colony and a Knight of St.
Louis. This levee was merely a temporary one, but answered
its purpose. It was worked on each successive year, raised
and strengthened from time to time, being finally completed
under Perrier in 1727. It then presented an 18-foot crown
and 60-foot base, and was 5,400 feet, or slightly over a mile,
in length. This was more than the city front, and was ample
protection to it. Above the city for 18 miles a smaller levee
was continued, and another extended 14 miles below, both for
the protection of farmers and of the city.

The country around New Orleans was settled, levees were
constructed, and by 1735 they extended a distance of 42 miles,
from English Turn, " *Détour des Anglais* " to 30 miles above
the city. With the exception of the New Orleans levee, however, they were low and weak and fell an easy victim to the
great flood of that year, which lasted from the latter part of
December to the end of June, 1736. The levees were broken
in many places and New Orleans flooded from the crevasses
above. The overflow caused great loss and damage and prevented the planting of much of the land, as the water did not
go down until so late a day. The levees were patched up, but
so little was done towards properly restoring them and cre-
vassses continued so frequent that the government took the
matter in hand and issued an edict requiring the owners of
land fronting on the river, and all the parties in the colony so
fronted to improve their levees and have them in good condition by January 1, 1744, under penalty of confiscation. This
stringent law seems to have accomplished its purpose, and for
the next half century Louisiana escaped with comparatively
little damage from overflow, and the levees were gradually
extended and became the basis of the present levee system of
the lower Mississippi Valley — indeed, it is possible that some
of them exist to this day in those sections where there has been
little change in the course of the river.

In 1752 the levees extended along the river front 20 miles

below and 30 above New Orleans, from Concession to near Bonnet Cerre. The levee system was excellent, and no breaks occurred; and however defective the government of the colony may have been in other matters at that time, when it passed through many financial depressions, there could be no doubt of the efficiency with which it guarded the levees. These were constructed by the inhabitants themselves, but the government reserved revisory power, and allowed no planter to neglect his embankment and endanger the safety of his neighbors. All the land protected by levees was under a high state of cultivation, and nearly the entire population of the colony was concentrated in this narrow limit of less than 200 square miles. The cost of levee building was relatively higher than it is now, the planter, having no facilities for this work; this caused the slow settlement of the country, as the expense of protecting new land from overflow was many times greater than the cost of buying and stocking it. The levee, however, continued to advance slowly northward at the rate of a mile a year. In 1782, 1785, and 1796 the river rose to a very great height, but the people escaped any serious damage from overflow. There were slight crevasses, it is true, and in 1780, 1785, 1791 and 1799 New Orleans was flooded from them. The last overflow, which was the worst, being a break in the Macarté Levee, just above the then city limits, but at what is now known as Carrollton, or the seventh municipal district of New Orleans. But little injury was caused by these breaks, as the levees were soon repaired. The districts not protected by levles suffered severely.

The flood of 1782 was the greatest ever encountered during the century in which Louisiana had been settled, and the water from the Mississippi overflowed the entire Attakapas and Opelousas regions, including all the country west of the Mississippi to the central prairies, only a few high points escaping.

In 1785 some of the lower levees were slightly injured, but no great harm done.

This experience firmly convinced the inhabitants of the efficacy of levees, and the work of building them was energetically continued. In 1812 they extended, on the east bank of the river, from Pointe a la Hache to Bayou Manchac, the dividing line between Louisiana and West Florida, a distance of 155 miles; and on the west bank from the lower Plaquemines settlement to Pointe Coupée, a distance of 185 miles. There were also a few levees on the west bank of the river, between the mouths of the Red and Arkansas Rivers, to protect the settle-

ments. The total length of levees in 1812, therefore, was
340 miles, which at the then cost of labor, most of it being slave
labor, must have cost some $6,500,000, a very heavy expense
for so young a country

GRAND LEVEE AT POINT COUPEE.

But little had been done in the way of levee building in the
neighboring Territory of Mississippi. In 1809, when the river
rose, it swept over all the country around Natchez, which
section then contained more than half the population of the
Territory, and destroyed the crops. Governor Sargent, in his
notes, declares that the inhabitants, who could not understand
the flood, entertained the belief that the Great Lakes had forced
an outlet into the Upper Mississippi and were pouring down
on them. In 1813 came the first serious disaster to the Louis-
iani levees in the breaking of that at Pointe Coupée, since
known as the Grand levee, and which protects seven parishes
from overflow. This levee, which is the largest, the most important, and the most exposed in the State, has broken several
times, each time causing great damage, as it overflows the
basins of the Atchafalaya, Bayou Teche, and Grand Lake. In
this year (1813) the water in Grand Lake rose from 4 to 5
feet higher than any previous year it had attained since 1780.
There were a number of minor breaks in the river embankment
from Concordia down, and even New Orleans suffered slightly
from a cave in the Kenner levee, 12 miles above the city.
In 1816 followed a notable overflow, restricted however,
almost wholly to the city. The Macarté levee which was undermined by the powerful current which there strikes the bank,
again broke and four days afterwards the rear portion of the
suburbs or faubourgs, as they were called, of Montagu, La
Course, Gravier, Trémé, Saint John, and Saint Mary were
flooded to a depth of from 3 to 5 feet. Within twenty-five
days, however, the water had run off, and all damages had been
repaired.
In 1828 the line of levees along the Mississippi was continuous except where they were not needed, from New Orleans
to Red River Landing, just below the mouth of Red River, a
distance of 195 miles, and for 65 miles below the city. Above
Red River they were in an unfinished state to Napoleon. From
1828 to 1844 they were gradually extended on the west bank
from Red River to the mouth of the Arkansas. There were also
many levees along the Yazoo front, but they were not continuous. Above Napoleon little, if anything, had been done
in the way of levee building.

THE SWAMP-LAND ACT.

The Memphis river convention of 1845 made an earnest demand on the Federal Government to grant the farmers some assistance in the matter of levee building, without which, it was declared, the settlement of the Lower Mississippi Valley could not go on successfully. The planters had already expended many millions in constructing miles of dikes; and it was pointed out that with more levees millions of acres of fertile lands, then useless and valueless, because subject to overflow, could be reclaimed. The proposition was made that these flooded lands should be given to the States to aid in levee building and in reclaiming them; and this was warmly approved by the convention and recommended to Congress.

The convention was not without its effect. The improvement of the Mississippi received the attention of Congress, and a resolution was adopted authorizing a survey of the Mississippi for the purpose of ascertaining the best method of reclaiming the alluvial lands. The same year Congress gave, for the first time, assistance in the construction of levees. An act was passed in 1849 donating to Louisiana to " aid in constructing the necessary levees and drains to reclaim the swamps and overflowed lands there, the whole of these swamps and overflowed lands which may be, or are found unfit for cultivation."

The General Government, in the spirit of enlarged public policy, conceded this class of inundated lands to aid in the construction of permanent levees, with a view to secure private property, the theory being reclamation of the land through the State and also as a sanitary measure.

Then followed the law of September 28, 1850, extending grant so as to enable " the State of Arkansas to construct the necessary levees and drains to reclaim the swamps and overflowed lands thereon, the fourth and last section of which enlarged the grant so as to embrace in each of the other States in the Union on which such swamps and overflowed lands, known and designated as aforesaid, may be situated." The act provided that " the proceeds of said lands, whether from sale or direct appropriation in kind, shall be applied, exclusively, as far as necessary, to the reclaiming of said lands by means of levees and drains."

Among the largest recipients of this bounty were the three river States of Louisiana Arkansas, and Mississippi, which have received 18,545,270 acres of swamp overflowed lands.

THE CONDITION OF LEVEES IN 1860

The funds from the sale of these lands have been generally turned over to boards of swamp commissioners, to be used by them on levee building. Of the States Louisiana has secured the best results from this donation. It is still possessed of considerable revenue from this source, and the Morganza levee in Pointe Coupée was constructed in 1883 out of the funds derived from the sale of swamp lands.

The assistance thus given by the Federal Government encouraged levee building, and the next ten years were the most active and successful in the Lower Mississippi Valley. At the outbreak of the war, Louisiana, Mississippi, and Arkansas had a perfect system of levees. In 1860 there were 2,184 miles of embankments on the Mississippi, with an average height of from 8 to 10 feet and a width, at the base, of from 50 to 75 feet, their width at the top being somewhat less than their height. Some of them were of much greater size. That at Yazoo Pass, cut by the Union forces during the siege of Vicksburg was, for a distance of half a mile, 28 feet high and at some points 38 feet, and in places nearly if not quite 300 feet broad at its base. The levees at Bayou Manchac and the Grand Levee in Pointee Coupée were nearly as large.

PROTECTION OF LEVEES AND THEIR SIZE.

Under the French rule, and for a long period afterwards, the levees were built and kept in order by the front proprietors. At a later date the police juné, corresponding to the county commissioners in the other States, took charge of the levees in Louisiana; but in times of danger the riparien proprietors, occupying alluvial lands subject to overflow within 7 miles of the river, were compelled to lend a helping hand. When a crevasse was threatened the planters and farmers of the surrounding country met and decided on the line of action to be pursued. Each gave the labor of a number of his slaves. One would give ten slaves for twenty days or less, another thirty slaves for fifteen days, each in accordance with his means. Afterwards districts were formed and taxes levied for levee purposes.

In Mississippi the levees were placed in charge of the board of swamp commissioners, who expended the money derived from the sale of the lands granted by Congress. Here also, however, the bulk of the work was done by the owners of the plantations fronting on the river.

In Arkansas, immediately after the grant of the swamp and overflowed lands by the General Government, a board of commissioners was created to determine the necessary drains and the levees to be erected. This board was abolished in 1856, and in 1857 an act was passed allowing the letting out of contracts for building levees when there was sufficient money in the treasury to pay for it. The funds becoming exhausted, the counties made their own laws respecting these dikes.

THE COST OF THE LEVEES.

In view of the manner in which the work on the levees was done —mainly by slave labor — it is somewhat difficult to arrive at a calculation of the cost of these dikes previous to the war. Various estimates have been made of the number of cubic yards of earth in the levees then constructed, and the cost is calculated on this basis. The State engineer estimated that the levees standing in Louisiana in 1860 cost $12,500,000. This represented their actual value, the number of cubic yards of earth in them, at the price then ruling. Another report places the total cost of levees in all the river States, from the beginning of levee building to 1862, as follows: —

Louisiana	$25,600,000
Mississippi	14,750,000
Arkansas	1,200,000
Missouri	1,640,000
Other States	560,000
Total	**$43,750,000**

Work was begun anew. In Arkansas and Mississippi large amounts of bonds were voted for levee purposes. In Louisiana a levee company was formed, to which was confided the absolute control of the construction of all levees in the State until 1892, a tax of 2 mills on the dollar being voted for the purpose of raising the necessary funds. The tax was subsequently increased to 4 mills, and then dropped again to 3. The company was to build at least 3,000,000 cubic yards a year, at 50 and 60 cents per cubic yard, which would have made the annual axpense for levees $1,650,000. In 1876 the chief engineer of the State reported that the work done by the company for the previous three years had not been sufficient to replace the wear and tear of the levees, and that they were losing ground every year."

CHAPTER XXXVIII.

FIRST STEAMBOAT COMPANY FORMED IN NEW ORLEANS.

IN a newspaper published in New Orleans called *Monitor,* March 5th, 1812, has this advertisement:

"STEAMBOAT. — The persons who desire to take an interest in the steamboat held under the patent of Messrs. Livingston & Fulton, destined to navigate upon the Mississippi and Ohio and Cumberland, and to the Falls of Ohio, will please address the undersigned at the house of Messrs. Talcot & Bowers, from eleven o'clock until two. The subscription books are open every day until they are filled."

N. I. ROOSEVELT

From the *Louisiana Gazette and Advertiser* January 13th, 1812: "The steamboat New Orleans from Pittsburgh, arrived here Friday evening last. The Captain reports she has been under way not more than 259 hours from Pittsburgh to this place which gives about eight miles an hour. She was built at Pittsburgh by the Ohio Steamboat Company, under the patent granted to Messrs. Livingston & Fulton of New York. She is intended as a regular trader between this and Natchez, and will, it is generally believed, meet the most sanguine expectations of the company."

February 8th, 1812, the same paper remarks: "The steamboat was at Fort Andrews, 50 miles below Natchez on her way up, on Saturday last. She was detained by breaking one of her wheels."

Wednesday, Feb. 12, 1812, the same paper makes this announcement: "The steamboat left Natchez on Thursday afternoon and arrived here on Monday evening last, and will start again we are informed on Saturday next."

NICHOLAS BAKER, *Captain.*

In the same paper of Jan. 16, 1812, is this notice: —

"For the *English Turn.* — The steamboat New Orleans will run from the English Turn and back on Friday next, to start precisely at 10 a. m.

Tickets of admission may be procured at the two coffee houses, at three dollars each. It is expected the boat will return at 3 o'clock. All persons who desire to dine before that hour it is expected will carry their provisions with them."

January 18, 1812. Yesterday the citizens were gratified with the power of steam in this vessel. She left this place at 11 o'clock, went five leagues down, and returned at 4 o'clock. A number of gentlemen were on board. The day was fine and general satisfaction was given."

New Orleans *Daily Gazette*, of Jan. 21, 1812, has the following notice: —

"For Natchez, the steamboat New Orleans will leave this port on Thursday, 23d inst.

From a gentleman passenger of correct information we are enabled to state that she can stem the current at the rate of upwards of three miles an hour.

That she went from this city to Houmas, a distance of 25 miles, in twenty-one hours."

In the Louisiana *Gazette* of July, 1818, the following announcement is made: —

"NATCHEZ, July 25, 1818.

"The stockholders of the Natchez Steamboat Company met yesterday. The subscription to stock having been completed amounted to one hundred thousand dollars.

The company in November last purchased the substantial steamboats New Orleans and Vesuvius and propose to keep them engaged in the trade between this place and New Orleans.

These boats were originally built under the sanction of the New York patentees, Messrs. Livingston and Fulton, and will possess whatever advantages may be derived from the establishment of their rights."

REMINISCENCES OF STEAMBOATS AND CAPTAINS OF THE BATON ROUGE, BAYOU SARA AND UPPER COAST TRADE.

(The following list is not claimed to be correct, but the best that could be made out of the obscure records.)

The first regular packet in the Baton Rouge trade was the steamer Ramapo, Capt. Laurant, from 1820 to 1825; then he commanded the steamboat Packet; in 1829 he commanded the Florida, and the Clipper in 1842, when she exploded.

In 1822, Capt. Reed commanded the Feliciana; this was a low pressure boat built at New York. She was a very staunch boat and run for many years.

1823. Capt. Urton, steamer Leopold; Capt. Ward, steamer Telegraph; Capt. Bosworth, steamer Hope.

1824. Capt. Gray, steamer Henry Clay; Capt. Beckwith,

Steamer Courier; Capt. John De Hart, steamer Feliciana; Capt. Mahe, steamer Louisiana.

1826. Capt. Wood, steamer Caravan; Capt. Kimball, steamer Red River.

1827. Capt. Graham, steamer Lady of the Lake.

1828. Capt. Crane, steamer Columbus; Capt. Curry, steamer Attackapas.

The following steamboats and masters comprise the principal names that were engaged in the New Orleans, Baton Rouge and Bayou Sara trade from 1840 to 1861: —

In 1840. Steamer Brilliant, Capt. Jno. DeHart; steamer Baton Rouge, Capt. Sellock; steamer John Armstrong, Capt. F. M. Streck.

In 1842. Steamer Persian, Capt. Jno. DeHart; steamer Colorado, Capt. F. M. Streck; steamer Buckeye, Capt. Isaac Hooper; steamer Luda, Capt. Thos. Clark.

In 1843. Steamer Persian, Capt. Jno. DeHart; steamer Belle Air, Capt. F. M. Streck; steamer Colorado, Capt. James Noe.

In 1844. Steamer Belle Air, Capt. F. M. Streck; steamer Rainbow, Capt. Sellock; steamer Helen, Capt. James Noe; steamer St. Laundry, Capt. Dugas; steamer Eliska, Capt. Dugas.

In 1845. Steamer Brilliant No. 2, Capt, John DeHart; steamer Music No. 1, Capt. F. M. Streck; steamer Clinton, Capt. Wm. Baird; steamer F M. Streck, Capt. Wilson.

In 1846. Steamer Majestic, Capt. Jas. Noe; steamer Eliska; steamer Belle Creole, Capt. Champromere.

In 1848. Steamer Luna, Capt. Wm. Baird; steamer Mary Foley, Capt. Dalfares.

In 1849. Steamer Gipsey, Capt. James Noe; steamer Clinton.

In 1850. Steamer F. M. Streck, Capt. F. M. Streck; steamer Patrick Henry, Capt. Dugas; steamer Gross Tete, Capt. Hooper; steamer Music, Capt. Streck; steamer Mary T., Capt. Dalfares.

In 1851. Steamer Patrick Henry, Capt. Dugas; steamer Home, Capt. Dugas.

In 1852. Steamer Emperor, Capt. J. A. Cotton; steamer Laurel Hill, Capt. J. A. Cotton; steamer Brilliant No. 3, Capt. Jno. DeHart; steamer Doctor Batey.

In 1853. Steamer Music No. 2, Capt. F. M. Streck : steamer New Latona, Capt. F. M. Streck; steamer Bella Donna, Capt. I. H. Morrison.

In 1854. Steamers New Latona and Laurel Hill, Capt. Gross.

In 1855. Steamer New Latonia, Capt. J. A. Cotton.

In 1856. Steamer Capital, Capt. Baranco; steamer Silver Heels, Capt. Jno. I. Brown; steamer Golden Age; Capt. McCombs.

In 1857. Steamer Laurel Hill, Capt. Hooper.

In 1858. Steamer Music No. 3, Capt. F. M. Streck; steamer Laurel Hill, Capt. James Noe; steamer Gen'l Pike, Capt. Jno. I. Brown ; steamer Music, Capt. Jno. I. Brown.

In 1859. Steamer Gross Tete, Capt. Hooper.

In 1861. Steamers D. F. Kenner and Laurel Hill; steamer Lafouch, Capt. Jno. I. Brown; steamer Jno. A. Cotton ; Capt. Cotton.

The Jno. A. Cotton was converted into a ram or gunboat during the war and lost in Bayou Teche. She was one of the fastest and most powerful boats of her day, and the first and only boat ever built on the Ohio that attempted to supply her boilers with a syphon alone, and while she succeeded in reaching New Orleans, it was found that while the syphon would supply the boilers after steam was raised, a doctor or an auxiliary engine was necessary for convenience and safety.

NEW ORLEANS AND VICKSBURG PACKETS.

Among the early organizations to Vicksburg, there was in 1842, steamer Baton Rouge, Capt. Walworth; steamer Vicksburgh, Capt. W. R. Glover; steamer Sultana, Capt. A. W. Tufts; steamer Norma, Capt. W. A. Grice

In 1844, steamer J. M. White, J. M. Converse.

In 1846, Magnolia, Capt. St. Clair Thomasson; steamer Concordia, John Raine.

In 1849, Princess No. 2, T. P. Leathers.

In 1844, Ambassador, C. H. Brenham; Yazoo, Dameron.

NATCHEZ AND NEW ORLEANS.

1841. Princess No. 1, Capt. C. B. Sanford; Invincible, Capt. James Walworth.

1846. Natchez, Capt. T. P. Leathers; Princess, Capt. Wm. Leathers.

NEW ORLEANS AND OUACHITA RIVER PACKETS.

1849. Steamer Grant, Capt. E. Connery; Princeton, Capt. H. A. Ealer.

BOATS IN DIFFERENT TRADES FROM 1840 TO 1860.

1851. Trenton, Capt. John Kouns; Robt. Whiteman, Capt. Geo. S. Kouns; S. W. Downs, Capt. John Cannon.

NEW ORLEANS AND ALABAMA RIVER.

1851. Steamer Alabama, Capt. P. Roberts, Jr.; steamer Pearl, Capt. A. P. Boardman; steamer Georgia, Capt. S. F. Scale; steamer Beacon, Capt. D. H. Shaw.

RIO GRANDE STEAMBOAT LINE.

1852. Steamers Grampus, Mentona, and Camanche formed a line from Brazos DeSantiago to Brownsville, owned and managed by Messrs. Kennedy, King and Jas. O'Donnell.

NEW ORLEANS AND YAZOO CITY PACKETS.

1843. Steamer Republic, Capt. John Good; steamer Yazoo, Capt. R. C. Young; steamer M. B. Homer, Capt. P. C. Wallace; steamer Patriott, Capt. D. F. Rudd.

NEW ORLEANS AND RED RIVER.

A Short History of the First Navigation of Red River in 1715.

"In 1715, by order of Bienville, the French commander of the territory of Louisiana, the steamer St. Denis was dispatched to Red River to make the first exploration of that country. He penetrated the valley of that river as far as the country of the Natchitoche Indians, and established a fort, where he left a number of soldiers and colonists. This was the first town established by the French on the banks of Red River. The colonists immediately commenced a trade with the Indians and purchased by barter all the hides, skins, peltries, etc., which they would bring to them.

In 1716 the steamer St. Denis[1] returned to New Orleans with a fleet of bateaux loaded with valuable skins, furs, hides, peltries, etc. For many years this navigation, by means of pirogues and bateaux, was carried on upon Red River.

The second expedition to Red River was made in 1818, by the steamer De la Harp, which ascended also to Natchitoches.

---

[1] NOTE.—This steamboat St. Denis is evidently a myth, as she is never heard of before or since her advent in Red River in 1715 and 1716.

Leaving her bateaux at this place she commenced the exploration of the country to the west of Natchitoches. She penetrated into the country of the Caddo Indians, from whence she retraced her steps; arriving at Natchitoches she concluded to penetrate westward into the territory of Mexico. After passing the Sabine river and penetrating some distance into Mexican territory she again retraced her steps to Natchitoches.''

OLD TIMER.[1]

REMINISCENCES OF RED RIVER.

Its Early Navigation.

"Up to 1824 Red River was navigated almost entirely by keel-boats. The first steamboat to enter Red river was the Enterprise, in 1815. She was commanded by Capt. H. M. Shreve, and made two trips to the falls.

The second boat of which there is any record was the Newport, Capt. Wm. Waters, in 1819. The third, the Yankee; fourth, Beaver, and the fifth the Alexandria. Capt. John R. Kimball (uncle of Capt. P. F. Kimball,) and after these the Governor Shelby, Neptune and the Arkansas, all in 1820. They were all pretty much the same class of boats as the Alexandria, which was 106 feet long, drew seventeen inches and carried 100 tons.

In 1821 the Missouri ran to Red River in addition to the above; in 1822 the Venture and the Hope; in 1823 the Experiment, Expedition and the Natchitoches.

In 1824 and 1825 the Florence, Eliza, Louisville, Red River and the Superior.

In 1826 the Planter, Virginia, Miami, Spartan and the Dolphin.

In 1827 and 1828 the Phœnix, Pilot, Cherokee, Robert Burns, Rover, Belle, Creole, Cincinnati and Rapides.

In 1830 and 1831 the Gleaner, Paul Clifford and the Vermillion.

In 1832 and 1834 the Beaver, Planter, Lioness, Bravo, Caspian and the Waverly.

Between 1835 and 1840 thirty-six boats other than those named above ran to Red River; in 1838 Capt. Jesse Wright commanded his first boat in this trade, the Ticher; in 1839, Capt. P. Delma, the Velocipede; in 1840, Capt. Mike Welsh, the Creole and the Bogue Houma, and the same year Capt. Benj. Crooks, the Hunter. These captains all became promi-

---

[1] Old Timer fails to explain how the steamboat De la Harp penetrated. into " Mexican territory."

LAST OF THE RED RIVER TRANSPORTATION COMPANY.

nent men, and of which, with others, an old steamboat clerk, who dates from 1845, will have more to say anon.''

" The Ashland, leaving to-day (July, 1882), will be the last boat sent out by the New Orleans and Red River Transportation Company prior to its dissolution. The first boat sent out after its organization (in June, 1875,) was the Col. A. P. Kouns, Capt. Isaac H. Kouns. At that time the following boats comprised the line, viz.: The Col. A. P. Kouns, R. T. Bryarly, La Belle, Texas, Lorts No. 3, Belle Rowland, O. H. Durfee, W. J. Behan and the Maria Louise. All of these boats are things of the past, and no longer float upon the waters, except the W. J. Behan and the Maria Louise, which, together with the Jo Bryarly, Frank Williard Cornie Brandon, Ashland, John D. Scully, Alexandria, Silver City, Yazoo Valley, Jewel, Danube and the Jesse K. Bell, comprise the line to-day, and seven barges besides. The Laura Lee and the Kate Kinney were also in the line, but were withdrawn a short time previous to the election in June last. The dissolution of this company goes into effect next Tuesday at midnight, and then — and then — what! Ever so many people are curious to know.

SOURCE OF RED RIVER.

REMINISCENCES.

Under the above head we published in Saturday's *Democrat* some historical facts in connection with the early settlement of Natchitoches. To-day from the same source we give the discovery of the headwaters of Red River.

In 1806, three years after the cession of Louisiana to the United States an exploring party under Capt. Sparks entered Red River in boats, intending to ascend as far as possible to the Pawnee country, where they would purchase horses and proceed to the tops of the mountains. It was evident from this that they supposed Red River issued from the mountain country. They got as high as the great raft, where they were met by a Spanish force and ordered back, an order which, owing to their numbers, they had to obey.

In 1819 and 1820, Col. Long, of the United States Topographical Engineers, on his return from an exploration of the Missouri and the country between that river and the head of the Arkansas, undertook to descend Red River from its source. The Colonel says: We arrived at a creek having a westerly course, which we took to be a tributary of Red River. We traveled the valley of this stream several hundred miles, when to our disappointment we discovered it to be the Canadian, a tributary of the Arkansas instead of Red River. Our horses and men being exhausted, it was impossible to retrace our steps. Dr. James, who accompanied Col. Long, in his journal of this expedition says : " Several persons have recently ar- rived at St. Louis from Sante Fe, and among others a brother of Capt. Shreve, who gives information of a large and fre- quented road which runs nearly due east from this place and strikes one of the branches of the Canadian. That at a con- siderable distance south of this point is the big plains, which is the principal source of Red River."

The source of Red River remained a mystery for many years, and it was not known until discovered by Capt. Marcy in 1852. He left Fort Belknap May 2, 1852; struck the Little Wichita; descending that stream he entered Red River and ascended it. On the sixteenth he camped near the mouth of Cash Creek, this being the point at which he was directed to commence his exploration. June 26 the expedition reached the Staked Plains. It was very much elevated above the ad- joining country with almost vertical sides, covered with a scrubby growth of dwarf cedars, and from the summit the country spread out into a perfectly level plain as far as the eye could see. June 27 he reached the main south fork which he ascended, passing into the gorge of the great Llano Esta- cado. These lofty escarpments rise to a great height. As they rode along the bed of the stream, so near its source, they found the water very nauseating, owing to its passing through a bed of gypsum, and the men were made quite sick from drinking it. July 1, 1852, they reached the source of Red River. This spring is in the gorge of the Llano Estacado, and bursting out from its cavernous reservoir leaps down over the huge mass of rocks below, and there commences its long journey to the Mississippi. These gigantic escarpments of sand stone rising to the giddy height of eight hundred feet on each side, gradually close until they are only a few yards apart, and finally unite at the top, leaving a long narrow cor- ridor beneath, at the base of which the head spring of the principal or main branch of the Red River takes its rise. The water of this spring is as clear as crystal and perfectly pure. On climbing to the summit of this escarpment they found themselves on the level plains of the Llano Estacado, which spread from there in one uninterrupted descent to the base of the mountains in New Mexico. The geographical po- sition of this point was 34 min. 42 sec. north and longitude

FRENCH EXPEDITION TO RED RIVER IN 1714.

103 deg. 7 min 11 sec. west. The approximate elevation above the sea, as determined by frequent barometric observations, is 2,450 feet.

REMINISCENCES.

In 1714 the French, who then held Louisiana, sent an expedition to Red River as high as Natchitoches for the purpose of forming a settlement. They also explored the country westward as far as the Rio Grande, then occupied by the Spaniards, and who claimed jurisdiction east as far as Red River.

In 1730 the French Governor Perriere organized an expedition to drive the Natchez tribe of Indians from the Red and Black River districts. The rendezvous was at Bayou Goula; from there they proceeded to the mouth of Red River, the ship Prince of Conde having been sent ahead with supplies. They ascended Black River, a lake near Trinity, where they met and captured the Indians after a five days' fight, whom they subsequently sent to St. Domingo, where they were sold as slaves.

In 1749 the province of Natchitoches contained sixty whites and 200 negroes, who raised cattle, corn, rice and tobacco.

From 1745 to 1796 Spain held possession of Louisiana. Their settlements did not flourish, though communication with Red River was kept up. Natchitoches then contained a population of 800 white and black.

CHAPTER XXXIX.

OLD TIME STEAMBOATS — WHARFAGE DUES, ETC., AT THE PORT
OF NEW ORLEANS.

"THROUGH the kindness of Gen. John L. Lewis, I have
been permitted to examine a directory of this city published in 1823, of which I hand you extracts. The following
statement will show the arrivals of loaded steamboats, barges,
keel and flat-boats within the limits of the city in 1821, from
the upper country, together with the amount of wharfage or
levee duty paid to the city corporation :—

Steamboats, 287; barges and keel-boats, 174; flat-boats,
441. Levee duty, $8,272.

Each loaded flat-boat pays a duty of $6; boats or barges, 70
feet or more in length, $10, and keel boats or rafts, $3.
Steamboats pay a levee duty according to their tonnage as
follows: 100 tons and under, $6, 150 tons, $9; 200 tons, $12;
250 tons, $15; 300 tons, $18; 350 tons, $20; 400 tons, $22;
500 tons, $26; 600 tons, $30.

In the year ending October 1, 1817, 1,500 flat-boats and
500 barges and keel-boats came down the Mississippi to this
place loaded with produce.

The batture which was formed by deposits from the river,
which has a front of 3,400 feet, and an average depth of 470
feet. This property has been set aside for the purpose of
landing all steamboats, barges, keel and flat-boats. This batture, or landing place, extends from Wither's saw-mill to
Canal street. In this year New Levee street was laid out in a
straight line from Wither's saw-mill to Canal street, having a
space of 60 feet between the houses and the edge of the wharf.

One-half the batture next the city is exclusively appropriated for steamboats, of which there are sometimes thirty
or forty lying at a time. The activity of this commerce is astonishing, vessels of 645 tons are employed in it, and it is not
unusual for the voyage to Louisville and back to be performed
in thirty days, formerly forty men with great difficulty navigated a boat of 50 tons the same voyage in six months. All
this commerce centers on the batture, and it would be difficult
to select in any city in the world a spot in which more extensive business is done in the same space. From the Custom-
house down to Esplanade street the levee front is set apart for
the landing of ships, brigs and schooners."

STEAMBOAT ARRIVALS IN NEW ORLEANS FROM 1812 TO 1823.

" Gen. John L. Lewis says he has a distinct recollection of seeing the first steamboat, the New Orleans, that landed at this port in January, 1812. That the event was so wonderful that the Legislature adjourned for the purpose of giving her a grand reception; he also remembers the Vesuvius, the second steamboat, and that she unfortunately run aground in December, 1814, and therefore could not render any assistance at the time of the battle of New Orleans ; he also remembers the Etna, the third steamboat; he also says that the captains of these original boats were sailors or seamen and mentions that Capt. R. De Hart and John De Hart were sent out from New York by Livingston and Fulton to take command of their boats. It was only a few years after this when the barge men became captains of the Western steamboats.

NOTE. — The saw mill of Mr. Withers was situated just in front of where the old Turo infirmary was built.

" The following is an alphabetical list of all the boats that have been in the New Orleans trade. Those marked thus * are either sunk or unfit for service or out of the trade — from 1812 to 1823 : —

*Ætna.	Geo. Madison.	*Ohio.
Alabama.	Hecla.	Olive Branch.
Alexandria.	Hero.	Osage.
Bearer.	Harriet.	Paragon.
*Buffalo.	Henderson.	Post Boy.
Car of Commerce.	Hornet.	*Pike.
Cincinnati.	Henry Clay.	Providence.
Comet.	James Rose.	Rapide.
*Constitution.	*James Monroe.	Ramaps.
Courier.	Johnson.	Rifleman.
Expedition.	Independence.	Rocket.
Eagle.	*Kentucky.	Robert Fulton.
Elizabeth.	Louisiana.	*St. Louis.
Exchange.	Maid of Orleans.	Tamerlane.
Eliza.	Manhattan.	Tennessee.
Favourite.	Maysville.	Telegraph.
Fidelity.	Mississippi.	Thos. Jefferson.
*Franklin.	Missouri.	Teche.
Frankfort.	Murs.	United States.
Gen'l Clark.	Mobile.	Vesuvius.
Gen'l Green.	Mandan.	Volcano.
*Gen'l Jackson.	Napoleon.	*Vesta.
Gen'l Roberts.	Neptune.	Washington.
*Gen'l Harrison.	*Newport.	*Yankee
*Gov. Shelby.	*New Orleans.	

The steamboat United States was the largest, her tonnage being 645 tons. The smallest was the Pike. Her tonnage was only 31 tons. The averaged tonnage of all the boats was about 150 tons each.

NOTE.— You will see that from 1812 to 1823, that is, in eleven years, there were 75 steamboats landed at the port of New Orleans. This will make an average of about 7 new steamboats each year. I am under the impression that the list taken from the directory of 1823 is a perfect one, as the author must have had access to the Custom House records and also to the wharfage book. If you will make the calculation you will find that these 75 steamboats averaging 150 tons each amounted to only 11,250 tons. We have now upon the Mississippi six steamboats whose tonnage will average 2,440 tons each, or the six boats 12,400 tons."

OLD TIMER.

CHAPTER XL.

OLIVER EVANS CREDITED BY BRITISH AUTHORITY.

STEAM COACHES.

[From Niles' Register, September 22, 1828, vol. 35.]

The following account of steam coaches in Great Britian is of much interest at the present time.

That they will become *common things* we have long believed.

It was in America that steam was first successfully applied for the ordinary purposes of navigation of rivers.

The first steamboat that ventured on the ocean was American, and the first that crossed the Atlantic, that penetrated the Baltic, and arrived at the capital of Russia was also American. And in noticing the progress of perfection, in the applicability of steam for moving of bodies on land, while yielding all due credit to British ingenuity and talents, we wish to record the fact, that the first application of its powers to this purpose was made by an American, and in the City of Philadelphia, by *Oliver Evans*, who entertained the project in 1786, and communicated it to several persons as well as petitioned the Legislature of Pennsylvania concerning *steam wagons* for which he was thought *insane*. The State of Maryland, however, in 1782 granted him an exclusive right to make and use steam wagons for 14 years.

16

FIRST STEAM ENGINES BUILT IN THE WEST.

But Evans was poor and confidence was not placed in his theory, so he obtained no pecuniary assistance, and it was not until 1804, that he was enabled to apply steam to propel bodies on land.

He built a flat, or scow, a mile and half from the water, of the weight of about 20 tons, with a steam engine on board of only five horse power, for the purpose of cleansing docks, and when all was ready, he placed wheels under the flat, and by steam transported it to and launched it into the water, and with a paddle wheel, then navigated it down the Schuylkill to the Delaware and up the Delaware to Philadelphia, beating all the vessels on the river against a head wind.   In 1812, Oliver Evans said, "I do verily believe the time will come when carriages propelled by steam will be in *general use*, as well for the transportation of passengers as goods, traveling at the rate of 15 miles an hour or 300 miles per day."

THE FIRST ENGINE SHOP IN THE WEST.

About the year 1812, Oliver Evans, sent his son, George Evans, to Pittsburgh, for the purpose of establishing an iron foundry, steam engine manufactory, mould makers shop and blacksmith shop with ten or twelve smith's forges and more than fifty workmen for making steam engines and other machinery. This was in all probability the first engine building establishment erected upon the banks of the Western rivers. And most of the first high pressure engines for Western steamboats were built at this establishment.   There was also an engine building shop established at Brownsville, or Bridgeport, on the Monongahela river, about the same time.

All the engines for Fulton & Livingston's first boats were built at Pittsburgh, as follows: New Orleans, 1811; Etna, 1815; Vesuvius, 1816, and Buffalo, 1816, had low pressure engines, built on the Watt & Bolton plan; they were built at New York and transported across the Alleghany Mountains by wagons.

THE SECOND STEAMBOAT ENGINE BUILDERS

I find any account of at Cincinnati, were Goodloe & Borden. They commenced as early as 1816, as this was the date at which the first steamboat was built at that place. They were succeeded by Mess. Harkness & Co., who for many years built steamboat engines.

The first mention I find of a master ship carpenter at Cincinnati is Mr. William Parsons; he came originally from New York, where he had learned the trade of building ships. He built many of the original steamboats at Cincinnati.

Mr. Crippin was the first ship joiner who built cabins for the original steamboats at Cincinnati; he emigrated from New York and walked from that city to Cincinnati in 1816; He learned his trade at New York, working upon the cabins of ships. Among those he worked upon was the celebrated United States man-of-war Brandywine, which was sent out in 1814 to the Mediterranean Sea to suppress the Algerine and Barbary pirates.

The first master ship carpenter I find an account of at Jeffersonville, Indiana, is a Mr. Vandusen from New York, in 1818. He brought out with him from that city fifty ship carpenters for the purpose of building the first steamboat at that place, which has since become so famous for building magnificent steamboats. The first steamboat was named the United States, owned by Edmund Forestall of New Orleans, measured 645 82-95 tons, and was said to have been the largest steamboat in the world at that date. The next celebrated builder at this place was the ingenious Mr. William French, who was a master ship carpenter and engine builder, who in 1814 constructed two steamboats at Brownsville, Pa. He had the repution of placing the first high pressure engine upon a Western steamboat. He built many magnificent steamers at Jeffersonville from 1820 to 1840.

SNAG-BOATS.

The First Snagboats Built for the Removal of Snags.

The first appropriation for this purpose was made by Congress in 1828. Capt. Henry M. Shreve was appointed superintendent of the work. He immediately commenced building the two first snagboats at New Albany, Ind., assisted by Capts. Abraham Tyson and John Dillingham. These boats were double hulls, held together by immense cross beams and iron chains. The hulls, Capt. Moffet, inspector, says, were built by Dohrman & Humphries; the engines were built by John Curry, of Louisville, Ky. They had several kinds of appliances on board for pulling snags and cutting them up. Capt. Moffet did the blacksmith work of making chains and fastenings. The boats were named the Heliopolis, Capt. Moorehead, and Archimides, Capt. H. M. Shreve. Col. Long

CAPT. SHREVE AND THE SNAGBOATS IN 1830.

was the United States engineer in charge of the improvements upon the Mississippi River.

The first account of work done by the snagboats is as follows : 1830 and 1831 — A Western paper states that the
agent employed by the government, Capt. Shreve, has perfectly succeeded in rendering about 300 miles of river as
harmless as a mill-pond, and will in the course of a short period remove every obstruction from Trinity to Balize. His
plan is to run down the snags with a double steamboat; the
bows are connected by tremendous beams, plated with iron; he
puts on a heavy head of steam and runs the snag down; they
are found uniformly to break off at the point of junction with
the bottom of the river, and float away.

1831 — The captains and crews of the snagboats Archimides
and Heliopolis, under the superintendence of Capt. Shreve,
are progressing rapidly in removing obstructions to the navigation of the Western waters. The Heliopolis, Capt. Moorehead, has ascended the Arkansas River about 20 miles, and
after removing all the snags in that distance, on account of
low water has returned to the Mississippi, and it will in the
course of the week have cleared the channel of the Mississippi
between Helena and the mouth of the Arkansas River. The
business, as it now progresses, is effectually done. During
the year, 1831, Capt. Shreve continued on down the river,
and made the cut off at the mouth of Red River. Capt.
Moorehead continued during 1831 and 1832 to work down to
that river, removing all the snags that presented themselves.

In 1832, Capt. H. M. Shreve was ordered to proceed
to Red River for the purpose of removing the great raft. His
fleet of boats consisted of the snagboat Eradicator and two
tenders, the Pearl and Laurel. The raft commenced at that
time about Loggy Bayou and extended to Carolina Bluffs, a
distance of 165 miles. It took six years to accomplish the
work of removing this raft, so as to give good navigation between the lower and upper Red River.

Official report of Capt. Shreve, June 4, 1838, of the snag-
boats Eradicator, Pearl and Laurel: On March 1, 1838, the
first boat was enabled to force her way through the upper
section of the raft, and up to the 29th five merchant steamboats passed up through the raft. On May 1, the navigation
through the extent of the raft was considered safe. There
were two boats lost near the head of the raft — the Black

Hawk and Revenue. The amount expended in opening the raft has been $311,000.

Note.—The town of Trinity, mentioned in this account, was about six miles above the mouth of the Ohio, where the boats from the Ohio and Mississippi exchanged cargoes. It was many years after the establishment of this place, that Cairo was founded and became the port of exchanging freights.

CHAPTER XLI.

[From Sharfs' History of St. Louis.]

PARTIAL ACCOUNTS OF THE FLOODS IN THE MISSISSIPPI AND OHIO.

THE first unusual rise in the Mississippi of which we have any account, occurred in 1542.

In March of that year, while De Soto and his followers were at an Indian village on the west side of the " Rio Grande," as the early Spaniards called the Mississippi, which from its elevated position indicates the sight of *Helena*, in Arkansas, there was a rise in the river which covered all the surrounding country as far as the eye could reach.

In the village (represented to have been on high ground) the water rose from five to six feet above the earth, and the roofs of the Indian cabins were the only places of shelter. The river remained at this height for several days and then subsided rapidly.

The earliest authentic account of the "American Bottom" being submerged is that of the flood in 1724. A document is to be seen in the archives of Kaskaskia, Ill., which consists of a petition to the crown of France in 1725, for a grant of land in which the damage sustained the year before is mentioned. The villagers were driven to the bluffs on the opposite side of the Kaskaskia river. Their gardens and their crops were destroyed, and their buildings and their property much injured. We have no evidence of its exact height, but the whole American Bottom was submerged. This was probably in June.

There was a tradition among the old French people many years since that there was an extraordinary rise of the river between 1740 and 1750, but we find no written or printed account of it.

In the year 1772 another flood came and portions of the American Bottom were again covered. Fort Charter in 1756 stood half a mile from the Mississippi river. In 1776 it was

eighty yards.   Two years after Capt. Pittman, who surveyed
the Fort in 1768, states: "The bank of the Mississippi River
next the Fort is continually falling in, being worn away by
the current which has been turned from its course by a sand
bank now increased by considerable of an island, covered with
willows. Many experiments have been tried to stop this
growing evil, but to no purpose. Eight years ago the river
was fordable to the island. The channel is now forty feet
deep."

FORT CHARTER DESTROYED IN 1772.

About the year 1770, the river made further encroach-
ments. But in 1772, when it inundated portions of the
American Bottom, it swept away the land to the Fort, and undermined the wall which tumbled into the river. A large and
heavily timbered island now occupies the sand bar of Capt.
Pittman's time.

The next high water occurred in 1785, during which Kaskaskia and Cahokia and large portions of the American Bottom were submerged. Concerning this great inundation
there is but meager information. This year, however, is
known in the annals of Western history as the year of the
"great waters."

In 1844 it was contended by some of the old settlers of
Kaskaskia and Cahokia, who remembered the great flood of
1785, that the water attained a greater height than in the last
mentioned year.

It is certain at Kaskaskia the water attained a greater height
in 1844 than was reached in 1785.

This is not predicated upon the mere recollection of individuals, but was ascertained by existing marks of the height
of the flood of that year, after the subsidence of the water in
1844. It was then proved that in the last mentioned year,
the water rose *two feet and five inches* above high water of 1785.

The destruction of property by this freshet was comparatively small.

The mighty stream spread over a wilderness tenanted only
by wild beasts and birds, and the few inhabitants then residing
within the range of its destructive sweep, easily escaped with
small loss, to the high lands.

From 1785 to 1811, there were no destructive floods, although an occasional overflow, sufficient to fill the lake and
low grounds on the American Bottom.

This was in the year preceding the great "Shakes," as the
earthquakes were called. The river commenced rising at St.
Louis early in May, and by the 15th had spread over a large

portion of the American Bottom, and by the first of June it was out of its banks only in low places. On the sixth it again commenced to rise and continued to rise until the 14th, when it came to a stand. But the greater part of the bottom, Kaskaskia, Cahokia, Prairie Du Pont, Cantine, and nearly all the settlements in the bottom were under water and the inhabitants had fled to the high lands.

The " common fields " at St. Genevieve were entirely submerged, the corn was nearly covered.

A story is still told by the old inhabitants of the village that the panic-stricken people appealed to Father Maxwell, the village priest, to " pray away the water." It is said he gave no encouragement at first, until the water came to a stand. Then he proposed to the people to drive off the water by saying masses. This they did, and as the water fell rapidly, the ground was soon dry and a fine crop of corn was raised, which was divided with the priest in conformity to the agreement for saying the masses.

The flood of 1811 exceeded all others until 1823. In this year the water in the Mississippi commenced rising rapidly about the 8th of May. It continued to rise until 23d of the month, when it came to a stand at St. Louis. It had then entirely covered the American Bottom, and the people from all the towns had sought refuge on the bluffs, or in St. Louis.

The houses in the lower part of the city were entirely surrounded by water, and the store at the foot of Oak street, occupied by John Shackford, had five feet of water on the floor.

The loss of stock and other property on the bottom opposite the city was very large, but no estimate has ever been made of the loss.

Like the flood of 1811, no means are at hand to determine the height of the water, as compared with previous freshets.

In 1826 the American bottom was again submerged and the inhabitants in all the towns were compelled to flee to the bluffs, and St. Genevieve share the same fate as did all the settlers on the Mississippi Bottoms.

The amount of stock and crops lost was immense. By the 25th of June the flood had subsided and the people again sought their homes and anxiously awaited the next freshet, which occurred in 1844.

The winter of 1823 and 1824 was remarkable for the amount of rain-fall in the Northwest. The river began to raise early in 1844, and by the first of May, was nearly bank full. By the 6th the people at St. Louis began to be severely alarmed.

The water had already reached the stores on Front street, and the merchants had removed their stocks of goods to the second stories, and the bank opposite in Illinois and the whole American Bottom was submerged.

The water came to a stand on the 21st of May, and declined gradually until the 7th of June, when it had gotten within its banks.

A succession of violent rain storms commenced on the 3d of June, and continued until the 10th, and were general throughout the Northwest and all the streams were bank full. By the 12th the river was again breaking over the banks and the people in the bottoms were fleeing for their lives, leaving everything behind.

By the 5th the people of the whole valley were alarmed, and it was asserted an unprecedented flood was inevitable.

On the 12th the water was six inches higher than it had been a month before. On the 18th the steamer Missouri Mail arrived from the Missouri River, and reported the river rising at St. Joseph, at the rate of seven feet in 24 hours. All the tributaries were full and overflowing their banks. The whole country from Western to Glasgow was under water and on the *Camden Bottom* it was from six to eight feet deep.

In the St. Louis *Republican* of 19th June is an account of the situation: —

" We have taken some pains to ascertain with certainty the height of the present rise as compared with former freshets. But have been very unsuccessful. Within the memory of many of the oldest inhabitants there has been three extraordinary freshets, one in 1811, one in 1823 and the last one in 1826.

The one in 1811 seems to have been the highest. In that year, boats passed from Ste. Genevieve to Kaskaskia and the water covered the whole American Bottom to the depth of several feet."

On the 20th of June, 1844, the Mississippi at St. Louis was from three to six miles wide and in some places nine miles.

The water was two or three feet deep in the lower part of the city and at the corner or Front and Pine streets it was to the top of the doors on the first floors.

Soulard's addition and St. George were entirely submerged.

On the 23d the water rose fourteen inches and came to a stand, remained stationary until June 28th, when it began to recede, and by the middle of July had reached an ordinary stage.

During this freshet steamboats were employed as ferry boats, at many points in the valley of the Mississippi and Missouri, where ordinarily only horse and flat-boats were used. The rapidity of the current and the increased distance rendered the usual mode entirely inadequate. Frequently trips were made from St. Louis to Belleville a distance of twelve miles, across the American Bottom with small steamboats, and many persons availed themselves of the novelty of the excursions.

There is no evidence to prove the Mississippi or the Missouri have ever been as high since their discovery as in 1844, although some writers claim that in 1785 it exceeded 1844. The late Dr. B. W. Brooks, of Jonesboro, Ill., in writing of the flood in 1844, says: "This inundation was ten of twelve feet higher than that of 1811, or of 1826, and higher than ever known except in 1785, when it rose thirty feet above the common level and was the greatest flood known for one hundred and fifty years."

Mr. Cerré, the oldest French settler in St. Louis, says the inundation in 1785 was not as high by four or five feet, as in 1844. In which opinion all old settlers in Kaskaskia agree — claiming there was one point in the town that was not covered in 1785, which was five feet under water in 1844.

The steamer Indiana was chartered to take the *Nuns* from Kaskaskia to St. Louis and received them on board at Col. Menard's door. The boat followed the road the whole distance, leaving the river far to the left. Some two hundred citizens went up on the Indiana, leaving the town from ten to twenty feet under water. Many houses were floated from their foundations and barns, fences and stock were swept off.

The city engineer at St. Louis ascertained on the 22d of June that the water was three feet four inches over the city directrix. This gave *thirty-four feet nine inches* plumb water, above low water mark.

The next freshet in the Mississippi of importance occurred in 1851.

On the 30th of May it was fifteen feet below the high water mark of 1844 at St. Louis. The rise continued the most of June and on the 23d of that month it was only four feet nine inches below the high water mark of 1844.

From this date it commenced to fall, after having almost devastated all the bottom lands on the Missouri, Illinois, Wabash and Upper Mississippi.

In 1854 there was another damaging flood in the Mississippi in which an immense amount of loss occurred in Arkansas,

Mississippi and Louisiana, and almost the entire levee at St. Louis was submerged.

HIGH WATER YEARS.

In 1858 the Mississippi again was at flood height and reached the flood of 1844 less about two and a half feet. The Ohio being very high at the same time great destruction of property followed. Cairo and many other cities and towns in the valley was overflowed by the breaking of levees, caving of banks, etc.

In 1863 the river at St. Louis was again very high and the water came into stores on the levee.

In 1867, 1871, 1875 were high water years, and while but little damage was done in the upper river valleys great losses occurred in Arkansas, Mississippi and Louisiana in consequence of the combined waters of all the upper rivers coming out at about the same time. As a rule, fortunately, the Ohio and its tributaries throw out their great floods some months earlier than the Mississippi. But when they all come at once there is no escaping an overflow.

[From Internal Commerce of the United States.]

The destructive floods of the Mississippi Valley not only sweep over the alluvial lands of the lower valley between Cairo and the Gulf, but frequently occur in the valleys of the Upper Mississippi, the Missouri, Ohio, Red, Arkansas, Tennessee, Cumberland, Yazoo, and other rivers of this comprehensive system, carrying with them enormous destruction to crops, roads, railroads, postal routes, buildings, live stock, commerce and industries. They are often attended with the loss of life itself.

Mr. Morey, in his report to the House of Representatives during the Forty-second Congress, said of the floods of 1868 and 1871: "The destruction caused by the last two floods above named in the Ouachita Valley is almost incredible. A valley of almost unexampled fertility, capable of raising, beside corn and stock in great abundance, at least 75,000 bales of cotton, worth, at the average price of this season, more than $5,000,000, was inundated, plantations destroyed, buildings washed away, cattle and swine by the thousand starved or drowned," etc.

Another flood in 1874 was still more destructive. Mr. Ellis, in his report to the House in 1876, says of it: "The loss by the flood of 1874 was $13,000,000. This year, so far as it can be ascertained, it is $2,000,000. And this makes the total sum $15,000,000 in actual material wealth within three years."

"THE GREAT FLOOD OF 1881."

The great flood throughout the length and breadth of the Mississippi Valley in the spring of 1881 was unusually destructive, the damage amounting to many millions of dollars. As it is impossible to give an accurate estimate of the total damage, we will give a few illustrations by extracts from the press dispatches published in leading daily papers of that time: —

" *Omaha April 25.* — The flood still continues. The river rose 2 inches last night at this point, but it has done no further damage to manufacturing interests on the water front. Much lumber in the yards has been removed to higher ground. The Union Pacific shops and smelting works, Boyd's packing house and distillery are still under water, and 1,600 men are out of employment.

" At Council Bluffs one-half the city is under water, and 600 people are homeless. All passengers from eastern trains are transferred by boat to the Union Pacific depot.

" A dispatch from Sioux City announces a fall of 6 inches at that point.

" This morning high winds set in from the north and stirred up the vast body of water north of the long embankment leading up to the Union Pacific bridge on the east side, and the high waves dashing against it soon washed out the dirt close up to the ties. This was discovered just in time to prevent an accident, and a large force of men were put to work piling sand bags along the north side, thus breaking the force of the waves and saving the embankment. Two hours more and the water would have taken out a section of several hundred feet of the approach to the bridge. The transfer of passengers, baggage, and mails is continued by boat at Council Bluffs. There is no material change in affairs here since yesterday. The Union Pacific road is running regular trains.

" The village of Waterloo, near Elkhorn River, 25 miles west of Omaha, is flooded to a depth of 5 feet.

" The overflow which covers the country for many miles is doing considerable damage to farms in Elkhorn Valley.

" Some citizens of Waterloo claimed their town was flooded owing to the Union Pacific Railroad embankment holding the water back, and they threatened to open a channel through it, but were prevented by the timely appearance of a sheriff and posse of constables from Omaha. Six ice-houses, located in Omaha Bottoms, have been wrecked by high water and rendered a total loss. A large wagon-bridge came down the river to-day, landing on the east side of the smelting works.

HIGH WATER ON THE UPPER RIVER.

"*Hannibal, Mo., April 25.*— The Sny levee broke at 3 o'clock this morning, at a point about a mile and a half above East Hannibal. The crevasse is 130 feet wide, and the water is still cutting both below and above the break. Near East Hannibal there are several weak points liable to go at any moment. The river is 19 feet and 1 inch above low-water mark, and is still rising, but very slowly.

"Trains from Quincy to Hannibal, via the Chicago, Burlington and Quincy Railroad, are abandoned, the track between Fall Creek and East Hannibal inside the levee being under water. It is estimated that 30,000 acres of fall wheat had been sown inside the levee, all of which is now a total loss. There are nearer 10,000 acres, the yield of which heretofore had averaged 30 bushels to the acre. This season it stood finer than ever. The loss on wheat alone is placed at $1,000,000. The river is still slowly rising, and has now nearly reached the highest point of last year.

"*Saint Louis, April 25.*—The river is rising and rapidly approaching the danger line. A rise of another foot and the water will submerge some of the low lands in the northern part of the city, and inundate part of the bottoms on the Illinois side of the river. Much apprehension is felt for property on both sides of the river, and measures are being taken to protect it. Old steamboat men are predicting a flood of unusual magnitude, and say that if the present warm weather continues, and particularly if there is much rainfall in the north, a freshet equal to that of 1844 will probably follow.

"*Bismarck, April 25.*— One mile of track and thirty pile bridges washed away constitute the extent of damages on the Northern Pacific extension. Night and day forces are at work repairing, and trains to the end of the track are promised in a few days.

"*Kansas City, April 25.*—The levee which was built to protect the town of Harlem and the broad bottom lands opposite the city from overflowing gave way on Saturday night, and a strong current, 10 feet deep, is now running at the rate of 5 or 6 miles an hour over the tracks of the Hannibal and Saint Joseph, Council Bluffs, Chicago, Rock Island and Pacific, and Wabash roads. For nearly a mile all these tracks are supposed to be washed out. The levee gave way about 10 o'clock at night. The water is overflowing a large number of farms to the depth of from 4 to 6 feet.

"*Saint Paul, Minn., April 25.*—A special from Fergus Falls says the upper country is an unbroken sheet of water, beginning at a point about 25 miles below Saint Vincent and extending this way to the vicinity of Crookston. Twenty-five miles south of Stevenson the water has swept away the track of the St. Paul, Minneapolis and Manitoba Railroad, and all railroad travel is suspended.

"*Saint Paul, Minn., April 27.*—The flood at St. Paul, caused by the coming down of high water in the Minnesota River, continues. The water has now reached 18 feet in the channel—3 feet higher than during the June rise of last year, and the highest point reached since the great flood of 1867. There is to-day scarcely a foot of uncovered land in the entire country west of St. Paul, flat lands, over which the waters are not now running riot. Old residents there affirm that although they have frequently seen the water cover the low lands, they have never known the current so strong as to sweep over them with such overwhelming velocity as it is doing to-day. The current carried away the bank on which Fifth street is built this morning, and there is only a single road remaining uncovered between river and bluff. A visit to the scene to-day found hundreds of houses isolated by water and the occupants busy moving. The sides of the raised embankment were filled in many places with all manner of household effects, which had been brought in boats from the inundated residences, and around which were the owners watching and guarding the same while awaiting the arrival of vehicles to transport the goods to some place of safety.

"*Omaha, Neb., April 27.*—The river has fallen 10 inches here. A further fall of 18 inches is reported at Sioux City. Information having been received at Nebraska City that many people living on the river north of that city were in great peril, one of the ferry-boats started out yesterday and rescued nearly 200 men, women and children, some of whom had been without food two or three days, and were suffering extremely from hunger. These people were lodged in the opera house, the city hall, churches, and other public buildings. * * *

"East Nebraska, on the Iowa side of the river, is entirely flooded, and all the inhabitants have been compelled to abandon their homes and seek refuge in Nebraska City proper. Thousands of people along the river bottoms in Nebraska, Missouri, Iowa and Kansas are homeless and destitute. Passengers, mail, and baggage trains arrived here same as the last few days, only did it more rapidly than heretofore. It will be at least one week before the railroads get into the same shape as before the flood.

"*Saint, Joseph, Mo., April 27.*—The river at this point

is 22 feet 6 inches above low-water mark, and rising slowly. Many families have been rescued from their inundated houses in the bottom lands during the day, generally in destitute circumstances. All the available flat-boats have been in use removing people and stock. An old man and his wife, 76 to 80 years of age, were to-day rescued from the Elmwood bottom, where they were living in a small, one-story house, having been two or three days surrounded by the swift current, a mile from land, and the water 2 feet deep in the house. * * *

" *Atchison, Kans.*, *April 27.*— Contrary to expectations, the river has continued to rise steadily during the past twenty-four hours, and is now 22 feet 5 inches above low-water mark, and at least twenty inches above the level of the great flood of 1844. The Missouri Pacific road continues to afford the only connection with the East, and it has to send its passengers and mails around by way of Topeka.

" *Chicago, April 20.*— The total loss of property by the flood on the Missouri River and its tributaries between Sioux City and Bismarck is estimated at $2,500,000. Below Sioux City, including the damage done at Omaha, Council Bluffs, Kansas City, and the great overflow on both sides of the Missouri between these cities and St. Louis, the amount of loss is computed at $1,500,000."

DEBATE IN UNITED STATES SENATE ON FLOOD OF 1882.

"In the spring of 1882 another destructive flood spread over the lower Mississippi Valley. Its damage in the States of Mississippi and Arkansas was described in the following debate in the United States Senate, February 23, 1882: —

"Mr. GEORGE. Mr. President, I should like to be indulged in making a remark or two explanatory of the magnitude of the disaster referred to in the joint resolution.

"The district overflowed from the breaking of the levee embraces all the Mississippi Delta between Memphis and Vicksburg, about 15 miles in length and about 40 miles in breadth. All of it is either now under water or will be in a short time. I desire also to state, for the information of the Senate, that four-fifths of the population which inhabit that district is composed of colored laborers, who have not the means of support during the time when this overflow will necessarily interrupt labor.

"Mr. INGALLS. What is the estimated number of laborers who have been rendered destitute by this inundation?

"Mr. GEORGE. They inhabit a district about 150 miles

long by about 40 wide. I suppose there must be from 50,000 to 75,000 inhabitants in that district.

" Mr. TELLER. What proportion of them will be rendered destitute?

" Mr. GEORGE. Four-fifths. I desire also to state for the information of Senators who are not familiar with the length or duration of an overflow in the Mississippi bottoms, that it is not an affair of a day or a week. The overflows in that section of the Mississippi bottoms generally continue from four to six weeks before there is a subsidence of the waters; and during all that time there is a total suspension of all labor; the water gets all over the whole country.

" I have confined my statement to the destitution in Mississippi. There are contiguous districts on the western bank of the Mississippi River, in the State of Arkansas, that suffer from the same overflow. The Senator from Arkansas [Mr. Garland] will make a statement upon that subject.

" I shall ask to have the joint resolution referred to the Committee on the Improvement of the Mississippi River and its Tributaries, in the hope that that committee may act upon it with promptness, as the matter will not admit of delay.

" Mr. GARLAND. The information that the Senator from Mississippi gives in reference to his own State applies exactly to the State of Arkansas, which is in front of the overflowed Mississippi River. The intelligence that I receive from that portion of the State of Arkansas through telegrams, letters and newspapers, represents the destruction there as widespread, and as absolutely appalling and unprecedented. The overflow has taken barns and granaries, and has swept away the last stock the farmers and planters of that country owned and had to live upon.

" I am not prepared in my own mind to say just exactly what relief, or what measure of relief, Congress can or should afford, but certainly there is now a just demand for relief, if it is in the power of Congress to grant it. I hope the joint resolution will be referred to the committee indicated by the Senator from Mississippi, and that that committee may see proper to give it early consideration and report some measure for the relief of those suffering people.

" Mr. HAMPTON. I just came into the Senate when the joint resolution was sent to the Clerk's desk and read, and as I am very familiar with that section of country, having been there a great deal, I wish to make a statement in regard to it.

" The area of land which will be overflowed if the river rises as high as it has done formerly will cover the richest por-

tion of the Mississippi Valley on the Arkansas side and on the
Mississippi side. I am more familiar with it on the Mississippi side than on the Arkansas side; but it will cover the
most productive and finest cotton-growing territory in the
whole State. I have known the river to be at that point
sometimes nearly 150 miles wide, for it covers from the Yazoo
hills on the one side to the Arkansas bluffs on the other, and
in that whole section of country, if the river is as high as these
dispatches say it is, there will be hardly any land at all
above overflow. There are only a few spots in that great Mississippi bottom which are above overflow, and the destruction
not only of stock, but of the incoming crop will be so great
that I have no hesitation in saying the dispatches from the
governor of Mississippi give but a faint idea of the destitution
and starvation that will follow there.

" My friend from Mississippi thinks that there are 75,000
people in this area covered. I think he has underestimated
the number very much.

" Mr. GEORGE. I spoke of the Mississippi side.

" Mr. HAMPTON. On the Mississippi side I think the numbers would be very much larger than that. Nearly the whole
of those people are colored people ; they rent the land and
the loss will fall upon them. They have made no provisions
at all for immediate sustenance, and unless some aid can be
given promptly, I have no question that there will be starvation and infinite suffering in that whole country."

In the spring of 1832 an unusually destructive flood in the
Ohio River Valley submerged a large portion of the city of
Cincinnati which was very forcibly described in the follow-
ing dispatch from Murat Halstead, February 16, 1883 : —

" The loss of life has not been very great, but the destruction of household property is enormous, and clothing, shelter-
ing, and feeding the poor who have fled from their homes will
strain all resources. The care of property in the submerged
district is a great task, and our military companies are out at
night patroling the streets. The school-houses are crowded
with fugitives. The coal supply of the city is under water.
The water-works are overwhelmed. The gas-works are submerged. Our condition is in many respects critical, but nothing but a sudden and immense rainfall beyond all example can
prevent our relief by the fall of the river. There are remarkable coincidences between this monstrous rise in the Ohio and
the December overflows of the Rhine and Danube. The parallel between the Rhine especially and the Ohio in the origin,
progress, extent, and duration of the floods is very striking,

and the correspondence in the two cases may be traced also in the intelligent compassion and remarkable liberality with which the sufferings of those made homeless, whether on the Rhine or the Ohio, were regarded and relieved by the enlightened and the benevolent."

The above are but illustrations of the frequent and wholesale destruction and desolation caused by the floods throughout the length and breadth of the great valley. But they are sufficient to show that these floods pay no attention to State lines and that they are national in extent and magnitude.

EFFECT OF THE FLOODS.

CREVASSES.

" Despite all this work, however, the Lower Mississippi Valley has suffered severely from floods and crevasses due to defective levees, to crawfish or rat holes, to rotten or defective rice flumes, to caving banks, storms, or other causes. Besides these crevasses already noted in the early history of levees, the following are the more important and destructive of the past half century : —

Flood of 1828. — This flood occurred before the country above Red River Landing was much settled, and it is probable that its marks have been confounded with those of 1815 in many localities. The Saint Francis and Yazoo bottoms were deeply inundated, being entirely unprotected by levees.

Relative to this flood in the Tensas Bottom, it was the highest of which we have even traditions. The whole region was under water. In the western part of the Atchafalaya basin the flood was the greatest of which we have record, there being no levees for several miles below the mouth of Red River. The overflow extended to the extreme western limit of the alluvial formations instead of only 6 to 8 miles from Bayou Atchafalaya as in ordinary floods. The plantations along the upper part of the Teche were not flooded, but the crops were lost on those within the influence of the backwater from the Atchafalaya overflow.

The eastern part of the Atchafalaya basin, indeed, the whole region bordering upon the Mississippi below the head of this basin, seems to have nearly escaped damage, the only exception being the Grosse Tête region, which was deeply flooded by backwater from the Atchafalaya overflow and by a break in the Grand Levee of the parish of Point Coupée, near Morganza.

17

FLOOD OF '44, '49 AND '50 ON LOWER MISSISSIPPI.

Flood of 1844. —A considerable rise occurred in April from a freshet in Arkansas River. In May, however, before the lower river had subsided, another and much greater flood in the Arkansas occurred. Above the mouth of the Red River the country was more or less flooded, but Red River, being fortunately low, the Atchafalaya carried off enough water to protect the plantations below the mouth of that stream from serious damage. This was the condition of the river in June when the great combined flood of the Upper Mississippi and the Missouri, which has rendered this year memorable in river annals, occurred.

The country above the mouth of the Red River was generally flooded. The St. Francis and Yazoo bottoms were nearly unprotected by levees and the water had free entrance. The Tensas bottom was badly inundated through breaks in the levees. Below the Red River Landing the country escaped with but little injury, owing to the very low stage of the Red River, which allowed the Atchafalaya to carry off the greater part of the surplus discharge of the Mississippi.

Flood of 1849. — The gauge at Carrollton indicates that the river rose nearly to highwater mark in the latter part of January, and remained there with occasional oscillations until the middle of May.

Above Red River Landing the ravages occasioned by this flood were comparatively slight.

The St. Francis and Yazoo bottoms were inundated, but to an extent not unusual for great flood years. Below Red River Landing the injury done was so immense that the flood is justly classed among the most destructive ever known. On April 7 a crevasse broke on the west bank, about 15 miles above New Orleans, at Fortier's plantation. This flooded the country between the Mississippi and the Bayou La Fourche to a depth of about 4 feet, and this submerged the rear of many rich sugar plantations. The effect of this crevasse upon the bed of the river has been much discussed. On the left bank a crevasse occurred on May 3, at Sauve's plantation, 17 miles above New Orleans, by which the city was inundated. The break remained open forty-eight days, and did an immense amount of damage.

Flood of 1850. — It appears that there were four principal rises this year, of which the first and second produced very little, if any, damage. The third was the highest, in the latter part of March, and the fourth, in the middle of May. The damage occasioned by this flood was immense. The

Saint Francis and Yazoo bottoms were not protected by levees, and both were deeply flooded. The Tensas bottom was submerged more effectually than in any year subsequent to 1828. The principal breaks were above the Louisiana line, which flooded Bayou Macon.

The water rose steadily until March 15, then declined slowly until early in April, then rose again until the middle of May, when it attained its highest point, and then rapidly subsided. At the mouth of Black River, the flood was 3 feet above that of 1814, and 5 feet below that of 1828. It is needless to add that nearly the whole region was submerged and the crops destroyed. Below Red River Landing the country fared but little better.

The water pouring from Red River exceeded the discharging capacity of Bayou Atchafalaya, and the surplus forced its way into the Mississippi by both of the mouths of Old River. The flood from above, augmented by this new supply, maintained an elevation sufficient to keep the numerous crevasses below Red River Landing actively discharging for more than four months. The basin between Bayou La Fourche and the Mississippi escaped nearly uninjured.

The crops upon the left bank above New Orleans were much injured by the celebrated Bonnet Carré crevasse, which attained width of nearly 7,000 feet, and continued flowing for more than six months.

Flood of 1858. — In the flood of 1858 there were four great rises. The first, caused mainly by a flood in the Ohio, occurred in December, 1857. The second rise occurred in the latter part of March and the first part of April, 1858, and was caused by a general swelling of the lower tributaries of the Missouri, Upper Mississippi, and Ohio. The third great rise occurred in the latter part of April. The Tennessee was unusually high.

The last and greatest rise in the flood of 1858, occurred at the head of the alluvial regions in June. It inundated the city of Cairo. It washed away miles of levees along the Saint Francis front, and poured rapidly into the bottom lands of that river. In the White River swamps the same condition existed. The Yazoo and Tensas bottoms, on the contrary, were comparatively empty. The June rise terminated the flood.

Flood of 1862. — Beyond doubt this was one of the greatest floods which ever occurred on the Mississippi, but the war raging at the time has so obliterated all records that it must always remain classed with the traditional overflows of 1815 and 1825.

FLOODS OF 1867 AND 1874.

We know that there was a great flood in the Ohio River at Cincinnati, and also in the Cumberland some time in the spring of 1862, and a destructive overflow in the Wabash in February. At Cairo the highest water occurred May 2, and was 1.2 feet above the high water of 1858. It is believed that there was no flood in the Yazoo or Red Rivers at the date of the high water in 1862 (except water returning from the swamps), but the records are too defective to render this certain.

Flood of 1867. — In some respect its origin was peculiar. The heavy downfall of snow and rain in the Ohio Valley, a sudden thaw caused moderate floods in the Alleghany and Monongahela Rivers and a great flood in the Wabash, the combined effects of which caused a sudden rise in the Ohio.

At Helena the first rise culminated March 14, standing 1 foot above high water of 1858, and eight-tenths of a foot below that of 1862.

The river then subsided about three-tenths of a foot, but again swelled to the highest point on April 1, being two-tenths of a foot above first rise. There was a moderate freshet in both the Arkansas and White Rivers; the Yazoo discharged a considerable volume ; in the Red River there was a considerable flood in June, due chiefly from the Ouachita.

The Atchafalaya basin was deeply flooded through a break in the Grand levee near Morganza. The Teche country was under water. The actual water-mark of 1867 was, in general, a little higher than that of 1858.

Flood of 1874. — In February the rain-fall throughout the alluvial regions was not unusual, and the river was generally about at mid-stage.

In March heavy rains prevailed throughout the lowland below Cairo, thus filling the swamps and swamp-rivers, and rapidly raising the Mississippi. In April these rains became excessive, and extended eastward over the valley of the Tennessee and Cumberland Rivers. In Missouri the breaks were very numerous. Between Commerce, Mo., and the Louisiana line there were 136.5 miles of crevasses and breaks.

The flood of 1874 rose 1.2 feet higher at Helena than in 1858. There was no great flood, properly speaking, in the Arkansas, River in 1874. In the White River, there was a destructive overflow. In the Yazoo, there was the largest freshet on record, due to rain-water alone. The combined rain and crevasse water in the Yazoo raised the Mississippi at Vicksburg 3 feet, during the last three weeks of April. At Alexandria, the Red River rose 23 feet between February 1 and April 4.

In the Ouachita the greatest flood on record occurred. Bolivar County, Mississippi, suffered severely from a rise in the Arkansas and White Rivers in March. The bottom lands of the Tensas were flooded through the crevasse in Carroll Parish. The overflow of the Atchafalaya basin was extreme in this flood. Bayou Teche was deeply inundated from Saint Martinville down. The Bonnet Carré crevasse raised Lake Pontchartrain suddenly about 2 feet.

The suffering in lower Louisiana this year was great. Hundreds of persons were actually in danger of starvation. Aid was asked for, and large sums of money were raised in New York, Boston and other Northern cities and States for the benefit of those residing in the overflowed region in Louisiana. Boston alone contributed $230,000 to this fund.

Flood of 1882 — In the early part of the winter of 1881–82, the river was unusually high, due to frequent rains that had fallen throughout the valley, but no grave apprehensions then existed of an overflow. At the beginning of the year, however, a series of rains commenced falling, which continued, without cessation, throughout the month, particularly in the valleys of the Ohio, Tennessee, and around Vicksburg. The smaller tributaries, the Clinch and others, in East Tennessee, overflowed their banks about the middle of January, and caused heavy damages to the farmers; the Cumberland rose rapidly at Nashville, flooding a large portion of the town on January 14, and causing much loss, particularly to the lumber interests, and much suffering among the poorer people of the city, 1,000 of whom living near the river were driven from their homes. Floods occurred also at Kosciusko, Miss., overflowing the Chicago, Saint Louis, and New Orleans railroad at Aberdeen, and at various other points. The Ohio also began to boom about this time, flooding the lowlands between Cairo and Evansville, and drowning considerable quantities of stock. The rains continued to fall and the rivers to rise. On the 18th the Big Black was out of its banks, and communication between Memphis and the outside world was nearly severed by the freshets occurring in all the neighboring streams. The Atchafalaya overflowed its banks, causing a suspension of work on the New Orleans Pacific, and at Grenada and Durant, Miss., and on the Tombigbee and Warrior Rivers, in Alabama, serious floods were reported.

SUFFERING THROUGHOUT THE WHOLE VALLEY.

The situation now began to look threatening. Heavy rains were falling every day, and the river rising. A thorough inspection was made of the levees, and much work done on them. But the rain softened and washed away the dirt. On January 28, a break occurred in the levee at Delta, Madison Parish, and another at Tropical Bend, in Plaquemines Parish, below the city; on the 30th another break occurred at Lockport, on Bayou La Fourche. On February 2 Red River rose, flooding the bottom lands below Shreveport. On February 9 the levees in the Yazoo valley broke. From that time forward crevasses occurred daily.

On February 13, the Kempe levee, in Tensas Parish, broke. By the middle of February all the bottom lands in Mississippi, Arkansas, and much of northern Louisiana were under water.

On the 20th all the upper rivers, the Ohio, Missouri and Mississippi suddenly rose, with a " boom " beyond all precedent. The lower portions of Cincinnati and Louisville were flooded; Saint Louis was cut off from railroad communication with the rest of the world, and hardly a town on the Mississippi or Ohio escaped without some damage from the flood. The situation grew worse every day, and only a few points on the river between Vicksburg and Cairo were left above water. On March 1 occurred a violent storm, which caused a number of breaks in the Mississippi levees, inundating Bolivar, Issaquena, Sharkey, Leflore, and Washington Counties. At that date there were fifteen crevasses in Louisiana on the Mississippi, Atchafalaya, and La Fourche. Great destitution existed throughout the overflowed region, and appeals were made to the Government for aid from Illinois, Missouri, Tennessee, Arkansas and Louisiana, and Mississippi. The number of sufferers by the flood was then estimated at 43,000. On March 8, the Point Coupée levee was broken, and the scene of destruction was changed to Central Louisiana. Through these new breaks the water poured down the Atchafalaya and began overflowing the Attakapas district of Louisiana, and ruining the finest sugar plantations of the State.

The water on the land overflowed by the Mississippi began to run off during the last two week of March, but in lower Louisiana the flood rose and continued through the greater portion of April. Even when this rise stopped, the flood did not entirely subside. It was not until late in June that some of the plantations were free from overflow. The flood may, therefore, be considered to have lasted fully five months. Over a hundred breaks or crevasses were caused by it, and 22,000 square miles, with a population of over 400,000, were overflowed.

Early during the overflow the Government had established relief bureaus in the various inundated States, and several hundred thousand dollars were distributed in rations. This was supplemented by the State of Louisiana, which organized a relief commission and sent a fleet to upper Louisiana to remove the people in danger of overflow to safe land, and to furnish forage to the stock which was being destroyed in thousands. This fleet rescued many people from starvation and drowning.

LOSSES FROM OVERFLOW.

An attempt was made to find accurately the losses from the flood in 1882. The police juries of Lonisiana were requested by the governor to prepare reports on this subject, showing the land overflowed on the amount of damage done. For Mississippi and Arkansas estimates were made.

In Louisiana, 26 out of 58 parishes were overflowed either wholly or in part. The parishes suffering most were Morehouse, Ouachita, Caldwell, Richland, West Carroll, East Carroll, Madison, Tensas, Franklin, Catahoula, Concordia, Avoyelles, Rapides, Saint Landry, Pointe Coupée, West Baton Rouge, Saint Martin, Iberia, Iberville, Assumption, Saint Mary, Terre Bonne, La Fourche, Ascension, Saint Bernard and East Baton Rouge.

In Mississippi, the counties suffering most were Tunica, Coahoma, Panola, Tallahatchie, Bolivar, Washington, Sunflower, Leflore, Yazoo, Issaquena, Warren, Claiborne, and Adams.

In Arkansas, Mississippi, Poinsett, Cross, Crittenden, Saint Francis, Woodruff, Monroe, Phillips, Arkansas, Desha, Chicot, Drew, Ashley and Bradley counties suffered.

The following estimates were made of the actual damage inflicted by the overflow:

LOSSES IN LOUISIANA.

CROP.	AVERAGE CROP.	LOSS.	ACREAGE.	PER CENT. OF LOSS.	VALUE.
Cotton..............bales..	171,750	42,280	229,000	32	$3,114,000
Corn...............bushels..	2,800,000	560,000	140,000	20	504,000
Sugar............hogsheads..	78,300	65,970	77,000	90	6,286,000
Molasses...........gallons..	4,984,000	4,225,000			2,142,000
Other crops...............			52,000		362,000
Total...............					$11,408,000

Add to the total above...............	$11,408,000
Damage to—	
Stock...............	1,090,000
Fences, etc..............	530,000
Houses and household goods...............	685,000
Levees...............	561,000
Railroads...............	730,000
Total loss in Louisiana...............	$15,004,000

FLOOD OF 1884.

The only important crevasse of 1884, but a very serious one, was that at the Davis plantation, 22 miles above New Orleans, one of the largest and most destructive known. A rice flume cut in the old levee had been imperfectly refilled and the great rush of the river washed out the loose earth, and soon cut a gap 1,000 feet wide. Through this immense opening the spare water of the mighty river forced its way, forming a converging stream that ran several miles inland, and pounding out deep gullies and holes here and there along its destructive course.

The railroad tracks of the Texas and Pacific and of the Morgan lines soon became submerged and all traffic stopped. The two railroad companies, in conjunction, undertook to close this tremendous crevasse, but the driftwood and debris of the river, together with the powerful current that was setting in against the work, so impeded, blocked and prevented any available efforts that they were finally compelled to abandon the undertaking. The great gap then grew apace, the water spread out a vast sheet of demolition over the surrounding country, overflowing adjoining parishes, poured into the town of Gretna, submerging the streets, driving families from their homes, causing widespread misery, destruction and suffering. The water poured down on the richest sugar district in the State, causing destruction on the west bank of the river almost to the Gulf, and entailing a loss of over $5,000,000.

HIGH-WATER FLOODS.

What May be Expected Every Ten Years.

The following is the Mississippi River Commission's calculations of floods: —

"At Cairo, between 1862 and 1883, inclusive, four floods have reached or exceeded a reading on the gauge of 50.8 feet, the highest known reading being 52.4 feet, in 1883. A flood of 51.5 feet may then be booked for once in ten years.

At Memphis, between 1858 and 1883, inclusive, the gauge reading has equaled or exceeded 34 feet six times, the highest reading being 35.1 feet in 1882. A flood of 34.5 feet may be expected once in ten years.

At Helena, between 1868 and 1883, inclusive, floods have four times equaled or exceeded a gauge-reading of 45.8 feet, the maximum being 47.2 feet, in 1882. A flood of 46.5 feet may be expected once in ten years.

At the mouth of White River, between 1862 and 1883, inclusive, the floods have five times given a gauge-reading of 46.6 feet or more, the highest being 48.5 feet, in 1882. A flood of 47.5 feet may be expected once in ten years.

At Vicksburg, between 1858 and 1883, inclusive, floods have four times given gauge-readings of 48.8 feet or more, the highest being 51.1 feet, in 1862. In 1882 the flood only reached 48.8 feet, the maximum since 1867, and may have had its height diminished by the Vicksburg cut-off of 1876. A flood of 49 feet may be expected once in ten years.

At Natchez, between 1858 and 1883, floods reached a gauge-reading of 47.9 feet or more five times, the maximum being 50.3 feet, in 1862. A flood of 48 feet may be expected once in ten years.

At Red River Landing, between 1867 and 1883, the gauge has in three years had a flood reading of 46.3 feet or more, the maximum being 48.6 feet, in 1882. A flood of 47 feet may be expected once in ten years.

At Carrollton floods have reached a gauge-reading of 15.4 or more five times between 1859 and 1883, the highest being 15.9 feet in 1862. A flood of 16.6 feet may be expected once in ten years.

These statements refer to the river as it has been since 1858.

COST OF HIGH WATER.

The total losses from overflow in the States south of Memphis since 1866 is estimated at $71,827,000, the worst years being 1867, 1874, 1882 and 1884.

The account of the Lower Mississippi Valley with the river since the war will stand as follows: —

To the building and maintenance of levees...................$25,704,482 94
To crevasse and losses from flood......................... 71,827,600 00

Total cost of high water in twenty-one years.........$97,532,082 94 "

The great flood in the Mississippi in 1881 commenced early in May at St. Louis, and on the 4th the water had reached nearly to the curb-stone on the levee. Great apprehension was felt for East St. Louis, and the inhabitants living in the American Bottom, and only for the railroad embankments near and parallel with the river, was the town saved from entire inundation. As it was, great loss and inconvenience was realized by the citizens as well as by all the inhabitants in the American Bottom."

These losses must continue in all bottom lands every season of high water, until a more thorough system of leveeing is adopted.

Experience has shown the practicability of this mode of protecting lands on the border of rivers. This, together with the revetting of caving banks, would in a few years reclaim all the bottom lands in the Valley of the Mississippi.

HIGH WATER IN THE OHIO RIVER.

[From Floyd's Steamboat Directory.]

"In the year 1786, the Ohio River rose fifty-nine feet above low-water mark. As the surrounding country was but sparsely inhabited at that time, the damage done by this flood was comparatively trivial. In 1792, the Ohio rose sixty-three feet above low-water mark — four feet higher than the flood of 1786.

On the 11th of November, 1810, there was a great flood at Pittsburgh. A brig which had been built at Plumb Creek, near that city, and which was ready to be launched, was floated off her ways by this freshet, so that the common process of launching was unnecessary. Fortunately the vessel was secured and made fast, or she would probably have made a long voyage down the river without the usual equipments.

July 14, 1828, there was an extraordinary rise in the Ohio River, supposed to be as great as that of 1792. It carried desolation into the lower part of Wheeling, which was covered to a depth of six feet. There was a vast amount of property destroyed along the river.

In 1844 the houses at Cairo, at the confluence of the Ohio and Mississippi, were nearly submerged. The swollen rivers were fourteen miles wide between the opposite shores of Kentucky and Missouri. Movable property of every kind, fences, cattle, lumber, furniture, and entire houses, (wooden ones, of course), were floated down the Mississippi and other rivers. A building was sent driving down the Mississippi, while several persons from the windows were calling for assistance, which, on account of the torrent-like velocity of the stream, could not be afforded them. Many drowning people and dead bodies floated down the Mississippi. A house, with a whole family inside of it, went over the falls of Ohio. Boats passed over fields and plantations, far beyond the usual limits of the river, and took the frightened inhabitants from the upper stories of their houses, to which they had been driven for refuge from the waters. The levees or embankments made at different places as defenses against the river, were broken through. Red River was higher in January this year than ever it was before within the recollection of man, and higher than it ever has been since.. All the lands in the immediate neighborhood of that river were desolated, and every vestige of cultivation was destroyed. In June of this year, the Mississippi at St. Louis was eleven miles wide, and was on the level with the second story windows of the houses on the levee at that city. Many houses were swept away and great numbers of cattle were drowned. The loss of property was immense. An obelisk about twenty feet high has been erected on the levee below Market street, St. Louis, to designate the height of the water at the time of this flood.

In March, 1849, the water was ten feet deep in some of the streets of New Orleans. This was the most destructive flood that ever visited that city. The plantations above were overflowed, and the rush of the water over the fields, in some places, was perfectly irresistible, carrying away every thing which opposed the current, which was believed to move at the rate of sixty miles per hour. The damage sustained by planters and others was estimated at $60,000,000.

In April, 1852, the Ohio, at Wheeling and Pittsburgh, rose as high as it did in 1832. There was a great destruction of property along the river, and many lives were lost.''

In December of 1847, there was another destructive flood in the Ohio. At Louisville the water was within thirty inches of its extreme height in 1883, which was the highest water ever known in that river. On the 15th of February, 1883, it reached 66 feet 4 inches at Cincinnati, 44 feet 5 inches at Louisville and 52 feet at Cairo. There was said to have been 15,000 people in Cincinnati houseless and homeless. Far greater damage and loss of life occurred on the Ohio this year than ever before or since. Until this year, 1832 was always referred to as the great high-water year on the Ohio, the water at Cincinnati then reached 64 feet 3 inches. While the water at Pittsburgh was not so high as on some previous years, all the lower tributaries were higher from the incessant rains that prevailed.

The loss in 1883 was estimated at ten million dollars at Cincinnati, Covington and Newport alone. Probably a larger amount was lost at other points in the aggregate. There was a large number of lives lost of which no record could of course be kept. As it was early in the season no losses were sustained in the crops, but as the banks and the bottom lands are

much more settled than on the Mississippi, far greater losses
occured in stock, houses, and movable property, although
the previous year, 1882, the losses in levees and crops, in
Louisiana alone, amounted to fifteen million dollars, from the
overflow of that year.

CHAPTER XLII.

TRAGIC EVENTS IN THE MISSISSIPPI VALLEY.

"MURREL" AND HIS GANG.

SINCE the discovery of America by Columbus in 1492, no
country known to civilization has been the theater and the
battle-field of more tragic events and blood-curdling incidents
than has been this beautiful Valley of the Mississippi.

Succeeding the treachery and massacres from the Indians
and the bloody battles that so often followed, encouraged by
the French and English authorities, came *the outlaw, the
pirate, the escaped convict* and the *desperate highwayman*
from all parts of the world.

The sparsely settled country rendered arrest and conviction
difficult, if not impossible. The numerous water-courses contributed to the escape of all offenders, and to the rapid movement of such as harbored on their borders. The mountain
fastnesses of the North, the boundless prairies of the West,
and the impenetrable canebrakes of the South made this
valley a veritable *elysian field*, for the successful operation of
all outlaws.

They appeared singly, and in all forms of organizations.
Among the earlier ones was Mike Fink, Sam Grity and their
associates. A class known as "boat-wreckers" in which
"Colonel Plug," figured prominently, on the lower Ohio, in
command of a gang of pirates, previous to steamboat navigation, whose headquarters were in or about the mouth of Cash
Creek, just above Cairo, together with organized gangs on the
Mississippi, which became so destructive to the early commerce of that river that the Spanish government at New Orleans took official notice of them and organized means to
suppress them. Later, and after the introduction of steamboats, gangs of horse thieves, negro thieves, murderers and
every class of desperadoes continued to infest the South,

making the Mississippi and the bayous their general rendezvous. Among the noted ones, even within the memory of many who still live, was one known as "Murrel's gang."

In the very popular work known as "Mark Twain's Life on the Mississippi," is this graphic description of the above gang:—

"There is a tradition that Island 37 was one of the principal abiding places of the once celebrated "Murrel's Gang." This was a colossal combination of robbers, horse thieves, negro stealers and counterfeiters, engaged in business along the river, some fifty or sixty years ago.

While our journey across the country to St. Louis was in progress we had no end to *Jesse James* and his stirring history, for he had just been assassinated by an agent of the government of Missouri, and in consequence was occupying a good deal of space in the newspapers. Cheap histories of him were for sale by the boys on the train. According to these, he was one of the most marvelous creatures of his kind that had ever existed.

It was a mistake. Murrel was his equal in boldness, in pluck, in rapacity, in cruelty, in brutality, heartlessness, treachery and in general and comprehensive vileness and shamelessness. And very much his superior in some larger aspects.

James was a retail rascal. Murrel wholesale. James' modest genius dreamed of no loftier flight than planning of raids upon cars, coaches, and country banks. Murrel projected negro insurrections and the capture of New Orleans, and furthermore, on occasion, this Murrel could go into the pulpit and edify the congregation. What are James and his half dozen vulgar rascals compared with this stately old-time criminal, with his sermons, his meditated insurrections and city captures and his majestic following of ten hundred men, sworn to do his evil will.''

There is a paragraph or two concerning this big operator from a now forgotten book, published half a century ago, as follows :—

"He appears to have been a most dextrous as well as a consummate villain. When he traveled his disguise was that of an itinerant preacher, and it is said his discourses were very soul-stirring, interesting the hearers so much they forgot to look after their horses, which were carried away by his confederates while he was preaching. But the stealing of horses in one State and selling them in another was but a small portion of their business. The most lucrative was stealing

:slaves, to run away from their masters that they might sell them in another quarter. This was arranged as follows: —

They would tell a negro if he would run away from his master and allow them to sell him to another, he should secure a portion of the money paid for him, and that upon his re-' turn to them a second time, they would send him to a free State where he would be safe. The poor wretches complied with this request, hoping to obtain money and freedom. They would be sold to another master and run away again to their employers. Sometimes they would be sold in this manner three or four times, until they had realized three or four thousand dollars by them. But after this, the fear of detection, the usual custom was to get rid of the only witness, that could be produced against them, which was the negro himself, by murdering him and throwing his body into the Mississippi. Even if it was established that they had stolen a negro, before he was murdered, they were always prepared to evade punishment. For they concealed the negro that had run away, until he was advertised, and a reward offered to any man who would catch him.

An advertisement of this kind warrants the person to take the property, if found, and then the negro becomes their property, in trust. When, therefore, they sold the negro it only becomes a breach of trust, not stealing, and for a breach of trust the owner of the property can only have redress by civil action, which was useless, as the damages were never paid.

HOW MURREL ESCAPED LYNCH LAW.

It may be inquired how under these circumstances Murrel escaped *Lynch law?* This will be easily understood when it is stated that he had more than *one thousand sworn confederates,* all ready at any moment's notice to support any of the gang that were in trouble.

The names of all the principal confederates of Murrel were obtained in a manner which I shall presently explain.

This gang was composed of two classes. The heads or council as they were called, who planned and concerted, but seldom acted. They amounted to about four hundred. The other class acted as agents and were termed strikers, and numbered about six hundred and fifty. These were the tools in the hands of the others. They run all the risk and received but a small portion of the money.

They were in the power of the leaders of the gang who would sacrifice them at any time, by handing them over to justice or sinking their bodies in the Mississippi.

The general rendezvous of this gang of miscreants was on

the Arkansas side of the river, where they concealed their negroes in the morasses and cane-brakes. The depredations of this extensive combination were severely felt, but so well arranged were their plans that although Murrel, who was always active, was every where suspected, there was no proof to be obtained. It so happened, however, that a young man by the name of Stewart, who was looking after two slaves who Murrel had decoyed away, fell in with him and secured his confidence, took the oath, and was admitted into the gang as one of the General Council. By those means all was discovered, for Stewart turned traitor, although he had taken the oath, and having obtained every information, exposed the whole concern, the names of all the parties, and finally succeeded in bringing home sufficient evidence against Murrel to secure his conviction and sentence to the penitentiary. (Murrel was sentenced for fourteen years imprisonment.)

So many people who were supposed to be honest and bore a respectable name in different States were found to be among the list of the Grand Council as published by Stewart, that every attempt was made to throw discredit upon his assertions — his character was vilified, and more than one attempt was made to assassinate him.

He was obliged to quit the Southern States in consequence. It is however now well ascertained to have been all true, and although some blame Mr. Stewart for having violated his oath, they no longer attempt to deny that his revelations were correct. I will quote one or two of Murrel's confessions to Mr. Stewart, made to him when they were journeying together. I ought to have observed that the ultimate intentions of Murrel was on a large scale, as stated by himself. Having no less an object than raising the blacks against the whites, taking possession of New Orleans, plundering the city, and making themselves possessors of the territory. The following are a few extracts: —

DETAILED ACCOUNT OF THEIR OPERATIONS.

" I collected all my friends about New Orleans at one of our friend's houses at that place, and we sat in Council three days before we got all our plans to our notion. We then determined to undertake the rebellion at all hazards, and make as many friends as we could for that purpose, every man's business being assigned to him. I started to Natchez on foot, having sold my horse in New Orleans, with the intention of stealing another after I started. I walked four days with no opportunity for me to get a horse. The fifth day, about noon, I had tired and stopped at a creek to get some water and rest a little. While I was sitting on a log and looking down the road the way I had come, a man came in sight riding a good looking horse. The moment I saw him I was determined to have his horse if he was in the garb of a traveler. He rode up and I saw from his equipage that he was a traveler. I arose and drew an elegant rifle pistol on him, and ordered him to dismount. He did so, and I took his horse by the bridle and pointed down the creek and ordered him to walk before me.

He went a few hundred yards, and stopped. I hitched his horse and then made him undress himself, all to his shirt and drawers, and ordered him to turn his back to me. He said 'If you are determined to kill me let me have time to pray before I die.' I told him I had no time to hear him pray. He turned around and dropped on his knees, and I shot him through the back of the head. I ripped opened his belly and took out his entrails, and sunk him in the creek. I then searched his pockets and found four hundred dollars and thirty-seven cents, and a number of papers that I did not take time to examine. I sunk all his clothing and effects in the creek. His boots were bran new, and fitted me genteelly, and I put them on and sunk my old ones in the creek to atone for them. I mounted as fine a horse as I ever straddled, and directed my course for Natchez in much better style than I had been for five days. Myself and a fellow by the name of Crenshaw gathered four good horses and started for Georgia. We got in company with a young fellow from South Carolina just before we got to Cumberland mountains and Crenshaw soon knew all about his business. He had been to Tennessee to buy a drove of hogs. But when he got there pork was dearer than he had calculated and he declined purchasing. We concluded he was a prize.

Crenshaw winked at me. I understood his idea. He had traveled the road before, I never had. We had traveled several miles on the mountain road when we passed a great precipice. Just before passing it, Crenshaw asked me for my whip, which had a pound of lead in the butt. I handed it to him. He rode up along side of the Carolina and gave him a blow on the side of the head which tumbled him from his horse. We lit from our horses and fingered his pockets. We got $1,262.00.

Crenshaw said he knew a place to hide him. He gathered, him under his arms and I by his feet, and conveyed him to a deep crevice under the precipice and tumbled him into it and he went out of sight. We then threw in his saddle, and took his horse with us, which was worth two hundred dollars.

We were detained a few days and during that time our friend went to a little village in the neighborhood and saw the negro advertised (a negro in our possession) and a description of the two men of whom he had been purchased and giving his suspicion of the two men.

It was rather squally times, but any port in a storm. We took the negro that night on the bank of a creek, which runs by the farm of our friend, and Crenshaw shot him through the head. We took out his entrails, and sunk him in the creek. We had sold the other negro the third time, on the Arkansaw river for upwards of $500, and then stole him and delivered him into the hands of his friend and then conducted him to a swamp and veiled the tragic scene, and got the last gleanings and sacred pledge of secrecy, as a game of that kind will not do unless it ends in a mystery to all but the fraternity. We sold that negro first and last for $2,000, and then put him out of reach of all pursuers. They can never find that negro, for his carcass has fed many a cat-fish and the frogs sung many a day to the silent repose of his skeleton."

MASON, THE CELEBRATED HIGHWAYMAN OF THE NATCHEZ TRACE.

1802. His band was the terror of every trader. Traders in those days went down the river in flat-boats and sold their produce for dollars or doubloons which they packed on ponies and went through on foot in gangs of five or ten men to their homes in the West. Before leaving Natchez or New Orleans they supplied themselves with arms and ammunition to protect themselves against Mason and his gang, who infested this only great road, the Natchez trace at that time, and preyed upon weak parties of boatmen passing that route. Governor Claiborn issued the following order for the capture of Mason and his gang. I have information that a set of pirates and robbers who infest the river and the road have their rendezvous in the cane-brakes near Walnut Hills. They recently attempted to board the boat of Col. Joshua Baker between the mouth of the Yazoo and the Walnut Hills, but were deterred by his show of arms and preparation for defense. The men must be arrested. The crimes of Mason are many and atrocious.

18

THE GOVERNOR OFFERED A REWARD OF $2,000 FOR THEIR CAPTURE—MASON KILLED BY HIS MEN.

Shortly after this Mason had a quarrel with two of his men, and on this occasion, when only the chief and these two men were in camp and he was asleep, they shot him, cut off his head, and set out with it to claim the reward. The Circuit Court was in session in the old town of Greenville, Jefferson county, when they arrived. They went before the judge to make their affidavit and get a certificate to the Governor. The head was identified by parties who knew Mason well, but just as he was in the act of making out a certificate, a traveler stepped into the Court house and requested to have the two men arrested. He recognized the horses they rode as belonging to parties who had robbed him and killed one of his companions some two months previously on the Natchez trace; and going into the Court house he identified the two men. They were tried and executed at Greenville. With the death of their chief and the departure of Harp, one of his captains, the gang dispersed and for many years there were no more highway robbers or river pirates in the Territory of Mississippi.

When General Wilkinson was negotiating a treaty with the Choctaws at Fort Adams, 1801, after having permission to have a road opened to the Chickasaw line where it would intersect the road leading by Colbert's ferry on the Tennessee River to Nashville, he proposed that a certain number of white families be allowed to settle there to keep entertainment for travelers. This the Indians refused, but as soon as the road known as the old Natchez trace was opened La Fleurs and other half-cast families moved to it and made lots of money, keeping entertainment for travelers. — *Claiborne's History of New Orleans.*

CHAPTER XLIII.

AMONG the noted men that came to the front during the
early settlement of the Mississippi Valley, they were not
all freebooters, pirates or desperadoes.

While General Harmer, General St. Clair, General Wayne
and other officers of the government in charge of troops were
fighting the British and Indians on the north side of the Ohio,
in defense of the new settlements in the neighborhood of
Marietta, Chillicothe, Fort Washington (now Cincinnati),
and on the Miamas, Daniel Boone with a few adventurous
spirits from North Carolina and the east side of the Alleghany
Mountains, were fighting their way through Virginia and
across into what proved to most of them to be the " dark and
bloody ground " —Kentucky, then the home of hostile
Indians and every variety of wild beasts. But to men like
Boone, Harrod, Kenton, Logan, Ray — McAffee and others
no barrier was sufficient to intimidate them or danger to prevent their westward march.

The woods were full of bear, panther, deer, the "open-
ings," of buffalo, and the lakes and water-courses of fish,
ducks and geese.

To men who had been raised on the frontier these attractions could not be resisted, though an Indian was found
lurking in ambush in every hiding place.

Every reader acquainted with the history and settlement of
Kentucky, knows how dearly it was purchased, and the blood
that was shed to secure its possession. To no one man is so
much due, perhaps as to Daniel Boone, although others
sacrificed much, and many, very many, sacrificed all they
possessed and their lives included. He was born in 1746, in
Bucks County, Penn., near Bristol on the Delaware. At the
age of 13 he immigrated with his father to North Carolina,
who settled in the valley of South Bodkin.

After remaining there a few years he married, and removed
further into the wilderness, where the game was more abundant. That having been his occupation and the only employment he ever fancied. While his opportunities for an
education were not good, he never embraced even such as
offered, but preferred employing all his leisure time, when

he could be spared from the farm in which his father and
brother was engaged, to devote to his favorite pursuit — hunting. In this he excelled even when but a lad. His rifle was his
constant companion, and his home in the woods and a dog
all the company he desired.

BOONE'S FIRST TRIP TO KENTUCKY.

After his marriage he settled on a place of his own and embarked in agricultural pursuits for a few years. But his adventurous spirit and love of solitude soon induced him to
abandon his home, family and farm.

In 1769, he, in company with a kindred spirit, by the name
of Finley, who had made one trip across the mountains from
North Carolina to Kentucky, and who had inspired Boone
with his thrilling hair-breadth escapes and wonderful accounts
of game and adventures, in company with four others, whose
names were Stewart, Holden, Mooney and Cool, all pledged
to stand by each other in all emergencies, started for Kentucky
leaving their families until they should " spy out the land,"
make a location and return for them.

Their route lay through trackless wilderness. The slender
supply of food was soon exhausted, and a camp for the purpose of hunting was made and as game was abundant, no
difficulty was experienced in securing a supply of deer and
turkey which was prepared for future use.

Their custom was for two of the party to watch while the
others slept, and so they alternated through the nights, by
short watches.

They soon reached the foot and began the ascent of the
Alleghanies.

Several days were spent in reaching the summit of the Cumberland Mountains, the most Western span of these heights.
From this point the descent into the great Western valley began.

The grand view that lay spread out before them inspired
them to press forward into the beautiful valleys of the Ohio
and its tributaries, with renewed vigor, knowing from Finley's account they were soon to be among vast herds of
buffalo, elk, and other wild game. While Boone had followed
the occupation of a hunter for many years, he had never
before been within the " buffalo range," and his anxiety to
reach that long-looked for field may be imagined.

The first large drove came in sight the day the travelers
reached the foot of the mountains. The buffalo emerged from
a skirt of woods and the plain was soon covered with an immense moving mass of these huge animals. They were moving right in the direction of the travelers, who had not been

observed.   Finley knowing something of their habits cried out to the excited party, "They will not turn out for us and if we don't look sharp we will be crushed."   The party came to a stand within rifle distance, when Finley shot the file leader. The patriarch of the herd fell, which momentarily checked the moving mass.   But borne along by the pressure of the multitudes in the rear those in front separated at the point the leader had fallen.   The opening once made the chasm broadened and passed the travelers on either side at a distance of some thirty yards.   To prevent the rear from closing in on them, they killed another, which falling in the track, secured their safety until all had passed, leaving Boone and the other members of the party who had just witnessed their first buffalo exhibition in wonder and amazement.   After this, buffalo were often seen like herds of domestic cattle, and were so easily captured they were passed without attracting special attention, unless their stock of provisions needed replenishing or their skins were necessary for protection.   Once across the mountains they were in the beautiful valleys on the head waters of the streams emptying into the Ohio, and by following the paths of the buffalo, deer, bear and other animals, they discovered the *sabines* or *licks* from which the salt was obtained, used by the settlers for many succeeding generations.

Thus surrounded, Boone and his companions had reached what seemed to be the "promised land."   The few Indians they met were disposed to be friendly, and they engaged in their favorite occupation of hunting, trapping, etc., with great success for several months, and accumulated a large quantity of skins and furs.   But the day of their trials was not long deferred, and what was to this small party of pioneers an *elysian field* at first, soon became the "Valley of Himnom, the shadow of death."   After numerous hardships and hairbreadth escapes such as would have deterred any less bold and adventurous spirit, Boone returned to North Carolina for his family.

From his representations and persuasive argument, after near two years effort, he succeeded in organizing a small party of emigrants, consisting of some eighty persons, men, women and children, and on the 26th of September, 1773, started across the mountains for the new El Dorado, *Kain-tuck-kee.*

For a detailed account of this perilous journey and of the subsequent trials and adventures of this wonderful man and not much less wonderful wife, see "Flint's Life of Daniel Boone," published in Cincinnati, in 1858.

In the same work may be found an interesting history of

another remarkable man who was cotemporary with Boone
and ought to be reckoned among the patriarchs of Kentucky.

DANIEL BOONE AND SIMON KENTON.

This was *Simon Kenton*, alias Butler. He was born in
Virginia, in 1753. He grew to manhood without learning to
read or write.

It is recorded of him at the age of nineteen he had a violent
contest with a competitor for the favor of a lady's hand.
She refused to make an election, and he, in disgust exiled
himself from his native home and located in Kentucky, where
he soon became a noted partisan against the Indians.

In 1774 he joined himself to Lord Dunsmore and was appointed one of the spies, where he performed important service in this employment. Subsequently he joined Colonel
Clark, in his gallant expedition against Vincennes and Kaskaskia. He passed through the streets of the former place
while in possession of the British Indians without discovery.
After performing many daring feats in this expedition, he was
employed to make a journey to Northern Ohio. He was then
captured by the Indians who painted him black, as was their
custom with those they intended to torture, and informed
him he was to be burned at Chillicothe. In the meantime,
for their amusement and as a prelude to his torture, they
manacled him hand and foot, and placed him on an unbridled
horse and turned the animal loose. After running through
the woods and brush in its fright without being able to shake
him off, the horse returned to the camp exhausted and worn
down, to the great amusement and shouts of the Indians for
the suffering and wounds that Butler had endured. Arriving
within a mile of Chillicothe, they took him from his horse,
tied him to a stake, where he remained 24 hours in one position. He was then taken from the stake to "run the gauntlet." This is the Indian mode for inflicting this torture.

The inhabitants of the tribe, old and young, are placed in
parallel lines, armed with clubs and switches. The victim is
made to make his way to the convict house through these lines,
every one endeavoring to strike him as hard a blow as possible
as he passes. If Butler reached the convict house alive he
was to be spared. In these lines were near 600 Indians, and
the distance was near a mile. He was started with a blow,
but soon broke through the lines, and was near the goal when
a stout buck Indian knocked him down with a club. After
beating him severely he was taken back again into custody and
marched through village after village to give all a chance to
see his sufferings. He made several unsuccessful attempts to

escape and run the gauntlet thirteen times. It was finally determined to *burn him* at Lower Sandusky, and but for a remarkable coincident that occurred while on his way to the stake, he would have been burned as proposed.

A notorious renegade by the name of *Girty*, who had united with the Iudians and was a moving spirit among them in all their cruelties and massacres of helpless whites, was then located at or near Lower Sandusky, which was a favorite resort with all Indians. After attacking Butler with the intention of killing him, Butler recognized him as an old acquaintance of his youth and managed to make himself known. Girty at once released him, and prevailed upon the Indians to forego the great pleasure they anticipated in burning him for the present. After five days they relented, and determined to carry out their cruel torture, in spite of all Girty could do.

By a fortunate coincident he met the Indian agent at Sandusky, from Detroit, who from motives of humanity exerted sufficient influence with the Indians to secure his release, and took him to Detroit, where he was paroled by the Governor. He escaped, and being endowed, like Daniel Boone, to be at home in the woods, by a march of thirty days through the wilderness he reached Kentucky, where he continued to devote his indomitable energies to the interest of all in the new settlements.

But it is not the object of this work to dwell at much length on subjects connected with the early settlements of the valley, which is not lacking competent historians. All who desire may find reliable and interesting authorities in every public library.

It is a subject of great regret, however, that so little has been recorded of that which relates to the early history of navigation of the great water-courses in the Valley, as it has been so intimately connected with the settlement of the country.

CHAPTER XLIV.

EARLY NAVIGATION OF THE ARKANSAS.

"THE first steamboat that ever ascended the Arkansas was the little old Buzzard, a worn-out rickety old craft that had lost all favor with every insurance company from Pittsburgh to New Orleans. Her machinery had been sunk in one boat, blown up in another, and pronounced unsafe and worthless by authorized inspectors, and instead of proceeding as it should have done, towards a junk shop to be sold for old iron.

In face of all these disadvantages, the captain had the audacity to stick hand-bills on the corners and other conspicuous places, announcing that the new, staunch, fast-sailing Buzzard, having splendid accommodations for passengers, etc., would leave for Little Rock, Van Buren and Fort Smith.

The owner of the Buzzard who had no other home was what might be termed an easy, shiftless, no account sort of a chap, fond of sleeping half the time and playing the fiddle the balance of the time.

The captain of the Buzzard was a different character, a wild, harum-scarum rough species of early rivermen. The owner was completely under his thumb, he had beaten him time and again for interfering in the management of the boat. Such was the captain, pilot, engineer; much of the same stripe, ever willing to fight, drink, deal faro, play poker or any other game.

One day the Buzzard entered the lower end of a long reach. The engineer now set his engine and proceeded to the cabin, took a smile of whisky and commenced to deal faro. The pilot lashed his wheel amidships, lit his pipe and proceeded to the cabin to bet against the engineer and captain.

The owner of the boat was seated aft in the cabin consoling himself with a plaintive air on the fiddle, he was great on Virginia hoe-downs.

The Buzzard, left to her own guidance, was going ahead finely on her own account when she entered a chute, took a sudden plunge into the bank with uncommon velocity, crushed in her bow, and knocked a hole in her as large as a hogshead.

"She's sinking," shouted an Arkansas man, "tomahawk me if she ain't, sinking shure." The owner heard it but fiddled, away with as little concern as Nero did at the burning of Rome.

"Three feet water in the hold," shouted the captain, "run the d——d old Buzzard ashore, if you can."

The owner heard these startling words, but continued to fiddle away. A passenger ran to him and bawled out,— "Did you know the boat was snagged."

"I suspected something of the kind," coolly answered the owner, as he laid his hand upon the violin.

"She'll be lost in five minutes" shouted the passenger.

"She's been a losing concern for five years," responded the owner, and went on playing his fiddle.

"I wish she would settle with me for what I have lost by her before she goes down, and be d——d to her," was the only answer from the owner as he moved the bow on his fiddle.

"But why don't you speak to the captain, give him some orders what to do in the emergency," said the passenger.

"Interfering with the officers of this boat is a very delicate matter," meekly remarked the owner, the next moment the cabin was half full of water. The Buzzard was a total loss.

The owner swam ashore with his fiddle under his arm, his bow in his mouth."

[From the Missouri Republican, August, 1822.]

"The distance from the mouth of the Arkansas River to Little Rock, the seat of government of the State, says the *National Intelligencer*, is computed at three hundred miles and the distance thence to the Cherokee Missionary establishment on the Arkansas at 130 miles.

Recently a steamboat, the Eagle, ascended the river the whole distance from the Mississippi River to within twelve miles of the Missionary establishment.

What a country is this where there are rivers navigable for hundreds of miles which we are just beginning to hear of. Surely the Arkansas is just becoming known abroad. If one steamboat trip to within twelve miles of the Cherokee Missionary establishment at Dwight, creates so much surprise among our Eastern brethren, how much more will they stare when they are told the steamboat Robert Thompson has actually made three passages this season to Fort Smith, about one hundred and twenty-five miles above Dwight, and upwards of five hundred miles from the Mississippi, and their astonishment will be considerably heightened undoubtedly, when we assert (and we do it from creditable authority) that she might have gone five hundred miles further without difficulty.

STEAMBOAT AT THE MISSIONARY STATION.

The sight of a steamboat gliding majestically through the waters of the Arkansas, in the very heart of the Osage nation, will be hailed with wonder and surprise by the aborigines of our country. And yet, however incredible it may appear to some, we have no doubt but that the time is not far distant when this sight will become familiar to them.

It is but little more than two years since we witnessed the sight of the first steamboat at the town of Arkansas, and not yet four months since we announced the arrival of the first steamboat that ever ascended the Arkansas to this place. But that which was a novelty to many of our citizens, a few months ago, has become familiar to them. They have already witnessed four passages made a great distance into the interior of our country by steamboats, and in future will look for their return with the same regularity that they look for the return of the seasons." — *Gazette*, *Little Rock.*

CHAPTER XLV.

FIRST STEAMBOAT TO ASCEND THE ALLEGHANY.

THE subjoined interesting account is from " An Old Boatman " who made the trip from Pittsburgh in 1830: —

It was several years after the introduction of steamboats on to the Ohio and other Western rivers before the commerce on the Alleghany warranted a great effort to navigate it with steam.

The current is strong and the water usually shallow and none but boats or light draft and large power are competent to navigate it successfully. Until the discovery of oil, there was but little for boats to do. The principal product on that stream for export was pine lumber. That was floated down on the spring floods and the lumber men's supplies was about all there was to transport for many years. After the opening of the oil wells an immense business was done on the river until the completion of some of the railroads, when it began rapidly to fall off, and was soon almost entirely monopolized by them, as are all water routes similarly situated.

An old boatman speaks of being on board the first regular stern-wheel boat, built at Pittsburgh in 1830, called the Alleghany. This boat was 90 feet long and 18 feet wide. She was worked by a double engine, two stern wheels extending 12 feet behind the boat. On May 14th she left Pittsburgh, stemming the current at the rate of four miles an hour. The first trouble she encountered was at Patterson Falls, 115 miles up the river. This is one of the worst rapids upon the river. Here a very useful improvement aided the engine, a poling machine, worked by the capstan or windlass in the bow of the boat, which drew her over with ease. Montgomery's Falls, five miles above, is nearly as bad.

We arrived at Warren, nearly two hundred miles above Pittsburgh on the 19th. It requires from 18 to 25 days for canoes and keel-boats manned in the best manner to perform this trip. On May 19th she departed from Warren for Olean, in the State of New York. Next day she arrived opposite the Indian village of Cornplanter. A deputation of gentlemen waited upon this ancient Indian king or chief and invited him on board this new, and to him, wonderful visitor, a steamboat.

The venerable old chief was a lad in the first French war of 1744 and was then nearly one hundred years old. We found many rapids and generally very strong water. On May 21st we landed at Olean Point, nearly four hundred miles from Pittsburgh.

The boat left Warren on the 23d and landed at Pittsburgh on the 24th. The time employed in running during the trip was seven days (running by day-light only).

FIRST MAIL ROUTE OVER THE ALLEGHANIES.

[Items, Niles' Register, vol. 14, 1818.]

"The Great Western mail and stages," says a Brownsville paper of August 10, 1818, "from Washington City to Wheeling, on the National Turnpike, arrived at Brownsville *for the first time*, on Wednesday last. It will pass three times a week.

A regular line of stages is also established by which passengers will be enabled to reach either extreme — a distance of 270 miles — in five days, in the following manner : —

From Washington to Hagerstown................................ 70 miles.
From Hagerstown to Pratts.................................... 20 "
From Pratt's to Big Crossing.................................. 20 "
From Big Crossing to Nichols, 12 miles beyond Brownsville...... 48 "
From Nichols to Wheeling...................................... 44 "

The promptitude with which this contract was undertaken leaves no doubt that this *mail route* will open facilities for

communication, and these stages will unite pleasure with
safety and expedition far superior to any other in this Western
country."

STAGE TRAVELING ON THE NATIONAL ROAD.

The above sketch will awaken early recollections and stirring
experiences in the minds of many old travelers, who used annually, and sometimes much oftener, to cross the Alleghanies
on business or pleasure, by the world renowned " National
Road." From this incipient opening in 1818, by the introduction of a single line of stages to run three times a week,
carrying the mail, there are thousands of persons yet living
who well remember the time when they crossed this same
" National turnpike," with a caravan of from five to fifteen
stage coaches in a line, filled with passengers and drawn by
four and six horses each. And they will not forget the excitement often caused by the break-neck speed in going
down the mountain slope, especially in winter, when the narrow tracks were covered with ice, and the only safety was by
putting the horses upon a run to prevent the coach from sliding off the track and down the mountain side. And even that
precaution did not always insure safety. Still that route was
so great an improvement over all others then available, that it
became very popular and was the principal route traveled between the East and the Great West for twenty years.

The opening of the Pennsylvania Canal was the first
successful competitor for this old stage route. But while
the canal route was much easier, and shorter, and afforded
many beautiful landscape and birds-eye views, the time required was much longer, and by business men was generally
avoided for the same reason that steamboats at the present
day are avoided.

But the canal was the favorite route for families, and thousands still live who remember among the most pleasant reminiscences of their lives, their experience in canal boat
traveling. And some of the most cherished acquaintances
ever formed was during these long canal-boat voyages.

ITEMS FROM NILES' REGISTER, VOL. XVII.

Steam — A London paper of July 17th, 1819, says: " The
Americans have applied the power of steam to supersede that
of horses in propelling stage coaches.

In the State of Kentucky a stage coach is now established
with a steam engine, which travels at the rate of twelve miles
the hour. It can be stopped instantly, and again set in motion with its former velocity, and is so constructed that the

passengers sit within two feet of the ground. The velocity
depends upon the size of the wheel.''

There is a steamboat in America of 2,200 tons burden. The
engine is of 1,000 horse power. It is called '' The Fulton the
First.''

'' The Erie Steamboat,'' from Buffalo, arrived on her first
trip to Detroit, 27 August, 1818.

The *Detroit Gazette* observes : '' Nothing could exceed the
surprise of the sons of the forests on seeing the *Walk in the
Water* moving majestically and rapidly against a strong current without the assistance of sails or oars. They lined the
banks above Waldon and expressed their surprise by repeated
shouts Tar-Tok-Nichee.

A report had been circulated among them that *a big canoe*
would soon come among them from '' noisy waters, '' which by
the order of the great Father of the Che-mo-komans would be
drawn through the great lakes and rivers by sturgeon. Of
the truth of the report they are now perfectly satisfied.'' —
Niles' Register, Vol. XVI. 1818.

CHAPTER XLVI.

THE PURCHASE AND SETTLEMENT OF LOUISIANA.

I.   HISTORICAL NOTES.

[From Internal Commerce of United States.]

IN the early days of European discoveries and rivalries in the
Mississippi Valley its comprehensive river system played
a prominent part on the stage of public affairs. The discovery of the river, in 1541, by DeSoto and his Spanish troops
was about a century later followed by explorations by the
French under the lead of Marquette, Joliet, La Salle, and
others, who entered the valley from the north. La Salle,
during the years 1679–1683, explored the river throughout its
whole length, took possession of the great valley in the name
of France, and called it Louisiana in honor of his king, Louis
XIV. Then resulted grand schemes for developing the resources of the valley, which a French writer characterized as
'' the regions watered by the Mississippi, immense unknown
virgin solitudes which the imagination filled with riches.''
One Crozat, in 1712, secured from the king a charter giving
him almost imperial control of the commerce of the whole
Mississippi Valley. There was at that date no European rival

to dispute French domination, for the English of New England and the other Atlantic colonies had not extended their settlements westward across the Alleghanies, and the Spanish inhabitants of New Spain or Mexico had not pushed their conquest farther north than New Mexico. Crozat's trading privileges covered an era many times larger than all France, and as fertile as any on the face of the earth. But he was unequal to the opportunity, and, failing in his efforts, soon surrendered the charter.

John Law, a Scotchman, at first a gambler, and subsequently a bold, visionary, but brilliant financier, succeeded Crozat in the privileges of this grand scheme, and secured from the successor of Louis XIV. a monopoly of the trade and development of the French possessions in the valley. In order to carry out his wild enterprise he organized a colossal stock company, called "The Western Company," but more generally known in history as "The Mississippi Bubble." According to the historian Monett "it was vested with the exclusive privilege of the entire commerce of Louisiana and New France, and with authority to enforce its rights. It was authorized to monopolize the trade of all the colonies in the provinces, and of all the Indian tribes within the limits of that extensive region, even to the remotest source of every stream tributary in anywise to the Mississippi." So skillful and daring were his manipulations that he bewitched the French people with the fascinations of stock gambling. The excitement in Paris is thus described by Thiers: "It was no longer the professional speculators and creditors of the government who frequented the rue Quincampoix; all classes of society mingled there, cherishing the same illusions — noblemen famous on the field of battle, distinguished in the government, churchmen, traders, quiet citizens, servants whom their suddenly-acquired fortune had filled with the hope of rivaling their masters."

The rue Quincampoix was called the Mississippi.

The month of December was the time of the greatest infatuation. The shares ended by raising to eighteen and twenty thousand francs — thirty-six and forty times the first price.

At the price which they had attained the six hundred thousand shares represented a capital of ten or twelve billions of francs.

But the bubble soon burst and its explosion upset the finances of the whole kingdom.

Some years later, in 1745, a French engineer named Deverges made a report to his government in favor of improving the mouth of the Mississippi, and stated that the bars there existing were a serious injury to commerce.

But France met with too powerful rivalry in the valley and in 1762 and 1763, after a supremacy of nearly a hundred years, was crowded out by the English from the Atlantic colonies, and the Spaniards from the southwest, the Mississippi River forming the dividing line between the regions thus acquired by those two nations.

The Spanish officials, for the purpose of promoting colonization, and to aid in establishing trading posts on the Mississippi, Missouri, Arkansas, Red and other rivers in the western half of the valley, granted to certain individuals, pioneers, and settlers, large tracts of land. They made little progress, however, in peopling their new territory.

But whatever progress was made under the successive supremacies of France and Spain, the Mississippi and its navigable tributaries supplied the only highways of communication and commerce.

In the year 1800, soon after Napoleon I. became the civil ruler of France, he sought to add to the commercial glory of his country by reacquiring the territory resting upon the Mississippi which his predecessors had parted with in 1763.

To quote the language of a French historian: "The cession that France made of Louisiana to Spain in 1763 had been considered in all our maritime and commercial cities as impolitic and injurious to the interests of our navigation, as well as to the French West Indies, and it was very generally wished that an opportunity might occur of recovering that colony. One of the first cares of Bonaparte was to renew with the court of Madrid a negotiation on that subject." He succeeded in these negotiations, and by the secret treaty of Ildefonso, in 1800, French domination was once more established over the great river.

Two years later the commerce of the river had grown to large proportions. Says Marbois, of that period, "No rivers of Europe are more frequented than the Mississippi and tributaries." A substantially correct idea of their patronage may be obtained from the record of the foreign commerce from the mouth of the Mississippi, for nearly all of the commodities collected there for export had first floated down the river. Of the year 1802, says Martin in his history of Louisiana: "There sailed from the Mississippi —

	No.	Tons
American vessels	158	21,388
Spanish vessels	104	9,753
French vessels	3	105
Total	265	31,241

"The tonnage of vessels that went in ballast, not that of public armed ones, is not included. The latter took off masts, yards, spars, and naval stores."

This growing commercial movement down the river of the products of the valley was checked by a foolish or arbitrary order issued on the 16th of October, 1802, by the Intendant Morales, "suspending the right of deposit" at the port of New Orleans.

Marbois well illustrates the intense indignation at this order on the part of the Western people by attributing to them the following language: "The Mississippi is ours by the law of nature; it belongs to us by our numbers, and by the labor which we bestowed on those spots which before our arrival were desert and barren. Our innumerable rivers swell it and flow with it into the Gulf Sea. Its mouth is the only issue which nature has given to our waters, and we wish to use it for our vessels. No power in the world shall deprive us of this right."

Of Morales's order James Madison, then Secretary of State, wrote to the official representative of the United States at the Court of Spain: "You are aware of the sensibility of our Western citizens to such an occurrence. This sensibility is justified by the interest they have at stake. The Mississippi to them is everything. It is the Hudson, the Deleware, the Potomac, and all the navigable rivers of the Atlantic States formed into one stream."

At this time, Thomas Jefferson was President, and in view of the uneasiness of the Western settlers he hastened to send to France a special embassador to negotiate for the purchase of Louisiana Territory. The opportunity was a favorable one, for France was then in danger of a conflict with Great Britain. The latter country had become alarmed at and jealous of Bonaparte's commiercial conquests, and he, apprehending war and fearing that he could not hold Louisiana, had about determined to do the next best thing — dispose of it to one of England's rivals.

Marbois, the historian of Louisiana, from whom we have above quoted, was chosen by Napoleon to represent France in the negotiations with the representative of the United States sent by Jefferson. His account of the cession — the consultation between Napoleon and his minister — and of his remarks and motives, forms one of the most instructive and interesting chapters of modern history. Napoleon foreshadowed his action by the following remark to one of his counselors: "To emancipate nations from the commercial tyranny of England it is necessary to balance her influence by a maritime power that may one day become her rival; that power is the United States.   The English aspire to dispose of all the riches of the world.   I shall be useful to the whole universe if I can prevent their ruling America as they do Asia."

In a subsequent conversation with two of his ministers, on the 10th of April, 1803, on the subject of the proposed cession, he said, in speaking of England: " They shall not have the Mississippi which they covet."

In accordance with this conclusion, on the 30th day of the same month the sale was made to the United States.   When informed that his instructions had been carried out and the treaty consummated, he remarked: " This accession of territory strengthens forever the power of the United States, and I have just given to England a maritime rival that will sooner or later humble her pride."

Under the stimulating influence of American enterprise the commerce of the valley rapidly developed.   In 1812 it entered upon a new era of progress by the introduction for the first time upon the waters of the Mississippi of steam transportation.

The river trade then grew from year to year, until the total domestic exports of its sole outlet at the seaboard — the port of New Orleans — had during the fiscal year 1855–56, reached the value of over $80,000,000.   Its prestige was then eclipsed by railways, the first line reaching the Upper Mississippi, at St. Louis, in 1857.   Says Poor: " The line first opened in this State from Chicago to the Mississippi was the Chicago and Rock Island, completed in February, 1854.   The completion of this road extended the railway system of the country to the Mississippi, up to this time the great route of commerce of the interior.   This work, in connection with the numerous other lines since opened, has almost wholly diverted this commerce from what may be termed its natural to artificial channels, so that no considerable portion of it now floats down the river to New Orleans."   The correctness of this assertion may be seen by reference to the statistics of the total domestic exports of New Orleans during the year ending June 30, 1879.   They were $63,794,000 in value, or sixteen millions less than in 1856, when the rivalry with railways began.

But since 1879 the river has entered upon a new and important era.   The successful completion of the jetties by Capt. James B. Eads inaugurated a new era of river commerce and regained for it some of its lost prestige.

19

Another step of great importance to the welfare of the Mississippi was taken about the same time. The control of its improvement was transferred by Congress to a board of skilled engineers known as the Mississippi River Commission. The various conflicting theories of improvement which have for years past done much to defeat the grand consummation desired will now be adjusted in a scientific and business-like manner."

IMPROVEMENT OF WESTERN WATERS.

In considering this mooted question of river improvement it may not be uninteresting to note some of the arguments and efforts that have been made from time to time during the earliest periods, since the agitation of the subject of " Internal Improvements," in Congress, on the ground of unconstitutionality.

After a partial acknowledgment of the right and duty of the Government to make appropriations for such purposes in the act instructing Capt. H. M. Shreve to remove the *Red River Raft*, and subsequently the snags and wrecks in navigable rivers, the first damper that was experienced came through a veto of President James K. Polk, of an appropriation bill, involving the question of *internal improvements*. He, with many others, at that time, taking the ground that the government could not constitutionally make appropriations for such works, and very strangely included that of -river improvements, while claiming exclusive jurisdiction over them and the "right to regulate commerce between the States." That put an end to all works of internal improvement by the government, laid the snag-boats to the bank, where they remained until they decayed and were then sold for a trifle.

After the expiration of Mr. Polk's administration and a more thorough discussion of the subject by the people, the conclusion prevailed that the government had the right and it was its duty to make the necessary appropriations to improve rivers, bays, harbors, etc.

From that time to the present the question has been what rivers should be improved, and how best to improve them.

The manner of improvement is still a mooted question, and conflicting opinions prevail. Every year, however, develops the fact that river navigation is not so necessary to the commerce of the valley as it was once supposed to be, and some large rivers are partially ignored, also many small ones, as being of no importance to the general commerce of the country — notably the Missouri, the Arkansas and some other streams. Later on, when the demand shall have largely increased for transportation, navigable waters will again become important factors, and it would seem a wise policy for the government to abandon for the time being the improvement of such streams, and devote its energies to the improvement of those now requiring it.

At the present time, 1889, there seems to be a general falling off in water transportation at the South as well as at the North, and a feeling pervades the whole Mississippi Valley that the decline is permanent, and never to be recovered.

This conclusion is based upon the observation and experience of the last few years, and has not been arrived at too soon.

It has arisen from natural causes, the result of the progress of the age, and demands a corresponding advance in the system of water transportation to meet it. This may require some years to perfect, but it is not too soon to recognize the necessity.

Fifty years was spent after the application of steam to navigation to arrive at the best mode of adopting it to commercial purposes. Modern science has made available a more expeditious, a more practicable mode of transportation for passengers and many kinds of freight, and it is only a question of time when the same agency will bring about a corresponding system of water transportation.

These great natural water ways in the Mississippi Valley, so convenient and so necessary to its commerce, will never be abandoned or left as mere sanatorians to the country through which they flow forever onward to the ocean.

The rapid development of the country is slowly awakening the government and the people who constitute the government, to a sense of the necessity of so improving these great arteries of commerce that they will be equal to the emergencies as soon as they arise, which will not be long deferred.

To the boatman of the present generation, to a superficial observer, the "good time coming" seems a great way off, and they are ready to exclaim, all is lost! "Othello's occupation is gone."

But when we contrast the situation now with what it was fifty years ago in this valley, what may not be realized five hundred years hence.

The present generation owe something to posterity, and although their occupation may be well nigh gone, their experience is of value and ought not to be lost.

There has long pervaded the minds of many experienced boatmen that the puny efforts of the government to improve

the navigation of Western rivers would prove abortive, that
no permanent good would result.

And such theories have not only been entertained, but often
expressed contrary to the opinions of long experienced government engineers.

This is unwise and damaging, and a little reflection ought
· to satisfy any one that the only way to make the best, the
most permanent improvement is through experiments. Hence,
if the government expends fifty million dollars and fifty years,
time in determining the best mode of improving the navigable
waters of this valley, who can say it was not well expended?

That there should be differences of opinion as to the best
mode of improving certain streams, there is no doubt.   But
to condemn any plan without being able to suggest a better
one, is absurd.   This is a sectional question and one upon
which this valley ought to be agreed, and to act in concert.
Otherwise we are liable to be combined against in any Congress and fail altogether.

To doubt the practicability of the plan of improving the
Mississippi River, as recommended and adopted by the Mississippi River Commission, would be impolitic, *provided* the
people of the valley stand by them and see that Congress
continues the necessary appropriations from year to year.
In the year 1872 the following communication appeared in the
St. Louis Republican: —

NAVIGATION BETWEEN ST. LOUIS AND CAIRO.

Editor Republican: From recent surveys and estimates
made by our present efficient and competent officer in charge
of " Western river improvements," Gen. Reynolds, it is satisfactorily determined that a seven-foot stage of water may be
obtained from here to Cairo during the lowest stages of the
river, at the small cost of $300,000.   (Greatly underesti-
mated.)

By the construction of dykes or wing-dams, of piles, brush,
or rock at twelve different points on the river, it is estimated
a permanent channel may be secured and with very little danger of being removed.

No one will doubt the expediency of the expenditure. And
if this object could be secured by the outlay of $3,000,000 the
merchants, underwriters and steamboat owners of this city
could well afford to pay the interest on that sum for all time
to come.   But it is not necessary for them to pay the interest
or principal on any sum to secure the object.

By a concert of action, prompt and decided, an appropriation may be obtained at the approaching session of Congress and the entire work completed within twelve months.

No argument is necessary to show the importance of the work. With a seven foot stage of water, flour was being carried to New Orleans for 40 cents per barrel freight; to-day, with a four-foot stage, freight is $1 per barrel.

The important question to determine is how to secure the appropriation for this specific work.

Since the government has recognized the necessity of resuming the further improvement of Western rivers, so signally interrupted by the veto power of a Western president, James K. Polk, various sums have been appropriated from year to year, to be expended under the direction of the engineer department of the government.

Last year the amount appropriated for the general improvement of the Mississippi was cut down by the manipulation of the committee on appropriations to $90,000, while it should have been at least $250,000, in order to have made available the snag and dredging boats the government had already in service, saying nothing about the iron boats it proposes to build for this particular kind of improvement.

A few thousand dollars expended at the present time between here and Cairo would be of incalculable service by a properly constructed dredging boat. But the meagre appropriation is all expended, the government boats all laid up and commerce crippled in consequence. We cannot afford to dispense with the general improvement appropriation. Neither would it be well to suggest it, as every one knows who is at all conversant with congressional legislation, that the appropriation bill, is an "omnibus bill," and subject to be manipulated by all who have any claims for appropriations. And all portions of the Mississippi valley have claims.

If we can secure the appropriation of $500,000 for the Mississippi, Missouri, Arkansas and Red Rivers, including the proposed improvement between here and Cairo, all interests may be pretty well served, and a large influence from all parts of the valley brought to bear upon the committee in making up the general appropriation bill.

It is fair to presume we can rely upon our Western members of Congress interesting themselves and doing what they can to secure this object, consistently with their other duties; but as their time is usually occupied in looking after the general interests of their constituents, it might be advisable to secure the services of some good, efficient man to go to Wash-

ington, and, in connection with our delegations, do what lobby-
ing may be necessary to secure that appropriation.

The object is worthy the effort, and no time should be lost
in putting the ball in motion.

A public meeting of those most interested should be called,
and the proper plan of proceeding agreed upon, and there can
be but little doubt of the result.   E. W. GOULD.

Two years previous to the foregoing communication, or in
1870, the following is an extract from the same paper referring to the necessity of protecting navigation against the en-
croachment of dangerous bridge piers, and the necessity of
larger appropriations for the protection of river commerce:

[For the Republican.]

RIVER APPROPRIATIONS, 1870.

Mr. Editor: It is a recognized fact that the public press
is the medium through which all great enterprises are inaugurated, all reforms introduced, and new ideas promulgated.   The
all-absorbing public enterprise of the present day seems to be
railroad building.   One can hardly look into a newspaper,
either city or country, without noticing one or more communications upon the importance of extending some railroad already built, or building a new one.   Then follows a long
editorial, setting forth in glowing terms the great benefits to
be derived by the city and country through which it is proposed
to run said road, winding up by an earnest appeal to the
philanthropy or interest of everybody, to contribute to the
great enterprise.

This is all right, and indicates the proper spirit.   And
whether it is all true or not, we want the railroads to develop
the country, and whether those that pay for them derive the
benefit or not, is a matter in which the public are not so much
interested.   But there is a matter in which the public are interested, and to this I wish particularly, Mr. Editor, to call
your attention, as well as that of your cotemporaries throughout the West and South.   I refer to our river improvement.
This may at first thought seem to be a stale subject, one that
has already been exhausted, and abandoned to the tender mer-
cies of Congress.   But let us see, before giving this matter
up, what the facts are, what has been accomplished and what
is proposed to be done.

The government, assuming control and jurisdiction over the
navigable waters of the country, is the only party to whom
we can look to foster and protect the commerce of our rivers.

And what has it done towards improving or protecting these mighty highways that float annually more commerce than our Atlantic ports combined? I apprehend it has done more to destroy the safe navigation of our rivers, by granting to railroads the privilege of erecting bridges over them, than it has ever done to improve them.

Seldom a week passes that we do not hear of the loss of some steamboat, coal boat, raft, or other water craft (saying nothing about the loss of life), while attempting to pass these railroad obstructions. It is contended they are necessary evils and must be endured. Although every man of ordinary intelligence knows they can be constructed just as safely, if not so economically, in a manner that will not materially interfere with navigation. It is only a matter of dollars and cents with the railroad companies. Not satisfied with granting to them subsidies by the million, in the shape of public lands, bonds, &c., Congress seems determined to sacrifice the commerce of the rivers by granting to them any privilege they may ask.

The question is not unfrequently asked by individuals as well as newspapers: Can not something be done to avoid the terrible marine disasters that are so frequently occurring on our rivers? Underwriters say, are we to be broken up, can nothing be done? Travelers hesitate, and often remark they would like to take a trip on one of those fine boats, but so many accidents occur they prefer staying at home, &c., &c.

Shippers complain of the exorbitant rates of freight boats are obliged to charge, in consequence of the dangerous navigation and the high rates of insurance they are compelled to pay, if indeed they can obtain insurance at all. Thus the whole community are directly or indirectly interested in the improvement of our rivers. And what measures of relief is the government proposing? What has it done to accomplish this entirely practical thing? Nothing, comparatively, nothing.

Three years ago Congress made a small appropriation, and ordered three snag-boats built. After much delay and perplexity in consequence of the red tape formality, the officer placed in charge of the work succeeded in completing the boats. Subsequently he was authorized to buy two or three more small boats for dredging, etc. With this little fleet he set to work to remove the snags and other obstructions from a given number of rivers, whose length embrace some 7,000 miles. But notwithstanding the inexperience of the officer in charge, as well as those of his officers and men, great good was accomplished. Thousands of snags and other dangerous obstructions were removed, besides many troublesome sand bars on the Upper Mississippi were excavated, and navigation much improved. But, unfortunately, about the time the officers and men engaged in the work had become familiar with it, and knew how to prosecute it to advantage, the appropriation of money was exhausted, and the whole fleet have been tied to the shore at Mound City for months, while the officer who had the work in charge has been removed to the Northern lakes, and the men scattered to the four quarters of the globe.

If Congress ever gets through with reconstruction, and should consent to take up the general appropriation bill, we may hope to get another appropriation, *provided* our Western delegation do not sacrifice us to some railroad scheme. If no appropriation is made, the snag boats will soon become worthless from decay, and will then be sold at auction, as were those built by the government under the direction of Capt. Shreve 35 years ago.

The question that naturally suggests itself here is: Why this neglect? Why are such important maritime interests left so long to suffer, while the government is appropriating millions for railroads and other purposes annually? To be sure, Congress has made two small appropriations for the improvement of the rapids of the Mississippi. But the canal at Louisville has been ten years under contract for enlargement, and not finished yet for want of means, while a railroad bridge has been built across the river at that point in less than three years — a work of greater magnitude than that of the canal — and will do more to obstruct the navigation of the river, than the canal will to improve it, except for the largest class of boats. So much for individual enterprise, and the influence of the press.

Now, Mr. Editor, if you and your cotemporaries through the Mississippi Valley will take up the subject of our river improvement, and ventilate it, and advocate its claims with half the zeal and determination you do that of a railroad or other public enterprizes, our delegations in Congress would never presume to return to their constituents until they had secured an appropriation that would render the navigation of our rivers as safe from obstructions as that of the lakes.

This is entirely practicable, as has been abundantly proven, and the appropriation of the insignificant sum of half a million annually, for a few years, will accomplish the object.

Can nothing be done to stimulate our representatives to move unanimously in this matter, and demand their rights? They have the power and ought to exercise it.

E. W. GOULD.

From about that time frequent conventions were held in different parts of the valley and the subject of river improvements were freely discussed and many communications were addressed through the papers in the valley. Among others were the following: —

"RIVER IMPROVEMENTS."

Editor Republican: In a recent number of the *Times* I notice an article over the signature of "Pilot" in which the writer joins issue with me on the consistency of criticising the work done at "Horsetail" and other points by government engineers.

I submit whether it is fair or consistent to indulge in any general denunciation without even an attempt at suggesting some better plan.

It is in effect saying the river cannot be improved, and this, coming from practical river men, who are supposed to know of what they speak so often and so confidently, may lead our representatives in Congress to conclude that it is not worth their time to urge so persistently, as they are obliged to (in order to secure anything) the necessity or utility of river improvements.

I am not an advocate of the present system of improving the river, if indeed there is any system. I have been of the opinion that the engineers having the work in charge have estimated from time to time what could be done, with the best results, with the small appropriations made — knowing from past experience that no large amounts need be expected, and have proceeded to make such improvements as in their judgment would most speedily improve navigation at the most difficult points.

That these have been the most judicious or the best that could have been made, I have no disposition to contend. I know of no precedents from which to judge. The character of the Mississippi is unlike that of any stream in this country where experiments have been made. And I doubt whether even our engineers know, except from theory, the effect that any given work will have upon the channel of the river.

They know, as we all do, that by contracting the channel, or the river sufficiently, they will secure deeper water. But the cost of building and maintaining works that will secure this result, must be for the present a matter of experiment. There is no doubt in my mind of the entire practicability of so improving the Mississippi as to secure a channel depth from St.

Louis to New Orleans of eight feet, except when the upper-
rivers are closed by ice.

If that were done but little embarrassment would ever be
felt from ice below St. Louis, and there would always be water
for all practicable purposes unless closed.

The best system to secure this result has never been submitted to my knowledge, or indeed any comprehensive one,
except the one proposed by Capt. J. B. Eads. Whether his
plan is practicable or not is not my purpose to discuss at present, but rather to urge the adoption of some practicable plan
to secure the necessary appropriation for the work.

I cannot agree with " Pilot " that by requiring from " can-
didates who offer themselves for Congress, a pledge to try
and secure justice to this great interest, we should get all we
want."

We can get those pledges all the time and without any combined effort.

Experience has shown that something more than a pledge
from members of Congress, elected upon a strict party platform, is necessary to secure the time and devotion the importance of this great work demands.

How many railroad subsidies and Credits Mobilier do you
think, Mr. Pilot, would ever have been secured by this pas-
sive policy, relying upon the justice of the case?

Congress is not a place to look for justice, and if we wait
for that our rivers will remain unimproved in the future as
they have in the past.

Our claim is certainly just, but in order to have it respected
we must send men to Congress not only pledged, but who
understand the tricks and are willing to devote their time and
influence to the promotion of the work.

We need not expect to effect it in one session. The public
mind must be educated up to the importance of the work.
Members of Congress from different sections of the country
must be secured and made to see that appropriations for this
great national work should not hinge upon the amount appropriated for small streams, bayous, inlets and unimportant
landings.

General appropriation bills are a kind of omnibus bill and
are open for all to ride who can get inside. And hence every
member is ready to jump in and load the thing down with unimportant measures, without regard to any general good.

So long as we look to the general appropriation bills for
means to improve our rivers, we shall never get enough to
amount to anything. That was fully illustrated at the last.

session of Congress. The bill was so loaded down with unimportant measures, the president assumes the right, when signing the bill, to cut off a large portion of it. This he very unfairly did by reducing the whole amount of the river and harbor appropriation three-fifths, instead of selecting the less important ones and leaving those he recognized as proper and legitimate to receive the benefit of the sums mamed in the bill.

But being upon the eve of a presidential election, he had not the moral courage to carry out his own convictions. Even in this case, if we had had the right man in Congress he would have stayed with the bill, and could have brought, in all probability, influence enough to bear upon the President to have induced him to have allowed the amounts appropriated to our rivers to have remained, as passed by Congress.

Now we are left with less than enough to remove the snags that have accumulated in the last six months, saying nothing about completing the works at "Horsetail" and other points.

It is now too late of course to expect to accomplish much in the next Congress. But if all in the river interest will unite upon some consistent plan of operation and push it as persistently as railroad men do their projects there is no doubt of the result.

At one of the early conventions of steamboat men, held at Cincinnati, I think, committees were appointed to confer with the Governors of States bordering upon navigable rivers, asking them to appoint commissioners — two civil engineers and two practical river men — (agreeably to my recollection) — from each State, to confer with two government engineers, as to the proper plan of improving all navigable rivers.

This, that then seemed to be a judicious plan of communing, fell still-born, I suppose, as most other things have, looking to the general good of river interests.

This or some more practical plan may be adopted, to set the ball in motion, and when once in motion it will only require the *votes* of its friends to keep it moving. Who will vote this ticket?   E. W. GOULD.
      1876.

THE JETTIES AT THE PASSES.

Editor Times: I find lying on my desk a marked copy of the Memphis *Avalanche*, of December 13, 1879, in which he following paragraphs are encircled: —

"It is a popular belief that the Eads jetties are a success."

"There is nothing really very wonderful in this popular policy, when it is considered that the influence of the press has been mainly exerted in behalf of this stupendous jetty fraud."

"The power of the newspapers is sufficiently great to make even the government solid for the jetty business."

"When the cash is all expended, and the contractors can see no prospect for any further subsidies, the dredge-boat will be broken up, the materials sold for old iron and fire wood, and the famous jetty channel will be allowed to fill up with Mississippi mud, unmixed by man's contrivances."

Now, Mr. Editor, if you can tell the object of this unceasing war upon the jetties after everything has been accomplished that was contemplated by the contractor and the government, you will confer a special favor upon our river improvement interests.

While there was yet any reason to doubt the success of this manner of improvement, it was not surprising that the plan, the contractor, and even Congress, should be critcised by those who thought some other mode of improvement preferable, or who felt envious towards Captain Eads.

Among the latter might of course be expected General Humphreys, engineer-in-chief of the corpse of government engineers, and his subalterns who had years previously reported against the jetty plan.

But at this late day, after the work has in the main been finished and the contemplated result secured, why this long continued opposition should be kept up, especially by those newspapers whose interests are so closely identified with everything connected with Southern and Western river navigation, seems passing strange.

The most charitable construction to be placed upon it is, they have said " the horse was sixteen feet high," and are not willing to admit that possibly he was not more than fifteen and a half.

Even if, as the *Avalanche* man suggests, the contractor breaks up his dredge-boat, and abandons the work when there are no more subsidies to be paid, the government can continue the work and secure the present depth of water, which is six feet more than has ever been in the Southwest pass, with all the dredging it has done, and at one-fourth the cost.

But according to my recollection, the government, by its contract, has agreed to pay $100,000 a year for twenty years, to maintain the present depth of water. And so long as that contract continues there is no reason to suppose the contractor will care to abandon it.

Of this no practical man who is at all acquainted with the character of the Mississippi, and who will take the trouble to go down to the jetties and examine the work, will doubt.

I am, therefore, forced to the conclusion that those who keep up this continued fight against this splendid achievement of Captain Eads are either ignorant of the facts or jealous of the result.

I have none but a common interest in the success of the jetties or in Captain Eads. But I think where a man has accomplished so great a good to navigation as this work has already proven itself to be, under so many embarrassing circumstances, sufficient time should at least be given to determine its value before condemning it or his motives.

But what is most to be deprecated in this connection, is the effect upon the public generally and upon members of Congress particularly.

While vigorous measures are being taken by those interested in river navigation to secure the co-operation of members of Congress, and suitable appropriations to insure the improvement of our great natural highways to the gulf, to have a continued tirade of abuse, suspicion and doubt in regard to what the government has done or is trying to do to improve our navigation, can but embarrass all efforts in that direction and prove to those members of Congress who are always too ready to interpose objections to appropriations for river improvements, that money voted for this object is being squandered and no benefits to navigation derived.

This, to some extent, may be true. But what work has the government ever undertaken that has not cost more than it ought to have done?

The various plans that have been advocated, and in some cases adopted, for the improvement of the Mississippi, are, of course, merely experiments, as there is no other river of its character known to navigation, where improvements have been made to any extent.

If the government should expend a few millions in determining the best mode of improving the navigation of the great rivers of the West and South, after having almost entirely neglected them for fifty years, it would be no great matter. And it comes with a bad grace from us here in the West, who are to be the recipients of the benefits sought, to be continually finding fault.

Let us accept with gratitude what we can get and make the best use of it we can.

If we don't strike the right plan at first, or some contractor

gets away with more than his share of it, or the work proves
a failure, we will try again.

The work to be accomplished is worthy of many trials, and
the expenditure of many millions. And it can hardly be expected that a system of improvements commensurate with the
demands of the commerce of this mighty valley can be successfully carried out without the expenditure of large sums in
surveying, in theorizing and in experiments.

E. W. GOULD.

St. Louis, December 17, 1879.

The following communication referring to debates in Congress on the subject of *too much* appropriation, is suggestive: —

RIVERS AND HARBORS.

To the Editor of the Republic:

St. Louis, July 5, 1888. — I see this "omnibus bill" is
again under consideration by Congress. But with what probable success of passing, "no fellow can tell." "Its log-
rolling" characteristics always endanger its passage, and
although it has passed the Senate, as it always does, with
some changes, it is by no means certain it will become a law.

And yet the friends of the Mississippi river, the main artery
of the commerce of this great valley; upon which hinge the
benefits accruing to all others in the valley, adhere to the time
honored custom of coupling its fate with that of all small
streams, creeks, harbors, etc.

The importance of this navigation, and the peculiar character of the soil through which the river runs, from the mouth
of the Missouri to the Balize is such that a claim for separate
and independent legislation by Congress, ought to be recognized
and if the delegations from the valley and the friends of the
measure would unite and step boldly to the front, and insist
upon this work standing upon its merits, there is but little
doubt of its being recognized. If not by the first effort, a
determined opposition to include it in the general appropriation bill, for river and harbors, would soon secure the necessary legislation, and insure regular appropriations, as the
work progressed. Even should this proposition be rejected
for years, but little would be lost to navigation. The meager
appropriations that are now being doled out from year to year
when any are made, is barely sufficient to show to practical
men and to engineers in charge of the work, what could be
accomplished by liberal annual appropriations.

The general public only know how little has been done towards permanently improving the navigation in all these years, without knowing *why more has not been accomplished* and are beginning to look with suspicion upon every appropriation that is asked for and to doubt the practicability of any attempt to improve the navigation of those great national highways.

Senator Plumb struck the keynote to the present system of river improvements in his speech in the Senate last Saturday in discussing Senator Vest's proposition to dissolve the Missouri river commission.

He said " while he had never voted for a river and harbor bill, he would be willing to vote an appropriation of $50,000,000 " if there was any guarantee that it would be judiciously expended. But he denounced the system of small and inadequate appropriations that could be of no permanent benefit to navigation.

He said he " was opposed to dumping it into small streams and insignificant harbors."

I think, however, the Senator from Kansas is in error in his estimation of the engineer corps of the government.

If correctly reported in *The Republic's* special of July 2 from Washington, " he (Mr. Plumb) handled the engineer corps without gloves, and declared they knew nothing whatever about civil engineering. They were fancy military men who employed practical engineers to do the work while they went into society," etc., etc.

That is probably true in many instances. But to charge that they know nothing about civil engineering, and employ others to do their work, is not true when applied to the engineers that have been in charge of the river improvements in the Mississippi valley for the last twenty years. The rules of the war department are such that it is necessary for the officials working under it to use a great amount of red tape, and work is often delayed in consequence. But that is not the fault of the engineers. So far as my acquaintance and observation goes the government engineers in charge of the work on the Mississippi river and its tributaries have been good business men, with large practical experience in engineering, and in knowledge of the wants of navigation, with quite the average ability to manage and utilize skilled and unskilled labor, in the prosecution of their work.

Failure on the part of the Congress to make sufficient provision to prosecute a system of works to a successful termination, or to fully test any proposed plan of improvement, should not be charged to the inefficiency of the engineers.

The truth is, the government has undertaken to do too much experimental work at one time. For as still as it is kept, the improvement of such rivers as the Lower Mississippi, the Missouri and the Arkansas, is yet an experiment, so far as the best, the most permanent and most practical method of doing it is concerned.

Although the system adopted by the Mississippi River Commission, so far as it has been fairly tried, seems probable to be entirely successful on such streams.

Senator Vest's proposition to dispense with the services of the Missouri River, Commission is undoubtedly a step in the right direction, and another one would be for him to move to strike out of the river and harbor bill the proposed appropriation for the improvement of the navigation of that stream. Although, considering his constituency and his own residence, it is not reasonable to suppose he would feel justified in making that effort now, even though the bill had not passed the Senate. But his observation for the last thirty years, I am satisfied, has been such that he could conscientiously oppose any more small appropriations, unless it was for the protection of the shores of some important cities and towns.

The Senator has seen in the time mentioned the river commerce of that stream fall off from the employment of sixty regular steamboats between St. Louis an Sioux City to none at all at the present time, except two or three small boats yet running at the lower end of the river, while the commerce of the Missouri valley has increased in that time probably 1,000 per cent.

Agreeable to the bureau of statistic at Washington, the government has expended a little less than $3,000,000 all told in its effort to improve and protect the navigation of this river, principally within the time specified above.

It is safe to say, however, that all the benefit that has accrued to navigation from the expenditure of this large amount of money has been counterbalanced by the damage produced by illy-constructed bridges.

It requires no further argument to show the fallacy of continuing the Missouri river Commission, or of the small appropriations that have heretofore been made.

If the experiments that are now being made on the Mississippi from the mouth of the Missouri to New Orleans are successful and secure good, permanent navigation the whole distance, it will establish the practicability of appropriating large and sufficient sums of money to make good and safe navigation on all streams of like character.

Then it may be possible, and even practicable, to secure appropriations sufficient to so improve the Missouri as to make it a competitor for the transportation of bulky freights, with the numerous railroads that are now monopolizing the entire commerce of that valley. But to persist in asking Congress to continue appropriations for the improvement of such rivers before they are absolutely necessary to accommodate the commerce of the country, or a plan has been determined upon by which they can be successfully improved, is unwise, and involves the liability of suspending work indefinitely on the Mississippi and other streams that are of great importance to commerce.

If the friends of the Western river improvements, both in Congress and out of it, would change their tactics to a less "log-rolling," or, as Senator Vest puts it, "a species of agreement," would probably secure in the end more satisfactory results.

E. W. GOULD.

"Capt. E. W. Gould is recognized by all as most competent authority upon all matters pertaining to our rivers and their commerce, and the following communication from him possesses much of interest to our merchants, shippers and steamboatmen:" —

PRACTICAL EFFECT OF DEEPENING THE MISSISSIPPI BETWEEN ST. LOUIS AND CAIRO.

Editor Republican: There seems no time so appropriate to awaken public interest, and especially that of business men, as when their business is being seriously embarrassed by any temporary cause.

That such cause now exists in consequence of the ice embargo there can be no doubt. I therefore propose, with your indulgence, to call the attention of shippers particularly to some facts connected with the suspension of navigation between here and Cairo.

It has now been nearly three weeks since navigation has been virtually suspended, and the probability is it will remain so for some weeks to come.

I question if there can be found a man in the city, whose opinion is entitled to consideration, that will not agree that if there were eight feet of water in the channel there would have been no serious interruption of navigation up to the present time.

I leave it to those most interested to determine the amount of damage that has already been sustained by the ice embargo this winter.

It is claimed by many good practical engineers that it is entirely within the possibility of modern science to so deepen the channel from here to Cairo to afford eight feet of water at all seasons.

If this is practicable, as I believe it to be, it would insure good and safe navigation the year round in some years, and but a short suspension in others. By deepening the channel and securing the banks, which must necessarily follow, if made permanent, the places where the ice usually blocks first would be easily removed by straightening the river at those points — thus removing in a great measure the liability of an ice blockade, except in very severe weather.

The principal liability would be in extreme high water in the Ohio, when the Mississippi is backed up and the current checked so that the ice will not run out. But as the water is always high at such times there need be no difficulty in keeping the river open at that point by moving a government snag boat, or any other boat, through it as often as might be found necessary and at small expense.

The only formidable objection that can be raised to this great enterprise is the cost of it, and I submit whether the damage to commerce is not (every winter navigation is suspended for two months) sufficient to pay the entire cost of the improvement — saying nothing of the great benefit to be derived during the usual low-water season.

The government has long since recognized the importance of this work, and has made many small inadequate appropriations to improve the navigation, but in consequence of not having first comprehended the magnitude of the work, and its great importance to commerce, the various appropriations have generally been frittered away without accomplishing much good.

The people of the valley have now so far waked up to the importance of water transportation there is a reasonable expectation that Congress will indorse the recommendations of the " commission " that was appointed by the President on the Mississippi River, and make the appropriation at this session to inaugurate the work.

This will be a great point gained, and will almost insure a continuance of the work to its ultimate completion.

But this proposition is confined to the river below Cairo, and will not be extended above that point for several years unless active measures are taken by citizens interested in the commerce of the river, living at St. Louis and in the country above.

The present blockade is very suggestive, and there is no doubt that a combined effort by all parties in interest at the present time, would do much to secure the favorable consideration of Congress to our pressing and immediate necessities.

It is only by active and vigorous measures that we can expect special attention to this part of the river in the near future.   E. W. GOULD.
ST. LOUIS, December 10, 1880.

IMPROVEMENT OF MISSOURI RIVER.

ST. LOUIS, Nov. 17, 1882.

Editor Republican: There seems to be some apprehension as to what disposition is to be made of the $800,000 appropriated by the last Congress for the improvement of this river. If it is proposed to enter upon a *general system* of improvement along the whole course of the river, from the mouth to Sioux City, a distance of 800 miles, according to plans submitted by Maj. Suter, leaving the bridges unprotected and other important work at the lower part of the river neglected, it will, in my opinion, be a grave mistake if not a blunder, and will demand an investigating committee from Congress far more than the works or the proposed work of improvement on the Lower Mississippi.

Agreeable to estimates made and submitted to the secretary of war by Maj. Suter, the engineer more especially in charge of this work, it was estimated to cost *eight millions of dollars*, to secure a minimum depth of water of 10 feet in the channel the whole distance; provided the whole amount was appropriated at one time, and subject to the draft of the engineer in charge of the work whenever called for.

This or any other sum might be considered a prudent estimate, upon that condition, as it is not among even the possibilities that any such sum can ever be secured at one time for this work. And if attempted to be done by appropriations, from time to time, agreeable to the caprice of Congress, it will undoubtedly cost double the amount of the estimate, if indeed it is ever done.

I doubt if there is a man living, whose opinions are valid upon this subject, who will not condemn any plan of improvement involving the probable cost of this

work — between Kansas City and Sioux City — certainly not
for many years to come.

A glance at the map will convince any one, who is not
blind, that the distance across the country to the lakes or to
tide water is so much less than by the meanderings of the
river that the commerce of that portion of the country will
never seek the river route whatever may be the character of
navigation.

HOW TO EXPEND $800,000.

The distance from the mouth of the river to Kansas City,.
or perhaps St. Joseph, is not so great but that with the bridge
piers, properly protected, the removal of snags, wrecks and
trees, with an occasional dredging at certain points, the navigation may be made equal to the demands of commerce for a
sum, probably consistent with the views of Congress.

There is no need of ten feet of water in that river. If six
feet is secured it will be quite sufficient for all practical purposes for twenty years to come.

Such is the competition with railroads even now, that freights
are carried as cheaply to and from all points on that river as
to most others the same distance to a market.

If the present appropriation of $800,000 is frittered away in
surveys, plants and preparations for a general system of improvement, nothing beneficial to the present navigation is
likely to result, and if we can judge anything from the present temper of the people, it is fair to presume that the next
appropriation for river and harbor improvements will be confined to strictly legitimate works. And there are too many of
them in the West and South to jeopardize them by asking for
appropriations for improvements not necessary to the commerce of the country for many years to come, if ever.

Would it not be far better and more consistent with the circumstances to economize in the use of the present appropriation and expend it in doing what is known to be practical work,
and very necessary too, than to launch out upon an untried.
and doubtful theory, involving millions of dollars?

It is well known the character of the Missouri and Mississippi, below the mouth of the Missouri, are very similar, and
as the system adopted by the " Mississippi River Commission "
is yet an experiment, prudence would certainly suggest the
wisdom of waiting until the result of these experiments is
known.

Members of Congress from Missouri, Kansas, Nebraska and
other Western States, who contributed so largely in securing

the appropriations for river improvements the last session, and who feel the necessity for improved navigation on the Missouri, will recognize the propriety of a judicious expenditure of this $800,000, well knowing that unless satisfactory results are secured, further appropriations will be withheld.

The whole amount of this appropriation can be judiciously expended between the mouth and Fort Benton, in the manner I have intimated, and good results secured for every dollar of it, and involve no risk or experiment.

E. W. GOULD.

CHAPTER XLVII.

FIRST IMPROVEMENT ON THE MISSISSIPPI.

IN 1699 and before any settlements had been made in the Valley, Bienville, the French explorer, found the river partially obstructed at one point by a drift pile which he removed and allowed the water free passage. This was probably the first attempt to improve the navigation of what were termed *Western Waters.*

In a statistical work recently issued by the Treasury Department under the direction of Colonel Wm. F. Switzler the following interesting statistical account is taken.

The great diversity of opinion on this important subject is sufficient apology for the extended quotations from this valuable work.

While it is principally local, and confined to the Lower Mississippi, it is still national in character and involves the question of river improvements throughout the entire Mississippi Valley.

"It is now recognized by the Mississippi River Commission that levees are an important factor in river improvement, and that whatever is done to restrain the volume of the river within its banks will enable it to cut out its channel and to give deeper water and better navigation. This doctrine was forcibly enunciated by the Commission in its first report, and it has since assisted liberally in the building of levees, recognizing them as important elements in river improvement. On this basis, therefore, the amount expended on levees by the several lower river States may be properly included among the expenditures for the improvement of navigation. They undoubtedly had that effect, as was well shown by the fact that in Louisiana, where the levees were maintained in the earliest day, the river was always deep and never troubled by bars, whereas above, there were frequent obstructions. As a matter of fact, however, these levees were created with no expectation or intention of deepening the Mississippi, nor, indeed, with any idea that they had that effect. They were constructed wholly for defensive purposes to protect the land from overflow.

The first work of the new settlers on the Mississippi in 1717 was to construct a levee for the purpose of protecting themselves from overflow, but without any idea of improving navigation.

FIRST WORK BY THE FRENCH.

The first regular river improvement was that attempted by the French Government in 1726, for the purpose of removing the bar from the mouth of the Mississippi, deepening its navigation, and allowing the easy entrance of its largest war vessels. At that time the Mississippi afforded a depth of only 6 or 8 feet, and while this was sufficient for the small vessels engaged in the colonial trade, it was not for the men-of-war seeking refuge in the river. The process adopted for removing the bar was one followed for many years afterward. It consisted simply in dragging iron harrows over the shallow places, stirring up the mud, which was carried away by the current. It was successful temporarily. The required depth was obtained, but it was only for a short time, and it had to be done over again repeatedly.

While some records exist of the work done on the levees under the French and Spanish regimes, there is very little said about river improvement. The only works undertaken were the leveeing of the banks, which had the effect of deepening the channel, the dredging at the bar to secure a better depth there, and the removal of snags and logs.

The Spanish Government, which devoted itself very assiduously to developing and improving the material resources of the country, cleared out the mouths of Bayous Manchac and La Fourche, and thus gave better connection between the Mississippi and these streams. As the clearing of the river banks gave a deep, navigable stream along all that portion of the Mississippi then settled (from Bayou Sara down), there was really nothing to be done save to keep the mouth of the river open and to clear it of floating drift. The first was done by the Government, the latter generally by the people, al-

though once or twice officers assisted in removing a troublesome raft where the logs and timber piled up in large masses,
affecting navigation more or less.

The cession of the country to the United States caused no
change. Nothing was done for the specific purpose of river
improvement, although that was incidentally obtained by the
levees constructed. About the time of the battle of New Orleans an important work was performed in the construction,
under the order of General Jackson, of a dike over Bayou
Manchac. Bayou Manchac connects the Mississippi River
with the Amite, or Iberville, and Lake Pontchartrain and the
Gulf, and is thus a short cut to the sea. It was frequently
used for purposes of navigation during the early days of the
colony, and it was by this route that Bienville and his men
entered the river from the settlements on the Mississippi
Sound coast, thus avoiding the danger of a trip through the
Gulf and passes and up the river. General Jackson's purpose
in closing the bayou was not river improvement, but military
defense, as this route offered the British an easy entrance into
the Mississippi above New Orleans. The work, however, in
the view now taken of river improvements by the Mississippi
River Commission was an important one, being the first step
towards closing outlets and thus confining the Mississippi to a
single channel and forcing it to cut out and deepen that channel.

The large number of people who about this time came pouring down the river from every portion of the upper country,
but particularly from Kentucky, Tennessee, Virginia, and
Pennsylvania, resulted in some improvement of the river, or
rather in the removal of the obstructions in the way of logs,
rafts, sawyers, etc., that had previously existed. The work
was done altogether by the boatmen. The States did nothing,
and the United States Government did not recognize its
obligations in this matter until about 1829, when it inaugurated, under Captain Shreve, the snag-boat system. Previous
to that time, the boatmen themselves had removed, in their
passage down stream, the numerous logs which obstructed
and rendered the navigation of the river dangerous. The settlers were everywhere felling the forests along its banks,
rafts and logs were being floated down, barges and flat-boats
sinking, and, as a consequence, the river was far more dangerous than to-day. When the first steamboat, the New Orleans,
contemplated making her trial trip to New Orleans, a special
agent was sent ahead to examine the route and see what were
the obstructions in the way and to remove them.

CAPT. SHREVE AND THE CUT-OFFS.

The snaggy condition of the Mississippi was such at the time that only three-fourths of the boats going down stream ever reached New Orleans, the others being shoaled or sunk on their way there. The losses were so heavy that the captains, pilots, and owners of river craft united in 1822 in a strong petition to Congress asking for the removal of snags. The petition received no attention for some years, but finally Congress recognized its obligations in the matter, and snag-boats were placed upon the river. Captain Shreve, who commanded the fleet, did good work. He invented a system of butting down the snags, and within a short time had cleared out the river. The work was one, however, that never had an end. New logs are constantly floating down, and the snagging branch of public service has ever since been fighting this danger, save during those few years when Congress failed to make an ap propriation for it. Captain Shreve, who was one of the earliest river experts, followed his good work in the way of snag removal by a very unfortunate act. At that time, the general idea of river improvements was to shorten the river — smooth out the wrinkles, as it were. With this idea in view he inaugurated his grand scheme by what is now known as Shreve's Cut-off, cutting off a bend. and thus shortening the Mississippi some 12 or 15 miles. The evil effects of this act are felt to the present day. The State of Louisiana endeavored to offset it soon afterwards by making a second cut-off across Raccourci Point. While these cut-offs did not affect the Mississippi itself seriously, they ruined the entrance to the Red, Ouachita, and Atchafalaya Rivers, and have caused the expenditure since of hundreds of thousands of dollars to set right this ill-advised attempt at river improvement.

Cut-offs became fashionable, and all along the river attempts were made to divert it from its ordinary course. To such an extent was this carried in the mad scheme to improve the river in this way that the legislatures of Arkansas and Louisiana declared it a felony to make an artificial cut-off of this kind.

Within six years of the recognition by the Federal Government of its obligations to the river States in the way of at least removing the snags, Louisiana organized a similar service and assisted in the work, and Mississippi did something towards improving the navigation of those of its streams emptying into the Mississippi. Both States had received donations of lands from Congress for internal improvements, and the proceeds coming from the sale of these lands were expended equally in the construction of public roads and in river improvement.

This, however, was far from all that the river States desired in the matter, and an agitation was begun in favor of river improvement by the Federal Government. The subject was discussed in the Southern and Western press for some time, and finally culminated in a convention, one of the first of its kind in the country.

MEMPHIS RIVER IMPROVEMENT CONVENTION, 1845.

In 1845 the great river improvement convention met in the city of Memphis, or rather there were two conventions that year in that city. At the first six States were represented, at the second twelve States, with about 500 delegates, and the president no less a personage than Hon. John C. Calhoun. This was not called specifically in the interest of the Mississippi River, but of internal improvements generally. In 1847 another river and harbor convention assembled at Chicago, at which were present many men who have since become noted in our country's history, as Abraham Lincoln, Charles Hempstead, Tom Corwin, Robert C. Schenck, Dudley Field, John C. Spencer, Horace Greeley, and many others. In 1851 a large convention was assembled at Burlington, Iowa, and was the initiative work in the improvement of the Rock Island and Des Moines Rapids of the Mississippi River. In 1866 another convention met at Dubuque, Iowa, and the following year witnessed another grand convention, and since that time there has scarcely a year passed that conventions have not been held at some of the principal cities in the valley of the Mississippi.

The four principal improvements demanded for the river were: —

(1) The improvement of the passes so as to allow vessels of larger draught to reach New Orleans from the Gulf.

(2) The improvement of the channel of the river so as to make it navigable at all seasons of the year, particularly that portion of the river lying between Saint Louis and New Orleans, for which a depth of 8 feet is demanded.

(3) The removal of obstructions in the river and its tributaries, as, for instance, the Rock Island Rapids, the falls in the Ohio opposite Louisville, the Raft in Red River, and similar obstructions to navigation.

(4) The prevention of overflows by crevasses, floods,

and freshets, whereby the fertile alluvial lands lying on the banks of the river were injured and damaged, and the course of the river itself obstructed with bars, etc.

These demands have all been more or less recognized; indeed, before the convention had met, the Federal Government had already recognized its obligations to the country in the removal of snags and obstructions, and had had its snag-boats at work for some years, and had spent some money in surveys at the mouth of the river and in attempts to remove the bars there.

SHIFTING OF THE CHANNEL AT THE PASSES.

The necessity for the improvement of the passes was admitted from the earliest days. The French and Spanish Governments had worked at them on the system of stirring up the mud at the bottom. The United States followed with the same system, and the first work on the passes was an ingenious but unsuccessful attempt to secure deeper water by dredging with buckets, a plan recommended by the board of United States engineers.

The Mississippi River, at its mouth, is constantly changing and shifting. This is especially so of the passes. Since La Salle discovered the mouth of the river, two centuries ago, the deepest pass through which vessels plying to and from New Orleans have sailed, has changed no less than four times. In 1750 the Northeast Pass was the one chiefly in use. Since then Pass à Loutre, Southwest, and South Pass have been successively employed.

In 1835 Congress appropriated $250,000 for the work, that being the first sum ever given by it for this improvement. A survey of the work and preparation for the dredging apparatus, however, nearly exhausted the appropriation, and several years elapsed before anything more was attempted.

The deepest mouth of the river at that time was Northeast Pass, which showed a depth of 12 feet of water, a depth whose inadequacy for the commercial needs of a near future was overlooked. Vessels built expressly for the carrying trade between New York and New Orleans did not, at that time, exceed 500 tons register. Surveys and reports of the passes were made in 1829, 1837, 1839, 1849, and 1851. Shortly after the survey of 1837 Northeast Pass, then the chosen commercial channel of New Orleans, shoaled up; but Southwest Pass was found to answer present purposes, being only less convenient of approach, and it continued to be used with tolerable facility until about 1850. Then the increasing draught of ships brought a new difficulty, and, "owing to pressing memorials of the citizens of New Orleans, Congress ordered an exploration of the region, and appropriated a large sum for the purpose of the deepening of the channel of the river." While various measures were being recommended, vessels of less than 1,000 tons were grounding on the bar.

In 1852 there were no less than forty ships aground on the bar from two days to eight weeks, many of them being compelled to lighter their goods, and some even to throw them overboard in order to get safely off the mud lumps. That year $75,000 was appropriated for the mouth of the river and a board of army officers appointed to suggest a proper plan of operations for increasing the depth of water on the bar.

The system of stirring up the bottom and dredging the river was recommended by the board; and, if that failed, the building of jetties at Southwest Pass 5 miles into the Gulf, and the closing of all the lateral outlets; finally, should this fail, the digging of a ship canal at Fort St. Philip, or some other convenient point, from the river to deep water in the Gulf. The system of dredging, by stirring up the bottom, recommended by the board, was approved by the War Department and a contract was accordingly entered into for deepening the Southwest Pass to 18 feet. The contract was successfully executed and a depth of 18 feet obtained in 1853. No further appropriation was made until 1856, when no trace of the former deepening of the channel was left. In that year $330,000 was appropriated for opening and keeping open, by contract, ship-channels through the bars at the mouths of Southwest Pass and Pass à Loutre   A contract was awarded to Messrs. Craig & Righter for opening both passes 20 feet deep and 300 feet wide, and for maintaining that channel four and a half years. They constructed on the east side of Southwest Pass a jetty about a mile long, which, with harrowing and dredging, deepened the channel to 18 feet, which depth was maintained during 1859 and 1860. The war then came on and the passes were neglected. In 1868 a system of dredging was again adopted by the government, and a steam-propeller dredge was constructed at a cost of $350,000; a short time afterward a second boat was built. These two boats worked for three years, but in 1873 the army engineers gave their opinion that this dredging could not maintain a depth of 18 feet.

The great loss occasioned by the detention of vessels at the mouth of the river at last called forth such loud demands for the deepening of the passes from the most influential organizations and men in the South and West that Congress, recognizing its responsibility, invited plans for the improvement of the mouth of the river. The two main plans suggested were:—

(1) The construction of a ship-canal from Fort St. Philip to the Gulf, as recommended by the commission of army engineers that had examined the mouth of the river in 1857, which, it was estimated, would cost $13,000,000.

(2) The building of jetties at the mouth of the river, a system of removing bars that had been tried successfully in Europe in deepening the Danube, Vistula, Oder, Dwina, and other important rivers. '

THE EADS JETTIES.

The jetty scheme was strongly advocated by Capt. James B. Eads, the great engineer, who had constructed the Saint Louis bridge, and had been engaged in other important engineering enterprises.

DIFFERENT PLANS PROPOSED.

In February, 1874, Mr. Eads made a formal proposition to Congress to open the mouth of the Mississippi River, by making and maintaining a channel 28 feet deep between the Southwest Pass and the Gulf of Mexico for the sum of $10,000,000 at the entire risk of himself and associates; not a dollar was to be paid by the Government until a depth of 20 feet had been secured when he was to receive $1,000,000, and afterward $1,000,000 for each additional 2 feet, or a total of $5,000,000 when 28 feet had been obtained. The remaining $5,000,000 was to be paid in annual installments of $500,000 each, conditional on the permanence of the channel during the ten years. This proposition at first met with vigorous opposition and denunciation.

When the matter was first submitted to Congress an appropriation of $8,000,000 was made for the Fort St. Philip Canal, which passed the House by a good majority, while at the same time the jetty plan was defeated. In the Senate, however, the canal scheme was crushed, Mr. Ead's arguments before the Select Committee on Transportation Routes to the Seaboard being so forcible that in the Senate the committee asked to be discharged from further consideration of the Fort St. Philip Canal bill, and to report as a substitute for it a bill authorizing the appointment by the President of a commission of seven engineers — three from the Army, three from civil life, and one from the United States Coast Survey — to whom this question as to the proper method of opening the mouth of the river should be referred, with instructions to report at the next session of Congress.

The report of this board was presented to Congress on January 13, 1875, by the Secretary of War, and it proved favorable to the jetty plan, the board recommending its application to South Pass. Soon after the report, Mr. Eads made a new proposition to Congress to make a channel 30 feet deep at the mouth of Southwest Pass. A bill embodying this proposition was presented to the House in February, 1875, and passed it ten days afterward. In the Senate, however, South Pass, as recommended by the board, was selected. The act became a law March 3, 1875.

The terms were that Captain Eads was to obtain a channel 20 feet deep and 200 feet wide at the bottom, in thirty months from the passage of the act, and having obtained such a channel, he was to receive $500,000 for every additional 2 feet in depth, with corresponding widths at the bottom until a depth of 30 feet and a width of 350 at the bottom were obtained. He was to receive $500,000, with additional payments, for maintaining the channel. Up to that period the payments of the Government would amount to $4,250,000, with $1,000,000 in addition, earned by Captain Eads, to be retained by the Government for a certain specified length of time as security that the jetties would maintain the channel secured. There was also a provision in the contract which gave Captain Eads $100,000 a year, for twenty years, for maintaining and keeping the jetty works in repair.

The jetties extend from South Pass across the bar into the Gulf. The total length of the east jetty as constructed was 12,100 feet, or nearly 2 1-3 miles; the west jetty terminates opposite the east jetty, but its total length is only about 1 1-2 miles, the difference being due to the greater extension of the natural banks on the west side of the pass. Without entering into a detailed account of the method of constructing the jetties, their mode of structure may be briefly stated to be with willow mattresses laid in layers and weighted with stone, and on this foundation a concrete wall is built. After successfully surmounting innumerable engineering difficulties and embarrassments of the most formidable character, Captain Eads achieved a glorious triumph in his great undertaking, and the jetties were practically completed in July, 1879. At the head of the passes a navigable channel 26 feet deep and 165 feet wide was obtained and certified to July 10, 1879. Since-

that date the semi-monthly surveys have shown constant increase both in depth and width. The bar at the head of South
Pass, with only 14 feet of water over it, which lay like a formidable dam in the entrance of the channel, was completely
removed, and the depth of water in South Pass was made
greater by 2 feet than that in the two larger passes on either
side of it. At the mouth of South Pass the current, which in
1875 struggled feebly against the frictional resistance of the
bar that obstructed it, became, by the construction of the jetties, a strong and living force, which, attacking the obstacle in
its way, swept it far into the great depths of the Gulf, and
carved out for itself a deep and wide channel more than equal
to the wants of commerce. The minimum depths through the
jetties at various dates since 1875 to date clearly indicate the
efficacy of the scouring process caused by the jetties. In
June, 1875, the water was 10.2 feet. In 1876 its greatest
depth was 23.5 feet in August; its least depth was 21.0 in
May. In 1877 it reached 24.2 from October 25 to December
14; its least depth was 22.0 in March. In 1878 it was 27.1
feet in December and 25.4 in March. In 1879 it was 31.7
feet in December and 27.0 in March. In 1880 the depths
were, June, 31.4; July, 30.8 ; August, 32.0; September, 30.6;
October, 30.3; November, 30.8; December, 30.8. In 1881
the greatest depth was 33.8 feet in January, and its least 30.4
feet in November. In 1882 it was deepest in September, being 31.9 feet ; its least was 30.5 in February, and 30.5 in
April. In 1883 the greatest depth was 33.4 in June ; its least,
30.2 in January.
   Since then the jetties have been put to the severest tests.
In 1883 the English cable ship, the *Silvertown*, put to sea with
the largest cargo ever leaving New Orleans: 10,618 bales of
cotton, 319 tons of ore, 24,193 bushels of grain, 10,750 staves,
1,000 tons of coal, and 275 of water ballast; a total of 5,020
tons, the vessel drawing 25 feet 4 inches. The *City of New
York* also went through, drawing 25 feet 10 inches. She was
a comparatively narrow ship, whereas the *Silvertown* had an
enormous breadth of beam and was nearly as broad at the bottom as at the top, being almost flat-bottomed. The saving to
the people of New Orleans and the Mississippi Valley by reason of the establishment of the Eads jetties, was plainly shown
by Hon. Joseph H. Burrows, of Missouri, in a speech on the
improvement of the Mississippi River, in which he stated that
the transportation rates on a bushel of wheat shipped from
the center of the Valley, at Saint Louis by river to the sea-

board at New Orleans during the three years 1877, 1878, and
1879, ranged all the way from 10 to 15 cents less than by rail
to the seaboard at New York. That, owing to the jetties,
half of the total grain produced in the 14 Valley States could
be shipped from Saint Louis to New Orleans, instead of by rail
to New York, with an annual saving to the seaboard at 10
cents per bushel, which would be $90,881,552, and at 15
cents per bushel, $135,572,328.

The following table is taken from the annual report of Major
Heuer, engineer in charge of the jetties, and gives the lowest
depth and width of the 26-foot and 30-foot channels through
the jetties, according to surveys made in May and June, 1887,
respectively : —

Distances from east point in feet.	Month.	Least width for—		Least depth.
		80 feet.	26 feet.	
0 to 2,000	May....	180	330	39.4
	June ...	190	350	39.0
2,000 to 4,000	May....	320	370	35.3
	June ...	280	330	35.4
4,000 to 6,000	May....	320	390	37.1
	June ...	330	380	37.5
6,000 to 8,000	May....	210	290	31.2
	June ...	210	280	32.3
8,000 to 10,000	May....	210	290	34.2
	June ...	180	250	34.1
10,000 to 12,000	May....	280	300	38.1
	June ...	190	270	35.2

Beyond the ends of the jetties there is a central depth of 30
feet on a direct course from the ends of the jetties to the sea;
the 26-foot channel is 210 feet wide and the 30-foot channel
60 feet wide.

At the head of South Pass, that is from the main river into
South Pass, there is a central depth of 29 feet, and the 26-
foot channel is very wide.

Above Goat Island the central depth is 29 feet, and the 26-
foot channel is 380 feet wide.

Near Grand Bayou the central depth is 28 feet, and the 26-
foot channel is 200 feet wide.

EXPENDITURES AT THE PASSES.

The following are the expenditures at various times of the Government on the improvement and deepening of the passes, other than the contract with Captain Eads for the jetties:—

Year.	For what expended.	Amount.
1829	Survey	$ 500
1836	Increasing depth	75,000
1837	Removal of obstructions	120,000
1850	Survey	50,000
1852	......do......	50,000
1852	Opening ship canal	75,000
1856	Improvement of South Pass and Pass à l'Outre	830,000
1866	Improving mouth of river	75,000
1867	......do......	200,000
1868	......do......	50,000
1869	......do......	85,181
1870	......do......	300,000
1871	......do......	125,000
1872	......do......	155,000
1873	......do......	125,000
1874	Improving mouth of river and survey	85,000
1875	Improving mouth of river	250,000
1876	Improving mouth of river and survey	115,000
1877	......do......	12,000
1878	Survey	15,000
1879	......do......	24,000
1880	......do......	10,000
1881	......do......	10,000
Total		$2,526,681
	Expended by the Government for the construction of the jetties under the contract with Capt. James B. Eads	5,950,000
Total		$8,476,681

MISSISSIPPI RIVER IMPROVEMENTS.

In respect to the improvement of the Mississippi River for purposes of navigation, little or anything was done save at the mouth before 1878. This was due to two reasons — because the Government did not fully recognize its obligations in the matter, and because the removal of snags and obstructions was deemed sufficient improvement. The first work undertaken on the Mississippi was on the upper course of that stream at the Des Moines.

In 1868 Congress made an appropriation of $40,000 for the removal of obstructions in the Mississippi River. It had previously set aside $3,352,040 for the snag-boats employed in

service on the Western waters.   This service was not confined
to the Mississippi alone, however, but included work on its
leading tributaries — the Ohio, Missouri, Red, and Arkansas.
About 40 per cent., or $1,340,800, may be counted on as
having been expended on the Mississippi below Memphis,
which, with the special appropriation of $40,000 in 1868,
makes the total for the removal of snags in that river $1,380,-
800 up to 1879.   Since 1879 the expenditures on the snag-boats
on the Mississippi and Missouri have been $495,349.77.   Al-
lowing 50 per cent. for the Mississippi, it gives $247,674.88
as the snag expenditures since 1879.

In 1878 the river and harbor bill included a number of items
for river improvements, mainly at the harbors of the chief
towns.

Memphis harbor received...$ 8,300
Vicksburg.. 184,000
New Orleans... 110,000
The mouth of Red River... 190,000

In 1880 the appropriations were: —

Memphis harbor..$15,000
Vicksburg... 20,000
Natchez and Vidalia.. 40,000
New Orleans... 75,000

In 1881, the following: —

Memphis.. 15,000
Vicksburg.. 75,000
Natchez.. 50,000
New Orleans.. 75,000
The Passes... 10,000

The following are the amounts expended on the improvement of the Mississippi previous to the creation of the River
Commission: —

Years.	For what expended.	Amount.
1871	Gauging...	$ 5,000
1874	Improvement of the alluvial basin......................	25,000
1776'-78-'79	Gauging...	15,000
1878-'79	Protection of harbor of Memphis........................	83,000
1878-'79	Protection of harbor of Vicksburg.....................	184,000
1878-'79	Protection of harbor of New Orleans...................	110,000
1880	Harbor of Memphis......................................	15,000
1880	Harbor of Vicksburg....................................	20,000
1880	Harbor of Natchez and Vidalia.........................	40,000
1880	Harbor of New Orleans..................................	75,000
1881	Harbor of Memphis......................................	15,000
1881	Harbor of Vicksburg....................................	75,000
1881	Harbor of Natchez......................................	50,000
1881	Harbor of New Orleans..................................	75,000

Total expended on river improvements previous to river
commission, except on passes and removal of snags $737,000

21

MISSISSIPPI RIVER COMMISSION.

In the meanwhile in 1879 Congress had passed the bill creating the Mississippi River Commission, of seven members, to suggest a plan for the general improvement of the river and to control and supervise the work done. Under that body the work has since been systematically carried on with much larger appropriations than formerly. The following are the amounts voted by Congress at different times to the improvement of the river under the Commission:

1881	$ 1,000,000
1882	4,123,000
1883	1,000,000
1884	2,065,000
1886	1,994,057
Total	$10,477,855

Of this there has been expended for channel work, as distinguished from levees, the following amounts: —

Location.	Amount.
Memphis harbor	$ 615,077
Helena reach	8,000
Choctaw reach	2,680
Repairs to plant	30,000
Greenville harbor	87,500
Vicksburg harbor	197,819
Lake Providence reach	2,415,902
Natchez and Vidalia harbors	8,253
Red and Atchafalaya Rivers	816,717
New Orleans harbor	283,195
Cubit's Gap	137
General service	114,259
Total	$3,979,539

The following is the levee work done in the same district by States: —

Tennessee: Lauderdale.

Mississippi: Tunica and Coahoma; Bolivar Riverton; Bolivar Hughes; Washington and Issequena; Ben Lemond.

Arkansas: Mississippi, Long Lake, Philips, 'Possum Fork.

Louisiana: East Carroll, Madison, Tensas, and Concordia; general protection of Tensas Basin; Point Coupée Morganza; general protection Atchafalaya Basin; Bonnet Carré.

The apportionment among the several States was as follows: —

Tennessee	$ 100,000
Mississippi	624,678
Arkansas	404,561
Louisiana	1,342,810
Total	$2,472,049
Total amount expended by river commission between Memphis and Gulf	$6,451,588.

LOUISIANA AND RIVER IMPROVEMENTS.

Among the river States, Louisiana has led by a long distance in the matter of river improvement. This was due largely to the fact that it was first settled, and was most dependent upon keeping open its water-courses. The settlements in Louisiana were almost altogether upon the streams. To secure, therefore, communication with markets, it was necessary to keep the interior rivers and bayous free from snags and other obstructions.

Louisiana, in consequence, expended more upon its levees and river improvements than all the other lower Mississippi States. There were some improvements attempted under the French and Spanish governments, especially at the passes, as already narrated. In 1814 the dike across Bayou Manchac was constructed to cut off that outlet.

In the early days of the State a large amount of work was done, but mainly by private individuals, the steamboat men and keel-boat men. The Mississippi and all its tributaries were at that time filled with logs and snags, and navigation rendered dangerous thereby. These obstructions the steamboat men gradually removed themselves, opening most of the streams. There are, of course, no figures attainable of the cost of this work. If, however, the work done in the way of removing the rafts, logs, and snags be estimated on the basis of that subsequently undertaken by the State boards of works and State engineers the expense of river improvement between 1800 and 1815 was from $12,000 to $15,000 a year; and from 1815 (when the steamboats began running) until 1833 from $25,000 to $30,000, or $490,000 for the whole period. This, however, is merely an estimate of its cost based on the work subsequently done by the State.

After 1833 the statistics are reliable and authentic as the board of public works and the various other boards carrying on the interior improvements upon which the State had entered, were required each year to present full itemized reports to the legislature. These reports give the various works under way and their cost. The great aim of the State government at that time was to give all portions of Louisiana a route to market, which was done partly by the improvement of the interior water-ways and partly by means of public roads.

In 1833 the legislature of Louisiana organized the board of public works, for the improvement of the State and particularly for cleaning out the streams, removal of snags and logs and other obstructions. The first work undertaken was the re-

moval of the rafts obstructing the Atchafalaya and Grand
Rivers, and Bayou Sorrel, in order to open the navigation
through these streams to the Attakapas.

WORK AT MOUTH OF RED RIVER.

It became, at the same time, necessary to improve the
mouth of Red River and the connection between that stream
and the Mississippi, which had been injuriously affected by the
cut-off made near its mouth by Captain Shreve, on behalf of
the United States, in 1831.

The board worked zealously at these two enterprises,
making, however, little progress with them, and fifteen years
afterwards, complaint was still made about the raft in the
Atchafalaya and its obstruction to navigation. The opening
of that stream moreover had an unfavorable effect on the
mouth of Red River. When the raft was partly broken and
removed the increased current velocity of the Atchafalaya soon
washed out the light deposits in the channel, and it was thus
able to carry off a large volume of the Red River and divert
that stream from the Mississippi.

The board of public works had complete charge of all the
public improvements going on in the State, the income being
derived from the public improvement fund, obtained from
the sale of lands granted Louisiana for its internal improvement. The work done was confined mainly to river improvement, the removal of rafts, dredging of the streams to give
them greater depth, and construction of canals to give intercourse between navigable rivers. The board had three boats
in the field, with crews of sixty men, and occasionally chartered
other vessels. The operations for the year 1840 show work
done on the Atchafalaya and Bayou Plaquemines, on Bayous
Bonfouca, Packet, Manchac Pass, which was opened; Bayou
Plaquemines opened to the Mississippi, where works were constructed to prevent the logs from drifting and causing the
Atchafalaya raft; on Bayou Bœuf, opened to Prairie Jefferson;
Tensas, to Bayou Roundaway; Macon, throughout Bayous
Bartholomew, Des Glaizes, and Courtableau. The United
States had undertaken the removal of the obstruction in the
navigation of the Red River, near Alexandria, known as the
"Rapids," or Falls. Loiusiaua also made an appropriation
for this purpose, and an arrangement was made with the
United States contractor to carry on the improvements under
the State specifications for slightly less than the legislature
had appropriated for this purpose.

The work was done mainly with slaves owned by the board
of works. A few convicts were employed, but were not found

satisfactory. The expense for labor, therefore, was small. The total expenditures for the year were $54,895.54. Of this, $5,000 was expended to Bayou Courtableau under a special appropriation of the legislature. All but $1,017 was expended on the Mississippi or tributary streams. The cost of the works at the junction of Bayou Plaquemines and the Mississippi to prevent the deflection of logs was $2,080. The floating boom proved to be of only temparary benefit and the State found it necessary each year to remove the logs gathered at the mouth of the bayou and to make changes and additions to the boom.

In 1846 the State had at work three boats and 114 men. It purchased that year a snag-boat and a dredging machine. The total expenditure, aside from work on the levees, that is the amount spent for the direct improvement of streams, the dredging of channels and removal of snags, $62,668. It ranged from $50,000 to $85,000 a year for the next ten years.

The State board of works continued actively on river improvement until the war broke out, with from three to six boats and from 50 to 150 men, most of them slaves, the principal work being done in Bayous Tensas, Grosse Tete, Courtableau, Macon, and the Mississippi, Red, Grand, and Atchafalaya Rivers. In 1847, under a special act of the legislature, a contract was made by the State with a Mr. Hoard to cut a canal across the Raccourci Bend, and thus cause a cut-off in the Mississippi River at that point. At that time great confidence was felt in cut-offs, and it was proposed in this way to straighten the river and reduce its length, and thus do away with levees. And as Captain Shreve had made his cut-off near the mouth of Red River for the United States so Mr. Hoard developed Raccourci Cut-off in the immediate neighborhood for the State of Louisiana. The work was done in defiance of the advice of the State engineer and cost $12,000. It consisted simply of a canal cut across the head of the Raccourci isthmus, through which the river poured, and in a very short time found its way, leaving its old bed a lake. It is now admitted that Louisiana made a grave mistake here. Instead of lowering the level of the river, as expected, it raised it, and the parish of Pointe Coupee below has suffered severely in consequence of these cut-offs, and has been compelled to raise its levees several feet until they are now the highest in Louisiana. Another effect of this work was to close up Old River, the connection between the Red and the Mississippi. This followed immediately after the making of Raccourci Cut-off, and in consequence of it and the removal of the raft in the Atchafalaya.

SWAMP LANDS DONATED BY THE GOVERNMENT.

The unsettled condition of a large portion of Louisiana and the immense number of logs and snags floating down the Mississippi from the new settlements being made above rendered it absolutely necessary to keep up this work of improvement. Thus, we find that the raft in the Atchafalaya and Grand Rivers and at the junction of Bayou Plaquemines and the Mississippi re-formed each year and had to be removed. Although the work of improvement was under the control of the State board of works and the State engineer, it was really directed by the legislature, which provided that such and such streams should be improved or cleaned, in much the same manner as Congress directs the United States engineers to-day. The legislature passed, for instance, in the six years between 1847 and 1853, no less than 132 different acts in regard to river improvement and affecting the State engineer and board of works, and providing for the cleaning out and improvement of streams aggregating over 5,000 miles in length.

In 1852 commissioners were appointed and money appropriated by the legislature for the removal of the falls in Red River. The work was let out, but nothing was accomplished nor did a second appropriation bring any permanent good, and the reports declared a lock absolutely necessary there. [The falls have since been removed by the United States.]

The donations made by the United States to the State of Louisiana in 1849 of all the swamp lands within its limits, to be used for the redemption of these lands, led to a great activity in levee building and in the improvement of the streams. The State was divided into four districts, in each of which was a commission in charge of the management of the swamp lands and of the various improvements going on there. The work undertaken was of a colossal character, and included the building of levees, the digging of canals, drainage of the swamp lands, and improvement of the streams. Most of the works undertaken were ordered by the legislature. Some idea of the magnitude of these operations may be arrived at by the fact in a single district, the second, in one year, appropriations aggregating $352,500 were made out of this swamp fund. It is true that the works cost less than the appropriations and that there was a handsome balance left to the credit of the fund, but the activity shown in public improvements may be imagined from this total. The bulk of the work done, however, was the building of levees and the digging of canals, not so much for the improvement of navigation as for the redemption of the swamp land by properly draining it.   The work of river improvement by the State continued actively through all this period.

In 1854, notwithstanding what had been already done in the improvement of the Atchafalaya, the legislature found it necessary to let the work of cleaning out that stream by contract, the price paid being $15,000.

In 1855 Louisiana undertook the improvement of the Ouachita, expending for that purpose $8,935, without securing any benefit therefrom beyond a survey of the river.   The special report on this subject calls attention to the increased danger of obstruction at the mouth of Red River, which entitled it, the report declared, to the constant service of a dredge boat at each high water, "since it is justly apprehended that at any season when the Red River shall have no rise subsequent to a rise in the Mississippi, the channel into it will most probably be barred up."

A timely warning this, for no other point on the Mississippi has given more trouble to the United States and Louisiana engineers than this.

In 1856 the State force at work included three snag-boats, two dredge-boats, and 95 slaves.   The State engineers were also allowed to use, for the space of a year, all the runaway slaves in the Baton Rouge depot.   The work to which this force was principally devoted was the cleaning out and improvement of the Atchafalaya, the removal of the falls in Red River opposite Alexandria, and keeping open the mouth of Red River where it joins the Mississippi.   Innumerable plans were suggested for these several improvements, dams, locks, etc.

In 1859 the State appropriated $35.000 for Old River and the mouth of Red River, which had by this time become a chronic nuisance.   Frequent appropriations had been made for this work — indeed, scarcely a year passed without it having been attended to and dredged; but the river was kept open in this way only a short time, and each report closes with the statement that the improvement secured was only temporary. On this point and the Atchafalaya, the bulk of the State river improvement fund was expended.   In 1860 the State finally came to the conclusion that the only way by which the connection could be maintained between the Red and the Mississippi was by constructing a dam or sill over the mouth of the Atchafalaya where it joins Old River — the plan proposed by the Mississippi River Commission to-day.   This work was ordered by an act of the legislature in 1860, but interrupted by the war. The cost was estimated at $996,000. Another plan proposed at the time was the closing of Bayou Plaquemines (since done) and its connection with the Mississippi by way of locks (reported on favoraly by the United States engineers) the cost of which was estimated at $226,000.

In 1860 the appropriation required for the execution of the several works, based upon the surveys called for under special acts of the legislature or under general order from the board of public works amounted to $1.288,765. Acts were passed by the legislature approving nearly all these schemes of improvement, and there is little reason to doubt that they would have been undertaken had not the war called a halt. None of them, however, were even begun; and during the few months intervening before the declaration of hostilities, the board of work confined its attention wholly to levees.

It is difficult to arrive at the amount expended by the State of Louisiana during this period for improvement. The appropriations of the legislature are far above the actual amount expended, running up some years to $500,000 and $600,000. The expenditures of the State board of works, State engineers, and the commissioners of the four swamp-lands districts were for the improvement of navigation, of drainage, for the opening of rivers, removal of snags, construction of levees and canals, and even of roads, and these are always very much mixed up with each other. It is possible, however, to disentangle them, but only by going over the expenditures item by item. The work was done mainly by negro slaves, the cost of whom was an important item, the slaves used for the dredging and snagging boats having cost the board of works no less than $275,500. In each report there is a demand for more slaves, and a request made that the State vote $250,000 for the purchase of extra negroes for this work. The engineer estimated in his report that the work could be done by slave labor at half the cost of free whites. In the following tables below, therefore, the estimates of the actual value of the improvements ought to be doubled — that is the work done is twice as much as the money value represents: In this cost is included the negro slaves purchased, as well as the dredge and snag-boats, lumber, and other expenses. These and the salaries of the State engineers and the actual cost of subsistence of the slaves employed on government work were the sole expenses, for there were no wages paid to hands. For a short period, the negro prisoners in the penitentiary were used in the State improvement works, but they were not found satisfactory. Later, the runaway slaves impounded at Baton

Rouge were required to labor twelve months on the government works before they were sold.

The following shows the amount expended by the State of
Louisiana, or its districts for divisions, for the improvement
of the navigation of the Mississippi and its immediate tributaries, aside from the amounts expended for levees, dikes, etc.,
and represents the expenditures for dredging the stream, removing rafts, logs, sawyers, and snags, for booms, dams, and
other constructions to regulate the outpour of the river, for
cleaning outlets, and in general for all works intended directly
and immediately for the improvement of the navigation of the
Mississippi and its tributaries, not including any amount expended for levees, for the protection of land from overflow, or
for any other drainage purposes.

EXPENDITURES FOR RIVER IMPROVEMENT BY LOUISIANA.

1833 to 1840...	$445,724
1840 to 1845...	302,120
1845 to 1850...	317,472
1850 to 1855...	212,264
1855 to 1861...	377,120
Total...	$1,654,700

The amount expended during this period for river improvements by the parishes and private individuals was small, as the
State boats went from stream to stream, clearing away all
obstructions. Only an estimate can be made of these expenses,
as about $60,000, or a little more than $2,000 a year.
There has, indeed, been scarcely a year when the steamboats
have not done something towards river improvement, and they
estimate their expenditures or time for this purpose, even to-
day, when the Federal Government has taken charge of the
rivers at $5,000 annually.

The war that followed interrupted all State work except a
little leveeing here and there. Nothing was done towards the
improvement of the Mississippi and its tributaries; indeed,
the aim was rather to close the streams and render them inaccessible to the Federal gunboats than to keep them open.

In 1865, immediately after peace came, an important work
was undertaken by the parish of Iberville and the planters of
the immediate neighborhood in the closing of Bayou Plaquemines. This had always been a troublesome point on the
Mississippi, and as early as 1840 the State engineers had taken
it in charge, for here the logs drifted from the Mississippi,
interfering with its navigation and filling up the Atchafalaya
with a raft. The river showed, moreover, a disposition to
cut in here, and it was deemed necessary both in the interest

of its navigation and the protection of the interior country, to
close this navigable stream. An attempt was made by the
State engineers some eight years later to reopen it, but they
were forcibly driven from the field by the people of Iberville.
A survey has since been made by the United States engineers looking to the reopening of the bayou with a lock.

A NEW POLICY.

With peace, the State did not return to the river improvement works it had on hand when the war broke out. Both
the levee board and the board of public works (recreated in
1868) confined themselves almost wholly to levees. The
United States had fully undertaken the work of removing the
snags and obstructions which had previously constituted so
large an element of the work done by the State in improving
the navigation of the Mississippi and its tributaries. The only
river improvements in which Louisiana interested itself were
at the head of the Atchafalaya, at Old River, giving the Red
entrance to the Mississippi and the Red River Falls. For Old
River an appropriation of $64,000 was made in 1869, but the
contract became involved in litigation and another contract
was subsequently made. In 1869 the improvement of the
navigation of the Teche was begun with a series of dams and
locks, but after the expenditure of a large sum it was abandoned *in toto*. An attempt was also made to cause a new cut-
off in the Mississippi at Waterproof, but without success.

The recognition by the Federal Government about this time
of the importance and duty of interior river improvement and
the appropriations for the chief rivers of Louisiana, in the
river and harbor bill, did away with the State work. The
only State river improvement or expenditures since have been
the construction of a dam across Ton'es Bayou in Red River,
which work was afterwards taken up by the Federal Government, and the improvement of Old River, connecting the Mississippi, Red, and Atchafalaya. The last work undertaken by
Louisiana was in 1877. Dissatisfied with what the Federal
Government had done at the mouth of the Red River, and in
deference to the requests of the steamboat people who found
themselves cut off from the Red, Ouachita and other streams,
the legislature voted $20,000 for the improvement of naviga-
tion at Old River. The work was undertaken by the State
engineers, assistance being given by the steamboats engaged
in the Red River trade; and at the expense of $7,220, the
river was opened to navigation.

Since then, the State has done nothing save in the work of

leveeing and draining. A considerable amount, however, has been expended by private citizens, principally by the steamboat men, to improve the navigation of the Red at Old River and the Falls at Little Devil's Bar, on the Courtableau, a tributary of the Atchafalaya. This cost, however, has been mainly in labor in the use of boats and men rather than in materials, and it is somewhat difficult to estimate it exactly. It can only be done on the basis of time consumed and men employed on the work. The expenditures from 1865 to 1887 for river improvement other than levees, has been $168,220 for the State and $115,500 for the parishes, planters, citizens, and steamboatmen, or a total of $283,720. During the greater portion of this period, the work of river improvement, snagging the river, was carried on by the United States engineers, and the State thus relieved from all except levee work.

The following table gives the amounts expended by the State or Territory of Louisiana in the improvement of its streams during the present century. It is restricted entirely to the improvements made for purpose of navigation, and includes none of the numerous works undertaken for drainage purposes, or for the protection of land from overflow or the redemption of swamp lands; and it is further restricted to the Mississippi and its immediate tributaries, which more or less affect it — the connection between the Red and "the Father of Waters," and the Atchafalaya, which plays so important a part in the improvement of the Mississippi: —

Estimated work done mainly by private individuals, steamboats, flat and keel-boats, with some assistance from the planters, 1808 to 1833... $490,000

Work done mainly by State and districts under boards of public works, engineers, etc., 1833 to 1861.......................... 1,714,700

Work done by State, parishes, and private individuals, mainly steamboatmen, 1861 to 1888................................... 287,220

Total... $2,491,920

As near as it can be divided these expenditures were: —

By State.. $1,826,235
By parishes, towns, and districts................................. 205,285
By private individuals, companies, steamboats and others........ 460,400

Total... $ 2,491,920

The five chief items in this total were: —

Dredging the mouth of the Mississippi.

Dredging and improving the connection of the Red and Mississippi, and the Atchafalaya.

Removing the Plaquemines and Atchafalaya raft, a work on which the State was engaged for nearly twenty years.

Removing snags and obstructions.

It is safe to say that three-fourths of this sum went for the specific purposes.

APPROPRIATIONS BY THE SPANISH AND FRENCH.

There are no records whatever of the expenditures for river improvement previous to the American dominion, although several references are made in the history of Louisiana to work done, particularly at the mouth of the river. Judging by the experience in later years, it would be safe to put the expense of the work at the passes under the Spanish and French Governments at $200,000. Of the other improvements, such as clearing away snags, there are no records whatever.

The other two lower river States have done little in the way of river improvement as compared with Louisiana. They were both settled many years afterwards, at a time when the Government recognized its obligation in the matter of the removal of snags. The State of Mississippi co-operated to a certain extent with Louisiana in the improvement of certain streams in which they were jointly interested, notably the Mississippi and the Pearl. Some work was done in the matter of snagging, but this was mainly by private individuals, by the planters and steamboatmen. Latterly, the town of Greenville has expended large sums for the purpose or holding the river bank there, a matter of equal importance to the town and to the maintenance of the river and the improvements of its channel. The Mississippi has been eating away the banks at Greenville for some time, destroying the front of the town. For over ten years the constant caving has destroyed the permanent value of real estate, 1,200 feet of valuable property having been swallowed up by the river. The Mississippi River Commission appropriated $37,500 to hold the bank at Greenville, regarding that as essential to the plan of river improvement it is carrying on. The appropriation was supplemented by the people of Greenville, who contributed $50,000 towards the work in the way of bonds. A survey was made and work begun in September, 1887."

COST OF REPAIRS.

The total sum expended by the General Government from March 4, 1789, to June 30, 1886 (a period of ninety-seven years), in the improvement of the Mississippi and its forty-four navigable tributaries, was in round numbers about $51,000,000.

The expenditures by rivers, compiled and re-arranged from

the official reports of the Treasury Department, are as
follows : —

Name.	Amount.
Mississippi	$29,785,666
Ohio	5,048,348
Missouri	2,866,965
Tennesssee	2,816,456
Kanawha	1,749,000
Red	1,443,793
Illinois	1,161,000
Cumberland	722,479
Kentucky	709,998
Wabash	487,500
Arkansas	420,076
Monongahela	808,600
Ouachita	290,000
Osage	189,994

CONSTRUCTION BY NATURE.

The next important consideration in a transportation line is
the cost of construction. Railway stockholders expect dividends, and if their roads be extravagantly built the burden is
soon shifted to the shoulders of the producer and consumer
along the way in the shape of excessive rates. Even if rightly
located and cheaply built, railroads represent enormous capital when contrasted with rivers made by nature at no expense
to the people.

The 16,090 miles of navigable water-ways which constitute
the commercial part of the Mississippi River system were constructed and presented by nature at no cost to the people.
But they are just as valuable as if artificially built. They are
the nation's property, and should, like its military roads, its
custom-houses, post-offices, and other property, be kept in repair. Congress is the board of management for this purpose,
and should, in guarding the people's transportation property,
exercise the same skill and observe the same laws of economy
as railway directors who are chosen to manage the railway
lines owned by individual stockholders.

COMMERCIAL VALUE.

There were, during the census year 1880, 87,782 miles of
railways in operation in the United States, built at a total cost,
for construction, of $4,112,367,176 or an average of $46,848
per mile.

Now, in view of the facts and figures showing the superior
and economical location of the Mississippi and its navigable
tributaries, their wonderful commercial capacity, their facili-

·ties for cheap transportation, the enormous annual products
·of the twenty-one States and Territories intersected, and the
colossal proportions of their internal commerce, it may not
be unreasonable to estimate their actual commercial value as
follows : —

MONEY VALUE OF WESTERN RIVERS.

The Lower Mississippi, from St. Louis to the Gulf, at
$468,480 per mile, or ten times the average cost per mile of
the railways of the United States.

The Upper Mississippi, from St. Louis to St. Anthony's
Falls, at $327,936 per mile, or seven times that of the average
railway.

The Ohio, from its mouth to Pittsburgh, the Missouri, from
its mouth to Sioux City, the Red River, from its mouth to
Shreveport, and the Cumberland, from its mouth to Nashville,
at $234,240 per mile, or five times that of the average
railway.

The remaining navigable tributaries of the Mississippi at
$46,848 per mile, or the same as that of the average railway.

We have then a total valuation as follows : —

The Lower Mississippi, from St. Louis to the Gulf (1,352 miles)	$633,387,664
The Upper Mississippi, from St. Louis to St. Anthony's Falls (809 miles)	265,300,224
The Ohio, from its mouth to Pittsburgh (1,021 miles)	239,159,040
The Missouri, from its mouth to Sioux City (1,019 miles)	238,690,560
The Red, from its mouth to Shreveport (456 miles)	106,813,440
The Cumberland, from its mouth to Nashville (209 miles)	48,956,160
The remaining navigable tributaries of the Mississippi (10,774 miles)	522,542,592
Total value	**$2,054,849,680**

In other words, the people of the United States have in the
Mississippi and its forty-four navigable tributaries, highways
·of commerce and cheap transportation to the seaboard to the
enormous value of $2,000,000,000. This property was a
present from nature. The question naturally arises, will
they manage it on business principles and keep it in an adequate state of repairs?

THE LEVEES.

" The delta or alluvial lands of the Mississippi are subject
to overflow unless protected by dikes or levees, the name
·originally given to these embankments of earth by the French
or creole settlers of Louisiana. This delta includes portions of
·seven States — Illinois, Missouri, Kentucky, Tennessee, Ar-

kansas, Mississippi, and Louisiana. It is calculated by the Mississippi River Commission to contain 29,790 square miles ·or 19,065,600 acres, as follows: —

[Compiled from the Alluvial Map of the Mississippi River Commission.]

Basin.	State	Square miles.	Acres.
St. Francis Basin and Mississippi River front.........................Illinois...........		65	41,600
	Missouri...........	2,874	1,839,360
	Kentucky.........	125	80,000
	Tennessee........	426	272,640
	Arkansas..........	3,216	2,058,240
	......do..........	956	611,840
White and Arkansas fronts...........Tennessee........		27	17,280
Yazoo basin.......................Mississippi........		6,621	4,237,440
	Arkansas..........	480	307,200
Macon, Bœuf, and Tensas basins.....Mississippi........		305	195,200
	Louisiana.........	4,475	2,864,000
Atchafalaya basin..............................do...........		6,195	3,964,800
Pontchartrain basin..............................do...........		2,001	1,280,640
La Fourche basin...............................do...........		2,024	1,295,360
Total...		29,790	19,065,600

BY STATES.

States.	Square miles.	Acres.
Illinois..	65	41,600
Missouri..	2,874	1,839,360
Kentucky...	125	80,000
Tennessee..	453	289,920
Arkansas...	4,652	2,977,280
Mississippi...	6,926	4,432,640
Louisiana	14,695	9,404,800
	29,790	19,065,600 "

COMPARATIVE EXPENDITURES BY THE GOVERNMENT.

To those who charge the government with too lavish appropriations for the improvement of Western water-ways may perhaps be enlightened by a recent debate in Congress on the subject of appropriations.

In discussing the Union Pacific Railroad indebtedness Mr. Edmunds of the Senate said: —

Mr. EDMUNDS. No, that is principal and interest down to the 1st of July, 1885. There is twelve years of interest yet on $33,000,000, which would be, at 6 per cent., 72 per cent.

on $33,000,000, which, in round numbers, is three-quarters
of that, which would be about $24,000,000 more, which added
to your $68,000,000, leaving off the odd hundred thousands,
would make $92,000,000, that within ten years from this date
will be due to the United States from this corporation for
actual cash that the United States will have paid out.

Now, what else did it get? Let us see. The land question
is stated in the same report. The net proceeds of land sales,
after deducting all expenses of management, commission, &c.,
to December 31, 1884, were $25,668,806.65. Add that
twenty-five million dollars to the ninety-odd. millions that I
had before and you have, in round numbers, just about $120,-
000,000 of cash that this company will have had from the
United States.

"The estimated value of the unsold lands is $13,602,-
696.25."

Take that to be a fair estimate of the value and add that
to your $120,000,000, and you have $134,000,000 that the
people of the United States have paid into this thousand
miles of road from Omaha to Ogden.

The amount appropriated for the improvement of the rivers
of the Mississippi Valley, as shown in the various reports
published in this work, sink into insignificance when compared with the subsidies granted this single road. And while
the latter is claimed to be a loan, in part, there are very grave
doubts whether the government will ever be able to collect
even the interest, much less the principal.

In discussing the subject of river and harbor appropriations, it was shown that out of $105,000,000 that had been ex-
pended up to 1882 — $19,000,000 had been expended on the
Mississippi River, and several millions have since been
absorbed.

The following table will surprise some who are not aware
of the distribution that has been made of the river and harbor appropriations up to 1882 by States. There is no comparative statement at hand by which it may be seen whether
the same proportionate division has been continued up to the
present time: —

There had been expended up to 1882 the sum of $105,000,-
000. Most of that has been expended since 1865. There has
been expended of this sum on the Mississippi River up to
1882, $19,536,000, and several millions have been expended
since. In other words, we have chiefly within the last fifteen
or twenty years made an expenditure of more than $125,000,-
000 on rivers and harbors, and each year we are continuing

to increase that amount by similar expenditures. The expenditure up to 1882 by States is as follows: —

Alabama	$ 956,142
Arkansas	315,000
California	1,493,428
Connecticut	1,527,448
Delaware	8,043,686
Florida	680,352
Georgia	1,364,064
Idaho Territory	10,000
Illinois	2,352,304
Indiana	786,198
Iowa	2,499
Kentucky	867,500
Louisiana	147,809
Maine	1,404,889
Maryland	1,485,769
Massachusetts	2,928,779
Michigan	7,828,356
Minnesota	447,500
Missouri	22,000
Mississippi	295,175
New Hampshire	175,500
New Jersey	987,496
New York	9,539,973
North Carolina	2,261,202
Ohio	2,857,031
Oregon	649,305
Pennsylvania	1,067,101
Rhode Island	733,613
South Carolina	931,342
Tennessee	85,500
Texas	2,166,133
Vermont	545,311
Virginia	1,683,375
Washington Territory	5,500
West Virginia	1,387,587
Wisconsin	4,616,495
District of Columbia	253,202
Miscellaneous	88,349,106
Sundries	
Total	**$105,796,403**

CUT-OFFS ON THE MISSISSIPPI.

"Old Timer" furnishes the New Orleans *Times-Democrat* with the following chronicles of cut-offs in the days of auld lang syne: —

The total number of cut-offs which have been made in the direction of the serpentine course of the Lower Mississippi by the shifting of its alluvial course at various times since 1699 are computed at no less than 180 miles. The channel is estimated to have been regularly changing for ages at the rate of two miles per year. It has probably thus traversed the whole alluvial surface of the States of Louisiana and Missis-

22

sippi, particularly the delta of the former, which is so low. The following are some of the cut-offs, commencing with the earliest of record: —

1. About 1699 it is supposed that the Yazoo cut-off took place and Old River was formed.

2. The first Homochitto cut-off in 1720, which saved a distance of thirty miles. Previously the river washed the highlands of the present county of Adams.

3. Point Coupee cut-off was made in 1721.

4. Great Cut Point. This cut-off is the one above latitude 33 degrees, and was made about the year 1747.

5. The second Homochitto cut-off in 1779. This burst through in one night while a boat ascending the stream lay just above it.

6. New cut-off, in 1817.

7. Red River cut-off, in 1831.

8. Bunch's cut-off in 1832.

Total extent of these cut-offs, 180 miles.

Niles' *Register*, October, 1836: The distance around the bend of the Mississippi, into which the Red River empties itself, is eighteen miles. On the 14th of January, 1831, Captain Shreve, the superintendent for improving the navigation of the Mississippi and Ohio Rivers, commenced making an excavation across the neck of land at the narrowest point. The object was effected by cutting a canal seventeen feet wide and twenty-two feet deep. The water was let through the canal about the 28th of January, fourteen days after the commencement of the work. In two days the water had excavated a channel to such an extent that the steamboat Belvidere passed up through it. On the same day the United States steamer Heliopolis passed up the same channel. In five days it was the main channel of the river. The excavation was made by the steam snag-boat Heliopolis. She used steam scrapers.

August 20, 1831, *Florida Gazette*, La., says "By shortening the river twenty leagues between Fort Adams and New Orleans you increase the rise of water at New Orleans, by 7 feet and 1 inch. Captain Shreve has therefore been tampering with a dangerous subject, and it is to be hoped that no more such experiments will be tried. It is well known that the levee is a heavy burden in lower Louisiana. In 1828 there was not, on an average, 6 inches of levee above the level of the river from Point Coupee to New Orleans. If the cut-off at Raccourei is

made, by which twenty-eight miles will be saved, the rise of
the river at the lower point will be about 3 feet 9 inches, and
the levee at New Orleans must be raised 5 feet higher.''

There has been since '' Old Timer's '' day or since the Red
River cut-off, the following : Agreeable to Captain Isaiah Seller's diary Horse Shoe cut-off was made in 1839. In 1847
Rackasee cut-off was made ; in 1858 Lake Port, then followed
in rapid succession the cut-offs at the mouth of Arkansas,
Terrapin and Davis cut-off. In 1876, the cut-offs at Commerce, Centennial or Island 32 was made, Vicksburg, Water
Proof and Kaskaskia about the same time. The latter is the
only cut-off above the mouth of the Ohio on the Mississippi
of which there is any record.

If '' Old Timer '' is correct in his calculations, and there
was saved in distance 180 miles in 132 years, by eight cut-offs,
we now find eleven cut-offs, from 1839 to about 1885, or say
46 years, some one has suggested that it would be an interesting problem for a curious mathematician to determine how
many years it will require to bring Cairo and the Gulf of
Mexico into close proximity.

The writer in the *Florida Gazette*, La., above quoted, is
doubtless in error about the effect of shortening the river,
although there is no doubt a cut-off raises the water immediately below. But the increase in the velocity of the current
and the increased scour on the bottom of the river corresponding with the velocity, very naturally modifies the rise, and it
soon adjusts itself, but renders necessary increased protection
to caving banks.

CHAPTER XLVIII.

IMPROVEMENT OF MISSISSIPPI ABOVE ST. LOUIS, OR UPPER MISSISSIPPI.

THE character of the river above the mouth of the Missouri differs so much from that below there seems necessary an entirely different system of improvement.

The plans adopted so far as executed, seem to have resulted successfully. The great natural obstructions " the lower and the upper rapids," as they are familiarly known, have been materially improved. The lower, or " DesMoine Rapids," by a canal of 8 miles. The upper or " Rock Island Rapids," by the excavation of rock from the channel. The system of dredging and wing dams seems adapted to the improvement of the low water embarrassment in other parts of the river and if continued may result in furnishing sufficient water in the channel for all navigable purposes. From present indications the sixteen railroad bridges across this river above St. Louis, so obstruct the navigation and restrict the commerce of the river, that the time is not far distant when the lumber traffic, the raft towing, will comprise its principal commerce. The careless and indifferent manner in which the government has allowed the railroad bridges to be built, seems to have pretty nearly accomplished two objects, whether intended or not, viz.: to change the course of trade from north and south, to east and west, and to so obstruct navigation as to destroy competition.

The first bridge across the Mississippi was at Rock Island. It was a draw-bridge and built without any legal authority, simply by a charter from the State of Illinois. It was commenced in 1853 and finished in 1856, and was the most dangerous obstruction to navigation ever constructed, on account of its being located over a chain of rocks, producing boils and cross-currents which were difficult to keep a boat in. Many lives were lost in passing through the draw, and under the bridge, and many rafts were broken up. One fine steamboat, the Effa Afton, was sunk and a large number of lives lost. An effort was made by the river interest to have the bridge removed as an illegal structure and dangerous to navigation. But such was the persistency of the proprietors they defeated every effort in the several courts to which it was carried, and after fighting the bridge for more than ten years with the money and influence of the Merchants' Exchange of St. Louis, as well as that of many citizens along the river, and the best legal talent that could be employed, the bridge remained until removed by act of Congress in 1872, when by a sort of compromise the government built another bridge higher up the river at the head of the Island, and removed the old one.

After the expenditure of more than $20,000 in litigation, of which the boatmen contributed very liberally, and to no purpose, they concluded it was not worth time or money to attempt to defeat a railroad in building bridges wherever they desired. Hence, whenever a road reached the bank of the river, they met with but little opposition in building any kind of a bridge they fancied. The result is, there is already 16 bridges on the Upper Mississippi, scarcely any one of which was built with any regard to the navigation of the river except the government bridge at Rock Island.

There has been expended by the government for improvement of navigation up to the present time, January, 1889, on the river above St. Louis, in round numbers, about eight million dollars, including the canal at the lower rapids which cost about $4,000,000. In 1837, the government undertook to make an improvement on the lower rapids under the direction of Lieutenant Robert E. Lee, of the Engineer Corps, by blasting out a channel through what is known as the " lower chain " or "Sucker Chute." It was a valuable improvement as far as it went, and is still used as the channel in low water. But the appropriation was soon exhausted and the work was abandoned. President James K. Polk's strict "construction" theory soon prevailed, and no more money for several years was appropriated for " Internal Improvements," among which was very inconsistently classed " *inland waters.*"

The theory that has more recently prevailed in the public mind, that all problems of cheap transportation would be solved by the introduction of *barges* as soon as navigation shall be so improved as to make the towing of them practicable, will probably never be realized on the Upper Mississippi.

From the earliest dates, since the settlement of the country required river transportation, barges or keel-boats have been important factors. Even before the introduction of steam they were here, as on other Western streams in general use, only of a little different character. They were known as " keel-boats " and the only change effected by the introduction of steamboats, was, they were towed instead of being floated and handled by sweeps, as formerly.

The great distance (some 30 miles), through which the rapids extend, with only 125 miles between the two, with some two feet less water across them than was found in the ordinary channel, rendered towing always practicable except in high water. The same custom still prevails, and while the canal and the deepening of the channel across the upper rapids have greatly improved the navigation, saying nothing about the other improvements still going on, the damage consequent upon the construction of so many badly protected bridge piers has done far more to destroy the safety of navigation than the eight million dollars expended by the government has done to improve it.

In this utilitarian age, it is hardly worth while to speculate or theorize upon the distant future or of what may occur. But there are a few old boatmen and citizens who still remember the beautiful scenery and picturesque views along the whole course of this river, from the foot of the lower rapids (Keokuk), to the Falls of St. Anthony, when the Indians were the sole occupants and owners on the west side, with but few white settlements on the east side of the river.

Even at that early day, before St. Paul was located, or Minneapolis thought of, an occasional tourist, attracted by the beauty of the scenery in its native wildness, would take passage on some of the few boats that annually made a trip to the forts and trading posts with soldiers and supplies.

Through the courtesy of the officers at Fort Snelling, the head of navigation, an additional pleasure was afforded them, and the officers of the boats by a trip in the government wagons, across the beautiful prairie, a distance of nine miles from the Falls St. Anthony, taking in on the route the picturesque little waterfall of " Minnehaha."

The only evidences of civilization then to be seen where the large city of Minneapolis now stands, was a little log grist mill built by the soldiers on the bank of the river in the midst of the falls from whence power was obtained to grind the corn for the use of the garrison nine miles distant.

While these wild native scenes are vividly remembered by the past and the present generations, what may not be anticipated by coming generations, when we contemplate the unsurpassed beauty and fertility of this valley and the grandeur and possibilities of this noble river which meanders a distance of 600 miles through this part of the valley in its course to the gulf.

No one mile through which it courses but what is susceptible of the highest cultivation and offers the rarest attractions for building hamlets, villas, towns and cities.

In anticipation of future events it is gratifying to know the

government has the power to remove or remodel these illy
constructed bridges. But from past experience it is well to
remember that the sentiment of the *people* must be *remodeled*
before it can be done. The practical question suggests itself.
Is it not wise to construct them properly at first? Of this
the government should consider.

The long intervals between boats at that early period,
sometimes rendered a resort to the canoe and pirogue necessary to travelers and tourists when it became important or
desirable for them to leave the country before the arrival of
the next steamboat.

This writer can speak knowingly and feelingly on this subject, he being desirious of attending the first sale of pine lands
on the Chippewa and Eau Claire rivers by the Chippewa Indians, in 1838.

The sale was advertised to take place at Fort Snelling on a
certain date. Having arrived there by steamboat a short time
previous to the day of sale, I concluded to remain with some
Indian traders living across the river from the fort whose acquaintance I had made.

Indians being a good deal like white men are often a " little
uncertain,'' and for some reason failed to arrive on the day
appointed for the sale, and as the sale was possible to be deferred from time to time, a small party of us who were there
for the same purpose concluded to buy two bark canoes and a
small outfit, and explore the country that was to be sold.

It lay about 150 miles east, by the way of the Mississippi
and Chippewa Rivers. Across the country it was much less.
But as there were no roads, guides, nor means of conveyance,
we took the natural route, packed our canoes and started down
the river.

When night came we had reached Red Wing, the Indian
village of the Sioux. But as their accommodations were only
sufficient for themselves, we made our camp on the bank of
the river where we entertained the whole village during the
evening.

There being four in our party we divided he night into four
watches, each standing two hours.

Tents had not then become so necessary to campers as they
are now, and we depended upon the clerk of the weather for
protection from storms in the absence of the Signal Service
Bureau. But having failed to provide ourselves with mosquito
bars, all other protection sunk into insignificance. We could
have withstood a hard storm, even a raid from the Indians,
anything that could have saved us from the persistency and

poisonous effects of these venomous insects.   Even in mid-day
or in a gale of wind it was all the same.   They seemed to have
existed so long on Indian diet that the blood of the white
man was a luxury they could not resist.   And still, judging
from the size to which they had attained, there could be no
doubt that their diet was at least strengthening.   The swamps
and morasses of Mississippi or Louisiana, where they feast
upon shrimps or alligators the year round, never produced such
bloodthirsty fiends as the Upper Mississippi did before the
white man squatted on its banks.   What effect civilization has
had upon them this deponent sayeth not.   After battling two
days with heavy winds through Lake Pepin, we at length
reached the mouth of the Chippewa.   Then came the tug of
war.   Recent rains had swollen that stream, so that in spite of
our efforts, after dropping one canoe and doubling our propelling power, we could only make about half a mile per
hour.   We were therefore compelled to the conclusion that we
did not care about buying pine lands any way.   And as we
were then some eighty miles from the fort down stream, we
ceased paddling our canoe and soon found ourselves floating
out on to the broad Mississippi, where we picked up our abandoned craft, re-arranged our cargo, and after persuading a
half-breed Frenchman, who was camping on the bank opposite
the mouth of the river, to part with his mosquito bar for our
remaining stock of whisky, we again shoved out and started
for civilization, satisfied that while we had the current in our
favor it was only a question of time when we should reach
there.

We divided our mosquito bar into hoods, or vails, by which
we protected our faces, necks, etc., and by long buck gloves
which we had supplied ourselves with, we bid defiance to the
gallenippers, except when eating our meals which we cooked
on shore.   After a few uneventful days of floating, paddling
and camping we reached Dubuque, wiser if not whiter men.

There we met the new steamer, Smelter, Capt. Smith
Harris, just from Cincinnati.   With all the applause and con-
gratulations that were being extended to the captain by the
citizens none were more ready or better prepared to appreciate the value of steam in navigation than we were.

CHAPTER XLIX.

IMPROVEMENT OF THE OHIO RIVER.

ON streams like the Ohio, the practicability of improving the navigation has never been questioned.

It is only as to the best mode of doing it and of the various plans proposed, most of which, so far as they have had a fair trial have resulted in some benefit.

For a period of six months each year, the Ohio furnishes as good, as safe navigation, or did previous to the building of bridges across it, as any stream in the known world. The banks are permanent, the bottom is of hard sand or gravel, the current is usually gentle, the channel varies but little.

In a very extended and able report made by Col. W. Milnor Roberts, civil engineer, in charge of Ohio River Improvements, to chief of engineers of the United States army, in 1870, various plans are considered in detail. Any one of which, if adopted by the government and vigorously prosecuted, would undoubtedly result in adding at least four months each year, making 10 months out of 12 of the best navigation on any river in America.

The following short extract from his report will be read with interest.

Those who are interested in the improvement of the Ohio will find in a work recently issued by the government, "International Commerce of the United States," extended quotations on the subject.

Wherever this river is improved as contemplated, and the bridges protected as they may and should be, there seems no good reason why certain classes of steamboats may not successfully compete with parallel lines of railroads in the transportation of all heavy and bulky freights. But never for a general passenger traffic, or for light, valuable merchandise.

The hope, then, for those engaged in river transportation lays within themselves. A united effort on their part may result in Congress making sufficient appropriations to so improve the navigation that the now rapidly declining commerce of the river may be practically, if not wholly, restored.

OHIO RIVER IMPROVEMENTS.

The following extracts, taken from a special report made in 1870 to the Chief of Engineers of the United States Army, by Col. W. Milnor Roberts, civil engineer in charge of Ohio River improvement, though voluminous, have such an intelligent and direct relation to this subject that the reader will find them perhaps the best exposition of the several modes proposed for river improvement possible under the circumstances. It will be sufficient to say before presenting these extracts that the main conclusions of this expert engineer have been generally approved by the General Government, and some of them — notably in the case of the Davis Island dam — carried into practical operation.

Colonel Roberts says : —

"Former reports to the Department made some years ago by different topographical engineers, and later reports made by myself, concur in the opinion that the system heretofore adopted to improve the navigation by means of riprap stone wing-dams concentrating and guiding the water into comparatively confined channels, although beneficial and useful, especially to the low-water navigation, does not meet the requirements understood as belonging to the radical improvement of the whole river. The present low-water system, it is true, does not involve a large expenditure of money. It does good and helps the navigation to a certain extent, at a small cost, and it can be effected in a short time, much of it in one or two favorable working seasons. But when finished, although it will be productive of public benefit more than commensurate with the outlay required, it will be no more than an amelioration of the present difficulty. All that has been promised or hoped for under this system, without the aid of artificial reservoirs, has been an increase of 12 to 18 inches in the depth of the low-water channels, making about $2\frac{1}{4}$ feet where there was only 12 to 18 inches in the natural river. It is important to effect even this, and the whole amount of money required for this purpose is comparatively insignificant. But the public now using and interested in the navigation of this river is a much greater and more influential and more national body than the public that was concerned in it twenty-five years ago; and such improvements as were then satisfactory are now believed to be inadequate, even for the present river business, and not at all such as ought to be established in view of its future augmentation. Hence the question of its radical improvement is much more important now than it was a quarter of a century ago. The present interests involved are manifold greater, and it is quite obvious that nothing is likely to occur to prevent or seriously retard their future further rapid development and extension. So that if there are now six hundred millions of dollars' value of river commerce, as compared with fifty millions of former times, a few years only in the national life will elapse till there may be a thousand millions in place of the six hundred millions of value at the present time. The permanent improvement of a natural channel of commerce of such vast present and future importance may well command the careful study and attention not only of the Engineer Department, but of Congress and of the whole country. Plans which years ago may have appeared gigantic or disproportioned to the extent of the trade then interested may now be regarded as no more than appropriate to the magnitude of the new commercial necessities of the river. Yet, forty years ago, in the infancy of the internal-improvement system in the great States of Pennsylvania and New York, these single States did not hesitate to invest over $60,000,000 for State public improvements, and this expenditure has been abundantly repaid in the consequent development not only of the resources of those States but of the resources of the great West. For unquestionably it was largely, indeed principally, owing to the construction of the great canal and railroad thoroughfares through Pennsylvania and New York (afterwards materially aided by the opening of the Baltimore and Ohio Railroad) that the West and North-west became so rapidly settled and developed in such an extraordinary manner. The fact, therefore, that it will cost a large sum to make the Ohio River all that ought to be made of it as a great national commercial artery is not and probably will not be generally considered to be of such vital consequence as in early times. The particular mode of improving it in order to secure the best attainable result is of more real consequence than the cost of effecting such result. It may be conceded and understood in the outset that to accomplish the complete, radical improvement of the Ohio River will require a large expenditure.

" Of the several plans proposed it is believed that only one would secure the proper depth of navigation at all times without aid from artificial supply from reservoirs. The plan of locks and dams, if the works were properly constructed, would, in my opinion, furnish the desired depth at all seasons, without any artificial aid from reservoirs. The reasons upon which this opinion is based will appear further on. It is not mentioned here in the way of an argument in favor of that particular plan, but merely as an ascertained fact. The merits and demerits of this plan will be exhibited in this report.

" The plan of reservoirs as the sole means of supplying the Ohio River at all times with an additional flow sufficient to insure in low-water periods a depth of 5 or even 6 feet originated with Charles Ellet, Jr., Esq., civil engineer, and was very beautifully elaborated by him in various publications, and thirteen years ago its adoption was strongly urged upon the country. His plan contemplated no work upon the river itself, the idea being to accumulate large quantities of water in reservoirs upon the headwaters, or on the main streams above the head of the Ohio, to be drawn off and allowed to flow when needed to maintain the proper depth of the main river. No special surveys were made for the purpose of determining the number and locations of the reservoirs contemplated on this plan. Daily observations had been made through a series of years of the depth of the flow in the channel at Wheeling. From these Mr. Ellet deduced by calculation the theory that enough water falls upon the territory drained above Wheeling, if it were equalized throughout the year, to make a constant depth of over 7 feet in that channel. He found by calculation the probable quantity of water required to be stored up in reservoirs sufficient to maintain a depth of 6 feet through the low-water periods. He also made some personal examinations along the upper portions of the Alleghany River and obtained considerable information from various sources respecting elevations of different parts of the region in question, all of which enabled him to present his views in very attractive forms, both to the scientific world and to the general public. The practical merits of this plan of reservoirs will be considered in another place in this report.

" A third plan for the improvement of the river was proposed by Herman Haupt, Esq., civil engineer, in 1855, which consists of a system of longtitudinal mounds and cross-dams so arranged as to make a canal on one side of the river about 200 feet wide, or a greater width, and reducing the flow to nearly an average of, say, about 6 inches per mile between Pittsburgh and Louisville. Thus, instead of a series of natural pools and ripples, which now constitute the general regimen of the river, this plan would change it, on a width of 200 feet or more, to an equable flow due to the general average declivity of the stream.

' Mr. Haupt's calculations showed that in extreme low-water stages there is not water enough flowing naturally to maintain the full required depth in such a channel; that some additional supply would be needed from reservoirs; very much less, however, than the quantity necessary to maintain a similar depth in the unobstructed river on Mr. Ellet's plan.

"A fourth plan has been proposed by Alonzo Livermore, Esq., civil engineer, the principle of which he secured by patent in 1860. It is a combination of dams and peculiar open chutes through the dams, arranged so as to retard the flow and lessen the velocity of the water from the upper to the lower pool without interfering with the free passage of boats through the chutes ; the chutes being substituted for locks. This may be regarded as another method or substitute for the open canal and dams which had been proposed by Mr. Haupt as a means of saving water on the reservoir plan. For a certain width of chute, say 100 feet, the natural low-water flow on Mr. Livermore's plan is deemed sufficient without the aid of artificial reservoirs.

"It is proposed to consider each of these four proposed methods of improving the river in the order in which they are already referred to, premising that this order or arrangement has no reference whatever to the respective merits of the different plans, but arises naturally in connection with the periods when the several plans were publicly promulgated. I should further remark here that although the writer early advocated the idea of the probable future construction of a lock-and-dam system for the Ohio, while engaged as engineer in constructing the Monongahela steamboat navigation in 1839, he has never been so wedded to that particular mode or to any one plan as to hinder him from presenting all plans in an impartial manner to the consideration of those who, with every wish to know their merits, could not be expected to take the time to examine fully for themselves. So that, in entering now upon a reinvestigation of this subject, I am by no means sure which plan, as a whole, may ultimately be deemed most advantageous. It is due to myself, in connection with so grave a question, to state further that at no time during former examinations into the merits of the different plans did the writer feel warranted in recommending without more investigation the adoption of either of the modes proposed."

CHAPTER L.

THE STEAM WHISTLE.

A GOOD deal of controversy has arisen at different periods by those claiming to know the invention and first use of the steam whistle. Without pretending to settle the question, the following paragraphs may throw some light on an unimportant matter. —

A paper published in St. Louis in 1838, called the *St. Louis Bulletin* makes this claim :—

" The steam whistle is an invention of the celebrated Mr. Watt many years ago. A correspondent of the *National Intelligencer* describes it as he saw it at the Chelsea Water Works as far back as 1820. It was an iron whistle, which, piercing the top of the boiler, descended into it, near to which the water could with safety be evaporated. The moment the water became exhausted below that level the steam would rush up into the whistle and ' pipe all hands ' giving the warning of danger."

Captain Wm. H. Fulton, an old river man living at Little Rock, Arkansas, writes to the *Marine Journal* in 1885 as follows: —

" We think we can settle the matter of the first steam whistle ever used on Western and Southern waters beyond the possibility of a dispute. In the spring of 1844, Capt. Abraham Bennett, of Wheeling, West Virginia, J. Stut Neal, of Indiana, and myself had a boat built at Pittsburgh, which was named, Revenue. While the boat was being finished Mr. Andrew Fulton, the great bell and brass foundry man, made a trip to Philadelphia on business. On his return he spoke of a great curiosity he had seen there in the way of a *steam whistle*, which could be screwed on the top of one of the boilers. Mr. Fulton described the whistle in such a manner that Mr. Neal, who was an engineer and one of the owners, ordered one to be put on the Revenue. I was to be clerk of the boat and induced the Captain to put into the staterooms rubber life preservers. I now state without fear of contradiction that the steamer Revenue was the first steamboat on Western waters to use a steam whistle or a life preserver."

Captain Joseph Wolff, formerly of Pittsburgh and an old river man, has this to say of the steam whistle: —

" The first steam whistle I ever heard or heard tell of, was on the two-boiler coast packet, Luda, in the year 1843. It was screwed into the top of the boiler, and the first time it was used was when she passed the fast Nashville and New Orleans packet, Talleyrand."

An old-time steamboat Captain thus expresses his views: — " The steamer St. Charles, built at Pittsburgh in 1844, for the Nashville and New Orleans trade, was the first boat ever to use a steam whistle. He came from Pittsburgh on the St. Charles and says Capt. Wolff is slightly mistaken. The boat was commanded by Capt. Mark Sterling, and owned by I. R. Yeatman & Co., of Nashville."

THE FIRST CALLIOPE ON A STEAMBOAT.

"The first introduction of the musical steam calliope on Southern waters was by the Ohio River steamer Unicorn, a little over thirty years ago. When the ear-splitting music began to play as the boat neared the wharf the people wondered, and the wonder grew as the airs changed. Up in the city the strains created a decided sensation, and many ran out of their houses, around the next corner expecting to see half a dozen brass bands march along. The farther the curious went the more distant seemed the sound, until at length word was spread that it was a steam calliope on a steamboat, and thousands went to the bluff to listen to it. Afterwards a calliope was put on Spaulding & Rogers' great show boat, the Floating Palace, and with a skilled musician to play it, together with a system of bell chimes. The peculiar music waked the natives on all the tributaries of the Mississippi as well as on the main river itself, and also on the Alabama and tributaries. The people of the Yazoo and Tallahatchie valleys were first treated to calliope music, in hand-organ style, on board of the steamer Dixie, a small craft built by Capt. S. H. Parisot and the late Capt. M. P. Dent, nearly thirty years ago. The swamps reverberated with the tones of the steam organ for many miles as the boat passed up and down the stream, and the darkies fairly howled with delight as they listened, while the white folks were almost equally excited. The steam whistle was first introduced on boats about 1845, and when the steamer Anthony Wayne ascended the Upper Mississippi and Minnesota Rivers with one a year or two after, a crowd of curious Chippewa Indians went overboard like didappers on the deep side at one of the landings, when the whistle was turned loose. The first boat built exclusively for passengers was the General Pike at Cincinnati, in 1818. The first boat

to use the steam capstan was the Tennessee River packet
Greek Slave in 1846, and the first steam freight hoister was
on the bayou Lafourche packet C. D. Jr., built at Louisville.
Before that, manual labor was the method.   The present system of swinging stages by steam was introduced a little over
twenty years ago, and the first electric light displayed at our
wharf, was on the iron steamer Chouteau less than ten years
ago."

THE FIRST U. S. MARINE HOSPITAL TAX.

[From De Bow's Review, 1846.]

By an act of Congress passed in 1798, a permanent fund
was provided out of the wages of seamen for hospital purposes, to the benefit of which boatmen were afterwards
admitted.

It has now been eighty-six years since the tax was first imposed upon seamen and boatmen. The tax has just been
removed during the present Congress and the government now
assumes the maintenance of this great institution.

In connection with the above we will state that some years
before the advent of steamboats upon the Western waters, or,
as early as 1804, at which time a U. S. Custom-house was
established at New Orleans, all barges and keel-boats entering
this port were enrolled and hospital dues collected, according
to the number of men composing the crews of these barges
and keel-boats, also all sea-going vessels entering this port.

CHAPTER LI.

THE WANTON DESTRUCTION OF VESSELS.

"MY attention has been drawn to this subject by an article published in one of the city papers. This refers to the steamboat Shanon. One of the principal charges is, that the clerk of the boat forged and uttered bills of lading for a large quantity of cotton which had never been shipped upon the boat. This was done for the purpose of defrauding the underwriters out of a large amount of money in case the boat sunk or was otherwise destroyed. This is one of the highest crimes known in the criminal law of England, punishable by transportation to the penal colonies for life.

I hope for the honorable and good reputation which the steamboatmen of the Mississippi and its tributaries have always borne, that this may not be true so far as the Shanon's officers are concerned.

I know of but one instance of this kind in the history of steamboating on the Western waters. This was the burning of the steamer Martha Washington in 1849 or '50, I think some place near Grand Gulf.

The steamer Martha Washington was commanded and owned by Capt. John Cummings, running between the ports of Cincinnati and New Orleans. A large amount of the cargo or the most valuable portion of it was shipped by Kassine & Co., Cincinnati, Ohio.

She was burned near Grand Gulf. The hull sunk before the entire cargo was burned. The wreckers took possession shortly after she sunk, and commenced to recover her cargo. They soon found that many of the boxes and packages shipped by Kassine & Co. contained only scraps, shavings, etc. Upon this the underwriters arrested Kassine, Capt. Cummings and some others.

Kassine was found guilty and sentenced for a long term of years to the penitentiary. Cummings was also tried, and I think on the first trial the jury could not agree. He was still under indictment and would have been tried again, but died, it is said, from the effects of his troubles."

The accompanying account of the same transaction as will be observed, locates the burning of the *Martha Washington*

23

at Island No. 65, instead of "near *Grand Gulf*," which is correct. The boat burned near Grand Gulf was the *Washington*, about the same time, hence the conflicting accounts.

REMINISCENCES OF CAPT. JNO. CUMMINGS AND THE BURNING OF THE STEAMBOAT MARTHA WASHINGTON, 1852.

" The writer knew Capt. Jno. Cummings in 1846, when he brought the steamboat New Brazil to Red River, and trade l with her between New Orleans and Shreveport. Cummings was a man of splendid physique, handsome and good address, he and his boat were very popular and did a good business. He only remained one season in Red River.

In 1847 I went down to the Rio Grande River, Mexico, with a small steamboat from Red River, as purser. The boat was chartered by the U. S. Quartermaster and we transported troops and munitions of war from the mouth to Comargo. Upon one of these trips I met Capt. Jno. Cummings in Matamoras and found that he was a partner in a large gambling house, the firm doing business under the name of Cole, Jim McCable & Cummings. Jim McCable was the faro dealer. He had also been a steamboat man upon the Mississippi and tributaries.

After the close of the Mexican War I did not hear of Captain Cummings until 1 read the following dispatch in the New Orleans *Daily Delta*, January 16, 1852: —

MEMPHIS, January 12, 1852. — The steamer Martha Washington, Captain John Cummings, bound from Cincinnati to New Orleans, was burned at Island No. 65 yesterday morning at half past one o'clock. Several lives were lost and the boat and cargo a total loss. The officers and crew were saved, some of whom were taken on board the Jas. Millenger, and some on the steamer Chas. Hammond. The books and papers were all lost. Sometime after this disaster I saw a notice of the arrest of Captain Cummings and William Kassine, charged with the crime of having burned the Martha Washington for the purpose of fraudulently obtaining a large amount of insurance on the boat and cargo. The next thing I heard was that the Cincinnati underwriters had sent a diving-bell boat and divers to make an examination and find the evidence of fraud. Shortly after the divers commenced to bring the cargo to the surface, they found that the boxes marked and shipped by Wm. Kassine as boots and shoes, saddlery and harness, dry goods, etc., contained only old scraps of leather and brickbats. With all this evidence of fraud on the part of Kassine & Co. the court was unable to convict them of the crime of having destroyed the boat purposely.

After this trial Captain John Cummings was arrested a second time by the authorities of the State of Arkansas and tried for murder and arson at Helena.   This second trial occupied a long time, and Cummings remained in prison for many months.   He was finally acquitted, but his long imprisonment destroyed his health and he died shortly after.

In the annals of steamboating upon the Mississippi River it has been but seldom that the captain of a steamer has ever been charged with barratry or destroying a steamer for the purpose of obtaining fraudulently money from the underwriters.   The Martha Washington is the only instance I know of where the boat was destroyed by fire."

                                                    F. C. F.

CHAPTER LII.

IRON STEAM VESSELS.

"THE first iron boat was built on the River Thames in 1822.   She was 106 feet long, seventeen feet wide, and was propelled by oars worked with steam.   She was called the Aaron.   The first iron steamer built in this country was the Valley Forge, in 1839.   She had four water-tight compartments, and was supposed to be proof against fire or sinking.   Nevertheless, she was snagged and sunk in her second or third year.   Capt. Jesse Hart owned and commanded the Valley Forge, and, from accounts, in finish she was the J. M. White of her day."

It does not appear who wrote the above article on the steamboat Valley Forge.   But the truth of history justifies this correction: The Valley Forge was built at Pittsburgh, Pennsylvania, by Roberson & Mimms, engine builders, and was owned by them, and commanded by Capt. Tom Baldwin. She had a good cabin for that period, but nothing superior.

Capt. Jesse Hart probably bought into her at a later date and took command of her.

But this boat, nor any of the few that have been built of iron, have succeeded on Western waters as a profitable investment, although there seems no good reason why they should not succeed as well as wood if properly built.

As *gunboats*, so far as they have been in service, they seem
to have given satisfaction.

Contrary to the above assertion, the Caledonia was
built on the Tay, in 1818, to run between Perth and Dundee,
and was undoubtedly the *first iron steamboat.*

THE FIRST IRON WAR STEAMER WAS BUILT AT PITTSBURGH, 1845.

" There is now on the stocks at Pittsburgh an iron forty-four
gun steam frigate, about 1,100 tons, to be ship-rigged and
propelled on Lieut. Hunter's plan.   This will be the largest
iron vessel ever built in the United States.

1847. The Alleghany, United States steamer, launched at
Pittsburgh, fitted out under the direction of Captain Hunter
at Memphis, Tennessee, with that gentleman's newly invented
machinery for propelling steam vessels.   This vessel is propelled by a submerged horizontal wheel.

The Alleghany sailed from Memphis navy yard on June 4th,
1847, under Lieut. Com. Hunter, for New Orleans.

Sept., 1847. The Alleghany sailed from New Orleans on a
cruise in the Gulf of Mexico.

1849. The United States steamer Alleghany, Commodore
Hunter, was off Belem, a suburb of Lisbon, on December 22d.

In an interview I had with the old Commodore Hunter,
yesterday, he informed me that the steamer Alleghany was
still afloat in the waters of the Indian Ocean.

April, 1847, during the Mexican war, Lieut. Hunter commanding the U. S. war steamer Scourge, captured the town of
Alvarado upon the Mexican coast.   When Commodore Perry
with his squadron arrived he found the place already under
the American flag.   He was greatly incensed against Lieut.
Hunter for making the capture, and a court-martial was ordered.   Lieut. Hunter was honorably acquitted.   Commodore Hunter resigned from the United States Navy on the
breaking out of the late war, and held a command in the Confederate States Navy until the close of the war.   He is probably the oldest living officer of the United States Navy.   He
is now one of the Harbor Masters at this port."

THE SECOND IRON STEAMBOAT BUILT FOR THE WESTERN WATERS, 1839.

June, 1839. The packet ship Edwina arrived at New Orleans from Liverpool, England.   She brought out in sections
an iron steamboat 180 feet long, 28 feet beam, 8 feet depth of

hold, and weighing sixty-five tons, intended to ply as a packet between Mobile and New Orleans.   This steamboat has been sent up the river to Pittsburgh, where she will be put together, receive her engines and return to her station.   The name of this boat was the W. W. Fry.   She sunk in the Alabama River about 1841. — *Ex. Niles' Register.*

[Niles' Register, Vol. 25, 1823.]

IRON BOAT IN ENGLAND.

From a late Liverpool paper: —

"The iron steamboat Commerce de Paris sailed last week for Paris."

"This boat is 112 feet long and 27 feet wide, including her wheels, which are only half the breadth of the common wheel. They are so placed that she is not in proper trim for going until she is loaded with 100 tons of merchandise.   She will then go eight miles an hour, and is capable of carrying 150 tons with very little diminution of speed, as the wheels work equally well, however deep they are in the water."

Soon after the great fire in Chicago in 1853, the people of St. Louis thought to avail themselves of that calamity, by inaugurating new enterprises, opening new avenues of trade, offering new inducements to manufacturers, and in short attempting to regain the prestige they had lost, by the greater enterprise of the people of Chicago.   Many suggestions were made and many schemes were proposed.

By the following communication, which is quoted from the *Missouri Republican* published at that date, it will be seen the subject of iron steamboats and barges was then just beginning to attract attention as being the thing to supersede wooden boats, in the near future, on Western waters.   But contrary to what then seemed sure to follow experiments in many parts of the country, and especially in Europe, with the exception of a few unimportant contracts, the efforts to introduce iron boats on the waters of the Mississippi Valley has proven a failure.   The reason of which does not seem so apparent.   The most probable cause is on account of the greatly increased cost of iron over wood.   The few boats that were built did not determine anything positively one way or the other, only that they cost more than double those of wood. Later, a yard for building iron hulls was opened at St. Louis, and quite a number of boats were built for the government, and seem to have given good satisfaction.

But soon after the establishment of this yard, it be-

came apparent that the days of the present system of steamboating were numbered, and no one had the nerve, if they had'
the means, to make experiments or to build expensive boats.

The falling off in the demand for wooden boats created'
great competition in those yards, and those that wanted a boat
built, could get it at almost any price.

This had much to do in preventing the use of iron undoubtedly, as well as closing up many boat yards.

The *mania* that prevailed about that time for barge transportation, filled the rivers with barges, and there was enough
built to supply the trade for many years or until they are
worn out.

Then it is possible, and there seems no good reason why
it may not be probable, that barge companies will try the use
of iron, or steel, in barges.

Contrary to what seemed probable ten or fifteen years ago,
iron or steel steamboats or barges have not been adopted.
But had the demand continued for any kind of boats, there is
but little doubt iron ones would at least have had a fair trial.

IRON STEAMBOAT JOHN T. MOORE.

In about 1880, Capt. Boardman, of New Orleans, built an
iron hull at Cincinnati for a stern-wheel boat for the Red
River trade.

She had capacity for about six or eight hundred tons and was a
good boat of her class. So far as her record goes she proved
satisfactory in every respect in which the hull was involved.

She was called "John T. Moore," and is probably still in use.

About that time Capt. Thorwegan, Chouteau, Maffitt and
others built the " Charles P. Chouteau " out of an iron hull
that had been used before.

She had a stern wheel and was one of the largest cotton
carriers on the Mississippi.

Her record is not conclusive as to the practicability of sub-
stituting iron for wood on Western waters.

The preponderance of opinion by those whose observation
entitles them to consideration, seems to be adverse to iron
hulls on shallow streams where hidden obstructions are liable
to be encountered.

At the present time, 1889, there is no iron boat yards in the
West, and but little use for any other kind.

BUILDING IRON STEAMBOATS.

" 1853.

Editor Republican: While our merchants, business men

and property holders are discussing how they shall best avail themselves of the present opportunity of securing the trade driven from Chicago by the recent calamity there, allow me to suggest that there are other and quite as legitimate enterprises that demand consideration at their hands.

And among them I would name that of a yard to build iron steamboats.

A yard with the proper facilities for that purpose can not be established for less than half a million of dollars. This would of course include all the necessary machinery for doing work with promptness and economy, and without such facilities, it would be useless to attempt to build iron steamboats.

The increased cost of building such boats over that of wood is the only objection that can be urged against their introduction. But with the proper facilities there is no reason why they can not be built nearly as cheap here as at Wilmington, Philadelphia, or even on the Clyde.

But without some material aid from the city or individuals, a yard of this kind will hardly be located here. As I understand there is a company already formed, who are looking about for the most favorable location to establish such a yard, there is no good reason why St. Louis should not have the benefit of it if our citizens show the proper spirit, and extend to the enterprise that degree of liberality it is entitled to, and which is already proffered from other points.

The great efforts that are being made to extend our trade and commerce in every direction is all very well and necessary; so, too, with the aid extended to railroads and other public enterprises. But here is a proposition to establish upon a permanent basis an enterprise that will do more to encourage manufacturers, and build up the city than all the increased trade that can be secured in consequence of the great Chicago fire.

Is there public spirit and liberality enough in our community to grasp this thing before the cities on the Ohio supersede us, and compel us to go there for *our iron boats*, as we have done for the last 40 years, for most of those built of wood.

Statistics would probably show that the citizens of St. Louis have paid ten millions of dollars to other ports for building their boats in the last 40 years, giving employment to thousands of mechanics, merchants, etc. And the reason for that, has principally been, that we have not had the building material to build them here. That can no longer be said in connection with iron boats. No one will doubt that we can

compete with any other point, in anything pertaining to iron.
If we cannot we had better appeal to our iron men to know
the reason why?

St. Louis, 1853.   E. W. Gould.

COST OF STEEL BOATS.

The present cost of steel would seem to suggest that as the
coming material for the use of vessels of all kinds, if wood
is to be superseded, as it is more ductile and lighter, in
addition to its superior strength, while the discrepancy in
cost is much less than a few years since. Among the last
regular steamboats built in the West, was one built of steel at
Dubuque, on the upper Mississippi, named Cherokee.

Why that location was selected does not appear, as it has
never been known as a boat-building point, or as offering any
peculiar advantages in the way of material or skillful
mechanics.

So far as reported, there seems no objection to the material
used in this boat. But it has been stated the cost of the hull
far exceeded the estimates of the builders and fully confirmed
the experience of all others who have figured on iron or steel
steamboats.

In Europe steel has been largely used in building steam
vessels for several years, as well as in America.

Whether the obstructions often encountered in river navigation will be found more serious to metal than wood hulls
probably yet remains to be tested. It is not one of strength
but of elasticity, the possibility of yielding a blow without
breaking.

LICENSED OFFICERS OF STEAM VESSELS.

1839. The first act of Congress relating to granting licenses
to steam vessels and steamboats was passed in 1839. Also an
act requiring all engineers, pilots and captains to be licensed.
The act reads as follows: All engineers before they shall be
allowed to act as such, shall be examined before a board of
persons appointed for that purpose. When upon being found
qualified shall obtain a certificate to that effect. Also all pilots
of steamboats shall be examined in like manner, and if found
qualified, upon such an examination, shall also obtain a certificate of his qualifications.

Also an act prohibiting any person acting as captain or
commander of any steamboat until he shall have served two
years in said business. Also requiring every applicant before

examination to bring forward testimonials as to his sober and industrious habits. — *Ex. Nile's Register, 1840.*

NOTE. — We would like to know if there are any captains, pilots, or engineers living in this city who held one of these original licenses.

The first fine imposed upon a Western steamboat for not having a license was in June, 1840. In the United States District Court, sitting at Columbus, Ohio, a judgment has been obtained against the steamboat Warrington, Capt. John Moore, for carrying passengers and freight on the Ohio river without a license. The verdict was for $500, the penalty. — *Ex. Hazard's Register, 1840.*

CHAPTER LIII.

TORNADO IN NATCHEZ, MISS., 1840.

UP to this date there is no record of any serious losses to steamboats in this valley from tornados, or cyclones, as they are now more familiarly known.

And even since that time there is no record of so great loss of life from that cause as was sustained then, if those on flat-boats laying at the landing are included.

In Floyd's "Steamboat Directory," published in Cincinnati in 1856, the following account is found :—

"On the 7th of May, 1840, the city of Natchez was visited by a tornado which occasioned immense destruction of life and property. Several steamboats were destroyed at the wharf and many persons who had embarked on them were drowned. A large number of flat-boats were wrecked and it was supposed 200 boatmen were lost. A heavy tax had been exacted of these trading flat-boats at Vicksburg and a large number of them had recently been dropped down to Natchez. So the number was much larger than usual, and at that time it was the great center of flat-boats any way.

The steamboat "Hinds" was blown out into the stream and sunk and all passengers and crew except four men were lost.

It is not known how many passengers were on the boat.

The wreck of the Hinds was afterwards found at Baton Rouge, with 51 dead bodies on board, 48 of which were males and three females.

The steamboat Prairie had just arrived from St. Louis loaded with lead. Her upper works, down to the deck, were swept off, and the whole of the passengers and crew are supposed to have been drowned.

The number of passengers is not known, but four ladies at least were seen on board a short time before the disaster.

The steamboat H. Lawrence and a sloop were in a somewhat sheltered position at the cotton press. They were severely damaged but not sunk. The steam ferry-boat was sunk, and the wharf-boat Mississippian, which was used as a hotel, grocery, etc.

Of 120 flat-boats which lay at the landing all were lost except four, but many of the men employed on board were saved."

The *facts* in this case were bad enough, but have been doubtless exaggerated by this reporter, whoever he may have been.

This writer left Natchez at 3 o'clock on the day of the storm, on the steamer Maid of Orleans, bound down stream, and had just made the turn going towards *Ellis Cliffs*, 15 miles below Natchez, when the cyclone passed up. While we were not within its direct course, the storm was so severe we landed and lay all night near the cliffs.

The first that was known of the severity of it was from the appearence of the Prairie, which passed down just after daylight, and before we started.

Her upper works were wrecked, chimneys down, pilot house gone, and a part of the hurricane roof. They had rigged up the stumps of the chimneys, one of which was about ten feet longer than the other, and the pilot stood out-doors.

As the machinery and wheels were not damaged they managed to get her to New Orleans, where she was repaired. I was well acquainted with the captain and most of the officers, and am under the impression there was no one lost on the Prairie instead of everybody as stated above.

The steamer Hinds was capsized at the landing and the hull was found several weeks later 150 miles below, or near Baton Rouge. It seems difficult to understand how so large a number as 51 dead bodies could have been found in the hold of the boat. But they must have been in the hold if anywhere, as it was found bottom-up with the upper works gone.

The Hinds was laying at Natchez taking in cargo, and instead of going into the hold the crew would have been more probable to have run on shore when the storm struck them; so too, with the flat-boats. One hundred is a great many.

but what there was of them were destroyed, with everything else " under the hill," and two entire squares of brick buildings on top of the hill, and many single buildings, trees, fences, etc., as well as many lives.

The storm seemed to have struck the foot of Natchez. Island first, which was then covered with a heavy growth of young cotton wood, from three to six inches in diameter. They were cut off 8 or 10 feet from the ground as clean and as evenly as could have been done with an ax, and at a little distance resembled a big field of corn, with the fodder just cut, much more than a young forest of cottonwood prostrated.

The uniformity with which the whole island was swept was the principal novelty.

There has been no storm on the Mississippi so destructive as this one at Natchez in 1840, until the great storm at New Orleans and vicinity in August, 1888.

This one continued for three days with more or less violence, rain falling in torrents most of the time.

Several steamboats were wrecked, some entirely lost, and 175 loaded coal boats sunk. These belonged principally to the Pittsburgh Southern Coal Co., and were valued at $250,000. Other property to an equally large amount was destroyed and several lives were lost.

The new steamboat Teche, Capt. L. T. Belt, was caught in the storm some sixty miles above New Orleans, and was for several hours at the mercy of the winds and badly wrecked. Nothing but the fact that she was new and a very staunch boat saved her and many lives from destruction.

CHOLERA AT ST. LOUIS — THE GREAT FIRE IN 1849.

[From Sketch Book of St. Louis.]

THE CHOLERA.

"Late in the fall, in 1848, that dreadful scourge — the cholera, made its appearance in our midst and began its work of death. The approach of cold weather stayed in a great measure, the ravages of the disease, although we heard during the winter occasionally of cases. But as the genial smiles of spring began to fall upon the city, the disease developed itself in full force, and like the famishing wolf, whose appetite is whetted by the taste of blood, it was doubly fierce and unsparing.

The general cry was: " Hush up ! Don't alarm the people.

You will frighten them into the disease. It is all humbug.
It is only a slight sickness among deck hands and poor
laborers, who eat poor food and live in badly ventilated
houses," etc., etc., and so it was determined to ignore and
discredit the existence of the disease.

But the formidable and insidious malady would not consent
to be ignored.

All the while it was furtively and gradually disseminating its
poison, sowing the seeds of a rich harvest of death — filling up
the wards of the city hospital and thinning the crowds of
laborers on the levee.

The very small number of our citizens who took the trouble
to examine the statistics began to be alarmed, but they were
frowned down as panic makers, and the disease — the existence of which was admitted, was pronounced to be ship fever,
which threatened only sailors and steamboat men.

The disease soon assumed a more bold and formidable
appearance, and instead of stalking through lanes and dirty
alleys it boldly walked the streets.

It was proclaimed in a thousand forms of gloom, sorrow,
desolation and death. Funeral processions crowded every
street. No vehicles could be seen except doctors' cabs and
coaches, passing to and fro from the cemeteries, and hearses,
often solitary, making their way to those gloomy destinations.
The hum of trade was hushed, the levee was a desert.

The streets wont to shine with fashion and beauty, were silent. The tombs, the homes of the dead, were the only places
where there was life — where crowds assembled, where the
incessant rumbling of carriages, the trampling of feet, the
murmur of voices and the signs of active, stirring life could
be seen and heard. Physicians were kept constantly on the
move — on visits of many going hither and thither, with no
hope of fee or reward, except that which will be awarded
them in an after world.

Some reeled through the streets like drunken men from
sheer fatigue and exhaustion. Many touched not a bed for
weeks. To realize the full horror and virulence of the pesti-
lence it was necessary to go into the crowded localities of
the laboring classes, where the emigrant classes cluster together in filth and without ventilation.

Here you would see the dead and the dying, the sick and
the convalescent in one and the same bed. Father, mother
child, dying in one another's arms.

Whole families were swept off in a few hours, with none
left to mourn or to procure burial.

Offensive odors often drew neighbors to witness such re-volting spectacles! What a terrible disease. Terrible in its insidious character, in its treachery, in the quiet, serpent-like manner in which it winds itself around its victim, beguiles him by its deceptive wiles, cheats him of his senses, and then con-signs to grim death. Not like the plague with its red spot, and maddening fever, its wild delirium, but with guise so de-ceptive that none fear the danger until it is too late—it marches on!

While the disease was raging at its fiercest, the city was doomed to another horror—the city was burnt—fifteen squares were laid in ashes. The fire commenced on the steamer White Cloud, laying between Wash and Cherry streets. The wind was blowing fiercely on shore, which fact contributed materially to the extent of the marine disaster, and although the lines of all the boats were cut and hauled in, and they shoved out into the current, the burning boat seemed to outstrip them all, with the speed with which she floated down the river, and in perhaps thirty minutes after the fire broke out, *twenty-three steamboats* had been abandoned to the prey of the flames and a half a million dollars' worth of property had been destroyed. So devastating a fire had never before been known in the United States.

It was a scene for a painter; which may not have been pre-served, but which may be pictured by any one having a taste for the wild and the wonderful—the fantastic forms and tracing presented in flaming boats, the island forest, the houses and the hills in the distance on the Illinois shore, the numberless warehouses, and the thousands of persons lining the wharf.

Fifteen blocks of houses were burned or seriously damaged, causing the loss of ten million dollars. The fire was finally extinguished by blowing up several houses with powder, but in doing that several lives were lost although great care was taken to give timely warning. The list of sufferers made eight or ten columns in the *Missouri Republican.*

The following are the names of the boats burned: —

American Eagle, Cossen, Master; Keokuk and Upper Mississippi packet; valued at $14,000; total loss; insured at Pittsburgh for $3,500; no cargo.

Alice, Kennett, Master; Missouri river packet; valued at $18,000; total loss; insured for $12,000—$9,000 in city offices, balance in the East; cargo valued at $1,000.

Alexander Hamilton, Hooper, Master; Missouri river packet; valued at $15,000; total loss; insured for $10,500 in. Eastern offices; no cargo.

Acadia, John Russell, Master; Illinois river packet; val-·ued $4,000; total loss; fully insured in Eastern offices; cargo valued at $1,000.

Boreas, Bernard, Master; Missouri river packet; valued at $14,500; total loss; insured for $11,500 in this city; no cargo.

Belle Isle, Smith, Master; New Orleans trade; valued at $10,000; total loss; insured at $8,000 in New Orleans offices; no cargo.

Eliza Stewart, H. McKee, Master; Missouri packet; val-·ued at $9,000; insured for near full value.

Eudora, Ealer, Master; St. Louis and New Orleans trade; valued at $16,000; total loss; insured for $10,500; no cargo.

Edward Bates, Randolph, Master; Keokuk packet; val-·ued at $22,500; insured for $15,000.

Frolic (Tow boat), Ringling, Master; valued at $15,000; no insurance.

Gen'l Brooke (Tow boat), Ringling, Master; valued at :$1,500; no insurance.

Kit Carson, Goddin, Master; Missouri river packet; valued at $16,000; insured for $8,000.

Mameluke, Smithers, Master; New Orleans and St. Louis trade; valued at $30,000; insured for $20,000; no cargo.

Mandan, Beers, Master; Missouri river; valued at $14,-·000; insured for $10,500; no cargo,

Montauk, Morehouse, Master; upper Mississippi; valued at $16,000; insured for $10,000; cargo valued at $8,000.

Martha, Finch, Master; Missouri river; valued at $10,000; fully insured; cargo valued at $30,000; also insured.

Prairie State, Baldwin, Master; Illinois river packet; val-·ued at $26,000; insured for $18,000; cargo valued at $3,000.

Red Wing, Barger, Master; Upper Mississippi trade; valued at $6,000; no insurance; cargo valued at $3,000.

St. Peters, Ward, Master; Upper Mississippi trade; val-ued at $12,000; insured for $9,000; no cargo.

Sarah, Young, Master; St. Louis and New Orleans trade; valued at $35,000; insured for $20,000; cargo valued at $30,000.

Tagliona, Marshall, Master; Pittsburg and St. Louis trade; valued at $20,000; insured for full value; cargo valued at $12,000.

Timore, Miller, Master; Missouri river trade; valued at $25,000; insured for $10,000; cargo valued at $6,000.

White Cloud, Adams, Master; St. Louis and New Or-·leans trade; valued at $3,000; fully insured; no cargo.

CHAPTER LIV.

STEAMBOATS AND PACKET COMPANIES.

THE writer of the following communication will be recognized by many old boatmen and citizens of Cincinnati as among the earlier boatmen running out of that port in the trades on the Ohio above that city. His recollections will, of course, revive that of the few of his associates who still remain and bring to mind some pleasant reminiscences of the past, and of many old boats long since fogotten.

All will unite with this writer in thanking Capt. D. F. Barker for his kind effort to awaken pleasant recollections of events half a century ago : —

CONCORD, MASS., Nov. 21st, 1888.

Capt. E. W. Gould, St. Louis:

DEAR SIR — My brother, J. H. Barker, tells me you propose publishing a history of old steamboat times, such as names of packets, when and by whom established, etc. As I was identified with some of the early packets in the Maysville and Portsmouth trade, my brother thinks I could give you some items that you might be able to use.

In June, 1836, Capt. Grafton Molen and James Walls bought of Jacob Strader the steamboat Swiftsure, and put her in the packet trade to Maysville. Previous to that time the trade had been supplied irregularly by several owners of boats, but the advent of Captain Molen with the Swiftsure may well be claimed as the beginning of what now is the widely known and influential packet line doing most of the business between Cincinnati, Maysville, Portsmouth and Big Sandy.

The Swiftsure was less than 100 tons measurement; built by Strader in 1835 for the Guyandotte trade ; but a short time before completed. Strader sold one of his Cincinnati and Louisville packets to go to Mobile, so he put the Swiftsure in the Louisville trade until the first double engine, Ben Franklin, could be finished. When Molen entered the Maysville trade with the Swiftsure, the Lady Scott, owned by the Woods of Maysville, had been in the trade for several months. The Lady Scott was originally a canal boat and left the trade in a short time after the Swiftsure entered it.

There were a number of boats built ostensibly for the trade between 1836 and 1840, but which did not continue long in it. The Casket, built at Ripley, by Capt. John Moore ; Rubicon, by a number of Maysville merchants ; Naples, by the Woods' family, and the Fairplay, by Capt. John Moore.

In 1839, Molen and Walls built the Mail, which proved too large and only ran a few months and was sold to Strader in 1840. In the fall of 1840, Molen put in the trade the second Swiftsure which remained until 1842, when she went into the Pittsburgh line, returning to the Maysville trade in 1844. From 1840 to 1844, besides the Swiftsure, there were the Fairplay, Capt. John Ellison; Indiana, Capt. John Harland ; the Pilot, Capt. Wm. McClain. In 1844, Molen built and put in the trade the Daniel Boone and McClain put in the Simon Kenton. McClain sold the Simon Kenton to Strader in 1847, and the Circassian, Capt. John Ballenger, took her place in the trade. In 1848, a stock company was formed called the Cincinnati and Maysville Packet Co., two new boats having been built for the trade — Boone, Capt. Molen, and Kenton, Capt. McClain. About 1855 or '56, the Scioto, No. 2, Capt. Keppner, then in the Portsmouth trade, was bought and the name of the company was changed to Cincinnati, Maysville and Portsmouth Packet Co., and so continued until 1859, when the company dissolved and the boats sold to individual members of the company who continued some of the boats in their respective trades.

My connection with the trades then ceased.

If you can make use of any of the above you are at liberty to do so.   Very respectfully,   D. F. BARKER.

NEW ORLEANS AND OHIO RIVER ORGANIZATIONS.

In 1858, there were more and better arrangements for regularity and punctuality in steamboat management than had ever before existed on all Western rivers.

In addition to the "Railroad Line" from St. Louis to New Orleans, there was organized to run from Louisville to New Orleans what was known as the "Lightning Line," consisting of some of the fastest and best boats then running, among which was the Robert J. Ward, Capt. Silas Miller ; Diana, E. T. Sturgon; Baltic, C. H. Meekin; John Raine, W. Underwood; Antelope, E. Brown; Pacific, A. McGill, Woodford, Moses Erwin; Jas. Montgomery ; Samuel Montgomery; Fanny Bullitt, S. B. Durham; E. H. Fairchild, I. H. B Fawcett

While this was only a joint arrangement and each boat was managed by its owner, it was well arranged and run with regularity and was very popular with the traveling public. It was maintained until the war, but never re-organized afterwards.

At Cincinnati a good line was organized on the same basis as the Louisville and New Orleans. It was known as the "Cincinnati and New Orleans Express Line" and was composed of the following boats: Switzerland, Captain J. P. Schenk; Ohio Belle, Captain John Sebastian: Monarch, Captain John A. Williamson; Tecumseh, Captain F. F. Logan; Judge Torrence, Captain R. M. Wade; Susquehanna, Captain O. C. Williamson; Madison, Captain G. D. Hoople; Universe, Captain Albert Stine; Nick Thomas, Captain John A. Duble; Queen of the West, Captain J. P. Wade.

These were what was known as short boats, and could pass the locks in the Louisiana canal — were not fast, but of large carrying capacity, with fine accommodations for passengers, and their tables were furnished equal to a first-class hotel. They were run on schedule time and maintained uniform rates of freight. Their regularity, promptness and good management was such an improvement upon the former style of running Cincinnati boats engaged in the New Orleans trade, that they soon secured a popularity that promised very satisfactory results. They were even an important factor in establishing rates of freight with the railroads and were really at that time the regulators of that traffic.

But two years later the war came, and not only destroyed all legitimate commerce between the North and South for four long years, but forever destroyed the hopes of that generation of boatmen of ever again establishing the supremacy of river transportation — from causes originating in the results of the war, which gave to railroads the ascendancy which they would not have attained in many years. The boats and the boatmen were alike scattered, and many of both destroyed, and when the war closed and government transportation no longer furnished employment, another and a more vital war was inaugurated — *a war for bread*. No industry suffered so much — no class in the community was so illy prepared to meet the emergency. From education and from habit, boatmen, as a rule, knew no other occupation — wanted to know no other. A few of the more enterprising embarked in other pursuits with varying degrees of success.

Another portion collected their exhausted energies and remaining resources and attempted to recover what was lost by purchasing from the government repairing and rebuilding

24

what remained of the old boats, and with them attempted to
re-establish what had once been legitimate and profitable lines
of boats.   In some few instances they succeeded, and are to-
day their own successors, after the lapse of many years and
many struggles and conflicts with their powerful rivals.   Another and perhaps the most numerous class that time has dealt
more gently with than has fortune, are still waiting and watching for the " shadows to a little longer grow " before attempting to launch their frail barques upon the unknown waters
across the river, while the well known waters upon which the
best years of their lives have been spent have proved so full
of wrecks, rocks and disasters.

CINCINNATI AND LOUISVILLE MAIL LINE.

Long previous to 1858, however, many flourishing steamboat organizations were in successful operation on the Ohio
and its tributaries.   The "Cincinnati and Louisville Mail
Line, "organized in 1818, the first steam packet company of
which there is any record.

In 1847 this company increased its stock and extended its
line from Louisville to St. Louis.   Adding the following boats :
Southerner (low pressure), Capt. Catterlin; Northerner (low
pressure), Capt. Erwin; Ben Franklin, Capt. Dollis ; Moses
McClellan, Capt. Barker; High Flyer, Capt. Wright ; Fashion No. 2, Capt. Reed ; Alvin Adams, Capt. Boies.

This constituted a daily line of first-class passenger boats between Cincinnati, Louisville and St. Louis.

The Jacob Strader (low pressure) and the Telegraph No. 3
were the connecting boats at Louisville.   The Strader was
the largest boat ever constructed to run above the falls, and
the most expensive.   Her cabin accommodations exceeded any
other boat ever built on the Western waters.   She would accommodate with state rooms some four hundred passengers.

The connecting boats below the falls were of large capacity,
and their recorded time was very fast.   Reducing the former
time between Louisville and St. Louis, from three days to 39
and 44 hours, and before the completion of a railroad the
travel on these boats was immense.

LOUISVILLE PACKET COMPANIES.

Louisville was also the home port for several lines of boats
beside that of the great and popular passenger line to New
Orleans.

Notably the "Henderson Packet Company," the Louisville
and Wheeling line of fast passenger boats, in connection with
the Baltimore and Ohio Railroad, known as the Union Packet

Company. This line was organized in 1852, and composed of the following elegant steamers: —
Alvin Adams, David White, Thomas Swan, Baltimore, Falls City, Virginia and City of Wheeling.

STEAMBOATS BUILT A LONG TIME AGO.

(From the Pittsburgh Dispatch, 18th.)

I have read with great pleasure a number of your old time boating items, our whole family of males having been engaged on the river, commencing with keel-boating, and when they disappeared, took to steamboating. The following list has never been in print : —

THE FIRST BOATS BUILT AT PITTSBURGH.

1811 — Orleans, built at Sucks Run, on the site where the Pan Handle Railroad bridge crosses the Monongahela River.

1814 — Vesuvius, Etna.

1815 — New Orleans ; only boat built that year.

1816 — James Monroe, Buffalo.

1817 — Franklin, James Madison, Gen. Jackson.

1818 — Alleghany, Expedition, James Ross, St. Louis, Tamerlane, Tom Jefferson.

1819 — Western Engineer, Telegraph, Rapides, Olive Branch, Dolphin, Cumberland, Car of Commerce, Balize Packet.

I have lost the record of building in 1820 and 1821.

1822 — Favorite, Gen. Neville.

1823 — Rambler, Phœnix, Pittsburgh and St. Louis Packet; Pittsburg, Pennsylvania.

1824 — American, Herald, President.

1825 — Bolivar, Friendship, Gen. Brown, Gen. Wayne, Lafayette, Pocahontas, Wm. Penn.

1826 — America, New York, Echo, Erie, Fame, Commerce, Columbus, Messenger, Liberator, Lady Washington, Jubilec, Illinois, Hercules, Gen. Coffee, Florida, De Witt Clinton.

1827 — Wm. D. Duncan, Pennsylvania, New Pennsylvania, Maryland, Essex.

1828 — Baltimore, Cumberland, Delaware, Missouri, Neptune, North America, Potomac, Phœnix, Star, Powhattan, Plaquemine, Red River, Stranger, Talisman. You will perceive that boat-building has steadily increased.

1829 — Citizen, Cora, Corsair, Caroline, Huntsville, Home, Huntsman, Hudson, Industry, Huron, James O'Hara, Kentucky, Link, Mohican, Monticello, Nile, Red Rover. The latter boat measured 500 tons, and was the largest boat built up to that time. Rhuhama, Talma, Trenton, Talgho, Tariff,

Uncle Sam, Victory, being twenty-four steamers built that year.

1830 — Sam Patch, Peruvian, Olive, Mobile, New Jersey, Hatchie, Eagle, Gleaner, Gondola, Enterprise, Abeona.

A. D. R.

PITTSBURGH BOATS AND BOATMEN.

Pittsburg Dispatch: In 1850–2, just prior to the opening of the railroad era at Pittsburgh, there were three principal packet lines running to Brownsville, Cincinnati and St. Louis. In the first line were the packets Louis McLain, Consul, Baltic and Atlantic, and the captains of that day were Adam Jacobs, Sam Clark, James Parkinson, Isaac Woodward and Elisha Bennett. Running in the Pittsburg and St. Louis trade were the John C. Fremont, Caledonia, Persia, Aliquippa, Anglo-Saxon, Alma, Niagara, Hindoo, Shenandoah, Arctic, Isaac Newton, Paul Anderson, Manchester, Keystone, Ben West, Honduras and Cambria. The captains were M. A. Cox, William Forsythe, Hiram Price, George W. Bowman, Hugh Campbell, Thomas and Robert Greenlee, Benjamin Hutchinson, James Gormley, Eph. Butcher, William Connelly, John and Henry Devinney, Jake Hazlett, George Cochran, Jake and Adam Poe, T. J. Stockdale, R. C. Gray, Dick Calhoon, Joseph Smith and A. G. Mason. The Cincinnati boats were the Monongahela, Keystone State, Alleghany, New England, Messenger, Brilliant, Crystal Palace, Clipper and Buckeye State, and the captains were Charles W. Batchelor, W. J. Kountz, R. C. Gray, Charles Stephen, Daniel Stone, John Klinefelter, R. J. Grace. Samuel Reno, Melchoir W. Beltzhoover and James Fisher. These boats, as a rule, drew four feet of water without cargo, and gray-haired rivermen say that in those days they always looked for boating at least ten months in the year, from September until June. They attribute the contraction of the boating season to its present limited period to the destruction of the forests and the absorption of the rainfall by the soil. Rivermen did not always believe in the expediency of building their boats to the length of 300 feet. Indeed in 1833 there was quite a rumpus about the length of the Wacousta, between Jake Arnold and Pete Dohrman, two of the pioneers. Jake wanted to make her 120 feet long. but Pete vowed he would never go into her wheel-house if she went over 110 feet, as she would surely capsize. How little foundation there was for good Peter's fears can be realized when he remembers that the Great Republic, built here in 1867, was 350 feet long, and 48-feet in the beam, or just three times the dimensions of the Wacousta. One could fill a volume of the most capaciou proportions with the stories of the old time river captains, and yet not adequately cover the subject. Many there are who will recall the disastrous fate of the steamboat Americus, that was launched on a Friday, thus setting at defiance one of the most firmly rooted superstitions of watermen of all climes. She was commanded by Capt. Charles W. Batchelor, and all went well with her until one day, while going up the Illinois River, Capt. Batchelor was standing in the wheel house with Pilot Jack Quick, a sad sea dog. There was a hail from the shore, and looking around, they descried a man sitting on a white horse. The nose of the boat was turned toward the bank, much against Jack Quick's inclination. Said he : " See here, Cap'n, if that 'ere man with the white hoss should be a preacher, this boat'll burn afore mornin'." And so the man turned out to be a preacher, and so, sure enough, the boat took fire and was burned, and it was all on account of her being launched on a Friday, and because she met a preacher with a white horse. So goes the tale, as reeled off by an ancient man of the wheel.

STEAMBOATS, KEEL-BOATS AND PETTIFOGGERS.

Portsmouth Tribune: Much has been written in newspapers about river men, and men applauded that started in where their fathers or some wealthy relative or friend left off, while men that commenced on the keel-boat, at the oar and setting-pole at fifty cents per day and came up to be men of wealth and standing amongst business men, have been entirely forgotten. The men that first opened up navigation on the Ohio river from Pittsburgh to Louisville, at the falls of the great Ohio, should not be allowed to die unseen, unheard of and forever forgotten. Such men as studied the channel of the river, marked it out by clumps of trees and by notches in the hills bordering on this beautiful river, many of whom lived to build, own and command good steamboats and navigated the Ohio and Mississippi and their tributaries. These men did not have the advantages that the captains (or bell-ringers) of the present day have. They had no wharfboats, no clean landing to discharge their cargoes on. They did not have any freight agent on shore to solicit freight and telegraph them at the different points on the river what was proper to do for their advantage, but they must go it alone and manage their own boat, get their freight, build up a good reputation for themselves and their boats by their industry, economy, fair dealing, and honesty. In those days there was not one suit against a steamboat and owners to 150 these days. We know that there was not so many boats in those days as now, nor half so

pressure), Philadelphia, (low pressure), Kentuckian, Bonnets, O'Blue, Samson, (without a p), Bellfast, Hudson, Constitution, Huntsman, Red River, Convoy, Scotland, Superior, Cincinnatian (low pressure), Ohio, Chesapeake, Reaper, Polander, Arab, Helen McGregor, Uncle Sam, Tuscarora. This boat was the first that made the trip from New Orleans to Louisville inside of eight days. Her time being seven days and sixteen hours. This voyage was made in spring of 1834.

There were quite a number of boats running from Pittsburgh to Cincinnati, Louisville and occasionally St. Louis, the latter city containing only 6,000 inhabitants in 1830. There were boats running to Nashville on the Cumberland and to Florence and Tuscumbia on the Tenuessee Rivers, and in the spring of the year boats would load to Lafayette, Terre Haute and Logansport on the Wabash. At that period Memphis had no boats running to it. Occasionally a boat would load for Little Rock.

The first combination or consolidation of steamboat stock was made at Louisville in the summer of 1832. A contract for carrying the mail between Louisville and New Orleans by the river was given to Charles M. Strader and others. Meetings were held for the attendance of owners of steamboat stock, suitable for New Orleans trade. The boats were valued by parties interested. Had their own agents at Cincinnati and Louisville.   Capt. Samuel Perry, and Levi James, at Cincinnati, and Chas. M. Strader and Henry Forsythe at Louisville. Supposing they had control of all boats, which were suitable for the New Orleans trade for carrying freight and passengers, they could be independent, and deemed it unnecessary to employ the old agents, Wm. D. Jones of Cincinnati, and J. C. Buckles at Louisville; were good business men, well liked and had been active steamboat agents for all trades on the river.   This was where the great monopoly made its first mistake.   In place of ignoring these men, they should have been made the agents of the "Ohio & Mississippi Mail Line Co."   "O. & M. Mail Line Co.," was on the side of their wheel houses.   Messrs. Levi James and Samuel Perry were old captains in the trades, their two sons were made captains.

The arrangement resulted in disaster, i. e., the line made no money for the reason that Messrs. Jones and Buckles would induce every owner of a steamboat of carrying capacity of 200 tons, and who were out of the " O. & M. Mail Line " to send or bring their boats to Cincinnati or Louisville, and load for New Orleans, that the monopoly was in bad odor with shippers, etc.

The consequence was that in place of pork paying $1.50 per barrel, it was carried for 37½ cts., everything else in proportion. At the end of the season the compact ended, and each and every owner took his boat back. The season following was successful, and boat owners did well till the panic in business which began in 1837 continued till the '40s.

The first regular boat in the trade between Cincinnati and Louisville was the General Pike, built at Cincinnati in 1818. Her first commander was Capt. Bliss. In 1821, Jacob Strader was made captain and James Gorman was clerk. The trade of this boat was between Cincinnati and Louisville, but occasionally her trips were extended as far as Maysville, Ky. In 1825 the (low pressure) Ben Franklin was built, commenced running in 1826, between Cincinnati and Louisville, not on regular days but as often as required. This being before the canal at Louisville was built, would load at Cincinnati with produce and reship at Louisville, wait at the latter city till an arrival of a New Orleans boat, then load for a return trip. The Ben Franklin was owned by Capt. Jacob Strader, James Gorman, Philip Grandon, James Kelly (engineer of boat), and others.

Capt. John Blair Summons, who for many subsequent years was a successful captain of the boats in the Cincinnati and Louisville Mail Line, was mate and pilot. John Wesley Brown was also a young pilot of the Ben Franklin. Messrs. Strader and Gorman retired from running as officers of steamboats in 1831. The boat being well along in years was sold to Robt. G. Ormsby, of Louisville, with Edward Carroll as captain, and James M. Noble (now living) was clerk.

Two Virginians, named Porter and Beldon, succeeded in obtaining contracts for carrying the mails in Virginia from Guyandotte on the river and from other points through Charlottesville, White Sulphur Springs, etc., to Richmond and Washington City, and by river to Cincinnati from Guyandotte four times a week, and intermediate points. Also from Cincinnati to Louisville and intermediate points daily. This was in 1830 and 1831. They also contracted to transport the mails between New Orleans and Mobile by steamboat. Two boats being built at Cincinnati for the purpose, one was named Star of the West, the other, William S. Barry, W. F. B. being the Postmaster-General.

Capt. Strader having retired from the river, but familiar with river business, was made the business manager of the boats, making regular trips four times a week between Cincinnati and Guyandotte and daily between Cincinnati and

Louisville. The United States Mail Line began running
every day in 1831. The contractors at this time owned only
two boats for this Ohio River service, the steamers Guyandotte and Portsmouth. The town of Portsmouth, 112 miles
above Cincinnati, had about this time become a very important point, it being the southern terminus of the Great Ohio
Canal, commencing at Cleveland and ending at Portsmouth, and
proved a valuable support of the boats. At this period there
were no railroads in the whole United States, except the one
from New Orleans to the lake, about four miles in length, and
one other — the Baltimore end of the Baltimore & Ohio road,
fifteen miles long to Ellicott's Mills. This much of the B. &
O. road was finished and put in use as early as 1827. Cars
being run by horse power. For the Guyandotte and Portsmouth trade two boats were built, the Guyandotte in 1831
and Portsmouth in 1832. The latter boat proved to be un-
necessarily large and expensive for the trade, and early in
1833 was placed in the Cincinnati and Louisville trade, the
Helen Marr taking her place to Guyandotte. The mail line
between Cincinnati and Louisville was maintained by boats
chartered or they were given a day in consideration of their
making no charge for carrying the mail. Until 1834 it required three boats to keep up a daily service. The Cham-
plain, Messenger, Robt. Fulton, and Portsmouth were mostly
in the trade till 1834. About this time Capt. Strader bought
all the interest of Messrs. Porter and Belden and became the
principal owner. Early this year (1834) a new boat was put
in the trade (I mean now the Cincinnati and Louisville Mail
Line), named Ben Franklin, was very fast, single engine, 5½
foot stroke, 27 inches diameter, hull 165 feet long, 18 foot
beam, 5 1-2 foot hold, 4 39 inch boilers, 18 feet long. This
boat made the trip from Louisville to Cincinnati in fourteen
hours twelve minutes.

This was more than 54 years ago. The Ben Franklin and
Portsmouth performed the service each, making the round trip
every two days. The trade proved to be profitable, the Ben
Franklin paid for herself in eight months. Jacob Strader and
J. B. Summons' the captain, were the sole owners of the Ben
Franklin, the writer being clerk. The Portsmouth was owned
same way, with the exception that Capt. I. D. Edmond had a
small interest. The Portsmouth was a good running boat,
though not as fast as Ben Franklin. In 1835 a new fast boat,
Gen'l Pike, took the place of the Portsmouth, was 168 feet long,
beam 19 feet, hold 5 feet 8 inches, single engine, 5 1-2 feet
long, 25 inch diameter, 4 boilers, 40 inch by 20 feet, made the

run from Louisville to Cincinnati in 13 hours, 40 minutes.
John D. Edmond, captain; Alfred Dunning, çlerk.

In June, 1836, another new boat took the place of the Ben
Franklin (the latter having been sold to Capt. Slade to go to
Mobile). This boat had double engine, 7 feet stroke, 6 feet
hold, 23 feet beam, was fast, having made the run from Louisville to Cincinnati in 12 hours and 8 minutes. Good passenger accommodations but poor freighter, was profitable to the
owners. In 1838, another double engine boat was placed on
the route to take the place of the single engine boat, Gen'l
Pike. This new boat was named Pike (Big Pike), 182
feet long (just filled the old locks), 28 feet beam, 7 foot
hold, 2 engines, 8 feet 25 inches, 6 boilers, 24 feet 40 inches.
This boat was built by Wm. French, Jeffersonville, about the
speed of Ben Franklin, but a larger carrier.

For low water boats the company built and owned boats   ⼗
suitable for the season named Little Ben, Little Pike,
Ben Franklin No. 7, Pike No. 8, etc. In 1840 the
United States Mail having been built by Mr. James Wall
for the Cincinnati and Maysville trade, which proved rather
expensive for the place, was sold to Capt. Strader. In the
spring of 1841 she was placed in the trade between Cincinnati
and Pittsburg leaving the former city every Monday morning
at 11. This was a fast boat, 2 engines, 18 inches 7 feet,
Stroke, 3 42-inch, boilers, 22 feet beam, 180 feet long,
etc. Carried a great many passengers, some freight, and did
very well. The writer was captain, James Summons clerk.

The apparent success of this boat during a rather short
season (water getting low by middle of June), suggested the
idea to the steamboat community of making it a tri-weekly
line. Linas Logan and P. Wilson Strader bought the "Mail"
for the purpose. William (Bill) Fuller put in the Swiftsure
No. 2. In the course of two years more, there were boats for
every day. The Messrs. Stone put in the Monongahela; Klinefelter, the Hibernia; Capt. Crooks, the Clipper; Capt. Grace,
the Brilliant; Capt. Dean, the Buckeye State; Capt. Kountz,
the Cincinnati, the Messenger was one of the boats, and Pittsburg, Capt. James McClew, Alleghany. It was in the '50's the
great "Wheeling and Louisville" line was established. At
about this time everybody wanted fine large fast boats. The
Pennsylvania Central was nearly completed to Pittsburgh and
the Baltimore and Ohio Railroad had almost reached Wheeling. Steamboatmen nor railroad men had at that time any
idea that railroads would be built to run from East to West
and North to South, over rivers, through and over mountains,

and all over the continent. The New York Central ended at
Albany and Buffalo. It was supposed the Pennsylvania
Central would end at Pittsburgh, and the Baltimore and Ohio
at Wheeling, otherwise the fine large steamers to ply between
Wheeling, Louisville and Pittsburgh and Cincinnati would not
have been built. They were, however, named as follows,
to-wit: Alvin Adams, David White, Thos. Swan, Baltimore,
Falls City, Virginia and City of Wheeling. The early
plans in building railroads were to place them so as to connect with steamboat routes.

EARLY PACKET LINES.

The result shows they didn't stop there, and steamboat enterprise has materially declined. This is quite a digression
from the original object. "Writing something about the
Mail Line" I will digress a little more, now I'm about it. It
was in the year 1832, Capt. Shrodes, of Pittsburgh, built the
largest boat ever constructed on the Western waters. This
boat was named Mediterranean. Was too long and too wide
to pass through the locks, drew about 6 feet light, 200 feet
long, 31 feet beam, 10 feet hold, 8 42-inch boilers 24 feet
long single engine, don't remember the size, passed down the
river in February, 1833, never returned as far as Cincinnati.
Capt. Shrodes afterwards built other large boats in 1834 and
1836. Three of them large carriers, Corinthian, Moravian,
and Peru. Double engines, lock length. As early as 1834
steamboat interest began to increase rapidly, many were built
at Pittsburgh. The trade with St. Louis and Upper Mississippi country was rapidly becoming of marked importance, and
it was not uncommon to see the signs for " St. Louis " on as
many as from 5 to 6 boats at the same time at the Cincinnati
wharf. There were lines formed. One : " The Pilot's Line,"
" The Good Intent Line," " The Red Letter Line," and later
a line of fast boats called the "Express Line." There were
five of them, named as follows : Tiber, Tribune, Susquehanna,
Paris, and London owned in Pittsburgh 175 feet long, 21 feet
wide, 5 1-2 feet hold 4 42-inch boilers 24 feet long, single
engines, disremember the size. I believe another of the same
class was in the line, named Glasgow, Capt. Wm. McClain.
I will now return to the " Mail Line." The second double
engine, Ben Franklin, was built in 1840, made two trips to New
Orleans in the winter of 1840–41. After returning to Cincinnati in February, 1841, carried General W. H. Harrison to
Pittsburg on his way to Washington to take his seat as President. This latter boat proving rather large for the Mail trade
was placed in the trade between St. Louis and New Orleans in
1842, Capt. Casey ; she was a fast runner, having left New

Orleans for St. Louis three times on regular trips in one
month, it was the month of May, 1842.   The Ben Franklin
No. 6 was built in 1843 and placed in the line.   The Pike No.
7 being the boat on the opposite days.   Ben Franklin No. 7
and Pike No. 8 being the low water boats.   Some time during the year 1840, Capt. John D. Edmond having resigned his
position as commander of the Pike, Capt. John Armstrong
was installed as captain of the "Pike side of the Line" and
Capt. Chas. P. Bacon, of Louisville, was placed in the office,
Alfred Dunning having retired as clerk with Capt. Edmond.
Capt. Bacon, in 1843, retired from Mail Line to engage as
captain in the trade between New Orleans and Louisville.
Capt. Fitzgerald, old "Two and a half and the door slides"
was clerk.   In all these years John Blair Summons was captain of the Ben Franklin and J. H. Barker was clerk.   James
Gorman became interested as owner on the "Pike side of the
Line;" also Capt. Armstrong became a stockholder in 1840,
each owning one-sixth.   Messrs. Summons and Barker holding
their stock in the "Franklin side," Jacob Strader being
owner of one-half of the "Franklin and two-thirds of the
Pikes."

The house of "Strader & Gorman," having been established about the year 1833 for the purpose of carrying on a general
produce and commission business, were agents for steamboats in the New Orleans trade as well as for the mail-boats.
Wm. Worsham was their confidential clerk and book-keeper
till 1840, at which time Ed. (Major) Tillotson succeeded Mr.
Worsham.   The old line continued until the year 1847 without any change in ownership.   When the property changed
hands, John B. Summons, Patrick Rogers, Thomas Sherlock,
C. G. Pearce, Philip Anschutz, Edward Montgomery and J.
H. Barker were the purchasers.   The Line since has continued
being the "United States Mail Line."   New owners have
been added and old ones have retired from time to time.   The
business increased, boats were built, some bought.   A daily
line at one time during the years before the war.   The Company owned and ran a boat every day to St. Louis.   Also a
tri-weekly line to Memphis.   Were interested as stockholders
in the "Great Mississippi and Atlantic Steam-ship Co."
and previous to the war in the line from Memphis to New
Orleans.

The names of the boats (some of them) owned by the com-
pany are somewhat familiar to the present generation.
Among which were Jacob Strader, Telegraph No. 3, Alvin
Adams, Fashion, The Pikes, Ben Franklin, United States,

America, Telegraphs, Nos. 1 and 2, Northerner, Southerner, Moses McLellan, Superior, Gen. Buell, Major Anderson, Pike No. 9, Lady Franklin, Lady Pike, High Flyer, Gen. Lytle, City of Madison.

ONE STOCKHOLDER 53 YEARS.

In May, 1884, the old company sold a majority of stock to the Big Sandy, Portsmouth and Pomeroy Packet Co., with Capt. C. M. Holloway, General Manager, Capt. John Kyle, President and Lee R. Keck, Secretary and Treasurer, of Cincinnati, and Capt. Frank Carter, Superintendent at Louisville. The steamers of the company at this time are the Fleetwood, City of Madison, Gen. Pike, City of Vevay and Minnie Bay.

One stockholder (J. H. B.) who become interested as an owner of the Ben Franklin in the year 1836, is now, in 1888, still one of the owners.

Hoping my humble effort may aid you somewhat in your undertaking, I am,

Yours sincerely,
(Signed)   JONATHAN H. BARKER.

CINCINNATI, O., Dec. 28th, 1888.

Capt. E. W. Gould, St. Louis. Mo.—

DEAR SIR: Yours of the 7th inst. was duly received, but an unusual press of official duties, together with indifferent health, prevented an earlier reply.

The following are the principal packet companies, with names of officers, as requested, but I regret my inability to give the respective dates of their organization: —

MEMPHIS AND CINCINNATI PACKET COMPANY.

James D. Parker, President; L. R. Keck, Secretary and Treasurer; R. W. Wise, Superintendent. Steamers — Ohio, DeSoto, Buckeye State, Granite State.

CINCINNATI, PORTSMOUTH, BIG SANDY, AND POMEROY PACKET COMPANY.

John Kyle, President; C. M. Holloway, Superintendent; L. R. Keck, Secretary and Treasurer; D. W. Shedd, General Freight Agent. Steamers — Bostona, Bonanza, Big Sandy, Telegraph, St. Lawrence, Louis A. Sherley.

OHIO RIVER PACKET COMPANY.

Cincinnati, New Richmond, Moscow and Chilo: David Gibson, President; N. C. Vanderbilt, Secretary. Steamers Tocoma and Lancaster.

MAYSVILLE AND VANCEBURG PACKET COMPANY.

David Gibson, President; Bruce Redden, Secretary; L. Redden, Superintendent. Steamer Handy No. 2.

WHEELING AND CINCINNATI PACKET COMPANY.

David Gibson, President; M. F. Noll, Secretary; Chas. Musselman, Superintendent. Steamer Andes.

Herewith inclosed please find P. O. order for my subscription for a copy of your forthcoming work.

Thanking you for the compliment paid me in your letter, which is scarcely warranted, I will close with kind regards and very many good wishes for the success of your worthy undertaking.

Sincerely yours,

HENRY H. DEVENNEY.

CHAPTER LV.

ST. LOUIS AND NEW ORLEANS PACKET COMPANY — "RAILROAD LINE," 1858.

THIS line comprised a number of the finest steamers on Western waters at the time. They consisted of the following boats, viz. : —

Imperial, Capt. Gould ; New Falls City, Capt. Montgomery ; Wm. M. Morrison, Capt. Bofinger; City of Memphis, Capt. Kountz ; James E. Woodruff, Capt. Rogers (the Woodruff was the first steamboat that ever published a daily paper on board; it was edited by Capt. G. W. Ford, the clerk); Pennsylvania, Capt. Klinefelter; A. T. Lacy, Capt. Rodney ; New Uncle Sam, Capt. Van Dusen ; J. C. Swan, Capt. Jones ; Alex. Scott, Capt. Switzer.

Ten steamers composed the line. They had an arrangement with the Illinois Central Railroad at Cairo, and with the Ohio and Mississippi at St. Louis, by which passengers and freight were contracted to all points reached by either road or the boats.

While this was not a joint stock company, the boats were run in joint interest, and with a regularity heretofore unknown in this trade and at uniform prices for the business they did.

Many forebodings were expressed as to its success, as it was among the first attempts to organize a regular line upon this principle.

But few months however elapsed before the line became very popular with the owners of boats, and with the traveling public and shippers everywhere.

A position in the railroad line, or a *"day in the line,"* as it was termed, was coveted by all who had a boat suitable for the trade, and commanded a large premium when offered for sale, and as high as $1,500 was paid in some instances.

But from the unfortunate *"unpleasantness"* that occurred between the North and the South, in 1861, the "railroad line of boats" promised a success that has not been excelled by any organization in the New Orleans trade since, and furnished a character of boats and a service to the public unrivaled before or since that time.

While their time was not as fast, their regularity and accommodations were as good.

ST. LOUIS AND TENNESSEE PACKET CO.

Before the close of the war the demand for transportation on the Tennessee river induced the establishment of a packet company between St. Louis and Johnsonville. Several boats found employment there in transporting government supplies, and a successful business was done for several years under the direction of Capt. Cafferes and other war captains of the time, as there was not a legitimate trade after the government transportation ceased, the boats were withdrawn and no regular boats ran there until the present company reopened the trade.

In 1881 a company known as the "St. Louis, Cincinnati, Huntington & Pittsburgh Packet Co.

Capt. I. M. Williamson, of Cincinnati, acted as superintendent at that port, and Capt. W. S. Evens filled the same position at Pittsburgh.

The company had some good boats and they were judiciously managed.

But it was soon discovered the distance was too long and the competition with railroads over a much shorter route could not be successfully maintained, and after a few months the boats were withdrawn.

ARKANSAS, RED RIVER, OUACHITA AND OTHER PACKET COMPANIES WERE FORMED AT ST. LOUIS.

Soon after the close of the war the trade of the South drifted towards St. Louis very rapidly, and suggested more and better facilities for transportation.

The result was the combination of the surplus boats that were left idle after the war into organizations, and were styled Arkansas River Packet Co., Red River Packet Co., Ouachita, Tennessee, etc., etc. They were simply associations with an agreement to run under certain prescribed rules, and under the direction of a board of directors and a president. Whenever, from any cause, the owners of a boat wanted to withdraw, they did so.

"The Merchants, St. Louis & Arkansas River Packet Co." was organized in 1870.

James A. Jackson was elected President; D. P. Rowland, Vice-President; G. D. Appleton, Treasurer; Sylvester, Secretary and Superintendent.

The company had several light draft boats which ran successfully a year or two. But low water and the Iron Mountain Railroad soon wore them out, and they were never replaced.

The Ouachita River Packet Co. was organized in 1870, with several good boats, owned at St. Louis, among which were the C. H. Durfee, Frank Dozier, master; Mary McDonald, John Greenough, master; Ida Stockdale, J. W. Jacobs, master; Hesper, J. Furgeson, master; C. V. Kountz, I. C. Vanhook, master; Tempest, D. H. Silver, master.

These boats were succeeded by others as they were lost or withdrawn, and it seemed for several years that a permanent trade by the river would be established. But like all other trades with St. Louis, on the tributaries of the Mississippi, it has only been a question of time, and that time has generally expired on the completion of every railroad.

A line of boats known as the "Carter Line," was established in 1869, to run between St. Louis and Red River. But its existence soon terminated, after an unsuccessful career of a few months.

A principal difficulty in this case was the great distance with no return cargo.

25

ATLANTIC AND MISSISSIPPI STEAMSHIP COMPANY AND IT
SUCCESSORS.

The great demand fór transportation after the second year
of the Civil War, for moving troops and munitions of war by
the government, induced the building of a large number of
boats and at fabulous prices. The result was, that at the
close of the war, or in 1866, it became a very serious question
with the owners, what could be done with them. It was painfully evident that the business of the country was so demoral-
ized that not half the tonnage then afloat on the Mississippi
and Ohio Rivers could be profitably employed. After various
plans had been considered and discussed by the large number
of owners, a joint stock company was agreed upon and the
assessed value of all the boats that were to be included in the
organization was to form the capital stock.

Three disinterested gentlemen were selected to value the
boats.

The aggregate value was fabulous — nearly two and a
quarter million dollars. It included some twenty boats,
many of them the largest and finest then afloat.

The company was christened the " *Atlantic and Mississippi
Steamship Co.*"

John J. Roe was elected first President, and John N.
Bofinger, Superintendent ; the principal office was in St. Louis.

It had the most extensive agencies and connections of any
steamboat company in the world. It had its own system of
coupon tickets, which was recognized and good on all railroads
in the country.

Freight and passengers contracted to and from all points.
Its connections at New Orleans with New York by steamships
were close, and large quantities of freight from Eastern cities
from all points on the Mississippi River were billed through
the line and *vice versa*.

The *first fatal mistake* was made in the organization, and
was probably the cause of its entire failure, within two years.
A majority of the best boats owned at St. Louis and in Cincinnati and some from other places were selected and appraised,
and stock issued agreeably to the valuation, which constituted
the capital stock of $2,000,000. Subsequently the company
purchased three or four boats which increased the capital stock
to $2,240,000 and the number of boats to about 25, leaving
about half that number of boats outside.

In this the mistake occurred.

These *outside* boats, while not as new or as valuable as most of those selected, were of large capacity, and when combined under an organization, at once presented a formidable competition.

Things went on swimmingly for a few months. The officers of the boats were generally selected from among those that had previously been employed by former owners, and were sometimes holders of small blocks of stock.

The war was over, and the country full of greenbacks. Everything was inflated, and prices of everything consumed by steamboats were fabulous. People at the North had become extravagant in everthing, and the only cheap commodity in the market was "greenbacks." The result was soon apparent, as many of the steamboats were in commission, manned by crews with but little interest, if any, beyond their salaries, each crew striving to excel the other in the elegance and luxury of their tables and in the speed of their boats, with no one to control or check their extravagance.

The wide-spreading limits of the company's business rendered it impossible for the executive officers (only two of which were receiving salaries) to do more than to give general supervision, leaving the detail and the result to the judgment and the caprice of those in charge of the boats. The result was as may be anticipated. While the company was doing an immense business, it was being done so extravagantly and with so little regard to permanent results, there was no margin for profits.

Although the war was now over and the volunteer forces had been returned to their homes, the government had yet a large amount of water transportation to be done, extending throughout the Mississippi valley, and advertised for bids to cover several months, and to include all its transportation. The directors of the Atlantic and Mississippi Steamship Co. decided that they had had enough government transportation before the "surrender" and declined to put in a bid.

This was another fatal mistake.

It left the field open for the organization of another company, which were not slow to avail themselves of it, and having secured the contract from the government all the outside boats that were suitable and desired to do so, were put into the new organization.

The government contract, although let at lower than the current rate at that time, formed the basis of a cargo in all directions, which gave another company a decided advantage over the A. & M. About this time, or early in 1867, adversity seems to have overshadowed the great company. Losses by the explosion of boilers was unprecedented. Several of their finest boats were burned. Three at one time, laying at the wharf at St. Louis. Some were sunk and in less than six months half the boats had disappeared. Many lives had been lost and damages had accrued from various sources. Suits had been commenced for damages in some cases and the stock which twelve months previous had been sold at par, was a drug in the market at any price. Debts were pressing, directors were indorsing paper to raise money and the boats making nothing. At length an assessment was made on the stockholders to pay off the indebtedness. A large portion of the stockholders responded. Some did not, thinking it was too late to save the "sinking ship."

They were wise. While a large sum was realized from the assessment, it only tided over the chasm that had been widening since the organization. It however enabled the company to liquidate its indebtedness to all except the stockholders. Later on they were relieved for their indorsements by the sale of the remains of the wreck. Every remedy known to the trade was resorted to at different periods during its short career to avoid the pending crash.

The directors were liberal, high-toned business men, and stood manfully by the company throughout all its embarrassments. Capt. John J. Roe resigned the presidency and was succeeded by E. W. Gould, Joseph Brown, and Wm. J. Lewis. But no amount of experience or financial ability could do more than defer the final catastrophe.

Thus perished one of the largest steamboat companies ever formed in the Mississippi Valley and with it vanished several fortunes, the accumulations from the result of the war.

One of the largest stockholders in this company had stock to the amount of $450,000, which represented the assessed value of the boats he put in. Others had very large amounts, perhaps not quite so much, but far more than they were able to lose, and never recovered from the loss.

St. Louis & New Orleans Packet Company succeeded the Atlantic & Mississippi Steamship Company. It was organized in 1869. Capt. John N. Bofinger was elected president. A large number of steamboats were included in the association, and controlled by the company, but were owned by individuals. When the A. & M. company collapsed several of their boats were purchased and put into the new line.

Having a contract with the government and each owner

managing his own boat, under the general rules of the company, the result was far more beneficial to the owners than had resulted to the owners of the stock in the Atlantic & Mississippi Company.

This organization continued with varied success for several years, and was succeeded by the " Merchant's Southern Line Packet Company " in which were included boats that had formerly been associated in the St. Louis & New Orleans Packet Company. Capt. I. F. Baker was elected president and B. R. Pegram, vice-president.

After a varied experience of two or three years the organization was not such as was satisfactory to shippers nor did it meet the demands of the commerce between St. Louis and New Orleans, neither was it profitable to the owners.

It was finally superseded by the " Anchor Line " which extended their Vicksburg line in part, and thus covered the whole territory from St. Louis to New Orleans.

" ANCHOR LINE."

By the addition of some outside boats this line was perfected and has been maintained for several years with profit, and has given general satisfaction to shippers and the traveling public. The promptness and regularity of the " Anchor Line " has given it a national reputation, which nothing but the overpowering competition from railroads will ever disturb. Certainly not so long as the company maintain the character of their boats and the regularity with which they are navigated, unless the withdrawal of so many boats from the New Orleans trade shall create dissatisfaction which may result in inducing competition from others beside the barge line.

It hardly seems possible to those who once knew of the large number of regular freight and passenger boats employed in this trade that *one boat per week* would at this date, 1889, be sufficient to accommodate that trade.

But those who have witnessed the result of railroad competition on other rivers need not be surprised at even this, notably from Pittsburgh to Cincinnati, from Louisville to New Orleans, from St. Louis to the Missouri River, where in less than thirty years the number of regular boats has been reduced from sixty to none at all.

CHAPTER LVI.

MEMPHIS STEAMBOAT ORGANIZATIONS.

AS early as 1844 as seen by reference to New Orleans papers an organization was formed to run a line of four boats to Memphis, composed of the following: —
Steamer Memphis, Capt. R. S. Fritz; steamer Joan of Arc, Capt. C. B. Church; steamer Louisiana, Capt. T. J. Casey; steamer Red Rover, Capt. M. G. Anders.

This was a temporary organization and was succeeded in 1849 by the steamer Autocrat, Capt. G. W. Gosler; steamer Magnolia, Capt. St. Clair Thommasson. These boats were continued in that trade several years and were succeeded in 1857 by the following boats, viz. : —
Steamer Ben Franklin, Capt. J. D. Clark; steamer Nebraska, Capt. A. R. Irwin; steamer Ingomar, Capt. Berditt Paras; steamer John Simonds, Capt. J. F. Smith; steamer Belfast, Capt. W. Wray; steamer H. R. W. Hill, Capt. T. H. Newell; steamer Capitol, Capt. J. D. Clark.

This was a well organized company and ran with regularity in connection with the Memphis & Charleston Railroad three or four seasons, ticketing passengers to all points in the West, North, and East.

It maintained an office in New Orleans and Memphis, and was really the first and most formidable steamboat organization that had existed up to that time. The boats were put in at a valuation which constituted the capital stock of the company. But the expenses more than absorbed the net earnings of the boats, and the owners preferred to sell the boats to pay off the indebtedness rather than to assess themselves to sustain the line.

The result was the boats were sold and the line discontinued, the owners having sunk nearly the value of the boats.

The officers of this company were James Gosley, President; C. B. Church, Superintendent; J. J. Rawlings, Secretary.

During this period there was a line of four boats from Memphis to Louisville, viz.: Tichomingo, Alvin Adams, Southerner, and Northerner; all fine boats, but there was not sufficient business to suport them, and the line was of but temporary duration.

OLD PROMINENT STEAMBOATMEN.

In the *Memphis Appeal* of September, 1888, one entire side of that paper is devoted to historical, amusing and interesting items relating to steamboats and steamboatmen more or less connected with that port, by W. S. Trask.

The following interesting items are from that elaborate article : —

"A number of very prominent men of the present day have passed a part of their career on boats plying the Western rivers in various employments. Ex-Governor Cameron, of Virginia, the predecessor of Fitzhugh Lee, was a clerk on the Wm. M. Morrison, less than thirty years ago, and Mark Twain, the humorist and author, was a pilot on the same craft. Wm. B. Bate, of the United States Senate, was a freight clerk on the steamer Tennessee, running between Nashville and New Orleans, over forty years ago. Many of the prominent bankers and insurance men of the Ohio River cities were captains or clerks in their earlier days, and ex-Congressman Hooper, of Utah, ran a boat called the Alexander Hamilton on the Upper Mississippi back in the forties and perhaps later. Charles E. Marshall, of the Red River packet B. L. Hodge, one of the most accomplished masters of thirty years ago, was a brother of the late gifted Humphrey Marshall, of Kentucky. The late Cornelius K. Garrison, the great railroad magnate of New York, ran the big side-wheel steamer Convoy in the Memphis and New Orleans trade, also to St. Louis, about '47 and '48, and Wm. Ralston, afterward a prominent San Francisco banker, was chief clerk on the same vessel. Both went to California in '49 and became millionaires several times over. Ex-river men now here in our midst include Mr. W. W. Schoolfield, the genial merchant, Mr. Samuel P. Read, the prominent banker, and several more not just now in mind. Last winter on one of the Ohio River flat-boats, which moored at our levee, a graduate of West Point was a hand at the sweeps, and Capt. Mallory, of flat-boat renown, is the auditor and treasurer of one of the richest counties of Southern Indiana, while another flat-boat captain, in the person of Mr. Espey, is a candidate for an equally responsible place in another Indiana county not far from the Ohio line. A host of others might be mentioned but these are enough to show that honor and fame from no condition rise.

The late William Bohlen, of this city, was identified with river interests for a full half century, covering the grand era of steamboating. He owned the steamer Alliquippa back in the forties, and for years the craft towed ice-loaded barges between the Upper Illinois River and Memphis, occasionally going to Vicksburg and as far as Baton Rouge, to supply the people's demands for ice. The steamer Capitol, built by the Howards at Louisville in 1854, for the New Orleans and Bayou Sara trade, where she had a most successful career, was afterward purchased by the Bohlens for their ice towing traffic, and this boat was sent from here to the Yazoo River in May, 1862, towing the war-boat Arkansas, which vessel afterward made havoc among the Federal fleet in front of Vicksburg. The Capitol had the reputation of being among the fastest boats of her day, and for an entire season, that of 1859, she made weekly trips between this port and New Orleans, carrying the mail and making fifty-six mail landings up, and as many on the down trip. The Capitol was 235 feet long, 35 feet beam, 8 feet hold and had six boilers with thirty-inch cylinders, nine feet stroke. She was contemporary and about the same size as the famous Southern Belle which ran in the New Orleans and Vicksburg trade between 1851 and 1858, commanded by Capt. J. M. White. A goodly number of pleasant stories are related of the late William Bohlen's success in various sports during the early history of this city. He was famed far and near as a most wonderful checker player, ranking in that way on a par with the great Creole chess king, Paul Morphy. It is related that on one occasion a visitor here from Vermont named Tinsley Kaye, brought with him an entire new kit of checker tools expressly to beat Mr. Bohlen at his favorite game, his renown in this sport having spread to the distant maple groves of the Green Mountain latitude. Mr. Kaye called on Mr. Bohlen, proposed a sitting, the couple repairing to a quiet room at the Gayoso for the indulgence, and after a four hour contest, the difference was only one game in favor of the Memphis player. Then an adjournment for supper ensued, and after it was over the play was renewed. It was kept up steady throughout the night and far along toward sunrise, at which time Mr. Bohlen was nearly forty games ahead. The visitor from Vermont packed his kit and went East, spreading the news about the Bluff City checker play as he traveled.

The surviving brother of the late Mr. Bohlen, now resident here, made his first voyage down the muddy Mississippi with coal and ice, going as low as Baton Rouge and trading off his stock by the barrel or cart-load as suited purchasers. He closed up the trip with $2,000 profit, all yellow gold coin, that being the favorite currency of time, and this he packed snugly in a box, taking passage for the Ohio River on the steamer Ben Sherrod. The boat took fire during the trip up, between Fort Adams and Natchez, at 2 o'clock on the morning of May 9, 1837, and was totally destroyed, over fifty lives being lost by the disaster. Among the lost was the father and two children of the boat's commander, Capt. Castlemar, but the latter saved his life as well as that of his wife by swimming ashore with her. Mr. P. R. Bohlen undertook to save himself as well as his treasure, but his efforts were only partially successful. He went overboard in deep water with the box of coin under one arm, held on to the burning boat by digging his finger nails into the oaken seams in the side of the hull, and finally when red-hot coals began to drop through the guard over his head, singeing his hair and scorching his ears, he took a notion it was time to drop the box and swim. He made the shore in safety, but lost his gold. Finally reaching his destination up the Ohio his friends staked him, and now in his advanced years he is comfortably fixed and leads a bachelor life at his ease on a farm in Central Illinois affording recreation and a chance for investing a share of the surplus earnings of his investments here.

The golden days of steamboating in the Memphis and New Orleans trade began about 1848, and the richest of this marine harvest time was the decade and a half preceding the interstate war. In those days several hundred thousand bales of cotton were annually carried South by boats from Memphis and points on the river below. Cotton, negroes and land comprised the wealth of the valley country and the cotton planters were the nabobs of the South. A negro in those days was worth a round $1,000, and a bale of cotton brought $50, the capacity of production being about ten bales of cotton and five acres of corn each year to a field hand. No railways penetrated the interior at the time, except for short distances, and the only means of transportation on our Western and Southern rivers was the stately steamboat, or the primitive keel or flat-boat, the latter being the exclusive method of conveying coal for use down South. It was away back beyond this period that the brave old warrior, Gen. Wm. O. Butler, who ran for the Vice-presidency with Cass in '44, and died at the advanced age of eighty-seven, wrote a poetical gem which will hold its place as long as time lasts, commencing —

> " O, boatman, wind that horn again,
> For never did the listening air
> Upon its lambent bosom bear
> So wild, so soft, so sweet a strain."

In those early days when the Convoy, Capt. C. K. Garrison, was the pioneer steam packet from Memphis to New Orleans, and the Autocrat, Capt. Goslee, soon after became her consort, most of the traffic was transacted on flat-boats moored at our landing. The best boarding place for single gentlemen was on the big wharf-boat always lying at the landing, and on which boat and bar stores were kept in abundance. Then it was that the respected Maj. J. J. Murphy sold groceries and ship chandlery from a flat-boat, the late C. W. Goyer dealt out side meat to country wagoners, Mr. Kinney and the Hon. John Johnson disposed of furniture in the same way; the Walt and Elliott brothers handled grain and produce, while many others had their trading boats floating at the front, filled with valuable stores to barter with the public. Flat-boating had been in years previous a perilous business, but it generally returned handsome profits, and a voyage southward was often full of romance as well as adventure. A three months' trip to New Orleans, floating lazily with the current, the scenery constantly changing, but ever wild and beautiful, was a thing never to be forgotten, and many of our early settlers laid the foundation of their fortunes while serving aboard of flat or keelboats. These gave place to the grander steamboat in due time, and as our little city grew in importance the packet steamers plying hence to New Orleans increased in number and capacity. The pioneer pair named above were followed by the first and second Bulletin, Capt. Charles B. Church; the Geo. Collier, Capt. Goslee; the Nebraska, Capt. Erwin; the Ben Franklin and Ingomar, Capt. J. D. Clark; the H. R. W. Hill, Capt. Newell; the R. W. Powell, Capt. Joseph Estes; the John Simonds, Capt. Frank Hicks; the Prince of Wales, Capt. James Lee, and several others of equal note, capacity and grandeur. All of the commanders and clerks of the boats named are now deceased except Capt. Frank Hicks and Capt. James Lee.

STEALING A STEAMBOAT.

Talent is essential to success, when it comes to stealing a steamboat, or a red-hot stove, for neither is easy to do, though both are known to have been done. A steamboat called the Sallie Robinson, that run, along in the fifties, on the Yazoo and Tallahatchie rivers, carrying 2,000 bales of cotton each trip in the active business season, was stolen outright twenty-five years ago by Edward Schiller, and he pocketed the proceeds of the sale, amounting to $20,000. The vessel belonged to a merchant of New Orleans named Joseph R. Shannon, but he had the craft registered in the name of his friend, Edward Schiller, at the time Commodore Farragut captured the Crescent City in 1862. Schiller managed to get hold of and destroy every paper relating to the ownership of the boat except the custom-house registration record. He sold the boat, gave a clear title and went West. Buying a farm near Fort Scott, Southern Kansas, then on the frontier, he lived in retirement for a dozen years; and, after that, Mr. Shannon found and began to worry him. A compromise proposed by Shannon was not accepted, and the bother began in earnest, as the rightful owner of the craft never let up until the other was penniless. Schiller had been a reporter on the New Orleans *True Delta*, at which time he wrote a book called "Cherry Blossom," that did not meet success. After he lost his Kansas farm he turned up here in Memphis while Greeley ran for the Presidency, and worked as a printer on the *Avalanche ;* also wrote for awhile for the same journal, and finally went off to Southern Texas, where he died in poverty some years later, leaving a son and a daughter. He was an eccentric individual, who, upon introducing himself into the *Avalanche* office, unloaded about a hand-cart of manuscript from his left shoulder and asked the editor, Mr. Brower, to examine it, with a view to publication. It is needless to say the matter was never printed, for it was not worth printing. The poor fellow could write very well, but his efforts were not appreciated by the public. He stole a steamboat, but could not hide the proceeds successfully — a common failing among pilferers.

The exploit of Schiller affords perhaps the only instance recorded where one man stole and sold a steamboat and made way with the gross proceeds, but numerous instances are related where boatmen have cut out vessels and run them off to get away from clamorous creditors and a burden of debt. One of the best remembered and most successful in this line was Capt. Abner Baird, formerly of this city. He rode recklessly at all hazards of life or limb when it came to running a steamboat, and he could pull the wool over the eyes of his creditors with much more ease than any one on the list. It was some fourteen years ago that he ran the steamer Glasgow off from the wharf here up the Ohio River, leaving debts due his crew and for supplies of a couple of thousand dollars. The captain had made several trips to the Ohio and also up White River, going out light and coming back empty. With no prospect of bettering his condition, he began to beat about to save his boat from attachment. One night he invited all hands and the cook to visit the spectacular Black Crook at the theater. After the play an oyster supper was discussed until an hour after midnight. The cost to the captain was a dozen dollars or so, which he borrowed from one of the victims. Meanwhile Capt. Selby, his partner, had steam raised on the boat, hired a few hands, and lit out for up the river. Old Si Dougherty, the pilot, John Darby, the clerk, Wm. Griffith, the steward, with Capt. Baird and half a dozen others, participated in the pleasures of the evening, but when they visited the wharf, foot of Jefferson street, their steamer was gone. To say they were mad would be putting it mild. Capt. Baird had run the sidewheel steamer Republic out of New Orleans in 1860, carrying a marshal and several deputies, afterward putting them ashore in a cypress swamp below Baton Rouge. He had flanked marshals, sheriffs and creditors when he ran the Admiral, the Sovereign and the Jno. D. Perry in previous years, but his best achievement was that of escorting the boys to the theater and making them have a good time while his partner took the boat away, leaving them in the lurch, with no money and no boarding house. Dozens of instances might be told where officers in charge of boats were circumvented, but none would beat the game played so cleverly by Capt. Baird.

Capt. James Lee, Sr., for whom the handsome steamer now running was named, and who now, in the evening of a well spent and active life, resides quietly with the family of his son in a pleasant home on Adams street, or rolls around in a big arm-chair on the steamer Rosa Lee, has been a notable character on the river for more than half a century. The captain began as a boatman in 1829, saw the rise of business, and participated in its most brilliant triumphs. He commanded some of the finest and best boats that ever floated the rivers, including the Old Hickory, the Prince of Wales, the Phil Allin, and as many as two dozen others. Capt. Lee is a great hand to tell stories, and he could keep his passengers in a state of merriment at all times when his duties would allow. One among his thousand or more of yarns ran about like this : "As odd a customer as you'll find in six States was old John Prewett, who lived in Stewart county, Tennessee. He was long and hungry looking, with his shoulder points away up between his ears, as if he'd been fixed up to be born over ; and he wore a coat with a pair of enormous buttons right between his shoulder blades. His head was sugar-loaf shaped, his eyes were small and close together, like a crawfish ; his

nose was long like a wedge, and his mouth looked like it
would hold a shovelful of potatoes. Prewett had powerful
lungs and he practiced with a bugle until he thought he was an
artist. When Stickney's circus went through, about the time
Polk was elected, Prewett visited Nashville and asked for a
job to blow the bugle. The boys had heard of his blowing
powers, and finally bantered him until he put up $40 as a bet
that he could blow the bridle bits out of a mule's mouth by
placing his own mouth under the animal's tail. Prewett won
the money, but he failed to secure an engagement as bugle
player with the circus.''

LOSS OF BULLETIN, NO. 2.

While lying at the Memphis wharf near the mouth of Wolf
River, then the public landing, the steamer Helen McGregor
exploded and a large number of people lost their lives. This
was the first recorded disaster of a long list that has since occurred in front or near our city. Among the most notable
was the loss of the Pennsylvania, Capt. Marshall, in June,
1858.[1] The boat was literally crowded with people, both cabin
and deck, and more than 100 persons were lost. In the list
was Judge Harris, the brother of Senator Isham G. Harris.
The judge occupied a state room over the boiler, in company
with Mr. Charles Stone, formerly of this city, and whose sons
reside with us. Both gentlemen were asleep, the disaster occurring about daylight, and Mr. Stone has related that when
he awoke he found himself in the river. He swam to a
tree in the overflow, the low country being submerged at the
time, and from that perch he was rescued. The locality was
near the mouth of St. Francis River, and the steamer Kate
Frisbee, Capt. John T. Shirley, came along shortly after and
brought the survivors to this port, where the wounded were
cared for, Odd Fellow's hall being converted into a temporary
hospital for their accommodation. Three years before that
the steamer Bulletin No. 2, Capt. Charles B. Church, was
burned near Transylvania landing, above Vicksburg, and
many perished, among the list being the father of Mr. George
Handwerker, the well known musician. Several survivors of
this disaster still live among us, although it happened thirty-
three years ago. Of these are Capt. Marsh Miller, a pilot of
the boat, Mr. App, the shoemaker, who leaped from the roof
of the boat into a coop of turkeys to save his legs from being

---

[1] Captain Klienfelter and not Captain Marshall was in charge of the Pennsylvania when lost. — ED.

broken, and others. Capt. J. H. Freligh, recently deceased,
was chief clerk at the time, and he was the recipient of a fine
silver set by our citizens, owing to his having successfully
cared for a round sum of money which was entrusted to his
keeping for account of our banks and their customers. Capt.
John T. Shirley, of this city, a passenger, was called upon by
Capt. Church to assist the other passengers ashore, and he
came near losing his own life in his efforts. Mr. Charles
Richards, one of the crew, saved the life of Capt. Shirley and
also that of Capt. Marsh Miller. Many acts of heroism were
recorded at the time. In April, 1859, the steamer St. Nicholas, Capt. Oliver McMullen exploded her boilers below this
city and many perished. A benefit was given the sufferers at
the theater here by M. W. Canning, the manager, on which
occasion Miss Vandenhoff recited an original poem. In
more recent years other disasters have occurred which surpassed them in horror and loss of life. The R. J. Lockwood
was blown up near President's Island over twenty years ago
and many perished.

EXPLOSION OF THE SULTANA.

The Sultana, carrying tubular boilers, exploded near Harrison's place, some fifteen miles above this city, in April,
1865, and 1,600 people, nearly all national soldiers going
home from the war, were lost. The boat floated down
to the head of the Island above Mound City and sunk, the
wreck now being covered with sand and a growth of willows and cottonwoods. The accident occurred before day,
and the first tidings had of it here was the cries of the people
as they floated by in the river on fragments of the wreck.
Nearly as bad was the explosion of the great steamer, W. R.
Arthur, in 1872, a short distance below Island 40. The
wreck floated several miles and then sank, destroying many
lives. Among the list of the lost was a man named Uhlen,
from near Golconda, Ill. He had been cotton planting near
Greenville, Miss., and after five years or so of hard labor had
accummulated $30,000, all of which he had with him. The
whole family and the money was lost by the disaster, also Dan
Stark, a well known flatboatman. The towboat Warner blew
up directly opposite the city about 1875, and half of the crew
were killed or crippled. One of the worst of the list of disasters was the burning of the Golden City, April, 30, 1884.
When about to make the landing at the foot of Beal street,
about daybreak, the boat was found to be in flames. The
pilot headed for shore, ran on a raft or flatboat and many

made their way ashore. The boat swung out into the river and a number were lost, several women and children being of the list.

As an evidence of the rapid decline of steamboating on Western rivers, the following figures will bear testimony: —
The tonnage built in 1881, was over 80,000. In 1883, it was only 26,000. In 1884, it was 16,000. In 1885, it was 10,000. In 1887, it was about the same.

The number of steamboats built in 1864 was greater than ever before or since, and aggregated 250, the tonnage of which was 148,000.

LARGEST CARGO OF COTTON.

The largest cargo of cotton ever floated on one bottom was carried into New Orleans April 2, 1881, by the steamer Henry Frank, Capt. Hicks, and amounted to 9,226 bales, with 250 tons of other freight. The Henry Frank made twelve trips that season, carrying into New Orleans a total of 76,009 bales of cotton, 28,218 sacks of seed, 13,675 sacks of oil cake, 1,225 barrels of oil and other freights. Her consort, the iron steamer Chouteau, carried the same season 76,950 bales of cotton, 30,088 sacks of seed, 15,335 sacks of oil cake and other freights. The two packets carried in two years into New Orleans 337,000 bales of cotton. Much of this cotton was shipped from Memphis direct. The iron steamer Chouteau carried in, next to the Frank, the heaviest single cargo of cotton — 8,841 bales; the James Howard, 7,700 bales; the Mary Bell, 7,108 bales; the Ed Richardson, 7,084 bales; the J. M. White, 6,765 bales; and the Natchez, 6,500 bales — a total by the eight boats of 61,033 bales. The Autocrat, a great steamer in the '40s, carried 5,000 bales into New Orleans, and her great achievement was pictured conspicuously on the canvas, painted by a celebrated artist of St. Louis, Leon Pomerede, who descended the Mississippi from St. Paul to New Orleans in a small boat, painting a panorama from sketches. This was afterward exhibited in the leading cities of Europe, as well as in this country. The Autocrat, Capt. J. W. Goslee, was a noted craft in her day, and her fame was added to by the picture of Pomerede. Up to the interstate war no cargo of more than 6,000 bales of cotton was ever carried at one time, and this was by the big Magnolia when she ran in the Vicksburg trade. Another Magnolia preceded the one mentioned, was a favorite passenger boat in the New Orleans and Vicksburg trade, and Capt. St. Clair Thomasson, her commander, was the most aristocratic boatman of that or any generation. More anecdotes were current on

Thomasson than any other boatman, unless exceptions be made of Capt. Billy Forsythe, of the Columbia, and Capt. James Lee. The two first named have long since been gathered to their fathers.

STEAMERS GRAND TURK AND JOHN SIMONDS.

The great passenger steamer, John Simonds, built at Pittsburgh in the year 1850, or thereabout, at a cost of not far from $100,000, was a mammoth three decker, at first commanded by Newman Robbirds, who had previously run with great success the Grand Turk, in the days when the best boats included a fleet, in part of which was the Mameluke, Sarah Bladen, Eudora, Glencoe, Marshal Ney, Josiah Lawrence, Alex Scott and a host of others. The John Simonds was first run in the St. Louis and New Orleans trade, but was sold to run between Memphis and New Orleans, and she was the banner boat of a fleet which for ten years preceding the interstate war was the pride of the people here and along the rich and productive valleys to the south of us as far as Vicksburg. These boats always went and came crowded with freight and people, and their traffic did not fall much below a round $10,000 per trip for each boat during the active business season. Capt. Church laid the foundation of the ample fortune he accumulated while running on this famous line of boats, and others of the fleet also lived and reared their families in good style among us. A balance sheet or trip report of the steamer John Simonds, made up by the boat's clerk, the late J. H. Freligh, for fifteen days from New Orleans to Memphis and return, March 21 and April 4, 1857, inclusive, reads as follows : —

	Up.	Down.	Total.
Receipts for freight	$2,817 20	$6,470 80	$ 9,288
Receipts for passage	1,322 50	748 50	2,066
Total for trip	$4,139 70	$7,214 30	$11,354

Expenditures —		
For wood	$2,036 60	
For crew's wages	2,498 15	
For stores	1,577 81	
Expense	1,575 67	$7,628 23
Net gain on the trip		$3,725 77

This, it will be seen, was thirty-one years ago, and the boat's expenses then was a little more than $500 per day, while receipts were slightly above $750 per day. The Simonds was destroyed during the war, during the early part of which she worked in the interest of the Southerners."

A line was also formed to run from Memphis to Cumberland River, a line of three boats, viz. : I. G. Cline, John Simpson, and City of Huntsville. They like the Louisville line was obliged to withdraw for the same reason.

There was at the same time running to Cincinnati, a line of five boats, viz. : Glendale, Josephine, Memphis, Silver Moon and John Swasey.

To Napoleon, Daniel Boone, Frisbee, H. D. Means, Kentucky and Victory.

To White River, the Kanawha Valley, Return, Admiral, A. W. Turner and General Pike. There was running to St. Francis River numbers one, two and three, Saint Francis.

It was claimed that during the palmy days of steamboats Memphis was represented by thirty boats, either owned or made that their home port, and the record confirms the claim.

MEMPHIS AND ST. LOUIS PACKET COMPANY

developed into the great *Anchor Line.*

Among the first and immediately succeeding the organization of the St. Louis and New Orleans "Railroad Line of Steamers," a line was organized to run between St. Louis and Memphis and was chartered in 1859 as the "Memphis and St. Louis Packet Company." Its stock was made up by the appraised value of the different boats that composed the line. Capt. Daniel Able was its first president. Succeeded in a few years by Wm. J. Lewis, who in turn was succeeded by John J. Roe. During this period the company added several new boats and did a large and prosperous business. Before Capt. Roe died the line was extended to Vicksburg, and greatly improved by adding some of the finest boats that had ever before been run in the trade.

Capt. Henry W. Smith was for several years acting as the Superintendent of the company and to his enterprise and perseverance great credit is due for the success and popularity of the line. He succeeded Capt. Roe to the presidency, and through his ability and practical steamboat knowledge, the company built and owned the finest and the fastest line of steamers that had ever run upon Western waters up to that time if not in the world.

26

ST. LOUIS ANCHOR LINE.

The Memphis Line was finally merged into the St. Louis and Vicksburg line, and as the railroads extended their lines south, the Packet Company gradually withdrew from the Memphis trade and extended their line to New Orleans, running a part of their boats to Vicksburg and part of them to New Orleans under the style and name of "Anchor Line."

As a practical steamboat and business man, Capt. Smith had no superiors and but few equals in the profession. And his death was not only a great loss to the company he had so long and ably managed, but a public calamity. His experience was varied as a business man, and his judgment of men and things rendered his councils of value upon many subjects besides that of a steamboatman. His ambition so far exceeded his vitality, that his life terminated in the midst of a useful career, lamented by all who knew him, in 1870.

Capt. Jno. A. Scudder succeeded to the presidency, after the death of Capt. Smith, and under his judicious management the reputation of the company has been sustained and has probably paid to the stockholders a larger amount in dividends than any other steamboat company in the world. Capt. John P. Keiser succeeded Capt. Smith as superintendent, and under his skill as a builder and a practical boatman, the company retained its prestige for fine boats, which were excelled by none, but improved by each additional boat, from the yard of the famous "Howards" at Jeffersonville.

In this connection it is proper to add that a principal cause for the improved excellence of this companys' boats arose from the fact that it was able to pay for everything that would contribute to an improvement, and having all of its work done at one yard, and by a firm pecuniarily reliable, each succeeding boat could easily be improved upon.

Mr. Scudder has been associated with the company as Secretary, President, or Vice-President, ever since the organization of the Memphis and St. Louis Company in 1859. For many years he was its chief officer, and only retired from the presidency one year to recuperate his energies, and during that time was relieved by Capt. Keiser, until 1888, when he resigned the presidency in favor of Capt. I. M. Mason.

This company still maintains its organization intact, and has the entire control of the passenger and freight business between St. Louis and points on the Mississippi River above New Orleans, so far as the river is concerned.

" The Barge Company " divide shipments to and from New Orleans with the Anchor Line, and bring from there the bulk of freight destined for St. Louis. The Anchor Line also continues to keep up its trade to Grand Tower, although often temporarily attacked by outside boats. This company is the only one running from St. Louis that has been able to withstand the railroad pressure unimpaired, or retain enough of its business to make dividends from, except the "Barge Line."

The phenomenal success that resulted to this company arose largely from the effects of the civil war. The trade that had heretofore sought New Orleans as its outlet and market was diverted to the North, even before the close of hostilities. The demoralization and bankruptcy of everything like business in the South was so universal that a change of base was rendered necessary for a time at least.

The Memphis Packet Company was partially intact, having been organized a year or two before the commencement of the war. As soon as Memphis was captured by the Federal forces, the trade between St. Louis and Memphis was renewed, with the addition that the immense transportation of troops and munitions of war gave to it. The same result occurred as the Federal authority gained possession of the country further South, and when the war terminated the field was opened for a commercial conquest second only to that which had been secured by the armies of the North politically.

This company was in position to avail itself of the opening. The stockholders being prominent business men and large provision dealers, were not slow to discover that the South needed more than all else, provisions, stock and farming utensils. These they had to dispose of, and abundant means to provide the boats to deliver them to the market that had been so literally stripped of all the necessaries of life by a devastating war of more than four years. Through the energy and foresight of the managers it proved itself equal to the emergency and reaped a rich reward, from which they have principally retired, except Mr. Scudder, who still stands as a sentry, watching the gradual approach of the devastating cyclone that has almost swept from the Mississippi Valley the immense fleets of "floating palaces" that so recently gave pleasure, profit and employment to so many persons.

Those that remain, beside this company, as a rule are only dragging out a miserable existence for the benefit of the few who can gain a subsistence in no other vocation, and it seems only a question of time when river transportation must be limited to heavy articles in bulk, on good navigable waters, and to short packet trades, where it is not practicable to build railroads.

On such streams as the Missouri and Arkansas, it is folly to ask Congress to appropriate large sums, with the expectation of making them permanent avenues for commerce. They can never compete with a railroad built along each bank, or near it.

It may seem a plausible argument at present, to urge that a water route serves to regulate and modify railroad tariffs. But the time will soon come, if not already here, when a water course that is frozen up one-fourth part of the time and dried up as much longer will not be considered a formidable regulator to anything.

It is a misfortune that this subject is not better understood by the people in the States bordering on the Mississippi, Missouri, and Arkansas Rivers.

FALLACY OF IMPROVING SOME RIVERS.

The more money the government is induced to expend in the improvement of the water-ways not possible to be made successful competitors with land carriage, the less probable it is to make appropriations for such streams as are susceptible of valuable improvements, as the result is sure to be made manifest sooner or later, even to those who have no practical knowledge or observation on the subject. The Mississippi River and the tributaries on the east side generally are susceptible of any amount of improvement that may be necessary to accommodate the commerce they control, and by united effort on the part of delegations in Congress from the Mississippi Valley as much money as can be judiciously expended may be secured.

CHAPTER LVII.

NATIONAL BOARD OF STEAM NAVIGATION, ITS ORIGIN AND ITS PURPOSES.

A N initiatory convention was held at Louisville on the 15th of November, 1871, in which representatives of water transportation from twenty States were present.

The aggregate amount of capital represented was estimated at *one billion six hundred million dollars*, which was invested in steam vessels operating on rivers, lakes and bays in the United States. This general uprising of steamboat owners from every part of the country was precipitated by the passage of a *new steamboat law*, enacted at the previous session of Congress.

It was substituted for the old law of 1851 and claimed to be an improvement on that law, which had failed to keep pace with the rapid development of steam navigation in the previous twenty years. The new law was prepared at the suggestion of the Secretary of the Treasury, Mr. Boutell, a Massachusetts man, who knew nothing of Western river navigation, and probably of no other. It was said the Board of Supervising Inspectors had much to do with the new provisions of that bill. But careful inquiry failed to divulge any connection of the Board with it, although they got the credit of it in some degree. But it bore the marks of bunglers rather than experts, and it was considered an insult to the thousands of those in the business who had spent a life time in acquiring a knowledge of its necessities.

To modify, or amend, this new law, and to make it practical and consistent in its operations, was the object of the convention.

After a session of three days, in which all the material points were discussed and the views of the convention well understood, a committee of five was appointed, representing the different sections of the country, to draft and prepare a new steamboat bill, or amend the existing law, to suit the necessities, as in their judgment might seem best.

The following names were selected on this committee: Chas. P. Coupland, of New York; T. G. Whiting, Detroit; T. G. Stockdale, Pittsburgh; Thomas Sherlock, Cincinnati; E. W. Gould, St. Louis. B. S. Osborn, of New York, was elected

Secretary. The committee agreed to meet at Pittsburgh a few weeks later, to carry out the instructions of the convention, which then adjourned, to meet at Washington, D. C. on the call of the committee.

The committee met at Pittsburgh early in December, and proceeded to the performance of the duty assigned them — which, as the sequel proved, was a task they were quite equal to, but enacting the bill into a law, was another matter.

After a session of eight or ten days they adjourned to meet at Washington a few days later, where their duties were resumed. Numerous interviews were had with members of Congress on the subject of the new law and the necessity for one. Mr. Conger, the member of Congress from Michigan, who had been employed by the Treasury Department to frame the new law, was at first antagonistic to the committee and their object, but was gradually won over by the arguments presented and subsequently became convinced that some amendments to the law were necessary. After much discussion it was decided to take the law as it then stood and proceed, section by section, to so amend each as to make it practical and consistent, so far as was possible.

The law contained over seventy sections, many of which were engrafted from the old steamboat law of 1851, when the character and condition of navigation and of commerce were very different and the law was not applicable to present necessities.

After close and careful application for several weeks the committee issued a call to the representatives at the National Convention held at Louisville the previous year, to again assemble at Washington.

The call was liberally responded to, and a large convention assembled.

The bill, as prepared by the committee, was submitted for indorsement or amendment by the convention. And after careful revision and such amendments as seemed to the convention necessary, it was approved and the convention adjourned, subject to call by the committee.

At this point the trouble commenced. The *vital mistake* had been made, but was not discovered until too late to overcome it. The convention had "counted without its host."

After the bill was completed and ready for introduction in Congress, as a matter of courtesy, the committee called at the Treasury office, to ask the indorsement and co-operation of the Secretary (Mr. Boutwell) in securing its passage. They were referred to the Assistant Secretary (Mr. Richardson), who later succeeded Mr. Boutwell, who appointed a meeting with the committee the next morning at 10 o'clock.

The committee called at the appointed time, and were cavalierly told the assistant had concluded not to see the committee.

Then the *mistake* begun to loom up. The committee had been in Washington some weeks and were known to be preparing an important bill to control a great industry which the Treasury Department had under its direction, and which by inference was a direct reflection upon the new law, which had so recently largely emanated from that department.

A consultation was at once had with members of Congress and those who were friends of the bill in both branches of Congress, without reference to the Treasury officials. Influential members contended it was not the duty nor the prerogative of the Treasury Department to make laws, but to execute them, and there was no doubt but that the bill could be passed and become a law in spite of Treasury officials.

Two bills were introduced. One in the Senate by Judge Thurman, of Ohio, one in the House by Gen. Negley, of Pennsylvania.

They were favorably received and referred to the appropriate committee — that on commerce.

The Chairman of the Senate committee was Mr. Conkling, of New York, who, at the request of Mr. Boutwell (it is charged) *put* the *bill* in *his pocket.*

The committee of the House proceeded to examine the bill and summoned experts from many places before them, to take testimony upon all points they needed to enable them to make an intelligent report on the bill.

No bill was ever more thoroughly discussed in committee or better understood.

It was unanimously indorsed by the committee and passed the House, almost unanimously, *three different times,* during as many succeeding Congresses.

No effort on the part of Senators ever succeeded in getting a report from the Senate Committee on the bill, although many attempts were made by Judge Thurman and others. Mr. Conkling remained Chairman of that committee as long as he remained in Congress. This factious opposition to a bill so generally indorsed induced, of course, many unkind, uncomplimentary remarks.

Those who remember Mr. Conkling in Congress, or out of it, know full well the effect of irritating remarks to him, or of him.

Unfortunately, perhaps, in this connection, the Secretary

of the Executive Committee who had prepared the bill, was the publisher of a marine newspaper in New York known as the *Nautical Gazette.*

Mr. Osbon, the editor, was a bright, vigorous writer, but it was often thought, with more zeal than discretion. In this instance it undoubtedly proved to be so. While he was fully alive to the interests of steam navigation, and understood perfectly the necessities and the rights of seamen (having been a sailor himself), he fearlessly defended their claims in his paper, and the invective of his pen cut both ways when defending his position. The exalted status of a United States Senator was no protection to him, if he crossed Osbon's path, and nothing suited him better than to have *carte blanche* to open his guns on any one who opposed him.

The experience at that early day of the Executive Committee had not convinced them that the influence of a small, factious minority in Congress, could not be overcome by outside pressure, and they did not attempt to restrain Mr. Osbon, their secretary. The result was, the breach between the Treasury Department and Mr. Conkling on the one side, and the steamboat interest on the other, was made wider instead of being healed.

EXECUTIVE COMMITTEE AND THE THIRD HOUSE.

The "steamboat bill" dragged its slow length along from one Congress to another for several years, always being represented in the *third house* by members of the Executive Committee, who lost no opportunity of urging its claims and discussing its merits, until it became as familiar to members of Congress as it was to the authors themselves.

Probably there has never been a bill introduced into any American Congress that has been more thoroughly discussed and better understood than this steamboat bill. Not because it was of more importance, but because it was so persistently oppposed and without the reason of the opposition being known to one in twenty of its friends.

In the first years of its advent in Congress it had as industrious and careful champions as there was in either body. Gen. James S. Negley in the House, acted as its chief champion and carried it triumphantly though almost unanimously. Judge Thurman did all that could he done to get a report on the bill, and had it been reported there was no doubt of its passage at that time, notwithstanding the opposition.

During all those years the National Convention continued to hold its adjourned annual meetings at different places, notably, Buffalo, Cleveland, Baltimore, Pittsburgh, Norfolk, Washington, New York, at which meetings the report of the Executive Committee, on the status of the "steamboat bill" and its prospects, was the principal subject of discussion.

New officers were elected and a new Executive Committee named, with instructions to again repair to Washington at the meeting of Congress, and resume the effort to secure the passage of the bill.

They were authorized to make, and did make, amendments and such changes as seemed to overcome all opposition to any and all the provisions of the bill, except that of the *liability clause* on inland waters, that was so manifestly a necessity that no amendment could be entertained, and it was referred to by those who had arrayed themselves under Mr. Conkling's lead more for the purpose of sustaining him and the interests he represented than for any harm that could result from the passage of the bill as proposed.

At a meeting of the convention at Cleveland it was determined to organize into a permanent association, and the "National Board of Steam Navigation" was the result. By-laws were enacted and officers elected and an executive committee appointed, whose duties, as prescribed, were about the same as that committee had been charged with by the first convention at Louisville. Some members of the original committee, notably Messrs Copeland, Shirlock and Whiting, stood boldly to the point for several years, and never a session of Congress convened that one or all of them was not present to insist upon the enactment of the "steamboat bill."

While the bill as a whole has not to this day become a law, sections of it have been enacted, and the old law in some parts has been so modified that less hardships are endured, and less inconveniences felt.

The National Board of Steam Navigation still maintains its organization, and holds its annual meetings in New York.

But so far as the Northern Lakes and the Mississippi Valley is concerned, it seems to have exhausted itself and lost its usefulness and its interest.

Although the ostensible object for which the organization was so long and so persistently maintained was not entirely successful, there is no doubt much good has resulted to navigation, if all the legislation that was asked was not secured, much damaging legislation was prevented and the wants of different parts of the country are better understood and a remedy for evils endured more easily provided.

If ever water transportation again comes to the front, and

national legislation is necessary to protect it, the long experience of the National Board, will be of signal service.

It is axiom in war never to underestimate the forces of
the enemy. It applies with equal force to factious legisla-
tors. In this struggle the doctrine of the "survival of the
fittest" has not been sustained, although the "National
Board of Steam Navigation" still lives as a practical factor
in national legislation.

NATIONAL BOARD OF STEAM NAVIGATION.

WASHINGTON, October 7, 1881.

To the Editor of the Post-Dispatch, St. Louis:

After a session of two days the National Board of Steam
Navigation adjourned last evening to meet at Cairo, Ill., with
the intention of holding their next annual meeting on board a
Mississippi River steamer, during her passage from that point
to New Orleans. The time was not definitely fixed, but
during the autumn or early winter of next year.

This proposition coming from Eastern members, it was considered by those from the West as a step in the right direction,
tending to awaken a more lively interest in the minds of
Western and Southern members in the objects of this organization, and to afford Eastern and Northern members a more
adequate idea of the importance of Western river commerce.

The report of standing committees, the appointment of
new ones, the election of officers and the appointment of delegates to attend the River Improvement Convention to be
held in St. Louis on 26th of October, together with the usual
routine business of similar organizations, were the principal
subjects brought before the board at this meeting.

The attendance from the West and South was small. But
a fair attendance from the East, many of the members having
their ladies with them.

It was evidently a mistake calling the meeting at so early a
day, especially at Washington. If called here at all it should
have been during the session of Congress, as this is the busiest
season of the year for all engaged in steam navigation.

The steamboat bill, as it is called, which has been hanging
fire in Congress for several years in charge of the Executive
Committee, elicited considerable discussion upon the reading of
the report of the chairman of the committee. But the opinion prevailed decidedly that a bill as carefully prepared and
so just and necessary for the promotion of steam navigation
as it, ought not to be abandoned without one more effort to
secure its passage by Congress.

Capt. John N. Bofinger, who has been chairman of the executive committee for the last two years, having tendered his resignation on account of not having the necessary leisure to devote, Gen. Jas. S. Negley, of Pittsburgh, was elected to fill the vacancy who, together with other members of the board, will be in attendance at Washington during the next session of Congress, when it is believed they will succeed in securing the passage of the bill, since the principal obstacle to its passage has recently passed under a cloud by resigning his position in the Senate.

A delegation from the board called to-day to pay their respects to the new President, who received them very courteously and assured them it would afford him great pleasure to contribute in any way he could consistently to the advancment of the objects of the board and to the interests of steam navigation.

After a brief interview the delegation retired with the full conviction that in the new President the business interests of the country had nothing to fear, but a very able advocate and fast friend. Respectfully yours,

E. W. GOULD.

[From the *Marine Journal*.]

LOS ANGELES, CAL., Aug. 16, 1886.

Editor Marine Journal:

I see Congress has at last adjourned, and, so far as I know, the committee to whom the bill for rebate of license fees was referred failed to report; and of course that measure, like hundreds of others of less merit, remains for future action.

There seems no good reason why a claim of that character and magnitude should not receive favorable consideration at the hands of Congress.

Pension claims are popular on the ground that the money is supposed to be paid to an indigent class of citizens, who have rendered valuable service to the Government.

The same class of citizens have paid an unjust tax to the Government which they ask to have refunded, and I believe it is only a question of time when it will be refunded, if the claimants press their claims with the same energy and determination that many other claims are urged. But it can only be done by a more unanimous effort by the individuals in interest, with their respective representatives in Congress.

The time is rapidly approaching for the annual meeting of

the National Board of Steam Navigation, and I regret to think circumstances may prevent my being present at that pleasant reunion.

It has so long been my privilege to meet with the board on these oft-returning anniversaries, I regret exceedingly my inability to attend this one — not that my presence will be missed or my counsels needed.

But it is pleasant to meet with old friends who have so long been engaged in the same object, and especially when success, long deferred, has to any extent been attained.

This I think the Board can congratulate itself upon having secured, after so many years of persistent effort.

While much has been accomplished there still remain important matters in which all interested in the great industry of steam navigation, are more or less interested, and for which the Board was organized.

The benefits are not alone for what has been accomplished in Congress, but for what has been prevented by damaging legislation in the interest of individuals ever since its organization.

I trust the interest that has sometimes lagged in the Board for want of success and on account of changes and the want of material aid, will be overcome by the present younger and more vigorous management, and that greater results may yet reward them for their very laudable and vigorous efforts.

As the season of the year is favorable and New York has many other attractions to draw a large number of visitors there, I hope to learn that a large and enthusiastic meeting of the Board has been held, and if so I have no doubt of the result.

The steam navigation of the country is largely dependent upon the public press for information and for avenues by which the public is made familiar with its wants and its acts.

If all that are interested in this great industry would give it the attention *The Marine Journal* does, it would not be so difficult to secure legitimate legislation or large and enthusiastic meetings of the National Board.

The principal steam navigation interests of *this coast* are owned by railroads, and is only a secondary consideration with them, consequently there never has been much interest felt in the efforts of the Board here.

Railroads, as you know, are parallel with all water routes, and steamboats are fast becoming things of the past, so far as inland navigation is concerned.

I trust my business relations here may be such that I can

consistently return to Washington this fall, and if the President desires a substitute for General Dumont's position, my services can be made available in the absence of all others.

E. W. GOULD.

In sketching the history of the National Board the following communications, extracted from papers of the day, may not, at this late day, be uninteresting to those who have been associated in its objects:—

We publish below a letter from Capt. E. W. Gould, who was one of the two representatives from St. Louis to the National Convention of the Board of Steam Navigation. It is but justice to Capt. Gould to say that to his untiring energy and perseverance in a forty-years' connection with the interests of Western waters that to him is due more than perhaps to any other one man whatever of river improvement has been instigated by general and State government. It was his zeal in the cause of the removal of obstructions in the Western waters that the government put the snag-boats to work, which though as yet incapable from the small number employed of doing all that boatmen could desire, yet, with the demonstrations of the utility of these appliances, and a few more live workers like Capt. Gould to battle for more river rights, we can yet have our water-courses free from obstructions, and deeper channels for the avenues of commerce. Capt. Gould was President of the Atlantic & Mississippi Steamship Company, also President of the Wrecking Company, formerly owned by Eads & Nelson, and is now the hard working President of the Missouri River Packet Company.— *St. Louis Republican.*

BUFFALO, Sept. 4, 1874.

RIVER EDITOR REPUBLICAN—*Dear Sir:* The "National Board of Steam Navagation" which adjourned from Philadelphia one year since to this place has just closed its annual session to meet again in New York on the first Wednesday of September next.

There were a large number of delegates present from nearly all important parts of the country excepting those on the Mississippi, representing some seven millions of capital.

Many regrets were expressed that St. Louis, Memphis and New Orleans had lost their interest in the important results anticipated from this organization, and failed almost entirely to be represented at the two last annual meetings.

Had it not been for the courtesy of the Pittsburgh delegation, the writer would have been the only representative from

the Mississippi river. Capt. R. C. Gray kindly volunteered
to act as my colleague. But for reasons unknown to me,
that delegation declined to give him up, but proposed Capt.
Wm. J. Kountz as a substitute. All those who know Capt.
Kountz as a delegate in any body in which he is interested,
know that he has courage, firmness and force of language
sufficient to protect any interest he represents, and in justice
to him I may add St. Louis was not left with a single representation, although their apparent indifference in sending delegates resulted in their being entirely ignored in the reorgan-
ization of the Board, or in the election of its officers the
ensuing year.

Thinking to revive the interest that was once felt on the
Mississippi, and give new life to the great interest we represented, we, the St. Louis delegation, assisted by other delegates from the West, made a vigorous effort to secure St.
Louis as the place for next annual meeting to be held.

But we had neither the numbers nor influence, and New
York was fixed as the place of meeting, although the East
was far behind the Mississippi in inaugurating any steps
towards reforming or amending the navigation laws of the
country, or of correcting the many abuses to which the navigation interests are subjected.

But the temporary cloud under which this great interest is
now suffering in the West is not the only one that is
depressed. I find the same stagnation upon the lakes, and,
to a great extent, at the East. And even the railroads, that
are charged with bringing upon us all our misfortunes, are
far from being happy. And when they fail to find foreign
capital to invest in their bonds, through such *patriots* as Jay
Cook & Co., and are obliged to build and run their roads as
steamboats are, a brighter day will dissipate the gloom that
now pervades navigation circles.

We have suffered long and seriously for the want of more
consistent legislation. We have been loaded down with exactions and expensive inspection laws, made by men who
know nothing and care less for the great marine commerce of
the nation.

Our rivers have been obstructed by railroad bridges, wrecks,
&c., until the cost of insurance of boats and cargo amounts
now almost to prohibition.

And yet when an organization is formed and placed under
the direction of some of the most practical ship and steamboat owners, engineers and business men in the country, for
the express purpose of relieving the embarrassments under

which we have been so long suffering, many of our people fold their hands and virtually say, we can do nothing, or that we have tried long enough, or that the railroads have got possession of the rivers as well as the public domain, &c., &c.

I speak with confidence when I say I believe, as far as legislation is concerned, that there never was a time when members of Congress were so well disposed, and so well aware of the necessity of doing something to protect and foster this great interest as at the present moment, and this is the result of the recent combined effort from all parts of the country through the organization of the National Board of Steam Navigation, which had its origin at a convention held at Louisville in 1870.

To be sure but little has yet been accomplished practically, although there is good reason to believe the way has been prepared by which great benefit may be realized, if those interested are true to themselves and the interest they represent.

All that is necessary for them to do is to unite their efforts and join with those already in the field in urging upon members of Congress the necessary reforms in the navigation and inspection laws, and also the importance of increased appropriations for the improvement of river navigation and the protection of these great arteries of commerce for present use as well as for the benefit of future generations. For the purpose of deriving some more immediate relief in the interest of Western transportation, the delegates from Western ports assumed the responsibility of issuing a call for a mass convention to be held in St. Louis on the 30th of the present month, hoping thereby to secure the attendance of large delegations from all parts of the South and West, with the hope of agreeing upon some plan by which the ruinous competition now existing may be avoided.

As this is a subject addressing itself directly to our present necessities it is to be hoped the call may be fully indorsed, and the convention largely attended.

I had intended to have written more at length upon the doings at the meeting of the National Board, and of its reception by the Buffalo local board. But having continued my letter upon incidental subjects so long, I must defer further remarks and refer those interested to the published proceedings.

I will say, however, in closing, that the meeting was entirely harmonious, and many subjects of interest were discussed and a most instructive and eloquent address was made by Geo. B. Hibbard, Esq., of Buffalo, upon the subject of maritime law. Mr. Hibbard is recognized as one of the best admiralty lawyers in the country, and entirely familiar with the present defective system of laws governing the navigation and transportation interests of this nation.

Before the final adjournment we were treated to a sumptuous repast on board one of their magnificent iron steamers, while making an excursion of several miles around the harbor, and in visiting their numerous elevators, iron-works, shipping, etc. During this elegant banquet, given by the hospitality of the Buffalo "local board" and the friends of navigation in this city, we have had the pleasure of listening to many eloquent speeches and suggestive remarks, inspired by the presence of a large number of ladies, and the influence of the prevailing *spirits* of the occasion.   E. W. GOULD.

CHAPTER LVIII.

MISSOURI RIVER PACKET COMPANIES.

THE Missouri River, although one of the most difficult and dangerous of all the rivers in the Mississippi Valley to navigate, from the large number of snags, sand bars, caving banks and rapid currents, saying nothing of the still more damaging obstructions authorized by Congress, in the form of railroad bridges, which are a modern innovation, of course, still the river has been navigated by steamboats ever since the first trip of the Franklin in 1819, and with more or less success — generally less, from the fact that so much was necessary for insurance and repair of boats.

The demand for transportation during the great rush of emigration to Missouri, Kansas, Iowa and Nebraska, saying nothing of the California crowds, in 1849 and '50, induced boat owners to take great risks and to add large numbers of new boats to the trade.

Such was the demand for pilots in that trade at one period that no price was too much for them to charge for their services, and the ability or skill of the pilot had but little to do with the compensation received.   This writer calls to mind one instance just after the war when he paid $800 for piloting a boat to St. Joe and return, and the trip was made in less than eight days.

In 1858 an organization similar in character to the "New Orleans Railroad Line," known as the "St. Louis and St. Joseph Union Packet Line," was formed, and was composed

of twelve Missouri River steamboats, viz.: Peerless, Capt.
Bissel; Morning Star, Capt. Burke; Silver Heels, Capt. Bar-
ron; A. B. Chambers, Capt. Gillham; D. A. January, Capt.
P. Gore; Minnehaha, Capt. C. Baker; Twilight, Capt. J.
Shaw; Hesperian, Capt. F. C. Kercheval; Southwestern,
Capt. DeHaven; Ben Lewis, Capt. Brierly; Sovereign, Capt.
Hutchinson; Kate Howard, Capt. Jos. Nanson.

This line was composed of good boats and run with regularity and gave great satisfaction to the business community,
and especially to the traveling public, and gave promise of
great success.   Their regularity of leaving port and arriving
at points along the river on schedule time was a new experience on that river, so far as any line of boats had previously
demonstrated, although individual boats had before that time
been run on regular time.

But the shortness of the navigation season and the dangers
of navigation, together with the long distance over such precarious navigation, soon developed the impracticability of trying to sustain the line, and as it was only necessary to withdraw
the boats at the option of the owners the organization did not
long continue its co-operation, but resolved itself back into individual interests.   Out of its integral parts other lines were
formed and the fatality that so universally befell all Missouri
steamboats at that period, soon disposed of the whole twelve
beautiful boats of which the line was composed.

In 1859 there was employed between St. Louis and Sioux
City sixty regular boats during the spring months.   Twenty-
nine years later there was not a single boat with the exception
of two or three small freight boats running at the extreme
lower part of the river.

MIAMI PACKET CO.

Soon after the close of the war the "St. Louis & Miami
Packet Company" was organized under the laws of the State
of Illinois and had their official office at East St. Louis,
business office on a wharf-boat at St. Louis.   This was the
first regularly organized joint stock company ever run on the
Missouri River (except one chartered by the Legislature
of Missouri known as the "Lightning Line," in 1856-7).
The officers were E. W. Gould, President; C. S. Rogers, Vice-
President; W. W. Ater, Secretary; Moses Hillard, Freight
Agent.

This company was organized to run from St. Louis to Miami.
Subsequently extending the line to Lexington and ultimately to
Kansas City — changing the name to "Missouri River Packet

27

Company," and adding more boats, and increasing the stock,
with a new board of directors and new officers, W. J. Lewis,
President. This was in 1871 and continued until the Kansas
City organization which succeeded it in 1878.

In 1870 the K. Line was organized to run with two boats,
under the direction and ownership of Capt. Jo. Kinney, from
St. Louis to Glasgow and Miami, in competition with the Missouri River Company. But a compromise was soon effected
and the two lines were merged, leaving the Kansas City Packet
Company in possession of the field. But the field was about
all there was left of what was once a good line of boats and a
remunerative business, although never able to make a dividend to the stockholders. The several companies that were
merged into each other from time to time built quite a number of boats and barges, besides purchasing many. That, together with the frequent losses and the expense of repairs,
absorbed the earnings, and the depreciation and insurance
finally absorbed the boats.

INTRODUCTION OF BARGES.

The only thing that kept the company alive during the last
few years of its existence was the introduction of barges,
which this company was the first to introduce in the Missouri,
and which enabled the boats to handle a large amount of business they never could have handled without them.

Before the extinction of the Kansas City Packet Company,
a part of the same owners formed what was known as the
" Belle St. Louis Transportation Company," and run their
boats in the lower end of the river. But the railroads en-
croached so rapidly upon the river commerce that it soon absorbed all that was of value in it, and closed the river to this
company as they had done to all others that preceded them.
Until the organization of the Miami Packet Company running
steamboats down stream at night was a thing seldom thought
of, except in clear weather and a good stage of water.

After this company started, laying up at night in any kind
of weather or water was the exception. So too, in the use of
barges. Before that period such a thing as towing barges in
the Missouri River was thought to be presumption, and it was
some years before the old boatmen and the underwriters could
be educated up to the necessity of towing barges, in order to
retain business enough on the river to compete with the railroads then running on either side of it. But it was only a
question of time, and only a very short time, developed the
fact that no steamboats need apply.

OMAHA PACKET CO.

In 1867 the St. Louis and Omaha Packet Co. was established. Joseph Nanson was the first President. The boats comprising the line were T. S. McGill, T. W. Shields, master; Silver Bow, T. W. Rea, master; Mary McDonald, Jno. Greenough, master; Cornelia, S. T. Belt, master; Columbia, Wm. Barnes, master; Glasgow, Wm. P. Lamoth, master; Kate Kinney, J. P. McKinney, master; H. S. Turner, James A. Yore, master. These boats were owned by individuals and run under a joint arrangement and on regular schedule time.

Its second president was Capt. Jno. B. Weaver, who filled that position during the continuance of the organization. During the first years of its existence it was a good line of boats and judiciously managed. But the character of the navigation and the long periods of low water were such that the railroad competition soon made it apparent that the line could not be sustained, and the boats drifted off into other trades, and the line was abandoned.

From that time forward the business that had heretofore been done by steamboats in that trade gradually found its way to the railroads, and has always been done by them since. And probably will always continue to be done by them, although Congressmen from that district, and some business men, persist in urging appropriations for the improvement of the Missouri River. But for all purposes of navigation it will prove a total loss, especially above Kansas City.

Farms in the bottom lands may be saved from washing, and landings at the towns and cities may be preserved, but the meanderings of the river so increase the distance, added to the character of the navigation naturally, that no improvement the government will ever make will render it possible for water transportation to compete with rail in this river. And the sooner its friends in Congress, and out of Congress abandon their effort to improve the navigation of the Missouri and devote their energies to the improvement of the Mississippi, and other streams that it is practical to improve, they will the sooner realize the advantages of river improvements to the commerce of the valley than they can ever expect to by attempting to improve the Missouri.

GREAT MAIL EXPRESS & PASSENGER ROUTE.

The Pacific Railroad Packet Line, known as the Lightning Line, was established in the summer of 1856 under a contract

entered into with the Pacific Railroad Company by Captain
Barton Able and Louis A. Welton, by which the latter parties
placed in connection with that road three steamers: The
Cataract, F. X. Anbry and Australia, forming a tri-weekly line
between St. Louis, Jefferson City, Kansas City and Western.

"On the opening of navigation in 1857 this line was increased to a daily, except Sundays, and met with a success
and patronage truly encouraging. The inducement offered by
this route appeals directly to the traveler, saving under the
most favorable circumstances which can surround steamers on
their trips from St. Louis, some thirty hours' time, beside the
many delays and annoyances incident upon a lengthened steamboat trip.

In the winter of 1856 and 1857 a very favorable charter
was granted by the Legislature of Missouri, to this company.
Incorporating it under the name of "Pacific Railroad Packet
Company," and the following summer Governor Brown, the
present Postmaster-General caused a contract to be made
with this company, by which the Western mails should be carried on their boats during the season of navigation and under
the same contract forwarded by express in winter.

The demand for transportation of government freight was
so great up the Missouri destined for the far West, and the
troops at Salt Lake, during the Mormon war, that a contract
was made with the Pacific Railroad and this steamboat line, by
the government, by which a large part of that business was
secured to them, and they soon became known as the "Great
Mail and Transportation Company of the West."

The following elegant steamers composed the line in 1858:
John H. Dickey, Dan Able, master; White Cloud, Jas.
O'Neal, master; Victoria, Ben V. Glime, master; Polar Star, O.
H. McMillin, master; Wm. H. Russel, J. McKenney, master;
St. Mary, P. Devinney, master, and are unsurpassed for speed
and accommodations, by any line on Western waters. Through
tickets can be purchased in all the principal ticket offices in
the East or North or in St. Louis."

Of all the packet companies ever organized on Western
waters I think this one was started on less capital, was boomed
into public notice with more gas, had the shortest lease of
life, went up with meteoric brilliancy and passed away into thin
air leaving many of its victims poorer and probably wiser
men, having learned, when it was too late, that the only use
railroads have for steamboats is to reach points until they
get there, which is not usually long delayed, and which was
the case with this packet company and the Pacific Railroad.

ST. JOE & OMAHA PACKET COMPANY.

Upon the completion of the Hannibal & St. Joe Railroad to the latter city, in 1859, a line of boats called the St. Joe & Omaha Packet Company was established to run in connection with the road from St. Joe to Omaha, under the management of Captain Rufus Ford, a good practical boatman, and under whose direction it was understood a successful business was done for several years for the benefit of the road who owned the boats or until the road was completed to Council Bluffs, or near there, when the boats were withdrawn and the business done by the road. In 1868 when that or some other connecting road was finished through to Sioux City, Capt. Joab Lawrence established a line of light draft boats to ply in connection with the road between that point and Fort Benton. This too was understood to be a successful enterprise and was continued until the Northern Pacific Railroad reached Bismarck. At that period, 1869, another line was formed by Captains Colson, Evens and others of Pittsburgh, Pa., and ran in connection with the road for several years with eminent success.

MOUNTAIN BOATS AND TRADE.

Capt. Wm. J. Kountz, of Pittsburgh, also had several boats in the "mountain trade" as it was called, at that time, and was a lively competitor for government transportation which furnished the basis for the trade between Bismarck and all points above, without which no great inducement remained for boats to contend. Hence the parties that had the best "friends at court," or could make the lowest rates, finally succeeded in retiring most of the large number of boats that had been employed on the Upper Missouri. Although the extension of the Northern Pacific road gradually diminished the river transportation until at the present time it assumes small proportions, as compared with what it was at an earlier date.

The fabulous prices obtained for freight to points on the Upper Missouri before any railroads were built, and upon the discovery of gold in Montana, induced a large number of boats into what was known as the "mountain trade." The nominal rate of freight from St. Louis to Fort Benton in 1863–4 was 12½ cents per pound, although that price was often shaded a little, as steamboat freights generally are.

But the margin for profits was several years sufficient to introduce the building of many boats expressly for that trade.

Some of them were the best low water boats, or boats of the greatest capacity as freight boats, ever built on the Western waters, and as the navigation of the Missouri river differs in the upper part so widely from the lower part, but little risk, comparatively, is involved in running light stern-wheel boats.

Hence every character of boat was introduced into the trade, and but few years elapsed before competition reduced the rate of freight from 12¼ cents per lb. to one cent per pound.

As soon as the railroad was finished to Bismarck, but little freight was shipped from St. Louis, and the trade was confined principally to points between Bismarck, the Yellowstone River and Fort Benton.

FATHER DE SMET AND SHOOTING OF M'KENZIE.

Previous to the discovery of gold in Montana, the American Fur Co. and its contemporaries and predecessors in the fur trade monopolized about all the traffic there was above Sioux City, commencing soon after the introduction of steam, in 1819, with one boat per annum, adding another from time to time as their trade extended up the river.

The arrival or departure from St. Louis of a "mountain boat" created about as much excitement and curiosity at that time as did that of a pirogue or Mackinaw boat loaded with skins and peltries at an earlier date. As the representative of that company, Mr. Chas. P. Chouteau in later years was the general manager of the transportation department and accompanied the boats on their long voyages to and from the mountains. Capts. Jos. and John LaBarge were the lieutenants of the company, and without one or both of them on board, or old "Black Dave" as pilot, the mountain crew was scarcely complete; and with them, but little apprehension from hostile Indians or dangerous navigation was felt. While the Indians were at peace with each other, the steamboat's annual trip was looked forward to by them with pleasure and great anxiety, as it was their source of supplies, and of them Indians are always short.

These annual trips for so many years made the Indians of the Missouri as familiar with the officers of the boat as with their own neighbors, and they often remained on the banks of the river for weeks waiting the arrival of *the boat*. The chiefs and head men were sure to be remembered by Mr. Chouteau or whoever is in charge of the expedition, and a grand spread was always anticipated and realized, at the principal trading posts, which consisted of coffee and hardtack, and, through the influence of some valued presents of buffalo robes and choice skins, not unfrequently small flasks of red-eye (whisky) might be seen walking off under the protection of an Indian blanket.

This practice, however, was not countenanced by the Fur Co., as it was from the effect of whisky that their losses in trade with Indians often occurred at that early day, as it does to-day in civilized communities and by a christianized people.

The Rev. Father DeSmet, for many years a missionary and general manager of Catholic missions among the Indians of the Northwest, was not unfrequently a passenger on these pioneer boats.

The black gown which he always wore in the presence of Indians inspired in them great veneration, as the representative of the Great Spirit. His amiable and suave manner always assured them, as it did every one else, that no evil could befall them in his presence, and he was, when known to be near, a constant check upon their habits of dissipation, quarrels and hostilities.

No matter how fierce the feuds between different tribes, he went fearlessly from one to the other to allay any commotion or fight and was always respected.

The writer saw this practically illustrated while at the mouth of Milk River, some 200 miles below Fort Benton, in 1864.

At that time the Sioux Indians were at war with the United States and with many tribes of Indians. Their country bordered the Missouri River for many miles and navigation was not considered very safe. Boats were occasionally fired into when running close to shore, and when lying up at night always kept a picket-guard, and the pilot was protected by shields of boiler-iron when under way. This was a low-water year and we were two months getting to the mouth of Milk River, where we were obliged to store our cargo. While lying there a tragic event occurred, through which, had it not been for the presence of Father DeSmet the steamer Nellie Rogers and probably some of the crew would have been sacrificed, for the cruel and unprovoked murder of young McKenzie, the son of a prominent merchant of St. Louis, whom many St. Louisans will remember as a very estimable gentleman. He at one time was an Indian trader on the Upper Missouri.

He had married a squaw, Indian fashion, and raised a family of half-breeds, a part of which he took to the States and educated. This young man, then about 30 years old, had returned to his tribe, "the Crows," married, and was living at Fort Peck, acting, perhaps, in the capacity of interpreter. He, with his wife and young child, together with a large number of Indians of both sexes and of all ages, had encamped on the bank opposite where the boat was discharging. They all had access to the boat and were constantly passing to and fro.

But as the bar on the boat had been closed by Mr. Chouteau's order, who had the boat under charter, no excessive drinking was allowed. There had been on board as a passenger all the way from St. Louis a Mr. Clark, formerly from Philadelphia a quiet gentlemanly man of education, who for the previous 10 or 12 years had been living among the Indians—principally at Benton.

After the boat had been lying there several hours Mc-Kenzie came on board with others and stepped into the cabin, and just as he got abreast of the stove in the hall, Clark stepped out of his state-room, which was one of the first rooms in the cabin, with pistol in hand, and without a word from either of them, instantly fired and McKenzie fell, shot through the heart.

His wife was one of the first who rushed on board, with many of her kindred and friends, and the excitement soon became intense — on the part of the Indians, for the sudden death of a prominent member of their tribe; on the part of the passengers and crew for fear of summary vengeance from the Indians, who were entirely masters of the situation. The fires were out and, of course, no steam could be had to move the boat for some hours. Father DeSmet and his black gown seemed about all that stood between an outraged body of fighting Indians and the Nellie Rogers, her passengers and crew, until Clark could be disposed of. While he was fearless and indifferent, it was evident there was no safety as long as he remained on board. Ponies were secured from the traders at Fort Peck, 12 miles distant, but who had come to see "the steamboat." Clark with two or three others, who were anxious to get to Fort Benton, started with very little preparation, and very little delay and stood "not upon the order of their going." And until they were well out of the Crow country it was thought no grass would grow under their horses' feet.

Before the Indians had gotten over their surprise and consternation, Clark, whom none of them knew personally, had gotten beyond the reach of their fastest horses, and through the influence of Father De Smet, it is probable they never pursued him. "Tom Dorris," a young man from St. Louis bound for the gold mines at Helena, then just beginning to attract attention, was one of Clark's traveling companions during that John Gilpin race. Subsequently it was learned that no halt was made until Fort Benton was reached, and the distance, 200 miles, covered inside of three days.

As there was no law and but little justice in that country then, no investigation was ever made, and no cause ever assigned for the sudden taking off of McKenzie.

It was believed an old grudge existed that was to be settled in that way whenever the parties met. It was afterwards said by Clark that he was the author of several similar tragedies previous to the one at the mouth of Milk River; although his appearance was anything but that of a murderer or an out- . law.

His subsequent history I have never heard.

Father DeSmet, who was on his annual tour to the missionary station among the Indians of the Northwest, together with the passengers who were bound for the gold mines of Montana, ultimately found their way to Fort Benton on foot or Indian ponies, and in wagons sent from the Fort, to transport the stores that were left on the bank, under the strong guard provided by the fur company. While the Nellie Rogers and her crew wended their slow return to St. Louis under all the embarrassments attendant upon a low water voyage, on that then but little known navigation.

According to Mr. Chouteau's recollection it was by far the the lowest stage of water that had been experienced on that river since his connection with it.

At that period and for several years subsequent the greatest drawback in that navigation, was the lack of fuel for steam, and boats had to depend entirely upon drift wood, and young cottonwood, growing sparsely on the banks of the river, in the narrow bottom lands, many times packing it a mile on the backs of the voyagers and half-breeds, who were generally shipped on all early boats for this purpose.

The practice of cutting down small cottonwood trees by the Indians to allow their ponies to forage from in the winter furnished the best fuel then obtainable, and was always first selected, as it only needed sufficient trimming to get it on board, after which it was cut into suitable lengths for the furnace while the boat pursued her voyage.

This foraging for fuel in the bottom lands had generally to be done in the daytime to avoid Indians in ambush. Hence most valuable time was consumed, as only in very low water could the "drift-pile" be depended upon for the necessary supply. In later years, when the settlement of Dakota and

Montana made it necessary for large numbers of boats to enter that trade, wood-choppers availed themselves of the law of "squatter sovereignty" and dropped on to every little patch of cottonwood timber on the whole Upper Missouri as well as on to the "pine-knot region" in the neighborhood of Fort Benton. This so increased the facilities of navigation that some boats made two trips in a season from St. Louis to Fort Benton and return; and it made it possible to run that large fleet of boats that was afterwards needed to accommodate the government in moving troops and munitions of war and for the transportation of miner's and settlers' supplies.

While young cotton wood cut and put on the bank was sold for $5 to $10 per cord, it was the cheapest fuel that could be had and no questions asked.

Notwithstanding the rush of miners to the gold fields of Montana, which set in just at that time, calling into use a large number of steamboats, the efforts of the government, the influence of Father DeSmet and other missionaries, nothing could induce the Sioux to remain on their reservations and be peaceful.

Sitting Bull and a few desperate young renegade braves were always on the warpath, committing all kinds of atrocities, inducing the restless and reckless of other tribes to join them in their brutal attacks upon settlers and all the defenseless far and near, until at length the government determined upon a more formidable movement to disperse them.

The following note explains itself:—

MALCOLM CLARKE'S FATE.

"FINDLAY, O., March 24, 1889.

"Reading in the Cincinnati *Enquirer* to-day an article taken from and credited to your paper purporting to be an extract from Capt. E. W. Gould's forthcoming book, I would like to know what became of Malcolm Clarke who killed McKenzie. I went to Fort Benton in '62 and left in '65, and was well acquainted with Clarke. He was a man to be feared, but quite a gentleman when not angry. He once placed his hand on his revolver to draw on me, but changed his mind. He was married to a beautiful half-breed girl with whom he seemed to live quite pleasantly. She had a brother named Isadore, who lived most of the time with Clarke and hunted or traded for him. In 1865 Clarke moved to Prickly Pear Creek and located a ranch just where Gillette's wagon road starts around Medicine Rock

Hill. For some reason Clarke became cruel and overbearing to his wife, and, after enduring it for a few months, she appealed to her brother for protection. He and Clarke had an altercation about it, and Isadore shot and killed Clarke. This happened, I think, in 1866. I do not wish my name published, but would not object to Gould's knowing it."

J. A. V.

Thanks.

CHAPTER LIX.

THE SECOND YELLOWSTONE EXPEDITION.

IN June, 1819, the government started an exploring expedition under the command of Major Long up the Missouri River to the mouth of the Yellowstone, a detailed account of which may be seen in another chapter of this work.

In May, 1873, the government having been several years trying to reconcile the Sioux Indians to pacific measures, and a more friendly intercourse without success, determined to try the virtue of *stones*, as *grass* did not seem to produce a lasting effect upon them.

The Northern Pacific Railroad was in course of construction through the Sioux country, very much to the disgust of that tribe, and required the strong arm of the government to protect the working forces.

It was determined to build two forts in the valley of the Yellowstone, and station troops enough there to compel submission and protect the railroad and the settlers.

In order to do that, a large amount of building material, ordinance stores and general supplies were necessary. A large number of troops were ordered through by land from Fort Abraham Lincoln and other frontier forts. In order to ascertain whether the Yellowstone River could be made available for transportation by steamboats, the steamer " Key West," under command of Capt. Grant Marsh, was dispatched by order of Genl. Sheridan, commanding the Military Division of the Missouri, to ascertain the practicability of attempting the navigation of that river.

Having proceeded under escort of Col. Fosythe and a small military guard to within three miles ot the mouth of Powder river, they returned to Bismarck with a favorable report.

During the following months of June and July steamers Key West, Far West and Peninah were employed by the Government in transporting supplies from Bismarck to Glendine.

In 1875, the government boat "Josephine," having been built expressly for this expedition, was dispatched from Bismarck to ascertain how far the Yellowstone could be navigated during the spring rise, which usually continues from the middle of May to July.

They proceeded to "Pompey's Pillar," thirty miles above mouth of the Big Horn, which is estimated to be 500 miles from Bismarck. Above that point the current was so strong and the channel so divided they could go no further and returned. The river being at an ordinary stage they explored the Big Horn for twelve miles from the mouth and then returned to Bismarck.

The following year, 1876, several boats were employed by the government in transporting supplies and munitions of war from Bismarck in connection with the military expedition.

In 1872, the government advertised for bids for freight, troops, horses, etc., per 100 lbs. per 100 miles, to extend from April 20th to August 15th.

A large number of competitors materialized and some friction was the consequence.

CONTRACTORS FOR GOVERNMENT FREIGHT.

Capt. John B. Davis, S. B. Coulson, A. H. Wilder, Joseph Lightner, Wm. J. Kountz and some others were interested in these contracts, and a large number of boats were employed for the next two or three years in transportation of government and private freights. During those years there was an immigration to the Valley of the Yellowstone, and it was understood the steamboats as a rule made a good deal of money. The defeat of General Custer's army in 1876, and the competition of the Northern Pacific Railroad terminated open hostilities from the Indians, and the principal business of steamboats. In 1880, the government made a small appropriation for the improvement of the channel of the river, and if it had been continued it could have been made a very navigable stream for several hundred miles.

It runs through a beautiful valley traversed in part by the Northern Pacific, and at the present time has a number of flourishing towns on its banks. It is estimated to discharge a greater volume of water into the Missouri than the Missouri itself carries above the junction. To have continued to make appropriations to improve the navigation, after the railroad was completed, would have been as futile as it is to attempt to improve the navigation of the Missouri with a railroad on each side of it, and a bridge across it every fifty miles.

Notwithstanding the attractive features of the Valley of the Yellowstone, and the value of its lands, its water-power and its parks, if the government estimates values as individuals do, it is very evident this expedition cost too much, far above its value in blood, if not in treasure.

The Northern Pacific Railroad seems to have been the only party deriving any direct benefit from it.

Whether the government had better or not to have furnished them all the protection they needed to build that road, by a small armed force, admits of no argument.

That the Sioux Indians were behaving badly and needed chastising there is no doubt. Nor that the battle of the Little Big Horn, although a most disastrous defeat to the government forces, practically ended the Sioux war and the career of Sitting Bull, although several battles occurred afterwards, will not be disputed. But that all, and much more, could have been secured through diplomacy and the lives of so many brave men, led by the intrepid Custer, been saved, there is but little doubt.

The unfortunate *partisan* political complications connected with that terrible tragedy, and the brave officers whose lives were sacrificed, has probably done much to deprive their families of the sympathy of the public, and the officers of the honor they were justly entitled to.

The charges that have so often been repeated that Custer's reckless impetuosity and lack of caution destroyed him and the troops under his immediate command is undoubtedly a misrepresentation, cruel and unjust.

That he was impulsive, sanguine and brave none can doubt; that he was frank, out-spoken and impolitic perhaps, will not be denied. But the record shows he was always ready and at the front when duty called.

He was a genial companion and warm friend, much beloved by those under him.

Promotion had not destroyed his high sense of duty towards those occupying subordinate positions. Nor did the attempt to prove him disloyal, to those higher in authority, intimidate him.

He had reason to believe there was irregularity in the office of the War Department, and he had the courage to say so, and although President Grant refused to recognize it at the time and dishonored Custer, subsequent developments proved General Custer was right in his suspicions.

This defeat at the battle of the Little Big Horn, where he lost his life, was in no way attributable to his recklessness or lack of judgment. The fatal mistake was in underestimating the number of warriors then in the field. In this Generals Crook and Terry, Major Reno and others agreed. And even the War Department, concurred in the opinion that there was not more than eight or ten hundred hostiles off of their reservations, agreeable to the reports from the agencies.

They also underestimated the prowess and the ability of Sitting Bull, as a war chief. No Indian of late years has developed so much skill and bravery as a fighting chief as he has. General Custer had but little love for an Indian, and less confidence in his integrity, and none in his courage in a square stand-up fight. He was always on the alert when in the neighborhood of hostile Indians for fear they would "run away."

CUSTER BEING LED INTO AMBUSH.

Even at this time, when he was rapidly approaching their camp, he reported to Reno "that the village was only two miles ahead and that the Indians were *running away.*"

Little suspecting he was being led into ambush and to meet 2,000 well armed warriors, under the command of one of the shrewdest and most desperate blood-thirsty savages of modern times. But such is the fate of war, and in less than an hour after the fight began, according to the best judgment of Major Reno and others in his command who were within sound of the firing, not one was left to tell the tale.

The Indians scattered in all directions and before the surprise and consternation had subsided and the other commands had been collected the Indians had left the valley.

A short time previous to the battle, General Custer had written to his wife at Fort Lincoln to come up on the next boat, as he apprehended no danger, and she had been left there very much against her will. It was her wish and generally her custom to accompany him wherever he went. The steamer that took the news of the defeat, the Far West, was to have taken Mrs. Custer and some other ladies up to join the expedition. In the expressive language of her journal, " the light of twenty-six hearts went out at the fort on the receipt of the heartrending news."

To Captain Joseph Todd, of St. Louis, whose experience in the navigation of the Upper Missouri and the Yellowstone is almost co-extensive with steam navigation, especially so on the latter stream, I am indebted for the foregoing information, and many other details not included. He being in command of one of the boats in the expedition was in position to know the facts and his account is corroborated by reports made at the time to the War Department.

CHAPTER LX.

CONDENSED LIST OF CASUALTIES ON STEAMBOATS.

IN *DeBow's Review*, of 1848, may be found one of the best histories extant of the many accidents and their causes that had occurred on Western waters up to that date, and while not absolutely correct in every particular, it is sufficiently so to be interesting and instructive.

Whole number of boats upon which explosions occurred, 233; passengers killed (enumerated in six cases), 140; officers killed (enumerated in 31 cases), 57; crew killed (enumerated in 25 cases), 103; whole number killed (enumerated in 164 cases), 1,805; whole number wounded (enumerated in 111 cases), 1,015; total amount of damages (enumerated in 75 cases), $925,650; average number of passengers killed in the enumerated cases, 23; average number of officers killed in the enumerated cases, 2; average number of crew killed in the enumerated cases, 4; average amount of damages, $13,302. The *cause* is stated in 98 cases, not stated in 125 cases, unknown in 10 cases; total, 233. Excessive pressure of steam, gradually increased, was the cause of 16; the pressure of unduly heated metals was the cause of 16; defective construction of boilers caused 33; carelessness or ignorance was the cause of 32; accidental rolling of the boat cause of 1.

NATURE OF THE ACCIDENTS.

Bursting boilers	101
Collapsing flues	71
Bursting steam pipes	9
Bursting steam chests	1
Bolt and boiler forced out	1
Struck by lightning	1
Boiler head blown out	4
Breaking cylinder head	1
Breaking Flange of steam pipe	2
Bridge wall exploded	1
Unknown	3
Not stated	38
Total	233

DATES AND NUMBERS OF EXPLOSIONS.

In 1816	3	In 1834	7
" 1817	4	" 1835	10
" 1819	1	" 1836	13
" 1820	1	" 1837	13
" 1821	1	" 1838	11
" 1822	1	" 1839	3
" 1825	2	" 1840	8
" 1826	3	" 1841	7
" 1827	2	" 1842	7
" 1828	1	" 1843	9
" 1829	4	" 1844	4
" 1830	12	" 1845	11
" 1831	2	" 1846	7
" 1832	1	" 1847	12
" 1833	5	" 1848	12

TOTAL IN 233 CASES.

Pecuniary loss	$3,090,366
Loss of life in 233 cases	2,568
Wounded in 233 cases	2,092
Total killed and wounded	4,660

The *Western Boatman*, for 1848, makes the following estimate of the fatality of steamboats up to that period : —

354 Worn out or abandoned	50½ per cent.
238 Snagged or otherwise sunk	34½ per cent.
68 Burnt	10 per cent.
17 Lost by collision	2½ per cent.
17 By explosions	2½ per cent.

Average age of boats worn out or abandoned, five years, or nearly so ; average age of those sunk, burnt or otherwise lost, four years, or nearly four.

There were built in the Pittsburgh District, 304 boats ; in the Cincinnati District, 221 ; Louisville, 103 ; Nashville, 19 ; other places, 37. Total, 684.

NUMBER OF BOATS BUILT IN EACH OF THE FOLLOWING YEARS.

In 1811	1	In 1825	32
" 1812	0	" 1826	60
" 1813	1	" 1827	24
" 1814	2	" 1828	35
" 1816	5	" 1829	55
" 1817	8	" 1830	43
" 1818	31	" 1831	68
" 1819	34	" 1832	80
" 1820	9	" 1833	48
" 1821	7	" 1834	59
" 1822	10	" 1835	52
" 1823	14		
" 1824	13	Total	684

The following compilation shows the number of boats lost and the aggregation of capital:—

From 1811 to 1820...	3
" 1820 to 1830...	37
" 1830 to 1840...	184
" 1840 to 1850...	270
Boats whose dates of loss is unknown......................	80
Total..	576
Total original cost...................................	$7,113,940
Depreciation in value while in service.................	3,665,890
Final loss..	3,681,292

Subsequent, and not included in the foregoing list of losses, among the many that followed in rapid succession. In "Sharf's history of St. Louis," to which I am indebted for many items of interest, are the following total losses — omitting the partial ones:

Andrew Jackson, destroyed by fire while laying at Illinoistown, August 7, 1850. She was an old boat; insured for $6,000.

The Sultana was burned the 12th of June, 1851, laying at Mullanphy street, St. Louis. Loss $75,000, on boat and cargo.

April 4, 1852, the Glenco blowed up at the landing directly after arriving from New Orleans, by which a large number of lives were lost.

On the 18th of January, 1853, steamers New England, New Lucy and Brunette were burned laying at the St. Louis wharf.

The steamer Bluff City was burned the 27th July, at the wharf in St. Louis.

The Doctor Franklin and the Highland Mary were greatly damaged by the same fire.

The Montauk, Robert Cambell and Lunette were burned at the landing 13th of October, 1853.

The Twin City, Prairie City and Parthenia were burned at the St. Louis wharf 7th of December, 1855.

A loss of nearly $100,000 was caused by the burning of the St. Clair, Paul Anderson, James Stockwell, Southerner and the Savanna, and the damage to Monongahela, Pennsylvania and Mattie Wayne.

The steamer Australia was burned April 1, 1859, and the New Monongahela and Edenburgh, laying at Bloody Island on the 15th of May, same year.

A loss of $200,000 was sustained by the burning of the H. D. Bacon, T. L. McGill, Estella, A. McDowell and the W. H. Russel, on the 27th of October, 1863.

Steamers Imperial, valued at $60,000; Hiawatha, valued at the same; Jesse K. Bell, valued at $20,000, and the Post

28

Boy, valued at $35,000, were bured 13th of September, 1863.

The Chancellor, Forest Queen and the Catahoula were burned on the 4th of October, 1863.

The steamer Maria, having on board a part of the Third Iowa and Fourth Missouri Cavalry, was blown up at Carondelet, in December, 1864, by which many lives were lost.

The steamer Jennie Lewis and the ferryboat Illinois, No. 2, were sunk in the ice at St. Louis, November 19, 1864.

The Carondelet and Marine Railway Docks, together with steamer Jennie Deans were totally destroyed by fire on 12th of May, 1866.

Steamers Ida Handy (valued at $75,000), Bostona, and James Raymond, were burned on 2d of June, 1866.

Steamer Magnolia, valued at $150,000, was burned at St. Louis on 13th June. On the 7th of April, 1866, steamer Fanny Ogden, Frank Bates, Nevada, Alex. Majors, and Effa Deans, all with some cargo on board, were burned, involving a loss of over $500,000.

On 26th of February, 1866, the Leviathan, Luna, Petona, and Dictator were burned at the wharf at St. Louis with an estimated loss of $750,000. On December 19, steamer Gray Eagle was sunk at St. Louis.

LOST FROM BREAKING UP OF ICE.

Breaking up of the ice gorge in the winter of 1865-6 caused a loss of nearly a million dollars to owners and underwriters at St. Louis.

This was the most disastrous *break up* that has ever occurred on Western waters.

The following is the estimate with the names of the boats lost :—

	Value.
New Admiral	$ 60,000
Sioux City	10,000
Empire City	20,000
Calypso (about)	30,000
Hylander	20,000
Geneva	28,000
Metropolitan (about)	18,000
Four Wharf Boats (about)	15,000
Two Barges (about)	25,000

ON THE SECOND BREAK OR MOVEMENT OF THE ICE ON FRIDAY, 12TH JANUARY, 1866.

	Value.
Belle Memphis	$ 85,000
John Trendly ferryboat	50,000
Prairie Rose	15,000
India	16,000
Warsaw	35,000
Underwriter, No 8	20,000
Omaha	12,000

Nebraska	20,000
City of Pekin	82,000
Hattle May	80,000
Diadem	22,000
Viola Belle	30,000
Reserve	80,000
Rosalie	45,000
Five Rock boats (about)	18,000
Memphis Wharf-boat	5,000
Alton Wharf-boat	2,500
Total	**\$692,500**

In the above estimate there is no calculation for the damage to boats not entirely lost. This is variously estimated from \$150,000 to \$175,000.

In 1860 there was lost and partially lost or damaged on Western waters 299 steamboat.

Totally destroyed, 120.

For some years after the bridge was completed, but few serious casualties occurred, and it was thought the bridge piers would so protect the harbor that the breaking up of the ice in the river would not hence forward cause serious losses. But the winter of 1887–8 proved more disastrous to floating property than any winter since the great break up in 1866.

All that remains for the protection of that harbor seems to be an appropriation from the government to build an ice harbor for the protection of boats in winter. Several efforts have already been made in that direction and an inadequate amount has once been appropriated, but for some reason used for another purpose.

The following is a list of steamboats lost and partially so, at or near St. Louis from 1862 to 1881, inclusive: —

1867—January 20, steamer Mexico, burned at St. Louis; total loss.

January 26, R. C. Wood, sunk opposite Carondelet.

January 26, E. H. Fairchild, sunk opposite Carondelet.

February 6, Tom Storms, sunk near St. Louis.

February 13, White Cloud, sunk at St. Louis; total loss.

June 13, Governor Sharkey, sunk at St. Louis; total loss.

September 10, G. W. Graham, burned at St. Louis; total loss.

September 10, Yellowstone, burned at St. Louis; total loss.

September 27, Illinois exploded at St. Louis, and repaired.

1868 — February 4, Annie White, sunk by ice at St. Louis; Clara Donolson burned at St. Louis.

February 22, Kate Putnam, sunk near St. Louis. **Raised** and repaired.

February 29, Paragon, sunk near Cape Girardeau.

March 2, M. S. Mespham, burned at St. Louis; **Fannie** Scott, burned at St. Louis; Kate Kinney, partially burned. April 18, George D. Palmer, partially burned.

December 18, George McPorter, sunk at St. Louis.

1869 — March 29, Carrie V. Kountz, Gerard B. Allen, Ben Johnston, Henry Adkins, Jennie Lewis and Fannie Scott, burned at St. Louis. Loss nearly half a million.

October 28, Stonewall, burned on lower Mississippi. Large number of lives lost.

1870 — January 17, Lady Gay, sunk near Chester; valued at $50,000. Belonged at the time to St. Louis & New Orleans Packet Co. Capt. I. H. Jones, master. Insured for $24,000.

January 27, W. R. Arthur, from New Orleans to St. Louis, exploded her boilers about twenty miles above Memphis. Was totally destroyed by burning, and about sixty people lost their lives.

1871 — March 8, Mollie Able was badly damaged by a cyclone while laying at East St. Louis. Several other boats were severely damaged by the same storm.

1876 — December 13. The following boats were destroyed, and partially so, by the breaking of an ice gorge in St. Louis harbor: —

Centennial, Jennie Baldwin, Bayard, Rock Island, Davenport, Alexander Mitchell. War Eagle, Andy Johnston. The Fannie Keener was sunk same year. Also South Shore and Southern Belle.

1877 — September 19, steamer Grand Republic, laying in the harbor of St. Louis, burned to the water's edge. She was said to have cost $300,000, and was insured for $50,000, and just previous to the disaster had been extensively repaired at a cost of $25,000. The steamer Carondelet, laying alongside, was burned at the same time.

1878 — March 8, steamer Colossal was burned to the water's edge laying in St Louis harbor.

June 9, steamer Exchange, burned at St. Louis.

1880 — March 27, steamer Daisy, sunk at South St Louis.

1881 — March 13, steamer James Howard, burned at the wharf with cargo of sugar on board valued at $65,000. Boat valued at $75,000.

The above list embraces some fifty boats lost in and near St. Louis in fourteen years, principally owned in that city.

This list does not embrace all, nor does it embrace barges, canal-boats, nor flat-boats, of which many were destroyed.

There seems to be a singular fatality attending this kind of property in and around St. Louis.

It can only be partially accounted for from the exposed condition of the harbor in the season of ice, and that must continue until the government provides an ice harbor.

Steamboat explosions for 50 years, commencing in 1816 to 1871 inclusive:—

Year.	Name of Boat.	Lives Lost.	Year.	Name of Boat.	Lives Lost.
1816	Washington	9	1857	Forest Rose	12
1817	Constitution	30	1857	Kentucky	3
1825	Teche	20	1857	Fannie Fern	20
1830	Helen McGregor	60	1857	Cataract	12
1836	Ben. Franklin	29	1857	Buckeye Belle	8
1836	Rob Roy	17	1858	Titonia	1
1837	Chariton	9	1859	Princess	70
1837	Dubuque	21	1859	St. Nicholas	45
1837	Black Hawk	50	1859	Hiawatha	2
1838	Moselle	85	1860	John Calhoun	8
1838	Oronoco	100	1860	Sam Gaty	2
1838	Gen'l Brown	55	1860	Ben Lewis	23
1838	Augusta	7	1860	H. T. Gilmore	2
1839	Geo. Collier	26	1861	Madonna	4
1839	Wellington	25	1861	Ben Shervod	80
1839	Walker	9	1862	Pennsylvania	,150
1840	Persia	23	1862	Monongahela	4
1844	Lucy Walker	25	1862	Com'd Perry	1
1845	Elizabeth	6	1862	Advance	3
1845	Wyoming	13	1862	Iago	1
1845	Marquette	30	1862	Ollie Sullivan	3
1846	H. W. Johnston	74	1863	Marion	4
1847	Edward Bates	53	1864	Ben Levi	5
1848	Concordia	28	1864	Sultana	1,647
1849	Virginia	14	1865	Nimrod	5
1849	Cutter	6	1865	R. I. Lockwood	11
1849	Louisiana	150	1865	W. R. Carter	18
1850	St. Joseph	13	1865	Gen'l Lytle	12
1850	Anglo Norman	100	1866	Missouri	7
1850	Kate Fleming	9	1866	Phantom	11
1850	Knoxville	19	1866	Cumberland	8
1851	Oregon	18	1866	Harry Dean	5
1852	Pocahontas	8	1867	Eclipse	22
1852	Thomas Stone	40	1868	Magnolia	31
1852	Glenco	60	1870	City of Memphis	11
1852	Saluda	27	1870	David White	5
1852	Franklin	20	1870	Silver Spray	36
1853	Bee	3	1870	Maggie Hays	13
1854	Kate Kinney	15	1870	Iberville	7
1854	Timore	19	1871	Judge Wheeler	9
1854	Reindeer	40	1871	W. R. Arthur	60
1855	Lexington	30	1871	Rob Roy	1
1855	Lancaster	5	1871	Raven	7
1855	Heroine	3	1871	New State	1
1856	Metropolis	14			

The above table was carefully revised by Capts. James McCord and S. L. Fisher, of St. Louis, in 1871, and as they were both practicable boatmen of large experience and extensive observation, it is safe to assume it embraces about all the casualties during the first fifty years, arising from explosions of steam boilers.

While the number is large, and the aggregate of lives lost is startling, when the circumstances are considered it will seem less surprising. In another chapter of this work the causes for the failure of steam transportation to prove remunerative to owners is considerated, in which the losses from explosions of boilers is included.

With the exception of the Sultana, they all seem to have occurred from natural causes, either from bad material, carelessness, or ignorance on the part of engineers.

The unprecedented loss of life on the Sultana arose from there being almost an unprecedented number of persons on board. They were soldiers returning from the enemy's country, and it was charged that explosives of some kind had been secreted in the coal or in some other way contributed to the terrible result, but it was not proven.

CHAPTER LXI.

TERRIFIC EXPLOSION AND LOSS OF LIFE ON BOARD THE STEAM-BOAT WASHINGTON.

THE following account of steamboat casualties are quoted from "Floyd's Steamboat Directory," an old work published in 1856, which contained illustrations of all these explosions, etc., and many others which are omitted, but are of no less importance or interest to those individuals who may notice their absence.

They simply illustrate the horrible results of such accidents that were once so common on our waters, and which are still occasionally occurring, although much less frequently than formerly, not alone from the fact that the number of boats is largely reduced, but the appliances for avoiding and overcoming these accidents are much more effectual.

The illustrations are also omitted, as of course they are purely the production of the imagination of the writer. While the description is sometimes over-wrought, it is generally from the observation of some one present, and is often far more terrible and revolting than can be described.

To those who have been compelled to witness such scenes, the sooner they are blotted from memory the better.

In a previous chapter in this work is an imperfect list of the principal casualties of this character, covering a period of fifty years of the earlier experience of steam navigation.

This is deemed sufficient, with the quotations which follow, to secure the objects of the work, without attempting to chronicle in detail even the names or the experience of other boats.

"This deplorable accident took place on the Ohio River on the 9th day of June, 1816. The Washington was the largest and finest boat which had hitherto floated on any Western stream. Her commander, Capt. Shreve, was skilled and experienced in all the duties of his calling; her machinery was all presumed to be in the best possible order, and no human foresight could have anticipated the fatal event. The boat left Pittsburgh, on Monday, June 7, and on the afternoon of the following day came safely to anchor off Point Hamar, where she remained until Wednesday morning. The fires were now kindled, and other preparations made for continuing the voyage down the Ohio, but a difficulty occurred in getting the boat into a proper position to start the machinery. While laboring to effect this object — the boat having in the meantime been carried by the force of the current near the Virginia shore — it became necessary to throw out a kedge anchor at the stern. Soon after all hands were summoned aft to haul in the kedge, and while they were collected on the quarter for that purpose, by a singular and most unfortunate chance, the end of the cylinder nearest the stern was blown off, and a column of scalding water was thrown among the crowd, inflicting the most frightful injuries on nearly all of the boat's crew, and killing a number on the spot. The cry of consternation and anguish which then arose might have been heard for miles. The captain, mate and several others were thrown overboard ; but all of these, with the exception of one man, were afterward rescued from the water, but were found to be more or less injured, either by the fragments of the cylinder or the scalding water.

The inhabitants of the neighboring town, now called Harmar, were universally alarmed by the sound of the explosion, which appeared to shake the solid earth to a considerable distance. A number of physicians and many other citizens crowded into the boat to ascertain the extent of the calamity, but no language can describe the scene of misery and torture which then presented itself to the view of the spectators. The deck was strewn with mangled and writhing human beings, uttering screams and groans of intense suffering. Some, more fortunate than their companions, lay still in the embrace of death. Among the wounded, six or eight, under the influence of their maddening torments, had torn off their clothes, to which the skin of their limbs or bodies adhered; the eyes of others had been put out, and their faces were changed to an undistinguishable mass of flesh by the scalding water. But the greatest sufferers, apparently, were those who had been internally injured by inhaling the scalding steam, the effect of which on the lungs is agonizing beyond all the powers of imagination to conceive. The whole scene was too horrible for description, and it made an impression on the minds of those who witnessed it which could never be obliterated.

The cause of the explosion was a disarrangement of the safety valve, which had become immovable in consequence of the accidental slipping of the weight to the extremity of the lever.

Mr. Williams, of Kentucky, while lying in the cabin of the Washington, in his last moments, offered one of the cabin-boys all his money if he would knock him on the head to put a speedy end to his misery. The boy who received this offer, and who relates the incident, is now Captain Hiram Burch, of Marietta, Ohio.

Joseph ———, one of the hands, was missing; he is supposed to have been blown overboard, and carried down by the current. Several of the wounded died a short time afterwards in consequence of their injuries. At a meeting of the citizens of Marietta, a committee was appointed to provide for the sufferers, and to make arrangements for the burial of the dead.

This first steamboat accident in the West produced a great excitement among the inhabitants of that region, and occasioned, for some time, a strong prejudice against steamboat travel, the people being oblivious of the fact, that when the water conveyances was confined to barges and keel-boats, there was more real danger and more actual loss of life than may be classed among the incidents of steamboat navigation.

"On the 4th of May, 1817, while the steamboat Constitution was ascending the Mississippi River, and when she was off Point Coupee, the boiler exploded, making the whole front part of the cabin a perfect wreck, and killing and wounding thirty persons, eleven of whom perished instantly. As soon as the terrific report of the explosion was heard on board, numbers of the excited passengers threw themselves into the rapid current, and many were drowned or wafted down the stream before assistance could reach them. The shrieks of the wounded and dying were reverberated from the distant shores, and many a ghastly and heart-sickening spectacle presented itself on the deck of the ill-fated vessel. One man had been completely submerged in the boiling liquid which inundated the cabin, and in his removal to the deck, the skin had separated from the entire surface of his body. The unfortunate wretch was literally boiled alive, yet although his flesh parted from his bones, and his agonies were most intense, he survived and retained consciousness for several hours. Another passenger was found lying aft of the wheel with an arm and a leg blown off, and as no surgical aid could be rendered him, death from loss of blood soon ended his sufferings.

The Constitution, formerly called the Oliver Evans, was built at Pittsburgh only a short time before this fatal explosion. At that period she was one of the finest boats on the river."

SINKING OF THE STEAMER TENNESSEE.

"About ten o'clock on a dark night, in the midst of a tremendous snow storm, on the 8th of February, 1823, when the
steamer Tennessee, under a full pressure of steam, was ploughing her way up the turbulent Mississippi River near Natchez,
she struck a snag, and immediately commenced filling with
water. The Tennessee was crowded with passengers, and the
confusion and excitement were great among them all. The
deck passengers had retired to bed. Most of those in the
cabin were spending a cheerful evening together, in the
enjoyment of social intercourse. The shock was great,
and called every one instantly to the deck. Some supposed the boat had run into the bank, and would bound off
again without injury. But the fatal truth was soon known,
and in the confusion many leaped overboard. Capt. Campbell gave orders instantly to stop the leak, but the pilot, who
had been down to examine the damage, with difficulty escaped
from the hold, in consequence of the water so rapidly rushing
in. A hole as large as a common door was torn in the hulk,
and the truth was soon told — the Tennessee was going down.
The shrieks of the women were heartrending at this awful
news. The night was dark, and the wind howling around in
its fury made the scene doubly terrible. Every one inquired
of his neighbor what was to be done, and every one was anxious to provide for his own safety. The yawl and long boat
were lowered, and into it the passengers, nearly two hundred
in number, crowded, till it was on the eve of sinking. Those
in the boat shoved off, and with one oar could not reach the
shore in time to return to assist those left behind. Some,
finding there was no chance in the long boat, jumped into the
river and swam ashore; others pulled off the cabin doors and
floated on them; some got among the fire wood, and were
lost by slipping through and being covered by it; some clung
to parts of the boat, which floated off with them. Mr. Keiser
got upon the carpenter's bench, and a Mr. A. Logan, who had
fallen into the water and sunk nearly to the bottom, on coming up fortunately caught hold of the way-plank, which formed
a raft, and on which he floated down stream. Mr. Keiser
soon came up with him, and leaving the work bench joined
him on his raft. They floated in company for about eight
miles, when, seeing a light on shore, they called for aid, and
were taken up by a young man named Gibson, who conveyed
them to the house of Mr. Randolph, where they were kindly

treated. One man swam with his hat and cloak on, until he reached the willows, when he deliberately relieved himself from the burden of those outside garments, leaving them on a tree till next morning, and swimming safely to shore. Another passenger swam out with a small bag in his mouth, containing $3,000 in gold, which proved of essential service to him; for on getting off a plank, and throwing his arm over it, he found the weight of his specie, which he then carried in his hand, admirably calculated to preserve his equilibrium. One man was sick in his berth, and being told of his danger, observed that he was too weak to save himself from drowning, and appeared reluctant to get up; but on being reminded that his father was on board, and required his assistance, he sprang from his bed, and not only saved his own life, but was instrumental in saving others. A young married lady, when her husband was about recklessly to throw himself into the Mississippi, caught hold of him, and by her presence of mind took off some shutters and made a raft, upon which they both floated down the river, and were picked up by a skiff.

The boat floated down the river a short distance and lodged near some willows, upon which many of the deck passengers clung until daylight, when they were relieved from their perilous situation.

Scarcely any property was saved from the wreck; a few trunks and other light things floated off, and were picked up. Some were pilfered by a mean wretch living in the neighborhood, named Charles Goodwin, others were preserved and afterwards reclaimed by the owners. The survivors speak in the highest praise of Mrs. Blanton, formerly of Kentucky, who in the absence of her husband, Mr. William Blanton, made every exertion for the comfort of the sufferers. By this disaster there were no less than sixty lives lost; the names of many will never be known.

This was one of the early disasters, and was the theme of conversation for months after the fatal calamity. Indeed, people, for a long time after this accident, were almost afraid to go on a steamboat; but it was soon forgotten in the narratives of the more heart-rendering disasters that followed after, in rapid succession."

EXPLOSION AND BURNING OF THE STEAMBOAT TECHE ON THE MISSISSIPPI RIVER, MAY 5TH, 1825.

" The steamboat Teche left Natchez on the evening of May 4th, 1825, heavily laden with cotton, and carrying about seventy passengers, many of whom came on board at the moment of departure and were unknown to each other. Her course was down the river, and she proceeded about ten miles, when the night became so excessively dark and hazy that her commander, Capt. Campbell, deemed it unsafe to proceed further, and concluded to come to anchor. At two o'clock on the following morning, May 5th, the anchor was weighed, and the steam having previously been raised, the boat had just begun to pursue her voyage, when the passengers, many of whom had been sleeping in their berths, were startled by a shock which seemed sufficient to separate every plank and timber in the vessel, accompanied by a report which sounded like a discharge of a whole broadside of the heaviest artillery. Every light on board was immediately extinguished, either by the escape of steam or the concussion of the air. As the day had not yet dawned, an impenetrable darkness now hung over the scene of the disaster, the extent of which could only be imagined by the affrighted and horrified crowd collected on the deck; but at that moment an appalling danger and still more dreadful uncertainty, was heard a cry that the boat was on fire! Then followed a scene of indescribable confusion; the passengers in the very insanity of terror, were rushing hither and thither, through the dense and ominous gloom, and many anticipated their doom in their erring endeavor to avoid it.

The number of lives lost by this accident could never be ascertained. Several persons were instantly killed by the explosion, and others were so badly injured by scalding, or otherwise, that they died soon afterwards. It is thought that not less than twenty or thirty were drowned."

EXPLOSION OF THE STEAMBOAT GRAMPUS, ON THE MISSISSIPPI, AUGUST 12, 1828.

The Grampus was engaged in towing three brigs and a sloop up to New Orleans, and was about nine miles from that city, when the explosion took place. This accident was one of the most remarkable in the whole catalogue of steamboat disasters, on account of the extensive wreck which was made of the machinery. The boat had six boilers, all of which were blown to minute fragments. The same complete destruction was made of the flues, and various other parts of the steam apparatus; and the boat itself was (as an eye-witness reports), "torn to pieces."

The Captain (Morrison) and Mr. Wederstrand, a passenger, were sitting by the wheel at the time of the explosion; both were blown to a part of the forward deck fifty feet distant, where they were afterwards found, very much bruised, among a mass of ruins. The pilot at the wheel was precipitated into the water and drowned. Another pilot, who was walking the deck off of the wheel, had a leg broken, and received other injuries, which caused his death. The brig in tow on the larboard side of the Grampus had both topmasts cut away by the fragments of the machinery, and her standing rigging was much damaged. A piece of the pipe fell across this brig's tiller, carried it away, and slightly injured the man at the helm. The brig on the other side of the steamer had her bottom perforated by a piece of the boiler. The other vessels, being astern, escaped without any damage.

The cause of this accident requires particular notice. It appears, from a statement of a passenger, that the chief engineer had "turned in," leaving his assistant in charge of the engine. This assistant, as it is supposed, went to sleep at his post, after partially shutting off the water. The consequence was a deficiency of water in the boilers ; and the assistant engineer, on waking, when he discovered that the boilers were nearly exhausted, ignorantly, or imprudently, put the force pumps in operation to furnish a supply. At this time the iron must have acquired a white heat, and the contact of the water produced such an excess of steam, that the explosion naturally followed.

Nine were killed on the spot, or died soon afterwards, in consequence of their injuries. Four others were wounded.

EXPLOSION OF THE HELEN M'GREGOR, AT MEMPHIS, TENNESSEE, FEBRUARY 24, 1830.

The steamboat Helen McGregor, Capt. Tyson, on her way from New Orleans to Louisville, stopped at Memphis, on Wednesday morning, February 24, 1830. She had been lying at the wharf about thirty minutes, when one or more of her boilers exploded, with the usual destructive and melancholy effects. The loss of life by this accident was at that time unprecedented in the records of steam navigation. In the bustle incident to the landing and receiving of passengers, a part of the deck near the boilers was crowded with people, all of whom were either killed instantaneously or more or less injured. No person in the cabin was hurt. The number of those who perished at the moment of the explosion is variously estimated at from thirty to sixty. As many of them were were strangers whose homes were far distant, and whose bodies were never recovered from the water, into which they were projected, it is very plain that an accurate account of the victims is not to be expected.

EXPLOSION OF THE STEAMBOAT ROB ROY ON THE MISSISSIPPI JUNE 9, 1836.

"The Rob Roy was on her route from New Orleans to Louisville, and was under way at 8 o'clock p. m. June 9, 1836, near the town of Columbia, Arkansas, when the fatal catastrophe we are about to record took place. The engine was stopped for the purpose of oiling some part of the machinery; and although this necessary operation did not occupy more than two minutes, the accumulation of steam was sufficient to cause an explosion. As soon as the accident occurred, preparations were made to run the boat ashore, which was happily reached within a few minutes. By this judicious measure many lives were undoubtedly saved. None were lost by drowning, and the only victims and sufferers were those who were killed or wounded at the moment of the explosion."

TERRIFIC EXPLOSION OF THE STEAMBOAT BEN FRANKLIN, AT MOBILE, ALABAMA, MARCH 13, 1836.

The steamboat Ben Franklin, on the day of this awful occurrence, was backing out from her wharf at Mobile, in order to make her regular trip to Montgomery. Scarcely had she disengaged herself from the wharf when the explosion took place, producing a concussion which seemed to shake the whole city to its foundations. The entire population of Mobile, alarmed by the terrific detonation was drawn to the spot to witness a spectacle which must have harrowed every soul with astonishment and horror. This fine boat, which had on that very morning floated so gallantly on the bosom of the lake, was now a shattered wreck, while numbers of her passengers and crew were lying on the decks, either motionless and mutilated corpses, or agonized sufferers panting and struggling in the grasp of death. Many others had been hurled overboard at the moment of the explosion, and such were the number of drowning people who called for assistance, that the crowd of sympathizing spectators were distracted and irresolute, not knowing where or how to begin the work of rescue. Many — how many, it is impossible to say — perished in the turbid waters before any human succor could reach them.

Apart from the loss of life, which at that time was unexampled, the destruction produced by this accident was very extensive. The boiler-deck, the boilers, the chimneys, and

other parts of the machinery, besides much of the lading, were
blown overboard and scattered into fragments over the wharf
and the surface of the river. Mr. Isaac Williams, a passenger,
was blown at least one hundred and fifty yards from the
boat.

The cause of this accident is believed to have been a deficiency of water in the boiler. The boat was injured to that
degree that repairs were out of the question, and she was never
afterwards brought into service."

EXPLOSION OF THE DUBUQUE, AUGUST 15, 1837.

"This distressing accident, by which sixteen persons were
instantly killed, and several others were badly scalded, took
place on the Mississippi, while the boat was on her voyage
from St. Louis to Galena. The locality of the dreadful event
was off Muscatine Bar, eight miles below Bloomington. The
Dubuque was running under a moderate pressure of steam at
the time, when the flue of the larboard boiler, probably on account of some defect in the material or workmanship, collapsed, throwing a torrent of scalding water over the deck.
The pilot immediately steered for the shore and effected a
landing.

When the consternation and dismay occasioned by the explosion had in some measure subsided, Captain Smoker, the
commander of the Dubuque, and such of his crew as were not
disabled by this accident, made their way with considerable
difficulty through the ruins to the afterpart of the boiler-deck,
when it was found that the whole of the freight and every
other article which had been there deposited, was cleared off
and wafted far away into the water. The unfortunate deck
passengers, together with the cooks and several of the crew,
were severely scalded either by the hot water or the escaped
steam. Many of these wretched people in their agony fled to
the shore uttering the most appalling shrieks, and tearing off
their clothes, which in some cases brought away the skin and
even the flesh with them. Humanity shudders at the recollection of the scene. It was several hours before any of them
died ; nor could medical relief be obtained until a boat, which
had been dispatched from Bloomington, returned with several
physicians who resided at that place. At 10 o'clock p. m.,
eight hours after the explosion, the steamboat Adventure,
Captain Van Houten, came up with the wreck and took it in
tow as far as Bloomington."

EXPLOSION AND BURNING OF THE LIONESS, ON RED RIVER, MAY 19, 1833.

"The destruction of the Lioness was caused by the explosion of several barrels of gunpowder which were stowed among other freight in the hold. The accident, therefore, cannot be attributed to any defect in the steam apparatus or to any mismanagement thereof. The catastrophe took place at an early hour on a calm and beautiful Sabbath morning in spring. Many of the passengers had not left their berths. Among those that had embarked in the Lioness at New Orleans were the Hon. Josiah S. Johnson, of the United States Senate, and several other distinguished citizens of Louisiana. The boat was commanded by Captain William L. Crockerell; her place of destination was Nachitoches, on Red River. She had accomplished a considerable part of the voyage and reached the mouth of a small stream called Ragolet Bon Dieu, when, on the morning referred to above, the mate and several of the crew were arranging some part of the cargo in the hold, and as the place was dark they found it necessary to use a lighted candle. It is conjectured that a spark from the candle in some way found access to one of the kegs of powder; but as every person who had been at work in the hold was killed by the explosion, the mode in which the powder became ignited could never be ascertained. It is reported that some articles of a very combustible nature, such as crates containing a quantity of dry straw and several casks of oil, were stowed in dangerous proximity to the powder. It was stated by some of the passengers that three distinct explosions were heard. The fore-cabin, the boiler-deck and the hold immediately under them, were literally torn to pieces and the fragments were scattered over the surrounding waters to a surprising distance. A part of the hurricane deck and a portion or the ladies' cabin were likewise detached, and this proved to be a favorable circumstance, as the hull almost immediately sunk and in all likelihood every female on board and many other persons would have been drowned had they not been sustained on the detached pieces of the wreck just spoken of. As it was, all the women were saved and the loss of life, though terrible enough, indeed, was less than might have been expected in view of all the circumstances of the disaster. The hull of the vessel was on fire almost from stem to stern at the time she went down. All of the crew and passengers who survived saved themselves by swimming or were floated to the shore on fragments of the wreck."

EXPLOSION OF THE BLACK HAWK, DECEMBER 27, 1837.

" This awful calamity, which hurried more than fifty human beings into eternity, occurred on a cold, wintry night, while the Black Hawk was about to ascend the Red River, on her passage from Natchez to Natchitoches.   The boat had a full load of passengers and freight, including ninety thousand dollars in specie belonging to the United States Government. She had just reached the mouth of the Red River, the boiler exploded, blowing off all of the upper works forward of the wheels.   The pilot and engineer were instantly killed.

The number of passengers on board is stated to have been about one hundred, nearly half of whom were women and children.   No estimate of the number killed was ever published, but it appears from the best accounts we have that a majority of the passengers and crew perished.   A large portion of the passengers on Western steamboats are persons from distant parts of the country, or emigrants, perhaps, from the old world, whose journeyings are unknown to their friends, and whose fate often excites inquiry.   When such persons are the victims of a steamboat calamity, their names and frequently their numbers, are beyond all powers of research.   So it appears to have been in the case now under consideration. Instead of a list of the slain, we are furnished only with a catalogue of the survivors, and these, alas, appear to have been merely a forlorn remnant."

EXPLOSION OF THE MOSELLE, NEAR CINCINNATI, OHIO, APRIL 25, 1838.

" We are now to relate the particulars of an event which seemed for a time to shroud the whole country in mourning ; an event which is still believed to be almost without parallel in the annals of steamboat calamities.   The Moselle was regarded as the very paragon of Western steamboats; she was perfect in form and construction, elegant and superb in all her equipments, and enjoyed a reputation for speed which admitted of no rivalship.   Her commander and proprietor, Capt. Perrin, was a young gentleman of great ambition and enterprise, who prided himself, above all things, in that celebrity which his boat had acquired, and who resolved to maintain, at all hazards, the character of the Moselle as " the swiftest steamboat in America."   This character she unquestionably deserved; for her " quick trips " were without competition at that time, and are rarely equaled at the present day.   To

give two examples — her first voyage from Portsmouth to
Cincinnati, a distance of one hundred and ten miles, was made
in seven hours and fifty-five minutes ; and her last trip, from
St. Louis to Cincinnati, seven hundred and fifty miles, was
performed in two days and sixteen hours; the quickest trip,
by several hours, that had ever been made between the two
places.

On the afternoon of April 25, 1838, between four and five
o'clock, the Moselle left the landing at Cincinnati, bound for
St. Louis with an unusually large number of passengers, supposed to be not less than two hundred and eighty ; or according to some accounts, three hundred. It was a pleasant
afternoon, and all on board probably anticipated a delightful
voyage. Passengers continued to crowd in up to the moment
of departure, for the superior accommodations of this steamer,
and her renown as the finest and swiftest boat on the river,
were great attractions for the traveling public, with whom
safety is too often but a secondary consideration. The Moselle proceeded about a mile up the river to take on board
some German immigrants. At this time, it was observed by an
experienced engineer on board that the steam had been raised
to an unusual height; and when the boat stopped for the purpose just mentioned, it was reported that one man, who was
apprehensive of danger, went ashore, after protesting against
the injudicious management of the steam apparatus. When
the object for which the Moselle had landed was accomplished,
the bow of the boat was shoved from the shore, and at that
instant the explosion took place. The whole of the vessel
forward of the wheels was blown to splinters ; every timber
(as an eye witness declares), " appeared to be twisted, as trees
sometimes are when struck by lightning." As soon as the
accident occurred, the boat floated down the stream for about
one hundred yards, where she sunk, leaving the upper part
of the cabin out of the water, and the baggage, together with
struggling human beings, floating on the surface of the river.

It was remarkable that the force of the explosion was unprecedented in the history of steam ; its effect was like that
of a mine of gunpowder. All the boilers, four in number,
burst simultaneously; the deck was blown into the air, and
the human beings who crowded it were doomed to instant destruction. Fragments of the boiler and of human bodies were
thrown both to the Kentucky and Ohio shores, although the
distance to the former was a quarter of a mile. Captain Perrin, master of the Moselle, at the time of the accident was
standing on the deck above the boiler, in conversation with

another person. He was thrown to a considerable height on the steep embankment of the river and killed, while his companion was merely prostrated on the deck, and escaped without injury. Another person was blown to the distance of a hundred yards, with such force according to the report of a reliable witness, that a part of his body penetrated the roof of a house. Some of the passengers who were in the after part of the boat, and who were uninjured by the explosion, jumped overboard. An eye-witness says that he saw sixty or seventy in the water at one time, of whom not a dozen reached the shore.

It happened, unfortunately, that the larger number of passengers were collected on the upper deck, to which the balmy air and delicious weather seemed to invite them in order to expose them to more certain destruction. It was understood, too, that the captain of the ill-fated steamer had expressed his determination to outstrip an opposition boat which had just started; the people on shore were cheering the Moselle in anticipation of her success in the race, and the passengers and crew on the upper deck responded to these acclamations, which were soon changed to sounds of mourning and distress.

Intelligence of the awful calamity spread rapidly through the city; thousands rushed to the spot, and the most benevolent aid was promptly extended to the suffers, or, as we should rather say, to such as were within reach of human assistance, for the majority had perished. A gentleman who was among those who hastened to the wreck, declares that he witnessed a scene so sad and distressing that no language can depict it with fidelity. On the shore lay twenty or thirty mangled and bleeding corpses, while many persons were engaged in dragging others of the dead or wounded from the wreck of water. But, says the same witness, the survivors presented the most touching objects of distress, as their mental anguish seemed more insupportable than the most intense bodily suffering. Death had torn asunder the most tender ties; but the rupture had been so sudden and violent that none knew certainly who had been taken or who had been spared. Fathers were distractedly inquiring for children, children for parents, husbands and wives for each other. One man had saved a son, but lost a wife and five children. A father, partially demented by grief, lay with a wounded child on one side, his dead daughter on the other, and his expiring wife at his feet. One gentleman sought his wife and children, who were as eagerly seeking him in the same crowd. They met and were re-united.

A female deck passenger who had been saved seemed inconsolable for the loss of her relatives. Her constant exclamations were " Oh, my father! my mother! my sisters!" A little boy about five years old, whose head was much bruised, appeared to be regardless of his wounds, and cried continually for a lost father; while another lad, a little older, was weeping for his whole family.

One venerable looking man wept for the loss of wife and five children. Another was bereft of his whole family, consisting of nine persons. A touching display of maternal affection was evinced by a lady, who, on being brought to the shore, clasped her hands and exclaimed "Thank God, I am safe," but instantly recollecting herself, she ejaculated in a voice of piercing agony, " where is my child?" The infant, which had also been saved, was brought to her and she fainted at sight of it.

Many of the passengers who entered the boat at Cincinnati had not registered their names, but the lowest estimated number of persons on board was two hundred and eighty; of these, eighty-one were known to be killed, fifty-five were missing, and thirteen badly wounded.

The Moselle was built at Cincinnati and she reflected great credit on the mechanical genius of that city, as she was truly a superior boat, and, under more favorable auspices, might have been the pride of the waters for many years. She was quite a new boat, having been begun on the 1st of December, 1838, and finished on the 31st of March, less than one month before the time of her destruction.

BURNING OF THE BEN SHERROD, MAY 8, 1837.

On the 8th of May, 1837, the large Louisville and New Orleans packet, the Ben Sherrod, caught fire on her upward trip, while she was engaged in an exciting race with the steamer Prairie. It was one o'clock at night, and the boat was about fourteen miles above Fort Adams, ploughing her way up the Mississippi with great velocity. The Prairie was just ahead of her, in sight, and the crew of the Ben Sherrod were determined, if possible, to go by her. The firemen were shoving in the pine knots, and sprinkling rosin over the coal, and doing their best to raise more steam. They had a barrel of whisky before them, from which they drank often and freely until they were beastly drunk. The boilers became so hot that they set fire to the sixty cords of wood on board, and the Ben Sherrod was soon completely enveloped in flames. The passengers, three hundred in number, were sound asleep, not thinking of the awful doom that awaited them. When the deck hands discovered the fire, they basely left their posts and ran for the yawl, without giving the alarm to the passengers. Capt. Castleman attempted for a time to allay the excitement and confusion by telling them that the fire was extinguished. Twice he forbade the lowering of the yawl which was attempted. The shrieks of nearly three hundred and fifty persons now on board, rose wild and dreadful, which might have been heard at a distance of several miles. The cry was " To the shore! to the shore!" and the boat made for the starboard shore, but did not gain it, as the wheel ropes soon burnt. The steam was not let off and the boat kept on up the river. The scene of horror now beggared all description. The yawl, which had been filled with the crew, had sunk, drowning nearly all who were in it; and the passengers had no other alternative than to jump overboard, without taking time even to dress. There were ten ladies who all went overboard without uttering a single scream; some drowned instantly, and others clung to planks; two of the number were all that were saved. Several passengers were burnt alive. One man by the name of Ray, from Louisville, Kentucky, jumped overboard, and hung to a rope at the bow of the boat, until rescued by the yawl of the steamer Columbus, which arrived at the scene half an hour after the boat took fire. Mr. Ray's face and arms were much burnt while clinging to the boat. He lost twenty thousand dollars in specie. The steamer Alton arrived half an hour after the Columbus, but from the carelessness or indiscretion of those on her, was the means of drowning many persons who were floating on the water. She came down under full headway among the exhausted sufferers, who were too weak to make any further exertion, and by the commotion occasioned by her wheels drowned a large number. A gentleman by the name of Hamilton, from Limestone county, Alabama, was floating on a barrel, and sustaining also a lady, when the Alton came up, washing them both under. The lady was drowned, but Mr. Hamilton came up and floated down the river fifteen miles, when he was rescued by the steamer Statesman. Mr. McDowell sustained himself some time against the current, so that he floated only two miles down the river, and then swam ashore. His wife, who was floating on a plank, was drowned by the steamer Alton. Mr. Rundell floated down the river ten miles, and was taken up by a flat-boat at the mouth of Buffalo creek; he saved his money in his pantaloons' pocket.

Mr. McDowell lost his wife, son, and a lady named Miss Frances Few, who was under his protection; also a negro servant. Of those who escaped we have seen and conversed with James P. Wilkinson, Esq., Mr. Stanfield, of Richmond, Virginia, and Daniel Marshall, Esq., of Moscow, Indiana. The scene, as described by them, was truly heartrending; while some were confined to their berths and consumed by the flames, others plunged into the river to find watery graves. One lady, who attached herself to Mr. Marshall, had clung to him while they floated four or five miles, was at length drowned by the waves of the Alton, after imploring the boat's crew for assistance and mercy. Mr. Marshall was supported by a flour barrel. Only two ladies out of ten who were on board were saved; one of these was Mrs. Castleman, the captain's wife; the other Mrs. Smith, of New Orleans.

It was said by some of the passengers, that the captain of the Alton did not hear the cries of those who implored him for assistance as he passed, it being midnight; but there can be no excuse for the monster who commanded the Prairie, for leaving a boat in flames without turning around and affording the sufferers relief. He reported her on fire at Natchez and Vicksburg.

EIGHT DIFFERENT REPORTS.

A man in a canoe near the scene of disaster refused to save any who were floating in the water, unless they promised to pay him handsomely for his services. So rapid were the flames that not even the register of the boat was saved; hence it was impossible to get a full list of the lost. One of the officers of the boat informed us, that out of seventy-eight passengers not more than six were saved. This was one of the most serious calamities that ever occurred on the Mississippi River, there being at least one hundred and seventy families deprived by it of some dear and beloved member, and over two hundred souls being hurried by it out of time into eternity, with scarce a moment's warning. During the burning of the Ben Sherrod eight different explosions occurred; first, barrels of whisky, brandy, etc.; then the boilers blew up with a fearful explosion, and lastly, forty barrels of gunpowder exploded, which made a noise that was heard many miles distant, scattering fragments of the wreck in all directions, and producing the grandest sight ever seen. Immediately after, the wreck sunk out of sight just above Fort Adams. A large quantity of specie, which was on its way to the Tennessee banks, was lost. One gentleman placed his pocket-book, containing thirty-eight thousand dollars, under his pillow, and though he managed to escape he lost all his money.   One scene was distressing in the extreme; a young and beautiful lady, whose name was Mary Ann Walker, on hearing the cry of fire, rushed out of the ladies' cabin in her loose night clothes in search of her husband, at the same time holding her infant to her bosom ; in her endeavors to get forward, her dress caught fire, and was torn from her back to save her life.   After witnessing her husband fall into the flames in the forward part of the boat, and unable to reach him, she rushed with her child into the water, seized a plank, and was carried by the current within forty yards of the Columbus, but just as she seized a rope thrown to her, both. mother and child sank to rise no more.   One young man, who had reached the hurricane deck in safety, hearing the cries of his sister, rushed back to the cabin, clasped her in his arms, and both were burnt to death.   One of the clerks, one of the pilots, and the mate were burnt to death.   All the chambermaids and women employed on the boat perished; only two negroes escaped out of thirty-five that were on the boat."

BURNING OF THE BRANDYWINE, APRIL 9, 1832.

"The steamboat Brandywine, Captain Hamilton, left New Orleans on the evening of April 3d, 1832.   Her place of destination was Louisville, Kentucky.   Her voyage was prosperous until the evening of the 9th, at seven o'clock.   When the boat was about thirty miles above Memphis, she was discovered to be on fire.   Among the lading it appears there was a number of carriage wheels wrapped in straw, as articles of that kind are usually put up for transportation on the river. These wheels were piled on the boiler deck near the officer's rooms and under the hurricane roof.   It was supposed that the fire was communicated from the furnaces to the highly combustible envelope of these wheels ; the wind blew hard at the time and the sparks were ascending very rapidly through the apertures in the boiler-deck which were occupied by the chimneys, these not being closely fitted to the wood-work.   It appears too, that the Brandywine was racing with the steamboat Hudson at the time the fire broke out, and, that for the purpose of producing more intense heat and thus accelerating the boat's speed, a large quantity of rosin had been thrown into the furnaces.   This fatal ruse was resorted to because the Brandywine had been compelled to stop and make some repairs, and the Hudson in the meantime had gained considerable headway.   Soon after the Brandywine had resumed her course, the pilot who was steering discovered that the straw covering of the carriage wheels was on fire.   Strenuous efforts were made to extinguish the flames and to throw the burning articles overboard, but it was found that their removal allowed the wind to have free access to the ignited mass, from which cause, as Captain Hamilton reports, the fire began to spread with almost incredible rapidity, and in less than five minutes from the time the alarm was first given the whole boat was wrapped in a bright sheet of flame.

The state of affairs on board may be imagined when it is understood that the Brandywine was crowded with passengers, and the only means of escape from a death of fiery torture which presented itself was the yawl, in which scarcely a tenth part of the affrighted people could be conveyed to the shore at a single trip.   But even the faint hope of deliverance which this single mode of escape offered them, soon terminated in disappointment and despair.   In the attempt to launch the boat it was upset and sunk.   The heat and smoke had now become so insupportable that not less than one hundred persons, made desperate by fear and suffering, threw themselves into the water.

75 SAVED OUT OF 230 PASSENGERS.

The number of passengers on board, according to some reports, was not less than two hundred and thirty ; of these only about seventy-five were saved ; the rest were either drowned or burned to death.   Among those who perished were nine women and about an equal number of children.

As soon as all hopes of extinguishing the flames was abandoned, an attempt was made to run the boat on shore, but she struck on a sand-bar in nine feet of water, and about a quarter of a mile from the nearest bank of the river, where she remained immovable until she was burned to the water's edge. Those passengers and other persons belonging to the boat who had the good fortune to escape, saved themselves by swimming or floating on detached pieces of timber to the nearest island.   It is reported to the honor of Captain Hamilton and his crew, that they remained on the burning boat to the last possible moment, exerting themselves to the utmost to save the lives which had been entrusted to their charge."

EXPLOSION OF THE ORONOKO, APRIL 21, 1838.

" On Saturday morning, at six o'clock, April 21st, 1838, the steamboat Oronoko, Capt. John Crawford, came to anchor in the Mississippi, opposite Princeton, one hundred miles above Vicksburg, where she stopped for the purpose of sending her yawl ashore to receive some passengers. In less than five minutes after the machinery ceased moving, a flue collapsed, spreading death and devastation throughout the boat. This accident occurred before the people on board were aroused from their slumbers. The deck passengers were lodged on the lower deck, abaft the engine, where, as is customary in Western steamboats, berths were provided for their accommodation. On this occasion the number of berths were insufficient, as the boat was thronged with emigrants, and mattresses had been spread over the floor for the use of those who could not be lodged in the berths. This apartment between decks was densely crowded with sleeping passengers, when the flue collapsed, as aforesaid, and the steam swept through the whole length of the boat with a force of a tornado, carrying everything before it. Many of the crew, whom duty had called on deck at that early hour, were blown overboard; and as the scalding vapor penetrated every part and recess of the cabin and space between decks the slumbering population of the boat, with scarcely an individual exception, were either killed on the spot or injured in a manner more terrible than death itself. Some of these unfortunates were completely excoriated, some shockingly mangled and torn, while others were cast among masses of ruins, fragments of wood and iron, piled up in inextricable confusion.

The deck was strewn with more than fifty helpless sufferers; the river was all alive with those that had been hurled overboard by the force of the explosion, and those who, frantic with pain and terror, had cast themselves into the water. Some of those who had been scalded swam to the bank, and then in the wildest frenzy, occasioned by intolerable agony, leaped back into the water and were drowned.

Those persons who occupied the cabin generally escaped before the steam reached that department; but one gentleman, Mr. Myers, of Wheeling, while making his way forward with his child in his arms, became alarmed at the scene of confusion and distress which presented itself, and rushing back to the cabin, which was by this time filled with steam, he and the child were both badly burned and died soon afterwards.

Nearly one hundred deck passengers are supposed to have been sacrificed, the names of a great majority of whom were not known, and therefore are not inserted.''

CHAPTER LXII.

BURNING OF THE ERIE.

THIS magnificent steamer, Capt. Titus, commander, was destroyed by fire, on Lake Erie, on the 16th day of August, 1841, by which calamity more than one hundred and seventy persons lost their lives. The following account is given of the origin of this disaster. Among the passengers on board were six painters, who were going to Erie, to paint the steamboat Madison. They had with them several large demijohns filled with spirits of turpentine and varnish, which, known to Capt. Titus, they had placed on the boiler deck, directly over the boilers. One of the firemen who survived the accident, asserts that he discovered the dangerous position of these demijohns, a short time after the boat left the wharf, and removed them to a safer locality; but some person must have replaced them, without being aware of the inflammable nature of the contents. Immediately before the fire broke out a slight explosion was heard; the sound is said to have resembled that which is made by a single puff of a high-pressure steam engine. The supposition is that one of the demijohns bursted, in consequence of its exposure to the heat. The liquid poured out on the boiler deck instantly took fire, and within a few minutes all that part of the boat was in flames. The steamer had recently been painted and varnished, and owing to this circumstance, the whole of the wood-work was very soon in a blaze. There were two hundred persons on board the Erie, and of that number only twenty-seven were saved.

COLLISION OF THE STEAMBOAT MONMOUTH AND THE SHIP TREMONT.

The steamer Monmouth left New Orleans, October 23d, 1837, for Arkansas river, having been chartered by the United States Government to convey about seven hundred Indians, a portion of the emigrant Creek tribe, to the region which had been selected for their future abode. On the night of the 30th, the Monmouth, on her upward trip, had reached that part of the Mississippi called Prophet Island Bend, where she encountered the ship Tremont, which the steamer Warren was then towing down the river. Owing partly to the dense obscurity of the night, but much more to the mismanagement of the officers of the Monmouth, a collision took place between

that vessel and the Tremont, and such was the violence of the
concussion, that the Monmouth instantly sunk.   The unhappy
red men, with their wives and children, were precipitated into
the water; and such was the confusion which prevailed at the
time, such was the number of the drowning people, who probably clung to each other in their struggles for life, that, notwithstanding that the Indians, men, women, and children, are
generally expert swimmers, more than half of the unfortunate
Creeks perished. The captains and crews of the steamers
Warren and Yazoo, by dint of great exertion, succeeded in
saving about three hundred of the poor Indians, the remainder,
four hundred, had become accusing spirits before the tribunal
of a just God, where they whose criminal negligence was the
cause of this calamnity will certainly be held accountable.

The cabin of the Monmouth parted from the hull, and
drifted down the stream, when it broke into two parts, and
emptied its living contents into the river. The stem of the
ship came into contact with the side of the steamer, therefore the former received but little damage, while the latter
was broken up, to that degree that the hull, as previously
stated, almost immediately went to the bottom. The ship
nearly lost her cut-water.

The mishap, as we have hinted before, may be ascribed to
the mismanagement of the officers of the Monmouth. This
boat was running in a part of the river where, by the usages
of the river and the rules adopted for the better regulation of
steam navigation on the Mississippi, she had no right to go,
and where, of course, the descending vessels did not expect to
to meet with any boat coming in an opposite direction. The
only persons attached to the Monmouth who lost their lives
were the bar-keeper and fireman.

It is not without some feeling of indignation that we
mention the circumstance that the drowning of four hundred
Indians, the largest number of human beings ever sacrificed
in a steamboat disaster, attracted but little attention (comparatively speaking) in any part of the country. Even the
journalists and news collectors of that region, on the waters of
which this horrible affair took place, appeared to have regarded the event as of too little importance to deserve any
particular detail; and accordingly the best accounts we have
of the matter merely state the outlines of the story, with
scarcely a word of commiseration for the sufferers, or a single
expression of rebuke for the heartless villains who wantonly
exposed the lives of so many artless and confiding people to
eminent peril or almost certain destruction.

SINKING OF THE SHEPHERDESS.

On the 3d of January, 1844, the whole city of St. Louis was thrown into consternation and feverish excitement by the intelligence that the steamboat Shepherdess had been wrecked in Cahokia Bend, only three miles from the center of that city, and that many lives had been lost. Several boats were immediately dispatched to the scene of the reported disaster, and the worst rumors were unhappily verified. The particulars of the sad event are given below :

The Shepherdess, while ascending the Mississippi River on her way from Cincinnati to St. Louis, and at 11 o'clock, in a dark and stormy night, struck a snag just above the mouth of Cahokia Creek. The concussion was very severe, and it is believed that several planks must have been torn from the bottom of the boat. According to the report of the officers, the number of passengers was between sixty and seventy. Most of those who were in the gentlemen's cabin had retired to their berths; four or five gentlemen in this cabin were sitting up by the stove, as it was cold winter weather. The ladies were generally undressed for the night.

In less than two minutes after the boat struck, the water rose to the lower deck, where most of the passengers in that part of the boat were asleep. The captain, who was on duty, ran to the cabin occupied by the ladies, and assured them that there was no danger; he then returned to the forecastle, and is supposed to have been washed overboard, as nothing was seen or heard of him afterwards. As soon as the shock was felt on board, one of the pilots attempted to descend into the hold for the purpose of examining the leak, but he had scarcely entered when the rush of water drove him back.

About this time shrieks and exclamations of affright and distress arose from the deck below, and several ladies, who hastened to the stern railing, reported that they saw a number of persons struggling in the river. Certain it is that the water rushed in with tremendous rapidity, and before three minutes had elapsed it had risen to the floor of the upper cabin. Some of those persons who were on deck saved themselves by getting into the yawl, which was cut loose and rowed to the shore with a broom. The water rose so rapidly that it soon became necessary for all to seek safety on the hurricane deck. This position was not attained without great difficulty, for the bow had sunk so deep in the water that the only access was via the stern. However, it is believed that all the people from the cabin succeeded in reaching the hurricane roof. In the meanwhile the boat was drifting down the stream, and a few hundred yards below, she struck another snag which rose above the surface. This threw the steamer nearly on her beam ends on the larboard side. Drifting from this snag, she again lurched to starboard. At each lurch several persons were washed off; some of them reached the shore, but many were drowned. A short distance below, just above the first shot tower, the hull struck a bluff bank, which again careened the boat nearly on her side. Here the hull and cabin parted; the former sunk and lodged on a bar above Carondelet, while the cabin floated down to the point of the bar below that place, where it lodged and became stationary.

The steamer Henry Bry was lying at the shot tower above Carondelet, and as the cabin passed, the captain of that vessel being aroused by the cries of the passengers, took his yawl to their rescue. This little boat could only take off a few at a time, but by the strenuous exertions of the captain of the Bry many were saved. This humane gentleman almost sacrificed himself in the work of benevolence, and did not desist until he was covered with a mass of ice, and benumbed to that degree that further effort was impossible. About three o'clock the ferry-boat Icelander came down, and took off all who remained in the detached cabin.

We have thus given a general history of this calamity, but some particular incidents deserve the reader's attention. A young man, Robert Bullock, of Maysville, Ky., was one of the passengers. With heroic devotion to the cause of humanity, he took no measures for his own safety, but directed all his efforts to the preservation of the women and children. When every other male person of mature age had deserted the cabin, he went from state-room to state-room, and wherever he heard a child cry took it out and passed it to the hurricane deck. In this way he saved a number of women and children. His last effort was to rescue Col. Wood's "Ohio Fat Girl," who happened to be on board. Her weight was four hundred and forty pounds, but with the assistance of several persons on the hurricane deck, he succeeded in raising her to that place of security. A short time after, the boat made a lurch, and Bullock was thrown into the water. He swam to the Illinois shore, having previously given his coat to a lady on the wreck who was suffering excessively from the cold. On reaching the land this young hero found two young ladies, who had been put ashore in a skiff and who were nearly frozen. They were about falling asleep, which would have been fatal in such circumstances, when Bullock, aroused them, and with great exertions succeeded in getting them to Cahokia, where they met with the attention which their half frozen condition required. An English family, from the neighborhood of Manchester, ten in number, were all saved. Five of them succeeded in getting to the Illinois shore, four to the Missouri side of the river, and one was taken off the wreck by the ferry-boat. They were all re-united on this boat at Cahokia, at a moment when each party supposed the other to be dead. A spectator of that re-union avers that he never witnessed a more affecting scene.

Mr. Muir, of Virginia, and his brother, were on board, with their mother and nine of their slaves, all of these persons were saved. Levi Craddock, from Davidson Co., Tenn., lost three children; himself, his wife, and two children were saved. Mr. Green, of the same county and State, lost his wife and three children, and was left with two helpless infants, the youngest only three months old. Mr. Snell, formerly of Louisville, Ky., lost a son and daughter. Mr. Wright, of Mecklenburg Co., Va., and two of his children, were drowned. His wife, who survived, was in a state of distraction. The captain, A. Howell, of Covington, Ky., was undoubtedly lost. He was in the act of ringing the bell, when the boat made a lurch, by which the boilers, and part of the engine and the chimneys, were carried overboard, Capt. H. being overwhelmed among the ruins, and he sunk with them. He left a wife and eleven children, the eldest of whom, a son, was with him on the wreck.

The bodies of two children who had perished with cold were brought up to St. Louis. Considering how many children were on board, it is surprising that more of these helpless beings were not lost. The Mayor of St. Louis, who personally assisted in relieving the sufferers, caused all who were saved alive to be taken to the Virginia hotel, where they were amply provided for. Forty persons are believed to have perished in this wreck. The Rev. Mr. Peck, of Illinois, who was on board at the time, makes the estimate much larger. One of the St. Louis papers averred that the number of persons lost was not less than seventy.

Capt. Howell had bought the Shepherdess, and this was her first trip after she became his property.

EXPLOSION OF THE ANGLO-NORMAN.

The new and beautiful steamer Anglo-Norman left New Orleans December 14, 1850, on an experimental trip, having

on board a large " pleasure party," consisting of two hundred
and ten persons. She proceeded in admirable style some distance up the river, satisfying all on board that she was a first-
rate sailer, and giving the promise of a brilliant career in the
future; but having tacked and directed her course back to the
city, all of her boilers exploded at the same moment, shatter-
ing a considerable part of the boat, and killing and wounding
nearly half of the people on board.

Mr. H. A. Kidd, editor of the New Orleans *Crescent*, was
one of the excursionists, and was reported among the killed;
but he lived to give a graphic account of his miraculous escape
from death, which account he somewhat eccentrically entitled
" The Experience of a Blown-up Man." Mr. Kidd says: —

Mr. Bigny, one of the editors of the *Delta* and myself, took
the only two chairs remaining unoccupied on the deck; his chair
having the back towards the pilot house, and mine with its
back to the chimney. It will be seen at once that we had
seated ourselves immediately over the monster boilers of the
boat.

We had been engaged in conversation but a very few minutes, when a jet of hot water, accompanied with steam, was
forced out of the main pipe just aft the chimney, and fell
near us in a considerable shower. I had never noticed anything of the kind before, and thought the occurrence very
extraordinary. Just as I was about remarking this to Mr.
Bigny, I was suddenly lifted high in the air, how high it is
impossible for me to say. I have a distinct recollection of
passing rather irregularly through the air, enveloped, as it
seemed to me, in a dense cloud, through which no object was
discernible. There was a sufficient lapse of time for me to
have a distinct impression on my mind that I must inevitably
be lost. In what position I went into the water, and to what
depth I went, I have not the slightest idea. When I arose to
the surface I wiped the water from my face, and attempted to
obtain a view of things around me, but this I was prevented
from doing by the vapor of steam, which enveloped every
thing as a cloud. This obscuration, however, lasted but a
short time, and when it had passed away, I had a clear conception of my situation. I found myself in possession of my
senses, and my limbs in good working order. I looked
around in every direction, and discovered that I was not far
from the center of the river, and in the neighborhood of some
twenty or thirty people, who seemed to have been thrown into
the water somewhat in a heap. They were sustaining themselves on the surface as best they could, many of them en-

deavoring to get possession of floating pieces of the wreck. I could see nothing of the exploded boat, and was fully satisfied in my mind that she was blown all to pieces, and that all my fellow passengers were lost, except those who, like myself, were struggling in the water. I will do myself the simple justice to say that, from the time at which I had arisen to the surface, I had no apprehension of drowning, though to a more disinterested spectator the chances might have appeared to have been against me. I never felt more buoyant, or swam with greater ease. Still I thought it well enough to appropriate whatever aid was within my reach; so like others, I began a race, which proved to be a tedious one, after a shattered piece of plank. I finally reached it, and putting my hands rather rudely upon it, I got a sousing for my pains. The piece was too small to render me any material service. I abandoned it, and turned in the direction of a steamboat, which I preceived advancing toward us. To keep my face towards the approaching steamer, I found that I had to oppose the strong current of the river. This, together with the coldness of the water, so exhausted my physical energies, that, for a brief space, I felt that I should not be able to keep afloat until the boat should reach me. As the steamer came near, there was a cry from my unfortunate neighbors in the water. " Stop the boat ! stop the boat !"

HOLD ON, PARTNER ! HOLD ON !

There was, indeed great danger of our being run over by it. I had, however, no fears on this point, and made no effort to get out of its way. Fortunately for myself, I was one of the first which the boat approached. A sailor threw out to me a large rope, which I succeeded in grasping at the first effort. I was drawn to the boat's guards, which was several feet above the water. While drawing me up, the kind-hearted sailor cried, " Hold on, partner ! hold on !" But I could not, my strength being exhausted, the rope was slipping through my hands, and I should certainly have fallen back into the water, and been irreeoverably lost under the boat's guards, had not another sailor quickly reached down and seized hold of my arms! I was drawn on board as nearly lifeless as any one could be without being actually dead. Two stout men assisted me to reach the cabin. My chest as I discovered from its soreness and my spitting of blood, had been somewhat bruised, but a little bathing with whisky soon gave me relief. My friend Bigny was one of the first I met on board."

Both these editors had been in the most dangerous part of

the boat, and their escape, almost without injury, was a remarkable instance of good fortune. One of the passengers who escaped remarked, that of the immense boilers, weighing many tons, not a scrap as large as a man's head remained. Very few of the names of those who were killed could be ascertained, but the general opinion was that the number of victims could not be less than one hundred. Mr. Perry, who was attached to the office of the New Orleans *Bulletin*, was one of the killed. The Hon. James Bebee, a member of the Missouri State Legislature, was believed to have been lost.

CHAPTER LXIII.

SINKING OF THE JOHN L. AVERY.

THE John L. Avery, J. L. Robertson, commander, was a new boat, built in the most substantial manner, and furnished with every necessary equipment for a first class passenger boat, being designed as a regular packet between New Orleans and Natchez. She left New Orleans, on her customary trip up the river, on March 7th, 1854. She stopped at Point Coupee and took in a large quantity of sugar and molasses; and on the 9th she passed the steamer Sultana, off Black Hawk point, forty miles below Natchez; and having left the Sultana (with which she appears to have been racing), about a mile astern, she struck what was supposed to be a tree, washed from the shore by a recent freshet. A very large leak in the bottom of the boat was the consequence of this accident, and although the pilot immediately steered for the shore, the steamer sunk before she could get near enough to land the passengers. Mr. J. V. Guthrie, an engineer, and the carpenter, were standing just forward of the boilers when they heard the crash — the boat at the same time making a sudden surge to one side. The carpenter immediately lifted the scuttle-hatch and leaped into the hold, but finding the water pouring in too fast to admit of any attempt at repairing the damage, he made haste to get out again, in the same time giving notice to the engineer that the boat had snagged. Mr. Guthrie, perceiving that the boat was going down, hastened to the engine, but before he got there, he was up to his knees in water. The cabin passengers were hurried up to the hurricane deck. Soon after, the boat righted, and the hull separated from the cabin and sunk in sixty feet of water.

As the hull parted from the upper works the surging of the waters caused the cabin floor to rise up against the hurricane roof, and six persons who remained in the cabin were dragged out the skylight by Capt. Robertson and his two clerks.

Mrs. Parnin, one of the six passengers rescued from that perilous situation, had her eldest child in her arms at the time, and was with difficulty prevented from plunging in again, as her babe was left asleep on the bed. But the situation of the deck passengers was the most calamitous; there was a large number of them crowded in their alloted place, where they were walled in by hogsheads of sugar, which would have prevented their escape, if escape had been otherwise possible. Those unfortunate people were nearly all drowned.

There were many Irish emigrants on board, whose names were unregistered, and there is a great deal of uncertainty respecting the number of those who perished. Eye-witnesses testify that a large number of men, women and children could be seen drowning at one time. Of twenty firemen on board, twelve were drowned. The second mate and another person launched the life-boat, but it was almost immediately upset, probably by the eager and ill-directed efforts of the drowning people to get into it. The steamer Sultana, with which the Avery had been racing, promptly came to the rescue of the drowning crew and passengers, and was the means of saving some of them; but the number lost is believed to be at least eighty or ninety.

Mrs. Seymour, one of the passengers who escaped, relates the following incidents of the wreck: —

While the passengers were at dinner, it was remarked that the atmosphere of the cabin was too overheated, a circumstance which one of the party accounted for by stating that some unusual means had been used to get up extra steam, as the officers of the Avery were resolved to outrun the rival steamer, Sultana. Mrs. Seymour had retired to her state-room for an afternoon nap, from which she was aroused by the concussion when the boat struck; and soon after she found herself in the water. She was drawn up into the floating cabin by one of the waiters, named John Anderson, who, as Mrs. Seymour testifies, was instrumental in saving the lives of several other passengers. She states that her pocket-book, containing nine hundred dollars, which she had placed under her pillow, was lost. She also lost a manuscript which she was preparing for the press, and which she valued still more highly than her pocket-book.

Mrs. Seymour continues: I cast my eyes upon the water,

which was covered with fragments of the cabin. To these frail supports human hands were clinging, while many human voices were crying, "Save me! oh, save me!" The water at first was dotted with human heads, sinking and rising, and then sinking to rise no more. A sudden splash drew my attention to the side of the boat, and I saw that a young lady, who had been drawn from the inundated cabin through the skylight and placed in safety on the floating deck, in the delirium of the moment had plunged again into the water, from which she never again emerged. Several others followed her example, but appearing again on the surface, they were rescued by the waiter Anderson and two or three others of the boat's crew, who never slacked in their efforts to save human life. Two or three gentlemen leaped into the water and swam to land. A fine Texan pony, belonging to Mrs. Emerson, escaped from the deck and endeavored to save himself by swimming. He reached the shore, but not being able to climb the bank, he fell back into the water and was drowned. In a faint but earnest tone, I heard a female voice say, "Oh, William, do save her!" On directing my gaze to the place from whence the voice came, I saw a woman sinking in the river. At the same time the child's voice exclaimed, "Oh, mother, he cannot save me!" I saw her fair hair, all wet, fall back from her young face as her little arms loosened their grasp on the neck of her brother, and the mother and her two children sank together.

BURNING OF THE ORLINE ST. JOHN.

The steamboat Orline St. John left Mobile for Montgomery, Ala., on Monday evening, March 2d, 1850. On the fourth of the same month, when within four miles of her place of destination, she was discovered to be on fire on the larboard side, near the boilers. In less than three minutes from the time in which the first alarm was given, the whole cabin was enveloped in a sheet of flame. There were about one hundred and twenty human beings on board, and it is reported that no more than fifty of that number survived the destruction of the boat. As soon as the fire was discovered, the pilot steered for the shore, which the steamer fortunately reached before tiller-ropes were severed by the flames. The boat was run ashore in a dense cane-brake on which her bow and waist rested, while the stern projected into the river. A few persons who happened to be on the forward part of the boat were landed without any difficulty, but the greater number of pas-

sengers ran aft, with the hope of getting into the yawl.   But
the deck passengers and a part of the crew got possession of
this small boat and had already left the steamer.   More than
one hundred people were now collected at the stern, which,
as mentioned above, projected into the deep water, which
effectually cut off all means of escape in that quarter ; and to
go forward was now impossible, as the whole of the middle of
the boat was completely wrapped in flames.   To make the situation of these people still more critical, the cabin threatened to
fall on them.   " As the flames spread aft (says an eye-witness),
the scene was indeed terrible.   The ladies and children had
gathered in the extreme after-part of the boat, and their
screams for help can never be erased from my memory."
   If the yawl had been brought back, all might have been
saved ; but the deck hands who had taken possession of it ran
it ashore in the cane-brake, and before the captain and second
mate could bring it back, all who remained on the steamer,
without a single exception, were drowned or burned to death.
Every woman and child who had been in the boat was lost ;
the only persons saved were those few who escaped over the
bow when the boat struck, and the five or six deck hands who
ran off with the yawl.   There were a number of returned
California gold diggers on board; such of them as saved their
lives lost all the produce of their toils.   No property of any
kind was saved, except a trunk belonging to Col. Preston,
which his servant threw over the bow into the cane-brake.

EXPLOSION OF THE CLIPPER.

   " This explosion, of which a very vague account has been
preserved, took place on Wednesday, September 19th, 1843,
at about a quarter past twelve o'clock, m.   One of the passengers who lived to relate the story, and who appears to have
powers of description peculiar to himself, states that the
Clipper " blew up with a report that shook earth, air and
heaven, as though the walls of the world were tumbling to
pieces around our ears.   All the boilers burst simultaneously ;
vast fragments of machinery, huge beams of timber, articles
of furniture, and human bodies, were shot up perpendicularly,
as it seemed, hundreds of fathoms in the air, and fell like the
jets of a fountain in various directions ; some dropping on the
neighboring shore, some on the roofs of the houses, some into
the river, and some on the deck of the boat.   Some large fragments of the boilers, etc., were blown at least two hundred
and fifty yards from the scene of the destruction.   The hap-

less victims were scalded, crushed and torn, mangled and scattered in every possible direction; some were thrown into the streets of the neighboring town (Bayou Sara), some on the other side of the bayou, three hundred yards distant, and some into the river. Several of these unfortunates were torn in pieces by coming in contact with pickets or posts, and I myself (says the same credible witness), saw pieces of human bodies which had been shot like cannon balls through the solid walls of houses at a considerable distance from the boat."

Every object in front of the wheel-house was swept away as if by a whirlwind. A gentleman who visited the place where the killed and wounded had been deposited, at Bayou Sara, says: "The scene was such as we never hope to look upon again. The floors of the two large ware-rooms were literally strewn with the wounded and dying, and others were pouring in as fast as it was possible to convey them to the spot. The sufferers were praying, groaning and writhing in every contortion of physical agony."

EXPLOSION OF THE LOUISIANA — ONE OF THE MOST FATAL ON RECORD.

"A few minutes after five o'clock, on the evening of November 15, 1849, the steamboat Louisiana, Captain Cannon, lying at the foot of Gravier street, New Orleans, had completed all the preparations for her departure for St. Louis. She was laden with a valuable cargo, and had on board a large number of passengers. The last bell had rung, the machinery set in motion; but at that moment the boat disengaged herself from the wharf and began to back out into the river, all the boilers exploded with a concussion which shook all the houses for many squares around to their very foundations. The Louisiana was lying between two other steamers — the Bostona and Storm — the upper works of which were completely wrecked; their chimneys were carried away, and their cabins were shattered to small fragments. The violence of the explosion was such, that large pieces of the boilers were blown hundreds of yards from the wharf, falling on the levee and in different parts of the city. One of these iron fragments cut a mule in two, and then struck a horse and dray, killing both driver and horse instantly.

Another mass of iron, of considerable size, was projected into the corner of Canal and Front streets, two hundred yards from the exploded steamer, where it threw down three large iron pillars which supported the roof of the portico of a coffee-

house.   Before it reached the iron pillar, this fragment passed
through several bales of cotton, which lay in its passage.

The tremendous detonation gave notice of the accident to
the whole city, and soon all the levee near Gravier street was
thronged with anxious and sympathizing spectators.   A
number of bodies, in every conceivable state of mutilation,
had been dragged from the wreck, and were surrounded by
the immense crowd which had assembled.   Hacks and furniture cars were sent for, and the wounded were conveyed with
as much dispatch as possible to the hospital.   The sight of the
mangled bodies on every side, the groans of the dying, and
the shrieks of the agonized sufferers, produced a general thrill
of horror among the crowd.   The body of a man was seen,
with the head and one leg off, and the entrails torn out.   A
woman, whose long hair lay wet and matted by her side, had
one leg off, and her body was shockingly mangled.   A large
man having his skull mashed in, lay dead on the levee; his
face looked as though it had been painted red, having been
flayed by the scalding water.   Others of both sexes, crushed,
scalded, burned, mutilated and dismembered, lay about in
every direction.   Two bodies were found locked together,
brought by death into a sudden and long embrace.

But it is utterly impossible to describe all the revolting objects which presented themselves to the view of the beholders,
suffice it to say, that death was there exhibited in all its most
hideous forms ;   and yet the fate of many who still lived was
more shocking and distressing than the ghastly and disfigured
corpses of those whose sufferings were terminated by death.

A gentleman who was a passenger on the Louisiana, says that
he was standing on the hurricane deck, abaft the wheel house,
at the time of the explosion, and though his position was most
perilous, he fortunately escaped unhurt.   He distinctly saw
the faces and arms of several ladies and gentlemen who were
vainly struggling to free themselves from the falling planks and
timbers.   They were carried down with the boat when she
sunk.   The steamer went down within ten minutes after the
explosion ; and it is thought that many citizens who went aboard
to assist the wounded, sunk with the boat.   The passenger
mentioned above succeeded in saving a little negro boy.   The
river was covered with fragments of the wreck, to many of
which persons who had been thrown overboard were clinging,
and a number of small boats were engaged in taking them up.
The confusion was so great that it was quite impossible to ascertain the names of one quarter of those who were killed;
and as a promiscuous crowd of strangers, emigrants, &c., were

on board, the greater number of them could not be identified. It is generally admitted that this disaster caused a greater loss of life than ever took place on the Mississippi, before or since. The most authentic accounts make the number of killed one hundred and fifty, and some estimates extend to two hundred. The mayor of New Orleans judged from his own observations and diligent inquiries on the spot, that one hundred and fifty lives were lost, at the lowest calculation.

The steamer Storm, which lay in close proximity to the Louisiana, was as almost completely wrecked as the last named boat itself, and was driven out fifty yards from the wharf by the concussion. Several persons on board the Storm were killed or wounded. The captain himself was severely injured, but appeared on deck, his face covered with blood, and calmly gave directions for clearing the wreck, and bringing his boat back to the wharf.

The fragments of iron, and blocks and splinters of wood, which were sent with the rapidity of lighting from the ill-fated Louisiana, carried death and destruction in all directions. Persons were killed or wounded at the distance of two hundred yards from the boat. There were many miraculous escapes. Dr. Testut, of New Orleans, was standing on the wharf, having just parted from his friend Dr. Blondine, of Point Coupee, who had embarked in the Louisiana, and was killed by the explosion. A fragment of iron struck a man at Dr. Testut's feet; the poor fellow while falling stretched out his hands and convulsively grasped the doctor's paletot, tearing a pocket nearly out. His grasp was soon relaxed by death. Among the citizens who received severe injuries from the flying pieces of the wreck was Mr. Wray, a clerk in the house of Moses Greenwood & Co., who had been on board of the steamer Knoxville, lying below the ferry landing, and was .passing up at the time. He was struck on the thigh by a piece of wood, and so badly wounded that amputation was necessary. Several newsboys, who had been selling papers on the Louisiana, and had just gone ashore, were killed.

The bodies of persons who had been in the steamer were, in some instances, blown to the height of two hundred feet in the air, some of them falling on the wharf and some into the river. Legs, arms, and the dismembered trunks of human bodies, were scattered over the levee. One man, it is said, was blown through the pilot house of the steamer Bostona, making a hole through the panels which looked like the work of a cannon ball.

Among those who were killed on board of the Storm was

Mrs. Moody, wife of the first clerk, who was standing
on the guard opposite the ladies' cabin. Twelve or fifteen
other persons were killed in this boat, and several others
were wounded, some of them mortally. The Storm had just
arrived with passengers from Cincinnati, none of whom had
been landed.

During the night thirty bodies, all strangers, were brought
to the watch house of the Second municipality. Capt. Cannon, of the Louisiana, was on the wharf at the time of the explosion. He had stopped for a moment to speak to an
acquaintance and this delay probably saved his life. A lady
and her two children escaped from the wreck of the boat as it
was sinking.

The effects of this disaster, unexampled in the history of
steam navigation, were visible in every circle of society at
New Orleans. Dismay was in every countenance, and the
whole city seemed to be in mourning for the numerous dead ;
while every heart was deeply affected with sympathy for the
surviving friends, and for all who were suffering in body or
mind from the effects of the dreadful catastrophe."

EXPLOSION OF THE ST. JAMES.

" The St. James was a high pressure boat owned by Capt.
W. H. Wright. She was built at Cincinnati in 1850, and was
employed on the Mississippi River until about a month before
her destruction, at which time she was engaged on Lake Pontchartrain. The accident took place on that Lake, at Point
Aux Herbes. The St. James left Bay St. Louis on Sunday
night, July 4th, 1852, in company with the steamboat California, having on board a large number of persons who had
been spending the anniversary of independence at the water-
ing places. Between two and three o'clock on the morning
of the fifth, the St. James stopped at the point designated
above, fifteen miles from the Pontchartrain railway landing,
and having taken in several passengers, started again on her
course. Her companion, the California, was at this time a
short distance astern; each boat, probably, was endeavoring
to out-run the other, and it is conjectured that the officers of
the St. James, in their eagerness to beat their rival, exposed the
lives of their passengers to very obvious danger.

The St. James had run scarcely two hundred yards from the
point where she had stopped, when all the boilers exploded,
and nearly at the same moment the boat took fire. The
stanchions being torn away at the explosion, the whole of

the boiler deck fell upon the boilers and machinery, precipitating a great many persons into the lower part of the boat, which was now flooded with scalding water, or strewn with the ignited fuel, which had been scattered abroad. Owing to this circumstance, a number of passengers who had not been injured by the explosion itself were severely scalded or burned when the deck fell in. As the time at which the disaster took place was long before daylight, many of the passengers were asleep. Some of them awoke in eternity, without knowing, perhaps, what cause had hurried them thither, and others were aroused from their slumbers by a sense of intolerable bodily anguish. Vainly would we attempt to picture the scene which now presented itself on the burning steamer. The shrieks of the affrighted passengers were heard on board the California, and Captain Ensign, of that steamer, immediately steered for the wreck. The space between the two boats was lighted up by the conflagration to the brightness of mid-day, and the spectators from the California could see the terrified men and women on board of the St. James hurrying to and fro, wringing their hands, or seizing on such articles as they could use for temporary support, and jumping into the lake. The screams were awfully distinct and harrowing, as they arose not from the burning boat alone, but from the water in all directions, where many human beings were shouting for help, or gasping in the last agony. Voices were calling from all points as the boats of the California went about swiftly picking up all who could be reached. The horrified eyes of the people on the California could see men cease to struggle and go down, while those who saw them perish had no power to save. It was a scene to harrow the soul of humanity, a scene which could not be remembered without horror, and one that could never be forgotten.

As the California approached the burning wreck, the heat was so great that Captain Ensign was compelled by a due regard for the persons under his charge, to haul off a short distance. The boats belonging to the California were launched, manned and sent to the aid of the sufferers. The flames arose from the center of the St. James, and Captain Ensign, while making a second attempt to reach the persons on the wreck, succeeded by nice management, in getting under the stern, and a large number of ladies and gentlemen from the St. James were thus enabled to reach the deck of the California. All who were saved owe the preservation of their lives to Captain Ensign.''

BURNING OF THE GEORGIA.

"On Saturday night, January 28, 1854, the steamboat Georgia was burnt on Alabama River, between Montgomery and Mobile. She had two hundred and thirty passengers on board, thirty or forty of whom are believed to have perished. When the fire was discovered, the boat was run ashore as speedily as possible. The scene which followed was one of indescribable confusion. One who saw it declares that women and children were "pitched on the shore like logs of wood;" the necessity of getting them out of the burning boat with the greatest dispatch seemed to require such rough and unceremonious handling. Several who were thus thrown out of the boat fell into the water and were drowned, and others struck the ground with such violence as to cause serious injuries. Mr. Jackson, of Barbour County, Ala., and one of his children, were lost. His widow and eight surviving children, who were on board with him, were left at Mobile, in destitute circumstances. Mr. Jackson had on his person checks and drafts to a considerable amount, which were also lost. Mr. Jolley and his family, of Randolph County, Georgia, were on the boat. The wife of this gentleman and one of his children were drowned. He lost besides $900 dollars in specie, and was left penniless. B. F. Lofton, of Lenoir County, N. C., lost two slaves. Rev. J. M. Carter, of Clinton, Ga., lost three negroes. His wife was badly burned. Dr. J. M. Young, of Hancock, Ga., lost a valuable slave, all his medical books, surgical instruments, and everything, in short, except the clothing which he wore at the time of the disaster. Mrs. Davidson, from Macon County, Ala., lost several negroes. Mr. Graham, from Williamsburgh, S. C., lost two negroes and $500 in gold. Thos. J. McLanathan, of Bristol, Conn., was drowned. A gentleman from Stewart County, Ga., lost several slaves. A woman who fell or leaped from the cabin floor to the main deck was caught on the horns of an infuriated ox, and thereby received several severe wounds, but the animal threw her into the water and she was saved. A father, who had rescued his wife and six children, went back into the blazing wreck, hoping to save the seventh, but lost his own life. A young man who had escaped to the shore, returned to the boat to bring away his sister, but he was seen to fall into the blazing hull, from which he never emerged. Another man saved three of his children, but his wife and six of his other children were consumed on this funeral pyre. A young man who had lost his wife in the wreck, sat on the wharf to all appearances an indifferent spectator of the frightful scene. It appeared afterwards that his grief had reduced him to melancholy madness, or idiotic apathy. Another young man who had seen his father and mother perish in the boat, loudly lamented the loss of $1,000 which the old gentleman had deposited in the safe. This bereavement seemed to be the only one which occupied his thoughts. W. B. Rhenn, of Newbern, N. C., saved himself, his wife, and his five children, but lost nine slaves.

Of the forty persons who perished in this conflagration twenty-two were negroes belonging to the cabin passengers, and more than half of the others were children. From the moment that the flames broke out until the fate of each person on board, for life or death, was decided, only three minutes elapsed; so quick was the work of destruction.

LOSS OF THE STEAMBOAT MECHANIC.

The steamboat Mechanic had been chartered at Nashville for the conveyance of General Lafayette and suite to Marietta, Ohio. She departed from the former place on Friday morning, May 6th, 1825, having on board, besides her officers and crew, General Lafayette, General Carroll and staff, Governor Coles, of Illinois, General O'Fallon, Major Nash, of Missouri, and several other gentlemen as passengers. On the following Sunday, about 12 o'clock, midnight, while the steamer was ascending the Ohio, and when near the mouth of Deer Creek, about one hundred and twenty-five miles below Louisville, a severe shock was felt by the persons on board, and it was soon ascertained that the boat had struck some object under the surface of the water. The commander, Capt. Hall, presently announced to the passengers in the cabin that the boat had snagged. Capt. Hall then caused the yawl to be made ready to convey General Lafayette and the passengers ashore. In the meanwhile, the General had been aroused from his slumbers and was soon prepared to leave the steamer.

As the night was very dark, and great confusion prevailed on board, General Lafayette, while attempting to descend into the yawl, was precipitated into the river and would have been drowned but for the assistance of one of the deckhands, whose name we have been unable to ascertain. The General, although far advanced in years, was able to keep himself above water until help arrived. He lost eight thou-

sand dollars in money, besides his carriage, clothing, etc., but
finally reached the shore in safety.

While Capt. Hall was devoting all his attention to the preservation of his passengers, his desk, containing one thousand
three hundred dollars, was lost overboard and was never
recovered.

SINKING OF THE BELLE ZANE.

"On the eighth of January, 1845, the steamboat Belle Zane,
while on her way from Zanesville, Ohio, to New Orleans,
struck a snag in the Mississippi, about twelve miles below the
mouth of the White River, and immediately turned bottom
upward. This terrible accident took place in the middle of
an exceedingly cold night. Of ninety persons who were on
board a moment before the disaster, only fifty escaped drowning — and many of those who succeeded in reaching the shore
were afterwards frozen to death. At the time the boat was
snagged, the passengers were all in their berths; those who
were able to extricate themselves when the boat suddenly
turned over, had scarcely any clothing to protect them from
the inclemency of the weather. No situation could be more
wretched than that of the people who escaped to the beach,
almost naked, unsheltered and drenched with water on a
freezing night in December. They remained in this miserable
situation for nearly two hours, when the steamboat Diamond
came down and took off all who remained alive, sixteen in
number. There were five ladies on board, all of whom were
saved in the yawl. The feet and hands of some of the survivors were so badly frozen that amputation was necessary."

EXPLOSION OF THE GLENCOE.

"On the 3d day of April, 1852, the Glencoe, Captain Lee,
from New Orleans, arrived at St. Louis, and had just been
moored at the levee, foot of Chestnut Street, when three of
her boilers exploded, with the most appalling and destructive
effects. The sound of the explosion was heard in the most
remote quarters of the city ; in the neighborhood of the levee
the shock was like an earthquake, the houses for several
squares around appeared to reel under the force of the concussion. The boat was crowded with people at the time;
the passengers were engaged in looking after their baggage,
and numbers of citizens, hotel-runners, hackmen, etc., had
pressed into the boat. There was a fearful loss of life, but

the names and numbers of the killed are beyond the scope of inquiry, as many of the victims were strangers; the bodies of a large number blown overboard were not recovered from the water, and many of the dead were so shockingly disfigured or torn to pieces that all recognition was out of the question. Fragments of wood, iron, and dead bodies were thrown to a surprising distance.

The shock of the explosion drove the steamer far out into the river, and immediately afterwards she took fire, the furnaces having been dismantled, and the burning fuel scattered over the decks. As the Glencoe floated down the stream, she presented a frightful spectacle. The whole forward part of the boat to the wheel-house, and down to the water line, had been swept away, all the after-part was a commingled mass of timbers, freight, and bodies heaped together in the wildest confusion. The fire burned fiercely and spread rapidly. The spectators on shore beheld men, women and children running, with frenzied gestures, from one part of the burning steamer to another, seeking some means of escape from the dreadful death with threatened them — some who had been caught between the falling timbers were writhing in agony, making ineffectual efforts to extricate themselves, imploring others to assist them. Numbers of the crew and passengers were compelled by the advancing flames to throw themselves overboard, some of these succeeded in reaching the shore, but many of them were drowned.

In the meantime several small boats were actively engaged in rescuing the drowning people, and a considerable number were saved in this manner. The wreck finally lodged at the foot of Poplar Street, where it burned to the water's edge, and then sunk, carrying down with it the ashes and the bones of the dead. Near the spot where the explosion took place many dead bodies and dying persons were extended on the levee. Thirteen mutilated corpses were soon after removed to the office of the Board of Health, that being the most convenient place where they could be deposited. Twenty or thirty of the wounded were conveyed to the Sisters' Hospital. Others who were less injured were running about the levee in a frantic manner, crying for assistance. The dead bodies of five persons who had been blown from the deck of the Glencoe were found on the steamer Cataract. They were dreadfully mangled, the limbs in some cases being torn from the trunk, heads were mashed and disfigured to a degree which defied all attempts at identification. The body of a woman was found on the levee stretched across a marble slab (the top of a table which had also been blown from the boat), every bone in this corpse was broken, and "the limbs," says an eye witness, "were so badly mangled that they could scarcely hang together."

The body of Mr. John Denny, first clerk of the Glencoe, was found on the hurricane deck of the steamer Western World. Few external injuries were found on his body, but life was totally extinct. The body of a little girl, with the legs torn off, was recovered from the river. The dissevered leg of a man was picked up on the sidewalk in Commercial street ; the boot, which remained on the limb, led to the recognition thereof as a part of the mortal remains of William Brennan, one of the engineers. Of thirteen wounded persons who were sent to the hospital, three died during the night, and scarcely any of the others were believed to be curable.

Capt. Lee, his lady and one of his children, left the boat as soon as she landed, and a very few minutes before the explosion. The Captain's little son, ten years of age, who remained on board, was killed. Mr. A. R. Jones, a merchant of St. Louis, was instrumental in saving a great number of lives. He obtained a yawl, and approached the burning boat near enough to take off a great many passengers. As an acknowledgment of his humane services in the time of danger and affliction, the steamboatmen of St. Louis presented Mr. Jones with a handsome silver mug, bearing a suitable inscription."

EXPLOSION OF THE SALUDA.

"The Saluda exploded on Missouri River, near Lexington, April 9th, 1852. It appears that this boat had been detained in the neighborhood of Lexington for four days, by a strong tide. Several of her passengers left her to seek other conveyances. On the day above mentioned, the captain made another effort to stem the current. The steamer left the landing at half-past one o'clock a. m., and five minutes after the boilers exploded with such tremendous effect that the cabin and all the wood-work forward of the wheel-house were completely demolished, and not a piece of timber was left above the guards. The boat sunk within a few minutes. The books were all lost, and the names of all the passengers who were killed by the explosion or who sunk with the boat could not be ascertained. The number of those who perished is estimated at one hundred.

The commander, Capt. Belt, who was on the hurricane

roof, was blown high in the air, and fell against the side of a hill in Lexington, at least one hundred feet from the wreck. The second clerk, Mr. John Blackburn, was standing on the boiler deck, and was also blown on shore, to a considerable distance from the boat.   He was taken up dead.   It may be mentioned as a melancholy coincidence, that a brother of this gentleman (E. C. Blackburn) was killed by the accident on the Pacific Railroad in November, 1855.   They were both highly esteemed by all who knew them.   The mutilated bodies of a large number of passengers of the Saluda were found in the streets of Lexington.   Charles Labarge and Louis Gareth, the pilots, and Messrs. Clancy and Evans, the engineers, were lost.   Their bodies were blown into the river, and were never recovered.   One of the surviving passengers lost his wife and seven children.   A lady was deprived of her husband and three children.   Such was the force of the explosion that a part of the boiler passed through a warehouse on the wharf, and quite demolished it.   The citizens of Lexington subscribed $1,000 for the relief of the sufferers.   The accident is ascribed to the negligence of the engineer.''

BURNING OF THE BULLETIN NO. 2.

The steamboat Bulletin No. 2, Capt. C. B. Church, was burned on the Mississippi River, near Islands No. 96, 97, March 24th, 1855.   A large quantity of cotton was among the freight, and this highly combustible article caused the flames to spread rapidly.   The boat was run ashore as quickly as possible; but as soon as she struck the bank, she bounded back again, and floated down the river until consumed to the level of the water.   The surface of the river was covered with floating bales of ignited cotton; and many persons who leaped overboard, while attempting to save themselves by clinging to these fiery masses, were severely burned.   One of the cabin passengers stated that he was sitting on the hurricane deck, when the fire first appeared, and before he could get a bucket of water to throw on it, the whole boat was in a blaze.   If the force pumps had been in good order (which was not the case), the flames could easily have been suppressed.   An eye witness thinks that the boat and the lives of many passengers could have been saved, if gum elastic hose had been provided for such an emergency.   Certainly it shows shameful and criminal neglect on the part of the captain or owners, when a steamer is without such apparatus.   While the boat was burning, the passengers were greatly excited and dismayed; but we have one instance of surprising coolness, whether it proceeded from courage or stupidity, we will not pretend to say. A gentleman was standing in the cabin with perfect composure and apparent unconcern while the fire was making rapid progress in every direction. Capt. Church advised this stoical person to take off the door of a state-room and endeavor to save himself thereon. "Make yourself easy, Captain," was the calm response; "I am safe enough." And, sure enough, he was saved. This anecdote reminds us of one which is told of a celebrated gambler, who leaped from a burning boat into the Mississippi, exclaiming: "Now, gallows, save your own!"

Some of the passengers of the Bulletin succeeded in leaping on shore from the forecastle at the moment the steamer struck the land, but a large majority, who were in the afterpart of the boat, were cut off from this means of escape. Capt. Church and all the other officers of the boat faithfully used every effort to save the passengers, and the Captain remained so long on board for this purpose that his own life nearly became the sacrifice of his fidelity. When driven to the last refuge on the wreck, by the flames, he threw himself into the water. The boat had drifted out to such a distance from the shore, that he would infallibly have been drowned, had not a skiff, which happened to be near, come to his assistance.

BURNING OF THREE STEAMERS.

Between the hours of 12 and 1 o'clock, on Monday morning, December 3d, 1855, a fire broke out on board the steam packet, George Collier, Captain Burdett Paris, lying at the lower landing, Memphis, Tenn. The steamer had just arrived, and had not been made fast, when the mate discovered the fire in a small closet under a flight of steps in the forward part of the boat. From this small beginning, the flames spread to every part of the steamer, in less than five minutes, all efforts to arrest the progress proving ineffectual.

Captain Burdett, perceiving that the total destruction of the boat was inevitable, gave the alarm to the passengers of the cabin. His first efforts were directed to the ladies, and in this, by almost superhuman exertions, he succeeded. The male passengers and some of the officers of the crew were compelled to save themselves by jumping off, some into the river and some on the lower deck of the wharf-boat, which lay near the Collier. This fine wharf-boat was called the Mary Hunt, together with the Mayflower, Capt. Jos. Brown, which lay on the other side, was soon involved in the fate of the Collier, and the three burning vessels are said to have presented one of the most magnificent and terrible spectacles ever witnessed in that locality. A flood of light, even at that hour, made every object distinctly visible for a great distance around the conflagration. Crowds of people rushed to the wharves, all in the most intense excitement and anxiety for the fate of many people who were known to be on board the blazing steamer. There were more than forty passengers on the George Collier, who, together with the officers and crew, made a total of sixty-five or seventy people, all of whom, for a time, appeared to be doomed to agonizing death. The register of the passengers names were destroyed with the boat. It is impossible, therefore, to state how many lives were lost, but twelve persons, at least, are known to have perished.

The George Collier had just completed her trip from New Orleans to Memphis, with a valuable cargo, all of which was destroyed. None of the passengers had landed.''

THE MARTHA WASHINGTON.

"The loss of the steamer Martha Washington, with its attendant circumstances, is one of the most extraordinary events in the records of marine disasters, a cloud of mystery hanging over the whole subject, will probably never be cleared away. This steamer, Captain Cummins, commander, was on her way from Cincinnati to New Orleans, when she took fire on the Mississippi River, near Island No. 65, at about half-past one o'clock, on the morning of January 14, 1852. The boat was entirely consumed. Several passengers lost their lives, but all the officers and crew, except the carpenter, were saved. The work of destruction was completed within three minutes. A whole family, consisting of a man, his wife and two children, perished in the flames. Two or three other persons were either burned to death or drowned while attempting to escape from the fire. The books and papers of the boat were lost.

The burning of this boat has given occasion for several lawsuits and criminal prosecutions. A charge of conspiring to burn the boat has been made by Sidney C. Burton, of Cleveland, Ohio, against Wm. Kissane, L. L. Filley, the brothers Chapin, Lyman Cole, Alfred Nicholson, the clerk of the Martha Washington, and several others. It was alleged that a heavy insurance on the cargo was obtained from several offices, and that the boat had been fraudulently laden with boxes con-

31

taining nothing more valuable than bricks, stones, and rubbish. It is said that in the summer of 1852, L. L. Filley, of Cincinnati, one of the persons implicated in the crime, confessed on his death-bed that there had been no merchandise shipped on the Martha Washington, and that the boat had been designedly set on fire to defraud the insurance companies. Sidney C. Burton states that he shipped on this boat a quantity of leather valued at $1,500, and that he was unable to obtain the insurance money, because the insurance officers protested that the boat had been fraudulently set on fire. At the suit of Mr. Burton, the persons named were arrested on the charge of conspiring to burn the boat, which involved the charge of murdering the passengers who were lost. Kissane was tried at Lebanon, Ohio, and afterwards at Cincinnati, and was convicted; he obtained a new trial and was acquitted. All the persons implicated were afterwards tried at Columbus, Ohio, for conspiracy, forgery, &c., but the jury brought in a verdict of "not guilty." Burton then obtained a requisition from the Governor of Arkansas on the authorities of Ohio, and had all the accused parties arrested by Officer Bruen, at the Walnut Street House, Cincinnati, in 1854. They were hurried into an omnibus, heavily ironed and ill-treated, and conveyed down to one of the wharves below Cincinnati, placed on a boat, and carried away to Jeffersonville, Ind., and from thence to Helena, Ark., to be tried for murder, arson, &c., where they were confined in a miserable jail three months.

They were again acquitted in the court of Arkansas. But the determined prosecutor again returned to the charge. Kissane, one of the defenders, in order to raise money to defray the expenses of his legal defense, committed a forgery on the Chemical Bank of New York in the summer of 1854. Some of his friends and advocates assert that he committed this deed in mere desperation, having been driven to the last extremity by the prosecution or persecutions of Burton. Kissane was arrested for this forgery, but while in the custody of an officer he contrived to make his escape from the railroad car by creeping through an aperture in the water closet. After concealing himself for some time, he was retaken, tried and sentenced to the State's prison, at Sing Sing, two and a half years; but in December, 1855, he was pardoned by Governor Clark, of New York. In the same month and year the grand jury of Hamilton County, Ohio, found a true bill against Burton, the prosecutor of Kissane, &c., and another person named Coons, for perjury. Coons acknowledged that Burton had paid him for giving in false evidence at the trial of the persons charged with burning the Martha Washington.

Such being the facts of the case, there are many conflicting opinions in relation to the guilt or innocence of the parties charged with the horrid crime of setting fire to the steamer and sacrificing the lives of several persons, for the purpose of obtaining a sum of money from the insurance companies. Several other instances of a mysterious and romantic character are related in connection with this narrative. Sidney C. Burton, the prosecutor of Kissane, etc., lately died (December 11th, 1855), at Cleveland, Ohio, in circumstances which gave a color of probability to a prevailing suspicion that he was poisoned. It is mentioned also that an attempt was before made to poison him at a hotel in Columbus, Ohio. The whole affair presents a tangled web which it would require a good deal of ingenuity to unravel.

CHAPTER LXIV.

WESTERN RIVER IMPROVEMENT AND WRECKING COMPANY.

[From Sketch Book, 1858.]

"THE first diving-bell boat on the Mississippi, we believe, was constructed and used by Wm. Thomas, formerly proprietor of the Sectional Docks, in this city, upon the wreck of a steamboat sunk between St. Louis and Alton about 1838.

His efforts were only partially successful, the diving-bell boats used being only flat-boats.

These boats, with some few extra contrivances of Mr. Thomas were all the public had to depend upon until 1842, when the Submarine No. 1 was built. She was considered quite a prodigy in her day and was built by Eads, Nelson & Case. The latter estimable gentleman lost his life at the unfortunate calamity of the "Gasconade bridge."

This boat was used only for the purpose of raising cargo from sunken boats. In 1845 Messrs. Eads and Case retired from the firm, and the business was conducted by Mr. Nelson alone, until the year 1847, when a company was formed, composed of Messrs. Nelson, Eads & McDowell. The latter partner, however, soon withdrew, and the business was conducted for ten years by Messrs. Eads & Nelson.

In 1848 the Submarine No. 2, was built at Cairo, and was eminently successful.

In 1849 the No. 3 was completed, and her first efforts were
spent in clearing the St. Louis harbor of 28 wrecks of steamboats from the great fire of that spring.

In 1851 the Submarine No. 4 was built at Paducah, Kentucky, and inaugurated a new era in the business of wrecking
on Western rivers. She was provided with one of " *Grimes'*
patent pumps," which was one of the most powerful ones
that had ever been invented, and this company had the sole
right to use it on all waters of the Mississippi Valley. Since
1851, they have raised by the use of this pump some 50
steamboats, a thing before thought to be impossible in many
cases.

In 1855, the five snag-boats built by the government for removing the Red River raft, and which cost $185,000, were
bought by Eads and Nelson, and converted into submarine
boats, and used for wrecking purposes.

In 1856 and '7, the No. 7 was built at a cost of $80,000,
and was undoubtedly the most complete boat of the kind in
the world, and was capable of raising the largest vessels.
After the purchase of these snag-boats a proposition was
made by this company to the government in 1856, to remove
the snags, stumps, rocks and sunken boats from the channel of the river for a fixed sum per annum for a term of
years. But from the hostility that then was entertained by
President Pierce and his advisers against the " internal improvement " system, the proposition was not accepted. In
1857 a liberal charter was secured from the Missouri Legislature under the name and style of Western River Improvement
and Wrecking Company, with a capital of $250,000, which
was readily subscribed by many of the best business men in
St. Louis. The affairs of the company were conducted by
seven directors, viz.: Charles K. Dickson, Thomas H. Larkin,
T. A. Buckland, S. H. Laflin, Charles Tilden, E. W. Gould.

This company is a standing rebuke to the government of
the United States. Instead of removing the obstructions
which offer constant peril to the entire commerce of the West,
it leaves to private enterprise to do that which justice and
right clearly point out as its duty. While millions of acres of
land are donated for building railroads, which in the end
mainly benefit speculators in lands and railroad stocks, not a
dollar is appropriated to improve the navigation of the rivers
that the whole West are compelled to use as the highway to
the markets of the world, at a cost largely increased in consequence of the excessive rates of insurance.

This company has a standing salvage contract with all

the principal insurance companies in the United States by which they are authorized to proceed at once to save any property wrecked on Western rivers, in which they are interested, at a stipulated rate of salvage.

In this way many steamboats are raised without removing the cargo and taken to the nearest dry docks and repaired, even before the underwriters are made aware of their loss, and consequently the company occupies a very important position in commercial circles, and one from which they are undoubtedly reaping a handsome reward."

This wrecking company was the avenue through which James B. Eads and his mechanical and financial ability became known to history and the world.

It was in these earlier, these minor transactions, that his genius and his financial ability were first developed to those who were intimately associated with him. This writer calls vividly to mind the cold rough morning in March, 1839, when young Eads, not out of his teens, stepped on board the old steamboat Knickerbocker, laying at the wharf at St. Louis, enroute from Cincinnati to "Galena and Dubuque."

Under a large circular cape he wore, he exhibited a miniature steamboat, complete in all its parts, and ready to raise steam on a tin boiler, ingeniously and systematically arranged.

He inquired where he could deposit his boat. Being shown the second clerk's room, as he had come on board to act in that capacity, he established himself and was duly enrolled as one of the crew for the then ensuing season. Previous to which he had been employed as an errand boy and a boy of all work, in the retail dry goods store of Henry During, on Main street, between Olive and Locust.

It was under the counter, in this store, during his leisure moments, when his genius developed the perfect specimen of a steamboat referred to.

This was his first practical introduction to the Mississippi River, a stream he afterwards became so familiar with.

After remaining one or two seasons in that capacity, a more active field for the development of his genius and ambition induced him to associate himself in a salvage company above referred to for the purpose of saving property wrecked on the Mississippi.

At the present time, 1889, that industry is not one that would have attractions for one of an ordinary ambition, much less for one with the towering ambition Capt. Eads possessed. But at the time he embarked in it, when it was not an unusual thing to note the sinking of a steamer with a valuable cargo on board in the daily papers, each day in the week, during the low water season, and it was conclusive evidence to his clear judgment that there was money in the *diving bell boat.*

The crude and unwieldy boats at first used presented a field for his mechanical genius, which soon resulted in improved boats, and machinery, commensurate with the rapidly increasing demand for their use. But few years was necessary to develop an immense collection of working stock, of every improved construction and every piece of it bore evidence of Capt. Eads' genius and master mind.

The whole culminated in the construction of the Submarine No. 7 (which many years later became the powerful gunboat, Benton.) While she was not the last boat the company built, and perhaps not the most profitable, she was the most expensive to build and to navigate. But for ingenuity of devise, and concentration of mechanical power, for which she was designed, she excelled all predecessors and anything that has been constructed since her day.

But it was not alone in the inception and materializing of this large and wealthy incorporation, that Captain Eads' genius and financial ability was made most prominent. The disposition of the stock, just at the moment when the tide of its success was about to turn, when its stock was thought to be a profitable investment, when all that was known of its value was from representations of interested parties, that he induced his friends to become interested in the "wrecking company." The result of this investment is still fresh in the recollection of many of Capt. Eads' contemporaries, as it was the means of wrecking some of them and in time was itself wrecked a few years later from many causes not necessary to enumerate.

The enterprise and zeal manifested by Capt. Eads in the rapid completion of so many gunboats for the government at the breaking out of the war was alone sufficient to give him a national reputation as one of the master minds in its service, and second to none in mechanical ingenuity, and *superior* to all in *perseverance.*

The construction of the St. Louis bridge and deepening of the channel at the mouth of the Mississippi are monuments to his public spirit, to his genius, and above all, to his financial ability.

Whatever credit is due him as an engineer, or for his mechanical and inventive genius, all sink into insignificance when compared to his ability as a *financier.*

Upon that all his success depended.

His ability to avail himself of the skill, of the experience and the brains of all with whom he came in contact, was phenomenal and enabled him to succeed in any mechanical proposition suggested.

The very able assistants and engineers he had employed in building the St. Louis bridge left him very little to do of the detail in construction; but to plan and execute, no man was his equal.

But only from his transcendent ability as a *financier* would there have been to this day so splendid a structure at St. Louis as the "Ead's bridge."

So, too, with the jetties at the mouth of the Mississippi.

No man with less ability as a lobbyist, or with less perseverance, or less knowledge of man and legistators, would have ever succeeded in securing the necessary appropriation for doing the work, with nearly the entire government force of engineers opposed to him and his plans.

The terms and conditions upon which he contracted to do that work were so stringent that not another man in America had the financial ability to have raised the means to do the work unless he had been a millionaire himself.

If Capt. Eads had lived, there is but little doubt but what he would have built a ship railroad across the Isthmus long before De Lessups or any one else would have finished a canal. There has never been but one *James B. Eads* in America.

By the following extract from the *Post*, published in San Francisco March 12th, 1882, it will be seen that the first proposition to build a ship railroad across the isthmus of Tehuantepec came from Dr. Wm. F. Channing, several years before Capt. Eads undertook the enterprise.

But genius in this case, as in most others, is of but little value without the financial ability to make it available. While Capt. Eads had genius in no small degree, his great success was achieved from his transcendent financial ability.

CAPTAIN EADS.

" Capt. Eads was a man of remarkable energy and fertility, and his work on the Mississippi jetties, if as effective as at present it seems to be, will assure him a permanent renown among civil engineers.

He was, indeed, so large a man that there should be no temptation for him to wear trophies rightfully belonging to another. We allude to the unique project of the Tehuantepec Ship Railroad. For years it has been allied with his name, and

much credit has been awarded to him for the ingenuity which
the scheme displays, a credit whioh Capt. Eads did not seem
to disclaim with much energy.

Yet, as a matter of fact, the whole conception and device of
a ship-railway across the isthmus originated in the brain of
that ingenious man, Dr. William F. Channing, now of California. Twelve or fifteen years ago he brought his idea to
maturity, wrote it out in Washington in an elaborate explanatory pamphlet, illustrated it with excellent cuts, similar in
scope to those with which the country is now familiar, and
applied to Congress for a charter. He was not able to expend upon it the large sums of money required for the development of the enterprise, and on returning to the city later
discovered that it had found a step-father in Capt. Eads. In
spite of many protests the thriving infant adopted its step-
father's name, who spent some hundreds of thousands of
dollars on its development.

Captain Eads was before a Senate committee only three
weeks ago, and his sudden death will seriously affect the
gigantic project for wedding the two oceans, with which his
name became indissolubly connected.''

CHAPTER LXV.

WESTERN RIVER PILOTS.

WITHOUT presuming to criticise unjustly the occupation or character of any class of men engaged in the navigation of Western rivers, the importance of the position of a pilot will justify the appropriation of one chapter to that subject.

"Mark Twain's" brief experience as a pilot on the Mississippi, entitles his remarks to some consideration.

Not that they are always just or truthful. But from his standpoint, and the time in which his *notes* were taken (which was several years before he wrote his "Life on the Mississippi"), strangers are liable to get a false impression of the facts.

True, at the time of his experience steamboating was at the height of its prosperity, and what seemed to him law, or universal custom, was only the result of the then prevailing circumstances.

No wonder he was charmed with the occupation, and "loved it better than any profession he has followed since," if what he says was true. "The reason is plain, a pilot in those days was the only unfettered and entirely independent human being that lived on the earth."

"Kings are but the hampered servants of parliament and people—parliaments sit in thrones forged by their constituents."

"The editor of a newspaper cannot be independent, but must work with one hand tied behind him by party and patrons, and be content to utter only half or two-thirds of his mind."

No clergyman is a free man and may speak the whole truth, regardless of his parishioners opinions. Writers of all kinds are manacled servants of the public.

In truth, every man, woman and child has a master, and worries and frets in servitude. But in the day I write of, the Mississippi pilot had *none*.

The captain could stand upon the hurricane deck in the pomp of very brief authority, and give five or six orders while the vessel backed into the stream, and then that skipper's reign was over. The moment the boat was under way in the river, she was under the sole and unquestioned control of the pilot.

He could do with her exactly as he pleased, run her when
and whither he chose, and tie her up to the bank whenever
his judgment said that was best.
His movements were entirely free.   He consulted no one,
he received commands from nobody; he promptly *resented*
the merest suggestions.   Indeed the law of the United States
forbade him to listen to commands or suggestions, rightly
considering that the pilot necessarily knew better how   to
handle the boat than any one could tell him.   So here was
the novelty of a king without a keeper, an absolute monarch,
who was absolute in sober truth, and not by a fiction of words.
I have seen a boy of 18 years of age taking a great steamer
serenely into what seemed almost certain destruction, and
the aged captain standing masterly by, filled with apprehension, but powerless to interfere.

His interference in that particular instance might have been
an excellent thing, but to permit it would have been to establish a most pernicious precedent.   It will easily be guessed,
considering the pilot's boundless authority, that he was a great
personage in the old steamboating days.   He was treated
with marked courtesy by the captain and with marked deference by the officers and the servants, and this deferential
spirit was quickly communicated to the passengers.   By
long habit, pilots came to put all their wishes in the form of
commands.   It "gravels" me to this day to put my will in
the shape of a request instead of launching it in the crisp
language of an order."

It is very apparent from the foregoing extract, that Mr.
"Twain" either magnified the authority he possessed as a
pilot very largely, or that he was fortunate enough to get
on to boats which were under the control of incompetent milk
and water masters.   *Probably both.*

There is no law of Congress, nor never has been, which
places a river steamboat under the control of a pilot.

When, from darkness of the night, or from any other cause,
the pilot considers it dangerous to life to run, he is authorized
by law to lay the boat up, *and then his authority ends.*   And
even in such cases, he seldom will exercise that authority
without consulting the master of the boat.   In fact, very few
pilots care to take the responsibility of laying a boat up, contrary to the judgment and wishes of the master, and are willing to run when in their judgment it is not altogether prudent
to do so if the captain will take the responsibility, which is
often done.

There was a short period before the war when pilots were

in great demand, and a certain *class* of them took the advantage of the situation and not only extorted extravagant wages, but often made themselves disagreeable by usurping authority they did not possess. The captain, recognizing his situation, yielded temporarily to the necessity. But there was always two sides to that situation and the captain's side was sure to win at the end of the trip.

Good sensible pilots and those who desired to retain the respect of their employers and their positions, never assumed the authority they did not possess, nor arrogated to themselves the right to command the boat.

To the few that took Mr. "Twain's" view of it, if the effect upon them was so severe as it was upon him when he lost that brief authority, they must have suffered great mortification, for lo these many years they have often been " *graveled* " since they have been obliged to " put their will in the weak shape of a request instead of launching it in the crisp language of an order."

But to resume the quotation : —

" Here is a conversation of that day : —

" A chap out of the Illinois River, with a little stern-wheel tub, accosts a couple of ornate and gilded Missouri River pilots : ' Gentlemen, I have got a pretty good trip for the up country, and shall want you for about a month. How much will it be?

" ' Eighteen hundred dollars a piece? "

" ' Heavens and earth ! You take my boat, let me have your wages, and I will divide.' "

I will remark in passing that Mississippi steamboatmen were important in landsmen's eyes (and in their own, too, in a degree), according to the dignity of the boat they were on.

For instance, it was a proud thing to be of the crew of such stately craft as the Alex Scott' or the Grand Turk.

Negro firemen, deck hands and barbers belonging to those boats were distinguished personages in their grade in life, and they were well aware of that fact, too.

A stalwart darkey once gave offense at a negro ball in New Orleans by putting on a good many airs. Finally one of the managers bristled up to him and said : " Who is you any way? Who is you? dat's what I want to know?"

The offender was not disconcerted in the least, but swelled himself up and threw that into his voice which showed he knew was not putting on all those airs on a stinted capital: " Who is I? Who is I? I let you know mighty quick who I is. I want you niggers to understan' dat I fires de middle do (door) on de Alex Scott."

That was sufficient.

"My reference a moment ago to the fact that a pilot's peculiar official position placed him out of the reach of criticism or command, brings Stephen W—— naturally to my mind. He was a gifted pilot, a good fellow, a tireless talker, and had both wit and humor in him. He had a most irreverent independence, too, and was deliciously easy-going and comfortable in the presence of age, official dignity and even the most august wealth.

He always had work, but never saved a penny. He was the most persuasive borrower, he was in debt to every pilot on the river, and to the majority of the captains.

He could throw a sort of splendor around a bit of harumscarum, devil-may-care piloting that made it almost fascinating — but not to everybody. He made a trip with good old Capt. Z—— once, and was relieved from duty when the boat got to New Orleans. Some one expressed surprise at the discharge. Capt. Z—— almost shuddered at the name of Stephen.

Then his poor thin old voice piped out something like this :

Why bless me, I would not have such a wild creature on my boat for the whole world. Not for the whole world. He swears, he sings, he whistles, he yells, I never saw such an Ingin to yell. All times in the night, it never made any difference to him. He would just yell that way, not for anything in particular, but on account of devilish comfort he got out of it. I never could get into a sound sleep, but he would fetch me out of bed all in a cold sweat, with one of those dreadful war whoops, queer being, very queer being. No respect for any thing or any body. Sometimes he called me *Johney*. He kept a fiddle and a cat, he played execrably. This seemed to distress the cat, and so the cat would howl. No man could sleep where that man and his family was, and reckless ; there never was any thing like it. Now, you may believe it or not, but as sure as I am sitting here, he brought my boat down through those awful snags at Chicot, with a rattling head of steam, and the wind a blowing like the very nation, at that. My officers will tell you so. They saw it, and, I tell you, sir, while he was tearing right down through those snags, and I a shaking in my shoes, and a praying, I wish I may never speak again if he didn't pucker up his mouth and go to whistling. Yes, sir; whistling 'Buffalo gals can't you come out to-night, can't you come out to-night, can't you come out to night,' and doing it as calmly as if we were attending a funeral and nearest relative to the corpse. And when I remonstrated with him about it he smiled down on me as if I was a child and told me to run in the house and try to be good, and not be meddling with my "superiors."

Once a pretty mean captain caught Stephen in New Orleans out of work and as usual, out of money. He laid steady siege to Stephen, who was in a very close place, and finally persuaded him to go with him, at $125 per month, just half wages, the captain agreeing not to divulge the secret and so bring down the contempt of the whole guild upon the poor fellow. But the boat was not more than a day out of New Orleans, before Stephen discovered that the captain was boasting of his exploit and that all the officers had been told. Stephen winced but said nothing.

About the middle of the afternoon the captain stepped out on the hurricane deck, cast his eye around and looked a good deal surprised. He glanced inquiringly aloft at Stephen, but Stephen was whistling placidly, and attending to business. The captain stood around awhile in evident discomfort, and once or twice seemed about to make a suggestion, but the etiquette of the river taught him to avoid such rashness, and so he managed to hold his peace. He chafed and puzzled a few moments then returned to his apartments.

But soon he was out again and apparently more perplexed than ever. Presently he ventured to remark with reverence, "Pretty good stage of the river now, is it not, sir?" "Well, I should say so. Bank full *is* a pretty good stage." "Seems to be a good deal of current here." "Good deal don't describe it. It is worse than a mill race." "Is it not easier in near shore than it is out here in the middle?" "Yes, I reckon it is, but a person can't be too careful with a steamboat. It is pretty safe out here; can't strike any bottom here, you can depend on that." The captain departed looking rueful enough. At this rate he would probably die of old age before getting his boat to St. Louis. Next day he appeared on deck again, found Stephen standing faithfully out in the middle of the river, fighting the whole force of the Mississippi River and whistling the same old tune in the same place and manner. This thing was becoming serious. In shore was a slower boat slipping along in the easy water gaining steadily. She began to make for an island chute; Stephen stuck to the middle of the river. Speech was moving from the captain. He said, "Mr. W——, don't that chute cut off a good deal of distance?" "I think it does, but I don't know." "Don't know! Well,

isn't there water enough to go through?"   "I expect there is,
but I am not certain."   "Upon my word this is odd!   Why
those pilots on that boat are going to try it.   Do you mean to
say you do not know as much as they do?"   "They! why,
they are $250 pilots.   But don't you be uneasy, I know as
much as any man can afford to know for $125."   The captain
surrendered. Five minutes later, Stephen was bowling through
the chute and showing the rival boat a two hundred and fifty
dollar pair of heels.   •

   "Most of the pilots and the captains held Stephen's note
for borrowed sums ranging from $250 upward.   Stephen
never paid one of these notes, but he was very prompt and
very zealous about renewing them every twelve months.

   Of course, there came a time at last when Stephen could
not borrow of his ancient creditors. So he was obliged to
lay in wait for new men, who did not know him. Such a
victim was good, simple-natured young Yates. I use a fictitious name.   But the real name began as this one with a (Y).
Young Yates graduated as a pilot, got a berth, and when the
month was ended he stepped to the clerk's office and got $250
in crisp new bills.

   Stephen was there.   His silvery tongue began to wag, and
in a very little while Yates' $250 had changed hands.

   The fact was soon known at pilot headquarters, and the
amusement and satisfaction of the old creditors were large
and generous. But innocent Yates never suspected that
Stephen's promise to pay promptly at the end of the week was
a worthless one.

   Yates called for his money at the stipulated time. Stephen
sweetened him up and put him off another week. He called
then, according to agreement, and came away sugar-coated, but
suffering under another postponement.

   Yates haunted Stephen from week to week to no purpose,
and at last gave it up. And then, straightway, Stephen began to hunt Yates. Wherever Yates appeared there was the
inevitable Stephen. By and by, whenever Yates saw
Stephen coming, he would turn and fly, and drag his companion with him if he had company. But it was no use. His
debtor would run him down and corner him.

   Panting and red-faced Stephen would come with out-
stretched hands and eager eyes, would invade the conversation, shake both of Yates' arms lose in their sockets — and
begin, "My, what a race I have had.   I saw you didn't see
me, and so I clapped on all steam for fear I would miss you
entirely; and here you are!   There, just stand so, and let me

look at you. Just the same old noble countenance; (to Yates'
friend). Isn't it? Just look at him. Ain't it just good to
look at him! ain't it now? Ain't he just a picture? Some
call him a picture. I call him a panorama! That's what he
is; an entire panorama. And now I am reminded; how I
do wish I could have seen you an hour earlier.

For twenty-four hours I have been saving up that $250 for
you, been looking for you every where. I waited at the
Planters' House from six yesterday evening till two o'clock
this morning, without rest or food. My wife says, Where have
you been all night? I said this debt lies heavy on my mind.
She says in all my life I never saw a man take a debt to heart
the way you do. I said it is my nature, how can I change
it? She says, Do go to bed and get some rest. I said, not
till that poor, noble young man gets his money. So I set up
all night and this morning out I put and the first man I
struck told me you had shipped on the " Grand Turk " and
had gone to New Orleans. Well, sir, I had to lean up against
a building, I was so sick, and began to cry. So help me
goodness, I could not help it. The man that owned the
place came out, cleaning up with a rag, and said he didn't
like to have people cry against his building, and then it seemed
to me as if the whole world had turned against me, and it
wasn't any use to live any more and coming along an hour ago
suffering, no man knows what agony, I met John Wilson
and paid him the $250 on account, and to think that here
you are now, and I haven't got a cent! And as sure as I am
standing here on this ground, on this particular brick — there
I have scratched a mark on the brick to remember it by — I'll
borrow that money and pay it over to you at twelve o'clock
sharp, to-morrow! Now, stand so, let me look at you just
once more.''

Bogart's saloon was a great resort for pilots in those days.
They met there about as much to exchange river news as to
play. One morning Yates was there, Stephen was there too,
but kept out of sight. By-and-by when about all the pilots
had arrived who were in town, Stephen suddenly arrived in
the midst, and rushed for Yates as for a long lost brother.
Oh, I am so glad to see you. Oh, on my soul, the sight of
you is such a comfort to my eyes!

" Gentlemen, I owe all of you money. Among you I owe
probably forty thousand dollars. I want to pay it, I intend
to pay it, every last cent of it. You all know without my
telling you, what sorrow it has cost me to remain so long
under such obligations to such patient, to such generous

friends. But the sharpest pang I suffer — by far the sharpest — is the debt I owe to this noble young man here, and I have
come to this place especially this morning to make this announcement, that I have at last found a method whereby I
can pay off all my debts, and most especially I wanted *him*
to be here when I announced it.

"Yes, my faithful friend, my benefactor, I have found the
method! I have found the method to pay off *all* my debts,
and you will get your money."

Hope dawned in Yates' eyes. Then Stephen beaming be-
nignantly, and placing his hand on Yates' head added: —

"I am going to pay them off in alphabetical order."   Then
he turned and disappeared.

The full significance of Stephen's method did not dawn
upon the perplexed and amused crowd for some two minutes.
Then Yates murmured with a sigh: —

"Well, the Y's stand a gaudy chance. He won't get any
further than the C's in *this* world, and I reckon after a good
deal of eternity has wasted away in the next one, I will still
be referred to up there, as ' that poor, ragged pilot that came
here from St. Louis in the early days.' "

These fictitious names that are introduced by " Mark
Twain " in the foregoing quotations from his life on the
Mississippi, so clearly illustrate the character of individuals
who most boatmen in the St. Louis and New Orleans trade
will recognize, that they are quoted more to show the genius
of Mr. Twain as an inimitable burlesque writer than for the
literal occurrences, as claimed by him. These peculiar characters are not alone found on steamboats, but in every walk
in life, and many persons will call to mind a Stephen, more
familiarly known as a " dead beat."

The cases referred to are clearly taken from real life,
although slightly embellished, and will be painfully recognized
by some confiding Yates.

CHAPTER LXVI.

PITTSBURGH COAL TRADE IN 1885.

"**D**URING the week which followed the rise in the river in the middle of November last, there was sent from the landing on the opposite side of the Monongahela river, from Jones ferry to Saw Mill farm, about 75 boat loads of coal — carrying 245,000 bushels. Boats and cargoes valued at $18,000. About the same quantity came down from the country along the Monongahela. The total value of coal annually shipped south from the Monongahela and from the mines opposite Pittsburgh may be estimated at about $100,-000."

COAL TOWING AND COAL TRADE.

In the New Orleans *Times-Democrat* of 1883 the following interesting account of moving, towing and floating coal on the Ohio and Mississippi rivers is given :—

THE JOSEPH B. WILLIAMS — HER CHAMPION TOW AND OTHER INTERESTING DATA IN CONNECTION THEREWITH.

" The Joseph B. Williams, that arrived at Bayou Sara a few days ago and turned back up the river from that point, brought from the Ohio the largest tow ever handled by a towboat. Her tow consisted of eight boats and one barge of coal, left at the mouth of Red River ; 25 boats of coal for Bayou Sara — in all 700,000 bushels ; a barge of hay, and a barge of fuel ; the total tonnage of which — coal, hay and fuel — amounted to 30,000 tons. An idea of the magnitude of this cargo can be had when we state that, if sent by railroad, 2,000 cars would be required for its transportation ; that would take 66 engines to haul, and which, if hitched together in one continuous train, would extend a distance of twelve miles. If the coal was heaped in a pile, it would cover a space 300 feet square and eleven feet high. The Joseph B. Williams has been distinguished for being the largest and most powerful towboat ever built, and for handling successfully great tows. On her last trip up she made the run from Helena to Memphis in the remarkable time of four hours thirteen and a half minutes, the fastest ever made, and now she has topped the pinnacle of her fame by bringing down the river the greatest of tows. The coal brought by the Williams belongs to the Grand Lake

32

Coal Company, for which Messrs. Desforges, Montagnet & Co., of this city, are the agents. In connection with this same subject we present some facts about coal that will prove interesting :—

THE EARLY HISTORY AND DEVELOPMENT OF COAL

is very obscure. It appears to have been used by the ancients to a limited extent. The American Cyclopædia says : "The first notice we find in official records of the development of coal in England — the first country in which the mining of coal became a commercial industry — is the receipt of twelve cart-loads of 'fossil fuel' by the Abbey of Peterborough in 850. The first evidence, however, of regular mining operations is found in the books of the Bishop of Durham, by whom, in 1180, several leases were issued for mining 'pit coal,' a term since common among the English miners and writers on coal."

THE FIRST MINING AND USE OF COAL IN THE WEST,

of which we have record, was in 1811, and is as follows:—

The attention of Robert Fulton and his friend, Chancellor Livingston, after their great success upon the Hudson River, was turned toward the great rivers of the West — the Ohio and Mississippi — and in April of this year (1811) they made an arrangement with Mr. Roosevelt, of New York, to visit these rivers and make an exploration of them for the purpose of forming an opinion whether they admitted of steamboat navigation or not.

Mr. Roosevelt surveyed the rivers from Pittsburgh to New Orleans, and his report being favorable it was decided to build a steamboat at this time. This was done under the direction and superintendence of Mr. Roosevelt, and in the course of the year 1811 the first boat was launched on the Ohio. It was called the New Orleans and intended to ply between the city of Natchez and the city of New Orleans. In the month of October it left Pittsburgh upon its experimental voyage.

Upon his first voyage of exploration Mr. Roosevelt had discovered two beds of coal about 120 miles below the falls of the Ohio. He took with him upon this second voyage tools and implements to work the coal mines, intending to take enough to make the downward voyage.

The first coal fleet to descend the Mississippi on record was that of two flats in 1829. The coal was mined at Bon Harbor, three miles below Owensboro, Ky., and was shipped in two flats eighty feet long, fifteen feet wide, and loaded to draw four feet. This coal was sold to the Labranche sugar plantation in this State, just this side of the Red Church. One of the men who helped to build these flats, load the coal and boat it to its destination, was Capt. George (Natural) Miller, now running the Saline to Bœuf River.

The first coal to arrive in this city in tow of a steamboat was in February, 1854, and the following mention was made of its arrival by a paper published in this city at that time: "The towboat Crescent City, Capt. Cochran, arrived on Wednesday, the 1st, from Pittsburg, with three barges coal, and one barge coke, in all 64,000 bushels. The Crescent City belongs to Mr. George Leadlie, of Pittsburgh, and is consigned to Mr. C. A. Miltenberger. She brings the first coal ever towed to this market, and will easily bring eight barges on a trip."

SECOND TOW-BOAT WITH COAL AT NEW ORLEANS.

The second tow to arrive here was ten barges of about 100,000 bushels, brought by the towboat James Guthrie, in April, 1854. The Guthrie was owned by Simpson Hornor and —— Hyatt, of Pittsburgh, and came through with her tow from Louisville in four days.

A statement before us, published in Pittsburgh, reports that, "During the week which followed the rise of the river in November (1834) there was sent from the landing on the opposite side of the Monongahela River from Jones' Ferry to Saw Mill Run about seventy-five boats, carrying 245,000 bushels of coal. About the same amount passed down from the country along the Monongahela above Pittsburgh. The total value of coal from the banks around Pittsburgh may be estimated at about $100,000. It is rapidly increasing in amount as it becomes more generally used upon the lower rivers."

Some idea of how rapidly the consumption of coal has increased, as above predicted, forty-nine years ago, may be had from the following paragraph from a recent coal statement published at Pittsburgh, (May 5, 1883): "One thing is very certain, at the present rate of export the day will come when Pittsburgh will have to shut down on such heavy shipments if we intend to retain our place as a cheap manufacturing center."

In 1869 the coal shipments from Pittsburg amounted to 4,670,000 bushels; this year, up to the present day, over 25,000,000 bushels have been shipped."

Respecting the recent coal run from Pittsburgh the *Commercial-Gazette* of the 13th gives some facts that speak eloquently of the great facility and economy of river in contradistinction to rail transportation.

The first of the run of the 10,000,000 bushels of coal coming out on the recent rise in the river will arrive this evening, and the coal fleet will be arriving and passing for two or three days. About one-third of it is intended for this market; the balance goes to points below. This immense amount of coal, because of the fact that it cannot come in advance of the rise in the river, will be about one week making the voyage from Pittsburgh to Cincinnati. When there is abundant water all the way the voyage is usually made in about four days.

In these 10,000,000 bushels there are 360,C00 tons. If it were piled up on the square bounded by Fourth, Vine, Fifth and Race streets, it would be a fraction over ninety-seven feet high or seven feet higher than the *Commercial-Gazette* office. It would cover an area of fifty acres, by many considered a fair sized farm — eight feet deep.

HANDLING COAL BY RAIL AND WATER.

A comparison of the facility and cost of transportation of such a mass, as between the river and rail, presents not only some interesting, but surprising results. The average coal car carries fifteen tons, so that it would require 24,000 cars to transport this 360,000 tons. Twenty-two cars, each laden with fifteen tons, is the full capacity of the average freight locomotive, so that 1,091 trains would be necessary. The cars average in length thirty feet, and with the locomotive and a caboose, each train of twenty-two cars would be 700 feet long. The 1,091 trains, placed close one after the other, would make a line of 144 miles, which is only eight miles less than one-half the distance between Cincinnati and Pittsburgh by the Panhandle road.

The Panhandle road changes its freight locomotives at Dennison and Columbus, so that three locomotives are used in the trip between Cincinnati and Pittsburgh. This would make necessary 3,273 changes of locomotives to haul the 1,091 trains. The Panhandle road could probably send twenty coal trains over its road daily if they were loaded and ready to be started, though it would take thirty-six hours for each train to pass between the two cities. It would take fifty-five days, upon this estimate, to bring as much coal to the city as is now coming on this rise.

The cost of towing this 10,000,000 bushels of coal to this city will not exceed $125,000. One cent per ton per mile is considered as low as railroads can afford to carry freight. The distance between Pittsburgh and Cincinnati by rail is 313 miles. Suppose coal could be carried at three-fourths of one cent per

ton per mile, each ton would cost $2.35, and the 360,000 tons
would cost $846,000, or $721,000 more than the cost by
river — nearly seven times as much.

THE COAL TRADE.

"A writer upon the subject estimates that the bituminous
coal field by which Pittsburgh is closely surrounded and from
which her gigantic coal traffic is derived is equal to 15,000
square miles, and its money value at five cents per bushel
is nearly $75,000,000,000, and that $75,000,000 worth
could be realized from sales of this coal annually for a thousand years, and then only exhaust the upper seam of the
measures.

In 1817 the transportation of coal in flat-boats down the
Ohio river from Pittsburgh was begun from French Creek,
where the mines were then located. These boats were loaded with from 4,000 to 6,000 bushels, lashed in pairs with ropes,
and floated as far down as Cincinnati under charge of a crew
of five men.

With the increase of trade and the development of the coal
lands along the Monongahela River this method of floating the
product to an equally growing market became too slow and
inadequate, and the application of steam for towing purposes
was made. The history of this enterprise has been admirably
told by Colonel Thurston, one of the best informed citizens of
Pittsburgh on all important commercial events in which the
city has been concerned during her wonderful career. He
says:

"The writer recollects well how the proposition to tow the
unwieldy 'French Creeks' was received by the coal boatmen
and was ridiculed. The term 'crank' had not then been coin-
ed, but those who talked of towing coal as a feasible thing
were at that day spoken of as such under a more common
name, and conservative business men shook their heads wisely
and smiled dubiously. As the coal boats had to be floated to
market on flood waters, it did, to those acquainted with the
rapid currents of the Ohio in the spring and fall rises and the
June freshets, seem a dangerous business to attempt to tow
those huge unwieldy bulks of coal in flat-bottomed, box-
shaped boats through the crooked channel and sharp bends of
the river. But in 1845 Daniel Bushnell began towing coal
down the Ohio with a small stern-wheel boat called the Walter Forward, making a trip to Cincinnati as an experiment
with three coal-flats loaded with 2,000 bushels each. In the

same year Judge Thomas·H. Baird began towing coal to Hanging Rock, Ohio, with a side-wheel boat called the Harlem and
two 'model' barges, bringing back pig metal.   In the fall of
1849 Hugh Smith began to tow coal to the lower markets with
the steam tow-boat Lake Erie.   During 1849 David Bushnell
built the Black Diamond tow-boat to tow coal to Cincinnati
and to New Orleans in 1850, from which date towing coal,
as it was called, superseded altogether the floating system.

THE WALTER FORWARD FIRST COAL TOW-BOAT.

"The term 'towing' is a misnomer, as the boats and barges
containing the coal are propelled instead of towed.   Although
this is an old song to Pittsburghers and many along the river,
yet to others it may not be uninteresting to be told that a tow,
as it is called, is made up of one tow-boat and from ten to
fourteen barges, coal boats and flats, and from one to four fuel
boats filled with slack coal for boiler fuel during the trip.
These boats are all placed in front of the tow-boat, except one
on each side of the steamer, all securely lashed together,
forming a compact mass about 350 feet long and 150 feet
wide, and holding from 500,000 to 700,000 bushels, or about
an average of 24,000 tons, being the yield of from five to seven
acres of coal land, according to the size of the tow, so called.
Of such tows from eight to ten in a day in the coal-boating
stages of the Ohio leave the harbor of Pittsburgh for all points
below as far as New Orleans, and there are now from ninety
to one hundred tow-boats, varying in cost from $8,000 to
$30,000, employed in thus propelling coal, being the outgrowth
in forty years from the little Walter Forward with her three
flat-boats, holding 6,000 bushels, or about 240 tons of coal.
As explanatory to those who are not familiar with the terms
of 'barge,' 'coal-boat' 'flat,' being the 'packages,' as the
trade term is, in which the coal is carried, a word or two of
description of these 'packages' may be of interest. Coal
boats are built 170 feet long by 26 feet wide, of 1 1-2 inch
plank, with about 18 inches rake at each end.   They carry
24,000 bushels and draw 7 feet when loaded.   They are only
used to convey the coal to its point of destination, and go
with the coal in the sale.   They cost about $600 each.
A barge is 130 feet long by 25 feet wide, constructed somewhat similar to the hull of a steam boat, but with stern and prow
alike, having bottom planking of 3-inch thickness and gunwales 6 inches.   The loading capacity of barges is about 13,-
000 bushels, and they draw 6 feet water when loaded.   They

cost from $1,000 to $1,100, and last from nine to ten years, being *towed* back from the point where the coal is sold, going by the technical term of ' empties ' on the return trip. Fuel boats are similar to barges, only smaller, being 95 by 20 feet, and draw 4 feet water loaded. They cost $600, and will last ten years in service, and carry 7,000 bushels. Flats are 90 by 16 feet, built same as barges, carry 4,000 bushels, and draw loaded 4 1-4 feet water, costing about $400.

"A tow of coal made up of these various descriptions of boats to the number, as before stated, of eighteen barges, coal-boats and flats, with the tow-boat, and loaded with the average of 600,000 bushels, or 24,000 tons coal, represents a value of $80,000 as it leaves the harbor at Pittsburgh. As before stated, eight or ten of such massive islands, as it were, of coal, equal in surface to 1 1-4 acres, floating the coal product of from 6 to 7 acres of coal land, depart in the boating stages of the Ohio from Pittsburgh. The ' driving,' for such it almost seems to be, in its handling by the deft pilot, who with sinewy arms whirls and rewhirls the wheel that guides the boat and this mass of coal, is a task to which only those brought up to the trade are competent. Skill, judgment, nerve are all called into play as this ponderous bulk, borne along on a river at flood height, running at a current of 8 to 10 miles an hour, sweeps onward. Through narrow channels, round sharp bends, between the stone piers of bridges, where a misturn of the wheel, a failure of judgment, a miscalculation of distance means disaster and wreck, the pilot guides the tow, now backing, now flanking, now pushing, now floating, watchful and cool the pilot does his work. There is probably no such boatsmanship shown anywhere else in the world as is displayed by the Pittsburgh coal tow-boat pilot. Watching one of these ponderous tows surging down the river with the little tow-boat of perhaps 90 to 100 feet in length and 20 to 25 feet in width at its rear, turning it round bends, flanking it past points, backing and checking it in narrow channels, one can but think of the old joke of the tail wagging the dog, and here it does it, and does it well. It is a wonderful exhibit of skillful navigation, and thus handling by the nervy grip of one man on a wheel a bulk of 30,000 tons, moving at a speed of from 12 to 15 miles an hour down such a tortuous stream as the Ohio, and with perhaps not 5 feet to spare of channel width or 2 feet of water depth."

The coal thus transported down the river from Pittsburgh is almost wholly drawn from the four "pools" of the Monongahela river that are stocked by fifty-nine firms of operators, employing the services of 8,860 hands, at annual wages averaging $3,177,000, and producing an output averaging 98,-580,000 bushels per year.

These figures are not precise, of course, being subject to the very important disturbing elements of "strikes," unremunerative markets and difficulties in running coal caused by low stages of water in the river; but the amounts stated form a fair average for the operations of a good season when the mines are productive up to their ordinary capacity.

The amounts passing the locks of the Monongahela Navigation Company represents the totals taken out of that stream and actually consumed in Pittsburgh and shipped to markets along the Ohio River and below. The following are statistics from the records of the company named : —

STATEMENT, IN BUSHELS OF COAL AND SLACK SHIPPED FROM THE SEVERAL POOLS OF THE MONONGAHELA SLACK-WATER ANNUALLY FOR THE YEARS NAMED.

Year.	Bushels.	Year.	Bushels.	Year.	Bushels.
1844	7,17,15?	1859	28,286,671	1874	67,821,300
1845	4,?05,1??	1860	37,947,782	1875	63,707,500
1846	7,778,91?	1861	20,865,722	1876	68,481,000
1847	?,645,127	1862	18,583,956	1877	79,480,918
1848	9,813,36?	1863	26,444,352	1878	76,895,355
1849	?,708,5?7	1864	35,070,917	1879	65,588,000
1850	12,297,5?7	1865	39,522,792	1880	84,048,350
1851	12,521,22?	1866	42,615,300	1881	88,954,660
1852	14,680,341	1867	30,072,700	1882	101,434,700
1853	15,710,367	1868	45,301,000	1883	108,487,800
1854	17,331,346	1869	52,512,600	1884	79,269,100
1855	12,234,069	1870	57,596,400	1885	83,459,050
1856	8,584,095	1871	48,621,300	1886	109,895,147
1857	29,971,53?	1872	54,208,900		
1858	25,036,069	1873	58,276,995	Total	1,869,980,776

In addition to the coal produced along the Monongahela and handled by water, the collieries along the railways diverging from Pittsburgh produce nearly 150,000,000 bushels in every ordinary year, of which 60 per cent. is probably consumed by Pittsburgh, and the remainder is shipped by rail directly from the mines to interior Western markets. There are no official statistics of the consumption of coal in Pittsburgh, so that it is impossible to state with precision what proportion of the total outputs of the mines goes to other markets.

Concerning the effect of introducing natural gas as a manufacturing fuel, Colonel Thurston, above quoted as an intelligent writer, while on the subject of coal in connection with Pittsburgh's industrial resources, has to say :—

" At first it would seem to threaten a decadence of the coal trade. But it is not unlikely it may increase the consumption of coal and thus even enhance the value of coal lands around Pittsburgh and the returns therefrom. While natural gas has almost entirely supplanted coal as a manufacturing fuel at Pittsburgh, this is possibly only a forerunner of a greater use of coal. The advantage in thus using gas is so great that even were the supply of natural gas to fail, the commercial manufacturing world would still require gas fuel from coal and preclude the return to crude coal heat. Ignoring the question of cheapness of gas over coal where the consumption is made at or in the near adjacencies to the well, the other advantages of gas fuel already established would enforce its use under a similarity of cost. The use of gas, whether of nature's production or from artificial supply, being primary, its obtainment from such material as will produce it most satisfactory in all respects follows. Of all substances bituminous coal, and of all coals that of the Pittsburgh seam, is pre-eminent. If artificial gas is to be had, the best quality and at the least cost is imperative. Where the gas is not in a vicinage artificial methods of conducting it there will be tried. At present the means of piping natural gas long distances are not economical, and its natural progress of flow seems limited, the appliances of artificial propulsion so far seeming to add so much to its cost as to overcome its desirability over coal fuel.

" The transportation of coal and its cost are fixed commercial facts. Where manufacturing facilities exist coal can easily be laid down in proximity to the fires to be fed. The coal of the Pittsburgh seam can therefore be made easily available at whatever point manufacturing fuel is demanded, and the great storage of the gas therein, cheaply transported, unlocked and used, while the coal fuel in form of coke, of a value quite equal to the coal, remains for other fuel uses, not to take into account other products which result from the distillation of coal for the production of gas. Of these latter there are a number; and skillful chemical handling and economical management would evolve other marketable residuums. It is, therefore, very probable that while the use of natural gas may decrease the consumption of coal at Pittsburgh, it will increase it in other localities, and the coal seams of Pittsburgh be more than ever valuable. For the carriage of coal, water highways are the cheapest, and the unsurpassed system of rivers by which the coal trade of Pittsburgh reaches the West and South is unrivaled, even enabling, when tonnage is wanted in interiors where the rivers do not reach, long distances of

railway transportation to be cut off, and such carriage reduced to short hauls."

THE COKE TRADE.

The coke business of Pittsburgh depends for its supplies
upon the Connellsville region, as only a small amount of this
article is produced in the city itself. All the great coke companies have their principal offices here, however, and their
financial transactions make no unimportant part of the daily
clearing-house returns. The Connellsville coke has made
Pittsburgh manufacturers what they are, and the product is in
demand all over the United States where metal working or
smelting is engaged in.

The first market consignment of this coke to a distance was
made in 1842, when two boat-loads, aggregating 1,600 bushels, were taken to Cincinnati. Since then the business has
absorbed nearly $7,000,000 in plants alone, and the annual
product taken by the general market will now average over
4,000,000 tons. Specifically the business engages 77 separate
firms and corporations, representing 10,788 ovens, consuming
annually in average years 180,000,000 bushels of coal, or
7,500,000 tons, and the wages disbursed amount to over $4,000,-
000 annually. The value of the product varies, like any other
stable commodity, with the current market price, but a safe estimate of value for each year's output would be $6,000,000.

In summing up these subjects of coal and coke, and they
should be mentioned together since the cokeries mine their own
coal, there are, in all the divisions of the business, 204 collieries, employing 27,680 hands, at wages amounting yearly to $11,-
150,000 ; the value of improvements, exclusive of cost of coal
lands, is $12,000,000, and the sales reach about $25,000,000 on
on the 430,000,000 bushels, or 17,200,000 tons mined annually.

Of this enormous aggregate fully 40 per cent. finds a market through the medium of the river transportation lines far
more cheaply than would otherwise be possible.

THE RIVER INTERESTS.

· Upon this material subject, as related to Pittsburgh trade,
Superintendent Follansbee, the chief executive officer of the
Pittsburgh Chamber of Commerce says: —

"Steam towing on the rivers of the United States has been
very largely the means of resuscitating the river trade, threatened with almost extinction by the construction of railroads.
By it Pittsburgh has sent forth hundreds of millions of tons of
coal, iron, and general merchandise throughout the entire Ohio

and Mississippi Valleys.   Her position in commerce has thus
been maintained and an economic check imposed upon the transportation charges in this vast territory of paramount influence."

As an example of what is claimed, Mr. Follansbee cites the
trip made in February, 1882, by the steamer Jos. B. Williams,
that left Louisville for New Orleans with a tow of 26 coal-
boats and barges, containing 600,000 bushels of coal, or 22,-
300 tons, a load far greater than any ever carried by the Great
Eastern and without parallel in the transportation annals of any
country.   The charges for carriage of this immense tonnage
from Pittsburgh to New Orleans, a distance of 2,000 miles,
were at the rate of 4 cents per bushel, or cne-twentieth of 1
cent per ton per mile, a freight rate that, as the writer remarks, "would bankrupt any railroad in the United States."

In 1881 the boating interests of Pittsburgh were represented
as follows : —

	Tons.
168 steam passenger and tow boats.............................	86,846
45 model barges...	16,243
1,500 coal-barges...	
500 coal-boats.. }	1,306,884
1,000 coal-flats..	
3,208 vessels, with tonnage of.................................	1,359,972
Capital invested...	$7,447,000
Hands employed..	3,260
Freight earnings during the year..............................	$2,400,000

Since the year named, with the exception noted below,
when the above statistics were gathered for a special report,
no precise figures have been preserved or are now attainable,
and reference is directed to the port list of boats at Pittsburgh
for the year 1866 for later figures, although the Government
does not include in its port registers the barges, boats, and
flats used in the carrying trade.   An estimate made in 1884,
however, places the tonnage of Pittsburgh in this latter class
at 2,000 barges, 60 model barges, 1,200 coal-boats, and 900
flats, valued at about $7,000,000.   These figures will not, it
is believed, vary much from the present tonnage of these
transports.   In this year above given (1884) the port list of
Pittsburgh shows 163 steam vessels registered, having a total
tonnage of 32,914.07, employing a capital of $9,740,000,
3,500 hands, and producing revenues from freights amounting to about $3,000,000.

The completion of the Davis Island Dam, at Pittsburgh,
will add greatly to the harbor facilities of the city.   This
work has cost the United States Government nearly $1,000,-
000, and furnishes a pool 7 feet deep, covering an area of

1.62 square miles, sufficient for the harborage of over 12,000 steamboats and barges. The lock length of this dam is 600 feet, with a width of 110 feet, thus making it the largest and longest lock in the world.

From the date of the construction of the New Orleans, in 1811 up to the present, steamboat building has been an important feature in Pittsburgh's industrial career. It is estimated that one complete steamer has been turned out from her shops and boat-yards weekly for more than a quarter of a century, beginning with the year 1842. During this period not only have a number of iron and steel steamers of light draught been built for foreign river navigation, but fully one-half of the steam fleet navigating Western waters has been constructed here. Steamboats for general freight and passenger service are turned out at these yards requiring only a draught of 2 feet, with a tonnage capacity enabling owners to make handsome profits at half the tolls customarily charged upon railroads for like service.

For Pittsburgh alone it is estimated that the average tonnage to the account of each steamer conveying coal and coke in tows is 5,500 per half trip.

REPORT FROM CHAMBER OF COMMERCE.

Approaching the subject of Pittsburgh's carrying trade by river and rail, any full statement of tonnage, classification, and direction of shipments for a series of years is found to be well-nigh impracticable, owing to the lack of procurable definite data. The only statement pretending to accuracy or official character is that made for the year 1881 by Superintendent Follansbee, of the Chamber of Commerce of Pittsburgh, in a report upon the "Commerce, Industrial and Transportation interests of the city of Pittsburgh," published as an appendix to the Report of the Chief of the Bureau of Statistics, Treasury Department, on the internal commerce of the United States in December, 1882.

Mr. Follansbee says : —

"The shipments from this city to points below, reaching as far South as New Orleans, for the year 1881, we find to be :

	Tons.
Coal and coke, 75,000,000 bushels, or.............................	2,884,610
Shipped by Saint Louis lines:	
Steel rails..	56,576
Bar-iron, sheet-iron, splices, glassware, etc............	18,827
	75,403
By Cincinnati, Portsmouth and Louisville boats:	
Shipments composed principally of iron, steel, nails, window-glass, glass-ware, plows, etc....................	33,750

CHAPTER LXVII.

BEACON LIGHT SERVICE ON WESTERN RIVERS.

BY an act of Congress approved June 23d, 1874, the jurisdiction of the Light House Board was extended over
the Mississippi, Missouri and Ohio rivers, for the establishment
of such " Beacon Lights, " day beacons and buoys as may be
necessary for the use of vessels navigating those streams.
The rivers were divided in two districts. The 14th, from
Pittsburgh, Pa., to New Orleans. The 15th, from St. Paul,
Minn., to Cairo, Ill., and Missouri River from Kansas City to
its mouth. The first beacon established on the Mississippi
River was on the dike below River Des Peres on December
4th, 1874. The work in the 15th district was then in charge
of Commander R. R. Wallace, U. S. N. The 14th district
was in charge of Commander Jos. Fyffe, U. S. N.

The work in the 15th district coming more directly under
the observation of the writer can say without any disparage-
ment to other inspectors that, after numerous experiments,
aided by the advice of masters and pilots generally, Commander Wallace soon overcame the difficulties of this new
work and had his most important aid to navigation fully recognized as invaluable.

On April 1st, 1876, the boundaries of the two river districts
were changed. The 14th, from Cairo, Ill., to Pittsburgh.
The 15th, from St. Paul to New Orleans, including the Missouri river. On January 1st, 1887, owing to the great increase
of the number of light stations the 16th district was formed
by dividing the 15th. The territory of the 16th being from
Cairo, Ill., to New Orleans.

Since 1874 there has been added the Great Kanawha, Tennessee, Illinois and mouth of Red River, all of which are now
well lighted.

The number of stations in the different streams are as follows : —

Mississippi River from St. Paul to Cairo	359
" " " Cairo to New Orleans	320
Mouth of Red River	7
Ohio River from Pittsburgh to Cairo	453
Kanawha River	27
Tennessee River	37
Illinois River	37
Missouri River	27

Total number of stations on Western rivers 1,276

The lighting of Western rivers has been under the immediate supervision of naval officers detailed for that purpose. Their work has given entire satisfaction, though the smallness of appropriations has prevented them from establishing as many beacon lights as are required. They have lighted all the dangerous crossings and navigation is made comparatively easy.

Frequent trips are made over the territory of the different districts by their respective inspectors, and the stations moved to suit changed channels, keepers paid, supplied, &c.

The appropriations for this service have been increased from time to time, commencing in 1874 with $50,000, the last one in 1888 was $225,000.

COST OF EACH BEACON LIGHT.

It is estimated that it costs a little less than $10 each per month to maintain these lights, in addition to the cost of the tender for visiting the different stations.

There are 1,226 stations in the three districts. If those on the Missouri River were discontinued and added to those which need more lights, it would be the proper thing to do, as they are no longer of any service on the Missouri; but it requires an act of Congress to do it. And it is presumed members of Congress from that State would object. For as long as they continue to appropriate money to improve the navigation of the stream, to be consistent, they must insist upon its being lighted, although it has been virtually abandoned by steamboats, without any probability of their ever finding profitable employment upon it again.

All who know anything practically of navigation are aware of the great benefit these lights are to navigators, and especially in dark stormy nights and shifting channels. No one knows the relief it affords under such circumstances to the anxious officers on watch unless they have experienced it.

Going down the Mississippi with a deeply laden boat, drawing nearly all the water, on a dark stormy night, with the leadsman crying no bottom — deep four, half three, marked three, half twain, mark twain, quarter less twain, nine feet, with every optic strained to catch sight of a "big break" on the one side, and a snag on the other, and the *beacon light* so long coming in sight, places one in a good state of mind to appreciate its illuminating power when it looms up in the distance, and he wonders how we ever managed to get along without them. And yet, if they are not located just where he thinks they ought to be, or for any reason the keeper has failed to light up in time or the Tender has been delayed in its constant rounds, the complaints are long and loud of neglect, inefficiency, failure of the system, etc.

And yet all are ready to admit that no other adjunct to our navigation has resulted in half the benefit for the money invested that this has. Still the system is by no means perfect, nor is it to be supposed the officers in charge are always above criticism.

The following quotation from the New Orleans *Times-Democrat* over the signature Pilot may be read with interest and is undoubtedly a just criticism : —

THE BEACON LIGHT SERVICE.

To the Editor Times-Democrat.

Next to the work of improving the channels of the rivers, unless we except the snag-boat service, the greatest aid to better and safer navigation given by the government is the establishment of the Beacon Light Service. An ever present ·and true monitor, they point us to the ways we should follow or avoid in the time of floods as well as low water, and turning night into day, as it were, they lessen delays and add to safety. But like the fickle river, which brooks not restraint and obeys but its own whim in its progress to the sea, the beacon that assures safety as we pass up, may lead to danger as we return down, and their station can no more be fixed than can the currents by which they stand as sentinels be controlled, and in acknowledgment of this is not only the fact that information from masters and pilots as to changes of locality that may have become necessary is sought and acted upon by the officials in charge, but the further fact that Congress, at its last session, subdivided the district to the end that the recognized and increasing needs of the service might be the better met. But in making appropriations therefor Congress was guided almost solely by the estimates submitted of the amount needed for its proper maintenance, and while it was surely expected that no part of the appropriation would be needlessly spent, it was just as surely intended that its disbursement would be made in accordance with the demands of the service, limited only by honest judgment, and uninfluenced by motives of parsimony or mistaken economy. And this leads me to speak of an act of omission and commission on the part of Lieut. O'Kane, of which it is to be earnestly hoped his successor, Commander Bridgman, now in charge, will not prove guilty. Lieut. O'Kane, while a conscientious and capable officer, was possessed with the idea that, happen

what might, his expenditures must remain well and safely
within his allowance, and so rigidly and invariably did he live
up to that idea, it is said, that the year before last he reported
an unexpended balance of $10,000, and last year $5,000, a result the fruit of which was to the immediate and serious im-
pairment of the service in two ways at least.

1. Because when the necessity of another and new light at a
given locality became apparent, instead of placing it there at
once, that overruling fear of such an outlay would manifest
itself, and to avoid this called-for increase in the number of
lights, one would, very often, be discontinued at some other
point and established instead at the new locality; thus happily (?) meeting an exigency without additional cost, though
at the expense may be of some other locality; as much as to
say, in other words, we know that new and additional lights
are needed from time to time, and we have the money with
which to supply them, but we don't want to spend it, and,
therefore, you must manage, through changing the lights from
place to place, to get along with what you have. 2. Because
by the saving of such balances from year to year the lie is
given to the estimates upon which the appropriation is based,
and justification given to Congress in cutting them down because of the fact made so patent thereby that the amount
asked for will not be needed. This, I believe, is not the kind
of service the government intended, and I am certain the exigencies require, and if any one will tell me that Congress in
making a specific appropriation for a specified object, contemplated or would approve of such a rule, I'll not believe
it. And if Lieut. Bridgman would do justice to himself and
to the Beacon Light Service, he must avoid the rule of his
predecessor in this particular, and be guided and controlled
only by the exigency of the demand and the means at his dis-
posal.   Respectfully,

                                         PILOT.

CHAPTER LXVIII.

UPPER MISSISSIPPI PACKET COMPANIES.

[From Sharf's History of St. Louis.]

"THE St. Louis & Keokuk Packet Company was formed January 1, 1842. John S. McCune and Jas. E. Yateman were the principal stockholders. The Di Vernon was their first boat. She was built at St. Louis at a cost of $16,000, and started on her first trip to Keokuk in the autumn of that year.

"In the spring of 1843 she commenced running regularly, and, with two other transient boats, made a daily line, except Sundays, which continued throughout the season.

"During the following winter the Laclede was built and the Boreas was purchased. With these three boats they opened the season of 1844, and secured a contract for carrying the mail."

"During this season an opposition line was organized with three boats—the Swallow, the Anthony Wayne, and the Edward Bates.

"They continued to run until mid-summer, when the opposition line was withdrawn, and the Edward Bates, a fine new boat was purchased by the old company.

"In the spring of 1846, the Lucy Bertram, a new boat, was added to the line, and in 1847 the Kate Kerney was built.

"In 1850, another Di Vernon was built at St. Louis, at a cost of $49,000, a sum that was considered fabulous at that time for a steamboat.

"In the spring of that year another opposition line was started with three steamers—Monongahela, New England and Mary Stephens."

The two lines continued nearly throughout the season. One boat of each line left St. Louis every week day evening, side by side doing the best they could, and sparing no expense for fuel or other expenses, and carrying freight and passengers at any price they could get. The contest continued until they had lost some $50,000, when the opposition was withdrawn, and the boats sold at auction, the old company buying the New England.

The Jennie Deans was built in the summer of 1852, and the New Lucy in the fall of the same year. She was burned at the wharf about six weeks after she was finished.

In 1853 the Westerner was built, and another Kate Kerney. Subsequently those were added to the line. From time to time

Sam Gaty, Keokuk, Quincy, Ben Campbell, Prairie State, G. McGee, Glaucus, Regulator, Jennie Lind, Connawago, Winchester, York State, Thomas Swan, and others.

In 1852, the company established a line from St. Louis to Quincy. Running one to Keokuk, and one to Quincy, daily, except Sundays. They were known as the Quincy Packets and the Keokuk Mail Packets.

The eminent success of this, the first organized packet company on the Upper Mississippi, was so great, and the result so satisfactory to the owners and the public, that other companies were soon organized, not only on the Mississippi above St. Louis, but on the Missouri and Illinois, as well as on most navigable rivers in the valley.

While the Cincinnati & Louisville Mail line antedated the Keokuk Packet Co. by more than twenty years, such was the popularity of the latter, that it was about as well known at this time (1857) as was the former, which was established in 1818.

POPULARITY OF THIS LINE.

The regularity and promptness with which it started from port and made its trips, soon became known, and was so satisfactory to the public and its patrons, and was such an improvement over the usual custom, of delaying departure for hours after the advertised time, and sometimes for days, that it grew rapidly into favor, and its patronage was unprecedented, and probably did more to advance the commercial interest of St. Louis, and for the settlement of the country bordering on that portion through which it run, than all other causes combined.

The stockholders of this company, of whom John S. McCune was one of the principal, and furnished the *brain power* and the energy for the whole, were equal to the times and to its opportunity, and the line was provided with the best boats, and managed in such a way that its popularity continued to increase until the stock of the Keokuk Packet company was considered the best in the market, and very little of it for sale for several years

The extinguishing of Indian titles, and the opening of the Northwest to settlement, stimulated emigration, and the rush to the Upper Mississippi, to "spy out the land," was immense about this time, or a little earlier. The result was a rapid increase of the number and character of steamboats on the Upper Mississippi, and while for several years a profitable business was done by all, the supply soon exceeded the demand, as it usually has in all steamboat business on Western waters.

Before attempting a description of the various packet companies which followed, it may be proper to refer to this part of the river before any companies were formed.

The Keokuk trade was recognized as such, many years prior to the organization of any steamboat company.

All early settlers, as well as old boatmen, will remember the Rosalie, Capt. Mike Littelton; the Quincy, Capt. Cameron; the Boreas, Capt Fitheon; the Knickerbocker, Capt. Gould, and many others long since forgotten.

BOATS AND BOATMEN ON UPPER MISSISSIPPI.

There was also many boats running above the rapids from St. Louis. Among which will be recollected the Warrior, Capt.Throckmorton; the Winnebago, Capt.Atchinson; the Joe Davis, Capt. Scribe Harris; the Pizarro, Capt. Smith Harris; the Rolla, Capt. Reynolds; the Gypsy, Capt. Gray; the St. Croix, Capt. Bersie; the Illinois, Capt.McCalister; the Rapids, Capt. Cole; the Fulton, Capt. Orrin Smith; the Brazil, the Irene, the Ione, the Time and Tide, the Falcon, the St. Peters, the Montauk, and many others. Stimulated by the success of the Keokuk company, which succeeded in holding its business in spite of the effort made by so large a number of boats running through its territory to divide it, determined to organize into companies, and manage their business in a more systematic manner.

The result was the formation of several companies in rapid succession. Among the first was one from Galena to St. Paul, known as the "Galen, Dubuque & Minnesota Packet Co," Orrin Smith, President. Minnesota was then the great point of attraction for immigrants, and the pine lands of Wisconsin had just come into notice, which gave to this company an immense business, and they at once commenced building boats to accommodate their trade, and could hardly supply the demand fast enough.

They bought everything that offered, that was at all suited to the trade, and built as many as five or six boats in one season, the largest and finest that had ever been above St. Louis, not excepting the famous Keokuk packets.

Soon after this organization, or about 1857-8, the boats in the trade between St. Louis and St. Paul decided it was necessary to do something to protect themselves against the excessive competition existing between them, and decided to make a joint arrangement and run their boats regularly, and on stated days — dividing the time and the business as judiciously and as fairly as they could. The result was, there was some ten or more boats included in this arrangement, which after running some two years, organized a *joint stock company,* known as the Northern Line Packet Co., and elected Capt. James Ward, President, and Capt. Thomas H. Griffith, Secretary and Treasurer. This was a good line of boats, and ran successfully for several years through from St. Louis to St. Paul. Before the completion of the canal at Keokuk, during low water, they divided their boats and ran a part from the head of the Rapids to St. Paul, and a part from Keokuk to St. Louis.   Thus affording acceptable facilities to the public, and the commerce of the Upper Mississippi, as could be expected until the completion of the canal, and the improvement of the upper rapids.

These important improvements added greatly to the facilities of transportation in that trade, and created an inducement to increase the size of boats, and to run them through from St. Louis to St. Paul.

About that time, or in 1864, CAPT. WM. F. DAVIDSON, who had been largly interested in boats, engaged in running to St. Paul from La Crosse, and from the Minnesota River, and had established what was known as the North-west Union Packet Co., by combining the interests of several other companies that had been driven from their respective trades by the extention of railroads, proposed to run his boats through to St. Louis.   Thus becoming an active competitor for the business of the Northern Line Co., and also of the Keokuk Co.

But in 1868, the Northern Line and the North-west Union Packet Co. consolidated, and the next season all ran under the joint arrangement, and ran through to St. Louis, with Thmas B. Rhodes, President, and Thos. H. Griffith, Secretary.

There was some twenty boats and many barges belonging to this organization.   Many of them large, fine boats, and they proved strong competitors for the business of the Keokuk line.   But after running one season a compromise was effected with the Keokuk Packet Company, and a new organization was created, which was known as the " Keokuk Northern Line Packet Company," with a capital stock of $750,000 made up by the aggregation of the appraised value of the stock of both companies.   John S. McCune was made President, and T. H. Griffith, Secretary.

It was an immense corporation, and with much more stock than they had business for.   But as long as Mr. McCune lived, the company was so well managed it seemed prosperous.

Although the depreciation of so much idle stock, and the

competition with railroads that had now reached almost every point on the river seemed to threaten the company with annihilation sooner or later. It probably never declared a dividend to the holders of stock of the new company.

Unfortunately Mr. McCune died about that time or in 1874.

Soon after his death a serious difficulty arose about his successor, Capt. Davidson being the opposing candidate for the succession. But the mantle from Mr. McCune was, after a long and bitter struggle, finally thrown upon the shoulders of David Hawkins, one of the directors, and a stockholder in the old Northern Line Company.

But from that time to the death of Capt. Davidson and Capt. R. C. Gray, of Pittsburgh, who was a large stockholder, and always a director, the company was in litigation, and in the courts some fifteen years, sufficiently long to absorb the value of a company's stock of far more value than that of the Keokuk Northern Line at the time it was closed out.

Here were two agencies, either of which was quite sufficient to consume and blot from existence any steamboat company at work, to destroy one of the most favorably located and well organized companies on Western waters — a *bitter feud* between stockholders· on the one side, and a *combination* of *railroads* on the other, and the result was as it always is and always will be in similar cases.

In 1881, the St. Louis & St. Paul Packet Company was organized as a successor to the Keokuk Northern Line Company, Wm. F. Davidson, President, F. S. Johnston, Secretary, with a capital of $100,000. It still continues, 1889,* to maintain the trade between St. Louis and St. Paul, in conjunction with a line known as the "Diamond Joe Line." But the prestige and the fame that so long attached to the numerous Upper Mississippi Packet Companies, and rendered them the pride and the boast of the whole Mississippi Valley, as well as of the thousands of tourists that annually resort to this beautiful river, seems to have passed under a cloud, and become obscured or nearly so, by the overpowering influence of railroads.

But those who are familiar with the picturesque scenery and the delights of a passage on this, the most beautiful of all American rivers, will never believe it will be abandoned or lose its attraction, at least for summer travelers and tourists, unless the navigation shall become so difficult and dangerous from the multiplication of railroad bridges as to render steamboat traveling unsafe or unpleasant.

---

* St. Louis & St. Paul Packet Co. since sold out.

In 1880, the " St. Louis & St. Paul Passenger and Freight Line," was incorporated under the laws of Wisconsin. The general office was located at LaCrosse, with Capt. P. L. Davidson, President, and Lafayette Holmes, Secretary. Its boats were of large capacity and light draft, and did a large freighting business.

DIAMOND JOE AND OTHER LINES.

The Diamond Joe Line was established in 1867 by Joseph Reynolds, with a single boat, and used principally in handling his own freight, at points on the Mississippi above Dubuque. Mr. Reynolds continued to increase his stock, by adding boats and barges until the Diamond Joe Line has become a successful competitor for a large proportion of the trade above St. Louis. The principal office is at Dubuque, with Joseph Reynolds manager and owner and Capt. E. M. Dickey general agent.

The Eagle Packet Co., originally the St. Louis & Alton Packet Co., has increased its stock and extended its business to Clarksville, 75 miles further up the Mississippi. It has several boats and barges engaged in towing rock, railroad ties, lumber, etc. Capt. Williams, President; Capt. Henry Lyhe, General Manager; principal office, Alton, Ill.

The St. Louis & Alton Packet Co. was one of the first companies organized, to run above St. Louis, and has been continued under numerous administrations with varied success. Before the completion of the railroads from Alton to St. Louis, the trade was large and prosperous and some of the finest and fastest boats running to St. Louis were in the Alton trade.

MINNESOTA PACKET COMPANY.

The following concise history from Capt. R. Blakeley, a veteran of St. Paul, one of the original organizers of the famous Minnesota Packet Co., embraces the names of so many well known steamboats and individuals still living, that a more detailed account than is usual in this work may prove of interest, and serve to awaken pleasant recollections of perhaps the most active period in the history of this great industry.

While many of the prominent actors have launched their frail barques on more peaceful waters, those that remain may remember with much satisfaction the stirring times on the Upper Mississippi during the existence of the world-renowned Galena, Dubuque and Minnesota Packet Co.

This Company was organized June 8th, 1847. During the winter M. W. Lodwick and R. Blakeley went to Cincinnati and bought the steamboat Dr. Franklin which was put on the river from Galena to St. Paul in the spring of the year 1848, M. W. Lodwick, captain, and R. Blakely, clerk.

In the spring of the year 1849, the steamer Senator, Captain Orrin Smith, was added and in 1850 the Nominee, Capt. Smith, replaced the Senator. In the fall of 1851 Capt. M. W. Lodwick went to the Ohio River and built the steamer Ben Campbell, which was added to the list. In the year 1852 the company bought some other boats for freight and low water purposes also.

During the years 1850-1-2 and 3, Capt. D. S. and R. S. Harris and their friends ran the steamer West Newton, Dr. Franklin No. 2 and some other boats in what was called or known as the opposition line from Galena to St. Paul. The business was regarded a very lively one, if not very profitable, and almost every one in Galena, Dubuque and St. Paul took sides with either one line or the other during this contest.

In the fall of the year 1853 the interest of all was consolidated under the name of the Galena and Minnesota Packet Company, Capt. Orrin Smith, President, and J. R. Jones, Secretary, and in the spring of the year 1854, the business opened with the following boats as the passenger boats of the line: Nominee, Captain R. Blakeley; War Eagle, Captain D. S. Harris; Galena, Captain D. B. Morehouse; Royal Arch, E. H. Gleim.

The War Eagle and Galena were new boats which were built during the fall and winter of the years 1853 and 1854, and were regarded as the best boats for high water, speed and first class accommodations. They were about 225 feet long and 27 or 28 feet beam, and very beautiful side-wheel packets and were a pride of the owners and patrons.

In the summer of 1855, the beautiful new packet Northern Belle, Capt. Preston Lodwick, was added to the list and proved a very popular and profitable addition to the fleet.

During this season the Illinois Central Railroad was completed to Dunleith, on the Mississippi River, and the packet Company made an arrangement, to run in connection with the railroad leaving Dunleith, morning and evening.

On the opening of navigation in the year 1856 the line was run as the Galena, Dunleith and Minnesota Packet Company, and the following boats composed the line, War Eagle, D. L. Harris, Galena, Capt. Kennedy Lodwick; Northern Belle, Capt. Preston Lodwick; Golden Era, Capt. J. W. Parker; Lady Franklin, Capt. M. E. Lucas; Ocean Wave, Capt. E. H. Gleim; Lily Belle, Capt. W. H. Laughton; Granite State, J. Y. Hurd; Alhambra, Capt. W. II. Gabbert.

Royal Arch, Capt. J. J. Smith, and Greek Slave, Capt.

Cephas Goll, ran to Rock Island to connect with the Chicago and Rock Island Railroad. This was a year of immense emigration and proved a profitable as well as a very active season and too much of a temptation to the people of Dubuque to be resisted and the business men, under the lead of Mr. J. B. Farley as manager, bought the Fanny Harris, Capt. Jones Worden, and probably two other boats were run during the seasons and they also made contracts to build two first class side-wheel boats for the year 1857.

GALENA, DUNLEITH & MINNESOTA PACKET COMPANY.

The Galena, Dunleith and Minnesota Packet Co., had also contracted for their new boats to be ready for the year 1857.

During the winter of 1856-7 the parties interested in the Galena, Dunleith and Minnesota Packet Co. and the Dubuque Co., formed a new or consolidated line for the coming season, under the name of the Galena, Dubuque, Dunleith and Minnesota Packet Co., Capt Orrin Smith, President; J. R. Jones, Secretary, and R. Blakeley, General Agent at Dunleith.

The new boats arrived early in the season and were as follows: Grey Eagle, Capt. D. S. Harris; Northern Light, Capt. Preston Lodwick; Milwaukee, Stephen Hewitt; Key City, Jones Worden; Itasca, David Whitten. The Grey Eagle was 250 feet long and 35 feet beam. The Milwaukee was 250 feet long, and 35 feet beam. The Northern Light was 240 feet long and 40 feet beam. The Key City and Itasca, were 220 feet long and 35 feet beam. These boats were very light draft and were built without regard to expense and were in all respects the best boats of their size and class that ran on the Mississippi River.

During the fall and winter of 1856-7 an arrangement was made with the Milwaukee & Prairie du Chien Railroad to put on a line of boats, to run in connection with the road from Prairie du Chien to St. Paul, to be called the Prairie du Chien and St. Paul Packet Line. The Milwaukee, Capt. Stephen Hewitt; Itasca, Capt. David Whitten; Ocean Wave, Capt. E. H. Gleim, composed this line.

In the summer of 1858 a line of boats belonging to the company ran from LaCrosse to St. Paul in connection with the Milwaukee & LaCrosse Railroad; the War Eagle, Northern Belle and probably another composed this line.

The boats above named continued to run on the river above Galena and Dubuque until the summer of 1862, when the property was sold and the Galena, Dubuque, Dunleith & Minnesota Packet Co. was dissolved.

Among the many and popular clerks who were employed on the line during its operation may be mentioned : John H. Mateland, John Brooks, A. L. Monfort, John Pieu, John Cochran, Jos. DuBois, Geo. H. Hamilton, Ed. Halliday, Chas. Hinde, Chas. Hargus, Geo. S. Prince and many others too numerous to mention.

CHAPTER LXIX.

EARLY STEAMBOATS ON THE ILLINOIS RIVER.

AMONG the first of which there was any regularity may be mentioned the Friendship, Mungo Park, Tiskilwa, Daniel Hillman, Wyoming, Sygnet, LaSalle, Alvarado, Princeton, Avalaunch, Pearl, Beardstown, Movestar.

Later they were succeeded by a little larger class, among which was the Herald, Excelsior, Timolian, Lehigh, Mountaineer, Planter, Eureka, Kingston, Ocean Wave, Pekin, Schuyler, Martha, Prairie State, Illinois.

Until 1835 there was but few boats on the Illinois River. Occasionally a boat bound for the Ohio, or for New Orleans would go up for a load, and a few ran irregularly, or when they could get a trip, and their advertisements were continued from day to day in the papers until they were loaded.

Among such boats may be found the names of Criterion in 1828, Orion and Express in 1832, Miner in 1833, Lady Jackson, Wisconsin, Cold Water, Utility, American, Springfield, Champion in 1834 ; Banner, Winnebago, Adventure, Illinois, in 1835.

NAPLES PACKET COMPANY.

This company was organized in 1848 by E. W. Gould and C. S. Rogers, of St. Louis, and Messrs Mather, Lamb & Ridgeley, of Springfield, Illinois, to run between St. Louis and Naples on the Illinois River, and in connection with the Sangamon & Morgan Railroad, then running from Springfield to Naples. That was among the first railroads in the West, and at that time the rails were made of *flat bar iron.*

Afterwards it was relaid with the ordinary T rail, and the road extended to Decatur, and then to Danville, and finally to the State line, and the name changed to Great Western.

The packet company was organized with two boats, the Time and Tide and the Anthony Wayne, both light draft side-wheel boats, each boat making three trips a week from St. Louis.

It was soon apparent the trade would not support two boats, and the Anthony Wayne was withdrawn, and returned to the Upper Mississippi, where both boats had previously been engaged. The Time and Tide was continued in the trade for several years, until withdrawn to make room for a boat of more speed and capacity.

The Niagara was purchased by the company and ran for several years, and was superseded by a new boat built by the company called Cataract. As this was the only route from Springfield and the interior of the State to St. Louis, except by stage, it soon became very popular, and was liberally patronized, and frequent accessions in the capacity of the boats was necessary.

THE FIVE-DAY LINE.

About this time, or in 1852, what was known as the "*five day line*" was organized, to run between St. Louis and La Salle, the head of navigation, on the Illinois river, and the terminus of the "Illinois and Michigan Canal."

This was rendered necessary to accommodate the rapidly increasing travel between the East and the West, a large portion of which selected the "lake route" from Buffalo to Chicago. The lake boats were then of great capacity for passengers, and very elegant and fast.

The canal was provided with packet boats which were fitted up in fine style for the accommodation of passengers, and would accommodate from 75 to 100 with sleeping berths, and although not capacious, was a great improvement over stage traveling, especially at night, and the meals provided were proverbially good.

This route soon became popular and the patronage of the *five-day line* continued to increase, until railroad facilities were such as to furnish more direct and rapid transit between the East and West.

This line was owned by individual companies, each boat being run on its owner's account. There was some of the finest and fastest boats of that day engaged in this trade, and the time made from St. Louis to LaSalle, by some of them, has never been excelled on the Illinois River, and not often on any tributary of the Mississippi.

The familiar names of Garden City, Amazon, Cataract, Messenger, Prairie Bird, Belle Gould, Aunt Lettie, Alma and others, belonging to that line, will awaken pleasant recollections of early steamboat days, and canal-boat experiences, in many who still survive the wreck of time, and the *result* of railroad *collisions*, etc.

The name of *"five-day line"* originated in the fact that heretofore weekly trips had been the universal custom of all boats in that trade, and it was a great innovation upon traditional usages to reduce the time to five days, and it was only through great persuasion the change was made, and then only under protest by the older navigators.   But it was in accordance with the spirit of the times, and soon adjusted itself to the inevitable.

The Naples Packet Company saw the necessity and the demand for increased facilities in the upper part of the river, and at the risk of its own trade, joined in the effort to secure faster and better boats for the through trade, adding two of their own boats to the through line.

A few years of railroad competition destroyed the famous *five day line* and all other lines on that river, except the Naples packets, and only from their connection with a railroad, which terminated at the river, it would probably have succumbed long years since.   But by extending its business to points further up the river, it still lingers under another name, as it has for years, through hope and fear, and unless the government comes to its relief, by completing the improvements of the river, it is only a question of time when it will yield its remaining business to the great monopoly.

Captains Rogers and Abrams are the only members of the old organization that still retain positions occupied in the old company for near forty years.   Their names and faces have so long been honored and recognized as the principal factors in the Naples Packet Co., that without them the new organization would hardly be identified.

In 1858 under the general incorporation act of the State of Illinois, the Illinois River Packet Co. was organized.   D. J. Hancock was elected President and Wm. Mullen Secretary, L. T. Belt, Superintendent.

The stock was made up by a valuation of the several steamboats intended for the line.   Among the masters of the boats the names of Belt, Devinney, Rhodes, Hicks, Clay, Stackpole, Scott, Sargeant, Russell and others will be remembered by the older citizens of Illinois and the merchants of St. Louis, as good boatmen commanding a good line of boats, deserving a better result, considering the great improvement they introduced by a combination of what had heretofore been an irregular and unsatisfactory manner of running their boats.   After a varied experience and a vigorous effort to meet the competition from the common enemy of all inland

water transportation, the company succumbed and the boats
that remained were sold to a new organization over which Mr.
John S. McCune was elected President and Capt. E. A. Shible
Superintendent.

This organization had ample facilities, and was prepared to
win fame and fortune, in spite of railroad competition. But
about two years was sufficient to satisfy the company that
unless the government would improve the navigation of the
river, longer effort was useless.

About that time Mr. McCune died, and the Naples Packet
Co. was all that was left to represent what once promised to
be one of the great arteries of the commerce of the valley of
the Illinois and a large contribution to the trade of St. Louis.

STEAMBOAT OTTAWA.

In Sharf's History of St. Louis, among other items relating
to early steamboats, is this one: —

"The steamboat Ottawa was the first boat built on the
Illinois. She was constructed in part at Ottawa, added to at
Peru, and finished at St. Louis. She was of the very
lightest draught, seventeen inches, and had a powerful engine ;
the design being to take two keels in tow in low water, the
steamer herself being light, so that whenever there was seventeen inches of water on the bars she would be able to reach
St. Louis with one 100 tons of freight weekly.

Her length was one 100 feet, breadth, 20 feet, and the cabin
laid off entirely in state rooms. The owners resided in
Ottawa."

There is no date by which to determine the appearance of
this specimen of marine architecture. It must, however, have
been pretty early, as none of the present generation of "old
boatmen" know anything of the "tow-boat" Ottawa.

As early as 1844, Capt. Samuel Rider, one of the most
mechanical and inventive boatmen ever on the Illinois River,
built at Griggsville landing a sort of nondescript boat he
called Olitippa, which was propelled by horses upon an
endless chain. The boat had no cabin or cargo box and the
hold was too shallow to stow freight in.

She was designed expressly to carry freight in low water
which, of course, had to be stowed on the main deck, as she
had no other, and the cook, the officers, and the men occupied
the same location. The clerk's office was carried in the
captain's hat, and as there was but few ladies traveling on
the Illinois at that early day, a chamber-maid was dispensed

with. Later on when accidents on the rivers were more frequent from fires, and bursting of boilers, the Olitippa would doubtless have become very popular, as but little apprehension could have been felt from either cause on her.

She proved to be what she was designed for, a light draught boat (only ten inches) for the Illinois River. But when she drifted out of her home element into the strong currents of the Mississippi, she was at sea without a rudder, or without power to avoid snags or lee-shores. Consequently after making one trip to St. Louis, she retired from the placid waters of the Illinois, and emigrated with the ducks and geese, to a more genial climate.

After the departure of the Olitippa the experience and the genius of Captain Rider led him to design and construct two steamboats at the same place, (Griggsville Landing), that excelled all steamboats in point of capacity on shoal water that had been built up to that date, 1847. While not a boat builder, but a sea-going sailor (all the way from Cape Cod), the model of the hull was unexceptionable, the power, although light, was well applied and the cabin finish and accommodations were about equal to any boats of the time, wherever built. The first one was called Timolian and the second was called Prairie State.

Capt. Rider was a careful, obliging commander and popular with all who knew him. No one knew better how to relieve a boat in difficulty than he did.

He crossed the unknown river in 1881, leaving four daughters and one son and many friends but no enemies. This can be said of but few men who so often meet the adverse side of society, as do the boatmen on Western waters.

CHAPTER LXX.

A FAST AGE—PASSION FOR RACING—A CELEBRATED FOUR-MILE-HEATS RACE—FAST TIME MADE ON THE MISSISSIPPI RIVER.

NOTHING so much interests the average American as rapid motion, and it is not confined to our nationality altogether either.

The fastest sailing vessel, even a merchantman, always got the preference in the early days, if known to excel in speed.

Then followed the clipper ships, which excited the admiration of the civilized world, because of their speed.

Steam had no sooner been applied to navigation than the genius of the best mechanical skill was challenged to produce the best results in speed from a combination of steam power and model of vessels.

Then followed individual rivalry for the championship in rowing, sculling,etc. Then yachting and sail-boating attracted great attention, and the rivalry between this country and Europe was such that in order to test the speed of some of their favorites, voyages have been made across the Atlantic and large sums of money staked on the result of a yacht race.

In the meantime railroads have been developing rates of speed unheard of by any other practical mode of locomotion yet discovered, and the road that has the fastest trains always has the preference, even though not so good a track or so good accommodations.

And antedating all these, was the ancient custom of trials of speed in foot-racing, horse-racing, etc. The last named seems even to increase in interest, and faster time in harness, if not under the saddle, is made than in former times.

In the New York *Evening Post* of May 23, 1823, the following account of the great race between *Eclipse* and *Henry* is published, and while on the subject of fast time, a report of this world-renowned race may be admissible, as no horse race in this country has ever created so much interest before or since as that did, and there is no record to show that so large a sum of money had ever before been staked on the result of any race.

REPORT OF THE RACE.

" Yesterday the match race between Eclipse and a Southern horse, called Henry, was won over the Union course.

It will be recollected that the gentlemen from New York in attendance at the match race last fall at Washington City between Eclipse and Sir Charles offered to run the Eclipse this spring on the ' Long Island course ' for twenty thousand dollars ($20,000) against any horse that could be produced in the United States or elsewhere, and gave the Southern gentlemen from that time, November 22, to the time of meeting to look around and name their horse.

The challenge was readily accepted, and the $3,000 forfeit that was agreed upon in case either party declined to run the race, was deposited.

A number of horses were put in training for the occasion, but only two, viz., Henry and Betsey Richards, were brought on from the South, who, it was thought, could contend with Eclipse, and which of these two were to run the race was kept a secret until the signal was given from the judges' stand to bring up the horse, when Henry made his appearance and Eclipse soon after.

The doubts that had heretofore been entertained (and they were many), that the Southern sportsman would pay the forfeit and there would be no race, vanished at once and all was anxiety to see the result of the contest.

The hour of starting soon arrived, but such was the immense crowd on the course in solid column for near a quarter of a mile, both right and left of the judges' box, that some minutes were consumed by the officers in clearing it. Nor was it effected without much difficulty.

About 1:10 o'clock both horses set off at the tap of the drum, Henry taking the lead, and keeping it the whole four miles, and came in about a half-length ahead. Although several efforts were made by the rider of Eclipse, a young man, whose name we do not recollect, to pass his antagonist, but still he could not do it. The result of this heat was so different from what Northern sportsmen had expected, that the mercury fell below the freezing point instantly. Bets 3 to 1 that Eclipse would loose the second heat were loudly offered, but few takers. Time in winning the heat was seven minutes and forty seconds.

SECOND HEAT.

Time having elapsed for breathing the horses were again brought up for the second heat. It had been determined in the interim to change Eclipse's rider, a thing that has often been done, and who should appear but our old friend Proody, who was greeted with tremendous cheers by the multitude. He soon mounted and at the word, went off. Henry took the lead, as in the first heat, and kept it until about two-thirds around on the third mile. Proody seized with a quickness and dexterity peculiar to himself the favorable moment that presented when appearing to aim at the outside he might gain the inside. Accordingly he made a dash and passed on to the left and maintained the ground he had gained to the end of the second race, coming out about two lengths ahead. The air was now made to resound from every quarter, with Proody forever, and as soon as he had been weighed, the populace bore him off on their shoulders, across the course, in spite of all entreaties he could make to the contrary.

The mercury in the sporting thermometer immediately rose to a pleasant summer heat, and the backers of Eclipse were now ready for anything that offered.

They proposed to bet even, but there were no takers. Several offers to draw were made by gentlemen who had bet on Henry, but not accepted. Confidence was fully restored to the friends of Eclipse.

Time on the second heat 7 minutes and 49 seconds.

THIRD HEAT.

When the horses were brought up for this heat, a jockey by the name of Taylor known for several years on Southern courses for his great success, and whose skill was acknowledged to be inferior to no one, made his appearance and was announced as the rider of Henry in the third heat, instead of the boy who had rode him in the former heats.

The course was once more cleared, and off they went, Proody taking the lead and keeping it to the end of the race, coming in about three lengths ahead.

The air was now rent with shouts by New Yorkers and the press around the judges' stand was so great for a few moments that nothing could overcome it.

The whole course was blocked up by a solid mass of men, 10,000 deep, leaving no room to bring the horses to the stand so the riders could dismount and be weighed. Order, however, was at length restored, the riders weighed and everything found correct and Eclipse pronounced the victor. He was then marched off the course to the popular tune of "See the Conquering Hero Comes."

Thus has ended the greatest race that has ever been run in this country. The result has shown that the challenge may again be repeated : " Long Island Eclipse against the world."

We hope, however, that Mr. Van Ranst will never again suffer him to run, but let the country have the benefit of his stock.

' He has now proved himself beyond all cavil to be a horse of both speed and bottom, unequaled in this country or perhaps any other at this time.

Time of third and last heat was 8 minutes and 24 seconds.

Thus the event has shown that the opinion of Northern sportsmen is better than that of Southern — that size and bone are essential to strength and ought to be taken into the calculation, and, supposing blood and bottom to be equal, must always win. It is supposed there was upwards of 50,000 spectators on the field.

It was claimed that Henry carried 12 pounds more weight than is allowed on any horse of his age — that being the regulation on the Union course. Under the usual regulations he would have distanced Eclipse in the first heat.

About the time this race between Eclipse and Henry was agitating the whole sporting world (1823) the application of steam to navigation was beginning to develop great possibilities of speed from steamboats. From 1811 there had been built in the Valley of the Mississippi up to that time 112 steamboats, and they were rapidly increasing. One of the problems to be solved by this new factor on Western rivers, as well as on tide waters, was the speed that could be obtained.

The popular stage coach, the keel-boat and the barge, the more modern canal-boat, were all too slow for the age and must be superseded. The principal question to be determined by all who had embarked in steam navigation was how much speed could be obtained. In this the whole country were in sympathy, and every town and city where suitable timber could be secured, on the Ohio or tributaries, undertook to build, and did build at least one boat.

Machinery was even brought from the East, and in some cases from England, to put in them. The result showed a wonderful increase in speed, as may be seen from the record.

In 1815 the steamer Enterprise made the trip from New Orleans to Louisville in 25 days 2 hours and 40 minutes.

In 1817 the Washington made it in 25 days. The Shelby made it the same year in 20 days 4 hours and 20 minutes.

In 1819 the Paragon made it in 18 days and 10 hours.

34

Each succeeding year reduced the time, and in 1828 the Tecumseh made the same run in 8 days and 4 hours.

In 1834 the Tuscarora made it in 7 days and 18 hours. In 1837 it was made inside of 7 days by the Gen. Brown, Randolph, Empress and Sultana.

In 1840 the Edward Shippen made it in 5 days and 14 hours. In 1852 the Eclipse made it in 4 days and 18 hours. In 1853 the A. S. Shotwell reduced it to 4 days 10 hours and 20 minutes.

Up to about this time everything designed to run on the Mississippi was sacrificed to gain speed. But it began to be seen there were some other things to be considered in order to secure the best results to stockholders. It was demonstrated that fast time was an expensive luxury, and while it was very enjoyable to the officers and crew and popular with passengers, the expense for fuel and often the neglect of business and other necessary contingents induced the building of a different class of boats, and more carrying capacity and less speed came gradually into favor on Western waters. But it was greatly accelerated by the building of railroads, which at once divided the trade, and was always a strong competitor for freight.

With the exception of the few boats that have been built to run on the lower part of the Mississippi, no effort has been made to secure speed at the sacrifice of other advantages since the days of the fast boats between Louisville and New Orleans and Louisville, Cincinnati and Pittsburgh.

The same may be said on the Northern lakes, where great efforts and great results were often obtained in this connection.

THE FASTEST BOAT.

The maximum of speed on the Western waters was pretty nearly attained, if not quite, in the steamer J. M. White, as early as 1844. And it is questionable whether the time made by her has ever been beaten, when it is recollected that several cut-offs were made in the river between the time she ran and the time the great match race between the Robert E. Lee and the Natchez 24 years later.

An evidence of the White's superior speed is seen in the further fact that she made three consecutive trips inside of four and one-half days each, and attended to her regular business both up and down, except on the one trip.

As a rule very little money was ever bet on steamboat racing by the owners, although large sums were often bet by the friends of either boat.

In the race of the Lee and Natchez it is not known that
any bets were made by the owners, although it is presumed
by some that as much money changed hands on that race as
on the great race between Eclipse and Henry, as reported
above.

Steamboat racing has never been popular with the traveling
public, and always expensive to the owners; hence, very little
racing has been done on the rivers and lakes since the enactment of the steamboat law in 1851.   The principal objection
urged by the public is the greater liability to accidents, although long and careful observation shows that to be an error,
for the reason that much greater care and watchfulness is observed by all on board when racing.

While a race or trial of speed is no longer heard of on inland waters, we are constantly noting the fast time and the
great speed of the ocean racers.   A steamer that cannot cross
the ocean in seven days is not up to the standard, and is considered only second class in point of speed, and consequently
second choice with the traveling community.

Speed seems to be the great desideratum with "young
America."   Not content with fast horses, fast steamboats,
fast railroad trains, the elements of the atmosphere and the air
are brought into subjection, to contribute to the speed of the
distant message, while the human voice is made to instantly
echo to all parts of a large city.   Go on to the marts of trade
anywhere, into the exchange, along the thoroughfares of the
city, and the impression arises at once in your mind, there
must be a fire in the neighborhood.

Go into a country town about dinner time, and when the
bell rings at the hotel to announce dinner the first thought is
a fight or a fire.

Go to a place of amusement, night or day, and when the
exhibition is near its close you will be sure the whole audience
either live out of the city or in the remote suburbs, and the
time of the last train is nearly up, such is the rush and anxiety
to get on to the street.

Everybody and everything seems to be in a hurry, except
horse cars on city railroads, and dudes and loafers on the
street corners of "retail streets" of a city.

No more striking contrast of this peculiarity in Young
America can be seen than in a visit to our sister republic,
Mexico.

There is no one in a hurry except the mule drivers on the
street cars.

CHAPTER LXXI.

ON the 9th of May, 1844, the *St. Louis Republican* made the following announcement : —

" What has heretofore been merely the speculation of enthusiasts has been realized. New Orleans has been brought within less than four days' travel of St. Louis, in immediate propinquity.

The J. M. White has been the first to accomplish this extraordinary trip.

The J. M. White left this port on Monday, April 29th, at 3 o'clock p. m., with 600 tons of freight, and arrived in New Orleans Friday eve, 3d inst., being three days and sixteen hours on her downward trip.

She left New Orleans for St. Louis on Saturday, May 4th, 1844, at forty minutes after 5 o'clock p. m., and arrived on the 8th, having made the trip up in three days and twenty-three hours, having been but nine days on the voyage out and home, including all detentions."

The following are the runs up, from wharf to wharf, it being the best time ever made by any steamboat on Western waters : —

" From New Orleans to Natchez, 300 miles, 20 hours and 40 minutes ; Vicksburg, 410 miles, 29 hours and 55 minutes ; Montgomery. 625 miles, 1 day, 13 hours, 8 minutes ; Memphis, 775 miles, 2 days, 12 hours, 8 minutes ; Cairo, 1,000 miles, 3 days, 6 hours, 44 minutes ; St. Louis, 1,200 miles, 3 days, 23 hours, 9 minutes."

The time of the J. M. White was not excelled to St. Louis until 1869. when the Natchez beat it one hour, 49 minutes, and the Robert E. Lee, in 1870, three hours, 44 minutes. Although at Cairo and Memphis and at other points below, the difference was much less, as may be seen by the annexed tables.

The race between the Lee and the Natchez, at least as far as Cairo, seems to have been a fair test of speed. From fog or some other cause, the Natchez claims to have been detained from there to St. Louis.

The claim that the Lee was assisted by the Pargoud while coaling, does not seem substantiated from their subsequent runs. The 26 years that elapsed between the time the White made her quick trip (1844) and the time of the Lee and Nat-

chez (1870) had made so many changes in the river, in the
character of the fuel, in the manner of handling it, in the
size of the boats and in the different stages of water, it is
difficult to make a fair comparison. Running against time
does not test the speed of steamboats like that of horses.
Circumstances so easily affect the former, that the only way
to determine the relative speed of boats is, to start them together, or at least the same day.

So far as the record goes, the most remarkable feature in
the White's trip is the time she made the round trip in. It
shows not only fast time for the boat, but fast work for the
crew, and good management by the officers. It has never
been excelled nor equaled by several days. Nine days from
St. Louis to New Orleans and return, handling 600 tons of
freight on the down trip, will probably never be excelled by
any steamboat.

The stage of water has so much to do with making fast
time, both up and down stream, as well as the weather, that
the boat striking both will show a far better record than one
even faster that is less fortunate.

Probably there has been no year since 1844, the time the
White made her great run, when the river has continued high
so long. Agreeable to my recollection it rained forty days
and nights, consecutively, although it was not until later in
the season, about the 17th of June, that the water was the
highest at St. Louis. But it was high all the season, and
more favorable for fast time before it became the highest.

The subjoined tables, although not supposed to be absolutely correct in all cases, will be read with interest by many
who still survive the wreck of time and that of the splendid
boats they were once connected with, as well as by those who
still remember with pleasure the excitement incident to a
quick trip by a favorite boat, to say nothing of the thousands
along the shores and even in distant States who bet large
sums of money on the *wrong boat*.

While making quick trips was always an expensive luxury,
during the time of the great passenger travel on the rivers of
the West, it was generally thought to pay, although as a rule
the ambition of officers and of owners to beat the time of some
other boat had more to do with *quick trips* than had the hope
of increased profits.

The charges so often made, especially in the East and
abroad, of the great danger to travelers from reckless steamboat racing on Western rivers, had very little foundation in
fact. The fewest accidents have ever occurred during a race

or a trial of speed against time for the most obvious reasons. Every one on board at such times is doing his duty, and when such is the case comparatively few accidents occur.

A proverbial fact on our rivers is that, as a rule, the fastest boats have not been profitable, and of late years the effort has been to build them for general capacity rather than great speed.

CONVERSE VS. SWAN.

An anecdote in point is told of Capt. J. C. Swan, one of the oldest and most respected of the few remaining old boatmen of the West.

There had existed for some years a commendable rivalry between him and Capt. Joe Converse as to the speed of their respective boats.

Capt. Converse had always managed to have the fastest boat. Finally Capt. Swan lost one of his boats by accident, I think, perhaps the first Alex Scott, when he bought Capt. Converse's interest in the J. M. White, which had then established a record of being the fastest boat in the West, if not in the world. After running her a few trips, Capt. Swan remarked to some friends : —

"Converse has often beaten me in the speed of his boats, but he never before has beaten me half as badly as when he sold me the White."

Among the races of former years none was more famous or exciting than that between the Baltic and Diana, from New Orleans to Louisville, about the year 1854. During that period a number of handsome steamers were engaged in the trade from Louisville to New Orleans, which would generally go into the latter city fully laden, take enough freight for ballast and all the passengers that wanted to go and hurry back to Louisville for another cargo. They kept out of the way of each other as much as possible by leaving Louisville on different days, but sometimes it would happen that two would leave New Orleans on the same day. The Baltic and Diana left New Orleans together, the Baltic slightly in the lead. Capt. Frank Carter, afterward superintendent at Louisville of the United States Mail Line Company, commanded the Baltic, and Capt. E. T. Sturgeon commanded the Diana. Neither of the boats had ever exhibited remarkable speed, and while this was what might be called a slow race, it was the longest race that was ever contested, and very exciting to the passengers and crews of both. The distance is 1,382 miles, and there was not an hour of the time occupied by the trip that the two boats were not in sight or hearing of each other. An artist was on board the Baltic at the time, and he immortalized the event by transfixing to canvas in oil a night scene, in which were depicted the two imposing steamers in the foreground. The Baltic won the race, but steamboatmen were always of the opinion that it was more by reason of mismanagement on the Diana than because the Baltic was the faster of the two.

In 1838 the steamer Diana received from the Post-office Department of the United States a prize of $500 in gold, which had been offered to the first boat that would make the run from New Orleans to Louisville inside of six days. Her time was five days, twenty-three hours and fifteen minutes. The quickest time, it is said, ever made from New Orleans to Cincinnati was five days and eighteen hours, in 1843, by the Duke of Orleans. The fastest trip after that was made by the Charles Morgan, in June, 1877. She made the time to Cincinnati in six days and eleven hours, having made forty-two landings and lost three and a half hours in getting through the canal at Louisville. In April of the same year the Thompson Dean made the run in six days and nineteen hours, and had lost fourteen hours in the canal and seventeen hours at way landings. The R. R. Springer went through in 1881 from New Orleans to Cincinnati in five days, twelve hours and forty-five minutes running time. Her best time was made while in the Mississippi River. From the time she reached the mouth of the Ohio until she arrived at Cincinnati her speed decreased. She consumed twenty-two hours and five minutes more time from New Orleans to Cairo than did the R. E. Lee in 1870. In March, 1881, the Will S. Hayes made the run in six days, seventeen hours and ten minutes from port to port, having made fifty-one landings and met with other detentions.

In May, 1882, four quick trips were made from Helena to Memphis. The first was made by the Belle Memphis in five hours and fifty-three minutes ; the second by the City of Cairo in five hours and fifty-two minutes ; the third by the City of Providence in five hours and forty-nine and a half minutes, and the last by the James Lee in five hours and fourteen minutes. In March, 1883, the Kate Adams made the run in five hours and eighteen and a half minutes. The time of the R. E. Lee between these points in 1870, in the great Lee-Natchez race, was six hours and forty-three minutes, and this had been beaten in May, 1853, by the Eclipse, which made the run in six hours and seventeen minutes, and by the Peytona previously, in six hours and thirty-six minutes. But cut-offs in the stretch of river from Helena to Memphis between 1870 and 1882 had shortened the distance about fifteen miles. However, it must be understood that this shortening of distance by cut-offs is not of much advantage to au ascending steamer, as the diminished distance is balanced by the more rapid current.

GREATEST STEAMBOAT RACE EVER RUN.

The greatest steamboat race that was ever run in the world, however, was that which occurred in June, 1870, from New Orleans to St. Louis between the Robert E. Lee and the Natchez. The latter was built at Cincinnati and was commanded by Captain T. P. Leathers, and in June of the above year made the fastest time on record from New Orleans to St. Louis, 1,278 miles, in three days, twenty-one hours and fifty-eight minutes. The Robert E. Lee was built at New Albany soon after the war and was towed across the river to the Kentucky side to have her name painted on her wheelhouses, a matter that was deemed prudent in those exciting times. She was commanded by Captain John W. Cannon, who died in Frankfort, Ky., in 1882. There was great rivalry between the boats, and when the Natchez made her great run Captain Cannon determined to beat it. He stripped the Lee for the race, removed all parts of her upper works which were calculated to catch the wind, removed all rigging and outfit that could be dispensed with to lighten her; engaged the steamer Frank Pargoud to precede her a hundred miles up the river to supply coal; arranged with coal yards to have fuel flats awaiting her in the middle of the river at given points and be taken in tow under way until the coal could be transferred to the decks of the Lee, and then to cut loose and float back. He refused all business of every kind and would receive no passengers. The Natchez returned to New Orleans and received a few tons of freight and a few passengers and was advertised to leave for St. Louis on June 30. In the afternoon the Robert E. Lee backed out from the levee, and five minutes later the Natchez followed her. The whole country watched the race with breathless interest, as it had been extensively advertised by the press, and the telegraph attended its progress along the river at every point. At all the principal cities — Natchez, Vicksburg, Helena and Memphis — people for many miles were present to see the racers pass, and the time of passing was cabled to Europe. When Cairo was reached the race was virtually ended, but the Lee proceeded to St. Louis, arriving there in three days, eighteen hours and fourteen minutes from the time she left New Orleans, beating by thirty-three minutes the previous record of the Natchez. The latter steamer run into a fog between St. Louis and Cairo, which delayed her more than six hours. It is said that 50,000 people crowded the wharf, the windows and the housetops to welcome the Lee on her arrival in St. Louis. Captain Cannon was tendered a banquet by the business men of the city and was generally lionized while he remained here. It was estimated that more than $1,000,000 changed hands on the result of the great race. Many of the bets were withdrawn, however, on the ground that the Lee had been assisted the first 100 miles of the trip by the power of the Frank Pargoud added to her own, and many steamboatmen have ever since regarded the Natchez as the faster boat of the two, but think she was outgeneraled in the race by the Lee. There was so much adverse comment afterward by the press that there has been no attempt since to repeat such a performance. — *St. Louis Globe-Democrat.*

CHAPTER LXXII.

BELOW are the tables of time of the Lee, Natchez and other boats as published in the papers of the period, and presumed to be correct.

NATCHEZ.

	DAYS.	HOURS.	MIN.
From New Orleans to the city of Natchez.........	..	17	52
Vicksburg..	..	26	..
Head of Thresherfield...........................	..	28	4
Napoleon..	1	18	15
White River.....................................	1	19	30
Helena..	2	2	35
Memphis	2	9	40
Head of Island No. 10...........................	3	..	..
Hickman...	3	1	43
Cairo...	3	4	24
St. Louis.......................................	3	21	58

ROBERT E. LEE, JULY 1870.

	DAYS.	HOURS.	MIN.
From New Orleans to Carrollton	..	..	27½
Harry Hill's	..	1	½
Red Church......................................	..	1	39
Bonnet Carre....................................	..	2	38
College Point...................................	..	3	50
Donaldsonville..................................	..	4	59
Plaquemine	..	7	5
Baton Rogue	..	8	25
Bayou Sara......................................	..	10	26
Red River	..	12	56
Stamps..	..	13	56
Briers	..	15	51½

	DAYS.	HOURS.	MIN.
Ashley..	..	16	29
Natchez..	..	17	11
Cole's Creek.......................................	..	19	21
Water Proof........ ....,.........................	..	19	53
Rodney..	..	20	45
St. Joseph...	..	21	2
Grand Gulf..	..	22	6
Hard Times.......................................	..	22	18
Vicksburg	1	..	38
Milliken's Bend...................................	1	2	37
Railey's	1	3	49
Lake Providence...................................	1	5	47
Greenville..	1	10	55
Napoleon..	1	16	22
White River.......................................	1	16	56
Australia... ....₄	1	19	..
Helena..	1	23	25
Memphis..	2	6	9
Island No. 37......................................	2	9	..
Island No. 26.....................................	2	15	30
Island No. 14......................................	2	17	23
New Madrid.......................................	2	19	50
Island No. 10......................................	2	20	37
Island No. 8.......................................	2	21	45
Lucas Bend.......................................	3	..	..
Cairo...	3	1	..
St. Louis..	3	18	14

Subsequent trials of speed by these boats against time between New Orleans and Natchez did not materially change
their previous record.   16 hours 36 minutes 47 seconds was
claimed by the Lee, which was about 11 minutes better than
the Natchez claimed.   The speed of the two boats developed
great uniformity in performance either in long or short distances and the friends of both claimed priority.

FROM NEW ORLEANS TO LOUISVILLE — 1,486 MILES.

	DAYS.	HOURS.	MINUTES.
May, 1815, steamer Enterprise made the trip in.....	25	2	40
April, 1817, steamer Washington made the trip in...	25	..	..
Sept., 1817, steamer Shelby made the trip in.........	20	4	20
May, 1819, steamer Paragon made the trip in.......	18	10	..
Nov., 1828, steamer Tecumseh made the trip in......	8	4	..
April, 1834, steamer Tuscarora made the trip in......	7	18	..
Nov., 1837, steamer General Brown made the trip in.	6	22	..
Nov., 1837, steamer Randolph made the trip in.......	6	28	..
Nov., 1837, steamer Empress made the trip in.......	6	17	..
Dec., 1837, steamer Sultana made the trip in	6	15	..
April, 1840, steamer Edward Shippen made the trip in	5	14	..
April, 1842, steamer Belle of the West made the trip in	6	14	..
April, 1843, steamer Duke of Orleans made the trip in	5	23	..
April, 1844, steamer Sultana made the trip in........	5	12	..
May, 1849, steamer Bostona made the trip in........	5	8	..
June, 1851, steamer Belle Key made the trip in.......	4	23	..
May, 1852, steamer Reindeer made the trip in.......	4	20	45
May, 1852, steamer Eclipse made the trip in.........	4	18	..
May, 1853, steamer A. L. Shotwell made the trip in..	4	10	20

The next year, the steamer Éclipse, E. T. Sturgeon, Master, made the quickest time on record; and when we take into consideration the low water, swift current, and other obstacles she met with, we may safely set her down as the fastest boat in the world.

ECLIPSE'S TIME IN 1853 FROM NEW ORLEANS TO —

	DAYS.	HOURS.	MINUTES.
Donaldsonville..	..	5	42
Baton Rouge...	..	9	27
Natchez..	..	19	46
Grand Gulf...	..	24	25
Vicksburg...	..	28	11
Columbia..	..	40	8
Napoleon..	..	44	12
Helena..	2	3	38
Memphis..	2	9	55
Cairo...	3	4	4
Evansville..	3	18	24
Louisville..	4	9	30

FROM NEW ORLEANS TO ST. LOUIS — DISTANCE 1,200 MILES.

	DAYS.	HOURS.	MINUTES.
1844, steamer J. M. White made the trip in.........	3	23	..

FROM NEW ORLEANS TO NATCHEZ — DISTANCE 300 MILES.

	DAYS.	HOURS.	MINUTES.
May, 1814, steamer New Orleans made the trip in...	6	6	40
July, 1814, steamer Comet made the trip in..........	5	10	..
May, 1815, steamer Enterprise made the trip in......	4	11	20
April, 1817, steamer Washington made the trip in...	4	..	..
Sept., 1817, steamer Shelby made the trip in........	3	20	..
May, 1819, steamer Paragon made the trip in........	3	8	..
Nov., 1828, steamer Tecumseh made the trip in.....	3	1	20
April, 1834, steamer Tuscarora made the trip in....	1	21	..
Aug., 1838, steamer Natchez made the trip in........	1	17	..
Aug., 1840, steamer Edward Shippen made the trip in.	1	8	..
Aug., 1842, steamer Belle of the West made the trip in.	1	18	..
Aug., 1844, steamer Old Sultana made the trip in....	..	19	45
Aug., 1851, steamer Magnolia made the trip in.......	..	19	50
May, 1853, steamer A. L. Shotwell made the trip in..	..	19	49
May, 1853, steamer Southern Belle made the trip in..	..	20	3
May, 1853, steamer Princess No. 4 made the trip in..	..	20	26
May, 1853, steamer Eclipse made the trip in.........	..	19	47
Aug., 1855, steamer New Princess made the trip in...	..	18	53
Aug., 1855, steamer New Natchez made the trip in...	..	17	30

FROM NEW ORLEANS TO CAIRO, SOUTH OF THE OHIO RIVER — DISTANCE 1,000 MILES.

	DAYS.	HOURS.	MINUTES.
May, 1853, steamer Eclipse made the trip in.........	3	4	4
May, 1853, steamer A. L. Shotwell made the trip in...	3	3	40

FROM LOUISVILLE TO CINCINNATI — DISTANCE 150 MILES.

	DAYS.	HOURS.	MINUTES.
1818, steamer General Pike made the trip in.........	1	16	..
1819, steamer Paragon made the trip in.............	1	14	20
1822, steamer Wheeling Packet made the trip in.....	1	10	..
1837, steamer Moselle made the trip in.............	..	12	..
1843, steamer Duke of Orleans made the trip in.....	..	12	..
1843, steamer Congress made the trip in............	..	12	20
1846, steamer Benj. Franklin No. 6 made the trip in.	..	11	45
1852, steamer Alleghany made the trip in...........	..	10	38
1852, steamer Pittsburgh made the trip in..........	..	10	23
1853, steamer Telegraph No. 3 made the trip in......	..	9	52

FROM LOUISVILLE TO ST. LOUIS — DISTANCE 750 MILES.

	DAYS.	HOURS.	MINUTES.
1843, steamer Congress made the trip in............	..	49	..
1854, steamer Pike made the trip in................	..	47	..
1854, steamer Northerner made the trip in..........	..	46	30
1855, steamer Southerner made the trip in	..	43	..

" The following table shows the progressive improvement in the speed of boats from New Orleans to Louisville, distance fourteen hundred and eighty miles, from 1815 to 1853: —

	DAYS.	HOURS.	MINUTES.
May, 1815 — Enterprise...........................	25	2	40
April, 1817 — Washington........................	25	..	..
September, 1817 — Shelby........................	20	4	20
May, 1819 — Paragon............................	18	10	..
November, 1828 — Tecumseh......................	8	4	..
April, 1834 — Tuscarora..........................	7	16	..
November, 1837 — General Brown.................	6	22	..
November, 1837 — Randolph......................	6	22	..
November, 1837 — Empress.......................	6	17	..
December, 1837 — Sultana........................	6	15	..
April, 1840 — Edward Shippen....................	5	14	..
April, 1842 — Belle of the West...................	6	14	..
April, 1843 — Duke of Orleans....................	5	23	..
April, 1844 — Sultana............................	5	12	..
May, 1849 — Bostona............................	5	8	..
June, 1851 — Belle Key..........................	4	23	..
May, 1852 — Reindeer...........................	4	20	45
May, 1852 — Eclipse.............................	4	19	..
May, 1853 — A. L. Shotwell......................	4	10	20
May, 1853 — Eclipse.............................	4	9	30

The Eclipse's was the best time up to that date, averaging fourteen miles an hour."

CHAPTER LXXIII.

IT was reserved to the steamboat Washington (says Commodore Preble), Captain Henry M. Shreve, to demonstrate by a second voyage of twenty-five days, from New Orleans to Louisville, that a steamboat could ascend this river in at least one-fourth the time required by the keel-boats and barges hitherto in exclusive use.

At a public dinner given to Captain Shreve at Louisville on his return, he predicted that the time would come when his twenty-five day trip would be made in ten. It has since been made in four days and nine hours."

" In 1823 there were public rejoicings at Louisville, Kentucky, when a steamboat arrived there in fifteen days and six hours from New Orleans.

The captain answering a complimentary toast gravely stated the voyage might be made in fifteen days, or six hours 'ess than he had just made. Within twenty years the voyage was actually performed in a few hours over four days."

FROM NEW ORLEANS TO NATCHEZ — 268 MILES.

	DAYS.	HOURS.	MINUTES.
1814, Orleans made the run	6	6	40
1844, Comet made the run,	5	10	..
1815, Enterprise made the run	4	11	20
1817, Washington.	4	..	..
1817, Shelby.	3	20	..
1819, Paragon.	3	8	..
1828, Tecumseh.	3	1	..
1834, Tuscarora.	1	21	..
1838, Natchez	1	17	..
1840, Edward Shippen	1	8	..
1842, Belle of the West	1	18	..
1844, Sultana.	..	19	45
1851, Magnolia.	..	19	50
1853, A. S. Shotwell.	..	19	49
1853, Southern Belle.	..	20	18
1853, Princess No. 4.	..	20	26
1853, Eclipse.	..	19	47
1855, Princess (new)	..	18	53
1855, Natchez (new).	..	17	30
1856, Princess (new)	..	17	30
1870, Natchez.	..	17	17
1880, Rob't E. Lee.	..	17	11

The third J. M. White has a record of 7 hours and 40 minutes to Baton Rouge — making landings at Donaldsonville and Plaquemine. This beats all other records.

FROM NEW ORLEANS TO CAIRO — 1,024 MILES.

	DAYS.	HOURS.	MINUTES.
1844, J. M. White made the run.	3	6	44
1852, Reindeer made the run.	3	12	45
1853, Eclipse made the run.	3	4	4
1853, A. S. Shotwell.	3	3	40
1869, Dexter.	3	6	20
1870, Natchez.	3	4	34
1870, R. E. Lee.	3	1	..

FROM NEW ORLEANS TO DONALDSONVILLE.

	HOURS.	MINUTES.
1852, A. S. Shotwell.	5	42
1852, Eclipse.	5	42
1854, Sultana,	5	12
1856, Princess.	4	51
1860, Atlantic.	5	11
1860, Gen'l Quitman.	5	6
1865, Ruth.	4	43
1870, R. E. Lee.	4	59

FROM NEW ORLEANS TO ST. LOUIS — 1,218 MILES.

	DAYS.	HOURS.	MINUTES.
1844, J. M. White.	3	23	9
1849, Missouri.	4	19	..
1859, Imperial.	4	17	..
1863, Ruth.	4	9	..
1866, City of Alton.	4	20	..
1869, Dexter.	4	9	..
1870, Natchez.	3	21	58
1870, R. E. Lee.	3	18	14

MEMPHIS TO CAIRO.

	HOURS.	MINUTES.
1865, Mollie Able.	19	25
1866, City of Alton,	17	41
1868, Rob't E. Lee.	16	37

FROM CINCINNATI TO PITTSBURGH — 490 MILES.

	DAYS.	HOURS.	MINUTES.
1850, Telegraph No. 2	1	17	..
1851, Buckeye State	1	16	..
1852, Pittsburgh	1	15	..

FROM ST. LOUIS TO ALTON — 25 MILES.

	DAYS.	HOURS.	MINUTES.
1853, Altouna	..	1	35
1876, Golden Eagle	..	1	37
1876, War Eagle	..	1	37

FROM ST. LOUIS TO KEOKUK — 214 MILES.

	DAYS.	HOURS.	MINUTES.
1859, Louisiana	..	16	20

LOUISVILLE TO MADISON.

	DAYS.	HOURS.	MINUTES.
Telegraph	..	3	24
Alvin Adams	..	3	27
Jacob Strader	..	3	12

FROM ST. LOUIS TO ST. PAUL — 800 MILES.

	DAYS.	HOURS.	MINUTES.
1868, Hawkeye State	2	20	..

ST. LOUIS TO LA SALLE.

	DAYS.	HOURS.	MINUTES.
1854, Steamer Cataract	..	23	45
(making five landings.)			
1854, Steamer Garden City	..	..	..

FROM ST LOUIS TO ST. JOSEPH — 600 MILES.

	DAYS.	HOURS.	MINUTES.
1853, Polar Star	2	16	..
1856, James H. Lucas	2	12	52

OLD TIME STEAMBOATS.

In the New Orleans *Picayune* of April, 1838, is the following paragraphs : —

UNPRECEDENTED SPEED.

" Who would believe that a boat could make a trip from this .port to Louisville and back in ten days and seventeen hours? Yet this has been done. That splendid steamer, the Empress, Capt. Robt. McConnell, arrived here yesterday from Louisville in four days and eight hours.

Her up trip was made in six days and nine hours. Deducting all delays for wooding, etc., the actual running time was only eight days and nine hours, a distance of 3,120 miles, averaging fifteen and one-half miles an hour.

On the 19th of June the same year the same paper makes this announcement : —

UNPRECEDENTED SPEED.—The steamer Monarch made her last trip from this port to Louisville in six days and one hour, that being eight hours quicker than ever before made. If the time of detention had been deducted the trip would have been made in five and one-half days."

On the 7th of July, same year, the same paper makes this announcement : —

THE FASTEST BOAT. — The steamboat Diana, Capt. Frank Carter, has eclipsed every other boat on Western waters, having made her last trip from this port to Louisville in five days and twenty-three hours and fifteen minutes, the quickest trip ever yet made. For this feat she gets a premium of $500 in gold from the Post-Office Department, that sum having been offered to the boat that should make the run within six days.

CHAPTER LXXIV.

MISSISSIPPI VALLEY TRANSPORTATION CO.

COTEMPORARY with the organization of the Atlantic and Mississippi Steamship Co. in 1866 the above company or the "Barge Line," as it is familiarly known, was formed, and Capt. Joab Lawrence and Barton Able, good practical boatmen, were elected its first Presidents.

It started its first tow of barges to New Orleans on the *first day of April*, 1866, and as its success was a matter of grave doubt in the minds of many, some were skeptical enough to say in derision, "the day was ominous of the result of the enterprise." But some of its projectors were more sanguine and persevered through the earlier embarrassments of a new mode of transportation, and as the times were prosperous and money was abundant from the results of the war, the company soon re-asserted itself and came to the front, with George H. Rea as its third President. H. C. Haarstick, Vice-President and Superintendent, Austin R. Moore, Secretary.

The shipments of bulk grain rapidly increased and the success of the company was so great another company was organized in 1880, called St. Louis and New Orleans Transportation Company, Capt. Henry Lowry, President.

At this time the bulk grain shipments had assumed such proportions the argus eye of Jay Gould and the Wabash system of railroads centering at St. Louis, with their usual sagacity and enterprise saw an opening they were not slow to avail themselves of. Consequently they joined Capt. Lowry and the result was the St. Louis and New Orleans Transportation Company, with a capital to at once enter the field of competitors for the business of the Mississippi Valley Co.

The foreign demand for the products of the Mississippi

Valley had increased the tow-boat and barge tonnage to such
an extent that as soon as that demand fell off, or short crops
of grain were realized, there was a collapse in the barge business and the stock that had been above par was soon a drug
in the market, and some companies with small capital were
sold out. The two principal companies located at St. Louis
soon recognized the result of a fierce competition, which
seemed imminent, and consolidated their stock and formed a
new company called the St. Louis and Mississippi Valley
Transportation Co., simply adding St. Louis to the former
name. This company was organized with a capital of
$2,000,000 and elected nine directors, four of which, R. S.
Hays, H. M. Hoxie, A. A. Talmage and George C. Gault,
represented the Wabash and Missouri Pacific Railroads.
Capt. Lowry was made Vice-President and H. C. Haarstick,
President. The company then owned some ten or twelve fine
powerful tow-boats, and about 100 barges, some of which had
a capacity of 1,500 tons.

This was about double the tonnage there was business for,
and of course, the surplus was retired which could not have
been easily done if under the control of two distinct companies. Thus was illustrated the secret of the success of this company. A system that would have saved from bankruptcy
many an organized steamboat company in the past as well as
individual companies. Under the shrewd and judicious management of Mr. Haarstick the company has continued to pros-
per and maintain an excellent line of boats and barges unequaled on any waters in the world of commerce — adequate
at all times to supply the demand on the Mississippi, except
when interrupted by ice or low water.

Although two of the company's original projectors and
large stockholders, Messrs. Rea and Lowrey, have crossed the
dark river and launched their "gilt-edged" barques on unknown waters, the company under the management of President Haarstick and his long tried and efficient corps of assistants, is conducting a legitimate and what seems to be a safe
and satisfactory business, with less to fear from ruinous competition than any other line of transportation on Western
waters.

About the time this barge company was organized there
was a great cry throughout the country for *cheap freights* and
many were visionary enough to suppose barge transportation
was the *panacea* that would forever settle that question and
establish a "thorough grain" system of transportation which
seemed to involve all problems in that connection. "If

35

barge transportation was practicable on the Mississippi and the Ohio Rivers there could be no reason why it should not be a success on all others," and in the imagination of enthusiasts, barges were to be used by every farmer living near a water-course, and by that mode of transportation every product of the country was to reach a market at a mere nominal cost.

Even business men living on the Missouri River were so sanguine of the success of this new idea that they could not be made to understand that the character of navigation had anything to do with it. And such was their enthusiasm and persistency coupled with the influence of newspapers, the St. Louis and New Orleans Barge Co. was induced to send a small tow of barges to Kansas City to take out a load of bulk grain. By great care and a favorable stage of water they succeeded in making *one trip*, but never ventured upon another nor did ever any other company attempt it.

The following extracts from newspapers of that day will, to some extent, illustrate the feeling that prevailed in some parts of the valley: —

BARGES VS. CHEAP FREIGHT.

Is it true, Mr. Editor, that the friends of the "barge movement" in this city, and the public generally, expected in the organization of that company to reduce the cost of transportation to a mere nominal sum, or say to "one-half what they are now charging."

By an article in the columns of the St. Louis *Democrat* of the 29th ult., I see "the public have been greatly disappointed because they assumed, and had a right to assume when this company was organized, that it meant *war to the knife* against high rates of freight."

If that was the case, I do not believe the public have been more disappointed than have the stockholders. I think the barge company have demonstrated — what the commercial editor of the *Democrat* seems incapable of understanding — that it costs money to transport freight, even in barges; and further, that the company was not organized entirely for the purpose of benefiting the farmer and the producer, or for " carrying out this through grain movement."

But as this writer proposes to "prepare an article which willnot only benefit the barge line, but be of much use in aiding on the through grain movement," they ought not to despair of success, even though the public are only " sympathizers."

But when they can make money for their stockholders by

carrying freight "*at half what they are now charging,*" on this stage of water, they will not only have the sympathy of the public, but their "overt acts," and will not present that "pitiable" appearance as when carrying freights "but *five cents* per barrel under steamboat rates."

The expose made by the Secretary of the barge company in his article in the *Democrat* of the 29th, does not seem to satisfy this champion of cheap freights, and he persists in knowing from him, in so.many words, why they do not *fix a low and uniform rate* and not play second fiddle to steamboats.

While I have no interest in the barge company I have some sympathy with them, and believe the statement made by the Secretary is quite explicit enough to suit the stockholders, if it does not satisfy this *expert* in cheap freights.   But I have no desire to provoke discussion with any one who has but a single idea upon the subject, or who can see but one side of it.

This writer seems to have the subject of cheap freights "upon the brain," and to him it makes no difference what other interests are sacrificed, if cheap freights are secured.   He would break down old and responsible packet companies, that have done more to build up the interests of this city, than a regiment of such writers would in a century.   He would destroy the business of our splendid freight and passenger steamers, and lay them to the shore to decay, while their owners and the thousands of employes and mechanics that are supported by them, are forced to leave the city they helped to build and seek new homes and new occupations.   Still his zeal is commendable, but zeal without knowledge, St. Paul concluded, — , was not profitable, and I believe it is equally true in the present day.

What is proposed to be gained to this city by cheap freight? Who are to be the especially benefited?   Upon general principles cheap freights are always desirable, all other things being equal.

Any man at all conversant with commercial transactions for the last two years will not contend for a moment that river transportation has been high in any direction, or comparatively so.   But on the contrary low, *too low*, much lower than it could profitably be done for, *even by the barge company* — and who has been benefited — not the consumer.   It has not reduced the cost of living, neither has it increased the profit of the merchant or the mechanic; but it has laid to the shore many fine boats and barges, and left in idleness thousands of builders and operatives upon all our rivers.

If the products of the country cannot afford to pay transportation to market, except by barges, which are expected to be run exclusively for the benefit of the farmer and producer, they certainly cannot afford to pay commissions and handling at intermediate ports, and hence cannot contribute very largely in building up the interests of "this beautiful, and is to be, mighty city" this writer speaks of.

The system of elevators that. is now being inaugurated along our rivers, will do much to reduce the cost of handling products of the country, as well as to reduce commissions and the labor heretofore necessary to handle it.

This, together with the rapidly increasing railroad facilities, and insane competition among steamboats, saying nothing about the barge competition, will be satisfactory to the producer and consumer, I presume, *even* though it does not succeed "in aiding this through grain movement" to pass down our river without some small portion of it being landed at our wharf and warehouses.   E. W. GOULD.

RIVER FREIGHTS — STEAMBOAT VS. BARGE TRANSPORTATION.

Editor of the Times: Can you tell " who killed the goose that laid the golden egg?" The *Times*, in common with its contemporaries, has for the last few years been laudably engaged in advocating the "through grain movement," as it is termed, by means of towboats and barges. That system has been adopted, and is now in successful operation, if we are to believe the half we read in the papers in regard to the expense of carrying grain in bulk.

And now let us see what has been the consequent result, so far as St. Louis is concerned. From the day the barge company was fully and systematically inaugurated, transportation to New Orleans by the ordinary steamboat mode has been rapidly declining, until now, and for the past two years, it has hardly been possible to load two boats per week, and them not with any regularity. Go where you may, among shippers in the city or along the whole line of the river, in Texas, or at ports receiving supplies through New Orleans, and you hear the same complaints: " What has become of the St. Louis boats?" " Will my freight never arrive?" " Why is there no regularity as in former times?" " You, the present class of boatmen, have no enterprise — no get up." " You are driving all our trade to the Ohio River and other places." " The trade we have so long enjoyed, and which St. Louis has grown rich from, is leaving us for the want of proper shipping facilities,'' etc.

Since the introduction of railroads, by which most of the travel goes, it is idle to talk about sending boats out regularly or frequently, unless they have something to go with — something to carry.

The cost of making a trip to New Orleans and return is no mean consideration, and there are but few men now in the business that are able, if disposed, to run their boats for the benefit of St. Louis or of the public.

Now, through the influence of the press and the indomitable perseverance of the very worthy representatives of the barge company, that enterprise has been placed upon a basis that is said to be beyond the possibility of failure so long as the country produces grain for export.

Now the practical question arises, Can the press, can shippers, do anything to restore the prestige once enjoyed by steamboats, and thereby secure the facilities all are clamoring for?

I contend they can do all that is necessary without injury to the barge interest or any other.

By reference to the receipts in New Orleans I think it will be seen that the barges deliver more package freight there, in addition to their bulk grain, than St. Louis steamboats do, while the price is the same by both modes.

Heretofore it has been claimed there was not enough bulk grain to make up a tow in reasonable time. That claim, if ever valid, is no longer so. It has also been pretended that barges could not be loaded with bulk grain alone; that it was necessary to have package freight to give them a load. This is a fallacy that needs no proof to practical men. To be sure, if it is admitted that all the barges that are brought here, and all that barge companies are disposed to buy or build, must be kept in use while steamboats are compelled to lay and wait for the accommodation of certain kinds of freight that barges do not want, or for landings they cannot profitably make, then indeed may shippers who desire to see revived and successfully continued the former regularity and promptness in the New Orleans trade forever abandon the expectation.

If this patronage, this preference for barge transportation, ever was necessary to insure its successful introduction, such is no longer the case. I am assured by parties in New Orleans and others, that the bulk grain trade is only limited by the supply and the facilities that are afforded for handling it.

Here, then, is a field quite large enough to satisfy the most

zealous advocate for "the through grain trade," and to give
employment to all the barge companies St. Louis has need of.
After what has been said the remedy for restoring the " old
goose " to life will readily suggest itself.   Let shippers and
business men remember that if they want prompt and reliable
facilities afforded, by which they can accommodate their southern patrons, they must unite in supporting such a class of
boats as experience has shown can and will do it.

                                                E. W. GOULD.

St. Louis, November 23, 1877.

BARGE TRANSPORTATION.

                                St. Louis, November 29, 1880.

Editor Times: " It never rains unless it pours " is an
old saying, and never more true than when applied to steamboatmen.

It may not be peculiar to them, but it certainly is true when
applied to them.

They are like sheep going over a fence. When one starts
they all follow without knowing where they are to land.

If any man can tell what use all the barges now built, and
under contract at the present time, are to be put to, he is
gifted, as Captain Beasley would say.

Every yard from Cairo to Pittsburgh is crowded with barge
building, or, in consequence, of the large number of barges
being built at other yards.

These barges are generally of the largest class, some of
which have a capacity of from 1,400 to 1,800 tons, which is as
much or more than the average Cincinnati and St. Louis and
New Orleans steamboats carry.

Including what barges have been built during the past summer and now under contract, the aggregate will be quite fifty,
probably more.

And what use is this 70,000 tons increased tonnage capacity
to be put to ? Transportation of bulk grain principally, of
course.

The last year has been one of the most productive ever
known in the West. And the short crop in Europe has
created a demand for this surplus. And a large amount of
this surplus grain has gone forward in bulk via New Orleans
and other ports.

Not being in the business I do not, of course, know how
much more than a fair margin of profit has been made by
those who have handled this grain.

But I do know that there has been no scarcity of tonnage except for a very small portion of the year. And the low rate of freight that has generally prevailed is conclusive evidence that an increase of 50 per cent. in the tonnage will reduce the rate below a possible margin, unless the demand for transportation is far beyond any reasonable expectation.

The large amount of railroad freight offering has of course tended to keep up prices by rail. Still statistics show that while exportations via New Orleans of bulk grain have been largely increased, by far the larger amount has been shipped via Northern ports, notwithstanding the high price of railroad and canal freights.

If railroad freights are scarce, it is fair to conclude they will always be strong competitors for bulk grain as well as for every other class of freight.

Ocean freights from Northern ports must always rule very much lower than from New Orleans; not so much on account of distance, as from the passenger travel and importations, of which New Orleans furnishes very little.

Hence the conclusion seems inevitable that notwithstanding the improvement at the mouth of the Mississippi, whereby vessels of the largest class can pass out to sea, fully loaded, there are many reasons for concluding the tonnage on the river may be increased far beyond any legitimate demand for many years to come.

"Cheap freights," is the commercial watchword, the world over, but why it should always be at the expense of those engaged in water transportation, remains for them to decide. With very few exceptions, from the earliest date of "steamboating" on the waters of the Mississippi Valley, to the present time, there has been no legitimate business that has paid so small a remuneration for the capital invested, as it has; and the indications are that barge transportation will form no exception, Jay Gould to the contrary notwithstanding.   E. W. Gould.

CHEAP TRANSPORTATION ON THE MISSOURI.

St. Louis, December 18, 1873.

To the Editor of the Globe:

In accordance with your request, I will attempt briefly to give you the result of my experience and observation in regard to the navigation of the Missouri river, and especially as to the practicability of establishing "barge lines" there, to create "cheap transportation." I have not unfrequently attempted to show the impracticability of that system of transportation under existing circumstances, but have been met with the accusation that my interests were prejudicial to the introduction of barge transportation, and hence no fair or unbiased conclusions need be expected from me.

The Missouri River Packet Company have built and navigated barges on that stream successfully, in the prosecution of their business, during low water; not with tow boats, but with their freight and passenger boats, for the purpose of lighting freight over shoal bars. But that does not prove the practicability of using barges as a system of cheap transportation.

This company could, and doubtless would, use regular tow-boats in their business if experience or observation showed them to be better adapted than those now in use.

Two things at least are now essentially necessary to warrant the success of barge transportation on the Missouri River. The first is the improvement of the river by the removal of snags, wrecks, etc., saying nothing about dredging the shoaler bars. Both of which are practicable, and demand the attention of our members of Congress. The second is, protection of those articles of commerce naturally seeking a market through water transportation.

At present railroad competition is such as to render it utterly impossible for any system of water transportation on this river to compete with it — as demonstrated by the prices charged during the latter year or two from St. Joseph, Council Bluffs and other points to St. Louis and Chicago. It is a well known fact that corn, oats and other heavy freights, have been carried by rail, during the whole summer, from these and other points, at twenty-five cents per 100 pounds, and for fifteen cents from Kansas City and other places. From the latter point to St. Louis by water is near 500 miles, and from St. Joe 660, and from Council Bluffs 800. If the cry of "cheap transportation" is not silenced by these rates, it is not necessary to look to the river for relief, under any condition of improvement. And until these cheap and bulky articles of freight shall have been largely increased in their production, or railroads find more profitable use for their stock, it would seem hardly necessary to inaugurate barge lines or any other cheaper mode of transportation.

In order to insure success in barge transportation, I apprehend a depth of at least five feet of water to be necessary on such streams as the Missouri, even after the snags, wrecks, etc., are removed. But out of the nine months of navigation, which is about the average time in that river, there are not

more than four months the water will average five feet in the
channel. The balance of the time it varies from three and
a half to four and a half feet, take one year with another.
While I am willing to admit the practicability and economy of
barge transportation on some rivers, and under some circumstances, I am not prepared to indorse it as the best or most
economical means of securing " cheap transportation," under
all circumstances.

I will venture the prediction, that when the Mississippi
River is so improved as to insure a channel depth of eight
feet water between St. Louis and New Orleans (which is considered practicable), the present system of transportation by
barges, for miscellaneous freights, will be considered among
that class of steamboats, the Hon. Henry T. Blow said before
the Windom Committee, " belonged to another age, and
ought to be burned up."

While I do not indorse Mr. Blow as to the disposition that
should be made of these boats or barges, yet I am satisfied that
they will be superseded by a class of steamboats better adapted
to insure cheap transportation than any system of barge
transportation yet known.

Did it ever occur to you, Mr. Editor, there were two sides
to this question of cheap transportation?

It sounds to me a good deal like a hobby, upon which
political aspirants, public speakers, and newspaper writers
generally, mount to catch the sympathy of those who so
generally respond to the sentiment of " cheap transportation."

As a rule, I admit the necessity of cheap transportation,
all things being equal. But there is a very important distinction between what might be considered cheap transportation
and a fair remunerative rate. It must be admitted that the carrier is as much entitled to a fair compensation for his capital
and labor as is the farmer or producer. We never hear the
latter abused for asking *two* or *three* prices for anything he
has to sell, if the market justifies it, however much it may
distress the poor family that is obliged to pay it.

But if the carrier advanced his rate under the law of supply
and demand, or to what he claims to be a remunerative rate,
there is no language too strong to express what the public
are pleased to call extortion and monopoly.

With very few exceptions, I am satisfied that the producing
classes of this country have been far better paid for their capital and labor than have any transportation companies in the
last five years. The evidence of that is too apparent to need
further demonstration.

Still the whole country is almost in arms for "cheaper transportation," and a war against public carriers is a popular sentiment to-day.

The carrying trade of this country is represented by hundreds of thousands, if not millions, of people. Look at the reports and balance sheets of this great interest, and at the number of idle railroad cars, steamboats and barges that are depreciating at the rate of from 15 to 20 per cent. per annum, saying nothing about the thousands of employes that are idle, and their families suffering for the necessaries of life. We hear of occasional "strikes" among these operatives, which are denounced by the public in unmeasured terms. But nothing is more popular than "farmers' granges" and "trade-unions" all over the country, and, agreeably to my understanding, the objects of both are about the same.

Surely, consistency, thou art a jewel. But I am digressing from the question, and if I have said enough for you to understand my views of barge transportation on the Missouri or other streams, your questions are answered. And I trust we may have the continued co-operation of the *Globe* in our efforts to secure such improvements on all our navigable rivers as will justify the public in demanding cheap transportation.

E. W. GOULD.

BARGE TRANSPORTATION ON THE MISSOURI RIVER.

Editor Republican. I am glad to again see the Kansas City papers teeming with articles on the subject of barge lines, barge companies and barge transportation from Kansas City South.

There has been a spasmodic effort periodically for several years past made by those papers to induce parties to establish such lines for the transportation of grain in bulk to St. Louis, and there has been no lack of encouragement from those claiming to be "old, practical steamboat, barge and flat-boat men," ready to indorse the entire practicability of such an enterprise.

I am also gratified to see that the *Republican* has taken up the subject and is contributing its influence to so important a matter.

Not that I have a particle of faith in any practical good that will result from this present effort, more than in all previous ones, so far as the establishing of a successful line of barges is concerned. But if persisted in, as I trust it will be, the object may be accomplished after a while. And why not now? you may ask.

If you will bear with me a little, I will repeat what I have often said before. Simply because it is entirely impracticable, and for several reasons, some of which I will briefly enumerate. The first and principal one is, the river is not in condition to make it possible to navigate a tow of loaded barges in an ordinary stage of water, much less in a low stage which usually prevails from the opening of navigation until the first of May, and from September 1, to the close of navigation.

I make this assertion without fear of successful contradiction from any practical tow-boatman or boat owners on the Missouri River whose opinion is entitled to consideration. I don't mean to say such a thing cannot be done if time and care enough is spent to work a single tow up and down. But no price will be paid for freight that will justify that.

That being admitted, further argument would seem unnecessary. But to further illustrate, let us see how about high water. That generally continues about three months out of the twelve; and if in every way adapted to barge navigation, no sane man will contend that the profits during that short period will justify establishing and running a line of barges; although from some estimates I have seen from these "old, practical boatmen," one might conclude there was a fortune in a single trip.

Every one acquainted with the navigation of the Missouri knows to their sorrow the difficulty and danger of passing the bridges, even in low water, which is doubly increased in high. In fact, it often occurs in high water that none but the most powerful boats in the river can pass those draws without a barge, and to attempt to take a tow of barges through them would be madness.

I doubt if a man of ordinary observation can be found, who has traveled on that river since those deadfalls have been built, that will dissent from this statement; and if there is a responsible insurance company that will underwrite on such tows, it will only be at a rate that will preclude the possibility of shipments.

The rate of insurance on that river is always so high that none but the cheapest character of freight can be shipped. The railroad rate of freight is often less than the insurance by river, on all classes of merchandise. Hence, as a matter of course, a line of barges would have to depend upon their down-stream freights principally, as steamboats do now.

After what I have said it is hardly necessary for me to attempt to show the lowest rate of freight at which a barge company could live, carrying freight one way only, or say from Kansas City to St. Louis.

With the large number of railroads that diverge from Kansas City, and the increased competition that would ensue, no price of freight could be had even from the most enthusiastic barge advocate that would pay a barge company under present circumstances.

But there may be a condition of things that will change these circumstances, and hence I said at first I was glad to see the interest the *Republican*, Kansas City and other papers were taking in this very laudable enterprise.

COMMENCING AT THE WRONG END.

But you have commenced at the wrong end, gentlemen, and will never succeed, until Congress shall have made sufficient provision, and improved the navigation.

With one-half the talk that has been made to establish a barge line, an influence might have been exerted upon our members of Congress that would have resulted in so far improving the rivers as high up as Kansas City as to make practical barge navigation. But with the exception of an occasional effort on the part of some member to introduce some impracticable measure for general improvement, we hear nothing said of the Missouri River, unless some railroad company presents a bill to bridge the river, which Congress is sure to grant and the people indorse and no questions asked until they want some compensation to "break up the pool combination" of these same railroads. Verily, "consistency, thou art a jewel."

But there is no use quarreling about what has been done — railroads and railroad bridges are good things. Both can and ought to be built — not to materially obstruct navigation, but across the Missouri they have not been so constructed.

But the practical question now is, What is the remedy? What can be done to so improve navigation at once, that our immediate necessities can be provided for?

I answer remove the snags and build cribs above and below the bridge piers at the draws, so that boats may drop or cordell through safely. This can and ought to be done at once, and will not cost to exceed $50,000. And it is all that is necessary to insure pretty safe navigation as high up as Kansas City for eight months in the year, or as long as good water continues.

But as snags are constantly accumulating, of course it will be necessary that one snag boat should be kept patrolling the river most of the time during the navigable season each year.

Now, gentlemen of the press, of the farm and the middle

men, if you mean business, and expect to accomplish anything, hitch your tow-line on the right end of your barge; trim your sails and bear down on your Congressmen. If you can't make the ripple through them you might as well give up the ship and the barge lines. E. W. GOULD.

BARGE TRANSPORTATION ON THE MISSOURI RIVER.

ST. LOUIS, March 1, 1873.

To the Editor of the Democrat:

Kansas City and other towns along the Missouri River have been alive with the " barge question " for some weeks past — all seeming to believe that if there were barge lines established their freight could be transported to Southern markets at less than half the present cost, besides being highly remunerative to the enterprising projectors. In this sentiment your commercial editor seems also to sympathize. My object at this time is not to attempt to show the fallacy of this proposition. Practical men know that at present it is nothing but a fallacy. And merchants of experience know that freights are carried to-day, by rail, cheaper from Omaha and many points between there and St. Louis than any water transportation in America, except ocean and lake. But it is claimed that Nebraska and Kansas are to be the great grain producing States of the nation, and must have increased facilities, and that barge lines can alone supply the demand. We will suppose that to be the case for the sake of the argument; for when the products of the country shall have increased sufficiently to give the roads what business they want, rates of freight will, of course, be greatly increased; and without a regulator, such as the river may be made, the rates of freight will undoubtedly be a subject of just complaint.

Now, right here, allow me to make a suggestion which, I believe, will do more to accomplish the object all these gentlemen have in view than the formation of a half dozen barge lines at the present time. Let them use half the effort to satisfy our members of Congress of the importance of *river transportation* that they have used to convince themselves and their readers of the necessity of barge lines, and they will very soon secure appropriations by Congress which will so improve the character of navigation on the Missouri that barge transportation will be a practical thing quite as soon as the demands of commerce require it. They have commenced at the wrong end of the rope. While their zeal is commendable, it is " zeal without knowledge." The great mania for railroad

building has entirely eclipsed the importance of river transportation until very recently, and the people have sat quietly
by and allowed these railroad corporations not only to
absorb millions of the public domain, and of the people's
hard-earned money, for which they have never returned a
dollar, but have absolutely allowed them to place obstructions
in the channels of our great navigable streams that will do
more to prevent barge and steamboat navigation, or cheap
transportation (which seems to be the great desideratum),
than all other causes combined. When these commercial
writers and "cheap transportation" advocates wake up to
the real issues, and learn what the first steps are that will
assure the object they so much desire, we may expect to find
them combating some of the numerous bridge schemes now
under contemplation, which, if not soon changed in character
will forever put a stop to not only barge transportation, but
to every other kind except railroad. We shall find them, too,
not only appealing to Congress for appropriations for the improvement of our rivers, but insisting that every candidate
who offers himself for Congress shall be pledged to use his
best endeavors to secure the necessary appropriations, from
year to year, until the great rivers of the country are made
navigable for all kinds of water transportation. When this
is accomplished, the barge question will be a more practical
one for discussion.

E. W. GOULD.

CHAPTER LXXV.

THE WAR RECORD OF STEAMBOATS.

PROBABLY no interest in the Mississippi Valley suffered so much from the effects of the war as did steamboating, especially at the South.

But as soon as hostilities ceased, those who still survived and had managed to save their boats, or could build or buy others, at once set to work with commendable zeal to recover their lost fortunes and to re-establish themselves in their respective trades, which were already being occupied to some extent by a class known as "carpetbaggers."

Such, however, was the demand for transportation that for a year or two all that recognized the situation and had provided themselves with boats, soon regained their former positions, and were doing a flourishing business. But in the meantime the war had given their natural enemy, the railroads, a long stride towards the front, and they were rapidly approaching the sources from whence steamboats draw their sustenance, and what seemed for a while a full return of former prosperity only revived hopes, to be disappointed in the near future.

There were but few of the regular transport steamboats at the South taken for gunboats. A few were purchased by the government and dismantled and their machinery used for purposes of defense in different parts of the country. Some were used for the transportation of troops and supplies, and a few continued to run in their legitimate trades as far north as Memphis, until New Orleans was captured and the Mississippi opened. Then all that could get away followed their predecessors into the Yazoo, Red River and the Bayous.

All that remained in the Yazoo were destroyed, either by one government or the other,—principally by the Confederates and the owners of the boats, to prevent their falling into Federal hands.

The boats that sought Red River and the Bayous were more fortunate, and many of them escaped destruction, and after the close of the war resumed their respective trades, as soon as they could be repaired, of which they were greatly in need, having been largely neglected for four years.

The first steamboat captured by either party during the war was a little transfer boat owned at Memphis by Captains

Frank Smith and Reese Pritchard, called S. H. Tucker, valued at two or three thousand dollars. She was captured by the Federal forces while laying at Columbus and taken to Cairo.

The following steamboats, tow-boats, tug-boats and one steamship constituted the material out of which the eight Confederate gunboats were constructed, that figured at Fort Pillow and Memphis, June 6th, 1862 : —

Tug Propeller (remodeled), called Little Rebel, commanded by Capt. Ed. Montgomery, Commodore of the fleet.

Steamship Mexico (remodeled), Gen. Bragg, commanded by Capt. Wm. Leonard.

Mary Kingsland, tow-boat (remodeled), Jeff Thompson, commanded by Capt. John Burke.

Julius Bebee, tow-boat (remodeled), Sumpter, commanded by Capt. Wallace Lamb.

Baltic, tow-boat (remodeled), Gen. Van Dorn, commanded by Capt. Isaac Fulkerson.

Milledon, tow-boat (remodeled), General Price, commanded by Capt. James Townsend.

Ocean, tow-boat (remodeled), Gen. Beauregard, commanded by Capt. Henry Hurt.

Hercules, tow-boat (remodeled), Col. Lovell, commanded by Capt. James Delacney.

The newspapers of the day are very destitute of detailed accounts of the performance of this fleet. But it is generally conceded their lives as gunboats were of short duration and barren of important results.

Some of them were powerful tow-boats and had previously been used in towing ships to and from New Orleans to the gulf.

They were bought by the Confederate government and paid for in their currency at par, which at that time would buy cotton or anything else the South produced. They were converted into gunboats at New Orleans and were thought to be equal to anything they were to come in conflict with from the North. But the result showed they were only principally useful in skirmishes, in running small batteries and in guerrilla warfare. Several of them were sunk in the little fight before Memphis. Others were destroyed by their officers to avoid falling into the hands of the enemy. One or two got away and were afterwards destroyed about Port Hudson or Baton Rouge.

The following is a partial list of boats which were destroyed during the war. While not complete, it is as perfect as present records furnish : —

Capital, transport, New Orleans and Bayou Sara packet.

Ivy, was made a gunboat. She was a low pressure tow-boat.

Gen. Polk (E. Howard), formerly transport, gunboat.

Lexington (ferry-boat), gunboat.

Mobile (propeller), gunboat.

Magnolia (transport), New Orleans and Vicksburg.

Magenta (transport), New Orleans and Vicksburg.

J. F. Pargoud (transport), New Orleans and Ouchita.

Prince of Wales (transport), New Orleans and Cairo.

Peytona (transport), New Orleans and Louisville.

Mary E. Keene (transport), New Orleans and Vicksburg.

Acadia (transport), New Orleans and Vicksburg.

Ferd. Kennett (transport), New Orleans and St. Louis.

Ed. J. Gay (transport), New Orleans and St. Louis.

Steamship Star of the West.

Hartford City, coal tow-boat, Memphis.

Hope, ———— (transport), Vicksburg and Yazoo City.

Cotton Plant (transport), Vicksburg and Yazoo City.

Scotland (transport), St. Louis and New Orleans.

Golden Age (transport), New Orleans and Fort Adams.

R. J. Lackland (transport), St. Louis and New Orleans.

John Walsh (transport), Memphis and New Orleans.

Natchez, gunboat (formerly transport), New Orleans and Vicksburg.

35th Parallel, gunboat (formerly transport).

Dew Drop (transport), Vicksburg and Yazoo River.

H. D. Means (transport), Vicksburg and Memphis.

Emma Betts (transport), Sun Flower River.

Ben McCullough (transport), Obion River.

Alonzo Child (transport), between New Orleans and St. Louis, was transformed into a Confederate gunboat.

Vicksburg (transport), between New Orleans and Vicksburg, was dismantled and her machinery used by the Confederates.

Lizzie Simmons (transport), New Orleans and Ouachita, converted into a gunboat or ram, lost, Arkansas River.

Wm. M. Morrison (transport), St. Louis and New Orleans, burned by the Confederates at the wharf, New Orleans, when the city surrendered.

New Falls City (transport), sunk in Red River by the Confederates, to prevent the expedition under Gen. Banks invading Upper Red River.

Many of the above boats were destroyed on Yazoo River, or its tributaries, by sinking or burning, generally, by order of the Confederate Government. They had been taken there by their owners as a place of safety. When the Yazoo Pass

36

was opened and Vicksburg taken, they were destroyed to prevent their falling into the hands of the Federals.

Among the larger and more valuable boats that were destroyed by the Confederates and those in sympathy with them and that belonged to owners outside of their lines, may be mentioned the following : —

Wm. M. Morrison, laying up, New Orleans.
Ruth, at Norfolk, loaded for New Orleans (incendiary).
New Falls City, sunk in Red River to obstruct channel.
Emma, lost on Red River.
Imperial, burned, wharf, St. Louis.
Sky Lark, ———, Tennessee River.
Claira Bell.
Callie, ———, Tennessee River.
Tigress, sunk, Vicksburg batteries.
Black Hawk.
Lebanon, ———, Old River.
Thomas E. Tutt, Red River, burned.
John W. Cheesman, burned, Tennessee River.
Dacotah, burned at Paducah.
City Belle, burned, Red River.
Julius H. Smith, burned, Cumberland River.
Ashland.
R. B. Hamelton, torpedo, Mobile Bay.
West Wind, burned at Glasgow, Mo.
Alice Dean, burned by Morgan at Brandenburg, Ky., after crossing his cavalry on their great raid.
Mazeppa and barges, burned on Tennessee River.
Rose Douglass, Little Rock, Chester Ashley, Daniel B. Miller, Violet, Cedar Rapids, all burned on the Arkansas, battle of Arkansas Post.
St. Francis No. 2, burned on White River.
Lake City, burned by guerrillas, Carson's Landing.
Henry Clay, destroyed at Vicksburg by the batteries at the time Forest Queen ran past them.

There were other boats destroyed on different streams in the South. But as yet there is no complete record, either in the South or West, of the results of the war so far as steamboats were concerned.

But under an act of Congress the War Department is preparing an exhaustive record of all transactions and incidents of the war in detail, both of the Federals and Confederates.

There is a War Records Bureau which has for several years been devoted entirely to collecting, compiling, and printing these war records. When completed there will probably be some forty or fifty large volumes.

As only boats of *loyal* citizens were employed by the government, except when seized and confiscated, this interest suffered much more at the South than in the West. Although in the value of the boats lost, if not in number, the West suffered most, principally from incendiarism and guerrillas, although by order of the Confederate government many were burned.

After the blockade was removed on the Mississippi there were many boats fired into from the Confederates along shore from masked batteries and guerrillas, and some narrow escapes and many lives lost.

Among the many attacks none are reported with more tragic results, or that made more narrow escapes, than did the large, new steamer Empress.

She was admirably calculated for the transportation of troops, horses and cavalry, equipage, etc., and consequently she was often in the service of the government.

On one trip from New Orleans in 1863 with 800 tons of sugar and molasses on board, Capt. John Molloy, master, when just above Island 82, she was fired into by the Confederates from shore, which killed Capt. Molloy and several others, and so disabled the machinery that only for the assistance of one of the *tin clads* that were patroling the river and happened to be within hearing, the Empress would have been captured and undoubtedly destroyed, as there was among the passengers Gen. John McNeil and many other Federal officers and soldiers but no organized command.

The boat being heavily loaded and with poor fuel was moving very slowly.

From some passengers who had landed at a point below, the Confederates learned that Gen. McNeil was on board and his record at Palmyra, Mo., made them anxious to become more intimately acquainted with him. The meanderings of the river enabled them to overtake the boat in the bend of the river below Gaine's Landing. Having planted their cannon in ambush, they waited behind the levee until the boat was abreast of them and not more than 300 yards distant.

Capt. Molloy stepped out of his room in front of the pilot house on the first report.

The second discharge took his head off and sent several shot and shell through the boat in different places.

As it was very warm weather several lady passengers and some children were in the pilot house. They immediately dropped on to the floor, and were partially shielded by the iron plates that were put up to protect the pilot.

Although they partially disabled one engine, through the quick action of the engineer, he shipped up the full stroke camrod in time to keep the boat going up the river, and she was soon out of range of their cannon.

But as the channel followed the shore for some distance their cavalry kept up with the boat and continued their rifle practice upon her until she was enabled to cross the river.

When, through the assistance of the *tin clad* that had come to her relief, she was landed on the opposite shore, where the dead were interred, the wounded cared for, and the machinery temporarily repaired, when she resumed her voyage.

This was probably the narrowest escape Gen. McNeil ever had. If the boat had been captured there would have been no exchange of prisoners in that case.

The Empress made many narrow escapes during the war.

On one trip from the South a battery at Bolivar, Mississippi, opened upon her when she was passing there in the fog. The fog lifted just as she was opposite, and before the guns could be got into range, she had gotten so far passed that the shot came in only at the stern, and did but little damage, although the boilers were closely shaved. One spent ball from the battery was picked up in the pilot house, and carried on the boat as a kind of trophy or memento until the close of the war.

After much valuable service in the Federal cause, and so many narrow escapes from Confederate batteries and guerrilla sharp-shooters, this splendid steamboat was ingloriously killed soon after the war by a more formidable battery in the shape of a sunken wreck at Island 34.

The following graphic account appeared in the St. Louis *Republican* soon after the occurrence. Many of his numerous friends will still recognize the signature of the corre-pondent.

It was from the pen of one of that paper's most reliable correspondents and one that was employed on Federal transports during the war. This writer is under many obligations to *Mr. Moore* for interesting items in this work : —

STEAMER EMPRESS FIRED INTO NEAR GAINES' LANDING, ARK. —
    TERRIBLE DAMAGE AND SLAUGHTER — GREAT CONSTERNATION
ON BOARD — FIVE PERSONS KILLED AND ELEVEN WOUNDED.

" The steamer Empress, en route for St. Louis, was fired into from the Arkansas shore, about one mile below Gaines' Landing, on Wednesday, the 10th inst., at 3:30 p. m.

The battery encountered comprised some eight guns, of six and twelve pound calibre, and of the most improved capacity for both accurate and terrible execution. The number of guns is derived from an estimate made by artillerists on board at the time.

The battery was doubtless supported by a large force of infantry, variously estimated at one to two thousand. However, of the strength of this force there could be no proper conjecture, except from limited information in possession of the gunboat officers in the vicinity. Certain it is that the boat encountered a perfect shower of musket balls, but which were seemingly regarded with but little terror amid the din and clash of the terrific, death-dealing missiles discharged from their artillery.

This battery was located in the bight of a deep bend, the body of water being confined to a narrow channel, while the rapidity of the current was proportionately increased; and to this list of well studied advantages, the fact that one among the first shots fired cut away the "camrod" to the larboard engine, while another shot or shell disabled the "doctor engine," and some idea, though indefinite, may be formed of the danger of the position. The larboard wheel being stopped caused the boat to be forced by the remaining wheel in the direction of the battery, and this disadvantage was made still more alarming by the fact of the boat not having sufficient headway to render her obedient to the rudder.

During this most desponding crisis the boat was almost stationary, and that, too, in the very mouth of the battery, and yet the engineers were braving every danger and striving with almost superhuman energy to effect temporary repairs, such as would enable them to work the engines, at least, until the supply of steam and water should be exhausted. They could not hope for anything beyond this, in consideration of the injury to the "doctor engine," by which the boilers are supplied. Their noble efforts were crowned with success, and many a drooping spirit leaped joyously with the first revolution of that engine.

The boat had just escaped the range of the battery when the tin-clad gunboat Romeo, or No. 3, came to her assistance and while rounding in alongside to take her in tow shelled the woods most furiously to silence the sharpshooters stationed along the banks.

The boat was under effective fire for over twenty minutes. Fifty or sixty artillery shots took effect in various portions of the boat; while the number of small shots is almost too numer-

ous to estimate. Many of the shots were evidently directed
at the boilers, and some conception of the accuracy may be
had when we state thirteen mules were killed immediately between the boilers and the battery.

Gen. McNeil having occasion to pass from the roof into and
through the cabin expressed it that he seemingly picked his
steps through a perfect "labyrinth of cannon balls."

At the time of the attack, there were some five hundred
persons on board, including passengers, about sixty of whom
were women and children. Words cannot express the consternation of that half hour. History will fail to record, or
canvas to portray, the horrors of such a scene. Men, women
and children running to and fro wringing their hands in utter
despair, or crouched behind some frail protection which fear
and terror had magnified into fancied security. To intensify
this scene of anguish, many passengers were hurrying about
the cabin and although unhurt themselves were literally
covered with blood received from the wounds of others near
by them.

After the gunboat had towed the Empress around the point
which shut out the locality of the battery from view, she
landed her and here she remained until the necessary repairs
could be completed. This required about eight hours, when
the lights on board were all extinguished, and under convoy of
the gunboat we proceeded up the river.

After the trying ordeal was passed, and notes and incidents
compared, we were enabled to bestow honor on whom honor
was due.

Among the bright stars in the galaxy, we beg to mention
the following names: Brig.-Gen. McNeil, Military Director;
Thos. Goslee and Enoch King, pilots; Hugh Davis, mate;
Geo. Bruce, Andrew Pendleton, Judd Weber and Wm. Ten-
nant, engineers and assistants.

The list of names of killed and wounded has doubtless, ere
this, reached you by telegraph.

When the attack was commenced Captain John Molloy was
sitting on the bed in his room, in the forward part of the
Texas. He immediately ran out the side door, and on the opposite side from the battery. He took hold on a small iron hog-
chain, by which he was endeavoring to swing himself out-
board to speak to the pilots, and while in this position a solid
shot passing through his room struck him, completely sever-
ing his head from his body.

Here let us pause while we pay a sad but fitting tribute to
the memory of a departed friend — Captain John Molloy had

been for a series of years an active steamboatman, hailing from this port — and in every position he was called to fill, he evinced a spirit of honor and integrity in the discharge of his duties, a pride in his profession, and a scrupulous regard for the interests of his employers, that endeared him to the hearts of all with whom he became associated.

We know of no higher or more deserving encomium when we say : " To know him was to love him." Many a stout heart among that crew bowed in sorrow and affliction on learning of the death of their commander.

A true friend — an agreeable companion — a high-toned gentleman. Who will wonder that many a bitter tear, on that sad occasion, bedimmed the eye of those " unused to weeping?"   " A. R. M."

OBITUARY.

Died, Wednesday, August 10th, on board steamer Empress, Captain John Molloy, in the 42d year of his age.

The subject of the above notice was a citizen of this city, long and favorably known throughout the community at large, but more especially to the steamboat fraternity, of which he had been for many years an esteemed and revered member. His parents emigrating to St Louis while he was yet in his infancy, he may be said to have " grown with the village," and being endowed by nature with these ennobling qualities of head and heart which ever attract the love and admiration of the circle, and unite, as with a silken bond, in friendship and sincerity, he had the gathering of long years to claim for his myriad of true friends and companions.

At an early age he selected for future pursuit a mercantile calling, and with this view entered the well-known house of Sproule & Buchanan, wholesale grocers and commission merchants. As evidence of worth he retained his position in this house for many years, and throughout all the varied changes to which the firm was subjected. About the year 1850 a river life claimed his attention, and we find him engaged as second clerk of the steamer Amaranth, a regular St. Louis and New Orleans trader. He was attached to this boat for over two years. Subsequently he was clerk of the steamers Aleck Scott, Shenandoah and J. C. Swon.

He was in command of the steamers Orleans and John Walsh, which latter boat he superintended during her building at Cincinnati. He also commanded the steamers Illinois, Planet, Champion, Mollie Able and Empress. He was an acknowledged competent boatman and thorough business man,

affable in his deportment to all, genial in his manners and much
given to social converse, a not uncommon sequence of river
life.

> " For what'er our mood
> In sooth, we love not solitude."

He was engaged with a friend in talk of home and the brighter
scenes of early youth but a single moment before he was summoned and called away from "earthly scenes."
He died as he had lived, with the words of duty upon his lips.
A loved companion has passed away, and we would fain
forget the scene or the occasion of his untimely death.   Yet in
after years, when the dread alarms of war are hushed and peace
shall lend its cheerful influence to home and fireside, remembrance will anon harrow up the retrospect and picture o'er
again the brief but sad hour that doomed a noble life.

> " Count life by virtues — these will last
> When life's short race is o'er —
> And these, when earthly joys are past
> Shall cheer us on a brighter shore."

Among other tragic events that occurred on transport boats
was one on the steamer Von Phul, on a trip from New Orleans to St. Louis in which Captain Gormon, her commander,
and the bar-keeper were instantly killed from a battery located
just above Bayou Sara on the opposite side of the river.

A STORY OF THE WAR — HOW THE ALICE DEAN WAS DESTROYED
DURING THE MORGAN RAID, FROM CINCINNATI "COMMERCIAL
GAZETTE" — CONFEDERATE GENERAL JOHNSON'S ACCOUNT RE-
LATED TO MRS. CAPTAIN JAMES H. PEPPER TWENTY-FIVE YEARS
AFTER.

APRIL 14, 1889.

"Previous to and in the early days of the war, the Cincinnati
and Memphis packet Alice Dean was one of the favorite and
most palatial of river steamers.   Her cabin was sumptuously
furnished, and she was one of the fast clippers, plying between
the Queen City and the now fast growing city on the Tennessee bluffs.   The Alice Dean was a favorite vessel for excursion parties from Cincinnati, and was commanded by Captain
Jas. H. Pepper, a mariner of prepossessing appearance, a re-
fined, well educated man, and whose urbane manners made
him a general favorite with the traveling public.   Captain
Pepper has long since gone to that bourne from whence no
traveler returns, and the grand floating palace during the war
was burned to the water's edge by the guerrilla, John Morgan,

near Brandenburg, while in the hospital service and en route from Memphis to Cincinnati.

The boat was hailed into shore by a distress signal, and John Morgan when she landed came aboard and demanded that he and his troops be transported to the other side of the river. Unbeknown to Captain Pepper at the time, Morgan was being hotly pursued by Generals Buford and Shackleford, and on the way up the river his men became very boisterous and threatened to burn the boat. Captain Pepper went to General Morgan, and, both being Masons, exacted a promise from Morgan that if the boat were landed and his men safely conveyed to shore the Alice Dean should not be in the least molested, and be permitted to continue on her trip toward Cincinnati. Hardly had the landing been made, however, before the boat was discovered on fire in several places, and soon burned to the water's edge."

The widow of Captain Pepper has for several years past been conducting a hotel at Temple, Texas, and recently wrote to a friend in this city relating a strange coincidence.

'The lady says: "You will, no doubt, remember the capture and burning of the Alice Dean. There has several times come to our house within the last three months a gentleman totally blind. His fine appearance and language excited one's attention and sympathy. A few weeks ago he registered with us again, and came here to meet some New York capitalists, who are projecting a railroad in this section. The name of the gentleman is General Johnson. One evening he and the New York gentlemen were in the office, and the General was relating some war reminiscences, when one of the party asked him if he had lost his sight during the war. He replied: 'Yes; I was with General Morgan, an officer at the time he made his raid through Ohio. We reached Brandenburg, Kentucky, where I captured a small stern-wheel boat, and, seeing a large steamer approaching from down the river, ran out into the river with the stern-wheel boat and began giving signals of distress. The captain of the large boat slowed up and came alongside, and in a few moments my men, at an order from me, had boarded her. I compelled the captain to carry all of Morgan's troops to the Indiana shore, where we safely landed, General Morgan going ahead with his men and I remaining on board with a small force, and then, it occurring to me and fearing that the captain of the captured boat might go back to the Kentucky side and carry over after us General Buford and his command, *I ordered my men to apply the torch, and burned her to the water's edge.*'

"All of this I heard, and not being able to longer contain my feelings, interrupted their conversation by saying, 'General Johnson, do you remember the name of the boat you burned?' 'Yes,' he said, 'let me see. I can see her in my mind.' I was too impatient to let him think, but exclaimed, 'Was it the Alice Dean?' 'Yes, yes, that was her name, and she was commanded by Captain Pepper.' 'Well, sir,' I said, 'do you know that Captain Pepper was my husband, and it was his property you destroyed?' 'Is it possible I am talking in the presence of Mrs. Pepper?' 'Yes, sir, you are.'

"There was a dead silence for a few moments, and then I left the office. I learned afterward from one of the gentlemen that they had had a skirmish with General Shackleford and General Johnson had been shot through both eyes, and was nursed by a family near Newbery, Indiana, named Sims. I have so often had a curiosity to know why the Alice Dean was burned, as I have heard Captain Pepper say General Morgan assured him as a Mason that his property should not be destroyed. Was it not strange that after so many years — over a quarter of a century — away here in far Texas, making my own bread and in my own house, I should hear a man say he applied the torch to my husband's boat?"

The name of the little stern-wheel boat referred to in the narrative was the John T. Macombs.

RIVER REMINISCENCES.

[Reported for the *Enquirer* from Memory by Captain A. H. Handlan.]

The following list of gunboats, rams and transports were at Shreveport, Red River, during the summer of 1863: Mary T, gunboat; Missouri, iron-clad, eleven guns; ram Webb, after New Orleans fell, came out of Red River, passing New Orleans flying the Stars and Stripes, and when opposite the point at Algiers pulled down the Stars and Stripes and displayed the Stars and Bars, and was fired at from a Union gunboat of Commodore Farragut's fleet, but she continued her course down the Mississippi fifty miles, where she met Commodore Farragut's flagship Hartford, when her crew ran her into the bank and deserted her after damaging her so that she sank. Above Shreveport: T. W. Roberts; the General Quitman came out with a cargo of cotton belonging to Captain John Cannon and went to St. Louis; Nina Sims, Anna Perrot; the Falls City was scuttled and sank crosswise in the river to prevent steamers from passing; the Twilight, Homer, Indian No.

2, Vigo, Trenton, ram and gunboat General Beauregard, afterward captured and sunk in the fight at Memphis: Charm, Andy Fulton, Eries Nos. 4, 6, 7, Doubloon, Countess, J. M. Ralph, Music, Lafourch, T. D. Hine, Cleon, Colona, Planter No. 2, Frolic, Morgan, Nelson, Dr. Beaty and others. None of the above were destroyed by the Union forces. But they blew up the gunboat Eastport to prevent her from being captured, beside losing some trnsports in that hornet's nest.

Memoranda. — Steamer John Walsh left New Orleans Monday, August 6th, at 5 o'clock, p. m.

We left in port for St. Louis, steamers Wm. M. Morrison, Imperial, New Uncle Sam, Jno. J. Roe and Hiawatha.   7th — Met T. L. McGill at Natchez.   8th — Met Edward Walsh at Vicksburg; City of Memphis just above; John Warner at Island 93.   9th — Met Gladiator at Greenville, and Skylark aground at same place.   10th — Met A. McDowell aground at Helena.   They had succeeded in sparring her straight with the current, and unless something should give way she would soon be afloat.   11th — Met Champion above Memphis; Choctaw still hard aground at Island 25; with Great Western alongside taking freight; L. M. Kennett just starting over the bar at the same place.   12th — Met Hannibal at No. 8; Arago at Cairo, loading for New Orleans and would leave same day; B. J. Adams, from Louisville, also loading to return from Cairo. She was about ready and only awaited the arrival of the Tempest with a lot of mules.   13th — Met Alonzo Child at Wittenburg.

When we passed Napoleon the wharf-boats were filled to their utmost capacity, and flat-boats were called into requisition for the storage of wet barrels and other descriptions of freight not liable to damage by exposure, To Little Rock there was a channel depth of only twenty inches, while above that point they report twenty-seven inches.

The Mississippi above Vicksburg is fast assuming what might be termed a very "ragged exterior."   The water on the principal bars may be set down as follows: Greenville, 7¼ feet; Bulletin, 8¼ feet; Island 34, 8 feet; above Cairo, 7 feet.

Yours truly,   E. T. C.

CHAPTER LXXVI.

STEAMBOAT vs. RAILROAD.

THE following paragraph is copied because it claims to be indorsed by a newspaper generally practical in all its suggestions — not because this writer indorses it for a moment.

True, the author of the paragraph, " R. F.," supposes a differently constructed wheel, and in fact what he terms " new methods" are to be applied. What they are or what may be the result of such " new methods," of course, no one can predict without knowing something of them.

But he claims that " methods *now* known " will insure much greater returns than have yet been obtained.

Without speculating upon the results of the new methods, his claims of what can be secured by those already known, are so impracticable, on the Mississippi River at least, that it is hardly worth while to discuss them. It is now more than seventy-five years since the best skill and mechanical ingenuity that this country and Europe have produced has been devoted to the study of the best methods in the application of steam to navigation. The last twenty-five years have certainly shown no improved methods, or if improved, no *new* methods. So far as the Mississippi River is concerned, there is no evidence to prove that there has been any improvement in the speed of steamboats in *forty-five years*.

When the circumstances are fairly considered, the time of the first J. M. White, in 1844, has never been equaled, and probably never will be, over the same course.

The proposition that passenger boats can and ought to be built to make the trip from New Orleans to St. Louis in seventy-two hours and back in forty-eight hours is too chimerical to talk of in the present condition of navigation, or in any other condition that is probable to exist.

No route, no circumstances in America, if in any other country, have as yet made it possible for a steamboat to compete with a railroad except in towing cheap freight, especially on such streams as those in the Mississippi Valley.

The route between Louisville and Cincinnati is a fair illustration. There was a wealthy corporation, well and extensively known for the excellence of their boats, almost entirely exempt from accidents, on a route free from snags, wrecks or other unknown obstructions, with a stage of water often extending through six or eight months, without interruption, and with a class of boats combining all known facilities for speed and comfort, with arrangements with all connecting lines of railroads — making sure connections at each end of the route — furnishing a good supper and a comfortable night's lodging at less than railroad cost.   The result is known to everybody — that ten passengers go' by rail where one travels by this fine line of boats.

The same may be said of the travel on the Hudson River, and a large part of the year even on Long Island Sound, and every other route where this competition exists.

Produce the *new methods* and if practicable there is plenty of capital to avail itself of the advantages developed.   But it is idle to flatter ourselves with methods or expectations long since exploded.

"*Editor of the Times:* I am glad to see that a suggestion of the *Times* to place exclusive passenger boats on the Mississippi from St. Louis to New Orleans is meeting with favor, because there is no doubt this is what is required to initiate a movement to recover steamboat interests from the depression caused by railroad competition.

Boats can be made to run quite as fast as average railroad trains, and if made and run over such a route within any time approaching railroad speed, would certainly be preferred.   Let the fast passenger boats be built, and the fast freight will soon follow.

On the time question, however, you do not aim as high as is within the reach of methods now known.   Two days for the down trip, and three up, is what should be aimed for.   And it is to be hoped that if there are any wide-awake men willing to go into such an enterprise, that they will be such as are also capable of entertaining some new ideas on the subject of marine propulsion; and who will before embarking examine into the merits of what may be shown and suggested to them.

That they will see that a few thousand dollars' expenditure in preliminary experiment would be a wiser measure than to risk all in old plans that have heretofore invariably failed to reach the results attempted.   It is also to be hoped that they will know enough never to expect any screw propeller is going to drive a large vessel against the current of the Mississippi River at the speed required; and that no paddle-wheel of the old pattern can yield a sufficient thrusting force.

Let them put no confidence in any engineer, who believes that a paddle-wheel properly constructed can have too broad

or wide a surface of paddle, and consequently too great resistance to its movement in the water. This is the power that
moves the boat, and when it moves the wheel turns and will
revolve as fast as the boat moves, and the boat moves just in
proportion to the amount of resistance the paddle encounters.
If it is more than the engine can overcome, it will move the
boat instead first, and the wheel will as surely keep up as the
wheels of a wagon keep pace with the motion of the load upon
them."   R. F.

From a recent letter over the signature of "A Clerk," published in the *Times-Democrat* of New Orleans, the subject is
considered from another standpoint:

                                        NEW ORLEANS, Jan. 13, 1889.
" *To the editor of the Times-Democrat:*
   " When the Ed. Richardson was sold to be wrecked we read
that she was the last but one of the river palaces which had
given so much fame to the Mississippi steamboat. Since the
sinking of the Natchez it is told that her loss is that also of the
last of the river palaces; that never again will we have such
fleet and elegant steamers as the Lee, White or Natchez; that
so largely has the traffic and travel by river fallen off there is
no longer need or profit for such boats, and that if the steam
boatmen are wise they will build in their places freight carriers
alone, and of the most economical kind. Now it has become
so common to speak thus of steamboats, to belittle their value,
to make it appear that they no longer serve a grand and useful
purpose, to so great an extent have they been supplanted, and so
uncommon is it for one to say a word in their praise or defense,
that I beg a hearing in behalf of the much maligned and misunder-
stood steamboat.   In the first place it is not the Lee, White, or
Natchez that made the Mississippi steamboat famous, for there
were boats before their day just as famous and widely known.
The Tecumseh was one, a boat which in 1828 went to Louisville from this city in 8 days and 4 hours, then considered a
marvelously fast run; the J. M. White of 1844 was another,
and whose time to St. Louis has been beaten but once since.
There was also the Hard Times, which boat in 1847 made
three trips in a month between this city and St. Louis.   There
was also the Duke of Orleans, whose time from here to Cincinnati in 1843 has not since been beaten.   Also the A. L. Shotwell and Eclipse, with the fastest of all records to Louisville, and the Princess and Natchez and other flyers of antebellum days.   It was feats and boats like these, and not the

record of any one or of three boats, that made the steamboat
of the Mississippi famous, and the glory of which will be but
added to in the future, as surely as time comes and goes. Nor
are all the "floating palaces" gone forever. Some yet remain, and the Oliver Beirne is one of them. The Beirne, so
far as "ginger-bread work" goes, is as elaborately finished
outside as was the Lee or White, and her cabin inside is
claimed by some to be more beautiful than was the White's,
and as to speed neither of the three great boats would have
had time to waste in keeping ahead of the Beirne.

There is also the Jesse K. Bell, though not so great in
size. Who can gainsay her beauty outside, or elegance
within? Both of these boats, belonging to the Planters and
Merchant's Packet Line, and running to Bayou Sara, have
done as much business this season as was done by any other
boat in the same time. There is also the St. Louis and New
Orleans Anchor line. When did the trade between this city
and St. Louis have the equal or superior of its boats, and if
such boats as the City of St. Louis, City of New Orleans, City
of Baton Rouge and others of the line are not floating palaces,
in size, finish, speed of elegance in cabin appointments, what
are they? Take the stern-wheel steamboats also. When was
there the superior of such boats as the Golden Rule, the
Pargoud and T. P. Leathers, the Warren, Teche, the
Lafourche, Whisper or the Paul Tulane of to-day! No, Mr.
Editor, the day of the fast and fine steamboat on the Mississippi river is not yet gone. Some remain to attract, others
will come, and all that is said or published to the contrary is
a wrong, in statement and effect.

It is true that we may never again see a *fac simile* of the
Lee, White or Natchez, but, though they were paying invest-
ments, there are those who believed that the building of such
large, heavy, costly and expensive boats was more in the
nature of pride and of ambition than necessity. They believed then, and do now, that he who had a boat that could be
run without loss eight months of the twelve was more to be
envied than him who had a boat that could be run but four
months. As a matter of course the railroads have diverted
business from the river, but the success of the railroads in
giving the same rapid transit for freight as in travel has done
greater harm than all. With the railroad results are more to
be considered than the means, and when their ways are more
nearly imitated; when steamboatmen realize, as they soon
must, that time is everything, even of greater importance than
the burning of a little more fuel; when instead of taxing his

and the ingenuity of others in planning the greatest carrying
for the smallest amount of power, he builds and runs to attract
and retain the custom he would have, then, and not before,
will he become a competitor against whom none may prevail.''

Respectfully,

A CLERK.''

If the following article from the *Railway Register* proves
anything, it seems difficult to tell what it is.   But as it has
been furnished by a friend to river transportation as an argument in its favor, it ought not to be lost sight of: —

THE RIVER BUSINESS.

"Undoubtedly the first glory of the great rivers has departed.
Time was when they monopolized the traffic of the country
from the days when the pioneer explorers of the new world
paddled their canoes down the Ohio to the comparatively
modern period when the only conveyance in the vast region
between the Rockies and the Alleghanies was the steamboat,
for the stage-coach then had but few traveled routes.

Of the important work done by the lake and river boats
historians, poets and novelists have spoken in a literature that
is world renowned. After the civil war river transportation
began to wane, for the railways were so much more convenient and speedy.

The great lakes have not lost the commerce they posessed
of old, but it has really increased right along as the traffic of
the Western States and the Northwestern regions grew into
such tremendous size.   All of the trunk lines and many of
the small railways have huge steamers which ply in close
alliance with them, to say nothing of the numberless small
and sailing crafts which crowd the ports all along the shores.

Water routes in the North and on the Atlantic coast are taking a more important part in the business of the country than
ever.   Before the railways came they possessed the entire
coast and much of the interior trade, but all of it was not a
tithe of what it is now.

The popular idea is that the steamboat trade on the interior
rivers has been on the wane until it is now comparatively unimportant.   This impression is far from correct.   In the
years, not so long ago, when the cotton of the South, and the
grain and other produce of the Mississippi Valley, as well as
the fur and other trade of the Upper Missouri, all was handled
by steamboats there was a greater show made, because most
of the passenger business went by river and light craft plied

on all of the smaller rivers. Unquestionably the railways have so successfully competed for the trade that the business of the boats seems unimportant to those who have not measured it or estimated it.

The proposed construction of new bridges across the Ohio has called forth earnest protests from the river interests, and some figures have been presented which are new and surprising. The rivers have always been the losers before the public on account of the lack of the full statistics which the railway companies furnish. The steamboat companies published no annual reports, stating the number of passengers and tons of freight carried, nor is their work constantly before the people like that of the railways.

But if the river trade could be calculated and measured its volume would surprise even those who are best acquainted with it. It is, of course, true that the multiplication of new railways has drawn away much of the custom of the steamboats and is constantly diverting more of certain portions of it. These new railways furnish facilities to towns which they did not enjoy before, and being speedier take away business from the boats.

But after all, a little reflection will show that in some departments the boats are actually gaining. One big steamboat will carry a trainload of freight, and so, though there are not many lines or boats, the aggregate of freight carried is immense. Then the system of barges towed by a steamer is gaining in favor. The bulk of the barge business consists of coal and grain.

One steamboat recently took out of Louisville a tow of 28,500 tons of coal, or enough to load a train of cars fourteen miles long. Pittsburgh alone sends out annually on the Ohio River 4,000,000 tons of coal, equal to 400,000 car loads of ten tons each. One statistician estimates that a double-tracked railway on each side of the Ohio River could not accommodate the traffic of the boats now plying on it.

The Mississippi barge line in 1884 made seventy-four round trips on the river, and carried 453,939 tons of freight. The Illinois Central, on its 2,000 miles of road, in 1885 carried 3,587,270 tons of freight, so the barge line business was nearly one-seventh as large as that of this great railway.

The demand of the times is for cheap transportation, and it stands to reason that boats plying on the river, without any expense for maintenance of way or stations, can handle freight cheaper than the railways. The rate of freight on the Mississippi barge line between St. Louis and New Orleans in 1883

was $2.37 per ton, and by rail it was $4.40. No doubt in
certain territory the difference is greater. Take the boats,
which run between St. Louis or Cincinnati and the interior
points on the Cumberland and Tennessee Rivers, and they
enable the merchants of the two cities to control a trade they
could not otherwise handle.

Freight by rail is being carried for a smaller rate than was
a few years ago believed possible, and on many roads it is
hard to see how many further reductions can be made without
cutting under the actual cost to the carriers of the transportation. As the competition between trade centers become
more intense it is probable that the rivers will be more than
ever relied on to help the merchants out. Expensive goods
may still go by rail, but all kinds of coarse freight will
choose the boats.

*   *   *   *   *   *   *   *   *

Whatever increases commerce is for the benefit of the railways, and so those interested in these carriers need not feel
concerned over the larger business of the river.''

Neither of the three foregoing extracts are based upon facts,
or upon the result of the experience of every one for the last
20 years so far as the waters of the Mississippi Valley are concerned. Of what value are arguments based upon sophistry?
Why consult our wishes and take counsel from our hopes,
when we have facts patent to every one from which to draw
our conclusions? Of what value is an opinion advanced in direct opposition to what is known to be true? It is like the
story of the "little boy who continued whistling while going
through the graveyard, to keep up his courage." Reference
is often made to the towboat J. B. Williams taking from
Louisville to New Orleans one tow of coal, amounting to 22,-
000 tons, enough to load a train of cars fourteen miles long,
as an evidence that railroads cannot compete with water transportation. In the article of coal and some other cheap and
bulky articles, no argument is necessary to prove that fact,
in a high stage of water, and over long distances.

But how many months in the year is there water enough
above Cairo for the Williams or any other boat to tow half
that amount?

That boat went through safely. But how often is it that
more or less of the boats in the tow are lost? How long would
any portion of that 22,000 tons of coal have lasted, in a storm
like that near New Orleans in 1888.

The experience of those engaged in the business may be of

value in estimating the ability of water transportation vs.
Railroad. Especially after there shall have been built another score of railroad bridges across the streams.

The correspondent in the "Times Democrat," over the signature of "A Clerk" insists that "the day of fast and fine
steamboats on the Mississippi River is not yet gone." "And
all that is said or published to the contrary is wrong in statement and effect." After referring to the Oliver Bevine, and
the Jessie K. Bell, as an evidence of his sagacity, he points to
the St. Louis Anchor Line, and says: "When did the trade
between this city and St. Louis have the equal or the superior
of its boats?" etc., etc.

This "Clerk" is probably from the interior, and not familiar
with the history of steamboats or of their number, and business
they once did. He has forgotten if ever he knew the time
when there was employed "between this city and St. Louis"
twenty to thirty regular boats, and some as fine and as fast as
the Anchor Line. He fails to state the melancholy and
damaging fact, that at the present time, 1889, that only *three
boats*, and those comparatively small ones, are now required
to do the business that formerly took twenty larger ones to
do. Why attempt to deceive ourselves and the public by a
fallacy patent to all?

In other chapters of this work this subject has been so
often referred to and the only possible means by which river
navigation can be partially restored has been so often discussed,
that further consideration of it at this time and place is
unnecessary.

CHAPTER LXXVII.

STEAMBOATING ON WESTERN WATERS — CAUSES OF FAILURE TO BECOME PROFITABLE.

IT seems a phenomenal fatality that has followed this great and legitimate industry from its introduction on to these waters to the present time.

There are many causes that have contributed to the general result. Perhaps none more prominent than the fascination the business has presented to the mind of young men, especially such as have not had the advantages of an education, and even to those, the free rollicking life of a boatman has often proven irresistible and disastrous in the end.

The fascination that enabled the early voyagers to meet and endure the dangers, the hardships and the privations of pirogue and flat-boat life, has never lost its attraction to the employes of steamboats to the present day. And yet none of them with the rarest exception, have ever laid up their earnings, and, as a rule, the higher their wages the less they save and the soooner their career terminates.

The officers of steamboats in later years have differed very materially from those that were the immediate successors of the old barge and keel-boatmen, many of which were transferred directly from those pioneer craft to the earlier steamboats. In fact it was from that class that all were obliged to look for their crews. And for several years, it was from them that the masters, the mates and the pilots were generally selected, and for many years their successors, as a rule, were not morally far in advance of them.

Another cause that has contributed largely to the want of success in this business is that of the facility with which boats could be built. At an earlier day they cost much less than at present, and a company, or even an individual, who represented any unencumbered real estate could easily secure sufficient credit to build a steamboat without any money. Thousands of men in the Mississippi Valley have lost their homes, their farms, and their all, by pledging them to pay for building a steamboat they had no use for. The result of course was to increase competition, and ruin those who were engaged in a legitimate business, although perhaps only making a fair living, and what was still more demoralizing, this was often done by men who had no knowledge of the business, nor in fact of any business.

From this custom, too, many, very many builders were broken up.

Another cause for the disastrous result to this great and important factor in the settlement of the valley was the dangerous character of the navigation.

It was not until about 1869 that the government could be induced to make the necessary appropriations to do anything towards improving navigation in a general way. Consequently the rate of insurance was so high that no price could be charged sufficient to pay the carrier a profit after paying his insurance and other legitimate expenses. And even then, very few underwriters made any money on hull insurance, and many of them were broken up that attempted it. And the rate was so high many steamboat owners declined to insure, and consequently many boats were lost with little or no insurance, which added to the general result.

The usual rate on hulls on the Ohio and tributaries, and the Mississippi and tributaries, except the Missouri, Arkansas and Red River, was from 10 to 12 per cent. per annum. On the excepted rivers, from 15 to 20 per cent.

A great amount of litigation arose in the settlement of losses, and in the earlier history of steam navigation the courts were often appealed to to adjust the differences. As the laws were not so well defined, and differently interpreted in different courts and different states, this was always expensive, and often produced crimination and recrimination between the owners and underwriters, each charging the other with attempt to defraud, etc., so that many owners declined to insure their boats on that account when they felt at all able to take the risk themselves. But the liability to loss was so great, but few were willing or able to take greater risks than the uninsurable ones.

The risk from bursting of boilers, breaking machinery or the escaping of steam were considered uninsurable accidents, and were generally excepted from policies of insurance, although a few companies issued a policy covering those risks. But in later years, since the inspection laws have been more rigidly enforced, and manufacturers of boiler iron and steel have found it necessary to pay more attention to the quality of that product, far less accidents have occurred from those causes. Much may be attributed, too, to the character and ability of engineers. Some of the most terrific casualties that have ever occurred on Western waters are undoubtedly attributable to too much whisky-instead of too much steam.

Referring to losses of life and of steamboats, no period during the history of steam navigation has compared with that immediately following the late war. This undoubtedly should be attributed to the poor quality of boiler iron.

The demand for boiler iron, to use in the construction of gunboats, was so great the demand could not be filled as fast as wanted. The result was a large quantity of bad iron was thrown upon the market and used indiscriminately.

The war having created an active demand for river transportation a demand for new boats in 1863, 1864, and 1865 was so great it was impossible to procure boilers enough made from suitable iron or steel. The consequence was many poor, unsafe boilers were put into steamboats, as "everything went" at that time, and very soon after many of the boats went, and as human life was considered cheap then, many were sacrificed on the altar of *avarice*.

Another prominent cause that has largely contributed in hastening the final result, and with drawing capital from this interest, is the lack of confidence those engaged in it extend towards their compeers. And this is incidental to the loose, unsystematic manner of doing business. The few well known good business men that have engaged in river transportation from time to time, have been unable to exercise sufficient influence over the great majority to introduce and maintain such systems and principles of business as will alone insure success in any business.

BENEFIT OF JOINT STOCK COMPANIES.

The persistent opposition against organized joint stock companies by many of those engaged in steamboating, tended to keep up an insane competition which not only destroyed profits, but confidence. And not until it was too late to secure the great benefits resulting from such organizations was it possible in many cases to induce their formation.

The opposition generally arose among the smaller stockholders in individual boats, and who were employed on those boats, fearing, very naturally, they might lose their position and their influence, but forgetting the necessity of more economy and less competition, which did result to all well constructed companies. But which finally were in many cases obliged to succumb to the overpowering element of railroad competition.

The following suggestive remarks are clipped from a St. Louis paper published in the *fifties*, by its correspondent, who evidently was engaged in the business, as he speaks feelingly and knowingly upon the subject.

"Never, until the present loose and unguarded system of

prosecuting the calling shall have been dissected, and each fractional part reached through some remediable agent, will it deserve to rank or be classed upon an equal footing with other business pursuits, but continue, as it is, a game of chance—a speculation—its successful issue dependent not upon the deal but upon the "turn up;" or you may confine it, if you will, to the juvenile pastime of "hide and seek," wherein one party, under the garb of friendly feeling, keeps secret his real intentions, until opportunity offers, aided by deception, to reach the goal in advance of other contestants.

The great importance attached, and, as well, the risk and capital involved, are wholly,lost sight of in the transaction of a business of such vast extent, while the weight of responsibility consequent upon the duties of a carrier, are treated lightly or oftentimes disregarded altogether; the result of either misconception, or an unwarrantable disinterestedness.

Some few facts, complied from a careful computation of the figures in our possession, and bearing directly upon the subject matter under consideration, may not prove inappropriate in the above connection; and, as the evil to be overcome is by far more apparent in the St. Louis and New Orleans trade, we have included only the boats engaged therein.

The number of boats belonging exclusively to the trade, we find to be 26, with the capacity for over 29,000 tons. The total valuation at the present day, regardless of original cost, may be safely estimated at $985,000. The calculation of 10 per cent. interest gives us $98,500. The insurance of two-thirds the valuation amounts to over seventy-eight thousand dollars. The yearly depreciation, allotting five years as an average lifetime of a boat, in this particular trade, and receiving the remains, after the term of service, as a compensation for the necessary outlay to keep up ordinary running repairs, is found to be 20 per cent. of the whole, and amounts in the aggregate to $197,000. Thus we have an annual expenditure, in liquidation alone of interest, insurance and depreciation of stock, of $374,000, or nearly 40 per cent. on the total amount of capital invested, and which amount varies little, if any, between running or remaining idle. These boats furnish employment for about 1600 men, at a monthly salary of $80,000.

Now, regard this matter in the light of a "joint stock," and what a magnified form would it assume. Yet should the fact of its distribution, in point of ownership, detract from its important mission, or render the common interest so rife with conflict!

In our honest conviction, the business referred to is upon the era of a most disastrous crisis, and one which no one individually can avert, however cautious or prudent ; but, on the contrary, a united effort on the part of the many interests must alone be looked for to arrest the impending danger.

The question very naturally arises, will they profit by their repeated failures heretofore, to establish some system consistent in its nature, and tending to the promotion of a combined interest, and institute some fully competent organization, one in no wise based upon either the "imaginary or hypothetical."

The dependence hitherto predicted upon the business between ports, and commonly termed "picking," was generally conceded remunerative, and continued to be so maintained, from the fact that it could not well be influenced by such direct competition as we find to be the invariable result of the presence of two or more boats at the same point.   Now, that a want of confidence between leading parties is the chief cause of all the trouble, cannot be denied ; and they ask, what course can we pursue to check the wanton spirit of rivalry discernable in the transaction of the river business ? We would answer this universal query by saying, if they will pardon the presumption, that they must adopt some policy to do away with the *necessity* for such a course."

In looking for the causes that have contributed to the failure of this great industry to be renumerative, we must not forget the vast amount that has been extorted from steamboats by individuals and by incorporations for the privilege of receiving and discharging freight and passengers, or in other words, *wharfage* and even where no freight or passengers have been received or discharged a tax has often been imposed for the privilege of landing to buy fuel or stoves.

The following, written several years ago on this subject, is yet in point, although there have been some modifications in those charges in late years.

THE WHARFAGE EXTORTION.

[*To the Editor of the Courier-Journal.*]

STEAMER WM. P. HALLIDAY, April 24, 1883.—I see that you are still warring against the unreasonable and inconsistent tax of your city government in their persistent determination to collect an exorbitant wharfage tax from steamboats. A small tax sufficient to keep the wharf in repair is recognized by all the courts where the issue has been made. I believe more than that is unjust and exorbitant, and ought to be resisted. Every one familiar with river navigation knows too well that every public landing in the valley of the Mississippi has been paid for many times over by the wharfage tax assessed against steamboats. And but comparatively few corporations have still the assurance of collecting so unjust a tax, simply because those most interested do not unite in resisting. They may with the same consistency be taxed for opening and repairing streets for the accommodation of citizens as wharves, which are as free to every one as are the streets. No one can consistently claim that they ought not to be allowed to use a public landing they have paid for building, if they keep the same in repair. But my object is not to complain of your city government. They have been very generous and accommodating to me — not having charged me wharfage at all for many new boats I have finished at their wharf. What I do want is to secure your efforts and influence, as well as that of every other public journal and individual interested in the marine commerce of this great valley, against the principle of this tax generally, and especially as indulged in at some points. For instance, at Cairo. Probably there is no other point in the Mississippi Valley where so many boats and barges land as at Cairo; nor where so large an amount of money is collected for wharfage. Why this soulless corporation has been countenanced so long in collecting an exorbitant tax from steamboats, which are so little benefited from the use of the wharf seems passing strange. The wharf at this point was built expressly to protect the town site, and to form a road-bed for the Illinois Central railroad and other individual purposes. Ninety-hundredths of all the business that is done there by boats is done on wharfboats, and never touches the improved wharf, and would be just as well accommodated if it was not there. And even if it was not necessary to accommodate the river commerce, one per cent. of the money collected would be more than enough to keep it in repair. It is an outrage that no class of men except steamboat owners would submit to. Memphis and Vicksburg may be referred to as further illustration of the same abuse, although not so entirely unwarranted as at Cairo. Still the amount charged is exorbitant and unjust. At Vicksburg no wharfage is charged unless a boat discharges or receives some cargo. A boat the size and tonnage of the Halliday is charged $12, if they are so unfortunate as to have $1 worth of freight to discharge or receive. To be sure boats are not obliged to land there. But it not unfrequently happens that a shipper has freight for many different landings and among them a little lot for Vicksburg. Of course, he wants to ship all or none, and boats are thus obliged to land there or abandon the business. If the

money that is collected for wharfage was even expended on
their wharf, there would be more justification. But judging
from appearances there is more money collected for wharfage
every year than has been spent on the wharf proper in ten
years. Of New Orleans I need not speak. Everybody familiar with our river commerce knows full well of the extortion
and robbery that have been practiced on water craft there for
many years. But I am glad to notice signs of reform when
the present lease of the wharf expires. The idea of leasing
out a public wharf to individual speculators, with the privilege
of fleecing the tonnage from which the city derives its principal existence, is, to say the least, suggestive. Please extend
your field of observation and give us a boom from the *Courier-
Journal*.   E. W. GOULD.

LETTERS TO THE NAUTICAL GAZETTE.

In 1875 this writer prepared for a New York paper, devoted
to marine interests (the *Nautical Gazette*), a series of letters
on the "early history of steam navigation on Western
waters," in which the subject of the *causes* of the decline of
water transportation were discusssd.

In a letter published in that paper January 12th, 1875, the
following passage occurs.

As it fairly illustrates the situation even at this late date,
it may not be uninteresting to quote it at some length : —

"The direct and immediate cause for the great decline in
this important branch of commerce is, of course, the construction of so large a number of railroads.

It is not necessary for me, in this connection, to enter into
the causes that have given rise to this railroad *mania* that has
permeated every section of the country for the last twenty-five
years. That it was unwarranted and visionary, the present
embarrassed condition of more than half the roads in the
country abundantly testify.

Such was the anxiety in every portion of the country for
railroads, that Congress, states, counties, cities, towns and individuals were besieged for subsidies and subscriptions to build
them.

The large profits and subsidies secured by the *projectors*
and *builders* were sufficient to induce all kinds of rings and
credit mobiliers to be organized, to fleece the country at large,
and especially the unsuspecting community through whose
section of country the proposed road was to run.

After exhausting all the arguments possible to be brought
forward to induce subscriptions, bonds were issued and forced

upon the market, through such agencies as Jay Cooke & Co.,
at any price. Hence the roads have cost double, and, in
many instances, more than double what they ought to have
cost. The result was what might have been expected. Some
one *punctured* Jay Cooke & Co., and the bubble burst, and the
whole country was thrown into consternation. Every one
was inquiring of his neighbor "What was the matter? What
was the cause of the panic?" And a good many people have
not found out yet that the country has expended more for
railroads in the last twenty years than will ever be made out
of them, and the payment of the interest alone that is paid to
European capitalists will keep the country poor for years to
come, saying nothing about the National debt.

Very naturally, every community, every interest is looking
for a remedy for the *hard times*. The agricultural community is looking to the Grangers to save them, and the
Grangers to the railroads for cheaper freights, while they
have already bankrupted their own stockholders by the ruinous competition and low freights. The manufacturer is looking to an increased tariff to save him, while the merchant seeks,
in a reduction of the tariff, his salvation.

In the absence of surplus earnings to pay dividends, railroad managers call a convention of connecting roads to find a
remedy, and if there is no competing *water route* to make war
upon, arrange a tariff of prices satisfactory to themselves, ad-
journ to meet again, as soon as a "cut" is discovered, which
generally occurs within twenty-four hours.

Various remedies and devices have been discussed and resorted to by those engaged in water transportation, but still
the interest languishes, and steamboat building has almost
ceased.

A few years since, an average of one hundred new steamboats per annum was a low estimate for all points on our
rivers. In 1874 there was but a single boat built of any considerable capacity, of the usual kind, for freight and passengers, and but very few tow-boats, or any other character of
boat.

The millions of money annually paid out for the encouragement of this great industry, in former years, has now been
directed into other channels, and I leave it for members of
Congress and political economists to determine whether the
ends have justified the means.

The popular sentiment of the day is cheap transportation,
and upon this pretense, one-half the railroads in the country
have been built. Of what advantage to the people is cheap

transportation, if they are taxed so heavily to procure that transportation, that they have nothing left to pay for the article transported? But you will say I am rather discussing results than causes. The two are so intimately connected, it is difficult to consider the one without the other.

Another important reason may be mentioned for the great falling off in water transportation — that of the great cost of navigating boats. Not that it is more so than formerly, but it has not been reduced in proportion to the reduction of prices of transportation, induced by the insane competition of railroads, nor can it be with the present cost of labor and supplies. While building is comparatively cheap, the cost of many articles of outfit are high. The numerous Government requirements, many of which are worse than useless, is a heavy tax, and ought to be removed.

While Congress is appropriating small sums of money annually, for removing natural obstructions from our rivers, it is granting railroad and bridge companies charters to place artificial obstructions in them, far more dangerous to navigation. And if a recent decision of the Supreme Court of the United States (that of insurance companies against the steamer Mollie Mollier, at St. Paul) is to determine future suits of a similar character, no other reasons may be sought for the abandonment of water transportation. In this case the court makes the monstrous assumption, that steamboatmen do not recognize the right of railroads to bridge the streams, and consequently run their boats against the piers (and, by inference, sacrifice their property, and endanger their own lives, and those of their passengers and crew, of course), with the hope that they will ultimately compel the removal of the bridge. I know nothing of the facts in the case, but am bound to suppose the verdict was in accordance with the law and the evidence. But the assumption of Judge Davis in giving the verdict of the court needs no comment. It is simply terrible to contemplate, in connection with the great number of bridges we are compelled to encounter, and those that are probably to be built.

These bridge obstructions greatly increase the danger of navigation, and render the cost of insurance much higher; in fact, it is very difficult to effect insurance in good companies, at the present time, on our best boats, running upon rivers, at any rate of premium. And the rates charged on cargoes gives to the railroads an unequal advantage in competing for freights.

There are many other causes that might be mentioned that

have contributed to the rapid decline of this great interest, but enough has been referred to to establish my assumption of a rapid decline. No one acquainted with the vast resources of this immense valley can suppose depression in water transportation can long continue. But until the country shall have been more fully developed, and the thousands of idle men that hang about the cities and towns shall be induced to remove to the country, and engage in producing, instead of consuming, and thus furnish a much larger supply for transportation, but little improvement can be anticipated. Then the intense anxiety of railroad men to secure freight at any price will be less apparent, as they will have what they can carry at remunerative rates, leaving a large surplus for water transportation.

With the necessary appropriations for the improvement of the mouth of the Mississippi and the navigable streams of the valley, there is no doubt but that the heavy and bulky products of the soil, as well as the coal and minerals, can be more cheaply transported by water than by any other means. And while we never need expect to see return to the river the immense passenger traffic it once accommodated, in its thousands of elegant steamers, we may expect to see the freight traffic increased a thousand fold greater than ever before witnessed.

Having written this much upon the subject of navigation on these waters, it would probably be interesting to many of your Western readers if I should devote another chapter to the notice of some of the more prominent individuals connected with this navigation, from its earliest history. If circumstances should render accessible to me such information as will enable me to do them justice, you may expect to hear from me once again.''   E. W. G.

Among the many reasons for the lack of success in steamboat business in the past, is from the fact that so many men engaged in it without any practical business knowledge, and the only rule that governed them in business transactions was that they " could afford to do business a little cheaper than their neighbors."

The very low price at which old, but insurable boats could often be purchased for, enabled a small number of idle or incompetent men to combine and buy an old boat with which they would cause the loss of a whole season to others who had a legitimate trade, and were doing it in a legitimate and honorable manner. This, of necessity, caused the organization of so many packet companies at one period, and postponed for a time the final collapse which has overtaken this great industry in all parts of the valley.

If what the *expert steamboat book-keeper* says in another chapter is true, and I am inclined to think it is, whatever else may be said of the character and ability of the earlier boatmen, no one will presume to doubt their *financial* ability, as demonstrated in the purchase of steamboats without money, and paying for them from their own earnings!" And still I understand that differs but little from the present popular mode of " option dealing," in which so many fortunes are made and lost, especially lost. The only difference perceptible is in the latter case, a small *margin* is deposited. But the law of evolution effects changes in customs, in modes of thinking and in results. Once such transactions were unsavory and considered "sharp practice," now they are legitimate and honorable. The old steamboat speculators lived too soon in the century.

CHAPTER LXXVIII.

LOW WATER TRAVELING ON THE OHIO.

PREVIOUS to the introduction of railroad traveling, long distances on the Ohio River was attended with much delay and discomfort, and only when it was absolutely necessary was the river resorted to by first-class passengers.

A great variety of water-craft was invented to facilitate this kind of travel, as those that were obliged to travel would pay extravagant prices by water rather than take stages.

This writer calls to mind a trip on the Ohio from Louisville to Cairo in 1838 or 1839 when there was but 16 inches of water in the channel at Rockport. This was an unusually low water year and all old boatmen on the lower Ohio will remember the difficulty of crossing the bar at Rockport, and many other places but little better. This was during the palmy days of the popular firm of Ludlow & Smith, the great theatrical men of the West and South. They, with their large company, star and stock actors, vibrated regularly between the North and South every year, spending the summer at Louisville, Cincinnati and St. Louis, and the winters at New Orleans and Mobile. The time was rapidly approaching when the "old St. Charles " at New Orleans must be opened. The company were all up the Ohio River and the means of getting to New Orleans was an important question. To think of going through by land was out of the question, and hence some kind of water-craft must be devised.

Boats that could run on 16 inches of water were not as plenty then as now. But a little side-wheel boat called Daisy was found that could be gotten over 16 inches of water by some persuasion.

The large (for that day) commodious passenger steamer Mediator, Captain Herculous Carroll, still in the flesh, God bless and continue him for ever, was laid up at Cairo, and the crew all up at Cincinnati where the boat was owned. They made an arrangement with captain Fox of the Daisy to fit up two little flat-boats, 16 feet wide and 60 feet long, covered with a tight roof with berths on either side to accomodate about 50 persons each, with sleeping apartments, leaving a wide passage-way between the berths for sitting-room purposes. These improvised cabins were furnished with bedding, chairs, tables, etc.

Thus was provided the means of transit from Louisville to New Orleans, *via* the Daisy to Cairo, and thence by the Mediator. Sixty dollars passage and no grumbling. Ludlow and Smith's theatrical company were first in say, and had the choice of *state rooms*.

They numbered about sixty, and as there was many passengers anxious to go South there was no difficulty in filling all the rooms. The Daisy was about 100 feet long and her cabin was appropriated to the officers of the boat, and the ladies in the company, and used for the general dining room. Among the passengers I call to mind, Mrs. Russel, — mother of Dick the comedian,— her daughter, Mrs. Farren, then just married to " old man Farren; " Miss Petre, once the pride of the stage ; Mrs. Ben DeBar,—together with DeBar, Farren and Mr. Parsons, who afterwards became a methodist preacher of much eloquence. All names familiar to old theater goers at that time, and many years since.

The gentlemen were allotted berths in the two flat-boats in tow of the Daisy. But as the dining room, the bar, and the ladies were all on the steamboat, it required the vigilance of two persuasive clerks, or marshals to keep the boat lighted up enough to run at all, and when crossing a very shoal bar, even the ladies were called upon to " lighten boat, " but when night came all were at liberty to roam over the fleet or on shore, as there was no running at night.

After the first day out, the two annex boats become so attractive that it was difficult for the few that wanted to sleep to do so.

Tables were improvised everywhere, and if there were any game at cards that was not represented it must have been entirely new, and even the cabin of the Daisy was often deserted in the evening to join the card parties.

But as all things terrestrial must have an end, Cairo was reached in about ten days, and all that were booked for New Orleans were transferred to the Mediator. But as the captain and watchman composed the whole crew of that boat, which had been laying up for some weeks, the passengers left the little Daisy with reluctance. But as the crew of the Mediator were on the Daisy, a day or two was sufficient to put things in order, and get the boat off for New Orleans.

ANOTHER MEMORABLE TRIP ON THE OHIO.

Twelve months later, or in July of the following year, the writer had a very different experience over the same course. Being on a trip from Galena and Dubuque to Cincinnati, with his own boat, the Knickerbocker, found at Cairo a boat from New Orleans bound to Louisville, with passengers. But as the water was reported too low for her to reach her destination the captain had decided to lay up at Cairo, and transfer his passengers. Fortunately there were but few passengers on board the Knickerbocker and those at Cairo were well accommodated.

At Paducah we came up with the Emperor, also from New Orleans with quite a number of passengers. She had also determined to go no further; not being able to get over Cumberland bar, had returned to Paducah. As all the rooms in the ladies' cabin of the Knickerbocker had been taken and but few of any kind remained, the inducement to leave nice rooms on a large boat like the Emperor and take cots on the floor on a much smaller boat, in hot weather, required a good deal of sacrifice of feeling and comfort. This the Southern families were not entirely prepared to do. But after much consultation and a thorough investigation of the accommodations that could be had on the Knickerbocker and the probable chances of doing better on the next boat, they determined to make the change at once. But when their effects, children and servants were gathered together and crowded into a much smaller cabin already comfortably filled, those only can appreciate the discomfort that have experienced it.

Unfortunately all travelers are not philosophers and it soon became apparent that we had the elements of discord on board, and that without great care and forbearance on the part of the officers of the boat an open rupture was inevitable. Nothing was satisfactory, nothing could be made right. The company was divided into four groups or circles, agreeable to the manner of their coming on board. There was the original party coming from St. Louis and the Upper Mississippi. The party that came on board at Cairo, the party at Paducah, with one more from some other boat not recollected, and they thus separated themselves in groups through the cabin, each watching and commenting upon the other, and as there were several children and servants of various nationalities on board there was no lack of material whereby to raise an issue at any moment.

After making many changes, appealing to the courtesy of some gentlemen who had more choice rooms to exchange them, and to others to vacate theirs, to accommodate ladies and take a cot on the floor, the threatening clouds seemed to break away a little and gave promise of a more harmonious feeling in the cabin and a more cheerful atmosphere on deck.

But alas, how deceptive appearances. It was only a calm before the storm. Even at that early day, that vital question of slavery, that culminated near a quarter of a century later, in the firing upon Fort Sumpter in Charleston harbor never failed to arouse the " Southern heart" whenever aggressively attacked, especially in the presence of the *chattel*.

As was customary at that time, for Southern families to travel with their servants and to those who were anxious, from either North or South, to raise an issue, a subject was never wanting.

There was, unfortunately, two gentlemen from the North occupying a state-room near the ladies cabin, who had been appealed to to vacate their room to accommodate a family who had none. This they did feel called upon to do, and consequently a sectional feeling was soon aroused from some unkind remark and lost nothing by being repeated.

The result was a general irritation all along the line, and an open rupture was possible, in which both sexes seemed eager for the fray. The clerks of the boat were often appealed to, and several times the captain was sent for to allay the excitement.

A little explanation and an appeal to the bar-keeper generally produced a soothing effect, although not always lasting.

The late Captain James B. Eads, then a young man of seventeen or eighteen, was second clerk on the boat, and with the suavity that characterized and popularized him in later years, did much to relieve the captain and quiet the irritation, especially in the ladies' cabin. The boat was drawing all the water in the river and the trip was slow and tedious.

But as we approached Louisville, which was on the 4th of

38

July, and there seemed a probable termination to the discomforts of a long low water voyage, a more agreeable atmosphere pervaded through the large company, and some of the more patriotic gentlemen proposed we should celebrate the day by having a Fourth of July dinner, with the usual accompaniments of an oration, toasts, songs, wines, etc.

That sentiment prevailed, and there was a reasonable hope that the trip that had been begun under so many forebodings and prosecuted under so much discomfort and ill-feeling would terminate pleasantly.

FOURTH OF JULY ORATION AND DINNER.

The dinner was prepared from the best that remained of the steward's stores, supplemented by a fresh supply from the barnyard of a well stocked farm on the bank of the river. The bar-keeper had replenished his exhausted stock at Evansville. The orator of the day had been selected from the legal fraternity on board — the toasts prepared and the songs arranged. At the hour named dinner was announced — the orator of the day, Judge ——— from Vicksburg, at the head of the long table, supported on either side by the ladies first, then supplemented by the rank and file, all ready to do battle to the long looked for *last meal* on the Knickerbocker.

Everything went without saying or ceremony, especially the champagne corks. The oration was patriotic and very enjoyable. The first regular toasts were rousingly responded to.

But as the wine began to inflame the brain and excite the imagination the volunteer toasts grew less patriotic and more sectional until at length they became personal and even descended to reference to the individual gentlemen who had declined to give up their stateroom in the early part of the trip. So violent did some of the party become that pistols and knives were drawn, and had it not been for the prompt and resolute action of some of the more conservative, the peace offering banquet would have resulted as did many similar ones from the same cause in the ante bellum times.

But as we were approaching the mouth of the canal at Louisville, where many of the passengers were to land, the excitement subsided and order was restored.

Thus ended the second low water trip on the Ohio River in one year.

Of the two, the first one was far the most enjoyable, free from trial, care or vexation of spirit, and when it comes to compensation no practical boatman will select low water to earn his money.

BIOGRAPHICAL.

CAPTAIN JACOB STRADER.

The following biographical sketch is from the pen of Capt.
J. H. Barker, who was for many years a cotemporary and an
associate with this old veteran: —
"Capt. Strader was born in Sussex County, N. J., 1788;
came to Cincinnati in 1810. J. H. Piatt was one of the
pioneer merchants of this young town of the West; came
from New Jersey in 1805. Mr. Piatt was Mr. Strader's
uncle; J. S. was his confidential clerk and book-keeper in the
office of Mr. Piatt. Later Mr. P. was a banker and the subject
of this article was installed in the institution, teller and cashier.
It was in the years immediately succeeding the war, 1812,
that many merchants and bankers, went down, making complete failures. Among the general crash the banking house
of J. H. Piatt was one of the number, and so the subject of
this sketch sought other business. In 1820 his river life began on the steamer Gen'l Pike. For about a year he was in
the office, with Mr. Bliss as captain. It was in 1821 his duties
as commander began, with James Gorman as clerk. Commercial Bank of Cincinnati having been established in 1831, Capt.
S. was made a director; was elected President in 1841, which
position he retained till his death, which occurred in 1860.
He was for many years President of the Little Miami Railroad. Had amassed an ample fortune. Left two children,
one Ben. F. and a daughter, who became the wife of Colin
Woolley, formerly of Lexington, Ky."
Capt. Strader was one of the few successful steamboatmen,
and had sufficient sagacity to retire from it in time to fall into
line with its great rival and more fortunate successor.
Coupled with his sagacity, his enterprise contributed largely
to the development of steam navigation in the West, and
especially in the establishment of that oldest of all steamboat
organizations known as the "Cincinnati & Louisville Mail
Line."

NEW ORLEANS & LOUISVILLE PACKET STEAMER TECUMSEH.

"Built 1826, at Cincinnati; launched with steam up and engine in working order.

She was 174 feet in length, twenty-three feet beam, nine feet hold; carried 242 tons.

Floor timbers 6x8, six inches apart, every fourth timber double. The frame forward solid. Bottom plank six inches thick.

Ladies' cabin in the hold, aft. Gents' cabin on the main deck.

Six boilers, eighteen feet long, thirty-six inches diameter. High pressure engines, eighteen inch cylinder; six feet stroke.

Time from New Orleans to Louisville, April, 1828, eight days, four hours.

Abe Tyson, Captain. Joe Arthern, Clerk.

She was owned by B. Hayden & Co. and Samuel and Joseph Perry, of Cincinnati."

CAPTAIN "ALEX" SCOTT.

Among the old and familiar names that the people of St. Louis and the Lower Mississippi will remember with pleasure in connection with early steamboatmen is that of Capt. Scott. He was universally respected as an enterprising, active business man and built several good boats which he ran in the St. Louis, Pittsburgh and New Orleans trades. Among his peculiarities as a boatman was that of always making a hand himself at whatever was to be done.

When the boat was under way he was always to be found on deck and about the fire doors, assisting the fireman. When landed, he was among the first on the forecastle, assisting the men in handling the freight. He never stood a regular watch and seldom slept when the boat was running. "By the Lord Harry" was his usual bye-word, and an exclamation he often used. His good nature and familiarity "about decks" subjected him to some practical jokes from the crew. Among others this is told, and well authenticated. A favorite position, and one he often resorted to when the boat was under way, was sitting on the capstan. One night when coming up the Mississippi on the Majestic, which was one of his large boats, and carried a large battery of boilers, he had located himself on the capstan as usual and dropped to sleep. By a concerted plan the boys had arranged a joke at the old man's expense. They carefully turned the capstan part way around,

which so reversed his position that he was facing the boilers
instead of the jack staff, as when he dropped to sleep. At a
given signal the firemen threw all the fire doors open at once,
and some one of the crew at the same moment aroused the captain, who upon opening his eyes was greatly alarmed in seeing so
glaring a light from the whole battery of boilers, which he supposed to be on a descending boat. He jumped from his perch
on the capstan and cried out at the top of his voice, " Stop
her, Mr. Pilot, or by the Lord Harry she will be into us."

The joke was so good that after discerning it, he joined in
the laugh, but never outlived it. I think the Madison was the
last boat Capt. Scott ever commanded.

While the old gentleman was not exorbitant in his views of
charges for the business he done he contended the competition was too great for him, and sold his boat and retired from
the river in about 1839. As an illustration of his views of
doing business, this writer, when in charge of the steamboat
Knickerbocker, met the Madison in New Orleans in the winter
of 1838 or 1839, and as the river above Cairo had been closed
by ice for some time, no other boats were in port. There were
several sugar buyers there from St. Louis all anxious to ship,
and it was presumed the river would be open by the time we
could get to Cairo.

The price of freight was at that time fixed by common consent at about 75 cents per 100 pounds. The Madison being
a large boat for that period, wanted a good deal of freight.
The merchants knew that, and they knew Capt. Scott's accommodating disposition and appealed for a reduction in
rates. The result was, the Captain said to me, "We had
better reduce the rate to 50 cents per 100, as these are all St.
Louis merchants," etc., etc. As freight was abundant, and
the Knickerbocker was not a large carrier, I objected. But
we finally compromised by charging 50 cents on sugar, and
75 on other goods, and filled up at once.

After leaving the river Capt. Scott removed to Pittsburgh
and engaged in the manufacture of iron, agreeable to my recollection.

In the *Missouri Republican* of March 20th, 1822, is this
notice :—

" The beautiful new steamboat, Pittsburgh & St. Louis
Packet, Capt. Alex. Scott, arrived here on Thursday last in
ten days from Pittsburgh. She left this place for Franklin,
and is now holding her way against the rapid current of the
Missouri."

CAPTAIN ISAIAH SELLERS.

This name will be recognized by all steamboat officers and many travelers on Western waters from the introduction of steamboats until the time of his death in 1864. He died at Memphis and was buried in Bellefontaine Cemetery, St. Louis. In manner and in character he differed widely from the large majority of his river associates. He was a strictly moral man, with a pronounced dignity that always commanded respect. He was a *pilot* by profession, and proud of his occupation, although sometimes in charge of boats. He had the confidence of business men as well as of the traveling public. And it was only necessary for either to know if "Sellers" was on board the boat, whether as master or pilot, all would be well. The boats he was on were always popular with passengers, and especially with ladies. If a gentleman wanted to send his wife and family to any point betweeen New Orleans and St. Louis, the boat that Captain Sellers was on always had the preference; and when he was in the pilot house the ladies' cabin was generally deserted.

"Mark Twain," in his very entertaining work of "Life on the Mississippi," has so correctly portrayed the characteristics of Capt. Sellers, that to attempt to improve upon them would be arrogance. In an interview with several pilots on the occasion of "Mark's" more recent return to the scenes of his earlier experience on the Mississippi, the conversation turned upon the lives and the history of their associates of an earlier date.

Among others, that of Capt. Sellers, as a sort of central figure, although he had several years previously become a central, or a prominent figure in the Bellefontaine Cemetery at St. Louis, where his body rests under a very beautiful marble monument with a full life-size figure of the Captain standing at the wheel of a steamboat, which had been prepared by himself some years before his death.

Those who had the privilege of Capt. Sellers' acquaintance will bear willing testimony to Mr. "Twain's" estimate of his characteristics and nothing "Mark Twain" has ever written more fully illustrates the genuine nobility of Mr. Clemens' nature than his closing remarks on *Captain Isaiah Sellers*.

TWAIN'S REMARKS.

"He was a fine man, a high-minded man, and greatly respected, both ashore and on the river. He was very tall,

well-built and handsome, and in his old age, as I remember
him, his hair was as black as an Indian's, and his eye and his
hand were as strong and steady, and his nerve and judgment
as clear as anybody's, young or old, among the fraternity of
pilots. He was the patriarch of the craft. He had been a
keel-boat pilot before the days of steamboats, and a steamboat pilot before any other steamboat pilot, still surviving at
the time I speak of, had ever turned a wheel — consequently,
his brethren held him in the sort of awe in which illustrious
survivors of a by-gone age are always held by their associates.
He knew how he was regarded, and perhaps this fact added
some trifle of stiffening to his natural dignity, which had been
sufficiently stiff in his original state.

He left a diary behind him, but apparently it did not date
back to his first steamboat trip, which was said to be in 1811,
the year the first steamboat disturbed the waters of the Mississippi. At the time of his death a correspondent of the St.
Louis *Republican* culled the following items from the diary :

"In February, 1825, he shipped on board the Rambler at
Florence, Alabama, and made during that year three trips to
New ·Orleans and back. Then the General Carroll, between
Nashville and New Orleans. It was during his stay on this
boat that Capt. Sellers introduced the tap of the bell as a signal
to heave the lead. Previous to which time, it was the custom
for the pilot to speak to the men below when soundings were
wanted. The proximity of the forecastle to the pilot house
no doubt rendered this an easy matter. But how different on
one of our palaces of the present day.

In 1827 we find him on the steamboat, President a boat
of 285 tons burden, and plying between Smithland and New
Orleans.

Thence he joined the Jubilee, in 1828, and on this boat he
did his first piloting in the St. Louis trade, his first watch extending from Herculaneum to St. Genevieve.

On May 26th, 1836, he completed, and left Pittsburgh in
charge of the the steamer Prairie, a boat of 400 tons, and the
first boat with a state room cabin, ever seen at St. Louis.

In 1857 he introduced the signal for meeting boats, and
which has with some slight change been the universal custom
to this day ; in fact, is rendered obligatory by act of Congress.

As general items of river history we quote the following
marginal notes from his general log : —

"In March, 1825, Gen. Lafayette left New Orleans for St.
Louis on the low pressure steamer Natchez. "In January,

1828, twenty-one steamers left New Orleans wharf, to celebrate Gen. Jackson's visit to that city."

" In 1830 the North American made the run from New Orleans to Memphis in six days. Best time on record to that date. It has since been made in two days and ten hours. In 1831, Red River cut off was made."

" In 1832 the steamer Hudson made the run, from White River to Helena, a distance of 75 miles in 12 hours. This was the theme of much talk and speculation among parties directly interested."

" In 1839, Great Horse Shoe Cut-off was made."

Up to the present time, a term of thirty-five years, we ascertain by a reference to the diary, he has made 460 round trips to New Orleans, which gives a distance of one million one hundred and four thousand miles, on an average of eighty-six miles per day.

Whenever Capt. Sellers approached a party of gossipy pilots, talking always ceased. For this reason, whenever six pilots were gathered together there would always be one or two newly fledged ones in the lot, and the elder ones would always be showing off before these poor fellows, making them sorrowfully feel how callow they were, how recent their nobility, and how humble their degree, by talking largely and vaporously of old time experiences on the river, always making it a point to date everything *back* as far as they could, so as to make the new men feel their newness to the sharpest degree possible, and envy the old stagers in like degree. And how complacent bald-heads would swell and brag, and lie and *date back*, ten and twenty years, and how they did enjoy the effect produced upon the marveling and envying youngsters, and perhaps just at this stage of the proceedings the stately figure of Capt. Isaiah Sellers, that real and only genuine son of antiquity, would drift solemnly into the midst. Imagine the size of the silence that would result on the instant and imagine the feelings of those bald-heads, and the exultation of their recent audience when the ancient Captain would begin to drop casual and indifferent remarks of a reminiscent nature about islands that had disappeared and cut-offs that had been made a generation before the oldest bald-head in the company had ever set his foot in a pilot-house.

Many and many a time did this ancient mariner appear on the scene in the above fashion, and spread disaster and humiliation around them. If one might believe the pilots, he always dated his islands back to the misty dawn of river history, and he never used the same island twice and never did he use one island that then existed, or give any one a name that any one present was old enough to have heard of before.

If you might believe the pilots, he was always conscientiously particular about little details. Never spoke of the State of Mississippi, for instance. No, he would say, when the State of Mississippi was where the State of Arkansas now is; and would never speak of the State of Louisiana or Missouri in a general way, but leave an incorrect impression on your mind.

No, he would say, when Louisiana was up the river further, or when the Missouri was on the Illinois side."

The old gentleman was not of literary turn or capacity, but he used to get down brief paragraphs of plain practical information about the river and sign them *Mark Twain* and give them to the *New Orleans Picayune.*

They related to the stage and condition of the river and were accurate and valuable, and thus far they contained no poison. But in speaking of the stage of the river to-day, at a given point, the Captain was pretty apt to drop in a little remark about this being the first time he had seen the water so high, or so low, at that particular point for forty nine years, and now and then he would mention Island so and so, and follow it with parentheses, with some such observation as "disappeared in 1807, if I remember rightly." In these antique interrogations lay poison and bitterness for the old pilots, and they used to chaff the "Mark Twain" paragraphs with unsparing mockery.

It so chanced that one of those paragraphs became the text for my first newspaper article.

I burlesqued it broadly, very broadly, stringing my fantastics out to the length of eight hundred or a thousand words.

I was a "cub" at the time; I showed my performance to some pilots, and they eagerly rushed it into print, in the New Orleans "True Delta." It was a great pity, for it did nobody any worthy service, and it sent a pang deep into a good man's great heart. There was no malice in my rubbish. But it laughed.

It laughed at a man to whom such a thing was new and strange and dreadful. I did not know then, though I do now, that there is no suffering comparable with that which a private person feels, when he is for the first time pilloried in print.

Captain Sellers did me the honor to profoundly detest me, from that day forth.

When I say he did me the honor, I am not using empty words. It was a very real honor to be in the thoughts of so great a man as Captain Sellers, and I had wit enough to appreciate it and be proud of it.

It was distinction to be loved by such a man. But it was a much greater distinction to be hated by him, because he loved scores of people, but he did not sit up nights to hate any one — but me.

He never printed another paragraph while he lived, and he never again signed " *Mark Twain*" to any thing.

At the time the telegraph brought the news of his death, I was on the Pacific Coast. I was a fresh, new journalist, and *nom de guerre*. So I confiscated the ancient mariner's discarded one, and have done my best to make it remain what it was in his hands—a sign and a symbol, and warrant whatever is found in its company may be found as the petrified truth. How I succeeded would not be modest in me to say.

The captain had an honest pride in his profession and an abiding love for it. He ordered his monument before he died, and kept it near him until he did die. It stands over his grave now in Bellefountaine Cemetery, St. Louis. It is his image in marble, standing on duty at the pilot wheel. And worthy to stand and confront criticism, for it represents a man who in life would have staid there until he burned to a cinder, if duty required it."

Captain John W. Keiser.

Among the few pioneer boatmen of the Missouri River, of which there is any public record attainable, the name of the gentleman at the head of this article will be recognized as one of the most prominent, worthy and persevering of all those that have made their last voyage over its turbulent waters,and cast anchor in a haven free from the cares and anxieties attendant upon the life of a Missouri river boatmen.

He was born in Fayette County,Kentucky, in 1801; moved to Missouri in 1828; located in Boone county. Built the *second steam mill* West of the Mississippi. (The first having been built at St. Charles.)

In 1837 or '8 his mill, which was built near Columbia, Mo., was burned.

He immediately went to St. Louis with the intention of procuring materials to rebuild his mill. His friends, Pierre Chouteau, Jr., and Capt. Sarpie, induced him to purchase an interest in the steamer St. Peters, a single engine boat, built by them for the *fur trade*, which was the largest commercial interest at that time on the Missouri River.

This was his first experience as a boatman. But at that early date his knowledge of steam machinery, and the versatility of his talent soon placed him in the front rank with many of much longer experience.

His next boat was the Antelope, which he purchased at St. Louis, and immediately took her to Pittsburgh; had her lengthened and her name changed to Trapper.

The American Fur Company bought the Trapper, and Capt. Keiser built the Shawnee, which was named by Mr. Chouteau in honor of that tribe of Indians, who were good customers of his and his personal friends. He built, in 1843, the Emelie, named in honor of Mrs. Chouteau.

In 1844 he retired, until 1847, when he purchased the Bertrand, and resumed his old trade in the Missouri.

The following year he purchased the Julia from Capt. Joe Converse.

She was destroyed in the great fire at St. Louis in 1849.

Soon after this Capt. Keiser was taken sick and retired to his home at Roachport, from which attack he never recovered, but crossed the river for the last time, in the vigor of manhood in 1849, leaving an interesting family, and a worthy example of strict integrity, honor, and indomitable perseverance, to which all that had the privilege of Captain Keiser's acquaintance will bear willing testimony.

CAPTAIN JOSEPH THROCKMORTON.

Among the old and prominent boatmen in the valley of the Mississippi whose names were long and familiarly connected with early navigation, none will be remembered with more pleasure to those acquainted on the rivers above St. Louis than that of Capt. Joseph Throckmorton.

Among the first steamboats he commanded was the Red Rover, engaged in the Galena and St. Louis trade.

Subsequently, or in 1830, he and Capt. G. W. Atcherson built the steamboat Winnebago, which they employed in the same trade.

In 1832 he built the warrior, which was a side-wheel boat, without cabin accommodations, but she towed a barge for the accommodation of passengers. During that year the Black Hawk war broke out, and the Warrior was employed to transport the government troops under Gen'l Atkinson. At the battle of Bad Axe, on the Mississippi, a short distance above Prairie du Chien, the Warrior and her crew took an active part and, while not seriously injured, the boat carried the scars

from Indian bullets for some months.   After continuing to
run the Warrior for several years on the Upper Mississippi,
he built the St. Peter in 1835, and in 1836 the Ariel, and in
the following year the Burlington, and in 1842 the Gen'l
Brooke.

Subsequently he built and purchased several boats which he
ran on the Missouri.

His experience in river navigation was no exception to the
general result.

While he was an exceedingly careful and competent commander, and popular with all who knew him, no qualifications
could overcome the embarrassments all had to contend with
in river navigation, and the few that have succeeded are the
exception.

For several years (about 1850) Captain Throckmorton represented in St. Louis a Tennessee Insurance Company and those
that had occasion to transact business with that company will
call to mind the agreeable suave manner in which they were always received, and their claims promptly, if they had such,
adjusted.

If that Insurance agency did not succeed in St. Louis it was
not the fault of the agent.

Subsequently Captain Throckmorton returned to the occupation he had so long and so honorably represented, but with
far less success than his long and useful career entitled him
to.   He crossed the river that ferries but one way in 1872 —
aged 72 years.

Captain George W. Atcherson

Was one of the pioneer boatmen on the Upper Mississippi.
While not the first, he was early engaged in the navigation of
steamboats.   The Winnebago came out in 1830, in which
he was interested with Captain Throckmorton, and continued
to run her on the Upper Mississippi for several years.   He
had three brothers, John, Mark and Samuel, all of whom were
engaged on the river at later periods and under his influence
and assistance.

His only child, George N., also followed the river as the
only profession he ever engaged in, but died before his
ability as a boatman was developed.   The father was not a
fast practical boatman, although an excellent builder and
built several of the best boats then afloat.   In fact the
Irene, the Ione, the Glaucus, the Governor Dodge, the
Amaranthe and before these, the Missouri Belle, are all

names that will revive pleasant recollections in the minds
of many travelers on Western waters in the earlier years of
steam navigation.

Captain Atcherson often commanded his own boats and
was one of the most genial and attentive masters to his
passengers that was then on the river and even up to the present day but few boats are more popular than were Captain G.
W. Atcherson's.

CAPTAIN C. K. GARRISON AND WM. C. RALSTON.

The subjects of the following comments can hardly be considered among the class known as "old boatmen." But as
there is no class to which they properly belong, we will associate them with a very worthy class of old boatmen and are
sure neither will be dishonored by the association.

It is to be regretted that the friends of many of those who
once figured so prominently, and have now crossed the river
for the last time, have not availed themselves of the opportunity presented in this work to bear testimony to the nobility
of character of many who once stood high in the estimation
of those with whom they were associated and are now only
remembered by their relatives and intimate friends.

Few of the present generation living in the Mississippi
Valley will recollect Wm. C. Ralston from personal acquaintance. Although his connection with river navigation was of
short duration, his subsequent life and brilliant career in
California entitle him to mention among the earliest prominent
boatmen of this valley.

While it is not possible to follow him through his short,
eventful life with the data at hand, a brief synopsis will recall him to the memory of many who knew something of his
later history.

This writer's acquaintance with Mr. Ralston dates from
about 1842, when he was acting as clerk on the Constitution.

When the California gold excitement broke out Capt. Garrison decided to sell his boat, the Convoy, and his interests
in St. Louis and proceeded at once to California, taking with
him a number of others, among whom was Mr. Ralston, then
a young man not over 25 years of age.

Capt. Garrison's sharp perceptive faculties, which made
him so prominent a figure in all his after life, had enabled him
to see in young Ralston the brains and the vim he admired.

Their trip across the isthmus was full of annoyances and
delays that all were subject to during that rush and until the

railroad was built. This suggested to Garrison that that was a point he could not afford to overlook, and while everybody was rushing on to California, believing that to be the El Dorado, he saw a sure thing on the Isthmus, if any one could be induced to locate there.

Ralston was his man; Garrison staked him, gave him an interest and he opened an exchange or banking house, and for two or three years did a very lucrative business. In the meantime Garrison went to San Francisco and soon climbed to the top round of the ladder, became Mayor of the city and was instrumental in introducing many greatly needed reforms in their municipal government, and was an important factor in many business enterprises, out of which he laid the foundation of a large fortune. He subsequently removed to New York where he died a few years since, leaving a fortune estimated at $3,000,000, and a young wife with no children.

Ralston subsequently located in San Francisco and engaged in banking, and became interested in mining and every new enterprise that promised success.

To no other man was San Francisco so much indebted for its rapid development and gigantic strides as to Wm. C. Ralston. No one appealed to him for assistance to open a mine, build a steamboat, a railroad, a hotel, or a manufactory without receiving it.

His financial ability placed him in the front rank among bankers, miners, brokers and business men.

He soon became president, director and cashier of the Bank of California, so far as its business was concerned, although he was nominally only the cashier. Our acquaintance was renewed 10 or 12 years after he left the Mississippi. He was the soul of generosity and his hospitality knew no bounds.

His residence, 25 miles from San Francisco, was palatial and accommodatd 50 guests sumptuously. A description of it has so often been given by tourists and reporters a repetition is unnecessary in this place. It was reached by railroad, although Mr. Ralston always drove his own team over the road twice a day in good weather, which is about 10 months out of 12. He always drove two and sometimes four horses in an open carriage, and his time was limited to two hours each way, with one change of horses half way.

His stables were stocked with the best horses that could be found, and anything less than a three-minute horse was of no use to him except on his ranch. Forty horses was not an unusual number for him to keep, and I have counted 52 different vehicles of his on the place at one time. His house was always open and the general rendezvous for all respectable visitors to the Pacific Coast.

His application to business was untiring, and however many visitors he might have at his house it did not interfere with his habits. He always started for the city in time to be at bank when it opened and left it in time to meet the guests remaining at his home at 6 o'clock dinner. Music and dancing, to those that enjoyed that recreation, were always on the programme and always participated in by himself. In fact his residence was more like a fine hotel at a fashionable wateringplace than a private house.

But at length a panic came, when he least expected it, and he was not able to bridge over the chasm his large drafts upon the bank had made. The run upon the bank was so great they were compelled to close the doors and call the police to clear the house. At no time since the famous vigilance committee was disbanded had the excitement in San Francisco run so high.

A casual examination of the bank's books revealed the fact that Ralston's account was overdrawn some $2,000,000. A meeting of the directors was called immediately, when he tendered all his stocks, real estate and everything he possessed in liquidation for his indebtedness, and it was said if a judicious disposition could be made of his effects, the bank *would* not be a heavy loser.

He had not intended to defraud the bank, but had failed *to* expose his over-drafts for several years, with the expectation of making them good when the tide of speculation turned in his favor.

After mature deliberation the directors determined to ask his resignation.

He was called to their room, and after hearing their decision, passed immediately out at the rear door of the bank and was never again seen alive by any one of his familiar acquaintances.

His body was found floating in the West Bay, about one mile from the bank, three hours later.

His proud spirit could not endure the mortification he *felt* when the directors discarded him. The announcement of his death produced greater excitement in the city than did the failure of the Bank of California, two days before.

The overdrawing of his account was the first mistake, although not done with the intention of robbing the stockholders.

The second and last act was a far more fatal mistake. Had he had the moral courage to withstand the disgrace he probably would not have been prosecuted, and within 12 months would have recovered the confidence of the public if not his position in the Bank of California, which soon made good its capital and resumed business.

Mr. Ralston's position in the bank was subsequently filled by his very worthy assistant cashier, Thomas Brown, who still occupies it, to the great satisfaction of all who have business with that bank or are casual visitors to the Pacific Slope.

He, too, was a graduate from the office of a Mississippi steamboat, and will be remembered with pleasure by the few who still survive and were thus connected in the *fifties*.

An incident is related in which the peculiar characteristics of Mr. Ralston are strikingly illustrated.

A Mr. Harrick Martin, living in St. Louis, became acquainted with Ralston before he went to California, and, having so much confidence in him, he lent him $500 to provide an outfit. Years passed on and Mr. Martin removed to New York with no correspondence between them. He subsequently became reduced and was in great want.

A mutual friend knowing the circumstances told Mr. Ralston of the situation. He expressed great sorrow at his benefactor's circumstances, and inquired for his address. A short time after this interview one of the banks in New York notified Mr. Martin that there was a credit there of $10,000 subject to his order.

Presuming there was some mistake he called at the request of the president, and greatly to his astonishment found it as stated. And also that his confidence in "Billy Ralston" had not been misplaced.

Among all the worthy and the unworthy and talented men that have ever graduated from the deck of a Mississippi River steamboat probably no two have ever developed so much financial ability and business enterprise as did Messrs. Garrison and Ralston.

Their connection with the river was not of long duration. But had it continued it is evident they would have left their impress upon its commerce. But their sagacity soon satisfied them that it must always be subject to a competition inherent in itself, if not from railroads (which had not in their time become so important factors), which must inevitably reduce the profits of transportation by river below a paying basis.

39

The Venerable "Davy Hiner."

(From an old timer.)

"A generation or so ago, there were but few steamboats that could carry 1,500 bales of cotton; few that drew less than five feet when light; few that were not heavy on fuel; few that could run from New Orleans to Vicksburg in four days; few that failed to make money—and lots of it; and few, if any, that had more than one captain at a time, either on board or ashore. Now, there are few that have not a full supply of captains from the agents to the chambermaids; the most prominent, generally, is the porter, each ones "runs the boat." Capt. David Hiner is of the old school. Once, in command of a fine boat, the mate wanted a new hawser; the steward wanted a new cooking stove; the engineer wanted a new doctor, the porter was bound to have a new badge for his hat; the chambermaid wanted a pane of glass in the window of her stateroom, and would have it. Capt. David wanted a new crew, and got it."

This manufacture of commodores by the dozen, cheap, too, and other toadyism, and again the gratification of personal enmity by epithets to boats, is entirely foreign to the province of this river department of a dignified daily newspaper and to the interest of the paper, the dignity of the public journal should not be prostituted in this way. Make yourself plentiful on the levee and useful to your employer. This river department of a paper should be manned by a skillful pilot, carefully guided down the channel, avoiding the "rocks and shoals" of poetry, politics and all that may lead to controversy."

Capt. Henry W. Smith.

No man in the period in which he was engaged on the river excelled him in enterprise, ingenuity, and perseverance.

His advent on the river, from a country store in Missouri, was in the year 1855.

The General Lane, a Missouri River boat, gave him a position as second clerk.

From that position he soon succeeded in elevating himself to the command of a boat in the Missouri, and soon after to the St. Louis and New Orleans trade, where he continued until the breaking out of the war.

Soon after that he was appointed inspector of hulls by the board of underwriters, which position he filled with credit and satisfaction until he was appointed to the office of Superintendent of the St. Louis & Memphis Packet Co.

At the death of Capt. John J. Roe, Capt. S. succeeded to the presidency, under whose administration the company developed into one of the great possibilities.

He comprehended the situation, and moved to the front, and the result was a better and a faster line of boats than had ever before been built on Western waters, except the boats owned by the Cincinnati & Louisville Mail Line, was built and put into the trade.

He had a mechanical eye and his genius enabled him to comprehend an improvement if suggested. He was quick to perceive, and had decision of character sufficient to decide without delay.

He was genial in temperament, and fraternal in his associations. All who knew him respected his judgement, and admired his frankness. His executive ability placed him in the front rank as a presiding officer in political or business organizations, and his good, practical, common sense made him a valuable anxiliary in all new enterprises.

The loss to the community of steam navigation interests in the West suffered more from the early death of Capt. Henry Smith than from that of any other that could have occurred.

He passed away in 1870, leaving an interesting family, and a host of friends and admirers.

CAPT. JOHN KLINFELTER.

"Mark Twain's" experience during his steamboat life on the Mississippi, whether real or ideal, portrays so much that is true to life and in accordance with facts known to many still living, no better illustration need be sought than is given in his very interesting narratives. I have therefore taken the liberty to make some quotations, which I am satisfied will be enjoyed by all who read them, although they may have read them before.

During his apprenticeship and while he was yet "Bixby's Cub," for some cause he was transferred to the steamer Pennsylvania, Capt. John Klinfelter, the subject of this sketch. A pilot by the name of Brown, who seems to have been a very disagreeable fellow, besides being a man of no education and destitute of principle, was employed on the boat at the time. Capt. Klinefelter's well known kindness and good nature subjected him to rudeness and imposition from this kind of ill-grained over-bearing men, although they were in his employ, and he would submit to almost anything, before he would discharge them.

The following incident so faithfully illustrates his character and that of a domineering, disageeable pilot of the olden time, whether his name is Brown, Jones or Smith, a repetition of it here will be excused. Mr. Twain continues: —

"Two trips later I got into serious trouble. Brown was steering, I was "pulling down." My younger brother appeared on the hurricane deck, and shouted to Brown to stop at some landing a mile or so below. Brown gave no intimation that he had heard anything. But that was his way, he never condescended to take any notice of an under clerk. The wind was blowing, Brown was deaf (although he always pretended he was not) and I very much doubted if he had heard the order. If I had had two heads I would have spoken. But as I had only one I thought it would be judicious to take care of it, so I kept still. Presently, sure enough, she went sailing past the plantation.

Capt. Klinefelter appeared on the deck and said: "Let her come around, sir, let her come around." Did not Henry tell you to land here? No, sir. I sent him up to do it. He did not come up, and that's all the good it done, the dod-derned fool. He never said anything. Didn't you hear him? asked the captain of me. Of course I did not want to be mixed up in the business, but there was no way to avoid it. So I said, "Yes, sir."

I knew what Brown's next remark would be before he uttered it, it was — "Shut your mouth, you never heard anything of the kind."

I closed my mouth according to instructions. An hour later Henry entered the pilot house unaware of what had been going on.

He was thoroughly an inoffensive boy and I was sorry to see him come, for I knew Brown would have no pity on him.

Brown began straightway, "Here, why didn't you tell me we had to land at the plantation?" "I did tell you, Mr. Brown." "Its a lie!" I said — "You lie yourself. He did tell you."

Brown glared at me in unaffected surprise and for as much as a moment he was entirely speechless. Then he shouted to me — "I will attend to your case in half a minute." Then to Henry — "and you leave the pilot house, out with you." It was pilot law and must be obeyed. The boy started out and had his foot on the upper step outside the door when Brown with a sudden access of fury picked up a ten pound lump of coal and sprang after him. But I was between, with a heavy stool, and I hit Brown a good honest blow which stretched him out.

I had committed the crime of crimes, I had lifted my hand against a pilot on duty. I supposed I was booked for the penitentiary sure, and could not be booked any sooner if I went on and squared my long account with this person while I had the chance. Consequently I stuck to him and pounded him with my fists a considerable time.

I do not know how long, the pleasure of it probably made it seem longer than it really was.

But in the end he struggled free and jumped up and sprang to the wheel — a very natural solicitude, for all this time there was this steamboat tearing down the river at the rate of fifteen miles an hour and nobody at the helm! However Eagle bend was two miles wide, at this bank full stage and correspondingly long and deep and the boat was steering herself straight down the river and taking no chances. Still that was only luck — a body *might* have found her charging into the woods.

Perceiving at a glance that the Pennsylvania was in no danger, Brown gathered up the big spy glass, war club fashion and ordered me out of the pilot house, with more than Camanche bluster. But I was not afraid of him now, so, instead of going, I tarried, and criticised his grammar, I reformed his precious speeches for him and put them into good English, calling his attention to the advantage of pure English over the bastard dialect of the Pennsylvanian colliers whence he was extracted, He could have done his part to admiration in a cross-fire of vituperation of course, but he was not equipped for this kind of controversy. So he presently laid aside his glass and took the wheel, muttering and shaking his head, and I retired to the bench.

The racket had brought everybody to the hurricane deck, and I tumbled when I saw the old captain looking up from the midst of the crowd. I said to myself, now *I am*, done for! For although as a rule he was so fatherly and indulgent towards the boat's family, and so patient of minor shortcomings, he could be stern enough when the fault was worth it. I tried to imagine what he *would* do to a cub pilot who had been guilty of such a crime as mine, committed on a boat guard deep with costly freight and alive with passengers. Our watch was nearly ended. I thought I would go and hide somewhere until I got a chance to slide ashore.

So I slipped out of the pilot house and ran down the steps and around to the Texas door — and was in the act of gliding within — when the captain confronted me. I dropped my head and he stood over me in silence a moment or two then said expressively, " Follow me."

I dropped into his wake and followed him into his parlor in the forward end of the Texas. We were alone now; he closed the doors and sat down. I stood before him.

He looked at me some little time, then said :

" So you have been fighting Mr. Brown? "

I answered meekly, " Yes, sir."

" Do you know that is a very serious matter? "

" Yes, sir."

"Are you aware this boat was plowing down the river fully *five minutes* with no one at the wheel? "

" Yes, sir."

" Did you strike him first? "

" Yes, sir."

" What with? "

" A stool, sir."

" Hard? "

" Middling, sir."

" Did it knock him down? "

" He — he fell, sir."

" Did you follow it up, did you do anything further? "

" Yes, sir."

" What did you do?"

" Pounded him, sir."

" Pounded him? "

" Yes, sir."

" Did you pound him much, that is severely? "

" One might call it that, sir; may be."

" I am deuced glad of it! Hark ye! Never mention that I said that. You have been guilty of a great crime, and don't you ever be guilty of it again on this boat. *But* lay for him ashore. Give him a good sound threshing, do you hear? I'll pay the expenses. Now go, and not a word of this to anybody. Clear out with you. You have been guilty of a great crime, you whelp."

I slid out, happy with the sense of a close shave and a mighty deliverance, and I heard him laughing to himself and slapping his fat legs after I closed his door.

When Brown came off watch he went straight to the captain, who was talking with some passengers on the boiler-deck, and demanded that I be put ashore at New Orleans, and added " I'll never turn another wheel on this boat while that cub

stays." The captain said — "but he need'nt come around
when you are on watch, Mr. Brown."

"I wont even stay on the same boat with him, one of us
has got to go ashore."

"Very well," said the captain, "*let it be yourself*," and resumed his talk with the passengers.

Any one who knew captain Klinfelter intimately will never
doubt the truth of this incident in Mr. Twain's narrative.

Nor should they doubt the untimely end of the unfortunate
Mr. Brown, or of the steamer Pennsylvania on the return
voyage, as described further along in the narrative. This
writer, with the steamer James E. Woodruff, on her way to
New Orleans, was the first to reach the wreck of the ill-fated
Pennsylvania after the explosion, as it lay at the Tennessee
shore at the little town of Austin some fifteen miles above
Helena, some four hours after the tragic event.

Mr. Clemens does not overdraw the picture. It required
a more graphic pen even than his to do it justice.

Many of the wounded who were able to be removed from
the *open flatboat* after the destruction of the steamboat and
desired to return South, from whence they came, were taken
on board of the Woodruff and made as comfortable as scalded
and dying people can be, stretched along the cabin floor on
mattresses, with the mercury at 100.

Those that survived were taken to New Orleans ; those that
did not were interred on the banks of the Mississippi (where
thousands have found a temporary resting place) until the
shifting and turbid currents of that treacherous stream shall
have invaded the sacred spot, and not only robbed the grave
of its treasure, but engulfed the grave and its surroundings.

Most of the passengers and the crew belonged at the North,
and were taken to Memphis on the first boat going up stream.

The A. T. Lacy was the first boat from New Orleans
to St. Louis, after his conflict with pilot Brown. This was
at a period which "Mark Twain" says pilots were entire masters of the situation, and were the autocrats on any boat upon
which they were employed. And it was not possible for any
captain to employ a pilot only at the option of the pilot's
association. Thus captain Klinfelter was obliged to retain
Mr. Brown, who declined to remain on the boat unless "Bixby's cub" was sent ashore, which was done, and his life
probably saved in consequence.

Mr. Brown with many others were never seen after the explosion of the Pennsylvania.

Captain Klinfelter continued on the river a few years after

the loss of the Pennsylvania. But subsequently retired and purchased a home in Bunker Hill, in Illinois, where he spent the remaining years of his life in the quiet enjoyment of his family, after a useful and varied experience in the precarious occupation of a boatman, beloved by all who knew him.

CAPTAIN D. SMITH HARRIS.

One of the oldest boatmen now living (1889) is Captain Harris, of Galena, Ills., if not in years, in the length of time he has been in active service either as a keel-boat or a steamboatman. In 1834, he, in company with a brother, R. Scribe Harris, built a little steamboat at Galena called Joe Davis which they ran from the lead mines to St. Louis for two or three years. She was a diminutive craft, with no accommodations for passengers and but little for any kind of business.

But the "lead mines" of Galena were then producing large quantities of ore and attracting a good deal of emigration. The Harris brothers were alive to the situation and with their characteristic energy, in 1837 built a much larger boat at Cincinnati called Smelter, which they designed, and ran in the trade between Cincinnati and Galena with flattering success.

No boat up to that time, on the upper Mississippi had equaled in speed or capacity the Smelter. She always had more passengers than she could well accommodate and was run with a kind of eclat that characterized all fast boats at a more recent date.

After the Smelter the two Harris brothers built several other good boats which they continued in the Upper Mississippi trade; among them was the Otter, the Pizzaro, the Preemption and some others.

They bought the West Newton after emigration set into Minnesota and ran her through from St. Louis to St. Paul, early in the history of that very active and profitable trade. They were cotemporary with Capt. Orrin Smith, who was the first President of the "Galena, Dubuque and Minnesota Packet Company," principal office at Galena. Captain Smith was among the pioneer boatmen in the Cincinnati, St. Louis and Galena trade. He built the Fulton, the Brazil, the New Brazil and ran them all in that trade and made for himself an enviable reputation as a good boatman and a high toned companionable gentleman. No man stood higher in the estimation of the public and in the hearts of those who knew him best, than did Captain Orrin Smith. His memory will live long and green in the recollection of his cotemporaries.

CAPTAIN ST. CLAIR THOMASSON.

Among the old boatmen in the antebellum period there is none that will be remembered with more pleasure than the subject of this sketch by those who had the pleasure of traveling on his boats.

Capt. Thomasson was born in Louisiana. His father was an American and his mother a French woman. By some infelicity in the family young St. Clair left his home at an early age and never after returned to it or claimed any kinship.

The best record extant of him places him in New Orleans in 1835, engaged with the late Capt. Theo. Shute in supplying plantation stores with dry goods, boots, shoes, etc. This trade they continued until 1843, when they embarked on the river and built the steamer Baton Rouge which they ran between New Orleans and that city. Their next boat was the Concordia, which they ran to Vicksburg. After disposing of her, they built consecutively within a few years, three boats named Magnolia. The last of the three was built without a passenger cabin, although she had accommodations of an inferior character for a few passengers. This boat was strictly speaking a *cotton boat* and a great carrier. She was burned in the Yazoo River during the war, to prevent her falling into the enemy's hands.

Subsequently Capt. Thomasson removed to St. Louis and took a position on the Great Republic, then the largest and finest boat that had ever been built, or has ever been built since with a few exceptions. He acted as a kind of cabin master on this boat and some others, but gradually retired from the river, the war having pretty nearly exhausted his resources and broke down his proud and genial spirit.

He passed from this life at Niagara Falls, August 2d, 1880, at the age of 75 years, and was interred within the sound of that sublime cataract that had for thirty-five years annually attracted his romantic tastes to its borders, and where he always expressed the hope his body might repose.

The *Niagara Gazette* of that date closes a worthy tribute to his memory thus: "He was a pure and noble man, unselfish and true, with a heart overflowing with kindness to all classes of people, loved and respected by all. Now that he has gone, sadness and sorrow will abide in many households."

Capt. Thomasson was never married and left no known relatives or heirs.

The late Capt. Shute and his daughter, who had been a life long friend and a partner, was with him when he passed the whirlpool for the last time, and contributed all that could be done to make the dark passage less gloomy.

Capt. Thomasson was an eccentric man, but his genial temperament and social habits made him a favorite with the traveling public.

In the spring and early summer, when the cotton season was over, before laying his boats up for the summer, it was customary for him to make two or three trips to Louisville, to accommodate the large passenger travel that always went North to spend the summer.

His boat, with many others at that time, advertised in the papers several weeks in advance the date of their departure. Whenever the register of his boat was full, and no more passengers could be accommodated with a stateroom, no more would be received on board.

Unlike many others, he would refuse all applications when his rooms were full.

The sumptuous fare that was provided, and the elegance with which it was served, enabled him to fill his staterooms with the best class of passengers at a price that few other boats presumed to charge.

Families, and ladies traveling by themselves, were a specialty with him.

He was known as a great ladies' man wherever he went, and he never seemed so happy as when he had a number of children hanging on to him, or was escorting a party of ladies.

His uniform politeness and suavity in the presence of ladies made him a great favorite, and his generosity was proverbial wherever known.

Capt. Shute, who always acted as clerk, or agent, on Thomasson's boats, was an exceedingly modest man, and if any credit was due to him for the good management and general policy on board, he never claimed it.

Although it was very evident to friends that he was really the "power behind the throne" in the cabin. The first two boats they owned were contracted for and superintended by Capt. Shute. He died in New Orleans in 1886, at the advanced age of eighty years, respected by all who knew him.

Thus, after contending with the turbid waters of the Mississippi, and the dangers incident to its navigation for so many years, two of the prominent "beacon lights" of earlier years made their last "crossing," and entered a haven where waters are lighted by the reflection of the noble deeds done while struggling with the reverses incident to the life of a boatman.

CAPTAIN CHARLES S. ROGERS
[Communicated.]

Was born in New Hampshire, 1816; was left an orphan at the age of four years, under the guardianship of an uncle, with whom he lived until he was eight years old, when he was removed to Portland, Maine, where he lived with another uncle until 1832, when he engaged in the dry goods business in the house of Hon. S. R. Lyman, where he remained until he accepted Horace Greeley's advice, and removed to St. Louis in 1838.

His first experience on the river was in the capacity of a clerk in 1842. From that time to the present he has been continuously engaged either as clerk, captain, or president of companies owning and running boats on the Mississippi, Missouri, or Illinois Rivers.

There are very few, if any, men engaged in steamboating at the present time that have been so long and so constantly engaged as has Capt. C. S. Rogers. He is the only surviving partner still in the business, that organized, and for more than forty years ran the Naples Packet Co.'s boats on the Illinois and other rivers.

In the forty two years the Naples Packet Company was in existence, it built, bought and operated of its own, twenty-three steamboats, beside numerous barges and wharf-boats.

They were of varied capacity — some of them of the largest class — some very fine and fast, and others very light draft.

They were built for different trades, and navigated nearly all the navigable waters of the Mississippi Valley.

Of the ten original stockholders in that company, with one exception, Captain Rogers is the only survivor.

His erect and robust form may always be seen during the Exchange hours, associating with the few remaining old landmarks that did business on the street before St. Louis had reached sufficient importance to require an Exchange. For one so long and constantly engaged in the arduous and exhausting duties of a river life, he is remarkably well preserved and there seems no good reason why he may not long survive the alloted time of " three score and ten."

If the declining interests he has so long and faithfully represented, or the reverses of fortune have failed to make him a millionare, it has not been from losses in wild speculations or neglect of duty, as all will testify who know him well. Ed.

CAPTAIN OWEN FINNEGAN.

MOBILE, ALA., April 22, 1889.

Capt. E. W. Gould, St. Louis, Mo.:

DEAR SIR — In compliance with the promise to tell you something about myself and the steamboat interest of this port for publication in your forthcoming work on steam navigation I will commence with myself.

I landed in Mobile in the year 1847, on the steamboat General Taylor, in the capacity of a watchman of the boat.

During the 42 years I have been constantly engaged in that business and have owned and commanded a large number of boats.

Among which I will name, Nyanza, R. E. Lee, John T. Moore, Maggie F. Burke, Lucy E. Gartrell, all of which, save the Maggie F. Burke have passed from view the way this kind of property generally goes.

The Burke I am still running as a weekly packet to Selma and Montgomery.

Capt. Jno. Quill and A. Newsmister own the Nettie Quill and the Carrier.

The Mary Elizabeth I own, with my associates. These four constitute the Alabama River boats.

The T, L. Tally, Mattie B. Moore, Hard Cash, C. W. Andrews and the Ruth are all engaged on the Bigbee and Marion Rivers at the present time.

In the ante bellum days, before the railroads invaded our territory, we had a large and profitable trade.

In 1852 or 3 we had a chartered company known as Cox Brainard & Co., that did an immense business and conducted the trade on all these rivers that are tributary to this city. We have good navigable waters during the winter and spring, nearly to the head of navigation, which is some 700 miles.

In 1857-8 the receipts of cotton in Mobile from these rivers amounted to 800,000 bales now it is but little over 100,000 bales.

Cox, Brainard & Co. owned many fine boats. Among those running to Montgomery I call to mind the Messenger, I. I. Cox, master; Magnolia, W. F. Jones, master; Cremonia, A. A. H. Johnston, master; Le Grand, G. W. Clondin, master; H. l. King, Owen Finnegan, master; Empress, G. H. Kirk, master; St. Nicholas, C. W. Locklier, master; St. Charles Robt. Otis, master.

These constituted a daily line, a part of which run as dispatch boats and only carried passengers and the mails.

Now two steamers a week is quite as many as we have business for.

During the war we lost several boats, which were burned by the Northern army.

At the surrender of Montgomery the Milner, the Cherokee, the Folly, the Iron King were all burned.

The Henry J. King, a fine side-wheel boat, valued at $75,000, with a part of a load of cotton belonging to myself and others, and of which I was in command, was burned by the Wilson raiders in 1865.

At the close of the war there was thousands of bales of cotton stored along the rivers, when it was selling in Mobile at 50 cents per lb.,and as high as forty dollars per bale freight was paid in some cases to get it to market. But that was owing to low stage of water and a scarcity of boats.

But from that time to the present the numerous railroads that have been constantly increasing have largely diverted our trade from the rivers and the business is no longer what it was as you will see by the foregoing brief account.

Trusting you may meet with the success your worthy enterprise merits,

I remain yours truly,

OWEN FINNEGAN.

CAPT. HENRY A. JONES, CINCINNATI.

NEWTON, MASS., Dec. 12, 1888.

Capt. E. W. Gould, St. Louis, Mo.:

Your favor of the 4th inst. was duly received. My earliest recollection of Capt. Henry A. Jones reaches back to the year 1832. At that time he was engaged in the then popular business of flat-boating between Cincinnati and New Orleans. Capt. Jones was a "regular trader," *i.e.*, he owned the boats and their cargoes, had no one interested with him, bought and paid for every article of merchandise, principally the produce of the country, before he pushed his boat from the wharf; was his own captain and supercargo. Having little faith in the banking institutions of that period, he never kept a " bank account," but always carried his money either in his pocket or in a belt buckled around his body. Born in Vermont in " 1808," but the family emigrated to the State of Ohio when the subject of this sketch was four years old. They settled in or near Zanesville. His father was a " mill-wright," but who died quite early in life. His mother married a second time, but Henry and two younger brothers never received much benefit from their step-father. Consequently they started out into the world early in life to care for and support themselves. The captain went to work near the salt works of their neighborhood at cutting cord-wood to be burned for making salt. For which he was paid 40 cents a cord for cutting, splitting and piling up.

For one of his years he did very well, could earn $1.00 per day, but his board, $1.25 per week, was deducted. At the age of nineteen he went to Cleveland, worked as a common laborer during the season for out-door work, made himself useful in the way of building houses, carried the bricks and mortar, while others did the work. Was at all times ready to make himself useful, especially if there was a prospect of making fair wages. In 1828 the Louisville & Portland canal was nearly completed, i.e., the excavation was about finished, but the bottom had to be smoothed off and the sides were to be paved. Capt. Jones got the job for paving two sections. He possesses the necessary articles for the work to be done, viz.: a willingness to work, a wheelbarrow, a hammer and his own strong arm.

The completion of the canal brings our friend to the time of life which made him a full citizen — the age of twenty-one. Though he had amassed a capital of six hundred dollars, he saw the necessity of adding more to it. And until something more desirable would offer, engaged as deckhand. There were no " roustabouts " in those days on steamboats in the New Orleans trade. This experience fitted him for the rugged life he was about to commence — that of a flat-boat or river trader on the Ohio and Mississippi Rivers. His first venture in this new line of life was in a " flat " 50 by 18 feet. Crew consisted of himself and one other man. Loaded with live sheep, flour, whisky, peach brandy, with some butter and cheese. With this craft full of produce, all paid for from his own earnings, he started from Cincinnati to New Orleans, unless fortune would enable him to dispose of his cargo at in-

termediate points, on both rivers and on the coast.
Everything was sold before reaching Natchez. Returning he
came on any good steamboat coming up the river. While he
followed the life of "flat-boating" he always returned in the
steerage as a deck passenger. He followed this mode of life
for six years, was always successful, never having met with
any serious accident or made a trip which caused pecuniary
loss. In the year 1836 his career as commander and owner of
steamboats began, and was so energetically and successfully followed until near the close of a useful and exemplary life, which
sad event occurred in the month of March, 1884. His first
steamboat was the Columbus. This was a vessel built at Rock-
ville, a point on the Ohio River, in Ohio, a few miles below
Portsmouth, in 1835, and bought by Capt. Jones in June,
1836. This was one of those old-time, heavy New Orleans
boats, such as were in use in those days. Length over all 181
feet; beam, 26 feet; depth of hold, 9 feet 6 inches; 6 42-
inch boilers, 24 feet long; single engine. Could carry 400
tons. Good runner, nice cabin, was a popular boat.

Second boat, Ohio Belle, then Henry Clay, Queen City,
2nd Ohio Belle, Europa, Hiram Powers, John Adams, Commodore Perry, Charles Hammond, Judge Torrence, Nicholas
Longworth, Niagara. The latter boat was put in the great
Mississippi and Atlantic Steamship Company of St. Louis,
valued at $120,000; this venture proving a total loss. Dur-
ing and since the war he built and was interested in a large
number of boats; some were sold to the government for
gunboats or transports. Three or four were put into
and helped to form a line from Cincinnati to Memphis, of
which line he was president for about six years. He was also
for a long period an owner and president of the Champion
Coal and Towboat Company, stockholder and director in several insurance companies, heavy holder of gas stock, director
and owner of National Bank stock. Also heavily interested
in real estate in Cincinnati and vicinity. With his fellowman
he was an agreeable companion; in conversation was most
entertaining, with a faculty for holding a *promptu* audience
(this is French), for hours at a time. It would usually require all of a forenoon and until three or four p. m. of the
same day in describing some of the interesting events of his
long and useful life. In common conversation he was superior to the large majority of mankind. All having the privilege of a listener felt they were very well paid for any loss of
time for such purpose. A full history of a trip to New Orleans on a flat-boat would usually consume a full half day.

40

Capt. Jones was most decidedly an agreeable gentleman to know, and to be his friend or he yours. I can recall but one lifelong friend now living. I refer to Captain Aaron S. Bowen. When Capt. Jones was engaged more than fifty years ago in buying a load of produce for his flatboats, Capt. Bowen was an active young man, clerk for one of Cincinnati's early merchants, C. W. Gazzam. He dealt in all manner of produce, and Jones would often buy of him, more on account of his friend Bowen than any other. During the latter period of his life they were very much together. They occupied the same office, in fact one desk was sufficient for both; were members of the same church, would indulge in long buggy rides through town and country. In short, where one was the other was sure to be.

We refer to Capt. Bowen for two reasons. First, because of long continued friendship between him and Captain Jones; second, on account of business matters in connection with steamboat affairs. Capt. Bowen was one of Cincinnati's earliest forwarding and commission merchants, doing business with Messrs. C. and J. Broadwell, also for many years steamboat agent — with one exception the oldest in that line of business now living. I refer to Capt. Ira Athern, now in the nineties.

Capt. Athern, as a steamboat agent does *not* reach back to as early a period as does Capt. Bowen, who for many years did business under the firm name of Bowen & Hibbard.

Captain Jones married late in life an estimable widow lady, Mrs. Stephens, which brought to their happy household three most beautiful daughters; one, the youngest, is a resident of your city, St Louis. She is the beloved wife of Mr. Bevis. The remaining daughters, married, and reside in Cincinnati : Mrs. Champlin and Mrs. McGregor.

I am very truly yours,

J. H. BARKER.

THE THREE J. M. WHITES.

Answer to Correspondent Y. A.—There were three steamboats named J. M. White.

The first of that name was built at Elizabethtown, Pa., and finished at Pittsburgh in 1842. Her dimensions: Length 250 feet, beam 32 feet, depth 8 feet. She was named in honor of J. M. White, a prominent merchant of St. Louis. She only ran one season, when she sunk on the Grand Chain, Upper Mississippi. Her engines were 25-inch cylinder 8 feet stroke.

STEAMER J. M. WHITE, No. 2, OR THE WHITE OF 1844.

The second J. M. White was built by Capt. J. W. Converse at Pittsburgh in 1843. Her dimensions were: Length 250 feet, 31 feet beam, 8½ feet hold. Her cylinders were 30 inches diameter, 10 feet stroke, with 7 boilers.

She proved to be the most extraordinary steamboat of her day in the way of speed. She made the run from New Orleans to St. Louis in 1844. Time — 3 days, 23 hours and 23 minutes. This time was not beaten until 1870, 26 years afterward. This was done by the celebrated steamers R. E. Lee and Natchez. The Lee's time was 3 days, 18 hours and 30 minutes. The Lee had two 40-inch cylinders diameter, 12 feet stroke, with immense boiler power. When we consider the difference in power of engines and the disadvantages which the White encountered, hers was the most wonderful run of the age. She had to take her fuel wood from the banks of the river, which caused great loss of time, while the R. E. Lee had coal barges stationed at regular intervals which she took in tow, thereby saving a great amount of time. It is still a mooted question among old steamboatmen as to whether the Lee really beat the White's time, if we allow the White her lost time in taking wood and screwing up her hemp packing.

The third J. M. White was built at Louisville, Ky., in 1878, and is considered the most magnificent steamboat in the world. Her dimensions are: Length 325 feet, beam 50 feet, depth forward 17½ feet, midship 11½ feet, width over all 90 feet, which is from the nosing on the outside of the wheel-house to that of the opposite side of the boat. Her carrying capacity is 8,500 bales of cotton. Her cylinders are 43 inches diameter, 11 feet stroke. The present White is thought to be the fastest steamboat that has ever navigated the Mississippi River, but she has never made a race against the time of other fast steamers, and, therefore, we cannot say positively that she is faster than other steamers which have made extraordinary time.

The saloon of the main cabin is 260 feet in length, 19 feet wide, and 16 feet in height. The state-rooms are all large, most of the rooms in the ladies' cabin being 10 feet by 14 feet, and 12 feet by 14 feet. The smallest rooms in the main cabin are 8 by 10 feet, with a wide guard or passageway around the whole extent of the cabin. It is to be fitted and furnished equal to if not superior to the finest hotels on the Continent. The upper cabin, the floor of which is 45 feet above the surface of the water, is 180 feet in length, and 28 feet wide; this too, with a guard all around it. This cabin, or texas, is

to be furnished with the best of everything, and will be larger and finer than the main cabin of most of the boats now in commission. "Comparisons," however, are odious." The weight of machinery and boilers exceeds 260 tons, and the stem band weighs 2,700 pounds, the largest ever made. These dimensions may impart a fair conception of the immense boat, the cost of which will exceed $200,000. She had 10 boilers 34 feet long, 42 inches diameter, 2 flues 16 inches diameter, water wheel 45 feet diameter, 19 feet bucket.

The John W. Cannon, for the New Orleans and Bayou Sara trade, is at the lower wharf, having her cabin finished the most magnificently ever yet put upon a steamer. The machinery and connections are nearly completed, and the boat is to be ready on or about the 1st of May. She is having frescoed ceilings, and a most elaborate cabin; the staterooms, 10 by 11 feet and 8 by 8 feet, all connected, and all with passageways on the outside. Captain Cannon is in ecstacies over the boat, pronouncing her the handiest and most roomy, with more deck-room, steam power and conveniences than any craft of her class yet built. The hull is 250 feet in length, with 43 feet beam, 9½ feet hold, heavily timbered, yet all model and sharp, knuckles rounded, and bound to be as fast as the fastest. She had 7 steel boilers, each 34 feet in length and 42 inches in diameter. Also, an extra boiler and extra engines. She also has four immense steam drums to retain full head of steam while making landings, as she runs by compass, the darkest nights or heavy fogs being no hindrance to her progress.

Captain Cannon is the veteran of the cotton trade, having more experience and having built more fine boats than any one else, this being the tenth boat built for him around the falls. The list of his ventures is as follows: The Louisiana in 1848, the S. W. Downs in 1852, the Bella Donna in 1853, the R. W. McRae in 1854, the Farmer in 1854, the Vicksburg in 1856, the Gov. Quitman in 1858, the first R. E. Lee in 1866 and the present R. E. Lee in 1876.

Since the above was in type the last J. M. White has been destroyed by fire in Morgan's Bend, La.

The only record obtainable of this boat's fastest time is as follows: "Left New Orleans at 5 o'clock p. m. on a regular business trip. Landed at Donaldsonville and Plaquemine and arrived at Baton Rouge twenty minutes before one the following morning, making the run in seven hours and forty minutes. Her usual time to Harry Hillsgate was fifty-six minutes. This is by far the best time on record.

CAPTAIN JAMES GOOD.

Below I take the liberty of inserting a private letter of a valued cotemporary, which is so unique and philosophic and so unlike the character and the experience of the large majority of my esteemed cotemporaries, that I am sure it will be appreciated by all who know the trials and the anxieties peculiar to the life of the master of river steamboats.

It must indeed be a man with a "happy heart" who can encounter the perils of navigation incident to high and low water, to storms and dark nights, to collisions with steamboats, snags, wrecks and railroad bridges, to explosions, sand bars and fires, to the liability of loss of life as well as the loss of money, to the insane competition he is always subject to, to the unjust exactions of those into whose hands he often falls, to the trials incident to careless and incompetent officers and unreliable hands.

One who has "spent forty years around and on the river and whose life has been all sunshine, not a cloud to shadow its pleasures" has certainly enjoyed a phenomenal experience and one that will be envied by all cotemporaries and yet those that know Captain Good best, bear willing testimony to his assertions.

Among many valued cotemporaries in the past, this writer calls to mind but two, and they have long since crossed to the shining river, and furled sail in less tempestuous waters, who resembled in character and disposition the subject of these remarks.

Captains Mortimer Kennett and Barton Able were philosophic steamboat masters, as well as good boatmen. The former was also master of the violin. No navigation was too difficult or night too dark to induce him to decline the very pleasant duty of entertaining his passengers with the sweet strains of his violin.

Even when crossing the lower rapids of the Mississippi, where steamboatmen in the earlier times did more hard work in low water than on any other river in the Mississippi Valley, having their entire cargoes to lighten across the rapids in flat boats, Captain Kennett never allowed himself to be disturbed, or to interfere with the duties of his mate or his pilot. There was often great strife and rivalry among the large number of boats accumulated at the foot and the head of the rapids to see which should get across and get away first. But the captain's philosophy was generally a good stand off for the

extra exertions of all others, and either that or his violin made
him the envy of his cotemporaries, of which this writer was
one.   Captain Able, while not a musician, was a good *politician*
and no circumstances were every so embarassing or trying
that he could not find time, and opportunity to entertain his
passengers and even his crew with a good story or a political
speech, and none enjoyed a hearty laugh and a good joke better
than Capt. Able.

There is no capital or stock in trade so valuable to the
master of a steamboat as a " happy heart " and a well balanced
head.   None others should embark in an occupation so *liable*
to conflicts and disappointment.

Captain Good says " Success means money."   While he
claims to have secured none of that, it is evident his success has
far surpassed that of many of his cotemporaries, as the duties
of his calling have always afforded him *pleasure*, however
laborious, and he is made happy by the reflection that " ease
and comfort will come when I go to that shining river
beyond."

OFFICE OF
St. Louis & Miss. Valley Trans. Co.,
St. Louis, May 22, 1889.

Capt. E. W. Gould:

"DEAR CAPTAIN — I am at a loss to communicate any event
of my life that would aid your work, or add to my posterity
any reading matter that they might be proud of.   Success in
life means money.   I have labored a lifetime for others, I
have nothing to show that would indicate success, except a
happy heart and a large family.   My " happy heart " tells
me that I have labored honestly, and all to my employers'
interest.   I was 60 years old 9th inst.   My life spent around
and on the river, has been all sunshine.   Not a cloud to shadow
its pleasures.   I am yet in the harness, a wheel-horse, next
the rider, and I receive many a lash that quiets pride and high
temper, and I pull with the rest of the team, awaiting another
lashing at the top of the hill.   I am up on the level now, and
I feel my heart beating hard, full of good blood, and veins
standing out.   Captain, I can boast on this theme only, and
if I can get a good square master that will give enough from
his lucre to secure me a good stall and provender, I will stand
up and fill the place I now hold for ten years yet.   Ease and
comfort will come when I go to that shining river beyond.

Your friend and well wisher,
JAMES GOOD."

CAPTAIN WILLIAM DEAN OF PITTSBURGH.

In a communication from St. Paul dated February, 1889, which is hereto appended, the Captain has related some of his experiences in early navigation which will undoubtedly be read with interest by many of his old associates who remember his urbane and gentlemanly manner as captain and pilot of many of the earlier boats on the Ohio.

It will be recollected that he was among the few masters of steamboats that were so conscientious they would not run a steamboat on Sunday.

He relates some incidents to prove that he made money by

laying up when Sunday came. But it is not charitable to suppose he done it for that purpose.

In 1837, the Captain says there were three opposition lines of steamboats between Pittsburgh, Cincinnati and Louisville.

" The Red Line, the Blue Line and an outside line, without a name. Then a pilot line was formed to break up all the other lines and monopolize the river. Out of nearly 100 pilots they were offered high wages not to work on the other lines."

" Your biographer did not bite at the offer and received $300 a month in the employment of the Red Line. I took stock, and gave my note, and never worked a day in the line.

It was not long before dishonest men were found managing the line. They took the money, kept the notes, and the line went to the devil."

But we will hear the Captain tell his experience.

ST. PAUL, Feb. 4th, 1889.

Dear Captain Gould:

Your biographer is attempting to talk a little to you in painful affliction. A native of Ohio. Born in New Lisbon in 1811. It was an exciting year in our country. Rumor of war with Great Britain and the earthquake at New Madrid which shook the solid earth for more than one thousand miles around.

My parents moved to the Ohio River or in sight. I was left to be bound to a merchant in New Lisbon; did not like the idea, a friend came up from my father's; I said, I would go home with you.

My first sight of the river was from 1823 to 1826; can't recall the date. I was greatly attracted at the sight. At this time only five steamers on the river — names to wit: Pennsylvania, Messenger, Bolivar, Mechanic and Velocipede.

Charley Basham was clerk of Velocipede. After years the great steamboat agent Captain Billy Forsyth said he was the best he ever had, never promised any business or gave any.

The state of morals was low at this time. Simon Girty, the half Indian desperado and terror to the community, had passed away. The run above the city emptying into the Monongahela River, was called Girty's run. He had his headquarters up the run north of the city, where he held carnival with the Indian savages and with devils. After he passed away another type of man — Mike Fink and Mike Wolf, of the keel-boatmen.

At this time no system of transit was inaugurated from Pittsburgh to ports below. The keel-boat, propelled by man, was a model one, 80 to 90 feet long, open hold, with cargo box and running boards, or guards cluted, for to put the foot against with his 12 foot pole. Iron socket at end, and large wood button at top and large sweeps on deck to propel it.

It was a slow system for transit. The time from Philadelphia to Pittsburgh was three weeks with large six horse road wagon, time from Pittsburgh to Cincinnati, Ohio, was three weeks by keel-boat. That was slow transit. Now the age of keel-boating Mike Fink, a type for vulgarity and profanity.

I must not fail to mention the keel-boat propulsion by manpower was 15 miles per day up stream, and down was paddled about 1½ miles through the water per hour. The accommodation was not of the best. If boat was loaded with pig metal that was the only bed — unless a board could be found — the living was not likely to give the gout — a wet hard tack or pilot bread, side bacon, full of creepers often, and potatoes, rice, coffee without sugar. Slow transit indeed. Now I drop the keel-boat.

The outfit of a keel-boat was not complete without a barrel of whisky on deck.

This was the mode, until the great Pennsylvania canal was built ; cost the State fifty millions. The canal commissioners' salary twenty thousand dollars yearly. Now the canal rushed the goods into Pittsburgh, the commission merchant urging to get goods to Cincinnati and Louisville. The keel-boat would not answer any longer ; the rivermen planning ways and means. Finally it was decided to build light boats, stern wheel, to have capacity for 60 tons and go safe on two foot water. Now this was the beginning of light stern-wheel boats, and answered the purpose for a series of years. It was schooling a grand lot of rivermen for after use.

Ways and means was employed by the boatmen. Finally light water stern wheel-boats were decided would answer. It was not long until the river was pretty well supplied.

This system answered for a series of years. But the cry was give us, an outlet by railroads. The Pittsburgh, Fort Wayne & Chicago was built. Stock was $50 par, went to $3 per share. I must tell of railroad speculation of mine. A friend came and said there is to be a road built to Connellsville, then to branch out into Virginia to the main B. & O. road. Like Col. Seller's mighty dollar, there is millions in it. Well, I bit at the bait and put my name down for 10 shares, paid in at time of subscription $12 per share.

The road appeared to drop out of sight in a year or two. I called at the Treasurer's office and inquired about my railroad to Connellsville, and the money paid. He said, your money is all eat up in oyster suppers; don't know anything about it at present. Well, in after years I had my steamer loaded for St. Louis, and ready to leave port. Law officers come and said there is a judgment against you and execution issued; it must be satisfied now. How much is the amount. About $600. But giving credit for $12 per share reduced it. I paid the judgment off and never knew more about it. Repudiated the whole matter. Never went into railroading again.

The light water stern-wheel boats answered until the PennsylvaniaRailroad was completed and finished toPittsburgh.

And now dawned the great steamboating on the Ohio River. The commission merchant wanted more rapid transit.

Your biographer had charge of the finest one of 23. The owners said, can you make weekly trips from Pittsburgh to Cincinnati and return in a week. I will try. Started and made 12 consecutive trips. It was hard boating, but was found possible. The owners said we will build you a fast boat; but I preferred to be so I could go where and when I pleased. Now was formed the grandest packet line of steamers in the world. We are now up in 1841 and had full control of river near 10 years, accommodating the Pennsylvania canal.

Pennsylvania Railroad now finished to Pittsburgh. Cry was give us, outlet by railroads. The P. F. W. & C. was pushed to completion, and Panhandle Railroad was being built bee line to Cincinnati. We had at this time nearly three-quarters of hundred fine steamers running out of port of Pittsburgh to every port or place below. (In 1888 only three stern-wheel boats between Pittsburgh and Cincinnati.)

And the grandest army of pilots and captains the world ever seen. Four Dean brothers, all pilots and captains. And now the Ohio River, with its grand packet line, and other transports. May state piloting was reduced to perfection for 700 miles — now Ichabod may be written, the glory departed.

Railroad on the bank of the Ohio River on both sides from Pittsburgh to Louisville. Three weeks to Cincinnati, and now 10 hours. *Rapid transit.*

Now your biographer is done, and you must accept all E. and O. I think I am the oldest living of that grand army of pilots and captains. In my 78th year and in suffering. Waiting for the time to hear the Master say, come up higher. As I live ye shall live also. Blessed hope.

I have written in great pain.

Respectfully submitted,

WM. DEAN,
Pilot and Captain, for more than 30 years.

The following supplemental notice is communicated by a friend : —

Captain Wm. Dean first came to Pittsburgh, Pa., in 1823, engaged in river pursuits, and became captain of the Wheeling packet Massillon in 1834.

Was captain of the Hunter, running to Cincinnati and Louisville in 1836; married to Miss Aurelia Butler in 1837.

Took command of the new steamer Boston in 1839; sunk her at Devil's Island, Mississippi River, in the winter of 1841.

The following spring, was captain and part owner of the single engine steamer Alleghany (this boat and the Lehigh were the pioneers in the Pittsburgh & Cincinnati Packet Line, making weekly trips); sold out to the late Capt. R. C. Gray in 1846.

Purchased an interest and was captain of the double engine steamer Brunette in the fall of 1846.

About this time contracted for and built the North River, with the idea of making ten day trips to Louisville. Sold out to Alex. Dean in 1848.

Built the stern wheel, open hold, light water boat called the Columbia, in 1849; had no cabin accommodations for passengers; sold to Thomas Greenlee in 1850, and the same year built the stern-wheel passenger steamer, of about 300 tons capacity, called the Navigator.

Built the Clara Dean, freight boat to run to Louisville, in 1853.

In the summer of 1854, built the light draft freight and passenger packet Louisville, for Alexander Dean. This boat had a phenomenally successful career. Built the steamer Saint Louis for Jesse Dean in 1855. This year sold interest in steamer Clara Dean to Sampson Cadmann.

In 1856 superintended and completed the following boats: Towboat, Tempest; packets, Rocket, Cambridge, Moderator, and Sam P. Hibberd.

In the interval up to the spring of 1859, was employed in piloting on the Upper Ohio. At that time was appointed general agent of the newly organized Alleghany Insurance Co., to take charge of the marine interests.

In 1861 bought the Bay City, and out of it built the second Navigator. Built the Camelia in 1862, America in 1863, Columbia in 1864, and Messenger in 1865.

Resigned the general agency of the Alleghany Insurance Co. in 1884, and became a member of the Fire and Marine Agency of Geo. W. Dean & Co.

CAPTAIN JAMES HOWARD — HIS FUNERAL YESTERDAY A SCENE
OF UNUSUAL GRIEF — THREE CITIES PARTICIPATING — RE-
MAINS CONVEYED FROM JEFFERSONVILLE TO CAVE HILL,
ATTENDED BY A GREAT CORTEGE — LIFE OF THE DECEASED.

CAPTAIN JAMES HOWARD.

[Courier-Journal, 1876.]

The funeral of the late Capt. James Howard took place yesterday, and such a sadly impressive and imposing scene was
never witnessed in this city. The three cities of the Falls
shared alike in the sorrow, and were largely represented at
the funeral. Upwards of 50,000 people took part in and witnessed the cortege as it passed up First street from the river.

The hour set for the funeral to take place was 12:30, but long before that time had come men, women and children were wending their way towards his residence in Jeffersonville. The three ferryboats from this side of the river were crowded with pedestrians and vehicles. The people went from this city, New Albany, and Jeffersonville. The steamers B. H. Cooke and Fawn, of the Henderson Packet Line, left the city wharf and carried people up to his residence and brought them back after the ceremonies at the house were over. The trains, too, from this city and New Albany carried crowds to the scene. Standing in large crowds in the neighborhood of the house were the workmen in his employ and those of Mr. D. S. Barmore and the employes of the car works. Business was entirely suspended in Jeffersonville, and the citizens, old and young, turned out to pay their last tribute of respect to the memory of a man whom they honored, loved and respected. All the steamers of our wharf and Jeffersonville had their colors half-mast and tolled their bells. Flags were at half-mast upon the public buildings in the three cities, and many business houses and private dwellings were draped in mourning, as was also the ship-yard of Mr. D. S. Barmore, brother-in-law of the deceased. A solemn silence seemed to pervade the whole face of nature. Upon the countenances of the masses could be seen the shadows of grief, and many a tear dimmed the eye, and sighs came from the lips of the multitude when they thought of the mission they had come to perform. Men of all ages, rank and vocation were there. The rich and poor met alike to share in each other's sorrows over the irreparable loss they had so suddenly sustained.

The services over, the procession was formed, and a quarter past 1 o'clock it moved its slow length along toward the ferry landing. The three first carriages contained the pall-bearers, were as follows: Capt. Frank Carter, Capt. Z. M. Sherley, Capt. W. C. Hite, Capt. A. H. Dugan, Capt. R. H. Woolfolk, Mr. W. R. Ray, Mr. Geo. Ainslie, of Louisville; Capt. Adams, Mr. W. H. Buckley, Mr. Daniel Anciskus, Mr. W. H. Fogg, Mr. W. H. Horr and Col. Jas. Keigwin, of Jeffersonville. Following these was the hearse containing the remains, which were in a casket mounted in silver, and upon the top of which were laid two beautiful anchors and a cross made of the choicest flowers. Then followed the carriages, buggies, omnibuses, men on horseback and footmen. The working men of the ship-yards — Howard's and Barmore's — together with those of the Ohio Falls Car Works and other establishments of Jeffersonville, walked upon each side of the procession until they reached the ferry docks. The procession moved down Old Market street to Fulton to Chestnut, down Chestnut and thence to the docks, where the ferry-boats Sherley ond Shallcross, lashed together, lay waiting to convey the funeral train across the river to this side. While the procession was moving from the house down Chestnut the children of St. Augustine church joined it, and proceeded with it to the ferry dock. The procession was marshaled by Colonel Jas. Keigwin. When the two ferry-boats were full of people and carriages they pushed away from the dock and steamed down the river, and the dark drapery, the tolling of the bells, the hearse, the sad faces of all on board, made it indeed a solemn picture. The two boats were unable to carry all, so the third ferry boat, Wathen, went back to Jeffersonville and brought over to this side the remainder of the procession and people. The Sherley and Shallcross landed at the foot of First street, and the procession marched up the hill, followed by those who came over upon the Wathen, and who joined it upon this side of the river.

Ever since the unfortunate accident on Saturday a number of men have been dragging the bottom of the river to recover the horse and buggy which were lost when the deceased was drowned. Yesterday when the lashed steamers reached a spot in the river near where the accident occurred the horse and buggy were recovered and brought to shore, near where the body was found.

Capt. James Howard was born within a stone's throw of the city of Manchester, England, December 1, 1814. His father emigrated to this country with his family in 1820, and settled in Cincinnati. Being a wool-carder and cloth-dresser, he engaged in the business in the latter city, and James worked with him in a small mill from the time he was eleven years of age until he was fifteen. He was then apprenticed to a steamboat builder, named William Hartshorn, who now lives in Cincinnati to serve his time at the trade until he was twenty-one years of age. In the year 1835 he commenced life and business without a dollar in the world, but being a good mechanic — a man of remarkable energy and ability — he soon overcame all obstacles in his way and worked himself up until he became the most famous steamboat builder in the United States With the exception of a few years he spent on the river as an engineer he has uninterruptedly engaged in boat building until the day of his lamentable and sudden death. In 1837 he went to Madison, Ind., and built sixteen boats. In 1844 he returned to Jeffersonville, Ind., where he had remained ever since. The business of boat-building grew to be of such vast extent during the latter days of his life that he associated with him in the building of boats his younger brother, John, and his (James) son, Edward. The firm then became James Howard & Co., or, as they were as familiarly known, the Howard Brothers. Before he took his brother and son into business, he alone built about fifty steamboats. He and the firm together have built about two hundred and fifty boats, among which may be mentioned the Robert Fulton, Tecumseh, Capitol, James Howard, Ruth, and last but not least, the new or last Robert E. Lee — she being the best and most beautiful of all they ever built. The Howards have built boats of all sizes and classes, and for nearly every river in the South and West, and no man's reputation outranked that of "Uncle Jim's " for a steamboat builder.

His family consisted of a wife, three daughters and one son, all married. He had three brothers, Daniel, John and Thomas. All were present yesterday at the funeral, save one married daughter, who recently went to California.

James Howard was a man of medium height and good figure. His head was large and long, with a high broad forehead, and all the other features prominent and expressive. In his manners he was unassuming, and cordial to all persons. He was strong in purpose and action. The whole energy of an active, comprehensive mind and of an almost tireless physical organization was given to whatever scheme or duty he ever had in view. His battle in life has been no easy one, but he stood true throughout to the principles of honor and integrity, and, having an industry and mechanical knowledge which he has suffered no man in his occupation to excel, he gained both success and distinction. An affectionate and loving wife has lost a noble husband; children are now fatherless; brothers are brotherless. The poor have lost a friend and the mechanic a benefactor.

He has launched his last boat and got in it alone,
 And sailed to that beautiful clime,
Where angels are waiting to welcome him home,
 On the banks of the river of Time,
He will land by himself in Eternity's port,
 Then pull the boat out on the shore,
And quietly walk through the beautiful Gates,
 And never come back any more.

We trust that some angel will show him the way,
 That leads to the great throne of Grace
Where God, in his mercy, will give him a seat
 And smile on his time-wrinkled face.
If ever a man was true, honest and kind,
 We think it was old " Uncle Jim,"
And if God has a home and a crown for good men,
 He will certainly give them to him.

EWD. F. HOWARD.

The subject of the sketch and the accompanying portrait is the only representative of the world renowned and popular boat yard known for the last half century as "Howard's Boat Yard," at Jeffersonville, Ind.

He is the son and former partner of the late James Howard, whose long and successful career as the "great boat builder of the Mississippi Valley," made his name familiar to all, and honored by all who knew him.

To say the mantle has fallen from a worthy sire upon the shoulders of a devoted and worthy son is recognized by all who have had the pleasure of knowing him.

His long association in the yard as draughtsman, foreman, and partner has made his name as familiar with the numerous patrons of the Howard Brothers as was those of the former partners and his long and well known skill as an expert draughtsman is a sufficient guarantee to all that want fine boats.

The honesty and integrity that has so long characterized all transactions of the " Howards " is still a prominent feature under the present management.

Up to the present time, January 1st, 1889, there has been built at this yard by the Messrs. Howard, 460 boats of all kinds, principally steamboats, commencing with the side wheelboat in 1834, Hesperion.

To attempt an enumeration even of the larger and finer boats of this immense fleet would transcend the limits of this sketch.

The history and national reputation of such boats as the two Ruths, the James Howard, the Robt. E. Lee, the John Cannon, the J. M. White and the large number of Anchor Line boats is sufficient to establish the skill and the genius of this, the largest steamboat yard in the world, so far as the number of boats is concerned.

Mr. Howard is a young man in vigorous health, born in 18—, with perhaps the best location on the Ohio River for a boat yard, with all the modern improvements in boat building, launching, etc., with an ample force of the best mechanics to perform all contracts at shortest notice.

CAPTAIN SAMUEL RIDER.

The following obituary notice appeared in a St. Louis paper soon after his decease, written by one who knew and appreciated him : —

In the death of this well-known and pure-minded gentleman the community will generally recognize how great the loss to those who knew him intimately, and especially to his own family circle.

In an experience of forty years of active life on Western and Southern rivers, occupying the prominent position of master of some of the finest boats navigating them, probably there is no position of civil life better calculated to develop a man's true character, or to afford the public a better opportunity to judge of it.

Capt. Rider commenced his career as a boatman in 1844,

agreeable to my recollection, and continued it uninterruptedly until 1878.   From that time until his death (August 19, 1881) he was an invalid, though not confined to his house but a few days before his death.   The disease of which he died (cancer) developed early and made slow but sure progress, indicating to him and his friends the certainty of the result in the near future.   But for one who had so often stood at his post on the hurricane deck of a steamer in the terrific storms to which boats are subject in navigating the waters of the

CAPTAIN SAMUEL RIDER.

West from the Balize to the Upper Missouri, and amidst the iron hail from masked batteries and the deadly aim of sharp-shooters for hundreds of miles along the Lower Mississippi and its tributaries, during the late war, saying nothing about the frequent contacts he had been subject to during seasons of malignant epidemic, cholera and yellow fever, the ap-proaching enemy had no terrors.   He had often seen his near approach before, but never shrank from duty to avoid him.

He desired to live for the benefit of his family and friends, and when he realized he could no longer serve them, the at-tractions on the other side of the dark river were sufficient to overcome all the embarrassment he had ever felt in launching his frail bark upon that dark but peaceful stream.

In our intimate business relationship of more than thirty years I never knew Capt. Rider to so far forget himself as to speak an unkind or a profane word. He was proverbially kind and generous to a fault, as will be testified to by thousands who have known him under all circumstances and in many of the most trying positions. Of his honesty none ever doubted who knew him.

To one so generally known as Capt. Rider was, it is hardly necessary to refer in detail to the numerous positions he has filled during his river life.

I will, however, as a matter of record, report the recollections of some of his old friends, who may feel an interest in reviewing earlier associations, by recalling the name of such boats as occur to me which were built or navigated by him.

His first steamboat was the Timolian, built and navigated by himself on the Illinois River. The second was the Prairie State, built by him at the same place and for the same trade. Both of these were good boats, well adapted for the trade for which they were designed, and established unmistakably the genius and the enterprise of the builder.

After disposing of these boats, he became associated with the St. Louis and Naples Packet Company, in which company he was still a highly esteemed member at the time of his death.

During his association with this company he was in command of the following named boats, together with several others, the names of which are not recollected, viz. :—

Niagara, Brunette, Time and Tide, Persia, Messenger, Cataract, Belle Gould, Adriatic, John B. Carson, Post Boy, James E. Woodruff, Fannie Lewis, Clara, Walter B. Dance, Alice, Time and Tide No. 2, Wm. J. Lewis, Post Boy No. 2, Marcella, Imperial, Belle of Pike, Empress, Mountaineer, Fannie Lewis, Joe Kinney, Calhoun, Mary Boyd, and Lady Lee.

In recalling the names of these boats, pleasant recollections will recur to thousands of passengers and to subordinate officers who have enjoyed the courtesy and kindness of their genial commander, whose memory will live fresh in their recollections among the pleasant things of life.

The Captain was raised at Truro, on the bleak shores of Massachusetts Bay, and it was there he received his first lessons in nautical life from his father, who for many years was known as one of the most successful commanders of sailing vessels out of New England ports to all parts of the commercial world.

While but a mere stripling of a boy the subject of this imperfect sketch spent his leisure hours in building and sailing
small water-craft on the waters of the bay, and not unfrequently ventured far out to sea in fishing smacks and
coasting vessels of which he was made master in
command. His enterprise and ambition soon turned
his mind to the then "far West," and, in company
with a few friends, he started to seek a fortune in the
great Mississippi Valley. After a short residence in
Michigan and Iowa he located in St. Louis, where he remained
but a few years and took up a prominent residence at Griggsville, Illinois, where he married and continued to live (when
at home) in the enjoyment of a fondly-cherished family, which
seemed to be the pride and only object for which he lived.
He left a family of four daughters and one son, all comfortably provided for, and this thought seemed to give him great
consolation during his last hours of consciousness. It was in
the domestic relations of life that his kindness and genial
temperament were best illustrated, and none but those who
enjoyed the privilege of that acquaintance can fully appreciate
the loss. He passed away at the age of sixty-six years. Born
October 31, 1814.

E. W. G.

St. Louis, August 24, 1881.

Commodore W. J. Kountz

was born in Columbiana County, Ohio, fifty miles below
Pittsburgh, on the Ohio River, in 1817. He commenced his
river career in 1827, on a keel-boat, owned and commanded
by his brother Hiram. He worked as a subordinate until October, 1832, when he was appointed captain of the keel-boat
Townsman. He continued to hold the positions of captain
and pilot of keel-boats till the fall of 1833, when he engaged
in business in Wellsville, Ohio. He soon tired of business
ashore, and in the spring of 1834, he engaged on coal boats
with Zachary Reno and made a trip, as linesman, to New Orleans. He met an old acquaintance there, and joined him in a
trip up the Yazoo River to cut and raft cypress lumber, for
the New Orleans market. After arriving at the head of the
Yazoo, he camped out, where he contracted the prevailing
diseases of that country, chills and fever, and being dissatisfied
with such experiences, he left this wilderness for Louisville,
where he engaged as an apprentice on a steamboat to learn en-

gineering. When he had mastered this trade he was not satisfied, but in the spring of 1835 he engaged with Johnson Marsh, who was captain of the Patrick Henry, to steer his watch and learn the river as pilot. In 1836 he engaged with Captain Robert Peer to pilot on one of the boats that he controlled, and, accordingly, was placed on the steamboat Ara-

COMMODORE W. J. KOUNTZ.

bian, with Captain Wm. Forsythe. He made one trip from Pittsburgh to Louisville, the boat being destined for St. Louis, and then returned to Pittsburgh, where he took command of the steamer Huntress, and ran her that season from Pittsburgh to Louisville. In 1837 he ran the Huntress from St.

Louis to Galena and Dubuque, which was then the outside of civilization. He gave up the command of the Huntress in the fall of 1837, and assumed the business of piloting. In the summer of 1838, he piloted three keel-boats from Pittsburgh to Louisville, owned by Wm. Vandegrift, and returned home by stage. In December, 1838, he married a daughter of David McKelvy, of Alleghany town, now city. In the spring of 1839, he again shipped as pilot of the steamer Troy, Captain Jas. Adams, and having made one trip to the Wabash River and return, he then shipped on the steamer Czar, Captain Wm. Hale. After piloting on various boats until 1842, he took command of the steamer Galant and ran her from Pittsburgh to Cincinnati, weekly trips, this being the first packet ever in the trade. He quit the river in 1843 and embarked in the grocery business in Alleghany, at which he remained for about 16 months. In 1844 he returned to the river as pilot with Captain John Vandegrift, on the steamer Pinta. He bought one-half of this boat from Clark & Thaw, but sold out in the spring of 1845, and took a position as pilot of the steamer Fulton, employing C. W. Batchellor as an apprentice. The same season he piloted the Prairie Bird, Captain John Vandergrift, with Batchellor accompanying him. He quit the Prairie Bird to take command of the steamer Pilot, the first boat he built. He advised Captain Vandergrift to place Batchellor as pilot of the Prairie Bird, which he did. He commanded the Pilot till the summer of 1846, when he bought the Financier and took command of her. In December, 1846, he bought the New England and took command of her, which boat was selected as the flag vessel of the first fleet of boats that took troops from Pittsburgh to New Orleans, en route to Mexico, General Wynkoop being first and Col. Sam Black, second in command. He commanded the New England during the winter and spring of 1847. During the year of 1847, he built the Yankee, bought the Wyoming and Mt. Vernon, and in turn commanded all of them. In 1849, he built the Aaron Hart and commanded her during the season of 1849, when she burned in New Orleans in October. He took command of the steamer Cincinnati in the spring of 1850. He built and took command of the steamer Luella No. 1, in this same year. He lost his wife in 1851 and afterwards married Miss Peninah Weaver. He took command of the Pittsburgh in November, 1851, and contracted for the Crystal Palace in 1852, and took command of her April, 1853. She was the finest steamboat that ever floated on the Western waters. He remained in command of her until 1856, when she was laid up at Pittsburgh to be dismantled. In 1856 he contracted for the famous steamer, City of Memphis, using the cabin and machinery of the Crystal Palace. It was the largest boat built up to that date. He left Pittsburgh on April 14, 1857, and commanded her with great success until 1858, when he was appointed freight agent of the Illinois Central Railroad at New Orleans, which position he held for one year. He then reassumed command of the City of Memphis, where he remained until the commencement of the war. The newspaper which was published daily on this boat was edited by Jas. Kerr, Jr., who was chief clerk on the City of Memphis. Every passenger found on his plate on the breakfast table this newspaper containing the bill of fare, with the events of the past twenty-four hours. He left New Orleans on the day that Fort Sumter was surrendered and arrived at Cairo, where the crew were paid off. The City of Memphis was laid up at Mound City, and he and his family went to Alleghany, their home. He then went to Cincinnati, where Gen. Geo. B. McClelland was in command of the troops of the State of Ohio, and volunteered his services without compensation to take charge of the river transportation. His services were accepted by McClellan, and at that time he received his title of Commodore. During the time he was in the service he purchased all the steamboats that were converted into gunboats, and also many other boats for transports, and occupied that position until the fall of 1861, when by order of Gen. McClellan, he was sent to St. Louis to take charge of river transportation there, and was ordered from there to Cairo, and from Cairo to Paducah. He resigned his commission, which was accepted April 1, 1862. He then took command of the City of Memphis until he sold her to John Bofinger and others in the fall of 1862. This ended his active service as steamboat captain.

He them bought the Eanny Bullett and Prairie Rose, and had then run in the government service. In 1863 he engaged in the banking business at Pittsburgh, the firm name being Kountz & Martz. In 1863 he built the steamer Carrie and in 1864 built the Katie. In 1865 built Luella No. 2 and bought the Nevada and Steven Bayard. In 1866 he bought the Urilda and Alleghany Belle No. 4. In 1864 retired from the banking business. In 1866 built the W. H. Osborn. In 1867 built Ida Stockdale and bought the Leni Leoti. In 1868 built the Peninah No. 1 and the Andrew Ackley. In 1869 built the Carrie V. Kountz, which burned on her first trip at St. Louis. Built Carrie V. Kountz No. 2 the same year. In 1870 built the Mollie Moore, Henry C. Yeager and rebuilt the Fontenell; 1871 built the John F. Tolle, May Lowry and Katie P. Kountz. In 1875 built the C. W. Meade. In 1879 built the Peninah No. 2 and the E. O. Stanard. In 1877 built the General Custer. In 1878 built the J. B. M. Kehlor, General D. H. Rucker, General Tompkins and John D. Scully.

He organized the Steamboat Captains' Benevolent Association of New Orleans in 1858. Also the Auxiliary Association in St. Louis, Cincinnati, Louisville and Pittsburgh. He held the position of President of the Pittsburgh, Alleghany and Manchester Passenger Railway Co. from 1866 to 1884; with eighteen years under his management the road was a great success.

He has built, owned and controlled more steamboats than any other man on Western and Southern rivers. And after a life of almost unrequiting hard labor, he is now enjoying his much deserved rest, at his home in Alleghany surrounded by a very devoted family.

[Communicated.]

CAPTAIN R. C. GRAY

was born in Alleghany City, Pennsylvania. on September 24th, 1822, and died at Fifth Avenue Hotel, New York, on May 28th, 1888. When he was quite young he went to St. Louis, Missouri, and was engaged with Collier, Pettis & Co. in the wholesale grocery business, and was there two or three years. Then he went as one of the clerks on the steamer Louisville running between St. Louis and New Orleans, and then returned to his old home in Alleghany City.

In 1841 he went on the river with his brother, U. C. Gray, one of the clerks of the steamer Lehigh, and ran from Pittsburgh to St. Louis and New Orleans, and in 1842 his brother U. C. Gray took command of the steamer Evaline and R. C. Gray went with him as clerk. In 1843 he went on the steamer Alleghany with Captain William Dean as clerk, running between Pittsburgh and St. Louis, for one season, and then he bought Captain Dean's interest and took command of the steamer Alleghany and ran here in the packet line between Pittsburgh and Cincinnati. In 1847 he built the steamer Pennsylvania and took charge of her and run her from Pittsburgh to St. Louis for a few years; sold her and built the Paul Anderson and run her from Pittsburgh to St. Louis and New Orleans. Then in 1856 he built the steamer Denmark and took her to St. Louis and run her between St. Louis and St. Paul, as one

ot the boats forming the line between St. Louis and St. Paul.
He also built the steamers Sam Young, Latrobe, and Altoona,
for low water boats between Pittsburgh and Cincinnati, to
connect with Pennsylvania Railroad. In 1860 he built the
steamer Hawkeye State at Pittsburgh and took her to St. Louis
and with the Denmark and Hawkeye State, in connection with
steamer Canada, owned and commanded by Captain James
Ward, Steamer Pembina, owned and commanded by Captain

CAPTAIN R. C. GRAY.

Thomas Griffith, and other steamers, they organized the
Northern Line Packet Co. running between St. Louis and St.
Paul. He then built for the same line the steamers Burling-
ton, Muscatine, Davenport, Minneapolis, Dubuque, Minnesota,
Dan Hine and Lake Superior.

In 1863 he, in connection with Captain M. W. Beltzhoover,
established Gray's Iron Line steamers Little Giant and Rover,
and then building the Ironsides, Iron Mountain, Iron Age,
Iron Duke and Resolute. These boats were engaged in towing

barges transporting iron and steel rails and Pittsburgh's manufactured articles on them from Pittsburgh to points on the Ohio and Mississippi River and tributaries, and iron ore on their return trips.

At the time of Captain Gray's death, he was president of the People's National Bank, Pittsburgh, and a director of the Keystone Bank and also director of the Boatman's Insurance Co., and M. and M. Insurance Co. and of the Pittsburgh Alleghany and Manchester Passenger Railway and of the Alleghany General Hospital and largely interested in the Black Diamond Steel Works."

None knew Captain Gray but to honor and admire his nobility of character and his genial sympathizing nature.

His record illustrates his enterprise, and those who knew him well, will bear willing testimony to his benevolence, of which he has left the best possible proof, in the liberal contribution for the support of the Alleghany General Hospital, as well as the many previous contributions to that and many other worthy objects of charity.

He was unostentatious and retiring and only those who knew him well could appreciate the quiet, genial exuberance of his nature.

He was firm and prsevering in his purposes and the large fortune he left abundantly proves the sagacity of his perceptions.

Among all the old boatmen who have launched their barges and spread their sails on the broad waters of eternity, I know of none that have left better evidence of their ability to safely and successfully resume and conduct the voyage which awaits all mariners who weigh anchor and cross the dark river.

Capt. Gray never married, but was a great admirer of ladies, and very popular with all and a genial companion.

He passed away at the age of 66, mourned by all who knew his many virtues.

CAPTAIN GRAY'S IRON LINE OF BARGES.

L. T. BELT.

The subject of this sketch was born March 19, 1825, in St. Clair County, Illinois, on the spot where now stands the town of Lebanon. His father, Horatio N. Belt, was born near Baltimore, Md., 1796, fought in the war of 1812, and took part in the battle of New Orleans under Gen. Andrew Jackson ; went to St. Clair County, Illinois, in 1819. The mother of L. T. Belt, Mary Jane West, born in South Carolina in 1805, moved to St. Clair County, Illinois, in 1822.

L. T. B.'S CAREER.

Early years passed on a farm, where he acquired habits of industry and economy, attending him through life. River experience commenced in 1840 on Illinois River, " keel-boating; commenced steamboating in 1845 on steamer " Tioga. In 1847, he and his brother, Francis T. Belt, purchased the steamer Planter, running her in the St. Louis and New Orleans

trade. Her boilers exploded February 3, 1848, at Twelve-mile
Island, Illinois River, killing or wounding most of her passengers and officers. Both owners were badly injured. Upon recovering they rebuilt this boat. She was afterwards blown
to pieces by a hurricane while lying up at St. Louis. In
January, 1850, Capt. Belt was married to Miss Elizabeth W.
Wolff of St. Louis, sister of M. A. Wolff, the noted real estate agent, and of Geo. C. Wolff, the most widely known
steamboatman of his time. In 1852 and 1853 Capt. Belt was
engaged in merchandising in the town of Fieldon, Illinois.
He then became connected with the Kingston Coal Co., on
the Illinois River, having charge of the transportation from
LaSalle to St. Louis. After engaging in many enterprises,
covering a long period, he became President of the St. Louis
and Illinois River Packet Company.

In 1879 he entered the Bayou Teche trade, Louisiana, with
the steamer Jno. M. Chambers. He has remained identified
with that trade up to the present time, being now President and
Superintendent of the New Orleans and Bayou Teche Packet
Company. His last and best boat, the steamer Teche, is the
most complete boat of her class in the South. During his
busy career, Capt. Belt has served, either as clerk, pilot, mas-
ter or owner of the following boats: Tioga, Planter, Kings-
ton, Movestar, Saluda, Ocean Wave, Challenge, Mary C.,
Americus, Sam Gaty, City of Pekin, Brazil, Beardstown, La-
Salle, Belle of Alton, Illinois, Tyrone, Isabel, Utah, Walter
B. Dance, Post Boy, Arabian, Iowa, Lady Lee, George C.
Wolff, City of Memphis, Edward Walsh, Olive Branch, Lady
Gay, Glencoe, Cornelia, Atlantic, P. W. Strader, Jas. H.
Whitelaw, J. M. Chambers, Key West, Ashland, Sunbeam and
Teche. Capt. B. served from 1873 to 1876 as County Treasurer of St. Louis, Missouri. Besides his steamboat interest,
he is engaged in the coal business, being senior member of
the firm of L. T. Belt & Co. Has not been out of active business a day in forty-five years, has lost only twenty-seven days
from sickness, and no man of his age is better preserved, men
tally and physically. Was one of eight brothers and four sisters, of whom four brothers and one sister are living. Filial
affection is a strong trait with Capt. B. For the twenty years
previous to her death he never, but once, no matter how great
the distance, failed to visit his aged mother on her birthday.
Is an active and honored member of the M. E. Church South,
being President of the Board of Trustees, member of the Board
of Stewards, and Superintendent of the Sabbath-school in
Rayne Memorial Church, New Orleans.   .

CLAIBORNE GREENE WOLFF,

familiarly called " George " by his friends, was born at Louis-
ville, Ky., March 17th, 1829. He was the son of Abraham
Wolff, a native of London, England, and of Susan Franklin,
of Louisville, Ky. The subject of this sketch was one of three
brothers, and four sisters. The only surviving brother is
Marcus A. Wolff, of St. Louis. The four sisters, Mrs. James
Hurley and Mrs. Josie Page, of St. Louis ; Mrs. George H.
Lee, of San Francisco, and Mrs. L. T. Belt, of New Orleans,
are all living at this time (1889). From his earliest years,
Mr. Wolff evinced a predilection for " the river," and this
fondness for river pursuits followed him through life. He
began his river career when a mere youth, and being faithful
and efficient, his services were in constant demand. In 1848

he served as pantryman on the famous steamboat Convoy, commanded by Captain, afterwards Commodore, C. K. Garrison. Mr. Wolff always alluded to this with pardonable pride. He left the latter position to accept that of steward on the ill-fated steamer Planter, where he remained until the vessel was wrecked by a storm in the summer of 1851. Mr. Wolff was one of the officers of the Ocean Spray, on the occasion of her celebrated race with the fleet Hannibal City. When the Ocean Spray took fire above St. Louis, at Bissell's Point, and burned to the water's edge, and a large number of lives were lost, Mr. Wolff proved himself a true hero, and, aided by his great swimming powers, he rescued many persons from what seemed certain death. He afterwards became associated with the Illinois River Packet Co., and remained with it until its dissolution. While he was with this company the steamer Geo. C. Wolff, named after him, was built and equipped under his supervision.

In 1861 he formed a copartnership with Mr. Geo. A. Hynes, of St. Louis, under the firm name of Wolff & Hynes, liquor dealers. This house transacted an enormous business at one time, owning the " bars " or thirty boats, including all those of the celebrated Atlantic and Mississippi S. S. Co.'s Line.

Several years before his death Mr. Wolff's health became impaired. Accompanied by his faithful brother " Mark," he passed one season in Colorado, in hope that the invigorating climate of that region would effect a cure. The insidious disease, consumption, could only be checked, however, and on October 18th, 1881, there passed away one of the bravest and gentlest spirits the world has ever known, at the age of 52, leaving a widow and one married daughter.

Mr. Wolff was a remarkable man in many ways. His memory was remarkable, and his mind was filled with steamboat statistics and reminiscences sufficient to fill volumes. Self-sacrificing to a fault, he never spared himself when a good deed was to be done. His highest delight was in alleviating the sorrows of others, while his own misfortunes were endured in silence. He was literally the poor man's friend. His great heart was easily moved to sympathy, and distress never appealed to him in vain. He was a consistent member of the Baptist Church, and died in the full belief of a blessed immortality.

He sleeps amid the peaceful shades of Bellefontaine Cemetery, St. Louis, and his ashes repose beneath a monument erected by his many friends. Carved thereon, in enduring marble, is the representation of a Mississippi River steamboat, fitting symbol of his chosen and idolized vocation. Surely the world is better for his having lived.

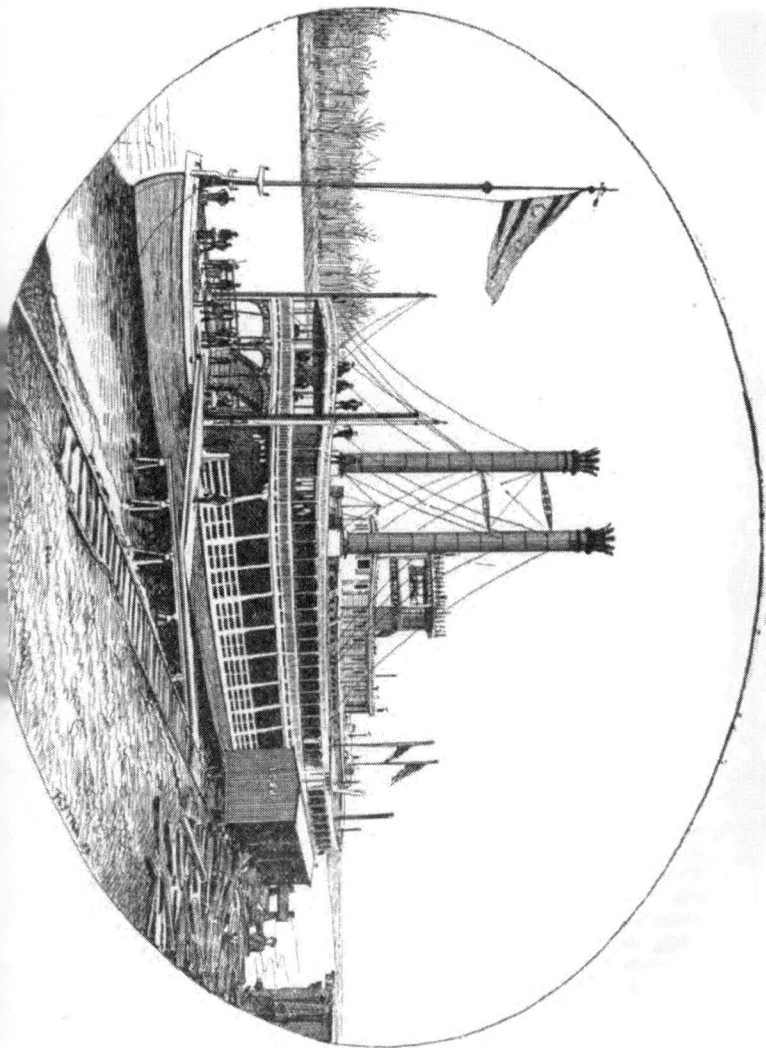

CAPTAIN JAMES DOZIER.

Capt. James Dozier was born in Nash County, N. C., Jan. 7, 1806, the son of Thomas Dozier, and descended from an old and well-known Virginia family. Of Capt. Dozier's boyhood little is recorded, but that he was of a stirring and adventurous spirit may be inferred from the fact that when but eighteen years old he migrated to the West, his only attendant being Peter, a negro boy, whom his father had given him. The journey, which was undertaken by land, was a toilsome one, there being no railroads then, and only a few primitive steamboats. He settled near Paris, Tenn., where, after a short season spent in farming, he commenced the mercantile business in a small way, and followed this pursuit several years with excellent success, having gained the confidence of all with whom he came in contact.

In 1826, Mr. Dozier married Miss Mary A. Dudgeon, the daughter of John Dudgeon, originally of Virginia, but later of near Lexington, Ky., where most of his family were born. In 1828, accompanied by his father-in-law and family, and two other families of that neighborhood, he emigrated to Missouri, settling in the upper part of St. Louis County, near the Virginia settlement of the Tylers and Colemans, families whose descendants are among the leading people of that locality. Here Capt. Dozier and Mr. Dudgeon, his father-in-law, leased the old McAllister tan-yard, and operated it with success for some years, when Capt. Dozier retired and resumed the mercantile business. He continued in this employment for a few years, and finally removed to the north side of the Missouri River, into St. Charles County, where he lived for many years. Here he laid the foundation of his subsequent fortune, conducting a flourishing business as a merchant and farmer, and became one of the leading men of that region. By frugality and industry he accumulated a large estate, consisting of lands, stock, etc., and in doing so was greatly aided by the most estimable of wives, of whom it was justly said that "she was a bee that brought a good deal of honey to that hive."

In 1844, Mr. Dozier engaged in the steamboat business, and owned and operated successively the Warsaw, Lake of the Woods, St. Louis Oak, Cora, Mary Blane, and Elvira (a boat of much reputation in her day, and named for his second daughter). Later, he or his sons owned the Rowena, Thomas E. Tutt, Mollie Dozier, etc. There are doubtless many old steamboatmen yet living in whom the mention of the names of these vessels will awaken the most interesting recollections. Those were the palmy days of steamboating on the Missouri River, and the vessels owned by Capt. Dozier made his name widely known along that stream and its tributaries, and everywhere respected as a synonym of all that was honest and straightforward. He was a contemporary and acquaintance of Capts. Roe, Throckmorton, La Barge, Eaton, Kaiser, and others, most of whom he survived.

In 1854, Capt. Dozier retired from the river to his country home, where he built a fine residence near the river bank. A more beautiful place or a better improved farm, or rather set of farms, could, perhaps, not have been found on the Missouri River than that of Capt. Dozier, at "Dozier's Landing." His house was ever open to his friends and neighbors, and for the twenty years he lived in St. Charles County was seldom without some visitors. His charities to the poor and orphans were of the most generous character, and his house at times

was the home of many unfortunates. In his numerous bene-
factions he was wholly free from ostentation, and the world
never knew of most of his deeds of benevolence. Capt.
Dozier was an owner of slaves, but a kind and thoughtful
master.

Immediately after the war he removed to St. Louis, and in
1867 formed a partnership with the long-established and well
known baker, Joseph Garneau, in the bakery business. In
1872 this firm was dissolved, and Capt. Dozier then founded
the present large baking establishment of the Dozier-Weyl
Cracker Company, than which perhaps no manufacturing establishment in America is better known, it being probably the
largest cracker-factory in the world.

Capt. Dozier died July 15, 1878, after but a few hour's
illness. For more than twenty years he had been a consistent member of the Methodist Episcopal Church South, and
enjoyed the confidence and respect of the members of that
communion, by whom his counsels were prized and his example is held in affectionate remembrance. As a citizen, he
stood very high, yet his real worth was appreciated only by
those who knew him intimately, for his nature was reserved,
and while his friends embraced all with whom he was ever
brought into business or social relations, comparatively few
were privileged to thoroughly know and comprehend his character. As a business man, though reticent, he was quick to
decide and equally quick to act, and his judgment was clear
and seldom at fault. Consequently he left to his family a
good heritage, the accumulation of a lifetime of economy and
upright dealing, but he bequeathed also what they prize far
more, the life record of a good citizen, a loving husband, and
a wise and tender father.

HENRY A. EALER.

NEW ORLEANS, March 24, 1889.

Captain E. W. Gould, St. Louis, Mo.:

Please find enclosed memorandum of names of the principal steamboats I have been engaged on as master or pilot
since my connection with the waters of the Mississippi Valley.

I was born in Allentown, Pennsylvania, in 1820. At the
age of twelve I sailed from Baltimore for Rio Janerio, on the
brig Sultan, with Capt. Willis. Returning from there in the
spring of 1835, I went to St. Louis and shipped on the steamboat John Nelson, with Capt. John P. Moore. Subsequently,

Capt. John Carlisle took command of the boat, and I made an arrangement with him to learn to be a pilot to New Orleans.

In 1839 I commenced standing a watch in the New Orleans trade.

In 1841 I was promoted to the captancy of the steamer Telegraph.

Later on I was pilot on the Alton, with Capt. John Simonds; on the Boonslick, with Capt. John R. Shaw; on the Maid

HENRY A. EALER.

of Orleans and the Harry of the West, with Capt. Van Houtan; on the Algonquin, with Capt. Hiram Kountz; Alex Scott, Capt. John C. Swan; Express Mail, Capt. Wm. Kountz; Convoy, Capt. C. K. Garrison; Joan of Arc, Bulletin and John Simonds, with Capt. C. B. Church; Duke of Orleans, with Capt. Holmes; Pawnee and Highlander, with Capt. E. H. Gleim.

I was master of the single engine steamer St. Louis, then on the Eudora, then on the Princeton, in the New Orleans and Ouachita River trade. In 1851 I built the H. D. Bacon, and in 1856 the steamer Planet and J. H. Oglesby.

Subsequently I resumed piloting, and have been pilot on more than one hundred different steamboats during my experience.

The Wyoming, Capt. Henry Keath, was the last boat I was engaged on in the capacity of a pilot.

I shall never forget the many pleasant years I have spent on the Mississippi River and its tributaries, nor the many genial officers of steamboats who it has been my privilege to associate with in all these long years.

I must not forget to say I was pilot on one of Admiral Faragut's gunboats that went up the Mississippi above Vicksburg, drawing eighteen feet of water, in 1862.

Trusting my recollections may awaken pleasant reminiscences in the minds of some of your readers

I remain yours truly,

HENRY A. EALER.

P. S. — Inclosed please find my *photo* which, if agreeable, I should like inserted in your forthcoming work.

H. A. E.

CAPTAIN JAMES WARD

was born at Southerly, Norfolk County, England, on the 22 of December, 1814.

His father was a boatman in the native place of the subject of this sketch.

His mother's maiden name was Hannah Porter. The early life of James presented but few advantages and to his own exertions, his habits of industry and strict integrity may be attributed his success in life.

To-day one of the prosperous merchants of St. Louis, honored and respected by his acquaintances, he stands deservedly high as a self-made man. He had but a small share of school advantages, and at the age of 12 was put to work in the ship-yard at Southerly, to learn boat-building with his elder brother. Here he remained nine years, when he emigrated to America, landing in New York, May 1st, 1836. He went to Brownsville, Penn., and worked in the ship yard until September 1837, when he shipped on the steamboat Fayette, as carpenter, where he continued in the Pittsburgh and Louisville

trade until the middle of the next summer, when he went to
Wheeling, Virginia, veiwing the lower trade as better suited
to his business, and as offering better facilities for rising in
the world. Mr. Ward moved to St. Louis in November,
1838, and settled there.

He first worked at his trade in the ship-yard, and afterwards shipped on the steamer Ione as carpenter.

CAPTAIN JAMES WARD.

He subsequently worked in the same capacity on the steamer
Amaranth, until the fall of 1843.

In the spring of 1844, in company with Hiram Berzie, Wm.
Cupps, and James Megan, he built the steamer St. Croix
and ran her in the Galena trade until 1847, serving all that
time as mate.

He then sold his interest in her and with two others, built
the steamer St. Peters and ran her in the Galena and

Dubuque trade. After the first year he served as captain and built up considerable reputation as an officer of first-class administrative ability. This steamer was burned at the levee in St. Louis in the great fire of 1849. That fall he purchased the steamer Financier and that winter bought and commanded the steamer Excelsior in the St. Louis and St. Paul trade until the fall of 1855. Selling her, he was captain on the York State, the same season but traded her for the Connestoga for the same trade in 1857.

The same summer he built two steamers, the Canada and the Pembina, at Pittsburgh, himself filling the position as captain on the Canada. These steamers he put in the same trade in 1858, and thus made the nucleus of the Northern Line Packet Co., whose boats ran from St. Louis to St. Paul.

For the immense trade that has sprung up from this beginning, and which has so materially added to the commercial prosperity of St. Louis, that city is indebted to Capt. Ward.

The directors were Thos. H. Griffith, Darins, Hunkins, R. C. Gray, T. B. Rhodes, Thos. Gordon, J. W. Parker, all being owners.

At this time they owned the Denmark, Henry Clay, Metropolitan, Wm. S. Ewing, Minnesota Belle, Hawkeye State, and Sucker State, and run three boats per week from St. Louis.

The Northern Line Packet Co. was organized under the laws of Illinois, in 1860, and had its principal office at East St. Louis, with a capital stock of $300,000. They then purchased boats enough to make a daily line. For the first three years Capt. Ward acted as president of the line. Subsequently he was superintendent. In 1868–69 he was again elected president, but soon after sold his stock, and retired from the river, and engaged in the ship chanderling business in St. Louis, in company with his son and another gentleman, under the firm name of Ward & Brady, where they still carry on an extensive business in the same line.

Capt. Ward congratulates himself upon the fact that in his long experience as master of many steamboats, no lives were lost, and but one boat, which was burned in the great fire in St. Louis in 1849. He has for many years been an active Mason and a member in good standing in the order of Knights Templar.

In 1847 he married Miss Annie Johnston, of St. Louis, whose parents emigrated from Ireland at an early day, and settled there. They have five children, viz.: Hannah, now Mrs. Wm. H. Owings ; Thomas H., now engaged in business

with his father; Mary E., Lillie H., and Ella S. now living
with their parents in St. Louis.

Capt. Ward has never been an active politician, but his
sympathies are with the Democratic party, to whose principals he still adheres. He was raised in the Episcopal church
and still associates with that denomination as a member in
good standing.

Burris D. Wood.

[Communicated.]

Capt. Burr. D. Wood was born in Pittsburgh, March 15,
1836. His father, Jonathan H. Wood, being a prominent
boat-builder of that city, whose death occurred in 1849. The
mother, Mrs. Wood, a grand old lady, is still living in the
homestead at Pittsburgh at the age of 75 years. Capt. Wood

has five brothers, John A., the wealthy coal operator of Pittsburgh; James O., associated in business with him; Jonathan H., a prominent tow-boatman; David D., who is blind, and W. Murph, in charge of a large tug and coal fleet in the New Orleans harbor. Capt. B. D. Wood, at 16 years, was apprenticed to a nail manufacturer, which trade he worked at for 13 years. In 1866 he went to New Orleans to establish the coal business, and in 1871 had established the firm of B. D. Wood & Bros., with a branch house at Baton Rouge, La. At this time, Capt. Wood is at the head of a large and flourishing coal business, with a branch house at Plaquemine, La., under the name of B. D. Wood & Sons, his sons, Will H. and Elmer E., being associated with him in business. Capt. Wood is the chairman of the executive committee on the improvement of the Western water-Ways, and was the moving spirit of the river improvement conventions held at St. Louis, New Orleans, St. Paul, Washington, D. C., Kansas City and Memphis, and in furtherance of the objects of which has appeared frequently before the committees of the United States Senate and House, to urge the propriety and necessity of appropriations for the improvements of rivers and harbors. Capt. Wood is also a member of the river improvement committee of the New Orleans Cotton Exchange and of the Board of Trade. He is also the first vice-president of the National Board of Steam Navigation, and has been diligent and conspicuous in the workings of that board. He was a member of the finance committee of the World's Industrial and Cotton Centennial Exposition of 1885, and Director-General of the North, South and Central Americas Exposition. Capt. Wood has been married twice, his first wife, deceased, was Miss Minnie Widney, daughter of the late Charles Widney, of Pittsburgh; his second wife, to whom he was married in 1877, was Miss Emma Phillips, daughter of Henry H. Phillips, a prominent citizen of Pennsylvania, who died at Baton Rouge in 1878. Mrs. Wood's untiring energy, intelligence, and refinement are always prominent in works of charity and temperance. She is the vice-president of the Woman's Christian Temperance Union, also one of the board of managers of the Christian Woman's Exchange, and of the Woman's Memorial Home. Capt. Wood is distinctly a self-made man, of high standing as a Mason, and who by his energy, integrity, manliness, genial warmth of nature, spirit of enterprise, and a studied regard for the prosperity of the city of his adoption, has become the center of a host of prominent river and business men of New Orleans.

CAPT. T. P. LEATHERS.

[From New Orleans *Picayune*, Dec., 1888.]

Captain Thomas P. Leathers was born in Kenton county, Ky., on May 24, 1816. He was the fourth son of a family of five boys and four girls. His father, John Leathers, one of the pioneers of Kentucky, was for years a tobacconist and farmer in Kenton county, five miles from the Ohio river, and owned a number of slaves.

Captain Leathers formed a liking for the river at an early age, and in 1836 he commenced his successful river career with his brother, Captain John Leathers, as mate on the Yazoo river steamer Sunflower, which position he held until 1840. He and his brother then built the Princess No. 1 and ran her in the Yazoo River trade, and later in the New Orleans, Natchez and Vicksburg trade. They then built the steamers Princess Nos. 2 and 3 for the same trade and ran them with great success for several years. In 1845 Captain T. P. Leathers built the first of the series of steamers Natchez at the mouth of Crawfish bayou, the hull by S. W. Hartshorne and the machinery by Anthony Harkness. She was a very fast two-boiler boat, with 20-inch cylinders, 8 feet stroke. This boat he ran in the New Orleans and Vicksburg trade as a Saturday packet until 1848, when finding that the increase of business demanded a larger boat, he sold her to Captain John Pierce. He then contracted with Burton Hazen of Cincinnati for the the Natchez No. 2. This boat had 3 boilers and 24-inch cylinders, with 8 feet stroke, and also proved very fast.

Captain Leathers ran the second Natchez until 1852, when he sold her and contracted with Cincinnati parties for a much larger and finer boat, the Natchez No. 3. She had 6 boilers and 34-inch cylinders, with 9 feet stroke, and had a carrying capacity of 4,000 bales of cotton. The career of the Natchez No. 3 was very short, as she had run only six weeks when she burned in February, 1853, during the great fire at the wharf in front of this city, which originated on the Belcher and destroyed some ten or twelve boats. Captain Leathers' brother James was asleep in the texas of the Natchez at the time the fire broke out and perished in the flames.

Soon after the destruction of the Natchez No. 3 Captain Leathers proceeded to Cincinnati and built the Natchez No. 4, a 6-boiler boat with 34-inch cylinders, 9 feet stroke. She had a capacity of 4,400 bales. The No. 4 Captain Leathers ran successfully until 1859, when he built at Cincinnati the Natchez No. 5, with the same power and a capacity of 5,000 bales of cotton. She was also very fast, and ran up to the eve of the surrender of New Orleans, when she was taken to the Yazoo River and was destroyed by the Confederates at Honey Island, 150 miles above Yazoo City. Captain Buchanan, after the war, wrecked what remained of this steamer, under instructions of Captain James B. Eads, and for which Captain Leathers got judgment against Captain Eads for $20,000. The money, however, he failed to collect.

During the war Captain Leathers remained away from the river. After the declaration of peace and the resumption of business Captain Leathers became interested successively in the Magenta and General Quitman, and ran them in the New Orleans and Vicksburg trade. The Quitman sunk in 1868 at Morgan's Landing. On top of the pilot-house of the steamer Quitman was a statue of General Quitman, which was saved from the wreck and now stands on the warehouse at New Texas Landing, a monument to the memory of the faithful craft. The steamer Magenta was destroyed by fire at this city while in charge of Captain J. Stut Neal.

Captain Leathers, in 1869, built the Natchez No. 6. Her hull was constructed by the Cincinnati Marine Ways, cabin by Elias Ealer, boilers by C. T. Dumont and machinery by the Niles works. She had eight boilers and 34-inch cylinders, 10 feet stroke, and had a capacity of 5,500 bales. During her career of nine and a half years in the New Orleans and Vicksburg trade she made 401 trips without an accident causing a single loss of life. This steamer was made famous by her great race with the steamer Robert E. Lee from New Orleans to St. Louis.

In 1879, the present steamer Natchez, which is the seventh of that name built by Captain Leathers, was launched at Cincinnati, and is one of the most substantial and elegant steamers ever constructed for the Western or Southern waters, and is reputed to be the fastest on the Mississippi River. Her dimensions are: length, 303½ feet; beam 46½ feet; depth of hold, 10 feet. She has eight steel boilers 36 feet long and 43 inches in diameter, containing two flues each, 15¾ inches in diameter. Her cylinders are 34 inches in diameter, with 10 feet stroke. Her boilers and machinery were furnished by C. T. Dumont. She has a carrying capacity of about 6,000 bales of cotton. This boat Captain Leathers ran successfully until about two years ago, when he laid her up owing to the falling off of river business, and built the steamer T. P. Leathers, a stern-wheel boat, to take her place as a Saturday packet in the Vicksburg trade. The T. P. Leathers is a 4500-bale boat and the fastest of her inches afloat. At the commencement of the busy season this year Captain Leathers, finding that the prospects were good for a fine trade, again started the Natchez out, and now has her running as a Tuesday packet to Greenville, the T. P. Leathers leaving here every Saturday for Vicksburg.

Captain Leathers for many years has been considered authority on all river matters, and his counsel has frequently been sought after by prominent men in the country. In

1874 he appeared before the committee on waterways in Washington, D. C., in 1875 before the senate committee, and in 1882 before the commerce committee, on which occasions his views on river improvements were asked and given.   At the waterways convention, held in this city during the late exposition, Captain Leathers also made a lengthy speech on the improvement of rivers.   Captain Leathers is over 6 feet in height and large in proportion, and though carrying the weight of over three score and ten winters, is still hale and hearty and looks good for many more years of usefulness.

NINE STEAMERS NAMED NATCHEZ.

The first steamboat named Natchez was built in New York in 1823 for the New Orleans and Natchez trade, where she continued to run until 1832.   She had a low pressure engine of the Watt & Burton type, with walking beam and condensor. She measured 366 tons.   She was commanded by Captain H. S. Buckner, of New Orleans.

The second boat called Natchez was also built in New York. She was a regular sea-going boat, intended to run between that city and Natchez.   She was built in 1836 and partially owned in Natchez, but proved to be too heavy draught for the trade and was finally sold to the Brazilian government and converted into a war steamer, for which she was better adapted.   This writer recollects finding her aground at Natchez Island on one occasion drawing 12 feet, which was more water than there was at that point.   After working to relieve her several hours with the steamer Knickerbocker, we produced no more effect than an ordinary tug boat would on the *Great Eastern* and left in disgust.   She was subsequently lighted off and retired from the trade.

The third Natchez was built by Captain Leathers in 1845, who subsequently built six others.

The last, or ninth one, sunk at Lake Providence, in February, 1889.

NEW ORLEANS AND VICKSBURG PACKET NATCHEZ

CAPTAIN JOSEPH BROWN.

ST. LOUIS, Mo., April, 1889.

Captain E. W. Gould:

MY DEAR SIR — I have your favor of the 19th inst, suggesting that I write for your forthcoming book, some of my experiences as a riverman.

I would willingly do anything in my power to assist you in your undertaking, but whether I shall be able to interest the general reader is the question.

However, at the risk of being thought egotistical, I will give a short outline of my early interest in, and subsequent connection with steamboating on the Mississippi River.

In 1834 my father moved West to St. Louis, bringing myself, then quite a small boy, with several other children; but not liking St. Louis, it being situated then in a slave State, and as Alton was at that time a rival of St. Louis, he moved there, taking me, of course, along with the family.

I early developed a great taste for the river, and though a small boy, spent much of my time on the wharf, noticing the boats, and their comings and goings.

At that time Alton was considered the head of navigation for New Orleans boats, and in some cases the upper river boats stopped at Alton and went back to Galena and other points without going to St. Louis at all, some of the New Orleans boats, as well as some of the up river boats, belonging exclusively to Alton. Nearly all the boats at that time had but one engine and no docter (so called) but pumped the water into the boilers with a pump attached to the main engine, which, when the boat was lying at the bank, the water wheels had to be unshipped, so as to let the engine work the pump, without moving the wheels while the boat was at the wharf; and it was this troublesome way of supplying water into the boilers together with the unchecked amount of steam carried that caused so many explosions.

At that time, say from 1836 to 1840, all traffic and travel was carried on by boat, there being no railroads in the West, and but one or two in the East, consequently the boats were generally crowded with freight and passengers, and particularly, as the largest boats of that day only carried about four or five hundred tons, and the cabin, if they had any, was on the main deck, and aft of the shaft back at the stern, and I can well remember when the first *upper cabin* steamers were built, that

they were advertised as "the splendid *upper cabin* steamers,"
&c.

About that time, and while I was still a boy, every boat had,
or gave out from the escapement of its steam, its own peculiar sound, and taking the deep interest in them that I did, I
could tell the name of nearly any boat in the night by the

CAPTAIN JOSEPH BROWN.

ound of the escapement. At that time there were no whistles
and no government regulations for boats meeting each other,
though the bell was unsatisfactorily used to designate which
side each boat wanted to take, and there was even a time when
hat was not used.

I remember in the years 1836-7, when still a boy, and alive
to all that pertained to steamboats, that two steamers more

43

particularly attracted my attention. One was the Paul Jones, and the other the Champion. The latter was a low-pressure steamer with a walking-beam engine, and as she would near the landing one of her firemen would mount the walking-beam and with a flag in his hand would wave it to the admiring crowd. I then thought if I could ever be in that man's place I would be the biggest man in the town.

The first steamer I became interested in was the Luella, a small boat only 100 feet long, but with an engine in her that had belonged to, or been in a New Orleans boat, and as the power was quite large for the Luella, it made her very fast, so that she was the fastest boat of her day running *above* St. Louis.

While interested in her, an opposition boat was put in the Alton and St. Louis trade against her, and the result was that the price of passage was put down by the Luella company from seventy-five cents each way to ten cents for twenty-five miles, with supper coming up.

That state of things lasted nine months, loosing a good deal of money by both parties, when a compromise was effected, and in a short time the far famed Altona was built.

I made the contracts and superintended the building of her, and when it was time to decide how much boiler power she was to have, the foundry men and engine builders said four boilers would make her the fastest boat above St. Louis. I said put in one more and make her the fastest boat on the river, and she was. I have landed her several times from Alton to St. Louis (25 miles) from wharf to wharf in fifty-six minutes, and she made the trip from St. Louis to Alton, against a five-mile current, in one hour and thirty-seven minutes, time that has never been beaten, and as there are now government restrictions on the amount of steam carried, her time never will be beaten.

I made it a point to run the steamer Altona from St. Louis to Alton just as long (in winter) as the ice floated, and often while the St. Louis ferry-boats were tied to the bank, and when no boat was arriving or leaving St. Louis but herself; and the result was, she paid for herself in just one year, at which time the Chicago & Alton Railroad purchased her at her original cost and run her in connection with that road, which then terminated at Alton. It would be hardly worth while to go into an account of all the steamers I have run, built, or been interested in, but among the most pleasurable trades that I ever ran in were the St. Louis & Keokuk and St. Louis & New Orleans trades. There was, during those years that I steamboated, not only a profit but a pleasure, — an exhilaration in the business, a constant change of scene, of faces and circumstances, and I knew then of nothing more exhilarating, or more enjoyable than to run one of the finest and fastest steamers on the Mississippi River. When, after a day or two's laborious work on the levee, probably in the broiling sun, I knew of no greater pleasure than to see the boat headed up stream with a good cargo and a full register of passengers and to stand on the hurricane roof and see her plow the water " like a thing of life."

Probably the finest boat that I ever built was the Mayflower, in 1854, a very large and fine steamer. She and the John Simonds were the only three-deckers ever built for the Mississippi River, the 3rd or middle deck being between the main and the boiler-deck, and intended for deck or steerage passengers, but emigration by New Orleans becoming checked, I afterwards altered her for a cotton boat, so that the middle deck was taken out and the boat put in the Memphis and New Orleans trade, where she was set on fire and burned, lying at the wharf at Memphis, by the steamer Geo. Collier, landing alongside of her while on fire, so as to save her own passengers.

It must not be understood, that during all the forty or fifty years of my life I did nothing but run steamboats, for both before and after I had satisfied my taste for steamboating, I was interested in *lines* of steamboats, the most notable of which was the Atlantic & Mississippi Steamship Company, in 1866, of which I was one of the Presidents; consisting of some 28 steamers that plied between St. Louis and New Orleans. This line consisted of many very splendid steamers, but the company was formed out of steamers owned by individuals who managed to put them into the company at very high prices, and the result was the company started under a load of debt which it never could pay, and that, together with the fact that the business of the South had not at that time sufficiently recovered from the effects of the war to sustain a line of that magnitude.

So that, after a struggle of three or four years to pay out, and failing, the line which had lost eleven steamers by explosion and other accidents, and without insurance, was placed in the hands of Mr. W. J. Lewis, now deceased, and myself to sell and pay the debts, which was fully done, but the stockholders got little or nothing, a stock of some two millions of dollars having been sunk. However, in justice to myself, I must say I was not connected with it as an officer at its inception or at its close, but was a loser as a stockholder to the extent of about seventy thousand dollars.

Nor must it be thought from what I have said, that steamboating in those days was all ease, comfort and pleasure. Far from it; I have run a steamboat into New Orleans (the St. Louis), when the death rate from yellow fever was over 100 a day, and that, too when, more than half the population had fled the city. I have been on a boat when over sixty died from cholera on the trip up (seven days). Of narrow escape I might fill a volume. I will relate one: I was commanding the Jennie Deans in the New Orleans trade when we carried 180 pounds of steam to the square inch, and had it at the time when she picked up a snag that came up through the lower guard, straddled the copper steam pipe and bent it up through the boiler-deck, until it hemmed in a man in his berth, so that when the boat was stopped he had to climb over the bent pipe to get out of his berth, and yet the pipe did not burst and we ran to St. Louis (800, miles) with the bent pipe, but not with 180 pounds of steam as may be supposed.

Writing of the Jennie Deans, it might be well to relate a feat that I accomplished with her that never was accomplished with or by any other boat in the palmiest days of steamboating.

She was built for the Keokuk trade, but I conceived the idea of running her to New Orleans in the winter months, and as she only carried about 750 tons she could not compete in carrying freight with boats carrying double her capacity and be as many days making the trip, so I conceived the notion of whipping her through both ways and made twelve trips to and from St. Louis and New Orleans in *eleven days* for the round trip, going into each port and coming out the same day and making 2,480 miles in eleven days. I have been on boats that have sunk and burned, but never on one that exploded, but I have come up with them soon after an explosion and seen their officers and passengers by the dozen, — yes, I might say by the hundred, almost flayed alive, and begging that their friends would shoot them. The class of men commanding steamboats on the Western rivers greatly improved in later years, not in goodness of heart, but in outward conduct and expression.

I will cite a conversation that occurred on a boat in the early times. It was the Autocrat, Captain Goslee.

It was while the boat was on her upward trip from New Orleans to Memphis, she being in the, cotton trade (so called).

The Autocrat was a *seven* boiler boat, and said to be a great wood consumer.

The boat happened to be lying at a "wood pile" on the Tennessee side, taking in a large lot of light cottonwood fuel when a country passenger came up to the captain, who was leisurely whittling a stick, and watching the deck hands take on the wood. The country passenger said to the captain, "Captain, how much wood will this boat burn in 24 hours," "O!" said the captain, "of good hard oak wood, about seventy cords." "O! well, but," said the countryman, "how much of *this* kind of wood, this dry cottonwood." "O!" said the captain, "of this kind of wood, it would be just like throwing shavings into h—l!" Another:—

Commodore Garrison, the millionaire, who died not long ago in New York, and brother of R. Garrison & Brothers in St. Louis, built partly with his own hands the Convoy, and ran her from St. Louis to New Orleans, and one trip we had a number of young ladies on board who played a trick on him, using a greenhorn to accomplish it, their object being to get the "drinks" for the crowd onto the captain, so they told the greenhorn to go to the captain and make a bargain with him, to let him ring the large bell for the next town, which happened to be Memphis, and when he got the privilege, not to stop ringing until they told him, and they would pay all the cost; so the captain, not suspecting the joke, agreed for $5 to let the greenhorn, as he thought, ring the bell on nearing Memphis; in the meantime the young ladies were standing around enjoying the joke, and after the captain had told the greenhorn to ring and thought he had rung enough to let the people of Memphis know a boat was coming, he turned to him and told him to stop, that that would do, but the greenhorn had been put up to it, and said, "O, no, I'm not ready to stop yet," when the young ladies set up a loud laugh. In the meantime a large crowd had collected on the wharf at Memphis to see why the boat continued so long ringing the bell.

The captain, seeing he was victimized, first offered him his money back to stop, then ten dollars, then twenty, and to treat the crowd on the boat besides, and finally a compromise was effected by including the crowd on the wharf.

It must be borne in mind that in the early days of steamboating there were few or no regular packets running in regular trades, and leaving on regular days; going on the principle of sailing for cork and a market as ships often do, and queer tricks were often resorted to, to get a trip of freight and passengers, when other boats were up for the same destination.

I have often and often known Ohio River boats lie at St.
Louis with steam up and all the appearances of starting in an
hour — lay there five or six days, and all the time the captain
and officers protesting they were going in as many hours.   If
some passengers were in sight, they would ring the big bell,
fire up so as to throw out a column of black smoke from the
chimneys, and work the wheels so as to give every indication
of starting, when they had not half a cargo and had no idea of
going.   One noted captain, nicknamed "Ephraim Smooth"
was in the habit of pulling out his watch and saying : "If you
are over an hour away from the boat you will be left."

There was another dodge resorted to by some, and as they
wanted to make all the show of starting by keeping up fire
without the expense and waste of fuel, or from keeping firemen, one captain full of inventive genius was caught by a
passenger who had been waiting three days in the delusive
hope of starting, building a fire in the breeching of the chimneys, and when asked "What he was doing that for," said :
"They were new kind of boilers, and had to be fired in that
way."

And so I might go on ad infinitum with stories of the early
days of steamboating, but will close, wishing you every success with your book.

Very truly your friend

JOSEPH BROWN.

CAPT. JOHN N. BOFINGER.

ST. LOUIS, May 1, 1889.

My Dear Capt. Gould:

My steamboat career commenced in the *forties* on the
steamboat Ben Franklin No. 7, as second clerk under that accomplished gentleman Jonathan H. Barker, who was first
clerk, and the veteran F. Blair Summons was the captain, the
genial Paul Houston, chief engineer, Captain James Hainer and
Capt. Jacob Remelin, pilots, and Captain Samuel Hildreth,
mate. This steamer, as well as the steamer Pike No. 7, belonged
to Strader & Gorman United States Mail Line running between
Cincinnati and Louisville up to this date. This line of
steamers was considered the best financially and otherwise on
the Western waters; after leaving Cincinnati the first morning
Mr. Barker called me into his office and said : "Now, John, you
have assumed the position as second clerk on this boat ; I wish
you always to treat passengers, shippers and the public pleas-

antly and gentlemanly, and when asked a question answer
them politely. You may be on the wharf busy receiving
freights, and interrupted by party, with an inquiry about
some other matter, entirely foreign to your calling. You give
in return an uncivil answer and turn abruptly away; in a short
time after this party may wish to go to Louisville, or ship

CAPTAIN JOHN N. BOFINGER.

some freight; he comes to the wharf and sees the Ben Franklin
lying there; he remembers the uncivil treatment he received
from its clerk and he goes to another steamer; but had you returned a civil answer to this man he might have forgotten that,
but he would not have harbored any feeling against the boat.

"In other words," he continued, "John, remember you can catch more flies with molasses than with vinegar," and I have never forgotten that. I remained over a year on that boat. Capt. Barker bought the steamers Mountaineer and North America. He placed Captain J. Ed. Montgomery in charge of the North America and put me in charge of the office. He took charge of the Mountaineer with Ira H. Gibbs as clerk, and the two steamers took their position as "opposition" to the Strader and Gorman United States Mail Line, the Mountaineer leaving an hour in advance of the Pike No. 7, and the North America in advance of the Ben Franklin No. 6. The "opposition" done the business, and kept the lead on every trip, when finally Captain Summons, of the Ben Franklin, conceived the idea to leave with the North America and to pass her underway in sight of Louisville. We heard of his intention, and prepared ourselves as best we could. During the night our crew "rolled" 25 barrels of rosin on board from Sherley's boat-store, and Sunday morning found our crew in fine spirits, and ready in all particulars for the race. The Ben Franklin, which lay at her wharf above the mouth of Bear Grass creek, to all appearances was ready, and only waiting to hear our big bell ring — but our captain kept his own council and made all inspection as to being ready. Pilot Bill Leonard in the pilot-house but not in sight — all ready — and the officers at their posts, no captain in sight, lines let go, and the engines moved ahead and the North America was "out and gone" and shot by the Ben Franklin before the "old veteran" of that steamer was aware that the North America had left. To get their lines in and ready took but a short time, but our boat was abreast of Jeffersonville before the Franklin got under way. A stern chase is a long one, as in this case; we landed nearly an hour ahead of the Franklin at the Cincinnati wharf, that night. The next day Mr. Barker bought out the Mail Line from Strader & Gorman, after one month opposition.

On the 8th day of April, 1848, I left Cincinnati for St. Louis on the good steamer Atlantic as clerk; Captain Jas. M. Broadwell was master. I was captain of this boat about three years when I left her in 1854 and took charge of the steamer L. M. Kennett. I brought out the steamer Wm. M. Morrison, February, 1857; bought the steamer Cora Anderson October, 1859. Sunk her January,1861; returned to the Morrison in March, 1861; made six trips from St. Louis to New Orleans and return in one hundred and one days. The last trip south May 14, 1861; left St. Louis with 150 cabin passengers, the majority of these had been captured at Camp Jackson, St. Louis, May 10th and paroled. The only freight on the boat was two bobtail street cars for New Orleans and thirty tombstones for New Madrid. 20,000 men at Cairo under Gen. Prentiss; but was not molested at Cairo. A large number of our passengers left the boat at Price's lending, above Cairo, fearing that the Federals might "gobble them up." They found the walking very bad to Columbus, Ky., where we found them, and where we commenced taking on cargo for New Orleans, and had a full load before reaching Fort Randolph where we found 5,000 Tennesseeans under Gen. Preston Smith who examined all steamers descending. On my return from New Orleans to Memphis, May 28, 1861, Gen. Gideon J. Pillow had stopped all steamers from ascending the river above Memphis. My passengers left for the North "overland," and the freight was stored, and the Morrison choked a stump on the Arkansas shore in care of two watchmen, May 30, 1861. Since this time I have not been engaged as master of steamers, but have ever been an owner in steamboats more than forty years. During the war of rebellion I had charge of moving the troops and supplies of Gen. W. T. Sherman from Memphis, and Gen. Fred Steele from Helena, over 35,000 men. In December, 1862, had 93 steamers employed, landing same on the Yazoo River, behind Vicksburg; no accident of any kind. Moved Gen. U. S. Grant and 25,500 men from Memphis to Vicksburg, January, 1863; attended to moving all the supplies and sending forward recruits from the North until the fall of Vicksburg, July, 1863, and as superintendent of the Atlantic and Mississippi Steamship Co., moved the army North; was president of the St. Louis and New Orleans Packet Co., after the war; held a contract, 1869, for transportation of troops and supplies from Fort Benton to New Orleans, 4,200 miles.

My relations with the river interest extends over forty years, and I have seen many changes. When I was a boy steamboats had their cabins on the stern. For gentlemen, on the main deck, for ladies, over same. No state rooms, but open berths with curtains, and with a carrying capacity not to exceed 500 tons. In 1870, we had steamboats of a carrying capacity of 2,000 to 2,800 tons, full length cabins, all state-rooms and furnished with all the elegance and luxury that money could buy. That class of steamboats are of the past, except as to packet lines and the barges with the towboats have taken their place. The time was, 1850, when forty or more boats were moored at the St. Louis wharf, loading or

unloading cargoes daily, and in 1869 there were eighty steamers
employed, running from St. Louis up the Missouri River.
Respectfully yours,   JOHN N. BOFINGER.

IS IT SUPERSTITION, FATALITY OR FACT?

"Capt. John N. Bofinger is an occasional contributor to
the St. Louis *Times*. His letters are full of interest and have
but the one fault — the time that elapses between them. In a
recent number of the *Times* Capt. B. makes the fatality that
attends the letter M the subject, and writes : "I do assert that,
with barely an exception, that all steamboats built and run on
the Mississippi River and its tributaries, whose name commenced with the letter M, were either burnt, sunk, exploded
or unsuccessful as an investment to their owners. You can
look over the long list of Missouri, Mississippi, Mary, Michigan, Marie, Monarch, Mediator, etc., and you will find that
they met the fate of one as above indicated. * * * Over
thirty years ago, Capt. John Pierce built the Metamora. I
tried my best to persuade the captain to name his boat some
other name, and gave him my reasons, going over a large number of boats whose name had commenced with the letter M.
He laughed at what he called a superstitious notion of mine
and called his boat the Metamora. She was a great success,
but sank above Choctaw island while she was in her prime.
Capt. Charley Davis, about the same time, built a splendid
Cincinnati and New Orleans boat. Davis, like his old partner,
Pierce, would not listen to my idea, launched and christened
her the Midas. She sank in the bend above Island 16. Capt.
Joe Brown built the Mayflower sometime during the fifties.
Long before she was launched I tried to talk him out of calling
the boat by that name — no use. She was burned at Memphis.
"Our old townsman, Norman Cutter, Esq., bought a hull
that had been built at Hannibal. Her cabin and machinery
was put on at St. Louis, where she was finished, and was then
(1852) the finest boat in the St. Louis and New Orleans trade.
It was the owner's intention that I should have taken charge
of the Charles Belcher, which was the name Mr. Cutter gave
her about a month before the Belcher was ready to start on
her first trip. I accidently found out from Emerson, who had
built the hull, that she had been launched and christened
Magnolia. That was enough for me. Nothing could have induced me to have taken charge of the Belcher. She was
burned on her sixth trip at New Orleans.
"I could name hundreds of instances to show the fatality

that seems to shroud the steamboats whose name commenced with the letter M, but will content myself with giving one more instance. I was in New Orleans in May, 1875, where I met Capt. Frank Hicks and his clerk, Mr. Alf. Grissom, who were at that time building a hull at Metropolis, Ill. They talked of calling her the Mary Bell. I did my level best to persuade them not to call her that name or any name that commenced with M; gave them my reason and recited many instances of losses, etc., all to no good; the boat was called Mary Bell, made but a few trips and burnt with a full load at Vicksburg. I do not pretend to give any reason why a steamboat's name commencing with the letter M should be any more unlucky than one commencing with any other letter, but the fact still remains, superstitious or not."

Others besides Capt. Bofinger entertain the same superstition, but, as with all other rules, there are exceptions, some of which come within our own recollection. For instance: Before the war the Majestic, Mary Hunt, Music (two of them), and Mary Foley were all coast packets. They lasted the usual life of a steamboat, say nine years, made money for their owners and were dismantled for their machinery. The last Magnolia, owned by Captains Shute and Thomasson, the largest cotton boat of ante bellum days, was purposely destroyed during the war. But the Magnolia before her ran nine years and was dismantled at New Albany for her machinery, the one before this having also been worn out. The Marsella lived to be about fourteen years old and was sold to Dave McCan & Son for her machinery and old iron. The Mary Houston ran for nine years and still lives in a sense, for her hull, after twelve years active employment, is now in use as a wharf-boat at Monroe. It is safe to suppose that when a boat runs for from 5 to 10 or more years without changing owners more than once in all this time, if at all, and then voluntary sale, she has proved herself a paying investment. Such instances we can give by mentioning among others the Mollie Moore, Minnie, Major White, Maria Louise and the Mary Ida. The Maria Louise is still owned by her builder, Capt. Brinker; has always been a successful boat, and is as staunch and serviceable and valuable to-day, perhaps more so, as she would be if her name commenced with a B instead of an M, and the same may be said of the Mollie Moore.

A general impression prevails among river men that any steamer's name commencing with M will either explode, sink or be wrecked. In numerous instances this has resulted. But this port had one with a double M, the rafter Mollie Mohler,

of the Schulenberg & Boeckeler Lumber Company's fleet.
She ran successfully for many years and was finally dismantled
and a new boat built on her hull. This, however, may be said
to be an exception.

CAPT. RUSSEL BLAKELY.

was born in North Adams, Berkshire County, Mass., April
19th, 1815, of Puritan descent from among the earliest families
of Plymouth, Mass., and New Haven, Conn.

In the year 1817 his parents, Denis Blakely and Sarah Samson Blakely, emigrated from North Adams to Le Roy, Genesee
County, New York, where he grew to manhood.

In the fall of the year 1836 his father and he took the Western fever and the only cure at that time was to emigrate, and
they selected Peoria, Illinois, as their objective point. He re-

mained in Peoria through the varying experiences of the eventful years of 1837 and 1838, and in the summer of 1839 again
made a new choice and moved to Galena, Ill., and became
engaged in mining and smelting in the employ of Capt. H. H.
Goar, in which he continued until the fall of 1844, when he
went to Wythe County, Southwestern Virginia, where he engaged in making lead, at what have long been known as the
Austinville Mines. In the summer of 1847 he returned to
Galena and became engaged in steamboating between Galena
and St. Paul, Minn., in which he was connected with what was
known as the Galena and Minnesota Packet Co., during its various changes to 1862, when it was sold out. In 1851 he was
married to Ellen L. Sheldon at Willow Springs, Wisconsin.

During the winter 1855–6 he became interested in the Northwestern Express Co., under the firm name of J. C. Burbank
& Co. and in the commission and general forwarding business at St. Paul with Mr. Burbank, under the firm name of
Blakely & Burbank. In the spring of 1862 he moved to
St. Paul, Minn., to take part in the management of the express and stage business. In the year 1858 J. C. Burbank
& Co. became contractors with the Government for the transportation of the mails very extensively in Minnesota
and the company was known as the Minnesota Stage and
Northwestern Express Co., and during the years 1858 to 1867
the business became very extensive, covering the entire State
and was extended to Fort Garry in Manitoba in 1870, and occupied and operated the several routes in the State until finally
superseded by the construction of the railroads on nearly all the
routes run by the company. When the gold mining excitement
opened up in the Black Hills in Dakota in the year 1876,
the stage, express and transportation business from
Bismarck on the Missouri River to the Black Hills,
seemed to promise to be very large and profitable, and the
business was then organized under the corporate name of the
Northwestern Express, Stage and Transportation Co. R.
Blakely, President, and C. W. Carpenter, Secretary and
Treasurer, and commenced in 1877 in connection with the
Northern Pacific R. R. Co. and carried passengers, mail and
express and transported merchandise. The stage running
daily carrying passengers, mail and express and the transportation of merchandise required a large amount of stock, horses,
mules and cattle in its operation. With the usual vicissitudes
of a new country, this route of operation continued until the
year 1888 when a railroad finally closed out the business of the
line.

Since the summer of 1847, when Capt. Blakely first landed
in St. Paul until the present time, he has been largely connected
with its interests and has helped to build up its railroad and
other interests. An active member of the Chamber of Commerce, acknowledged a very zealous and active member of
the Republican party from its origin. Capt. Blakely and wife
are in usual health and strength for persons of their age, and
have a family of six sons and two daughters grown to man
and womanhood.

CAPTAIN ISAAC L. FISHER.

[Communicated.]

Born in New Brunswick, New Jersey, in 1843, received a
common school education, was taught the science of navigation by his father, who was a shipmaster. His father afterwards becoming interested in inland navigation, Captain
Fisher, served an apprenticeship in the drawing department,
machine shop, boiler works, and shipyard, serving also as
engineer, pilot, and master of boats about the New York harbor, and is now the manager of one of the largest towing and
transportation lines in the United States. Capt. Fisher plans
himself and personally superintends the construction of all of
the boats of his line, even to the boilers and machinery, and
has probably done more work of this kind any than man of his
age in this country. Captain Fisher is a popular man with all
classes and conditions of people. He has held political offices,
and although a republican with a democratic constituency, was
never defeated. He served as alderman 6 years, chief of the
fire department 3 years, and three successive terms in the
New Jersey legislature, and was made speaker of the house,
though strongly opposed by combined railroad influences.
He was at that time the youngest man in any State to serve
as speaker. Captain Fisher was chairman of the Steam and
Sail Vessel Association, of New York City, for two years, and
represented that body in the National Board of Steam Navigation. For several years he held the office of president of the
National Board of Steam Navigation, is an active member of
the executive committee, and honorary president of the board.
In all matters of reform, and for the general good of the
steam vessel interests, local and national, Captain Fisher has
been an indefatigable and successful worker, and to his efforts
for the protection and promotion of those interests much is
due. He led in the movement before congress for the abol-

ishment of the steam recording gauge monopoly, the doing away of inspections and license fees, the repeal of the statute imposing a tax upon mariners for the support of the Marine Hospital, the modifications of the statutes relating to the liability of steam vessel owners, and other matters of a like nature.

CAPTAIN ISAAC L. FISHER.

Having an extensive acquaintanceship, and a thoroughly practical knowledge, he has been a spirited leader in every movement for the better safety of life and property upon the waters, and to secure to vessel owners and employes, just and adequate protection, and a proper reward. He served a term as private in the late civil war in New Jersey regiments.

CAPTAIN ISAAC M. MASON

was born in Brownsville, Penn., March 4th, 1831 — commenced
steamboating on the steamer Consul as second clerk in 1846 —
was clerk of the Atlantic in 1848-9. In 1850, at the age of 19
years, took charge of steamer Summit, and ran her in the
Louisville and Nashville trades.

The next fourteen years was acting as captain or clerk on the
following boats: Editor, Australia, Honduras, Alma, Bell
Golden, Vixen, Denmark, Fred Lorenz, Savanna, and Hawkeye State.

First trip to St. Louis was on the steamer Summit, in
April, 1851. Continued in active service until 1865, when he
was made general freight agent of the Northern Line Packet
Company, which position he retained for eleven years.

He was elected Marshal of the County of St. Louis, 1876,
and in 1880 and 1882 Sheriff of the City of St. Louis.

Although temporarily disengaged from the river, always maintained his interest in all that related to its improvement and to water transportation.

In 1884 he was appointed superintendent of the Anchor Line of boats between St. Louis and New Orleans, and president of the same in 1888.

All who know Captain Mason appreciate him for his moral worth, his integrity, his suavity and the courtesy with which all are treated who have occasion to meet him.

CAPTAIN MORGAN MASON.

ALEXANDRIA, Mo., 1889.

Capt. E. W. Gould, St. Louis:

DEAR SIR — In reply to your inquiry as to my steamboat experience, I respond briefly, as follows: —

My first introduction was in 1837, as first clerk on steamer Kentucky. She belonged to the " Good Intent Line," which had its principal office in Pittsburgh. We made our first trips between Pittsburgh and Louisville, afterwards extended them to Nashville and St. Louis.

We had a large number of emigrants, composed principally of Kentucky planters, going to the " Platt Purchase " with their slaves, to engage in raising hemp. At that time St. Louis was a small city, and extended but little west of Fourth street.

My next experience was on the Monongahela River, in 1843, on the steamer Consul, Captain Saml. Clark.

In November of that year the " slack water improvement " was completed to Brownsville, and Gen. I. K. Moorhead, with a large party of citizens from Pittsburgh, made an excursion to Brownsville, returning next day on the Consul.

I remained on the Consul as captain and clerk until she was worn out. Then I went on the Atlantic with Capt. Parkinson. After he retired I took command of her and remained until she was worn out. Then we built the Jefferson, and I run her three years. I was also on the Resolute until she was sold to parties at Madison.

My connection with river navigation continued for eleven years.

Wishing you much success in your very worthy enterprise,

I remain truly yours,

MORGAN MASON.

CHARLES C. KEENER.

The subject of this sketch is the principal representative of all that remains of the once famous Naples Packet Co. — one of the first organized steamboat companies on the Mississippi River.

After a varied experience of forty years the old company finally succumbed in 1887, and its effects were purchased by a new company, known as the St. Louis, Naples and Peoria Packet Co.

The old and well known Grain and Commission Merchants, T. and F. Keener, of Naples, had long been stockholders in the company, and through that connection the new company with Captain C. C. Keener, the son of the surviving partner of the old firm became the principal proprietor of the new organization, and was elected its president.

Having served a long apprenticeship in the grain and shipping business, and having a taste for navigation, he decided to extend the knowledge he had acquired from his experience in the management of a *fine steam tug-boat*, which he built for his own pleasure and convenience, he assumed command of the Steamer 'Calhoun and has devoted his personal attention to the management of the new company since its organization.

Although not a veteran in the service, the eminent success that has attended his efforts in navigation and in the fine condition in which he keeps his boats show conclusively that age and experience are not the only requisites to success.

The unlimited means and the large operations in grain of his firm, "Keener & Pike," secure to their boats a large business independent of shipments from others.

If the Government continues its appropriations even in small sums it will ultimately succeed in so improving the navigation of the Illinois River that what has for the last ten years seemed a foregone conclusion, may yet be recovered and the river again become an important factor in the commerce of that productive valley. Of all the tributaries of the Mississippi there is none so easily and cheaply made navigable for a good class of boats for nine months in the year as this stream, and had the demands of its commerce been heeded by the Government long years ago and the necessary improvements been made and railroad bridges properly constructed, a far different result would have been manifest. The towns and cities that were springing up all along its banks, would have continued to flourish, by the stimulating influences incident to shipping and receiving large consignments to and from the interior.

The lands along the bottoms would have continued to be cleared and cultivated, levees would have been built, and overflowed lands recovered, the most productive in the State, adding health and prosperity the whole length of the river.

Captain Keener is young, vigorous and enterprising, and what his predecessors have failed to realize may yet become a bonanza to him, and a great blessing to the inhabitants of that long neglected valley.

CAPTAIN JOSEPH S. NANSON

was born at Fayette, Howard County, Missouri, 22d of January, 1827.

His first adventure as a steamboat man was on the steamer Banner State, which he purchased in 1857 for the St. Louis and Glasgow trade.

On the third trip the boat sunk and was a total loss.

Nothing daunted he left his home at Glasgow, where he was engaged in the commission business with the late Theo. Bartholow, and went to St. Louis and purchased the steamer, which he ran in the same trade for one year. At the expiration of that time he sold his interest, and in company with his confidential friend and partner, Moses Hillard, went to Louisville and built the steamer N. J. Eaton.

This boat sunk in the Missouri on her first trip and was a total loss.

This disaster well nigh bankrupted the owners. But through the assistance of strong friends at Glasgow, he again repaired to Louisville and built the steamer Kate Howard, which he ran with great success for three seasons between St. Louis and St. Joseph, on the Missouri River. At the end of this period, or in 1859, the Kate Howard sunk, after having handsomely remunerated her owners for their investment.

At the close of her career, Capt. Nanson and his crew went on board the John D. Perry, where he remained until the close of that season.

In the spring of 1860 he formed a co-partnership with Logan D. Damoran, and opened a commission house at St. Louis under the name of Nanson, Damoran & Co., which did a successful business.

In 1864-5 Capt. Nanson, Henry Ames and Miles Sells purchased the steamer Shreveport, and took her to Red River to embark in cotton speculations under the care and protection of General Banks military expedition to that river. But at Alexandria the expedition was repulsed and compelled to return.

The result was that all the cotton that had been purchased, together with several boats, was destroyed by the Confederates, and the expedition, as well as the cotton speculations, was declared a failure.

In addition to Captain Nanson's commission business in St. Louis, New Orleans and New York which was large and attended with varied success, he was elected President in 1868 of the St. Louis and Omaha Packet Company, which was composed of nine first-class boats and extensively known as the "O Line."

In consequence of the great demand upon his time by the commercial transactions in which his house was engaged, in 1869 he resigned his position as President of the Packet Company.

As an evidence of the appreciation in which his services were held, the owners of the line presented him with an elegant carriage costing $1,000.

He was at one time director and owner in the Memphis Packet Company, and an owner in steamers Sultana, Ingomar, Kate Kinney, Wm. J. Lewis and other boats.

In 1872-3 he organized and acted as president of a short line of boats to run between Atcherson and Nebraska City, known as the Railroad Line, which connected with the Missouri Pacific at Atcheson; also another line from St. Joseph to Nebraska City, which was known as the Missouri, Kansas and Nebraska Line.

These later connections were more especially designed to afford shippers in that country facilities for reaching the St. Louis market, which they formerly enjoyed via water, but were now deprived of in consequence of the completion of several railroads across the country to Chicago and the East.

But low water and ice soon demonstrated the impossibility of that competition and the boats were soon retired, never more to return to so unequal a contest.

Later, or in 1879, Captain Nanson, in company with Messrs. Pegram and Hillard purchased the Laclede Hotel in St. Louis, and after a successful year or two in that enterprize, disposed of his interest and embarked with Messrs. Hillard, Buzard and Barnard in the purchase of a stock farm in Tevolla County, Texas, which has under iron fence 80,000 acres of land. The name of the firm at the present time is Buzard, Hillard and Barnard. They are feeding 50,000 head of cattle and devoting much care to the improvement of their breeds and to milch cows.

Captain Nanson was married in 1855 to Miss Belle Billingsly, of Glasgow, Mo., who still lives to cheer him on in his active and enterprizing career of usefulness and social life — together with two cultured daughters who are happily united in marriage with gentlemen in fine positions in society, and of high character.

JOHN W. BRYANT

was born in New Orleans, La., in 1841. From 1857 to the breaking out of the war was a discharging clerk on the levee. Discharged the cargo of the Magnolia, 6537 bales — the largest cotton trip of *ante bellum* days, served through the war, on the Confederate side. Was one of the besieged in Port Hudson, serving as acting assistant quartermaster on the staff of Col. W.!R. Miles, in command of the right wing of the defenses. Was paroled in 1865 at West Point, Ga., returned to New Orleans, and again became a discharging clerk. Was also a clerk in the Red River and other trades and cashier of the New Orleans Post-office. In 1874 was employed as a river reporter and is now filling that position on the New Orleans *Times-Democrat.* In 1885 was made secretary of the Executive Committee on the Improvement of the Western Waterways. Was also the assistant secretary of the Kansas City, New Orleans, Washington, D. C., and Memphis River Im-

provement Conventions. Served also on all of the committees appearing before the River's and Harbor's Committee
of Congress to present the resolutions of conventions and urge
appropriations. Was charged with the duty of presenting to
President Cleveland a copy of the resolutions adopted by the

JOHN W. BRYANT.

Memphis Convention. Is also secretary of the National
Board of Steam Navigation and has, with others, been a
prominent worker for the Board at Washington in the departments and before committees of the Senate and House, in securing modifications of, or preventing the adoption of statutes
that were to the injury of the steam interests.
    Is a Mason and an active worker in several benevolent or-

ganizations, of one of which he is the president. Was chosen
to represent the steamboat interests before the interstate commerce commission during their sittings at New Orleans, Memphis, and Washington.

The original of this fine picture, and the author of the foregoing sketch, has for several years been a representative in all
prominent efforts and organizations for the promotion of *water
transportation* in the Mississippi Valley, and for the protection and advancement of water transportation throughout the
country.

The Southern interests that he has so long and so ably represented could not have confided their interests to a more
competent or faithful representative. His efforts in numerous conventions, in the National Board of Steam Navigation,
before committees of Congress, and with individual members,
have been phenomenal. None but those who have had the
privilege of being associated with him in similar efforts can
appreciate the value of his labor.

His untiring energy and familiarity with all subjects connected with river navigation render his services and his experience invaluable to his constituents, and whenever they are
in position to elect a member to represent their interest in
Congress they cannot select a more competent or faithful representative. And why are they not always in position to do
so? No interest in America of half the importance that the
water transportation interests are, but what have not only one,
but many, direct and indirect members in Congress to represent them.

If ever this great and important interest has had an expo-
nent, a representative in Congress to protect, and to advance its
interests, there is no record of it.

Is it surprising the interest languishes? While its great
competitor, its opponent, has many members in both branches
of Congress, and on all special occasions a full quorum in the
"third house."

Who so competent to legislate as those who are entirely
familiar with all the facts, and who more familiar and competent to judge of them fairly and impartially than John W.
Bryant?

Through his kindness and industry this writer is indebted
for many interesting items selected from old papers, books,
&c., which will be read and enjoyed by all. And for which
he desires in this connection to return many thanks.

CAPTAIN B. R. PEGRAM.

COHASSET, MASS., January, 22d, 1889.

Capt. E. W. Gould, St. Louis, Mo.:

DEAR SIR : — In answer to your suggestion, I may say I am glad of the opportunity of putting myself on record with so many old friends as I am sure will avail themselves of the privilege your very laudable enterprise will afford them.

While my river experience was of shorter duration than that of many of my esteemed cotemporaries, it was an eventful one, and largely diversified.

Commencing on the Illinois River at the age of fifteen, as a ferry-man, with a horse-boat at the mouth of Apple creek; advancing from that to a pilot of a wood-boat engaged in boating wood to St. Louis for the next few years.

My father removed from Virginia, where I was born in 1828, and settled in Carrollton, Illinois, where he had an extensive practice as a physician. He died when I was eleven years old, and the family removed to Newport, on the Illinois River, from whence I graduated, although with but little education. I vibrated between the river and a farm in that neighborhood until 1849.

My first practical steamboating was on the steamboat Ruth, in the winter of 1862 and '63. In August of '63 she was burned, it was believed, by an incendiary rebel while laying at Norfolk, six miles below Cairo. She had a large number of people on board, and *three millions* of government greenbacks, which were destroyed, and some thirty-five lives.

The Ruth was a new boat, came out in the spring of that year and cost $65,000. She was 275 feet long, 41 feet beam, 8 feet hold. Her engines came out of the Peter Tellon and were 27 inches diameter and 9 feet stroke, with five 26 feet boilers 44 inches diameter. She was among the first boats burned after the breaking out of the war, and there was good reason for believing it was done by the rebels.

The second Ruth built a few years later, was 300 feet long, 48 feet beam, 10 feet hold. She had the engines of the H. R. W. Hill which were 30 inches, 10 feet stroke. Boiler (6), were 46 inches, 30 feet long. She cost $200,000 and was very fast and an immense carrier, and an elegant cabin. She was burned in 1868, at Pawpa Island; no lives lost.

After the burning of the first Ruth, I was in command of several boats, viz.: Olive Branch, Ida Handy, Clara Dolson, Lady Gay, and second Ruth. After the organization of the Atlantic & Mississippi Steamship Co., I was for 18 months acting as its agent in New Orleans.

After the collapse of that company, my brother George and myself built the James Howard, and I commanded her eight years. Sold her 1878, and retired from the river.

Wishing you merited success in the very difficult undertaking in which you have embarked, I remain, very truly yours,

B. R. PEGRAM.

HENRY C. HAARSTICK.

(COMMUNICATED.)

The salient points in the history of this sketch furnish a most remarkable example of what large results can be accomplished in the business world by the unaided, intelligent and indefatigable efforts of a single humble citizen, when directed towards a definite object.

Henry C. Haarstick, the President of the St. Louis & Mississippi Valley Transportation Company (Barge Line), was born in 1836 at Hohenhameln, near Hildesheim, in the Kingdom of Hanover, and emigrated to America with his parents when but 13 years old; the passage was a long one—being by sailing vessel from Hamburg to New York, and consuming 49 days; the destination of the family was St. Louis, and the route then lay as follows: from New York by steamer to Al-

bany; thence by canal to Buffalo; thence by steamer to Sandusky, Ohio; thence by rail to Cincinnati and thence by
steamer to St. Louis.

The young emigrant arrived at his destination on the 25th
of July, 1849 — a year memorable for the great fire and the
cholera which then visited the city.

After a few years of diligent application to study, young
Haarstick began his business career in February, 1853, as clerk
with the distilling firm of Malony & Tilton, passing ten years in
their employ and becoming their successor by purchase in 1863.
In 1867 he relinquished this business to Messrs. Card & Lawrence, and the following year, having his attention drawn to the
possibilities of success in the business done on the river, he purchased stock in the Mississippi Valley Transportation Co.'s
barge line, and directing his closest personal efforts toward
extricating the company from embarrassments which threatened its extinction, he had the satisfaction ere long of seeing
its business placed upon a firm and sure foundation.

In 1869 he was elected a director and vice-president of the
company, and, upon the death of Supt. Greenleaf in March
of that year, Mr. Haarstick was made general manager and
conducted the business thenceforward with signal success until
1881, during which year the entire property of the company
was sold to the St. Louis & Mississippi Valley Transportation
Co., a new and powerful organization with $2,000,000
cash capital, formed for the purpose of absorbing the four
barge lines then existing.

This new combination has been operated as a unit since its
establishment, under the presidency and direct personal management of Mr. Haarstick, and it goes without saying that it
has exerted a most potent influence for good, not only upon
the business done on Western waters, but upon the entire
grain producing area of the Mississippi Valley.

Recognizing the benefits of cheap transportation to the
growers of our cereals, and that efforts in this direction must
necessarily develop St. Louis as a market for European buyers. The most patient and persistent efforts were put forth to
build up and finally establish a line of grain carriers on the
river which should form a connecting link between the American farmer and the European consumer.

It need only be said by way of illustration that, during the
period of these efforts the river rate on bulk grain has been
reduced from 12 and 14 cents per bushel to 5 cents per bushel;
every cent of the difference inuring directly to the benefit of
the farmers of this country and aggregating millions of dol-

MISSISSIPPI VALLEY TRANSPORTATION COMPANY.—TOW-BOAT AND BARGES.

ars in their annual savings. Second only to this achievement have been Mr. Haarstick's efforts toward the stimulation of the direct importation of foreign commodities via New Orleans. He was the first to furnish the merchants of the interior with a bonded water route for imported goods, and his line has carried vast quantities of this description of freight without the loss of a single package, and without a complaint from the Government.

The resources of the St. L. & M. V. T. Co., embrace 12 powerful steamers, nearly 100 grain barges, (each of a capacity of 50,000 bushels), large and convenient stationary grain elevators at Belmont, Mo., and New Orleans, La., a well equipped Marine Railway and dockyard at Mound City, Ill., besides the necessary floating elevators for transferring bulk grain from barges into ocean vessels at New Orleans. The company is carrying about 12,000,000 bushels of grain annually besides about 150,000 tons of package freight.

Mr Haarstick is in the prime of life and vigorous manhood, and actively engaged in the management of the great corporation of which he is president. He is an ardent advocate and active supporter of all public improvements; has been president of the Merchants' Exchange during one of its most prosperous years, and is recognized in commercial circles as one of the most sagacious, far-seeing, progressive and influential citizens of St. Louis. His kindly, conservative manner, his unostentatious charities, his consideration for his business associates and competitors and his retiring modesty, all warrant the hope that so useful a life may be greatly prolonged.

John G. Prather

was born in Clermont County, Ohio, June 16th, 1834, His people were connected with the river and river interests from the earliest steamboating on the Ohio and Mississippi Rivers. At an unusually early age he cast his lot with that interest, occupying almost every position from the deck to the roof. Coming to St. Louis in 1850, and following the river in various capacities until 1852, when he went to California — returning in 1855. He associated himself with the late Daniel G. Taylor (his uncle) in the wholesale liquor business on the levee, where he still holds forth at the old stand, 516 N. Levee. His connection with the river continuing up to the present time. Was owner in whole or part of many steamers during this time, notably the steamers Des Moines, Bart Able, E. F. Dix,

Fannie Tatum, Westerner and others; has been twenty years associated with the famous Anchor Line; is now a director of that line; was a staunch Union man during the war; served as Lieutenant-Colonel of 5th Regiment Missouri Militia, and assisted in the organization of that regiment, is a Democrat and has taken an active and prominent part in the councils of the

JOHN G. PRATHER.

Democracy of Missouri; is a member of the National Democratic Committee; serving his third term in that capacity. Col. Prather's establishment is now the oldest on the Levee. His recollection of the primary days of boating in the Missouri, Upper Mississippi, Illinois, and Lower Mississippi Rivers would make an interesting history. Col. P. is vigorous and according to himself, feels as young as ever and expects to live to see Democracy vindicated by the national success in '92.

CAPT. O. P. SHINKLE. }

CINCINNATI, Feb. 14, 1889.

Captain E. W. Gould, St. Louis, Mo.:

Inclosed I send a photo of myself for insertion in the work you are preparing on the history of navigation of Western waters.

Appreciating your object, I desire to contribute as far as my experience goes whatever of interest it may possess.

I was born in Brown County, Ohio, August 31st, 1834, in the town of Higginsport.

45

I commenced my steamboat life in 1850 at the age of sixteen. In 1854, at the age of twenty, was placed in command of a tow-boat, and continued building and navigating steamboats from 1850 to the present time, with the exception of two years.

During this period I have built three steamboats, have been interested in eight and commanded them all at different periods on different rivers, viz.: Mississippi, Ohio, Cumberland, Tennessee, Arkansas and White Rivers, but principally on the Ohio and Mississippi.

I am at present running the steamer Golden Rule, from Cincinnati to New Orleans, where I have been engaged for several years past.

While the business is not what it once was, it still continues to pay such boats as are adapted to the trade and judiciously managed a small margin of profit. Although the time for expensive passenger boats in this trade seems to have passed, at least until the navigation shall have been further improved.

Trusting you will meet with success in your very laudable effort, I remain,

Yours truly,

O. P. SHINKLE.

CAPTAIN JOHN P. KEISER,

son of Captain Jno. W. Keiser, was born in Boone County, Missouri, 1833.

He, after receiving a good English education, concluded to follow in the footsteps of his father, and embarked on the river with Capt. Henry W. Smith on the steamer J. M. Clendenin in 1852, for the purpose of learning to be a pilot. In 1853 he was with Capt. Wm. B. Miller on the steamer Isabel. He obtained a license the same year, and his first piloting was in the fall of '53, on the government snag-boats. In 1854 he was engaged to pilot the N. J. Eaton, Capt. Joseph Nanson. The boat only made two trips and then sunk. The remainder of the season was pilot on the steamers Clara and Sam Cloon.

In 1856 he was engaged in piloting in the Lightning Line from Jefferson City to Western Missouri, on the steamer Cataract; salary $1,000 per month.

In 1857 he was master and pilot of the Cataract, in the same line; salary, $1,250 per month.

In 1858 he bought an interest in the Isabella, and was mas-

ter and pilot of her until 1861. After the war broke out he
sold her to Capt. Dozier & McPherson.

In 1862 he built the Esteller at Pittsburgh, which was lost
by fire at the St. Louis wharf.

The same year he built the Majestic, a large Lower Mississippi River steamer. She was lost by fire at Island No. 8,

CAPTAIN JOHN P. KEISER.

May 6th, 1863. He soon afterwards bought the Fannie Ogden, and sold her in February, 1864. The same year he
built the Waverly for Missouri River, and a steam ferry-boat
for Rocheport.

In 1865 he built the G. B. Allen for the Missouri River.
The Waverly was sunk in 1866, and the Allen burned at St.
Louis, March, '67.

He then retired from the river and went into the commission
and storage business with his brother. The firm was J. P. &
C. W. Keiser. Capt. James B. Eads was then building the

St. Louis bridge, and needed some one to purchase supplies and construct the boats to be used for laying stone in the piers, etc. Capt. Keiser was selected for the work. He served in that capacity for twelve months and resigned. Shortly afterwards he was made superintendent and general manager of the Carondelet docks, then doing a large business, and was with that company about twelve months when he resigned to take charge of as general superintendent of the Memphis and St. Louis Packet Company, and was superintendent and general manager of that company for 13 years, having built in the meantime $1,250,000 of steamboat property, viz.: steamer Grand Tower, City of Helena, Belle Memphis, Ste. Genevieve, Baton Rouge, Bayou Sara, Arkansas City, City of Vicksburg, City of Chester, City of Cairo, City of New Orleans, City of St. Louis, City of Greenville ; rebuilt James Howard.

Bought for said company: Capitol City, Emma C. Elliott, John B. Mande, W. T. Halliday, Will S. Hays, Illinois, Commonwealth, City of Alton, Annie P. Silver, Gold Dust. Built Package Elevator at Memphis, Tennessee, and Vicksburg, Mississippi.

In 1882 Capt. Scudder resigned his position as President of this company and Capt. Keiser was duly elected President and under his administration the St. Louis and Vicksburg Packet Company was consolidated into the New Orleans Anchor Line, and capitalized at $1,500,000. In December, 1884, he resigned his position of President and sold his steamboat stock. He was at this time a large holder of gas stock in the Laclede Gas Company of St. Louis, and was made President of the Company immediately on his resignation of the Presidency of the Anchor Line, where he now is, enjoying good health and the earnings of his successful career as a boatman for thirty years, having handled successfully as much, or more, steamboat property as any one man in the West.

L. M. Chipley.

St. Louis, Mo., 4th, 11th, 1889.

Capt. E. W. Gould: —

I herewith hand you a photo of the first steamer Post Boy built under your supervision, for the Illinois River trade (Naples Packet Co.) in 1859. The Post Boy as you will remember proved to be a very fast boat for her power. The average time made by this steamer from St. Louis was two hours and five minutes to Alton, and twelve hours to Naples, including stops for freight and passengers. Hugh Thomas, agent~at Florence, always claimed that the clock in his office

Yours, Truly,
L M Chipley

was the correct time, as he regulated it by the arrival of the Post Poy at the landing, as she was always there at 3 a. m. without fail every Tuesday, Thursday and Saturday morning. My first experience as a river man was on this boat in capacity of second clerk and I thought that I had reached the highest pinnacle in the ladder of fame when I was appointed by you to the position of an officer on this steamboat.   At that date, to be an officer on a fine steamer was the height of ambition with all young men living near the river, and even to this day there is an air of importance about a steamboat officer on duty that commands the admiration and respect of many passengers that travel on boats.

The Post Boy was in the government service during the war and was selected as dispatch boat for the fleet at Vicksburg during the siege, and also dispatch boat of the fleet at the siege and capture of Arkansaw Post, and served in same capacity on White River at Clarendon and Duvolls Bluff and returned to Saint Louis in the fall of 1863 and was destroyed by fire along with the steamers Jesse K. Bell, Hiawatha and last, but not least, the Steamer Imperial, the queen of all, and the fastest and finest steamboat that ever run in the St. Louis and New Orleans trade.   This boat was also built by you.

The officers of the Post Boy were Jas. Abrams, Master; O. S. Watt and L. M. Chipley, Clerks; Enoch P. King and T. B. Chipley, Pilots; Wash McCann and Wm. Mitchell, Engineers; Hugh Davis and Hosey Densmore, Mates; Feilding Corbin, Steward.   I often wonder how it is that boatmen did not become connected with railroading, that superseded the boats as the carriers of the commerce of the West, as they were more familiar with the details of the freighting business than strangers could possibly be.   The only reason or explanation I can offer is that they did not look on a four-foot railroad track, equipped with a forty-foot box car as a competitor worth considering in comparison with a two thousand ton steamer with a free river three thousand miles long and a mile wide.   But others saw the opportunity, and built, as it were, a fence of railroad iron around the rivers and abided their time for steamboats to be starved out of the business that had taken a lifetime to build up at the expense of millions of dollars to their owners who had not kept pace with times that demanded rapid transit for freight and passengers, a want that railroads filled to perfection.

Yours truly,

L. M. Chipley.

ST. LOUIS & NAPLES PACKET COMPANY'S STEAMER POST BOY.

CAPTAIN WILLIAM F. DAVIDSON,

long and favorably known in connection with the steamboat business of the Mississippi River and its tributaries. For a number of years he resided in St. Louis and was president and active manager of different steamboat lines, most notably The Northwestern Union Packet Company, and The Keokuk-Northern Line Packet Company.

His early career in steamboating began on the Ohio River, but his life's work extended over an area of the entire Mississippi Valley, and there is hardly a man who has been connected with the river interests of the valley during the past half century, who has obtained more prominence, or been better known than the late Commodore Davidson.

He was born at South Point, Lawrence County, Ohio, February 4th, 1825. His father — William W. Davidson — was a pioneer in that part of Ohio, and was very well known throughout the southern part of the State, Eastern Kentucky and West Virginia.

The subject of this sketch began his steamboat career when but a small boy by boating on the Big Sandy River, the Ohio River, the Sciota, and other tributaries of the Ohio. He accompanied his father, who did something in that line in the early days of boating along the Ohio and Sciota Rivers. When quite a young man he became interested as part owner in the steamboat Gondola; also, The Relief, and later on, The United States Aid, The Jacob Traber, The Frank Steel, Favorite, and other boats.

He married in Southern Ohio, in the winter of 1858-59, a daughter of Judge Benjamin Johnson, who survives him. He also leaves surviving him a son — Mr. Edward E. Davidson — of St. Paul, and a daughter — Miss Sallie Davidson — who makes her home with the mother in Southern Ohio.

Commodore Davidson visited St. Paul and the Upper Mississippi in 1855, and subsequently removed to St. Paul, and began steamboating on a large scale between LaCrosse and St. Paul. This business steadily increased until his line was extended from St. Paul to St. Louis, and his business became so large in the line of boating and transportation that in the spring of 1870 he found it desirable to reside in St. Louis, and so removed his family to that point, making it his home until about the year 1882. He was also very much interested in real estate in the city of St. Paul, which he held on to with great persistence, steadily improving it and building business blocks and structures thereon, up to the time of his death, which occurred at St. Paul on May 26th, 1887.

During his residence in St. Louis he was converted, and thereafter became an active worker in temperance and religious reforms. Perhaps the best work he did in this line was during his presidency of the St. Louis Bethel Association, where he was

CAPTAIN WILLIAM F. DAVIDSON.

the most active business manager in its financial interests. He was later also identified with the St. Paul Bethel Association, and was an officer of that organization at the time of his death.

After he became interested in religious work he abolished bars from the steamboats which he controlled, and did a great deal of personal work to reform the employes on the river from intemperance and immorality. He personally assisted and aided multitudes of men whom he had once employed, or in whom he had become interested while boating on the Mississippi River.

He was a very hard worker, giving his personal attention to all the details of his business up to a few days before his death. He led a very busy life, and never took time for pleasure, or the ordinary amusements which engross the attention of most men situated as he was financially.

His estate at the time of his death was quite large, and consisted mostly of real estate and business property well located in the heart of St. Paul. Much of this real estate was purchased as early as 1864 or 1865, and certainly prior to 1870, and had increased and multiplied in value so that it left a handsome fortune to his heirs.

He was identified with so many business enterprises of St. Paul that he was greatly missed from the community which he had done so much to build up and render prosperous by undertakings which he had inaugurated and pushed to success. Many of the business men of St. Louis, and other cities in the Mississippi Valley, will long remember him as a pleasant business acquaintance. An active, pushing man of business, he was always ready to do his share in bringing to a successful issue enterprises with which he became connected.

Like many of his associates — who have passed over to the majority during the last ten years — he is lying quietly at rest in Oakland Cemetery in the city of St. Paul.

CAPTAIN C. W. BATCHELOR.

Captain Chas. W. Batchelor was born in Steubenville, O., in 1823, and received his early education at private schools in his native town. His father was Jos. S. Batchelor, who moved from Philadelphia to Steubenville, in 1810, and engaged in the manufacture of furniture. In 1841, Captain Batchelor apprenticed himself to Captain Henry Mason, of Wheeling, on steamer Tioga, to learn to be a pilot. In 1845 he became a full pilot, and in 1849 he bought the interest of Captain John Klinefelter in the steamer Hibernia, No. 2, of Pittsburgh and Cincinnati Packet Line, and assumed command. In 1853, he took command of the famous Alleghany in the same line. In 1854, he sold his interest in the Alleghany, and built the Americus for the Pittsburgh and Nashville trade. In 1855 the Americus burned, and he left the river to become the active Vice-President of the Eureka Insurance Company, of Pittsburgh, and acted as the general agent in settling marine losses. In 1861 he was appointed, by President Lincoln, as surveyor of the Port and United States Depository at Pittsburgh, where he remained until September, 1866, when he was removed by President Johnson, because he would not be-

come a Johnson man. During his connection with the latter office, he disbursed over one hundred million dollars, and wound up with the Government in his debt. In 1867, he became president of the Eagle Cotton Mills Company, of Pittsburgh, where he continued until 1873. In 1868 he was made president of the Masonic Bank of Pittsburgh, where he continued until 1884, when he resigned, to become acting Vice-president of the Keystone Bank, and president of the Pittsburgh Petroleum Exchange. He continues his connection with the Keystone Bank, but resigned the presidency of the Oil Exchange. He is now the president of the Natural Gas Company of West Virginia, furnishing gas to the city of Wheeling, and secretary and treasurer of the Natural Gas Company, Limited, of Pittsburgh, the first gas company that ever handled natural gas for manufacturing purposes, which was in 1875, and president of the Manufacturers and Merchants Insurance Company of Pittsburgh. During his steamboat career, he owned in and built the most of the following steamers: Hibernia No. 2, Alleghany, Americus, W. I. Maclay, Eunice, Lucy Gwin, Paragon, Mary E. Forsyth, Geo. W. Graham, W. R. Arthur, Emma Duncan, Darling, Norman, Guidon, F. Y. Batchelor, and the Lac La Bell, of Cleveland, Ohio.

In 1885 he was made Chairman of the Committee of Arrangements and Commodore of the Fleet, for the celebration of the opening of Davis Island Dam, at Pittsburgh.

Captain Batchelor has been a prominent Mason for years, he having received the highest degree that can be conferred, and past Grand Commander, of the Grand Commandery of Knights Templar, of Pennsylvania.

LOUISVILLE, KY., June 20, 1889.

Capt. E. W. Gould, 1620 S. Grand Avenue, St. Louis, Mo.: —

DEAR SIR — I have been away from home a great deal since I received your favor of April 23d, and have neglected to send you biographies of the lives of Capt. Swagar and Capt. Sherley. Inclosed I send you a copy taken from the "Ohio Falls Cities and their Counties," which I trust will be in time; when your history is published I would be glad to have some copies of it.   Yours truly,

T. H. SHERLEY.

CAPT. Z. M. SHERLEY.

"This distinguished citizen of Kentucky was born in Virginia, in Louisa County, May 7th, 1811. He was removed to Kentucky at a very early period of his childhood, and had for a number of years to battle with the exactions of poverty. He was one of a pair of twins; his twin brother, Thomas Sherley, early embarked in the stock business, and while engaged in transporting cattle to a Southern market, was

drowned in the Mississippi River. The resemblance of the
twins was so perfect that when Z. M. Sherley approached
the house to inform the widow of the catastrophe, she was
confident that it was her husband. During a trip up the river
in 1832 the steamboat was hailed by a flat-boat on its way to
New Orleans with produce, with a request to take the sick
captain aboard and return him to his family at Portland. To

CAPTAIN Z. M. SHERLEY.

the horror of the captain and crew of the steamboat they discovered that the man was ill with cholera; at that time this
was supposed to be contagious, and the sick man was fastened
up in a room to battle with death by himself. All stood
aloof from him. In hunting some needed article, Captain
Sherley, a passenger on the boat, remembered that it was in
the room of the sick man, and he went into it with great fear
and trembling, in search of the missing implement, intending

to beat a very hurried retreat. The dying man spoke to him informing him that he had a wife and little boy at Portland whom he hoped to see before death terminated his sufferings. Captain Sherley could not leave the dying man, but remained by him until he died, ministering to his comfort and wants. He besought Captain Sherley to watch over the youthful life of his young son. When the boat reached Portland the captain went to the house of the dead man to convey the mournful tidings of the death. He found the widow was the daughter of John Tarascon, a gentleman who had acquired a great celebrity in his struggles in behalf of the prosperity of Louisville. He was a man of great enterprise.

In due course of time Captain Sherley married the widow of Captain Taylor, and commenced his career as a business man. His wife bore him two sons, when she died with consumption. She was one of the loveliest of her sex. She left the captain with four children to provide for, a son and daughter by Mr. Taylor, and two sons by Captain Sherley. No one was ever able to see any discrimination in his care of these children. They were well educated and the boys were trained to business pursuits, in which they prospered.

Captain Sherley engaged for a short time in the pork house business but retired from it retaining his interest in the property. He successfully run for some time a bout store, thus paving the way for that which was to be the master business of his life — the management of lines of transportation. No man was ever more gifted for any enterprise than he was for this great department. He became a prominent owner in the mail line between Louisville and Cincinnati, and his singular capacity for this great public interest was manifested conspicuously in every feature of its management. He was known throughout the country by his great success with everything of this kind with which he was connected. He owned an interest also in the line of packets running from Louisville to Evansville and Henderson. He became an owner in the ferry-boat interest between Louisville and Jeffersonville. Nowhere on the Ohio River were to be found boats that surpassed the equipments of the boats between Jeffersonville and Louisville, and he thus wielded an immense trade that widely extended his fame. He was well known from Maine to the far off borders of Texas, and from the Atlantic to the Pacific Coast. As the demands for business increased, he seemed to expand his capacity for every emergency.

During the civil war he was incessantly at his post, and no man was more relied on than he was by the military authorities. He was never found wanting in anything that was needed. His judgment was ripe, his advice at all times judicious, and when he was called upon for action he was always ready and fully equipped for duty. When, for example, it was necessary to move Gen. Buell's army from Louisville South, Captain Sherley at once furnished means for the transportation of the entire force by water. The boats made their appearance at the proper time as if by magic. This was accomplished by Captain Sherley. His knowledge, the wide acquaintance he enjoyed among steamboat men, their perfect reliance upon him, enabled him to supply the government with all it needed in this great emergency. This fullness, this promptitude, enabled Buell to reach Pittsburgh Landing in the very nick of time. In expediting comforts and supplies to the soldiers in the field, supplied often by the ton by soldiers' aid societies throughout the Northwest and the middle States, he was the master mind to whom all looked, and he never failed in a single instance in promptly furnishing the needed means to forward the supplies. In some of these emergencies he seemed at times to be endowed with a species of ubiquity. In all these matters he fulfilled to the letter, and in the fullness of its spirit, the apostolic injunction : to be " instant in season, out of season ! " It was remarkable how he met every emergency ; how successfully every one of these demands upon his capacity was carried out. He thus gave free and speedy transportation for supplies that would have footed up thousands of dollars if charges had been made. It was a consolation and reward to him to know that no suffering soldier was kept out of supplies by any remissness on his part.

When the last battle was fought, before its smoke cleared away, he became conspicuous in his active, enlarged and judicious spirit of conciliation. He at once evinced his desire that all should be blotted out, and that we, who had met as hostiles, should become one in all things. He carried this out in all his conduct ; he remembered in the calamities of the South, the gentle offices of mercy, kindness and beneficence. In these highest traits of humanity he was as active and unceasing as he had been during the war in doing all in his power to bring about this result — the peaceful solution of a perplexing problem. In the pursuit of this object he enjoyed the esteem and confidence of the chiefs of the governing authorities, and his advice was eagerly sought and usually obeyed. In this way Captain Sherley wielded an immense influence for the welfare of his country. It was very quietly exercised, but was not, thereby, the less effective.

In the city of Louisville his judgment and management were eagerly sought, and they were in the highest degree useful in their various exercises. He was a trustee of the medical department of the University of Louisville for a number of years, and was efficient and faithful in the performance of his duties of the trusteeship. For a number of years, indeed, up to the time of his death, he was a member of the Board of Trustees of the Kentucky Institution for educating the blind, and of the American Printing-house for the Blind. In the duties devolving upon him in these two trusts he was remarkable for the excellence of his services. In the heating apparatus for the institution, in the alterations of the building, in the stucco work on the house, his labors were altogether invaluable ; in these he has left testimonials that will be fitting monuments to his noble memory. He was for a number of years a trustee of Cave Hill Cemetery. Through his active agency a number of deforming obstructions were removed and graces of beauty and taste were substituted for them. We never see them without awakening memories in the mind that materially aid in evoking them into monuments that supply food to the taste and delight the eye by their beauty. In all these departments of duty Captain Sherley has left conspicuous traces of himself as imperishable as the material on which his tasteful and wise labors were expended. In all his business ways, his management of everything, he was remarkable for the quiet and unostentatious way in which he succeeded. No braying trumpet ever attended him in his movements.

Captain Sherley was married three times. The first wife was, as we have mentioned, Mrs. Taylor, a member of the celebrated Tarascon family. The second one was Miss Clara Jewell, of Louisiana ; the third, who survives him, was Miss Susan W. Cromwell, of Fayette County. A single son by each of these wives survives him. He left a large estate which was divided among these four heirs. The afflictive illness which carried him off was cancer of the stomach. This deprived him of appetite, and during the last twelve months of his life he rarely felt any disposition to take any kind of food. His mind was remarkably clear, and he attended to a variety of business with an unclouded intellect. This was very conspicuous in all his affairs long after his debility drove him to bed. Indeed, this was his condition up to near about the time the cancerous tumor of the stomach ate through his duodenum. At 2:15 o'clock on the morning of February 18, 1879, his long, beautiful life closed upon earth, amid a host of sorrowing friends and relatives. He had become a member of the Presbyterian Church some time before his death, and his hours of consciousness were, as his life had been, peaceful and calm. His funeral was attended by a multitude of his admirers, the Rev Messrs. Simpson, Wilson, Humphrey and Tyler officiating. His body reposes in the beautiful Cemetery of Cave Hill, which he did much to adorn and beautify.

Thus passed away from among us one of the most perfect types of manhood. He was a citizen of whom the commonwealth has just reason to be proud. In all the duties of good citizenship, he took a delight in advancing the welfare of his fellow-citizens. Calm, self-possessed, thoughtful and intelligent he rarely ever made a mistake in the conception of what it was right and proper to do, and he unwaveringly walked in the pathway which his judgment approved. He was greatly beloved, and he commanded an amount of confidence among those who sought his advice in their troubles, and we know of many hundreds of this kind that never were misplaced. It is incredible what multitudes of such cases went to him for guidance, and how cheerfully and calmly he aided and befriended them. He had a great number of relatives to whom his beneficence and kindness were unceasing. As a son, a brother, a husband and a father, he was a great exemplar. In his friendships he was rarely ever equaled: if he had any enmities, he kept them concealed.

Upon the occasion of his death, the various and numerous bodies of citizens with which he had long been connected in the transaction of public affairs, met and took action upon the great bereavement they had experienced, and expressed their sense of the great loss they had experienced in his death.''

Captain Joseph Swagar.

" The hero of this brief sketch enjoys the honor, doubtless, of being the oldest retired steamboat captain in the Mississippi Valley. Now, about to round his ninetieth year, he is still in marvelous health of mind and body, with his physical faculties almost unimpaired, save for some dullness of hearing. His clear and vivid recollections, stated in his graphic yet simple way, go back, as will be seen below, almost to the very dawn of the new era in river transportation in this Western World.

Captain Swagar is a native of the Keystone State, born in Montgomery county, then thirteen miles north of Philadelphia, on the 29th of October, 1792. When but eight years of age, when the glorious nineteenth century was coming in, he went with his parents to reside in the Quaker City. Five years more passed in the pleasant pursuits of home and the schools of that time, when, at the age of fourteen, he was apprenticed to a coppersmith, and in seven years became thoroughly mas-

CAPTAIN JOSEPH SWAGAR.

ter of the trade in all its branches, as then practiced. He then, late in 1815, decided to try his fortunes in the almost wilderness West, came across the mountains to the Ohio, and for lack of better conveyance just then, embarked in a flat-boat for a voyage down that stream. It was caught by cold weather and much ice at Maysville, and young Swagar pushed into the interior, spending the remainder of the winter at Lexington. The next spring — sixty-six years, two generations ago, be it noted — he reached Louisville, with which most of his busy life since has been identified. He shortly engaged to take two flat-boats, with cargoes of bacon, whisky and tobacco, to New Orleans, where he remained about three months, and then took ship for Richmond, Virginia. On this voyage he came near being shipwrecked on the Florida coast; but happily escaped, went on to Richmond, and reached Philadelphia again the same year (1816). He had taken a fancy, however, to the rising and hopeful village by the Falls of the Ohio ; and after a little rest at the old home, he started again toward the setting sun, to make a new one in Louisville. He tarried a little at Pittsburgh, and there, by arrangement with the owners, contracted for the copperwork to go into the Hope Distillery, then about to become the most flourishing industry in this place He engaged as an engineer in it upon his arrival, and completed its works by 1818.

There were few skilled mechanics of any kind then in town and Mr. Swagar found his services considerably in demand. Messrs. David Prentice and Thomas Bakewer, in the year before that last noted, started their foundry here, and turned over to him all their steamboat machinery that needed repairing. He served them profitably until 1821, by which time the foundrymen were considerably in his debt; and to extinguish this in part, he took an eighth interest in the new steamer Magnet, which they built the next year, and of which Captain J. Beckwith took command. Mr. Swagar's turn came the succeeding year (1823), when he mounted the deck of his first vessel as master. It was the well remembered Plowboy, built that year, of which he also owned an eighth. It was a very light-draught steamer, drawing only three feet when empty, and built after the pattern of a schooner. He accordingly, in 1824, took her up the Wabash to Terre Haute, and gave the wondering natives in that quarter and along shore their first glimpse of a real steamboat — a sign which some of them, it is said, went thirty miles to see. Until 1828 Captain Swagar was chief officer of the Plowboy. Then he went to Portsmouth at the mouth of the Scioto, bought the original Diana, and ran her two years. As one of her longer and more eventful trips he went up the Missouri with her to Council Bluffs in 1829, taking up the Sixth regiment of regular infantry to Fort Leavenworth, and returning with the Third regulars. Two years afterward he built a boat which made a yet more notable voyage for that period, which deserves to be permanently recorded in history. We will let him tell the story in his own words, as communicated to the *Courier-Journal* in the spring of 1880.

"After the total failure of the Colonel-Dick-Johnson expedition, up the Yellowstone in 1819 and 1820, the Missouri River was deemed unnavigable for steamers. The Fur Company sent all their supplies to the trading-posts on the Missouri River and Yellowstone, in barges or keel-boats until the building of the steamer Yellowstone in 1830–31. I had run the Diana up to Fort Leavenworth, with a keel-boat in tow, with perfect success the year before, and assured the Fur Company that I could build them a steamboat that would go to the mouth of the Yellowstone and back with as much certainty as to New Orleans and back; that all that was required was a boat of easy model, strong, plain engine of sufficient power, etc. The engine of the Yellowstone was at least fifty per cent. heavier than those usually built at that day. This steamer made one voyage a year to the Yellowstone and back to St. Louis, without breaking her engine or serious causalty, until the hull was deemed unsafe from decay. I superintended the building of this boat without pay or charge, as I had promised the boat builders that they should have at least one boat to build per year. My pride of citizenship induced me to labor to make Louisville famed for building steamboats and engines of a superior class for speed and safety."

In 1836–37 Captain Swagar built the steamer Antelope for the same company, which successfully navigated the turbulent Missouri. He had started the first ship-yard here in 1829, and the next year completed in it the first steamer built on this side of the Falls, after the Governor Shelby (the Don Juan), and also built the Yellowstone. Owning three-fourths of the vessel, he took personal command, and ran her for two years; sold out and built the Diana No. 2; ran her one and one-half years, and sold to the Fur Company; built the General Brown in 1836, for himself, Captain Frank Carter (now superintendent of the Cincinnati line of mail packets), and D. S. Benedict. This was the fastest boat of her time. The next year he sold her to his partners and others, and built the Diana No. 3; which, in 1838, at a time when a premium of five hundred dollars in gold was offered to the steamer which should get here from New Orleans inside of six days, brought the mails up in five days twenty-three hours and fifteen minutes. From 1842 the Captain himself ran the Diana No. 3, until she was somewhat worn, when he reconstructed her for the Diana No. 4, which he commanded one year and then sold. In 1845 he built the Homer, ran her two years, and then, in 1848, at the age of fifty-six, he retired permanently from the river.

In the year 1849 he made the overland trip with Bryant's company of emigrants to California, a trip of two thousand two hundred miles, with a pack-mule train; but returned the next year. In 1854* he was instrumental, with the late Capt. John Shallcross and others, in getting up the first law for the regulation of steamboat navigation through Congress. The next year he was appointed local inspector of hulls at Louisville, and held the post until 1861. Since that time he has been substantially retired from business, although for some time about 1865 he was President of the Franklin bank.

Capt. Swagar was married in 1819 to Miss Mary Walter, of Louisville, sister of Jacob Walter, well known in local history as a lively speculator of that age. She died in 1835, and he was remarried in 1839, his second wife being Rachel Moore, of Philadelphia, descendant of one of the emigrants with William Penn. She survived until February 1, 1870. His children living are but two — Frances, daughter of the former wife, now wife of Joseph Clement, long a hardware merchant in Philadelphia, and has three children; and Ella S., daughter of Mrs. Moore-Swagar, married Thomas H. Sherley, a prominent business man in Louisville, and they have five children — three daughters and two sons. Captain Swagar lost eight children, four by each marriage — among them a very talented and promising son, Charles M., who after a varied and eventful life, died in Paris in 1871."

CAPT. JOHN W. CANNON.

The following short letter from his son indicates the energy and perseverance so thoroughly prominent throughout Capt. Cannon's life that to those who knew him it is not necessary to add anything. Laudable ambition was his peculiarity. Honesty and integrity marked his course through life. Kindness, generosity and suavity were prominent virtues in his character.

His great ambition to excel all competitors involved his health and his fortune. And although a man of remarkable physique and of good judgment his ambition probably destroyed both.

To his enterprise and ambition the merchant marine of the Mississippi Valley is largely indebted for the world renowned elegance and speed of its steamboats in the past.

The accompanying cut is a photograph of the steamer Rob-

* This should probably be 1851.

ert E. Lee as she appeared on her arrival at St. Louis after her great race with the Natchez in 1870.

Capt. Cannon's name is so familiarly associated with that of the "Bob Lee," that to speak of the one involves that of the other.

It is claimed by the friends of the Lee that she was the champion of Western waters.

The record shows that she made the best time from New Orleans to St. Louis ever made and also to most of the points below St. Louis.

Whether the circumstances attending the great race against time, made by the first J. M. White in 1844, were such as to deprive that boat of the championship she so long enjoyed will probably always remain a moted question.

The last boat of that name left an imperfect record of speed, although there is no doubt she was the fastest and the most elegant steamboat ever built for Western waters.

NEW ORLEANS, April 10th, 1889.

Capt. E. W. Gould, St. Louis, Mo.:

" DEAR SIR— Agreeable to promise I now write you concerning my father. John W. Cannon was born June 17th, 1820, on a farm, two miles above Hawesville on the Ohio River in Hancock county, Ky.; his tution at school he paid with money earned by rail-splitting. When a young man he made a trip down the Mississippi with a flat-boat laden with coal and hoop-poles; then he went on the Ouachita boats as cub pilot, paying for that privilege by sundry work on the boat. After leaving the river, by strict economy saving his earnings, and with the aid of friends he built the steamer Louisiana, which boat was destroyed by the explosion of her boilers at the New Orleans wharf just on the eve of departure; a large number of persons were killed by the accident. Then he built the following boats: S. W. Downs, Bella Dona, W. W. Farmer, R. W. McRae, Gen. Quitman, Vicksburg, two R. E. Lee's, J. W. Cannon, Ed. Richardson. Owned the Rockaway, Anna, and interests in a number of boats that I have no knowledge of. Father was attacked in the prime of life by pneumonia brought on by neglected colds which settled on his lungs, and after many years of physical misery died at his home in Frankfort, Ky., April 18th, 1882, where he is buried.

I trust from the above you will be able to get what data you may need for the book to be published.

With my kindest regards and best wishes for your health. Respectfully yours, etc.,   W. L. CANNON.

THE BEST RECORDED TIME EVER MADE ON THE MISSISSIPPI.

NEW ORLEANS AND VICKSBURG STEAMER;ROBT. E. LEE.

PROMINENT NAMES THAT HAVE CROSSED THE RIVER.

Among the foregoing, whose biographies and auto-
biographies have been briefly sketched, will be missed the
names of many of their cotemporaries, the honorable mention
of which in this connection would awaken pleasant memories
of the past in the minds of thousands of their survivors, and
add much to the interest of these pages.

It was the hope and expectation of the author to enlist a
much larger number of contributors to this part of the work.

But the modesty of the survivors and the apparent apathy
of the part of those whose friends have crossed to the other
shore, leaves a vacancy in the history of this great factor of
Western civilization much to be regretted.

Among the many prominent names that will be recalled on
the Ohio River that are not mentioned in this work, are Captains
Forsythe, Jacobs, Beltzhoover, May, Wood, Campbell, Bennett,
Woodward, Smith, Stockdale, Reno, Poe, Hazlett, McLain,
Mason, List, Pierce, Rogers, Pepper, Stine, Summons, Kyle,
Shallcross, Bashum, Goslee, Sturgeon, Van Dusen, Woolfolk,
Hite, Montgomery, Mekin, Irwin, Benedict, McConnell, Hil-
dreth, Faucett and many others.

On the Upper Mississippi such familiar names as Taylor, Van
Houten, Reynolds, Loockwood, Able, Eaton, Miller, Fitheon,
Bernard, Warner, Whitney, Roe, Ranney, Moore, Hawk,
Jewett, Welton, Weaver, Cameron, Gorman, Ater, De Witt,
Sweeney, Middelton, McCune, Johnston, Freeland, Stettinius,
Price, Blood and many others no less worthy, will long be
remembered without an epitaph.

The Lower Mississippi too, has its mementoes of the past, in
such names as Holmes, Smoker, Hart, Cotten, Strecke, Hooper,
Kounz, Sinnott, Burdeau, Blanke, Tobin, Brown, Kennett,
Achin, Lee, all worthy of an epitaph in a history devoted
to the great industry in which they were among the prominent actors, the absence of which may suggest to their survivors the consistency of writing *their own epitaphs* before
crossing the river for the last time.

No profession in life is more frequently called upon to make
sacrifices and to contribute to the worthy and the unworthy
than the Western river boatman, and none are more ready to
contribute to the cause of humanity.

STEAMBOAT BOOK-KEEPING OF LONG AGO.

The following imaginary dialogue so well illustrates what many steamboat men and owners have been familiar with, it deserves a place in these reminiscences before the closing chapter.

It is from the Sketch Book of St. Louis, published in 1858.

"From the simplicity of the practical forms now in use for cash books, freight books, passage books, etc., the limited variety of transactions and the uniform manner of adjusting each trip's work in the ordinary routine consequent upon doing a cash business exclusively, many have been led to suppose steamboat book-keeping to be a very easy and simple thing. While to the thorough accountant and experienced steamboat clerks, such is the fact, but in a great majority of cases the reverse holds good.

That is, steamboat book-keeping without the knowledge of mercantile book-keeping, is more complex, varied and difficult than the latter. And why should it not be so? Steamboats incur responsibilities, contract debts, deliver goods without pay, just as merchants do.

They often speculate just as merchants speculate and not unfrequently negotiate bills of exchange "to raise the wind" or to make ends meet under circumstances that would make a levee merchant blush. I have known a man to purchase a steamboat without a dollar in hand, drop her down to the wharf, stick up his "shingle" for New Orleans, get a full cargo, step into one of our offices, effect an insurance on his freight list, negotiate a bill of exchange on his agent in New Orleans to pay charges and outfit here, make a successful trip or two, pay for his boat and in sixty days be on the lookout for another similar speculation.

Such, and three times as much more of a kindred nature, not unfrequently falls under the observation of any one whose duty calls him to wade through lots of books where such transactions have been involved.

Understanding *one account* an alternative is left him, that is to throw all transactions into his *cash account*.

Recapitulate and hand over a cash memorandum to his successor.

This clerk turns over a new leaf, counts the actual cash on hand and commences his work on a "clean sheet," but pays no further attention to the "cash memorandum." (It being no part of his business.)

The memorandum is soon misplaced or lost, debts due the boat remain uncollected and bills against the boat commence coming in, of which there is no entry in the books.

The season advancing and the receipts falling off, the owners conclude to "tie up." Whereupon the following interesting conversation occurs : —

Owner. Well, Cap, what is the word?

Captain. Gentlemen, we have had a fine run, a splendid business, carried more freight and passengers, made better time, burned less wood, carried less crew, had the best steward in the trade. Indeed, gentlemen, it is acknowledged by all hands in port and out of port, high water or low water, that she is emphatically *the boat.*

Owners. Good morning, Mr. Clerk, what's the good news with you?

Clerk. Good morning, gentlemen ; right side up ; only give this boat a good chance and "she'll stack you up a cord of it."

Owners. What do you mean by a good chance, Mr. Clerk?

Clerk. Get the owners to square off the old debts up to date ; put in an extra boiler ; paint up and put her in first-rate running order, and let Capt. ——— manage affairs to suit his own notion.

Owners. How far short will she be after paying off as far as she is now able?

Clerk. Can't tell exactly ; indeed, a Philadelphia lawyer could not tell from the manner in which those books have been kept, up to the time of my taking charge of them, bills are coming in every trip ; but, so far as known, about fourteen hundred dollars will be the pile.

Owners. Well, well, this will do pretty well for green hands at steamboating. A splendid boat ; a fine and popular captain ; an economical steward ; had a splendid run ; made lots of money, but no cash on board.

This might be thought a fancy sketch by some, with a few thousand dollars in spare cash, just ready to embark in a steamboat speculation. But it is our candid impression that if an infallible medium were to issue a narrative containing the history of steamboating, and the lives of steamboat owners, especially of those who are not familliar with steamboat accounts, the facts disclosed would prove that hundreds of captains, pilots, engineers, etc., had been ruined, or bankrupt, and thousands of dollars squandered by incompetent, inexperienced and careless steamboat clerks."

It must be recollected that this picture was drawn in 1858.

We have had a good deal of experience in the last thirty years : We have passed through four or five years of war, which developed a good deal of rough clerking; some fine specimens of speculation by contractors and star-routers; some loyal patriotism that thought Uncle Sam was an old goose and ought to be picked, and some magnificent specimens of stealing, that have entirely laid in the shade all the little shortings that have been developed by incompetent and unreliable steamboat clerks since the introduction of steam.

Then, again, we have seen the demoralizing effect of the love of money upon men in high position in civil life, aldermen, bank officers and confidential clerks. So while what the expert book-keeper of 1858 declared he believed was true, we have the satisfaction of thinking they were not of all men the greatest thieves.

We also have the satisfaction of knowing that steamboat clerks of the present day are competent, and as honest as the average of mankind, who are obliged to work for less money than will support them, and then only get employment half the time. Besides, if they were inclined to purloin, steamboats have not the money to steal they had at the time above referred to.

However, the picture of the expert is no ideal one, but will call to mind many cases where precisely the same state of facts, if not the same language, has existed in the experience of many men who have long been engaged in the business.

The failure or want of success does not, however, as this expert intimates, always or, indeed, in the majority of cases, arise from dishonest clerks, but from incompetent masters, not as sailors or practical boatmen, but as good business men.

There is no position in life where a more thorough knowledge of men, of general business transactions, of what is due to patrons, to the employed, and to politeness, than is necessary in a man in charge of a good business steamboat. The practice of placing a man in charge of a steamboat because he was a sailor, or familiar with the duties of a master, or what is known as a good boatman, without the other qualifications has done more to ruin the success of owners, and bring discredit upon the occupation, than the ignorance, or lack of integrity on the part of steamboat clerks.

FIFTY YEARS' OBSERVATIONS CONDENSED.

In the lifetime of a nation *fifty years* is but a span, a moment of time. But in the life of an individual, if an eventful life, how much is often crowded into it. How much of interest, if remembered, could be related of the events that have transpired under the observation of even a boatman on the Mississippi.

While these pages chronicle events covering a much longer period than *fifty years*, in closing this desultory history it may be interesting to note a few of the more striking changes that have occurred in the valley within the observation of one man, and will illustrate the changes that are rapidly being evolved.

A recent trip (1889) along the principal streams of the valley, has given the writer an excellent opportunity to contrast the situation, the condition of things *fifty years* ago with the present time or

THEN AND NOW.

Commencing at New Orleans, the natural culminating point of the principal river commerce of the great valley, from the deck of a steamboat one is struck with the great change that is presented to the eye of one who was familiar with the scene *fifty years* ago. Even thirty years perhaps has wrought a greater change.

Then, all was life and animation, no commercial scene probably in the world equaled that of New Orleans during the business season from 1840 to 1860.

No mart, or area devoted to commercial purposes, could excel the wharves in that city in the amount of business transacted, the number of vessels engaged, the number of drays that were employed, or the cosmopolitan character of the people that thronged them.

Now, how changed — instead of the moving panorama of human, animal, and vegetable life, revolving in quick succession throughout the immense space devoted to commerce, the iron horse with long trains of cars and numerous depots, sheds, etc., occupy the principal space on the levee, while the water front that was then occupied by so many steamboats, flatboats, and sailing vessels, is now occupied by comparatively few of either, but with many large steamships, grain-barges, tow-boats, coal-boats, sailing craft and a few steamboats.

There are no statistics at hand by which to determine the aggregate amount of business *now* and *then*. But while the city is supposed to have added 150,000 inhabitants to its population in *fifty years* it is evident its commerce has largely increased, although judging from a casual observation on the wharves one will naturally conclude there has been a large falling off from its most prosperous years.

Then there were no railroads. *Now* there are seven lines of roads centering at New Orleans.

Modern ideas are developing in every direction. Progress and evolution are written in bold relief in many parts of the city. Buildings that would do credit to any city are being erected, and many private residences indicate a degree of wealth and refinement unknown in the earlier days. Great improvement is observed in the sanitary condition of the city, resulting from paving the streets with granite blocks, and in a more perfect drainage.

Much yet remains to be done in that direction, and when properly done as now proposed, no city will present greater attractions to visitors or to business men.

Its system of street railroads is unequaled, many of its streets are wide and tastily shaded and its system of electric lights throughout the city surpasses that of any other. No greater change is observed than in the character and habits of the people. This arises largely from the change incident to the emancipation of the slaves and a more general adoption of American customs.

Its close proximity to the West India Islands, to Central and South America, to the Pacific Ocean, *via* the Isthmus routes which are soon to be opened to commerce; with extensively improved water communication extending to all parts of the valley, it can only be a question of a few years when New Orleans will realize greater changes than it has in the last *fifty years*.

In passing up the river from New Orleans *fifty years* has wrought many changes which are painfully apparent. Not so much perhaps in fifty as in forty years. This is evidently caused by a change in the system of labor too.

Many large, fine sugar plantations are much neglected. Some others are abandoned and overgrown with willows and weeds, many sugar houses are in ruins and elegant dwellings going to decay. Where once was seen rows of 20, 30, 40 and 50 neat comfortable cabins for negro quarters, many are gone or deserted while the occupants are scattered and many of them have become vagrants, wandering up and down the earth, while

others are squatting along the banks of the river in little
shanties, subsisting on crawfish, garden truck and an occasional day's work they can chance to get from   " ole massa "
or his more fortunate successor.   Even that universal resort
to which all poorer classes on the coast formerly claimed as a
common heritage, whether slave or free, no longer avails
them, as there is no sale for *drift-wood.*   Both sugar houses
and steamboats have substituted coal for fuel in a large degree.   If such was not the case, it is doubtful whether the
negroes have sufficient energy to catch the drift and prepare
it for fuel.   Most of the larger estates that owned and worked
from three to six hundred hands have changed owners or
been subdivided until they are no longer recognized as the
beautiful places of *fifty years ago.*

In many places may be seen along the banks of the river,
just in the rear of the levees, collections of small houses,
cabins and tents, among which one of larger proportions is
designated *the store,* occupied by a son of Abraham, dispens-
ing the necessaries of life to the children of Ham at the small
profit of one hundred per cent, " being zust what he cost me,
so help me gracious."

There have been since the war but few improvements, and no
new land added by clearing up the swamps.   This is not only
true on the coast, within the sugar-belt, but extends all the
way to Cairo ; nor does there appear much improvement in
the small towns and parishes even up to that point, and many
that were in embryo *fifty years* ago have disappeared
altogether.

Baton Rouge is the first point above New Orleans that seems
to have aroused itself and responded to the demand to " fall
in " and join in the march of improvement that its position
entitles it to do.

Leaving many towns in obscurity that had large pretensions
fifty years ago, Natchez is still found sitting upon a hill that
cannot be hidden, and while evidences of prosperity and progress are apparent, it has not made rapid strides commensurate with the beauty of its location or of its early promise.
One hundred years ago Natchez was an important point, and
the largest and best known town above New Orleans on the
Mississippi.

" Natchez under the hill " had a notoriety known to no other
point in the great valley.   But the great tornado in May, 1840,
swept from sight nearly all the buildings and flat-boats that
had so long served as a rendezvous for the thousands of
desperate and dissolute that congregated there.   That portion

of the city has never been re-built, but the destruction on the hill has long since been obliterated by new and improved dwellings and business houses.

Passing several which were embryo cities *fifty years* ago, Vicksburg, or what was known as the 3d *Chickasaw Bluff*, has survived the fierce onslaught of the Federal forces under General Grant, and the effects of Yankee shells from Young's Point, and still presents the most picturesque and beautiful view from the river to be seen from New Orleans to St. Louis. And notwithstanding, the river in its natural course has succeeded in doing what General Grant could not do, and has left the city a mile distant from its channel, through the capacity of Government engineers and the liberal appropriations from Congress, Vicksburg still maintains its commercial importance, and has high hopes of continued prosperity. The quiet and unpretending little city of Lake Providence, bordering on the shores of the picturesque lake of that name, seems to about hold its own, and serves to awaken pleasant recollections in the minds of travelers and navigators of *fifty years* ago. Fifty miles above is Greenville, a modern little city unknown to fame *fifty years* ago. But if the Government succeeds in arresting the city plat from its tendency to cave and float off, there seems good reason to believe the enterprise of the Hebrews and other nationalities there, will succeed in building a city of some magnitude. The once well-known towns of Columbia and Gaines Landing have ceased to attract attention and are only remembered for what they once were.

Arkansas City, fifty miles above Greenville, is a modern town, and at one time had high expectations, from the fact that a railroad connected it with Pine Bluff and other interior points in Arkansas. But the argus eye of Jay Gould was attracted by the volume of business arriving there by steamboat, and a branch road settled the question, leaving Arkansas City to wonder in amazement at the effect of one man's suggestion.

At the mouth of the Arkansas River where once stood the famous city of *Napoleon* nothing remains to mark the spot, and its classic grounds have long since floated into the Gulf of Mexico through the jetties.

The mouth of the White River or Montgomery's Point, the bloody ground of *fifty years* ago, and the resort and hiding place of *Murrel's gang*, and river pirates and desperadoes, has long since followed its rival, Napoleon, and deposited in the waters of the gulf the remains of a greater number of outlaws than any other point on the Mississippi can boast of.

Friar's Point has changed but little in appearance in *fifty years*, but *Delta* has disappeared.

Helena has " fought a good fight," and arisen from a submerged bed of river deposit, and the energy and enterprise of her citizens has excited the admiration and sympathy of the Government, which will probably result in more perfect protection in the near future.

Sterling, Austin and *Commerce* have but little left to indicate their importance *fifty years* ago.

Memphis stands out in bold relief, and in striking contrast with the 400 miles of what is yet often submerged bottomlands, that we have been passing since we left Vicksburg on the third Chickasaw Bluff.

Here, on what was familiarly known as the Second Chickasaw Bluff, in the early times, has sprung into life a beautiful city of 100,000 inhabitants, which *fifty years* ago could hardly boast of one-tenth that number.

After traveling hundreds of miles through the low wilderness country, destitute of even the thousands of cord-wood piles that lined its banks *fifty years* ago, and the numerous steamboats, and yet more numerous flat-boats that were never out of sight, Memphis rises like an oasis in the desert, to dispe the thought that we have retrograded — that we have been taking a Rip Van Winkle nap for the last *fifty years*.

Notwithstanding the absence of the large number of steam and flat-boats, that once crowded the levee in front of the city, and covered its limited wharf with cotton bales and the importations from all other countries, enough remains to contrast the progress in *fifty years*, and to note the fact that Memphis has caught the inspiration of the age, and is no longer wedded to the old ways of transportation, nor of the manner of doing business in ante bellum times.

New Orleans and other rival points must look well to their interests, or Memphis will eclipse their *cotton aspirations* and leave them in the shade.

What has been said of the country below Memphis will apply even up to Cairo. Leaving Memphis, the first old land mark, Randolph, is about " snowed under," and lost its importance, if it ever had any, as a shipping point. Osceola is obscured from view by the large tow-head in front of the town, although claiming to be among the progressive points in Arkansas.

The fleet of government boats laying at the upper landing is about all that changes the place in appearance now from *fifty years ago*, except the large tow-head in front of the

town. The same monotony continues, only intensified by the
absence of the immense piles of cord-wood, and wood-boats,
that formerly lined both shores, until reaching Mrs. Merry-
weathers (now Caruthersville), Point Pleasant and New Madrid.

These places occupy about the same position and importance
as formerly. The latter point, however, being still on wheels,
gracefully recedes as the river encroaches upon its sandy
foundation.

There is scarcely enough left of *Island Number Ten* to mark
that famous battle ground, in the early days of the rebellion,
when mortar practice with whistling shells, and rifle pits was
the chosen mode of warfare. Mills Point, or Hickman, as
it is now called, has increased in size and population slowly.
But when a railroad reached it, which was supposed to increase
its importance as a commercial point, the immense tobacco
trade, of which it had a monopoly, was directed to other points
and Hickman soon lost its pre-eminence as a shipping point.

The Chalk Banks and Columbus, or as formerly known, the
" first Chickasaw Bluff " still holds its own against the resist-
less force of the Mississippi, which has for long years can-
noned against its side, leaving the little town of Columbus
undisturbed; while its commercial importance was carried
off by the first train of cars that crossed the ferry to the Iron
Mountain Railroad many years since.

Fifty years has done much to bring Cairo to the front, and
to protect it from the floods of the two " River Gods " that
unite here and carry commerce and devastation on their way
to the gulf.

It is now just *fifty years*, or in 1839, this writer had an
eventful experience at Cairo, which then had but a single
house to mark the spot in high water, but many flat-boats
and water craft moored at the shore, with one larger one,
kept by a Mr. Falls, a very accommodating, agreeable Irish-
man, who lived across the river at Birds Point, in Missouri,
and did business at Cairo.

The channel of the Mississippi at that time was close down
the Illinois shore and very near where the " Haliday House "
now stands.

The two islands that have since occupied the bend above,
have each in turn been removed and deposited on the point at
Cairo, and in turn have again been washed down until at present the point and the channel are more than a mile below the
town.

The *one house* was located near the Mississippi, and stood
upon posts several feet above the ground. It was a two-

47

story frame, some 150 feet long, divided into compartments, and used for a hotel, a private dwelling, a store house, and in fact for anything that needed shelter.

In coming out of the Mississippi with the steamer Knickerbocker, she struck an obstruction on the bottom about two miles above the point, knocking a large hole in her knuckle and bottom, which, upon going into the hold, I at once saw would sink the boat very soon, perhaps before we could reach the shore at Cairo. But as the current was too strong, and the river too full of snags and trees, which were then just falling in with the bank and the island, I ran to the hurricane deck and instructed the pilot (Capt. John Carlisle), to get the boat around the point at Cairo, if possible, that being the only safe place we could reach to land the large number of passengers on board. In rounding the point he shaved the bank so closely one could have nearly reached dry land by jumping from the guards of the boat. She was landed among several flat-boats, with but little regard to the manner of landing, and the passengers and crew availed themselves of those floating craft to escape from the rapidly sinking boat. We had barely time to run a hauser to a big cotton-wood tree then standing on the bank, to prevent her sliding into deep water, when she went down.

The boat was loaded principally with lead, and sunk very quickly. There were no lives lost except that of stock, and of them but few could be unloosed in time to save them.

As is often the case in time of peril and excitement, some amusing incidents occurred which become indelibly fixed in my mind.

After the boat struck the snag and it was announced she was sinking, in going from the lower deck to the roof, I passed through the cabin to see that the passengers were all called, as it was then early in the morning. I found everybody up and in the cabin, but no one had finished their toilet, nor did they seem to know or care anything about toilets or clothing. One gentleman from Palmyra, Missouri, had a large number of slaves on board he was taking to New Orleans for sale. He came rushing forward from the after part of the cabin, with his pants and one suspender and one boot on, and a life-preserver in his hands, which he was trying to inflate, crying at the top of his voice: "Where are my niggers, where are my niggers?" But the negroes were saved and re-shipped, as were the other passengers, to the place of their destination.

The light freight and other movable things about the wreck

were soon disposed of by the river pirates, and others living along the shores.

As this was before the introduction of diving-bells and wrecking-boats, the cargo (lead) remained for many years in the hull, and was in after years a frequent resort of the diving-bell men in dull times, and proved a *lead mine* worth working.

A stay of some weeks at the wreck made a lasting impression upon my mind as to the accommodations of the *Cairo hotel* and the value of water lots.

Until the Illinois Central Railroad built its track along the bank of the Ohio in front of the town, the growth of Cairo was slow. Since that time it has made commendable progress, and if its business is not interrupted by the building of railroad bridges, in the near future, and the Government continues its protection of the river banks, there seems no good reason why Cairo should not show greater improvement in the next fifty years than it has in the last. So far as the improvement on the banks of the river above Cairo go, there is no advantage over those below Cairo. With the exception of Cape Girardeau and Chester, *fifty years* has made no change for the better, until St. Louis is reached. These two places seem to have overshadowed all others along the river, and made some advance; they being the principal railroad points may account in some degree for their improvement.

In all the changes that *fifty years* has produced between New Orleans and St. Louis, none are so marked as the changes in the number and character of the floating craft on the river and the changes incident thereto.

THEN AND NOW.

Then a steamboat of 1,000 tons capacity was never seen.

Now those of 1,500 tons are not uncommon.

Then a boat with two engines was unheard of.

Now it is not unusual for them to have six and sometimes even more.

Then a doctor or auxiliary engine for pumping water into the boilers was not thought of, and a steam whistle never heard.

Now they are universal.

Then the use of steam to work the capstan or to handle spars had not been adopted.

Now no boat is without them.

Then loose planks were used to construct a stage or gangway at every landing.

Now a substantial stage is always suspended and ready to launch into position for use by the power of steam by the time the boat strikes the landing.

Then the use of coal for steam on Mississippi River boats had not been adopted, and " wooding the boat " was an important feature which even the deck passengers were expected to take part in.

Now wood is seldom used except for culinary purposes ; not even torch-wood is required, as the almost universal electric light supersedes all other modes of artificial light, and is one of the greatest auxiliaries to safety, convenience and economy that has been introduced since the application of steam to navigation.

Then boats were constructed with the ladies' cabin in the hold of the boat, which was open, and in the afterpart. The gentlemen occupied a cabin overhead, located nearer forward, — state-rooms were not thought of, nor a Texas for the crew provided.

Then a tow-boat with barges of produce or merchandise, or a tow of coal boats was never seen.

Now a larger amount of both are thus transported than is carried on ordinary steamboats.

Then a steamboat was seldom out of sight, night or day, and to see twenty flat-boats at one time was no novel sight.

Now to meet or pass a steamboat attracts particular attention and a flat-boat or broad-horn with produce is seldom seen, while tow-boats with large tows of barges loaded with produce or merchandise are not unfrequently in sight.

In a good stage of water in the Ohio River a tow-boat with fifteen or twenty loaded coal boats going down the Mississippi, or the same number of empty boats going up, is no rare thing.

Then no *beacon light* was seen on the banks to assist a pilot in finding an obscure landmark in a dark stormy night, or relieve the anxiety of the captain who has been standing on the hurricane deck watching for an ugly snag, or a dangerous break he knew they were in the neighborhood of. ·

Now, through the watchful care of the light house board and the annual appropriation of the Government, all difficult crossings are well defined, and dark nights are robbed of their former gloom and uncertainty.

Then, to see fifty snags in the channel at one glance was no rare occurrence and the wreck of a steamboat was no novelty.

Now, through the ingenuity of Captain Henry M. Shreve, the Government is enabled to remove the snags as often as they make their appearance, and the genius of Captain J. B. Eads has rendered practicable the raising of many sunken boats, and the removal of all wrecks.

Then the custom of *card playing* was almost universal with passengers, in which the crew often participated, when off duty. As the rules of most boats did not restrict card players to " simple games for amusement " or require them to " retire at 10 o'clock," they were sometimes continued into the wee small hours, and not uufrequently until daylight — many old stewards can yet bear testimony to the fact that they have often found the same players still engaged in the fascinating old game of *draw* when they called their cabin crew at daylight in the morning, that were playing with their coats off when he retired the eveuing previous.

To find fifteen or twenty old decks of cards strewn over the floor of the *social hall* in the morning (the part of the cabin that was then appropriated to card playing and the officer's rooms, which was of course before the Texas or officer's quarters were introduced on to Western boats) was no uncommon thing.

Fabulous stories were told of the amount of money and valuables lost and won at these all-night sittings, and not unfrequently, negroes, then on the way to a Southern market, in charge of their owners, were staked on the result of the *winning hand.*

As an evidence that those games were sometimes indulged in by officers even though on duty, this writer has abundant testimony. A single case in point will illustrate, and it will not be necessary to call names, as many (not very old boatmen either) will recall the circumstance.

In the early spring of ———— the beautiful little side-wheel boat ———— belonging on the upper rivers, was returning to St. Louis from a trip to New Orleans, when she struck a snag at Ruckers Point, between Memphis and Cairo.

The boat and cargo were a total loss, but no other casualty. Later developments proved conclusively that the pilot on watch, or who should have been on watch, was in the hall below playing *poker* with the passengers, and a steersman was piloting the boat, when she struck a snag, being too far out on the bar.

Many such cases could doubtless be enumerated, but not many perhaps with such fatal results.

Now, all is changed. One may sometimes make a trip of several days on a steamboat and not see a game of any kind played. Gambling is an unusual occurrence, and when indulged in by passengers the game is closed at bed-time, in accordance with the rules of all good boats. Now, such a thing as the crew participating in any game on board, is of rare occurrence and never to the neglect of duty.

The cause of this change may be more difficult to determine; it certainly does not arise from a higher state of morals.

While there may be less public gambling with cards, there is evidently tenfold more gambling in business transactions than ever before. The principal difference in betting on who holds the best hand at cards, and on the price of corn or wheat next month, is simply the time and manner of settlement. As one has become a legitimate (?) occupation, and the other indulged in usually as a pasttime, or recreation, it may be an interesting question for the moralist to determine which is the least demoralizing.

UPPER MISSISSIPPI.

Leaving St. Louis and going up the Mississippi, *fifty years* has made but little change in the appearance of the country or of the river, until Keokuk is reached.

The few towns and cities that are passed show an improved condition generally, but not specially marked, considering the length of time between *then* and *now*.

Half a century has developed Keokuk from a small village of whites, half-breeds and Indians, to a prosperous city of 40,000.

From there to the falls of St. Anthony there has been a wonderful change, not only in the settlement and cultivation of the land on the banks of the river, but also in building cities and towns.

Fifty years has probably done more to develop and cultivate that portion of the valley than has been done in all other portions combined.

The first half of the fifty years developed an immense river commerce. Since that time it has been largely transferred to railroads and the tonnage of the river correspondingly reduced.

The large expenditures by the government for the improvement of navigation ought to have secured to the river a constantly increasing business.

The pine lumber business is probably the only one that has held its own since its development, which has been within the *fifty years*. It now emyloys some 100 tow-boats and many thousand men.

The only thing that seems possible to interfere with that river traffic is exhausting the supply of pine timber.

While the numerous bridges across the stream add largely to the expense of handling rafts, the introduction of steam still renders the river the cheapest mode of marketing the lumber.

Most of the large towns above St. Louis have been built, or largely so, through the profits of the lumber trade.

Less than *fifty years* has brought St. Paul and Minneapolis from nothing to their present prosperous condition. Many boatmen are still living who can remember the time when neither place had even a log cabin to mark their location ; so too with many of the towns lower down the river.

Fifty years has seen Nauvoo grow from a single stone house on the bank of the river to a city of 30,000 inhabitants and then dwindle away to less than one thousand.

The beautiful transparency of the water, as it floats gently along, washing the shores of the thousand islands — the picturesque beauty of the bold promontories and hills that slope gracefully down to the water's edge, added to the healthy invigorating climate, will always render this the most attractive portion of the great Mississippi Valley, and who will dare predict its development by generations yet unborn.

Among other great changes *fifty years* has made on this part of the great river none are more marked than the building of the canal at Keokuk has produced.

Then, no point on the river above St. Louis exhibited half the life and business appearance that Keokuk did, especially during the low water season.

To see 40 or 50 flat-boats or lighters engaged in receiving or discharging cargoes of merchandise or produce from steamboats to be lighted across the rapids by the use of horses, was no unusual thing, involving the labor of a large number of men and horses, beside the crews of a dozen steamboats there waiting to discharge or receive the cargo that was being lighted across the rapids for points above or below — presenting an animated scene unequaled at any interior point in the valley except the large cities.

Now, the canal has changed all that and the steamboat, with her cargo unbroken, passes immediately to or from the canal, leaving Keokuk like a way station on a railroad, or a big town on the river, after the completion of a railroad bridge. But Keokuk anticipated the result, made hay while the sun shone, and is now largely independent of either steamboat or railroad.

In nothing has *fifty years* made greater changes in the commerce of Western waters than the introduction of towboats and their uses. They are known under two classes, although used for the same purposes.

The *tug-boat*, with a screw propeller, and the regular *tow-boat*, or stern-wheel boat, with the paddle wheel, neither of which was known or used *fifty years* ago for the purpose to which they are now so largely devoted.

With the exception of towing ships to and from New Orleans, no tow-boats were used on these waters, and they were a powerful class of side-wheel boats built exclusively for that purpose. *Now* the number of tow-boats is legion, and are seen every where.

A far greater amount of capital is now invested in tow-boats than in freight and passenger boats. As high as $75,000 is sometimes invested in a single tow-boat.

There are at the present time (1889) about eighty tow-boats owned and operated from Pittsburgh, some of them of the largest class. About an equal number is owned at other points on the Ohio River.

There are about twenty owned at St. Louis employed on the Lower Mississippi, principally by the Mississippi Valley Barge Co. There are some 100 employed in the lumber trade on the Upper Mississippi.

There is also a large number of tug-boats which are found to be very useful in handling all kinds of water craft in the harbors and for short jobs of towing every where.

There has been nothing introduced within the *fifty years* that has contributed so much to the convenience and saving of labor as these little tugs.

From past experience and present indications it seems reasonable to predict that for the next *fifty years* the tow-boat will be the principal factor in river commerce, on all inland waters and in fact upon all waters. Coal, lumber, bulk grain, ice and rock, which constitute nine-tenths of the present river traffic are all largely dependent upon this mode of transportation and seem to defy competition.

CHANGES ON THE MISSOURI.

Fifty years have seen greater changes in the commerce and navigation of the Missouri and Illinois Rivers than is perceptible in the improvements upon their banks. As on the lower Mississippi, a few cities and towns have grown into prominence while by far the greater number have become obscure and almost forgotten. Less land is in cultivation on the banks of both these streams than was the case *fifty years* ago. While the commerce of the valleys has largely increased, that on the rivers has almost disappeared; although during the half century, the surface of these rivers have floated millions of tons of produce to the markets of the world.

The three millions of dollars the government has expended in useless efforts to improve the navigation of the Missouri has not done so much to improve it as the railroad bridges have to damage it, and it is not probable that *fifty years* more will restore to the river the amount of transportation it once enjoyed. It has required less than forty years to reduce the number of steamboats from sixty, at one time employed, to scarcely none at all at the present time.

CHANGES ON THE ILLINOIS.

Fifty years has reduced the trade on the Illinois, nearly in the same proportion, and while the commerce of both valleys is rapidly increasing there seems no reasonable expectation that water transportation will become a necessity for many years to come.

CHANGES ON THE OHIO AND TRIBUTARIES.

Fifty years has probably wrought less radical changes on the Ohio River and its tributaries than on the Mississippi.

While there has been but little change in the products of the soil, the increase of manufacturers has been very large; and yet for thirty years water transportation has been largely superseded by rail, except in the article of coal. That industry has increased so rapidly it is difficult to determine whether the falling off of the one has been counterbalanced by the increase of the other. It has certainly resulted in important changes. It is now (1889) about thirty-five years, since steam has been used in handling coal. *Fifty years* ago there was a very large number of steamboats and a larger number of flat or produce boats employed, but the business of steamboats did not reach the zenith of its prosperity until about 1858 or '9, and it culminated in 1861, when the war broke out. The efforts of the Government to improve the navigation has resulted favorably in most cases.

The character of the bed of the river and the shores are such there is no doubt of entire success in a few years, if continued.

If, in the meantime, illy-constructed bridges do not destroy the navigation, it seems probable that the rapid development of the valley will at no distant day even increase river transportation far beyond its present status; although the time is probably forever past when the splendid lines of passenger boats that were once the pride and the glory of the great West, will again be called into use.

The great danger is, that the railroad influence in national legislation and the present depressed condition of river interests, will result in withholding annual appropriations and destroying the interest in river improvements that has pervaded the West for the last few years. Strange as it may appear, there has often appeared an inclination on the part of those most interested in river improvements, a disposition to criticise the manner and the principle upon which the engineers were doing their work, instead of recognizing the fact that the work was necessarily experimental often, and that if not successful the first time, it was at the expense of the Government and would be remedied later, with the valuable experience of the engineer, who is a ward of the Government, and educated at its expence. However unintentional these criticisms may be, they are not without their influence on the public mind, which finds expression in Congress through our representatives.

Much, very much, depends in the future upon the Government's action in improving the navigation of the waters of the Mississippi Valley.

THE TRIBUTARY STREAMS.

What has been said of the Mississippi, the Missouri, the Illinois, the Ohio, will apply generally to the principal navigable tributaries; all seem in a transition state. *Fifty years* have served to develop their natural possibilities. Modern science and the progress of the age demand another step forward. Nature, always munificent in this great valley, requires the assistance of the mechanical genius of man to further develop the great natural highways of the valley so as to render them commensurate with the demands of its rapidly increasing commerce. If the Government is true to its great mission, *fifty years* more will see the whole delta of the Mississippi and the bottom lands of its tributaries securely protected from overflow, *which will result in maintaining a depth of water in the channels of the rivers equal to the demands of the commerce,* if not obstructed by artificial appliances erected by antagonistic interests.

MISSISSIPPI RIVER COMMISSION.

While the Mississippi River Commission has made commendable progress in its experimental work on the Mississippi, since its creation, under the adverse circumstances and unfair criticisms with which it has had to contend, it has developed a system of improvement which, if followed up, will undoubtedly insure a stage of water and the protection of the banks of the Mississippi commensurate with the demands of its commerce for long years to come.

In the fiftieth Congress a bill was introduced to create a Bureau of Harbors and Water Ways, which is to be known as the "Corps of United States Civil Engineers." If this bill becomes a law, which there is no reasonable doubt of, it will place river and harbor improvements on a more secure foundation, with a guarantee to the government against a useless expenditure of money on unimportant works, with the assurance that whatever is undertaken will be prosecuted with economy and with the advantage of the best skill and experience known to modern engineering.

It seems that the system contemplated by this bill, if adopted, will insure results in the Mississippi Valley which will give new life and importance to navigation.

CONCLUSION.

EVIDENCE OF PROGRESSION.

While the principal changes that have taken place in the last *fifty years* in this valley have been generally physical in character, the following anecdote from the *Arkansas Traveler* will fully prove that great moral and social progress has been made through the influence of emigration and contact with citizens from other parts of the world. No one who was familiar with the ignorance, lack of thrift and adaptability of the backwoodsman of the South in earlier years, but what will be surprised at the effect that even *less* than *fifty years* has had upon the American citizen of African descent, as illustrated in this anecdote :

[From the Arkansas Traveler.]

A party of Eastern capitalists were riding along a lonely wood in a wild district of Alabama. Suddenly, upon turning in the road, they saw a woman wringing her hands. One of them ordered the driver to stop.

"What's the matter, my good woman?" some one called.

"O, Lordy! O, Lordy! They have hung my poor husband!" Then, pointing, she showed the strangers the body of a man hanging from a tree.

"O, Lordy! they come to our house an' tuk him out an' hung him jest because he told the deputy marshals when they axed him that the Phillips boys was a makin' uv whisky. O, I don't know what I'm going to do. Thar ain't nothin' in the house fur the children to eat, an'——" here she broke down.

"Let us cut him down." exclaimed one of the capitalists, springing out of the wagon. "Perhaps he is not dead."

"O, yes, he is," the woman mourned. "They hung him this mawnin' about daylight and swore they'd shoot anybody that cut him down."

The capitalists climbed back into the wagon.

"My mother has gone airter a Justice uv the Peace," said the woman, "but I don't know what good he ken do. O, Lordy, what'll become uv my po' chillun. Gentlemen, ain't you got nothin' ter eat in yo' wagin. Ef you ain't got nothin, but a piece of bread, for the Lawd's sake let me have it."

"Madam," said a man who seemed to be the leader of the party, "we brought a lunch with us, but unfortunate

a few miles back; but we will see that you do not suffer.
Here, boys, I'll start the ball with $10. Chip in and help
this poor woman."

Pocket-books flew open. Each man contributed something,
and the woman, with many tears of gratitude, accepted the
contributions. The capitalists drove away, and when their
wagon was out of sight a lank man poked his head from behind a tree and said:

"How's the haul, Lize?"

"First rate," the woman replied.

"Lemme see," he said, approaching her. "Bled like a
stuck pig, didn't they?" he added, as he took the money.
"Times is improvin' slow, but shure."

"Sam, I hated to take this yere money. Them men
'peared to be teched."

"Oughter be teched ter see a pore man hangin' in the
woods thiser way. Hate ter take the money! W'y, it's my
pension, gal. The Gover'ment oughter give a man a pension,
no matter whut side he fout on, an' ef the Gover'ment won't
do it, w'y a man jest haster collect the best way he ken.
Reckon we'd better take down the gentleman," nodding at
the figure that hung from the tree, " an' move him away. O,
I tell you a pa'r uv ole boots, some ole clothes, an' a little
wheat straw pans out putty well sometimes."

"Sam, I still think we oughn't ter tuk it."

"W'y, gal, don't yer know they feel jest ez good ez ef that
thing hangin' thar wuz me, an' I know that I am better off, so
the thing has turned out all right. Ef they wuz so teched
they mout be glad to know that yore po' husband ain't dead.
It don't make no diffunce ter a man's feelin's whether he has
done good ur not, jes so he think's he has. They think
they've done good, an' we know we have. My daddy uster
say so, an' I'm beginnin' to b'leeve it, that this here thing uv
enterprise mighty nigh allus wins."

CORRECTIONS.

Page 243. — Tenth line from bottom; read *none of* the engines instead of *all*.

Page 359. — Tenth line from top; read *Island 37*, not *32*.

Page 369. — Third line from bottom; read *Louisville* canal, not *Louisiana* canal.

Page 405. — Fifteenth line from top; read *Boutwell*, not *Boutell*.

Same page. — Third line from bottom; read T. *J.* Whiting and T. *J.* Stockdale, not T. *G.*

Also sixteenth line from bottom; *1887*, not *1882*.

Page 517. — Tenth line from top, read *Darius Hunkins*, not *David Hawkins*.

Page 652. — Ninth line from bottom, read *barques*, not *barges*.

Page 742. — Fourth line from bottom; spell *employs* with a *p*.

ADDITIONS TO THE PREFACE.

New Orleans *Picayune*, Memphis *Appeal*, De Bow's *Review*.

CPSIA information can be obtained
at www.ICGtesting.com
Printed in the USA
BVHW010455131221
623890BV00024B/323